Home Improvement

ALL-IN-ONE

FOR

DUMMIES®

Home Improvement
ALL-IN-ONE
FOR
DUMMIES®

**by Roy Barnhart, James and Morris Carey,
Gene and Katie Hamilton, Don R. Prestly, Jeff Strong**

WILEY

Wiley Publishing, Inc.

Home Improvement All-in-One For Dummies®

Published by
Wiley Publishing, Inc.
111 River St.
Hoboken, NJ 07030-5774
www.wiley.com

Copyright © 2004 by Wiley Publishing, Inc., Indianapolis, Indiana

Published by Wiley Publishing, Inc., Indianapolis, Indiana

Published simultaneously in Canada

For general information on our other products and services or to obtain technical support, please contact our Customer Care Department within the U.S. at 800-762-2974, outside the U.S. at 317-572-3993, or fax 317-572-4002.

Wiley also publishes its books in a variety of electronic formats. Some content that appears in print may not be available in electronic books.

Library of Congress Control Number: 2004102437

ISBN: 0-7645-5680-0

Manufactured in the United States of America

10 9 8 7 6 5 4 3 2

1B/RU/QU/QU/IN

WILEY

About the Authors

Roy Barnhart is a lifelong do-it-yourselfer and former professional building and remodeling contractor. He enjoyed eight years as Senior Building and Remodeling Editor for two national home improvement magazines. As a freelance writer, editor, and consultant, Roy has contributed articles to more than a dozen home improvement magazines, including *Family Handyman* and *House Beautiful*. He has also contributed to four books.

James and Morris Carey, known as the Carey Brothers, are nationally recognized experts on home building and renovation. They share their 20-plus years of experience as award-winning, licensed contractors with millions nationwide through a weekly radio program, daily radio vignette, syndicated newspaper column, and comprehensive Web site (www.onthehouse.com), all titled "On the House." Morris and James continue to own and operate a successful home remodeling and construction firm, Carey Bros., and have been named to *Remodeling* magazine's Hall of Fame Big 50, which recognizes top achievers in the industry. They've also been honored as one of the nation's top 500 companies by *Qualified Remodeler* magazine.

Gene and Katie Hamilton have been working on houses and writing about home improvements for over 30 years. They've remodeled 14 houses and write a weekly newspaper column entitled "Do It Yourself . . . Or Not?" which appears in newspapers across the country and on Web sites. The Hamiltons are authors of 16 home improvement books, including *Home Improvement For Dummies, Carpentry For Dummies, Painting and Wallpapering For Dummies,* and *Plumbing For Dummies*. They're the founders of www.HouseNet.com, the first home improvement site on the Internet and America Online. You've seen these veteran do-it-yourselfers appear as home improvement experts on CNN, *Dateline,* the *Today* show, *Home Matters, Today at Home,* and *Our Home*.

Don R. Prestly is a former senior editor for *HANDY Magazine* for The Handyman Club of America, as well as a former associate editor for *Family Handyman* magazine. In addition to his nearly 20 years of writing and doing home improvement projects, he spent several years as a manager for one of the Midwest's largest home centers. Throw in the everyday upkeep needs of being a homeowner, dealing with the same problems and repairs as other homeowners, and it's obvious that he has the background and experience to help you make your kitchen dreams come true.

Jeff Strong began creating sawdust at a very young age while helping his father, a master craftsman, build fine furniture. An accomplished woodworker, Jeff has designed and built countless pieces of furniture and currently accepts commissions to build his creations. His woodworking style marries Arts and Crafts, Southwestern, and Asian influences. *Woodworking For Dummies* is his third book.

Publisher's Acknowledgments

We're proud of this book; please send us your comments through our Dummies online registration form located at www.dummies.com/register/.

Some of the people who helped bring this book to market include the following:

Acquisitions, Editorial, and Media Development

Compilation Editor: Pam Mourouzis

Senior Project Editor: Tim Gallan

Acquisitions Editor: Tracy Boggier

Copy Editors: Kristin DeMint, Esmeralda St. Clair, Laura K. Miller

Technical Editor: Roy Barnhart

Editorial Manager: Christine Meloy Beck

Editorial Assistants: Melissa S. Bennett, Elizabeth Rea

Cartoons: Rich Tennant, www.the5thwave.com

Illustrators: Tony Davis, George Retseck, Lisa Reed, Precision Graphics

Production

Project Coordinator: Nancee Reeves

Layout and Graphics: Andrea Dahl, Lauren Goddard, LeAndra Hosier, Stephanie D. Jumper, Michael Kruzil, Jacque Schneider, Julie Trippetti

Proofreaders: Arielle Carole Mennelle, Dwight Ryan Ramsey

Indexer: Infodex Indexing Services Inc.

Publishing and Editorial for Consumer Dummies

    Diane Graves Steele, Vice President and Publisher, Consumer Dummies

    Joyce Pepple, Acquisitions Director, Consumer Dummies

    Kristin A. Cocks, Product Development Director, Consumer Dummies

    Michael Spring, Vice President and Publisher, Travel

    Brice Gosnell, Associate Publisher, Travel

    Kelly Regan, Editorial Director, Travel

Publishing for Technology Dummies

    Andy Cummings, Vice President and Publisher, Dummies Technology/General User

Composition Services

    Gerry Fahey, Vice President of Production Services

    Debbie Stailey, Director of Composition Services

Contents at a Glance

Table of Contents

Introduction

$\mathcal{W}$elcome to *Home Improvement All-in-One For Dummies*, a whole-house repair manual. One glance through this book and you quickly see that it's not overloaded with technical details and obscure advice that you'll never want or need to know. Our goal was to compile a book that explains, in a fun and easy-to-understand style, how to complete a wide range of projects. This anybody-can-do-it approach appeals to fledging do-it-yourselfers and seasoned handymen and -women. We encourage you to dust off your toolbox and tackle simple repairs and improvements using our goof-proof instructions.

This book contains a combination of need-to-know techniques on topics from routine home maintenance to remodeling to plumbing. Basic steps and illustrations throughout the book walk you through the key points of maintaining and improving your home. These are tried-and-true solutions to everyday home repair and improvement questions.

Foolish Assumptions

You know what they say about the word *assume*. In any event, we do assume that you care about the appearance and condition of your home, and hence its value. We don't have this vision that you're a home improvement fanatic or that you're particularly handy — you don't need to be. All you need is a song in your heart, a smile on your face, and an insatiable desire to see your home be the best that it can be.

A few tools are of infinite value when it comes to home improvement. However, the most complicated tool you'll need is a cordless driver/drill for sinking a screw here and there. The tools that you'll find yourself needing most often are a scrub brush, a paintbrush, and plenty of patience.

Most important, we assume that you'll always seek help when needed, and that you'll always put safety first when attempting a home improvement project.

How to Use This Book

You can use this book in two ways:

- ✔ If you want information about a specific topic, such as plugging up cold drafts with weather-stripping or cleaning out gutters, flip to that section and get your answer pronto. (We promise to have you back on the couch in no time.) If you need help finding a particular piece of information, use the Table of Contents at the front of the book or the comprehensive Index at the back.

- ✔ If you want to be a home improvement guru, read the whole book from cover to cover, and a wealth of knowledge will spill forth from your lips whenever the word *house* comes up in conversation. You'll know so much that Bob Vila will be calling you for advice.

How This Book Is Organized

The book is actually six books in one. The chapters within each of those books cover specific topics in detail. You can read each chapter or book without reading what came before, so you don't have to waste time reading what doesn't apply to your situation. Occasionally, we refer you to another area in the book where you find more details on a particular subject.

Book 1: Planning Your Home Improvement Projects

Undertaking a home improvement project without planning is a recipe for disaster. This book walks you through the decision of whether to take on a task yourself or hire a professional, helps you gather the tools you need to do most home improvement projects, and gives you important tips for staying safe.

Book 11: Basic Home Maintenance and Improvement

This section walks you through the various parts of a home, from the foundation to the roof, and tells you how to make common repairs. You find information about your home's heating and cooling systems, its electrical system, and even its appliances.

Book III: Painting and Wallpapering

A simple coat of paint or layer of wallpaper can have an amazing impact on how a home looks. This book helps you choose the best materials for your situation and get them up onto your walls like a pro. The chapters on painting cover both the interior and the exterior of a house.

Book IV: Bathroom and Kitchen Remodeling

Although bathroom and kitchen remodels can be among the most costly home repairs to undertake, they also have been proven to add the most value to a home. This book walks you through the process of remodeling either type of room, from budgeting to choosing fixtures to putting in cabinets, sinks, and showers and tubs.

Book V: Carpentry, Woodworking, and Flooring

Working with wood is a sensual experience — it's addictive. And really, it isn't too difficult. This book talks about the basics of carpentry and woodworking, from affixing pieces together to sanding and finishing wood projects. It also walks you through the processes of repairing and installing new hardwood and other types of flooring.

Book VI: Plumbing

Plumbing may be an area that you've always found a little bit intimidating — many homeowners do. But when you understand how everything fits together, plumbing repairs aren't any more difficult than other home maintenance projects. In this book, you find information about two major, vexing plumbing problems: leaks and clogs. Before you call a plumber in a panic, check these chapters — you may be able to make a simple fix and save yourself a hundred bucks or more.

Icons Used in This Book

We use the familiar *For Dummies* icons to help guide you through the material in this book. Read on to find out what each icon means:

Get on target with these great time-saving, money-saving, and sanity-saving tips.

Commit to memory these key tidbits of information that come into play in various aspects of your home improvement adventures.

We don't want to scare you off, but some of the projects discussed in this book can be dangerous, even deadly, if approached improperly. This icon alerts you to potential hazards and signals information about how to steer clear of them. We also use this symbol to mark advice for making your home a safer place.

Some fixer-upper mistakes are so common that you can see them coming from a mile away. Let this icon serve as a warning that you're treading in trouble-prone waters. Why should you have to learn from your own mistakes when you can learn just as well from others'?

Some projects and repairs require the skills, experience, and know-how that only a professional can offer. Novices and weekend handymen (or women) just can't handle them. When we discuss these kinds of projects in the book, you'll see this icon.

Most people want their toilets to flush, but some folks aren't happy until they know how the toilet flushes. This book doesn't bombard you with a bunch of technical trivia, but some background tidbits are too good to leave out. If you're an engineer-type who craves obscure details that most normal people don't care about, seek out these icons. If you'd rather live in ignorant bliss, by all means, skip these little diversions.

Where to Go from Here

We don't care whether you start with the Table of Contents, the Index, Book V, or even Chapter 1 (what a novel idea!). What's important is that you get going. A better home is just around the corner!

Book I

Planning Your Home Improvement Projects

The 5th Wave   By Rich Tennant

"Oh Dave is very handy around the house. He manually entered the phone numbers for the electrician, the carpenter, and the plumber on our speed dial."

In this book . . .

Where do you start? Can you do it yourself? What materials, tools, and knowledge do you need? How much will it cost, and how do you keep from maiming yourself in the process? Dig into these chapters that frame answers to these knotty questions.

Collecting basic household tools and the right stuff for specific jobs doesn't have to be a struggle. Venturing into the local hardware store or home center need not signal safari time — although with the size of today's home centers, you may need to pack a lunch.

Whether you want to estimate the time and cost involved in a job or check out the possibility of adding more hands-on adventures to your to-do list, you can build comfort and confidence with a cruise through this book.

Here are the contents of Book I at a glance.

Chapter 1

Do It Yourself or Hire a Pro?

In This Chapter

▶ Sizing up costs, time, and skill level

▶ Choosing the right person for the job

▶ Getting down to business

*Y*ou can expect to save at least 20 percent and sometimes 100 percent of the cost of any job by doing the work yourself. What's more, you can enjoy the sense of pride and accomplishment that comes with a job well done. That said, you must remember that most people are hard-pressed for time and energy, and some projects require special skills and tools that the average Joe may not possess.

We're not suggesting that you tackle these really advanced jobs. But countless other projects, such as removing wallpaper or sanding wood, require little in the way of tools and talent. By beginning with unglamorous repairs, such as fixing a broken window screen or tightening a loose hinge, you can quickly build your do-it-yourself skills and confidence. The bonus is that doing these projects makes your house a better and more comfortable place — a convenience that won't go unnoticed by you or anyone else in the house. Install a ceiling fan, and everyone notices the balmy breezes; paint the garage, and your neighbors rave. The idea is to choose projects that make a difference in the livability of your house and, at the same time, build your skills and confidence.

Just how do you know your limitations? That's the $64 question. We know that there's nothing a handy homeowner can't do, but that's not the issue. When it comes to massive projects, such as replacing all the walls in a house or building a large addition, you have other factors to consider. As you gain experience, you'll develop a sixth sense to evaluate your limits and your situation. That's what this chapter is all about.

Taking Everything into Account

Three factors go into the decisions of whether and how to do a job yourself: time, money, and skills. If you have plenty of time, you can tackle almost any project, using only some basic tools and gaining the skills you need as you go. If you have lots of dough, you can purchase plenty of timesaving tools and gear, or even hire someone else to do the job for you. And if you already have a treasure trove of home improvement skills, you can do the job yourself quickly and for a moderate cost (maybe even without using this book).

But for most mere mortals, the question of to do or not to do the work all by yourself involves finding a balance of all three factors and then doing some soul-searching for a reasonable response.

Calculating the cost

First up, consider the cost of materials. Don't become another statistic of the do-it-yourself damage factor. If the materials are expensive, you're taking a big risk by doing the job yourself. If, for example, you're laying $30-a-yard wool carpeting, you're gambling with expensive dice. Make one miscut, and you suddenly find yourself in the carpet remnant business. You have to replace the damaged material, and you'll probably end up calling in a carpet installer to finish the job after all. Not much savings; plus, you wasted too much time in the process.

If you're considering a project and want to get a ballpark figure of the labor costs involved, go to a home center and ask whether an installation service is available. Many retailers feature this one-stop-shopping service, farming the work out to contractors. These stores often display materials, such as doors, windows, and ceiling fans, with two costs: a do-it-yourself price and an installed price. The difference between the two figures is the cost of the labor.

This figure gives you a starting point for looking objectively at the cost of tackling a project. But don't forget the other part of the equation — the cost of tools that you may need. Look at tools as a long-term investment: If you're a budding do-it-yourselfer, you want to add to your stash so that you have a complete workbench that can last a lifetime. However, if a project requires an expensive tool that you may only need once in your life, consider other options, such as renting or borrowing.

Although perfectly affordable rental tools are available for many jobs, some people love any excuse to buy their own new tools. And that's okay. In fact, you may even say that nurturing the home improvement market so that it continues to contribute generously to our national economy is your civic duty. We list our top tool and gadget picks in Chapter 2.

Tallying the time

Time is a real consideration when you're deciding whether to tackle home repairs and improvements yourself. Whether you're skilled or not, working around the house takes time, sometimes an amazing amount of it. For all handypersons — and wannabes — estimating the time to complete a job isn't an exact science. If you're new to the do-it-yourself realm, heed these words about estimating how long a job is likely to take: Bone up on what's involved, write down the process in step-by-step fashion (as you perceive it), and include the shopping time, working time, and cleanup time. Translate the work into numbers of hours . . . and then *triple it*. The result that you get is liable to be pretty close. The more projects you complete, the more you realize the value of estimating accurately.

Many novice do-it-yourselfers make the tragic mistake of underestimating the time commitment and then box themselves into an unrealistic deadline, such as painting the living room before Christmas or building a deck for the Fourth of July family reunion — both noble ideas, but they warrant considerably more time than initially imagined. The work takes much longer than you anticipated the first time that you do any job. Setting an inflexible deadline only adds more pressure to the project.

Scrutinizing your skills

Now for a touchy subject: recognizing your talent. This topic is sensitive because some people are born naturally handy — a fluke of nature like having blue eyes or red hair. Some people are innately gifted with an artistic or mechanical sense; the ability to hang wallpaper or repair a loose hinge seems to come naturally to them. Others are less gifted. For the mechanically challenged, these seemingly simple tasks are tantamount to building the Taj Mahal over a long weekend.

Remember when your gym teacher shared this wisdom: "You may be good at sports, but it takes a lot more than that to be a professional athlete"? Well, this is where the tide of fate flows in your favor. You may not have been born with a hammer in your hand, but you can develop the skills of a confident do-it-yourselfer and go on to accomplish amazing feats. You can gain and hone the skills of a handy homeowner — without the drudgery of running laps or lifting weights to stay in shape. It's true; as you get older, you get better. After you figure out how to install a dimmer switch, it's like riding a bicycle; you never forget.

Starting small

Even if you aren't a do-it-yourselfer and you have no desire to become one, you can participate in projects and save money by doing the grunt work. We're talking about simple jobs, such as removing wallpaper, tearing up old floors, scraping paint, and many other tasks that require more time and enthusiasm than talent.

The bottom line: If you're a first-timer, choose projects that are within your range of skills and don't require expensive materials and tools. Avoid boxing yourself in with unrealistic deadlines, and by all means invest your time as sweat equity and do the grunt work yourself.

Hiring Help the Smart Way

You can find entire books devoted to hiring a contractor, but we think that you need to know the basics. If a project is simple, such as replacing a closet door or repairing a faulty dishwasher, the plan is pretty straightforward. Get a couple of estimates and compare them, making sure to specify the full scope of the job and the quality of materials. Remember: You want estimates that compare apples to apples.

This advice becomes dicey when the project is more complex — say, bathroom remodeling that involves opening a wall, replacing the fixtures, and upgrading the flooring — all subject to surprises, hidden costs, and unexpected complications. Professionals have difficulty bidding on a job without knowing what they may find when the wall comes down or the old floor comes up. An accurate bid is based on complete and accurate information and the cost of fixtures, which can range from low-end to luxury. As a consumer, you have to spell out exact styles, models, and colors for a precise estimate.

Finding a good contractor

Shop 'til you drop . . . for the right contractor, that is. Spend as much time reviewing contractors as you do choosing a doctor. Start in your neighborhood and branch out to a network of friends and acquaintances who can provide referrals. Most contractors are listed in the Yellow Pages, but contractors rely on their reputations, not the phone company, for new customers.

Check out the service trucks that you see working in your neighborhood; the most familiar one probably has a good repeat business there. Stop by or call the neighbor (yes, be that bold!) and explain that you're looking for a contractor. Ask about your neighbor's experience. Is the homeowner pleased with the contractor's work? Most often, people are quick to share their thoughts, positive or otherwise.

This seat-of-the-pants screening process is the best way that we know to find competent contractors — it's direct, immediate, and tells you what you want to know from a reliable source, another homeowner just like you.

Whether you live in a suburban subdivision or a historic urban neighborhood, look for contractors who work on homes similar to yours. Kitchens and bathrooms in tract ranch houses are subjected to repeat remodeling, and the contractor who works in the neighborhood knows what to expect. Along the same lines, a carpenter who specializes in historic houses is more likely to know the intricacies of older homes, so he or she is your best choice for restoration.

For the same reasons you don't usually go to a proctologist for an earache, don't hire a rough carpenter to do fine woodworking. Sure the carpenter can do the work, but you get the biggest bang for your buck by hiring someone with skills and experience for the specific job. Take advantage of individual expertise — that's what you're paying for.

Know what you want before talking to a contractor. No, you don't have to know the serial number of the new faucet, but you do need to have an idea of the type, style, and features you want. First of all, a contractor can't bid on a job without knowing what you expect to have installed, repaired, or built. Second, the only accurate way to compare bids from different contractors is to be sure that the work is based on the same specifications.

Some people may tell you to get three bids from different contractors and choose the middle one — easier said than done. If you do your homework and are satisfied with the references and professional manner of a contractor, you may be hard-pressed or time-restricted to scour up two more. The bottom line is to use your best judgment and common sense, and don't let a schedule force you into making a decision. If you interview a contractor and are thrilled with what you find, don't balk at having to wait until he's available. Never rush a job and settle for someone you're not completely satisfied with. After all, you only build an addition or remodel your kitchen once in your lifetime — that is, if you get the job done right the first time.

When you meet with a contractor, ask for customer referrals of work similar to your project, and then check out those references. This task takes time, but you can benefit greatly by listening to someone with firsthand experience. Many people consult the Better Business Bureau as a resource or contact a local chamber of commerce for a list of referrals. Even if you find a contractor through one of these sources, you should still ask the contractor for a list of satisfied customers in your area whom you can call for recommendations.

Covering all your bases

After narrowing your search for the perfect contractor, you're ready to get down to business. At this point, it's critical to get everything in writing:

- ✔ **Liability:** Ask for a certificate of insurance and make sure that the contractor is licensed and bonded to cover any injuries that may occur on the job. Reputable contractors carry workers' compensation insurance and insurance that covers them in the event of personal liability or property damage. Checking out a contractor's liability is very important, because you may be held liable if the contractor or one of his workers is injured while working on your home. You may also be held liable if the contractor or one of his employees injures someone else. Check with your insurance agent about getting additional umbrella liability coverage for the duration of a major building or remodeling project.

- ✔ **Contract:** A complete contract includes a detailed description of the project with a listing of specific materials and products to be used. For a job that involves various stages of completion, a payment schedule itemizes when money is to be paid. A procedure for handling any disputes between you and the contractor is also important, along with directions for handling changes in plan due to an unforeseen need for additional work or materials.

  If the project involves removing debris or if it's intrinsically messy (hanging drywall, for example), make sure that the contract has a cleanup clause that clearly defines the contractor's responsibility to leave the work site "broom clean" and orderly. Also make sure that the contract spells out who's expected to apply and pay for the building permit and what's necessary to meet those requirements.

  Most states require a *recision clause* that allows you to cancel the agreement within three days of signing it. This arrangement gives you some time to think things over and helps to prevent you from being pressured into signing the contract.

- ✔ **Warranty:** If the contractor offers a warranty, be sure that the provisions include the name and address of the person or institution offering the warranty and the duration of the coverage. Read the document closely to be sure that it's written clearly and that you understand all the terms and conditions. A *full warranty* covers the repair or replacement of the product or a refund of your money within a certain period. If the warranty is *limited,* find out what those limitations are.

✔ **Building permit:** Most towns or counties require a permit to build on or change a property. The fee is based on the scope of the improvements and is either paid by the homeowner or included in the contractor's bid (which the homeowner pays eventually). If you're doing work that requires a building permit, you must fill out an application and pay a fee. If you hire contractors, you're better off having them apply for the permit because their license is on the line. During different stages of the job and at its completion, the work is inspected to ensure that it meets the building codes. These inspections are your best assurance that the work is done correctly or at least that it meets minimum government standards.

Chapter 2

Gearing Up for Your Home Improvement Adventures

. . . .

In This Chapter

▶ Stocking up your toolbox

▶ Investing in great gadgets

. . . .

*H*ow can you expect to create miracles without a magic wand? Of course, you can't. And by the same token, you can't expect to do projects around the house without reliable tools.

People take different approaches to owning tools. Tool-obsessed individuals look for any excuse to add to their collection — these folks simply can't own too many tools. More practical do-it-yourselfers want to own only what's required to do the job. Both approaches have their place, but whichever your persuasion, you need a stockpile of core tools — the essentials that you never want to be caught without.

If you think of every tool you buy as a long-term investment, you'll gradually acquire a reliable stash that can get you through most home repairs and improvements. In this chapter, we walk you through the basic tools that are essential to any toolbox, but we can't resist also tempting you with some of our favorite gadgets and gizmos designed to delight any do-it-yourselfer.

Sure, everyone dreams of a workshop like Norm's. But in the real world, most people are hard-pressed for the space. At a bare minimum, find room for a workbench somewhere in your house, garage, basement, or shed. Designate this space as a work area, where you can take a door lock apart or stir a can of paint, lay out a window frame that needs new screening or stow your tool tote and rechargeable power tools. Your workspace doesn't have to be fancy; anywhere with good lighting and electrical power will do. Lay a flat work surface across two sawhorses or, if space is at a premium, get a portable bench that you can fold up and store out of the way.

The Top Tools for Any Homebody

Shop for the tools you need in home centers, hardware stores, or any large mart. Don't try to buy all the tools that you'll ever need at one time; instead, buy tools as you need them. Focus on quality rather than quantity and buy the best-quality tool you can afford.

The tool-buying experience can be daunting for a first-timer. As you roam the aisles of megastores, don't let the overwhelming selection intimidate you. Ask a salesperson for help and explain that you're new to the do-it-yourself scene. A knowledgeable salesperson can help you make your decision by explaining how the wide range of prices reflects the quality, features, and materials of various tools.

So here it is, our list of the basic tools you need to get on the road to home improvement adventures:

- **⅜-inch variable speed reversible drill:** This tool, available as a plug-in or cordless, uses steel blades called *bits* to drive in or remove screws, drill holes, sand wood, mix piña coladas, and do other important home improvement tasks. See Figure 2-1.

- **Claw hammer:** We recommend a 16-ounce hammer with a fiberglass handle to cushion the blow to your hand. Watch out for *carpal tunnel syndrome,* an injury that can occur from repetitive motions, such as constantly hitting your thumb and then hopping around the room.

- **Pliers:** Slip-joint pliers have toothed jaws that enable you to grip various sized objects, like a water pipe, the top of a gallon of mineral spirits, or the tape measure that you accidentally dropped into the toilet. Because the jaws are adjustable, pliers give you leverage to open and firmly grip an object.

- **Toolbox saw:** A small, easy-to-use handsaw is useful for cutting such materials as paneling or shelving.

- **Assorted pack of screwdrivers:** Be sure that you have both slotted (flathead) and Phillips screwdrivers in a variety of sizes. The slotted type has a straight, flat blade; the Phillips blade has a cross or plus-sign that fits into the grooves of Phillips-head screws.

- **Utility knife:** Choose a compact knife with replaceable blades that's strong enough to open heavy cardboard boxes and precise enough for trimming wallpaper.

   Buy the type with a retractable blade; you'll appreciate it the first time that you squat down with the knife in your pocket. (Ouch!)

✔ **Staple gun:** You can use this tool for a variety of jobs, like securing insulation, ceiling tile, plastic sheeting, and fabrics.

✔ **Carpenter's level:** A straightedge tool that has a series of glass tubes containing liquid with a bubble of air. When the bubble in a single tube is framed between marks on the glass, it shows that the surface is *level* (horizontal) or *plumb* (vertical). See Figure 2-2.

✔ **Metal file:** Filing tools, such as those shown in Figure 2-3, are flat metal bars with shallow grooves that form teeth. Metal files are useful for sharpening the edges of scrapers, putty knives, and even shovels and garden trowels.

✔ **Allen wrenches:** These L-shaped metal bars, often sold in sets (see Figure 2-4), are designed for turning screws or bolts that have hexagonal sockets in their heads. This tool also goes by the name *hex-key* or *setscrew wrench*. Used to assemble everything from knock-down furniture to bicycles to gas grills, this tool was invented by a man named, umm, let's see . . . we'll have to get back to you on that one.

Book I

**Planning
Your Home
Improve-
ment
Projects**

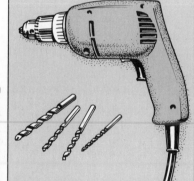

Figure 2-1:
An electric
drill with
a variety
of bits.

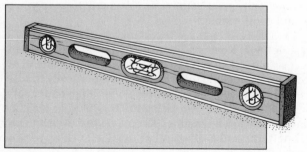

Figure 2-2:
A standard
carpenter's
level for
finding level
and plumb
lines.

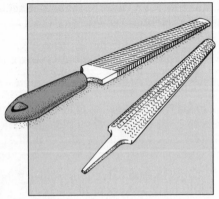

Figure 2-3:
Metal files
are good for
more than
breaking
out of jail.

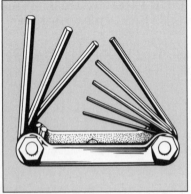

Figure 2-4:
Many
"assembly-
required"
items call
for a set
of Allen
wrenches.

Gizmos and Gear

Tools alone don't lead to a life of joyful home improvements. You gotta have gadgets, too. Some really great gadgets are available to keep you organized, efficient, safe, and comfortable:

- **Itty-bitty notebook:** Keep a reference of your home improvement needs in your car or purse and refer to it when you shop. Instead of jotting down notes on scraps of paper that you're more likely to lose than use, keep all this stuff in one place. Buying a new lampshade? Jot down the dimensions of the old one. Replacing the tray to your ice-cube maker? Make a note of the model number. Keep a record of paint colors and wallpaper patterns and a zillion other details (such as your wedding anniversary) in this little notebook.

- **Tool tote:** Keep a stash of the tools that you reach for most often in some kind of portable toolbox or crate. Be sure to include a stock of string, a pair of scissors, and other common household repair acces-sories. Many repairs must be done onsite, so having a tool tote that you can take with you to the project can be invaluable.

✔ **Kneepads:** Cushioned rubber pads, held in place with elastic strips, protect your knee joints from the impact of kneeling on hard surfaces. (Pretend that you're in-line skating, and you won't feel so silly.) Kneepads are especially important to wear when you're crawling around on hard, debris-strewn surfaces.

✔ **Goggles:** Remember how your mom always made you wear a hat when it was cold outside? Well, if she saw you with a hammer or chipping away at something with a chisel, she'd say, "Put on your safety goggles!" A tiny chip of wood or a speck of metal or hardened paint can seriously damage your eyes, so protect them at all costs. Mother knows best.

Goggles used to be clunky contraptions that only kids wanted to wear, but now they're available in designer styles (well, sort of). Goggles are an inexpensive investment that may save your eyesight. Just remember to put them on.

✔ **Gray duct tape:** Sure, this product was designed for taping heating ducts, but it's a national icon for do-it-yourselfers. Use it to seal window screens, patch old sneakers . . . heck, we've seen it patching dents in cars!

✔ **Neon circuit tester:** This two-buck item, pictured in Figure 2-5, can be a lifesaver whenever you have to work on an electrical switch, receptacle, or power source. Before you begin tinkering with a device, use this circuit tester to make sure that power isn't flowing to it.

✔ **Wire brush:** This item, shown in Figure 2-6, looks like a lethal toothbrush. It's useful for scraping blistered paint, removing rust from metal, and taking corrosion off spark plugs.

Figure 2-5: Electricity can be deadly. Use a circuit tester to make sure that wires are safe to handle.

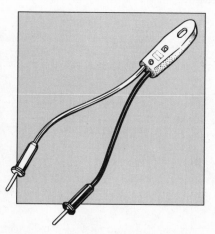

✔ **Stud finder:** No, this tool isn't for finding hunky guys (unless they're trapped in your walls). *Wall studs* are the vertical wood framing to which wallboard is fastened. A stud finder, shown in Figure 2-7, is an electronic device that locates the metal fasteners behind finished walls, which enables you to find a sturdy place to hang pictures, mirrors, and shelves.

✔ **Ladders:** Get a stepladder for household chores, such as changing light bulbs and painting rooms; get a taller self-supporting or extension-type ladder for outdoor maintenance like cleaning gutters and trimming trees. In general, aluminum ladders are lightweight and strong; wooden ladders are solid, heavy, and economical; and fiberglass ladders are strong, electrically nonconductive, and expensive. If you can afford it, fiberglass is the best choice.

Every ladder is given a *duty rating* — its maximum safe-load capacity. This weight includes you plus the weight of any tools and materials you wear and haul up the ladder with you.

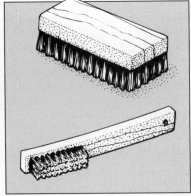

Figure 2-6:
This is one brush you don't want to take into the shower with you.

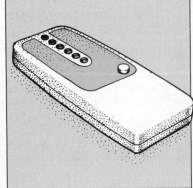

Figure 2-7:
Use a stud finder to avoid hanging heavy items over hollow wallboard.

Chapter 3

Safety and Preparedness

. . . .

In This Chapter

▶ Preventing household fires

▶ Protecting your home with smoke alarms, carbon monoxide detectors, and fire extinguishers

▶ Being prepared for general emergencies

▶ Gas line maintenance tips

▶ Tightening up security

▶ Garage door and electrical safety

. . . .

*I*n this chapter, we offer time-honored, proven safety practices blended with a host of new innovations, contemporary concepts, and the very best of today's high-tech electronic wizardry. When used all together, these measures ensure greater peace of mind for homeowners.

Practicing Fire Safety

Fire has been a number one household danger ever since the day, many eons ago, when our prehistoric ancestors got the idea of bringing fire indoors for cave heating and dinosaur cooking. Since then, accidents and total household destructions have occurred due to misunderstanding, miscalculations, and misuse of this powerful force of nature.

The following points are worth noting with regard to residential fires:

✔ Careless smoking is the leading cause of residential fire deaths.

✔ 25 percent of fires with child fatalities are caused by children playing with fire.

✔ Household fire hazards include overloaded electrical circuits, faulty wiring, unsafe appliances, wood- and coal-burning stoves and furnaces, electric and kerosene space heaters, unattended fireplaces, and the careless use of lighters and matches, especially by children.

Only you can prevent fires

REMEMBER

So what's your best defense against this household killer? Your best defense is quite simple — good old common sense:

✔ Exercise great care with all flammable materials, including fabrics (like drapes and furniture) near high heat sources (like stoves, space heaters, and open fireplaces) and especially combustible liquids (like solvents, cleaners, and fuels) — when both using and storing them.

✔ Don't overload electrical circuits or put too great a burden on individual outlets or lightweight extension cords. Overloading causes overheating, which leads to wire fatigue and a possible fire. Dimming or flickering lights, a power cord that's warm or hot to the touch, and fuses that repeatedly burn out or breakers in the electrical panel that frequently trip are sure signs of an overloaded circuit.

✔ Don't use bulbs with a higher wattage than a lamp or fixture is rated for because the lamp can seriously overheat. Most modern light fixtures and lamps have a label on the fixture that rates the maximum recommended bulb wattage for that fixture. If you can't find the label, bring the lamp or information on the fixture to a lighting store for recommendations on the wattage of bulb that should be used.

✔ Watch for faulty electronic equipment, malfunctioning appliances, frayed electrical cords, flickering lights, or fuses that blow and circuit breakers that trip repeatedly — they're all potential fire hazards.

✔ Never smoke cigarettes, cigars, or pipes in bed — or when you're tired or lying down.

✔ Make sure that any ashes have cooled before you throw them away. Many fires are started by the careless dumping of ashes that are not fully extinguished. This includes ashes from ashtrays, fireplaces, and barbeques. Hot embers can smolder undetected in the trash for hours before igniting.

✔ Keep space heaters at least 3 feet away from flammable items. Only buy units with tip-over shut-off switches and never operate one while sleeping.

Smoke alarms: Gotta have 'em

A smoke alarm is considered to be one of the least expensive, most popular, and best forms of life protection insurance you can buy. A working smoke detector doubles your chance of surviving a fire by warning you of a dangerous situation before it's too late.

For minimum coverage, have at least one smoke detector or alarm on every level of your home and in every sleeping area. You can also add alarms to hallways outside every bedroom, the top and bottom of all stairways, and often-forgotten places such as basements, attics, utility rooms, and garages.

Book I

**Planning
Your Home
Improve-
ment
Projects**

Smoke detectors can be either

- **Battery-operated:** These inexpensive units can easily be installed any-where. They require frequent inspection to determine the condition of the battery.

- **AC-powered:** Installed by an electrician (or those with a good working knowledge of electricity), these units are much more dependable over the long haul due to their direct-wired power source. But they should have an independent battery backup so that they continue to operate during a blackout or an electrical fire that temporarily interrupts power.

Some newer models have a hush-button feature that silences a nuisance false alarm and desensitizes the unit for a few minutes until the air clears, when it resets itself. Other high-end models have safety lights that come on when the alarm is activated.

Dealing with fire emergencies

After a smoke detector sounds — whether night or day — a quick response and preplanned actions are your two best lifesavers.

Before opening any doors, look for smoke seeping around edges and feel the surface with your hand. The doorknob is another reliable indicator as to whether fire exists on the other side because metal conducts heat faster and more efficiently than wood does.

If it feels safe, open the door slowly and be prepared to close it quickly if heat and smoke rush in. Don't stop to get dressed, find pets, or collect valuables. Wasted seconds can cost lives. Gather only family members and exit immediately. If smoke is extremely dense, crawl on your knees and keep your mouth covered with a towel or cloth, if possible.

Families should develop and rehearse a home escape plan, with two ways out of every room. Store a fold-up fire escape ladder in every second-floor bedroom. Also include plans for a designated meeting place where everyone should gather once safely outside. After you're out, stay put until help arrives and never re-enter the house under any circumstances.

Rehearse your family escape plan regularly. After everyone knows what to do, perform run-throughs with your eyes closed — simulating darkness or smoke-filled passages — counting and memorizing the number of steps to each and every turn and ultimately to safety.

PASSing on a fire

If you ever need to use a fire extinguisher, use the PASS method:

✓ **P**ull the pin.

✓ **A**im at the base of the fire.

✓ **S**queeze the handle.

✓ **S**weep the base of the fire from side to side, starting with the closest edge and working away from yourself.

Testing alarms and detectors

All smoke detectors and alarms have a test button that, when pushed, causes the alarm to sound. Also, most detectors have either a blinking or a solid light that glows to let you know that the alarm is getting power.

Once a month, get up on a chair or use a broom handle for extra reach and push the test button. If you don't hear anything, then your battery is dead. If after changing the battery, the smoke detector is still not working, immediately replace it with a new one.

The button test ensures that the batteries are working. However, it doesn't tell you whether the detector is operating properly. To find out, put two or three lighted matches together (the wood kitchen type is best) and then blow out the flame, holding the matches so that the smoke wafts up toward the unit.

While battery-operated units have a built-in device that chirps when batteries get low, signaling the need for replacement, common wisdom dictates not waiting until that point. Batteries should be replaced twice a year, once in the spring and once in the fall.

Never remove a battery from your smoke alarm for use in another item, such as a radio, toy, or TV remote. Many people do so with every intention of replacing them in short order, only to remember that they forgot while standing and watching their house burn down (if they were lucky enough to awaken and escape in time).

While you're up checking your battery every month, also brush or vacuum the alarm to keep dirt and dust out of the mechanism. Never use cleaning sprays or solvents that can enter the unit and contaminate sensors.

Book I

Planning
Your Home
Improve-
ment
Projects

Replacing alarms and detectors

After a period of ten years, a smoke detector has endured more than 87,000 hours of continuous operation, during which time the internal sensors have probably become contaminated with dust, dirt, and air pollutant residues. If your alarm or detector is more than ten years old, consider replacing it to maintain optimal detection capabilities of deadly smoke in your home.

Fire extinguishers

Most fires start out small. Often, they can easily and quickly be put out if you have a working fire extinguisher readily at hand. Manufacturers of home safety products recommend having one fire extinguisher for every 600 square feet of living area. The kitchen, garage, and basement each should have an extinguisher of its own. Keep one in your car, as well.

Fire extinguishers are rated according to force and how much firefighting agent they contain — both of which determine how long the extinguisher operates when it's used and discharged. With most home extinguishers, the duration is short — so quick action and good aim are important factors in quenching flames while a fire is still in its early stage. (See the sidebar "PASSing on a fire" for tips on using fire extinguishers.)

Always purchase fire extinguishers with pressure gauges. Check the pressure gauge at least once each month to ensure that it's ready for use at all times. If the fire extinguisher pressure is low and the model can't be recharged, dispose of it and replace it with a new unit.

Under no circumstances should you test the extinguisher by pulling the pin and squeezing the trigger. Doing so can result in premature loss of pressure.

Preventing Carbon Monoxide Danger in the Home

Carbon monoxide (CO) is the number one cause of poisoning deaths in America. CO is an invisible, odorless, poisonous gas produced by the incomplete combustion of fuel — such as gasoline, kerosene, propane, natural gas, oil, and even wood fires. In concentrated form, CO can be fatal when inhaled — killing in minutes or hours, depending on the level of CO in the air. In smaller doses, CO produces a wide range of flulike symptoms ranging from red eyes, dizziness, and headaches to nausea, fatigue, and upset stomach. One telltale sign of mild CO poisoning is flu symptoms without a fever.

Typical sources of CO in homes are malfunctioning gas furnaces, gas stoves, water heaters, clothes dryers, and even improperly vented fireplaces. Other major dangers include using a generator in or too near your home, cooking or heating with a barbeque unit indoors during a power outage, and letting a car run in a garage or carport where exhaust fumes can collect and enter the home. Many of today's energy-efficient, "tight" homes minimize outside air exchange and cross-ventilation, giving CO no chance to exit after it enters the home.

There are CO detectors and combination CO and smoke detectors for the home. The Consumer Product Safety Commission (CPSC) recommends that every home with a fuel-burning appliance of any kind be equipped with a least one CO detector.

If you have only one unit, place it in the hall outside the bedroom area of your home. Invisible CO in concentrated form is even less likely to awaken a sleeper than thick toxic smoke.

While heat and smoke rise toward the ceiling, CO wafts through a room like perfume — only you can't smell or see it. Place CO detectors from 14 inches off the floor to face height on the wall and never near a draft, such as a window, doorway, or stairwell.

As with smoke alarms, CO detectors can be battery operated, hard-wired-mounted directly onto an electrical wall outlet, or plugged into an electrical cord, allowing units to sit on a shelf or tabletop. Units that plug into a direct power source should have an independent battery backup in case of a power failure.

Your CO detector should have a digital display with memory that indicates and records a problem, even when it's too small to trigger the alarm. A normal low level of CO in a home is zero. Nada, zilch, zip. However, even a small reading — such as 25, 30, or 35 parts per million — indicates a problem that could escalate.

The care and maintenance of CO detectors is basically the same as for smoke alarms. (See the section "Smoke alarms" earlier in this chapter for more information.) However, unlike using kitchen matches to test a smoke alarm, a carbon monoxide detector can't be tested using an outside source. Therefore, it's imperative that the test buttons provided on the equipment be tested at least once each month.

Additionally, have your heating system, vents, chimney, and flue inspected (and cleaned if necessary) by a qualified technician. Always vent fuel-burning appliances.

Other important maintenance procedures include checking and correcting any signs that indicate potential CO problems, such as

✔ A noticeably decreasing hot water supply

✔ A furnace that runs constantly but doesn't heat your house

✔ Soot collecting on, under, and around any appliance

✔ An unfamiliar burning odor

✔ A loose or missing furnace panel or vent pipe

✔ Damaged brick, chimney discoloration, or a loose-fitting chimney pipe

Guarding Your Home against Natural Disasters

Natural emergencies can befall the average home and family without warning, anywhere in the world. Earthquakes, tornadoes, hurricanes, floods, mud-slides, blizzards, tidal waves, lightning, squalls, gales, downpours, monsoons, typhoons, whirlwinds, and zephyrs can come out of nowhere and cause sub-stantial damage to a home. Although you can't do anything about the weather, you can be prepared for such emergencies, which may save your life and avert damage to your home.

Shoring up your castle

The same things you do to maintain your home every day pull double duty because they also can prepare your home for a natural disaster. The best defense against becoming a victim of an earthquake, fire, flood, snowstorm, tornado, or other natural disaster is a strong offense — keeping your home in tip-top shape.

For example, maintaining your roof can prevent shingles from being blown off and a roof leak from occurring. Well-sealed masonry can prevent freeze-and-thaw damage brought about by bone-chilling cold. Plumbing pipe heaters can prevent hundreds or thousands of dollars in damage caused by a burst pipe due to freezing.

How strong is your offense?

Reacting appropriately in the face of disaster

When your castle comes under siege from any of Mother Nature's natural marauders, three defensive maneuvers should take place in rapid succession:

- ✔ **Go to your safe place.** Have a safe place in your home, such as a windowless room in the basement, ready and stock it with emergency survival supplies, including first aid equipment, a radio, bottled water, and emergency food provisions.

- ✔ **Stay in your safe place until you get the all clear.** That's why you need a portable radio with functioning batteries! A portable or cellular phone (with extra batteries) also comes in handy at this stage.

- ✔ **Check for damage.** Following any major disaster, first check the status and well-being of your family members and neighbors. Then begin a thorough home inspection to ascertain any damage that may create larger problems.

   Check especially for damaged power lines and dangerous gas leaks, which can cause fire and explosions. Then check for electrical system damage and downed power lines. If you see sparks, note exposed wiring, or smell overheated insulation on wiring, shut off the electricity at the main circuit breaker or fuse box. If water is present, be careful not to make contact if you suspect that it may be electrically charged.

   Also check for any damage to water pipes and sewer drain lines. If they're damaged, turn off the main water supply valve, avoid drinking tap or well water, and don't flush toilets or drain water into tubs and sinks.

Well in advance of any natural emergency, you should know where your valves and circuit breakers are located. Make sure that you know how to turn off all major supply lines, and show your family members how to do so, too. Many hardware stores and home centers sell an inexpensive combination dual-emergency wrench designed specifically for quick gas and water shutoffs.

Putting things back together

Follow these general guidelines for getting back underway after an emergency:

- ✔ Deal cautiously with structural damage, watching for physical dangers, ranging from broken glass and nails to water and wet surfaces that may be electrically charged after power resumes. According to the American

Red Cross, the number two flood killer after drowning is electrocution. Electrical current can travel through water. Report downed power lines to your utility company or emergency management office.

✔ Use a flashlight to inspect for damage. Don't smoke or use candles, lanterns, or open flames, unless you know the gas has been turned off and the area has been aired out.

✔ Prevent deadly carbon monoxide poisoning by using a generator or other gasoline-powered machine outdoors. The same goes for camping stoves and charcoal grills.

✔ Some appliances, such as televisions, keep electrical charges even after they have been unplugged. Don't use appliances or motors that have gotten wet unless they've been taken apart, cleaned, and dried.

✔ Watch for snakes and wild animals that have been flooded out of their homes and may seek shelter in yours.

✔ Discard contaminated foods and kitchen and bath products.

✔ Boil drinking water until you're absolutely sure that it's safe.

✔ Pump out flooded areas in your home as soon as possible to avoid permanent damage to the house's frame.

✔ Pump out flooded basements slowly over the course of several days to prevent the basement walls from caving in due to the excessive pressure being placed on the walls from water-logged soil on the opposite side.

✔ If hardwood floors get soaked, mop up excess water and debris immediately and dry the floors slowly to reduce warping. Don't use heat for drying. Open windows and doors and allow finishes to air-dry. Rent a high-volume fan such as those used by professional carpet cleaners to hasten the drying process.

Drying finishes out too quickly can cause warping, buckling, and cracking that can be avoided if finishes are allowed to air-dry more slowly.

✔ If carpeting gets soaked, don't remove it while it's wet — doing so can cause tearing. Instead, pick up excess water with a wet/dry vac or carpet cleaning machine, slowly peel back wet carpet, and discard the padding. Then set up a box fan or two to dry the area completely. In most cases, carpets can be cleaned and reused; just the padding needs to be replaced.

✔ Have a professional check all plumbing and service your septic tank, if you have one.

✔ Call your insurance agent to begin the claims process.

For more information about disaster preparedness and recovery, visit the Web site of the American Red Cross at www.redcross.org.

Additional emergency measures

When dealing with an emergency situation, after immediate dangers are dealt with and relatively under control, take photos to record all damage to your home and its contents for insurance purposes. All too often, taking photos only comes to mind once cleanup and repairs are well underway.

Also, keep emergency gear close at hand, including a pair of sturdy shoes (to prevent injuries from rubble and broken glass), heavy socks, heavy work gloves, and clothing for keeping warm and dry for an extended period, both day and night.

Emergency preparedness also includes putting together a full first-aid kit with a manual instructing you how to deal with most major situations and injuries step-by-step. Check this kit twice a year for expiration dates and freshness of the products it contains. Also, watch for free first-aid training classes in your area, often sponsored by local organizations, hospitals, or police and fire departments.

Immediately after a natural disaster, the power is often out. Thus your emergency preparedness should also include provisions for both portable and self-contained lighting, including flashlights, extra batteries, candles, a disposable butane lighter, and waterproof matches.

Playing It Safe with Gas Lines

Of all emergency preparedness topics, gas lines deserve extra consideration — both in the event of natural disasters and for day-to-day living. If not properly installed, monitored, and maintained, natural gas is without question the most potentially dangerous item in your home. Gas can cause instant flash fires and devastating explosions that can result from negligence and carelessness.

Don't pour concrete or put asphalt around the rigid gas delivery pipe leading to the meter. This pipe must remain in soft, pliable dirt to ride out any seismic activity safely.

An exposed gas meter is always susceptible to being damaged or dislodged by contact. For protection from housework and gardening and to keep gas meters near driveways and sidewalks from being hit, place two heavy metal pipes in concrete (much like you would set a fencepost) in front of and on both sides of the gas meter.

To keep the gas line shutoff wrench easily accessible in a gas emergency, attach it to the main line at the shutoff valve with a piece of chain and a hose clamp. If you ever have to close the main gas valve, rotate the bar on the valve only one-quarter turn so that it runs across the gas line (closed) rather than parallel to it (open).

Inspect all gas line connections in your home. Those leading to appliances, furnaces, and water heaters should be only corrugated stainless steel or new epoxy-coated flexible connectors with shutoff valves where they meet the solid gas delivery lines (unless the manufacturer or local building codes specify otherwise).

Always call before you dig. Many types of underground lines serve your home, ranging from gas and electricity to water, telephone, and cable TV — and they're often only a few feet beneath the surface. So before you dig a ditch, sink a fencepost, or plant a tree or shrub, call your local utility companies for location information.

Book I

Planning Your Home Improve- ment Projects

Maintaining Burglar Alarms

Not all household dangers derive from natural forces. You also need to take measures to protect your home against those who would storm the castle, scale the proverbial stone walls, and plunder the family jewels.

Have properly installed solid and secure window and door locks strong enough to deter the average burglar. Then be sure to use them. Sounds too mundane and simple, you say? Police report that 50 percent of all home burglaries are due to windows or doors being left unlocked.

One of the best ways to determine whether your home is secure from potential intruders is to lock yourself out and try to get in without using your house key. You'll either be surprised at how easy it is to gain entry, or you'll feel relieved at how tough it is to get into your Fort Knox. During this exercise, be on the lookout for loose doorknobs and deadlocks and shaky windows and doors (including the garage door).

Many break-ins can be averted. A number of whole-house alarm systems are available today, and — just as with smoke alarms and carbon monoxide detectors — they need occasional testing, checking, and tuning up. Most systems include a failsafe battery backup, which needs checking and replacing at regular intervals — at least twice annually. Many systems also have a fire-sensing capability that must be checked and maintained as outlined in "Smoke alarms" earlier in this chapter.

Most systems have a keypad for indicating system operation and points of intrusion, and a horn or siren installed indoors (in the attic) or outside under an overhang or eave. Follow the manufacturer's instructions for maintaining and checking these features at specified intervals — pay particular attention to all points that signal an intrusion when contact is broken.

Make sure that sensitivity levels are properly set to avoid both frequent false alarms (that eventually go unheeded) and a system that doesn't respond properly when it should.

Before ordering and installing an alarm, check with local law enforcement agencies to see if any restrictions or special ordinances apply to alarms in your area. Most police departments discourage homeowners from installing a dialer-type alarm system that automatically calls the police or sheriff's department when activated. They find that when a major disaster takes place, this type of alarm swamps incoming lines that are needed to field calls for specific individual emergency situations. A good alternative is to have your alarm monitored by a central reporting agency. Thus, if a false alarm occurs, the police or sheriff won't be summoned, and you'll be off the hook for a false alarm fee and the embarrassment of having the cops show up at your home only to find you in your bathrobe collecting the morning paper.

Keeping Automatic Garage-Door Openers in Working Order

As with all mechanical components in a home, an automatic garage-door opener requires periodic maintenance to ensure safe and efficient operation. In fact, because a garage door is often the heaviest and largest single piece of moving equipment around a home, frequent testing and maintenance are especially important.

One of the best resources for garage-door maintenance is the owner's manual. Lubrication requirements and adjustment details are typically found in this manual. If you don't have an owner's manual, you can usually order a replacement copy by contacting an installing dealer or the manufacturer. Some manufacturers even make owner's manuals available on the Internet. All you need is the brand and model number.

An inspection of the garage-door springs, cables, rollers, and other door hardware is a great place to begin. Look for signs of wear and for frayed or broken parts. A handy do-it-yourselfer can perform most minor repairs, such as roller replacement, but a qualified garage-door service technician should handle the more complicated tasks. The springs and related hardware are under high tension and can cause severe injury if handled improperly.

Rollers, springs, hinges, and tracks require periodic lubrication. Use **spray** sil-icone, lightweight household oil, or white lithium grease according to the instructions in your owner's manual.

Periodically test the balance of the door. Start with the door closed. Disconnect the automatic opener release mechanism so that the door can be operated by hand. The door should lift smoothly and with little resistance. It should stay open around 3 to 4 feet above the floor. If it doesn't, it's out of balance and should be adjusted by a professional.

In addition to extending its life, monthly inspection and testing of the automatic opener can prevent serious injuries and property damage. Careless operation and allowing children to play with or use garage-door opener controls are dangerous situations that can lead to tragic results. A few simple precautions can protect your family and friends from potential harm.

Never stand or walk under a moving door. Don't let children play "beat the door." Keep transmitters and remote controls out of the reach of children and teach them that they aren't toys. The push-button wall control should be out of the reach of children (at least 5 feet from the floor) and away from all moving parts. The button should always be mounted where you can clearly see the door in full operation.

Test the force setting of the opener by holding up the bottom of the door as it closes. If the door doesn't reverse readily, the force is excessive and needs adjusting. The owner's manual will explain how to adjust the force sensitivity.

To avoid entrapment, perform the 1-inch reversing test after any repairs or adjustments are made to the garage door or opener. Simply place a 2-x-4-inch block of wood flat on the floor in the door's path before activating the door. If the door fails to stop immediately and reverse when it strikes the wood, disconnect the opener and use the door manually until the system can be repaired or replaced.

Since April 1982, federal law has required that a closing garage door that's operated by an automatic opener must reverse off of a 2-inch block. Even with the safety improvements resulting from this legislation, injuries continue to occur, and safety is still an issue. Consequently, a second law enacted in 1993 requires that a garage-door opener must be equipped with a monitored non-contact safety reversing device or safety edge that stops and reverses a closing garage door. An example of such a safety device is an electronic beam sensor that's installed at either side of the door opening, which, when broken, causes the door to stop and reverse itself.

A second safety feature is a pressure-sensitive electronic rubber strip that attaches to the bottom of the door where it makes contact with the floor. As with the beam sensor, when engaged, this safety edge causes the door to stop and reverse itself, avoiding injury or damage to property.

Here are some of the most common garage door opener problems and their solutions:

- If the opener raises but won't close the door, the safety beam sensor may be faulty, misaligned, or unplugged.

- An opener that operates by remote control but not by the wall switch is a sign of a short in the wiring or a loose connection at the switch.

- A remote control that doesn't work may be something as simple as a weak or dead transmitter battery, an antenna wire on the opener that isn't properly exposed, or a dead transmitter.

- If the opener is operating but the door doesn't open, the problem may be due to a worn gear or chain-drive sprocket, a broken chain, or the door disengaging from the operator.

- A faulty transmitter, a short in the wall switch, a faulty circuit board, or a stray signal (which is very rare) can cause an opener to operate by itself.

- If the remote control only operates the door when it's located 25 feet or less from the opener, the battery in the remote is weak or the signal is poor.

- A door that reverses while closing or that doesn't completely open or close is usually obstructed or binding. This condition can also be caused when the open limit or sensitivity is set wrong.

- A straining opener usually occurs when safety reversing is activated or the close limit is set improperly.

Maintaining Electrical Safety

Leave most electrical work to a qualified electrician. A professional electrician gives you the power you need to keep from blowing a fuse of your own. It's time to call an electrician when you see any of the following signs:

- Habitually flickering lights
- A breaker that repeatedly pops
- A fuse that repeatedly burns out

Any of these signs can mean a loose connection or a circuit that's overloaded, which can cause a house fire.

Testing Ground Fault Circuit Interrupters

Book I

Planning
Your Home
Improve-
ment
Projects

The *Ground Fault Circuit Interrupter* (GFCI) was developed to help keep people from getting shocked. The easiest way to think of a GFCI is to remember that a normal circuit breaker protects property, while a GFCI protects people.

When a short or ground fault occurs, the GFCI detects it. Any variation indicates that some of the current is going where it's not supposed to go and is creating a shock hazard. When this occurs, the GFCI trips in one-fortieth of a second — a short enough period that most healthy people aren't injured.

GFCIs should be installed at all receptacles within 4 feet of a sink, at all exterior and garage receptacles, and at all electric fixtures over showers and tubs.

All GFCI receptacles have test buttons. Test each GFCI receptacle in your home at least once a month. If the test doesn't trip the breaker, replace the GFCI immediately.

Chapter 4

Working with (and within) a Budget

In This Chapter

▶ Working the numbers — sizing up the project and getting prices

▶ Financing the project

▶ Keeping yourself from overspending

*E*very home improvement project requires a budget. Whether you're painting a bedroom or gutting and remodeling a kitchen, you need to look at your current finances and make sure that you have enough money (or a way to get enough money) to pay for everything. Home improvement budgets can range from a few hundred dollars to tens of thousands, depending on the size and scope of the project. This chapter shows you how to establish a realistic budget that gives you a good shot at getting everything you want.

Establishing the Scope of the Project

Where do you begin? First, you need to decide what you don't like in the area(s) you plan to remodel. What doesn't meet your family's needs and lifestyle? What additional things do you need to make the area more livable? What have you seen in other homes (family's, friends', neighbors', and so on) that works for them and may work for you, too? Answering these questions gives you insight into what you want and need and helps get your creative juices flowing. Use Table 4-1 to jot down your ideas.

Table 4-1	Determining What You Like and Don't Like
What Works in the Room I Plan to Remodel	**What Needs to Be Changed in the Room**

Don't forget to list the existing things in your home that do work and things you want to retain in the remodeled area(s). In most cases, you don't need to totally gut the area. Yes, you may make major changes, but you probably don't need to tear everything back to the wall studs.

After you make your lists, prioritize the items from most to least important, which will help you in the decision-making process. You may not get everything you *want,* but make sure to include everything you *need.*

Looking at Things Room by Room

Remodeling projects take on many forms, depending on which room is being made over. The following list looks at the rooms in a typical house, one by one, and shows you what you need to cover when assessing the situation for a remodel.

- **Living room:** Call it a living room, a great room, or the room where you do your formal entertaining — it's an important part of your home. You need to analyze a couple of critical things within its area for a remodel:

  - Does the existing floor plan work? The original designer or architect had a specific layout in mind when designing the room, especially regarding traffic flow. You need to decide whether it works for you.

  - Is enough light getting into the room? Do the existing windows do the job when it comes to size, shape, and location? Visit today's model homes and you'll see all types of window shapes used not only to allow more light into the space but also to enhance the look of the room. Size is another area in which windows have improved. Rooms with huge, multiple-window walls allow in ample light. And more light makes a space seem larger and more inviting.

Book I

Planning
Your Home
Improve-
ment
Projects

✔ **Dining room:** People do a lot of entertaining in this area, like a living room. It needs to work both size-wise and layout-wise, or you won't want to use it. Most people remodel their dining rooms to increase space. Put in a dining table, eight to ten chairs, a china cabinet, and maybe a corner hutch, and you may not have enough room for your guests to sit down! Well, that may be a little extreme, but the room can feel mighty cramped and confined. For most folks, remodeling a dining room involves taking out a wall from an adjoining room or bumping out an area on the exterior wall to add floor space. Either way, this remodel is a major project and can cost you a substantial amount of money.

✔ **Family room:** Real life happens for most families in this room. It's where we watch TV, play video games, and work (or play) at the computer. It's also where we bring friends for a night of relaxing, playing games, or engaging in good conversation. An open floor plan, appropriate lighting, and maybe a fireplace make this room the most comfortable room in the house.

The number-one addition for most family rooms is the installation of a fireplace. Whether it's a fuel-efficient gas-fueled unit or one that burns real wood (still my favorite!), a fireplace brings warmth and coziness to a room like little else can.

✔ **Kitchen:** The kitchen is the number-one remodeled room in the house. It's also the one that gives you the best return on your remodeling dollar. You need to address cabinets, sinks, appliances, lighting, flooring, and decorating (paint and wallpaper) in a kitchen remodel. If you're replacing cabinets and flooring, be ready to spend thousands. After all, the cabinets are the most visible items in your kitchen, so you want them to look as nice as you can afford. The floor also needs special attention because it's likely the most used and abused floor in the house. Everything from daily dirt and grime to cooking residue and dropped dishes puts a kitchen floor through its paces.

Beyond the obvious visual items, you need to make sure that the layout works. If, for example, you have a small kitchen but are a multicook family, you may want to find a way to enlarge the kitchen space. This often means knocking out an adjacent wall or bumping out an area, as for a dining room. It also can be as easy as rearranging the kitchen's layout. A qualified kitchen designer can help you analyze your existing kitchen's layout, assess your wants for the new space, and create a new layout that gives you what you need.

✔ **Bathroom:** Most folks want a sink, toilet, and tub or shower to make a bathroom serviceable. But who wants only serviceable? Bigger is more comfortable, especially when two people are trying to get ready for work or a night on the town at the same time. A bathroom, like a kitchen, often necessitates a new floor plan to make things work better. Installing a whirlpool tub, repositioning a conventional tub, adding or enlarging a shower, repositioning the toilet, and even adding a second (or third) sink are possible remodeling steps. Yes, they involve a lot of work and planning, and a professional carpenter and plumber should probably handle them. However, making these moves will make your mornings less cramped and just may get your days off to a better start.

✔ **Bedrooms:** Most people remodel bedrooms to enlarge the space. Homeowners often take two small bedrooms and create one larger space by removing a wall. In some jobs, the homeowners add or enlarge closet space. Both remodeling projects are considered very doable but usually require at least some good, hard consulting with a building or design professional.

✔ **Basement:** For some homeowners, remodeling the basement isn't an option; they live in slab homes or in regions where basements aren't available. But if you're lucky enough to have a basement, consider finishing the space. It's a great place for a second family room, especially one that serves as a playroom for the kids, or a home office. Don't overlook an existing "finished" basement, either. What was good-looking and trendy 20 years ago doesn't cut it for most folks today. By making a few updates, you can make your basement part of your livable space with the right wall and ceiling finishes and flooring.

✔ **Porches and decks:** Don't forget about outdoor spaces when considering a remodel. Screened porches, four-season porches, and large decks are areas that increase a home's usable living space — not to mention increase its value. You can usually do these additions easily, structurally, because you add them to the outside of the house. A remodel requires a space for the door, but beyond that, most of the work occurs on the outside.

After you've taken a hard look at what you want to remodel, list all the materials and equipment you're likely to need. Table 4-2 provides a handy place for you to do so. You can't know everything you're going to need, and you'll probably forget a few things, but make as complete a list as possible so that you can proceed to the next step — looking at what the stuff's going to cost!

Table 4-2	Listing the Materials You Need
Room or Project	*Materials*

Getting Estimates and Prices

If your project involves major (or even minor) structural changes to your house, you need to involve an architect, a contractor, and possibly even an engineer. Any structural change can affect the integrity of your house, and it must meet local building codes to ensure that the house remains structurally safe to inhabit. You also need to engage inspectors from your city's various building departments — construction (building), plumbing, and electrical.

Choosing an architect or designer

If your project involves complex or detailed drawings and plans, don't plan on having two or three examples to compare. Architects and most design and construction people don't create elaborate plans without being compensated. It's not like getting a lumber or materials price bid from a couple of different retail stores. You need to select a single designer or architect to work with, so here's where you do your homework ahead of time.

Even though you won't get several drawings or bids to compare, you should meet with at least two designers or architects, and for two very good reasons:

- ✔ You need to see whether they can give you a rough plan that meets your wants and needs. If they can't understand what you're looking for, why would you hire them?

- ✔ You need to determine whether your personalities are compatible. This factor is critical to a successful remodel. You must be able to get along with the designer so that both of you can listen to and discuss suggestions and changes without becoming agitated. Homeowners too often fail to thoroughly feel out designers and architects before hiring them. Eventually, they end up having to make a switch halfway through the project. In all instances, the change in personnel costs not only time but also big money.

Pricing materials

A visit to a local lumberyard or home center is a great way to begin the step of pricing materials. Don't be afraid to visit a couple of different stores. Competition is fierce, and you may be surprised by what a particular retailer or supplier can do for you, especially if the store believes that it can get your entire order.

A thorough materials list is invaluable here. Providing the store with a complete list enables them to do a *take-off* (an estimate of materials needed and their total costs). Give the list that you created in the preceding section to each retailer and see which one gives you the best prices. Just make sure that you give out the same list each time so that you're comparing apples to apples.

Don't be afraid to ask one store to match a competitor's price. Most retailers are willing to drop a few dollars (sometimes just pennies per item!) to get your business.

Try to work with one person at each store. You don't want to explain your project to half a dozen people in the same store. Dealing with one person also helps you resolve any problems that may arise — for example, if a problem with your order pops up or if the materials don't arrive on time.

After you have a couple of estimates in hand, do your homework. Don't pick a product or material simply because it has the lowest price. Make sure that the prices are for the same product or for products of equal quality — the old apples-to-apples comparison. Check the brand, model, size, and so on to confirm that the products are comparable. If you're not sure about the differences between two brands, ask! If you get evasive or hesitant answers, ask to speak to someone who can give you the information you want.

If you're not familiar with a specific type or brand of product, ask to see it. Have your salesperson explain its various features. Listen to how the salesperson talks about the product, too. If he's not behind it 100 percent, consider a different brand or model for equipment and a different supplier for building materials. Don't be afraid to go with your gut. If the salesperson doesn't seem comfortable selling you the product, consider a different one or ask to speak with someone else. Any good salesperson is unafraid to ask an associate for product information if he doesn't know it well.

Another good source of product information is the Internet. Most manufacturers have Web sites to provide consumers with product information and evaluations, even if only their own evaluation. Also consider checking consumer advocacy magazines like *Consumer Reports* to see whether they've tested the type(s) of products you're looking at. Their reports are very fair at evaluating and rating all types of products, especially home products, such as appliances.

Many remodeling projects involve opening, moving, or even removing an entire wall or part of a wall. If plumbing is part of the project, you may need to move drain lines. Either of these scenarios is considered a complicated remodeling project and, for most people, means hiring professional help, so remember to factor in labor costs. A good way to get an estimate is, once again, to consult your local home center. Most home stores offer installation as an option with the products they sell, so you should be able to get the price of the product with and without installation and then do the simple math. This method is not 100 percent precise, but it gives you a good ballpark figure to work with.

You have value: Estimating what your time is worth

One area that too many people overlook is their own time. Your time is valuable not only to you but also to your family and friends, so it's critical that you figure out the best way to use your available time on a remodeling project. If the project's going to tie you up every weekend during the summer (or even through a winter), but you could hire a professional to complete the job in, say, a couple of weeks, doing it yourself may not be worth it. You need to weigh the cost of hiring a professional versus what your time is worth to you. Remember, professionals do remodeling jobs for a living and get things done right and as quickly as possible. That's how they make money. You, on the other hand, may have other things you would rather (or need to) do, so hiring a pro may make better sense.

If you do decide to handle some or all of the labor yourself, now's a good time to ask for help or to have a favor returned. Keep in mind that not all helpers have the experience to do a really good job, so if you hire beginners, you'll need to keep an eye on their work.

Making adjustments until everything fits

Establishing a workable budget usually means compromising on a few things. Here are a few ways to make your budget numbers add up to what you can afford to spend:

- ✔ When pricing new products — for example, a whirlpool tub, a stove, or a refrigerator — consider getting one that has only the features you need and no extra bells and whistles. It's sort of like buying a new car: The top-of-the-line model may be your dream machine, but the model a notch or two below probably does what you need it to do, and it's still nice.

- ✔ If you're remodeling a bathroom or kitchen, consider leaving the drain lines where they are, especially if your budget is tight. Moving drain lines is time-consuming, which means a lot of money in labor costs (it's usually best to leave this task to a professional plumber).

✔ Do as much of the work as possible yourself. If you're replacing kitchen cabinets, for example, why not tear out the old ones yourself? Most homeowners can do this part of the project; plus, it's a great way to relieve some pent-up frustration.

✔ If you're set on using some expensive materials, plan on paying a professional to do the installation rather than starting the project yourself and calling someone in midstream. In addition to the fact that you'll have to pay top dollar because you need help immediately, you may also have to pay to have someone correct your mistakes.

✔ Don't forget to figure in your time constraints. If the project is going to take longer than you can allow for your labor, budget for someone to do the work that you know you won't have time to do.

Allowing for fun (and your mental health!)

You alone can't wrap up many remodeling projects in a weekend or two. Even if you bring in the pros, you can expect your home and lifestyle to be disturbed for at least a short while. To avoid total chaos and keep family members acting civil to one another, allow room in your remodeling budget for eating out and maybe even sleeping away from the house.

Unless your remodeling project is off in some remote area of the house, preparing meals and finding a suitable place to enjoy them probably becomes a challenge, to say the least — especially if you're remodeling a kitchen. Meals can throw a budget way out of whack. Why? It's pretty simple, really. A family of four can easily spend $20 to $30 on an evening meal — and that's if you go the fast-food route. Go to a sit-down restaurant and you likely spend $15 to $20 per person. If you factor in breakfast and lunch, the family spends at least $100 a day to keep your strength up. So budget accordingly.

You may see this as a good time to take your family or friends up on a favor when they ask what they can do to help. Inviting your family over for dinner or bringing in an already-prepared meal is a huge help, so feel free to ask. Remember, feeding the troops is just as important as swinging a hammer!

If your project is going to last for a substantial length of time, plan a weekend away somewhere near the middle of the project's timeline. Go to a hotel for a couple of nights and relax. Take in a movie, see a play, go to a concert — just do something other than remodeling! This short break may be the best gift you give yourself during the project. Yes, you'll spend some money, but this hiatus will bring you home rested and energized, ready to get back at it and get your project completed.

If you do build in a mid-project retreat, try to schedule it around a part of the project that involves fumes or odors — for example, if you're having floors refinished or walls painted.

Considering Financing Options

After you determine how much money you want and can afford to spend, you need to find the funds. Finding the money to pay for a remodeling project may be the most important step in the project. After all, getting good prices on materials and fair estimates on labor doesn't do you any good if you can't pay for them.

You have several financing methods to choose from, depending on the scope of the project. What makes one better than the others? This section looks at the options that work for most folks and should work for you, too.

You shouldn't use the following information as financial or investment advice. I'm providing it as a starting point to help you find the best way to pay for your remodeling project. As you would with any financial matter, consult your personal banker, financial counselor, or tax advisor.

Don't start a remodeling project before getting your financing in order. Most lenders require that the house be appraised *before* they loan you money, and the house must be in sellable condition when it's appraised. It can't have walls being removed or a bathroom or kitchen being torn out when the appraiser comes to do the job.

Refinancing your home

For a remodeling project that's going to cost thousands or even tens of thousands of dollars, refinancing the home is a popular method of paying for things. Most homeowners have built up considerable equity in their homes. *Equity* is your home's current assessed value minus the total amount of mortgages or loans against its value. *Refinancing* is the process of paying off the existing mortgage(s) based on the current value of the house.

The best thing about refinancing is that the interest on the new loan is tax deductible. And with mortgage rates low (at least at the time of this writing), most homeowners can not only lower their monthly mortgage payment, but quite often put money in their pockets, even after paying for the remodel. Remember, all these figures depend on your home's value minus the outstanding balance on the mortgages and loans against it.

Finding a lender for refinancing isn't difficult, especially in today's competitive lending market. Your bank is a good place to begin your search. Contact your current mortgage holder, too. The lender will be glad to talk to you, and going this route may make things easier because the lender already knows your credit history and is familiar with the property (your home). You can also contact a local real estate office. Real estate agents are in constant touch with mortgage officers who can give you a competitive current interest rate on a home mortgage.

Keep in mind that refinancing your home is almost the same as purchasing it for the first time, so you need all the closing documents from the current loan, employment information, and so on. Most mortgage officers are true professionals and will work with you through this seemingly daunting process.

Getting a home improvement loan

Many homeowners have enough equity in their homes that a home improvement or second mortgage is a viable option. The security for the loan is the assessed value of your home versus the amount you want to borrow. Second mortgage rates are generally a few percentage points higher than current first mortgage rates; however, the interest on most second mortgages is tax deductible. Check with your current mortgage holder about getting a second mortgage through that company, or check with any mortgage officer. Most companies that provide first mortgages offer second mortgages, too. Make sure to consult with a competent mortgage officer or your tax advisor before entering into a second mortgage.

Some lenders may offer a second mortgage that's as high as 125 percent of your home's current value. Although that may seem like an easy way to get all the money you need for your project, I would never recommend borrowing more than the current value of the property. If you do borrow more than your home's value and the value suddenly drops, you could be in big trouble — especially if you find yourself having to sell your home and end up selling it for less (maybe a lot less!) than the amount of the mortgages or loans against it. When this happens, you, the seller, end up writing a check at closing to pay off the balance of the mortgages. I've seen this happen too many times, and it's not a pleasant experience for the seller, the buyer, or the loan closer!

Charging on low- or no-interest credit cards

An option available to some folks is to open new low- or no-interest credit card accounts. Yes, doing so means adding another creditor or two to your credit record, but these cards also enable you to purchase things immediately without having to go to the bank. This option is handy when, for example, you see the tub or stove you want on sale for less than your estimate bid and you decide that it makes sense to purchase it now, even if you don't need the item for several weeks.

Read the fine print that describes the card's rules and regulations. Most of these cards offer very attractive up-front rates but hit you hard if you miss the payment date even once. For example, I've seen a card that offers a 1 percent rate on all new purchases; however, if you make just one payment late (even one day late!), the interest rate soars to around 20 percent — and stays there! Whenever possible, make your payments as soon as you can. In our house, we turn our payments right around on the day the monthly statement arrives. This way, we virtually ensure that we'll never miss a payment due date.

Paying the old-fashioned way: Cash!

Most people don't have thousands of dollars lying around or buried in coffee cans in the backyard. But if you do have enough ready cash available, consider using it to pay for the project. You'll have the satisfaction of paying for the project completely, plus you may get discounts on materials if you don't need to charge things. Remember, the retailer is charged for using credit cards and has to pass on that cost somewhere — and you're that somewhere. Besides, the retailer gets its money immediately and doesn't have to hassle with financing forms and such.

If you do plan to pay cash, consider opening a separate checking account dedicated to the project. A separate account helps you track your spending on the project and keeps your everyday expenses separate.

Watching Every Penny to Avoid Overspending

The number-one problem with remodeling projects is going over budget. Most people don't consciously or intentionally overspend — it just happens. Most homeowners do their best to adhere to the budget they created, but unfortunately, a little overspending here and there adds up to going over budget. This section offers some suggestions to help you keep your spending in check.

Track and review expenses regularly

Getting cost estimates for materials and labor is only part of the financial picture. You need to set up a filing or tracking system so that you can check what you're spending versus what you've budgeted. You can find a number of budgeting and record-keeping computer programs available. If you're computer challenged or don't have a home computer, you can find home record-keeping plans at most bookstores.

No matter what record-keeping method you choose, (and you really do need to choose one!), use it regularly! Update your records as you make purchases instead of saying, "I'll take care of things on a weekly basis." Continued purchasing without recording and reviewing expenses against your budget numbers is a quick and easy way to go over — or completely blow — your budget.

Review your records weekly, even if you didn't spend anything that week. Besides seeing up-to-date numbers, you're more likely to catch mistakes or remember a purchase that may not have made it into the records. Think about tracking your project purchases the same way you keep your checkbook ledger and balance current. If you're like me, you hate finding one, two, or several items that you forgot to enter into the ledger. Boy, can that make your cash balance look bad, fast!

Looking out for sales

Shopping for remodeling materials is no different than shopping for everyday items. In other words, keep your eyes open for sale prices! For example, if you know that you're going to get new countertop appliances and they're on sale now, grab 'em! The same holds true for lumber and other building materials.

If you know you're going to need lumber, plywood, roofing, or other building materials, contact the retailer you plan to use and make sure that you can get those sale prices when it's time to order. You may need to pay for the materials now, but at least you'll get the sale price, even if the materials aren't delivered immediately.

Buying big-ticket items doesn't mean that you can't or won't find them at a good or sale price, so be vigilant about watching for sales.

Haul it yourself

One other area where you usually can save money is delivery. If the stuff isn't too tricky to haul and you have access to the right type of vehicle, consider hauling things home yourself. Just don't try to handle anything more than you can safely haul and then unload. Delivery drivers are usually skilled at maneuvering their vehicles in tight places, as well as unloading things quickly and safely.

If you do need to have things delivered and you're ordering all your materials from one store, see if they can reduce or even waive the delivery charge. If you need multiple deliveries, see if you can get one or two of the deliveries at no charge. If not, at least ask for the store's minimum delivery charge. Don't be afraid to try to wheel and deal — the worst they can say is no!

Book I

Planning Your Home Improvement Projects

Book II
Basic Home Maintenance and Improvement

The 5th Wave   By Rich Tennant

@RICHTENNANT

"You'd be surprised how much a fresh coat of polish and some new laces increase the resale value."

In this book . . .

*E*veryone knows that a bit of caulking or a coat of paint can make a home look better. What many folks don't realize, however, is that beauty isn't only skin deep. Both of these maintenance tasks, like most maintenance tasks, do more than meets the eye. This book helps you see beyond the obvious and shows you what to look for when it comes to keeping your home fit.

Here are the contents of Book II at a glance.

Chapter 1

Making Inside Repairs and Improvements

*I*f the social analysts who say that we're a nation of stay-at-homers are right, some of us had better spend a little time getting our nests in better shape. Who knows if we're really experiencing a cocooning phenomenon? Who cares? All we know is that these cozy little spaces that we call our homes have plenty of room for improvement. This chapter includes our best advice on how to fix up your corner of the cosmos.

Working on Walls

Practically speaking, the walls in your home provide barriers, make compartments of space, and create a floor plan that directs the flow of traffic. On an aesthetic level, walls deliver a palette of color and pattern that creates a mood and provides a backdrop for furniture, artwork, and such. And, of course, they also support the ceiling and roof. But just like every other part of a house, walls are susceptible to damage and the ravages of time. This section includes all you need to know to repair and decorate the walls that keep the roof over your head.

Filling cracks

In wallboard construction, two types of cracks occur in walls or ceilings: hairline and structural cracks. Faulty workmanship, defective material, or head banging cause hairline cracks. Movement in the structure or framing of the building causes structural cracks. The framing movement is the result of shrinking and swelling of the wooden structural members, such as studs or joists. This movement occurs seasonally, when changes in the temperature and humidity cause fluctuations in the moisture content of the framing lumber. Cracks filled with spackle or other brittle patching compound recur with these movements.

The following list tells you what you need to repair a crack:

- ✔ Hammer
- ✔ Screw gun
- ✔ 1-inch wallboard screws and/or 1¼-inch wallboard nails
- ✔ 6-inch-wide taping knife
- ✔ 10- or 12-inch-wide taping knife or plastering trowel
- ✔ Plastic wallboard mud pan to hold the taping compound
- ✔ Premixed wallboard compound and fiber (or paper) wallboard tape
- ✔ Fine sandpaper

Cracks at the joint of corners may be due to a buildup of taping compound or paint. These hairline cracks are in the excessively thick material; they don't extend through the reinforcing tape itself. To repair these surface cracks, fold a piece of sandpaper over the end of a 6-inch taping knife and carefully sand away the excess material. By folding the sandpaper over the knife blade, you can keep the sanded surface smooth and flat; if you sand a soft, flat surface like drywall with your fingers backing the sandpaper, you may leave an uneven surface. Do not sand through the wallboard tape. After removing the excess material, use a small paintbrush to touch up the corner. Avoid a buildup of paint in the joint; accumulated paint is likely to crack in the future.

Follow these steps, shown in Figure 1-1, to repair a deeper crack with wallboard tape:

1. **Clean out the interior of the crack so that no loose material is present.**

2. **Apply a light coating of wallboard compound to the crack.**

   Premixed wallboard compound contains about 50 percent water by volume, so it shrinks as it dries. For this reason, several applications are needed to build up a surface and overcome shrinkage.

3. **Embed the paper tape in the wallboard compound and scrape a 6-inch knife along the joint to remove excess wallboard compound.**

   Don't leave wrinkles in the tape: If the crack isn't straight, cut the tape where the crack zigzags and apply the tape so that it's centered over the crack.

4. **Apply a thin coat of wallboard compound over the wallboard tape and smooth it with a wide taping knife to minimize sanding.**

5. **Let the patch dry completely.**

6. **When the wallboard tape and first coat are dry, use a 10- or 12-inch taping knife or trowel to apply a second, smoothing coat.**

   This application is intended to smooth and conceal the tape. Don't pile wallboard compound in a thick coat over the tape; you're not decorating a cake.

7. **Let this application dry completely and repeat with a third coat.**

8. **Use a sanding block to smooth the repaired area.**

   TIP

   To avoid creating sanding dust, use a damp sponge or a special spongy wallboard sander to smooth repair areas. Sponge sanders work best if used after the wallboard compound has hardened but isn't completely dry. Remember that smoothing the wallboard compound with a trowel or knife during the repair process is much easier than sanding the compound after it dries rock-hard.

9. **Apply a coat of wallboard primer and let it dry.**

   The wallboard's now ready for decorating.

Book II

Basic Home Maintenance and Improvement

Figure 1-1:
Apply a light coat of wallboard compound over the crack and then smooth tape into place with a wide knife (left). When the first coat is dry, apply a thin second coat (right).

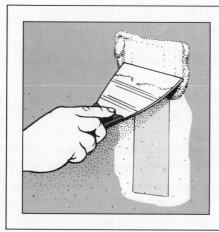

Repairing plaster cracks

The advice in this section for repairing cracks is intended for wallboard construction, but you can follow generally the same patch techniques for plaster cracks.

When patching plaster with wallboard tape, you don't have to cut a V-shape into the crack to retain patching plaster, nor do you need to clean out the inside of the crack. Use a 6-inch taping knife to clean away any broken plaster that's protruding out of the crack and then coat and tape as described for filling cracks in wallboard.

Repairing nail pops

Wallboard nails often work themselves loose from the wall framing and appear as small crescent-shaped cracks in the wall. This curious phenomenon, called *nail pop,* usually happens during the first year of a building's life, while the house framing is settling or drying out.

Nailing wallboard became outmoded the day that wallboard screws and screw-guns were invented. Fastening wallboard takes fewer screws than nails, and fewer fasteners mean fewer pops. Also, 1-inch-long wallboard screws provide the same holding power as 1¼-inch wallboard nails, but with less penetration of the wood framing. Less wood penetration equals less pop.

When you see a popped nailhead or a small crescent-shaped crack, press with the flat of your hand against the wall and notice how the framing has shrunk away from the wallboard. Shrinkage in framing lumber often causes nail pops. As lumber dries out, it shrinks away from the wallboard, leaving the nailheads or screwheads protruding from the wall.

Follow these steps, illustrated in Figure 1-2, to repair a nail pop:

1. **Drive new drywall screws a few inches above and below the popped fastener.**

   The wallboard pulls tight against the framing as you drive the screws into it. The screwhead should dimple, but not penetrate, the paper facing.

2. **Use a hammer and a nail set or large nail to drive the old fastener completely through the drywall and tight against the wall stud.**

3. **With a 6-inch taping knife, apply a coat of premixed taping compound over the dimpled heads of the old and the new fasteners.**

   Don't pile compound above the surface of the wall; smooth it so that it's flat on the surface.

4. When the compound is dry, sand it with a fine sandpaper, feathering it to blend in with the surface of the wall.

5. Apply a light second coat of compound in the same way and then sand it smooth to match the surface of the wall.

Figure 1-2:
Drive new drywall screws above and below a popped nail to pull the drywall back to the wall stud (left). Before you patch the nail pop, drive the loose nail through the wallboard.

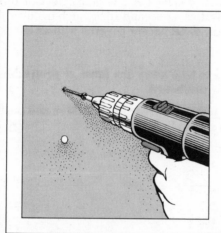

When you're patching popped nails, shine a strong light across the wall. The beam highlights any defects and reveals even the slightest nail pops. Set a floor lamp about a foot from the wall and use a 100-watt bulb with the lampshade removed. When subjected to strong side lighting, defects pop out like stars on a dark night.

Patching holes

Nail pops occur all by themselves. A hole in a wall is a whole other matter. You often find holes behind a swinging door, with a nice imprint of the doorknob, or where your dear child ran his tricycle into the wall. Whatever the cause, it's a simple fact of nature: Holes happen.

The challenge of patching holes in wallboard is bridging the gap of a small hole or anchoring a new piece of wallboard in a large hole. In times past, the only way to make those kinds of repairs was to cut away the damaged area to reveal the studs on either side and then nail the new patch into place on the studs. For years, people used the old cardboard-and-string trick (tying a string to a piece of cardboard and sticking it into the hole so that they could use the cardboard as a base for the patching compound), but that's ancient history. Try some of these new ways for dealing with this age-old problem.

A bridge for small gaps

If the wallboard hole is less than 4 inches in diameter, hang a picture over it. Not good enough? Oh, okay. Use a peel-and-stick patch to cover the hole. These patches consist of a stiff metal backer covered with an adhesive mesh. Here's what to do:

1. **Use a sharp utility knife to trim away any loose or protruding paper facing or loose pieces of wallboard.**

2. **Peel away the backing paper covering the adhesive and position the patch over the hole, as shown in Figure 1-3.**

   Make sure that the patch is smooth.

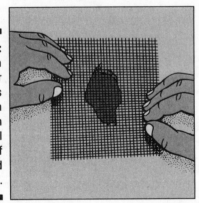

Figure 1-3:
Smooth a patch over small holes and then cover it with several coats of wallboard compound.

3. **Use a 6-inch taping knife to press the adhesive edges into place.**

4. **Apply two thin coats of wallboard compound, letting the compound dry between applications.**

5. **When the second coat is dry, sand the patch smooth so that it blends in with the surface of the wall.**

Wallboard clips for large holes

The key to repairing a large hole is to make a clean cutout of the patch area so that you can insert a same-size piece of wallboard into the hole. You then screw wallboard clips into the surface of the surrounding wall to hold the repair piece in place. After you screw in the clips, break the tabs off of the clips and apply wallboard compound as you would for other repairs.

Follow these steps, illustrated in Figure 1-4, to install wallboard repair clips:

1. **From a piece of scrap drywall, cut a patch that completely covers the hole in the wall.**

   Save yourself time and trouble — make the patch a square or rectangle, even though the hole may be a different shape.

2. **Place the patch over the hole and trace around it with a pencil.**

3. **Use a straightedge to guide your knife as you cut the wallboard along these layout lines.**

   If the patch is large, you can make the project go much faster by using a drywall saw, as shown in Figure 1-4, to cut the wall. Just be careful to avoid wiring and pipes that may be hidden behind the walls.

4. **With the sharp utility knife, cut away any protruding paper facing or crumbled gypsum core from the perimeter of the patch area.**

5. **Install wallboard clips on the sides of the hole and secure them on the edges of the damaged wall by using the screws supplied with the clips.**

   Space the clips no farther than 12 inches apart.

6. **Insert the wallboard patch into the hole and drive screws through the wallboard patch into each wallboard repair clip.**

7. **Snap off the temporary tabs from the repair clips.**

8. **Apply wallboard tape and wallboard compound to all four sides of the patch.**

9. **When the tape and first coat are dry, apply a second, smoothing coat.**

   This application is intended to smooth and conceal the tape. Don't pile taping compound in a thick coat over the tape. Otherwise, the repair will be as obvious as the hole was.

10. **Use a sanding block to smooth the repair area so that it blends with the surface of the surrounding wall.**

11. **Apply a coat of wallboard primer and let it dry.**

Book II

Basic Home Maintenance and Improvement

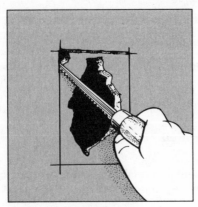

A. Using the replacement patch as a template, cut away the damaged drywall. (Step 3)

B. Push the wallboard clips over the edge of the sound wallboard and secure each clip with a wallboard screw. (Step 5)

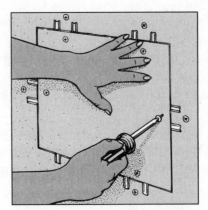

C. Place the wallboard patch in position and secure it by driving a wallboard screw into the wallboard clips. (Step 6)

Figure 1-4:
Repairing a large hole in a wall is easy with the help of wallboard clips.

Repairing sagging plaster on walls and ceilings

Older houses may have plaster walls and ceilings with wood lath for a base. The wood lath was installed with gaps, called *keys*, between each piece of lath. The plaster was forced between spaced lath, and this keying action held the plaster in place.

As plaster ages, these keys may break away from the lath, and the plaster coating can come loose and sag away from the lath. Sagging is usually visible to the eye. If you have sags in a plaster ceiling, press upward on the area with the flat of your hand. If the plaster feels spongy or gives under your hand pressure, it's a sign that the key strength has been lost. If it's not repaired, the plaster ceiling can collapse.

Whether you patch or replace the sagging plaster depends on the extent of the damage:

✔ If the sagging is severe, meaning that it's hanging an inch or more away from the lath base, or if it covers a large portion of the ceiling, your best bet is to remove the old plaster and replaster the ceiling, or cover it with wallboard. Not an easy do-it-yourself project.

✔ If the sagging is slight, or covers a small area, you can reattach the plaster to the wood lath by using long drywall screws fitted with plaster washers. A plaster washer is a thin metal disk that increases the size of the head of a drywall screw so that it doesn't pull through the plaster. You thread the drywall screw through a plaster washer and then drive it through the plaster and into the ceiling joists, wall studs, or wood lath. The screw and washer pull the loose plaster tight against the framing, restoring the ceiling. By surrounding the area with plaster washers, as shown in Figure 1-5, you can stabilize the plaster so that it doesn't sag any further.

You may find plaster washers at a hardware store in a neighborhood with very old houses. The only source we know of is Charles Street Supply Company in Boston. You can order through its toll-free phone number (800-382-4360) or online at or online at www.charlesstsupply.com.

To reattach the sagging plaster to the lath, drive the washer with a power screwdriver or drill so that it penetrates the wood lath, wall studs, or ceiling joists. To avoid cracking the plaster and creating an even bigger repair job, don't pull the plaster tight to the lath in a single motion. Instead, start a few washers around or across the sagged area and drive them snug against the plaster face. Then tighten each of them slowly, moving from one to another, so that the plaster gradually pulls tight against the lath.

To repair large sags, follow these steps:

1. **Remove the loose plaster.**

2. **Install drywall screws and plaster washers around the perimeter of the loose area, as shown in Figure 1-5.**

Book II

Basic Home Maintenance and Improvement

Figure 1-5:
Install
plaster
washers
around the
edge of the
damaged
area to pull
the plaster
tight against
the lath.

3. **Install a drywall patch over the exposed wood lath.**

   See the preceding section for instructions on patching wallboard.

4. **Apply primer and a coat of paint by following the directions earlier in this chapter in the section titled "Filling cracks."**

   Wallboard compound absorbs a lot of paint, so plan to give the patched area several coats of paint to make it blend in with the rest of the wall.

Decking the walls

When it comes to hanging something on a wall, you have to consider both the surface of the wall and the size and weight of the object that you're hanging. For example, a lightweight framed poster doesn't require the holding power that a heavy architectural plaque or a nifty moosehead does. And fastening a hanger into hollow wallboard is a whole different process from mounting something to a brick wall.

When you're shopping for hanger hardware, know the following:

   ✔ **The approximate weight of the object:** Put it on the bathroom scale.

   ✔ **The dimensions of the object:** Get out a measuring tape.

   ✔ **The type of wall surface:** Is it wallboard, plaster, or brick?

As you look at various types of hanger hardware, read the package instructions. They usually spell out weight and dimension requirements. Hanging very large or heavy pictures always requires anchoring the picture hanger into wood framing, and you may need two or more hangers for support.

Hollow walls

Most walls have cavities created by the wall studs. Builders use these cavities to run electrical and plumbing lines through the house. Building codes generally require that these lines be protected so that you can nail and drill into most walls and be pretty sure that you won't damage one of these lines.

But remember: Whenever you nail or drill into a wall, be careful. If, while drilling, you encounter unexpected resistance, STOP. Drywall, plaster, and wooden studs are rather soft compared to steel or copper pipes. Don't push harder on the drill; instead, back off and investigate the source of the resistance. You can't even begin to imagine the amount of damage you can cause if you drill into a copper water pipe.

Use the following items to hang lightweight objects on hollow walls:

- Small finishing nails and brads driven at a 45-degree angle into drywall or plaster
- Hook-type hangers that are held in place with a nail
- Adhesive hangers

Book II

Basic Home Maintenance and Improvement

Find the stud

Where possible, anchor hardware into the wall studs, not the space between them. Stud spacing is typically 16-inches, center-to-center. To find a stud, you can go the high-tech route and use an *electronic stud finder* — a gadget that locates studs in the wall by measuring the density of various points. When you pass the stud finder over a wall stud, a light signals the location.

For a low-tech approach, check at wall receptacles, removing the cover plate if necessary.

There's always a stud on one side or the other. Or remove the shade from a lamp and set the lamp with bare bulb about a foot away from the wall to highlight fastener locations. Or get down on your hands and knees and look at where the baseboard molding has nailheads showing. Wherever you see a nailhead, especially if they appear to be 16 inches apart, it's likely that there is a stud behind it.

To hang medium-weight objects, use one of these items (pictured in Figure 1-6):

- *Molly anchors,* or hollow-wall anchors, are combination screws surrounded by casing. As you tighten the screw, the casing around the screw collapses against the wall interior. Predrill a hole and insert and turn the screw to collapse and tighten.

- *Toggle bolts,* another type of hollow-wall anchor, have spring-loaded wings that expand inside the wall. Predrill a hole, remove the winged toggle from the screw, and place the screw through whatever you want to hang. Then replace the toggle and insert the assembly into the wall. Tighten the screw to pull the toggle tight against the inside of the wall.

- Plastic *expansion plugs* fit snugly into predrilled holes in the wallboard. As you drive a screw into the plastic plug, the slotted base of the plug spreads and locks against the perimeter of the hole.

┌Toggle bolt   Molly anchor┐

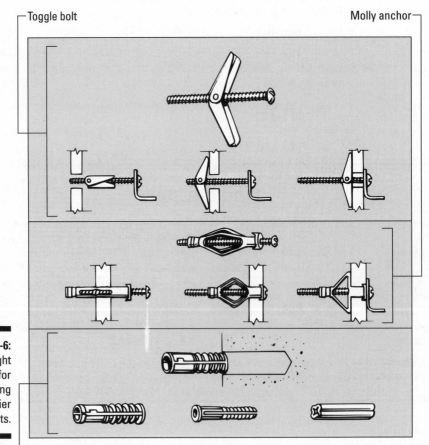

Figure 1-6: The right tools for hanging heavier objects.

└Plastic expansion plug

Brick and masonry surfaces

Penetrating hard surfaces, such as brick and concrete, is more difficult than getting through ordinary wallboard. For this job, you need an electric drill with a masonry bit to predrill a hole.

To hang lightweight items on a brick or masonry surface, follow these steps:

1. **Drill a hole in the masonry to the same depth and diameter as the anchor.**

2. **Tap the plastic plug or anchor into the hole.**

3. **Drive a screw through the fixture and into the plug to expand it and lock it inside the hole.**

To hang medium-weight items on a brick or masonry surface, do the following:

1. **Drill a hole in the masonry the same depth and diameter as the anchor.**

2. **Tap an expansion-type anchor into the hole.**

3. **Drive a screw into the anchor to expand it and lock it inside the hole.**

Book II

Basic Home Maintenance and Improvement

Building Shelves

A simple wall shelf adds form and function to a room. Use it to display a treasured collection or to store cookbooks in the kitchen. A shelving system that uses brackets and uprights to hold the shelves is a bit more costly and time-consuming to install, but it's a project worth tackling. And closet shelving is downright rewarding because it puts you on the road to peace and order, knowing that, when you open your closet door, you're not in danger of getting clobbered by falling objects. Whatever shelving you choose, it's always a treat to have a place for everything and everything in its place.

Putting up a simple wall shelf

A single small wall shelf like the one shown in Figure 1-7 consists of the shelf itself and brackets that are fastened to the wall. The shelf is either secured to the brackets or just rests on top of them. A wide shelf typically has at least two brackets fastened to the wall studs; more brackets are needed for longer shelves. Simple brackets are available at hardware stores or home centers, and a wide variety of decorative brackets are sold in all kinds of stores, catalogs, and just about anywhere household furnishings are available.

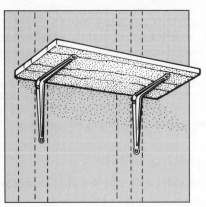

Figure 1-7:
Secure
shelving
brackets to
wall studs to
ensure that
the shelf
can safely
support a
heavy load.

Here's what's involved in installing an out-of-the-box decorative wall shelf with two brackets and one shelf:

1. **Locate a wall stud and mark the location for the first shelf bracket on the wall.**

   Follow the instructions in the "Find the stud" sidebar in this chapter to locate a stud in the wall. Then hold a shelf support bracket over the stud and use it as a template to mark the location of the mounting screws on the wall.

2. **Install the bracket with screws that are long enough to penetrate the wall stud by at least an inch or so.**

3. **Mark the location of the second stud.**

   Wall studs are usually placed 16 inches apart, so measure 16 inches from the bracket you just installed. Place a carpenter's level on the first bracket to extend a level line to the second stud and then hold the second bracket in position. Mark the location for the second set of mounting screws on the wall.

4. **Install the second bracket with screws that are long enough to penetrate the wall stud by at least an inch or so.**

5. **Install the shelf on the support brackets. Use short screws to secure the shelf to the brackets.**

Installing a shelving system

A shelving system is made up of three basic components: shelves, *standards* (long vertical slotted strips fastened to the wall), and brackets that fit into grooves along the length of the standards. Because the shelf sits on top of

these brackets, you can adjust the height of shelving for a variety of configurations, as shown in Figure 1-8.

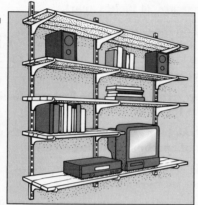

Figure 1-8:
Choose a
shelving
system
that's
flexible
enough
to hold
everything
you want
to store.

Book II

**Basic Home
Mainte-
nance and
Improvement**

Before you invest your hard-earned dollars in a shelving system, consider
these shopping tips:

- Make a preliminary shopping/learning expedition to select a shelving
  system and pick up a planning brochure with the system's standard and
  bracket specifications. Pack a lunch; this trip may take a while.

- Decide how many shelves you want and how you want to arrange them.
  Make a sketch of the wall, noting the location of wall studs so that you
  can plan the design.

- Choose the standard size and shelf depth and style to fit the items you
  plan to store and display, such as deep shelves for large items and narrower ones for smaller things. Plan to space the standards about 32 inches
  apart and allow a maximum overhang of one-sixth of the shelf length.

- If you must fasten the shelf to a hollow wall, choose mounting anchors
  based on their weight-bearing capacity. Don't be embarrassed to ask for
  help!

- Read the directions on the package, noting how many uprights and brackets and what width and length of shelves are included. Most systems have
  brackets for at least two widths of shelving, so make sure that you buy
  the correct sizes. Some systems include the mounting hardware; some
  don't. Don't leave the store without everything you need.

Follow these steps for installing a component shelf system with standards and brackets:

1. **Use a stud finder to locate the studs on the wall; they're usually placed 16 inches apart. (Some are 24 inches apart.)**

   Plan to install each standard on the center of the stud. Make light pencil marks on all the wall studs in the vicinity of the spot where you plan to install the shelving unit. (You may have to adjust the exact location slightly so that the standards are attached to the studs.)

2. **Mark the location for the top screw hole on the first standard and drill a small pilot hole through its top hole.**

3. **Use a carpenter's level to straighten the standard so that it's plumb and then mark the location of another mounting screw.**

   To mark the spot for the next screw, place a pencil on one of the mounting screw holes in the bracket, as shown in Figure 1-9.

4. **Swing the bracket to one side and then drill a pilot hole for the mounting screw.**

5. **Reposition the upright and install the mounting screw with a Phillips-head screwdriver.**

6. **Locate the proper position of the second standard.**

   To position the second standard, place a shelf support bracket in the standard hanging on the wall. Then install another shelf support bracket in the same slot of a second standard. Hold the second standard over the next wall stud and then place a level (alone or on a piece of shelving) on the brackets and move the new standard up or down until the shelf is level, as shown in Figure 1-9.

Figure 1-9:
A carpenter's level can ensure that the first standard is plumb (left) and that subsequent uprights are level with the first one (right).

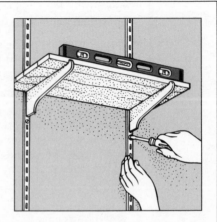

7. **Mark the location on the wall of one of the mounting screws for the second standard and install it as you did the first one.**

8. **Repeat with the remaining standards.**

9. **Install the shelf support brackets into the standards.**

   These brackets usually tap into slots that lock them in place.

10. **Install the shelves.**

Adding a wire shelf system to a closet

Book II

Basic Home Maintenance and Improvement

You can tame closet clutter by installing a closet organizer with ventilated wire shelves. You still have to hang up your clothes, but opening the closet door is far less intimidating when you don't face a potential avalanche. By reorganizing the inside of your closet, you can almost double your closet space, making the chore of sorting through your stuff to install shelving well worth the effort. The installation is the easy part; the real work is cleaning out the closet and realizing that you used to actually fit into some of those clothes.

These systems are sold as individual components to fit any size closet and as closet kits designed for various sizes. For example, a kit for an 8-foot closet includes four shelves, one support pole, a shoe rack, and mounting clips and screws.

Here's what you need to install a wire shelf system:

- ✔ A carpenter's level
- ✔ Screwdrivers
- ✔ Measuring tape and a pencil
- ✔ A hacksaw for cutting the metal shelving to length
- ✔ A free afternoon

Before you can install a closet wire-shelving system in your closet, you have to do the following prep work:

1. **Remove all the stuff inside the closet.**

   Just do it! Think of this as an opportunity to get rid of items that you don't wear or use. Donate the booty to charity or to anybody who can use it; just get rid of it.

2. **Remove the existing shelving and the clothes rod.**

   You may need a pry bar to remove the shelving if it's nailed to the walls; otherwise, it's a matter of unscrewing screws or fasteners or pulling out nails that hold the shelf and pole in place.

3. **Patch any nail holes that remain from the old shelving with a wall-board compound.**

   See the "Patching holes" section earlier in this chapter.

4. **If the walls are dirty and dingy, give them a quick coat of paint.**

   Trust us. The extra effort will pay off every time you open the closet door.

To install the shelving system, follow these steps:

1. **Read through the instructions that came with the shelving a few times.**

2. **Determine the height for the main shelf, hold a carpenter's level at the approximate height, and mark a level line on the wall with a pencil.**

3. **Mark the locations for the wall clips.**

   Make a mark 2½ inches in from either end of the shelf line and ½ inch above the shelf line. Then mark 1-foot intervals along a level line connecting the two marks.

4. **At each mark, drill a hole ¼ inch deep and insert the wall clip, as shown in Figure 1-10.**

5. **Insert a screw into each wall clip and tighten them into the wall.**

6. **Put the end caps on one end of the shelf and measure and cut the shelf to length on the other side.**

7. **Put the other end caps on the cut end.**

8. **Hang the shelf on the wall clips, as shown in Figure 1-10.**

9. **Hold the shelf level with the lip of the shelf toward you and facing down.**

10. **Position the wall brackets on the side walls so that the shelf lip fits into the U and mark the holes.**

11. **Lift up the shelf until it's level (perpendicular to the wall) and drill holes for the anchors.**

12. **Insert the anchors.**

13. **Position the wall bracket, insert the screws, and tighten.**

14. **When both ends are installed, tighten the screws of the wall mounting brackets.**

Figure 1-10: Installing a closet system is easy with special brackets that have a built-in wall anchor. The shelf snaps into the mounting bracket, and a screw threaded into the anchor locks it in place.

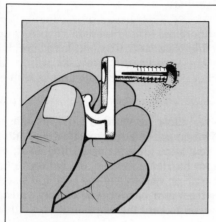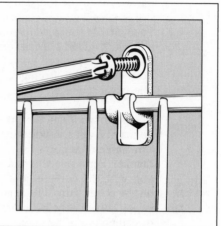

Insulating Your Home

One of the easiest jobs for a do-it-yourselfer is also one of the most valuable: adding attic insulation to cut down on heating bills. Admittedly, there isn't much glamour in crawling around in your attic, and visitors won't even be able to tell that you've done anything. But you'll enjoy the payback every month when your utility bill comes.

Be sure to wear safety goggles, a dust mask, and protective clothing when working with insulation.

Upgrading attic insulation

The longstanding popularity of fiberglass insulation is based on several important features: Fiberglass is inert, vermin resistant, and fireproof, and it has excellent R-value per inch of thickness. (*R-value* is a measurement of the resistance to heat flow. The higher the R-value, the more effective the insulation.)

The problem with fiberglass insulation is that handling the stuff is like petting a porcupine: The glass fibers produce an irritating itch when they contact bare skin. Plus, medical experts suspect that inhaling airborne glass fibers can be hazardous to the lungs. Imagine that!

To eliminate these problems, fiberglass insulation manufacturers developed a product called *polywrapped fiberglass batts*. The batt insulation is encapsulated in a perforated polyethylene covering that prevents airborne fibers and protects the skin from glass fiber contact. The product looks kind of like a fiberglass sausage.

The perforations in the polywrap allow moisture to pass through, so the poly does not form a vapor barrier when applied over existing insulation. This feature makes the polywrapped insulation ideal for upgrading an attic insulation blanket. For areas where a vapor barrier is desired, insulation batts are available with the perforated polywrap on one side of the batt and a solid polyfilm on the other side. When using the vapor-barrier type of poly, you apply the vapor barrier side with the barrier toward the warm-in-winter side of the wall or ceiling.

If your ceilings lack adequate insulation, choose polywrapped batts. You can install polywrapped batts on top of any type of existing insulation. The usual practice is to install the new polywrapped batts at right angles to the existing insulation, as shown in Figure 1-11. You can cut the batts with a sharp razor knife or large scissors.

Figure 1-11:
To add insulation to an attic, place fiberglass batts or rolls without a vapor barrier perpendicular to the floor joists.

Upgrading crawlspace insulation

If your house is built above a crawlspace, heat may be escaping downward through the floors. Information about required insulation performance, expressed in R-values, is available from your local building department. Whatever the R-value recommendations, it's a good idea to install insulation batts that are as thick as the floor joists are wide.

To upgrade crawlspace insulation, choose polywrapped fiberglass batts with a perforated polyfilm on one side and a poly vapor barrier on the other. Install the insulation batts with the poly vapor barrier toward the warm-in-winter side, in other words, facing up in all but the warmest climates.

To install the batts, press them into the cavities between the floor joists, as shown in Figure 1-12, and staple the insulation to the joists. You can also secure batts in place by stapling hardware cloth or chicken wire to the joists. While installing the batts, avoid wrinkles that can let warm air or moisture pass between the batts and the floor joists. Make sure that the vapor retarder is in full contact with the subfloor.

Book II

Basic Home Maintenance and Improvement

Figure 1-12: Install crawlspace insulation between floor joists with the vapor barrier facing up towards the warm area above.

Chapter 2

Windows Don't Have to Be a Pane

In This Chapter

▶ Keeping your windows in good working order

▶ Conserving energy with caulking and weather-stripping

▶ Treating your windows to shades, blinds, and curtains

The windows in a house are designed to bring sunshine and fresh air inside. Unfortunately, in some homes, windows have broken glass panes and rotted wood, or they rattle like a bag of bones and let in cold drafts. This chapter is a crash course in the basics of window maintenance and repair. Read on to discover how to improve or upgrade your windows and even how to decorate them with shades and miniblinds.

Know Your Windows

Not all windows look and work alike. Some slide, crank, or swing open and closed; others, such as picture windows, have no working parts. The window frame, which encloses all the basic parts of the window, may be made of wood, vinyl, or metal. Wooden window frames require painting, but those made of vinyl or aluminum are nearly maintenance free. Because metal conducts cold, wood windows are preferred in climates with cold winters.

The most popular window style is the *double-hung window,* shown in Figure 2-1. Double-hung windows have an upper and a lower *sash* (the inner frame that holds the glass panes in place) that move vertically in separate channels. The sashes are separated by a small piece of wood called a *parting strip.* The upper and lower sashes have *meeting rails* — that is, the top rail of the bottom sash and the bottom rail of the upper sash meet and are slanted and weather stripped to form a tight seal between the rails. A locking mechanism secures the sashes together at the two parting rails to create a tight seal and to minimize air infiltration and heat loss.

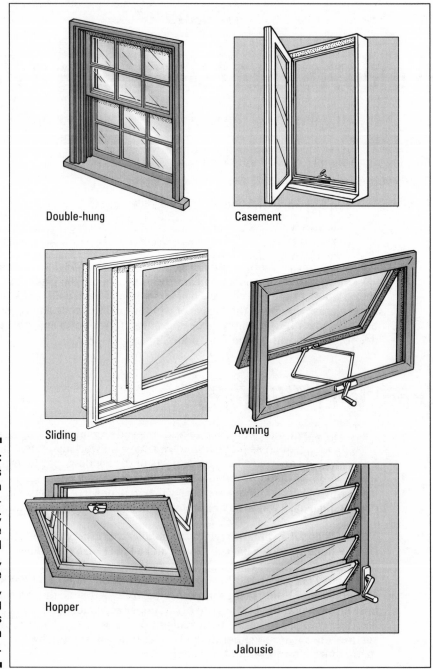

Double-hung

Casement

Sliding

Awning

Hopper

Jalousie

Figure 2-1:
Windows
aren't an
open-and-
shut case;
some slide
up and
down,
others side
to side,
some swing
out, others
open in
slats.

Other common window styles, shown in Figure 2-1, include the following:

- **Casement windows** have hinges on one side of the sash and swing outward when you activate a lever or crank. Because the entire casement sash swings outward, these kinds of windows provide full ventilation and unobstructed views. Casement windows are easy to open, so they're commonly used where humidity or heat can build up, such as above kitchen sinks, in bathrooms, and on walls that connect to porches.

- **Sliding windows** open horizontally and bypass each other in separate tracks mounted on the header jamb and sill.

- **Awning windows** are hinged at the top and swing outward via a crank or lever.

- **Hopper windows** are hinged at the bottom and swing inward.

- **Jalousie windows** are made of a series of horizontal glass slats that are joined so that all the glass slats open or close together when the crank is turned. The drawback to jalousie windows is that the cracks between the slats offer an avenue for air infiltration.

Although they differ in design, basic maintenance is the same for all types of windows. By figuring out how your windows are supposed to work, you can keep them in tiptop shape and detect problems before they become serious.

Book II

Basic Home Maintenance and Improvement

Window Maintenance

At least once a year, put together a maintenance kit and inspect, lubricate, and clean each window. We admit that window duty isn't a particularly pleasant way to spend a weekend, but annual maintenance adds years to the life of your windows. Be sure that your maintenance kit includes the following items:

- A small paintbrush for cleaning dirt and debris from the window channels

- A handheld, battery-powered vacuum for sucking up loose dirt

- A roll of paper towels

- An aerosol can of spray lubricant, such as WD-40, for lubricating channels and locks

- A selection of both Phillips and flat-head screwdrivers for tightening any loose screws

First, open the window and use a hand vacuum or small paintbrush to clean the debris from the windowsill. Then wet a paper towel and wipe down the sill to remove any residual dust.

Inspect the window unit for any loose hardware. Metal window channels or guides are attached to the side frames via small brads or screws. Renail or tighten loose guides. Check the window locks to be sure that screws are tight: If they aren't, retighten them. Lubricate the locks with a shot of spray lubricant.

If window locks are fouled with paint, remove the locks and soak them in paint remover; then clean, polish, lubricate, and replace the hardware. Use paper towels to wipe away any excess lubricant.

Modern double-hung windows don't have ropes and sash weights the way older model windows do. Instead, the sashes travel vertically in metal chan-nels that are positioned on either side of the window. The channel on one side is spring-loaded, and the spring tension holds the window in position. But when you move the window sash to the middle of the frame and then pull sharply to the spring-loaded side, the sashes slip out of the frame easily, ready for repair or cleaning. This easy-access feature has been available on double-hung windows for several decades. To check your windows, press against the metal channel on both sides of the frame. If one side yields to hand pressure, your window sash can be snapped out of the frame. Use graphite or any other dry lubricant to grease the metal window channels in double-hung windows.

Casement or awning windows are operated with a crank or lever. The win-dows open via an arm, which may be a single linkage arm, double sliding arms, or a scissors arm. By opening the windows fully, you can disengage the arm from the track, which permits you to lubricate the arm and track or to free the window sash for easier washing.

If you have casement windows that are hinged on one side and swing out via levers or crank handles, open the windows fully and use spray lubricant to oil the hardware, including the crank or lever, the hinges, and the lock.

With the arm disengaged, you can also service the operator mechanism. Check the owners' manual provided with the windows for instructions on removing the cranking mechanism cover. Of course, owners' manuals, like able-bodied teenagers, have a way of disappearing when you need them. If you can't find the official instructions, look for a couple of screws on the housing cover to which the crank or lever is attached and remove them. Lift off the cover, apply a bit of light grease to the crank gears or opening levers, and then replace the cover.

Unsticking a Stuck Window

If a window is stuck, the problem may be that the window channels need cleaning and lubrication, but the odds are that paint has run into the cracks between the window stops and the sash and is binding the window. Either problem usually yields to a simple solution.

The first rule of unsticking is this: If the window doesn't budge, *don't force it.* You may break the glass and cut yourself or damage the window beyond repair.

First, check to be sure that the window is unlocked and that you're not lifting up on the sill. If the window is unlocked, place a block of wood against the sash frame and, moving the block along the entire length of both stiles, tap the block lightly against the stiles with a hammer. This trick may loosen up the window so that you can open it. Whatever you do, don't pound on the block, or you may crack the glass.

Book II

Basic Home Mainte-nance and Improvement

If your double-hung window still refuses to open, remove the stops along both side stiles of the sash with a small pry bar. You can then remove the window sash. Use fine sandpaper or a paint scraper to clean the edges of the sash and the edges of the stops. To lubricate the sash, rub a block of paraffin or a wax candle stub along the edges of the window sash and the stop.

If the window resists your best open-sesame efforts, check for paint in the crack between the window sash and stops. Insert a serrated tool, called a *Paint Zipper,* into the crack, as shown in Figure 2-2. Using a light sawing motion, move the Paint Zipper in the crack along the entire length of the window sash on both sides. Then use the tool to cut any paint bond between the bottom rail and the sill. Now try again to open the window. In most cases, the window will open. (A pizza cutter has been known to work just as well as a Paint Zipper; don't hesitate to experiment!)

Figure 2-2:
Use a special tool with a serrated blade or a putty knife with a thin, flexible blade to open painted-shut windows.

Replacing Sash Cords

The sash weights in old double-hung windows are intended to provide balance so that, when the window is open to the desired position, it stays there. If the sash cord (or chain) breaks, the window can't stay in place. If you have to prop open your double-hung window with a stick, chances are that the sash cord is broken and the window operates with all the controlled restraint of a guillotine.

To replace the sash cord, follow these steps (illustrated in Figure 2-3):

1. **Use a razor knife to cut the paint line where the stop is attached to the frame.**

   Cutting this paint seal keeps the stop from breaking when you pry it off.

2. **Using a thin pry bar or a stiff putty knife, gently pry out the stop at each nail location.**

3. **At both sides of the frame along the upper sash, use the pry bar or putty knife to remove the parting strip.**

4. **Raise the lower sash so that it clears the sill; then swing out the sash.**

5. **Disconnect the sash cords from the slots at each side of the sash.**

   With the sash removed, you can see the sash weight access panels on either side of the jamb.

6. **Use a screwdriver to remove the retaining screws and then pull off the panel cover.**

7. **Remove the sash weight from its space.**

8. **Use an aerosol lubricant such as WD-40 to lubricate the pulley above each access panel.**

9. **Feed the new sash cord over the pulley and downward until you can see the end of the cord through the hole at the access panel.**

10. **Tie the sash cord to the weight.**

    Pass the end of the cord through the hole in the top of the sash weight and then tie a figure-eight knot in the end of the rope.

11. **Replace the weight in its compartment.**

    Pull the other end of the rope tight so that the sash weight stands up straight in the compartment.

12. **Attach the sash rope to the sash.**

The end of the rope that you have in your hand attaches to the window sash. Most sashes have a groove milled in the side that fits the diameter of the sash rope. At the end of the groove is a recess that holds the knot. Tie a knot in the cord so that the sash weight hangs about 3 inches above the bottom of the compartment when you put the knot into the recess and raise the sash all the way up.

A. Gently loosen the window stop before pulling out the nails. (Step 2)

B. Access the window weights by opening the small door in the base of the jamb. (Step 6)

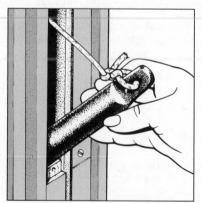

C. Remove the weight from the hollow area behind the window jamb. (Step 7)

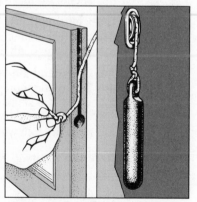

D. To reinstall the sash, tie a knot in the end of the cord and push the knot into the recess in the side of the sash. (Step 12)

Figure 2-3:
Replacing a damaged sash cord in a double-hung window.

Book II

Basic Home Maintenance and Improvement

While you have the window sash removed, replace *both* sash cords, not just the broken one. After you replace the cords, position the window sash back in the frame and renail the window stops.

Modern double-hung windows have metal channels in which the sash sides, or *stiles,* move. These channels are spring-loaded, and one channel has tension screws that can be adjusted to hold the window in any open position. If your double-hung window refuses to stay open at the chosen position, adjust the tension on the channel. Inspect the window channels to find the adjustment screws. To increase the tension on the stiles, turn the screws counterclockwise with a screwdriver. When properly adjusted, windows open easily but remain firmly in place at any open position.

Replacing a Broken Window Pane

Replacing window glass is not a difficult task. Repairing the damage is only slightly more difficult than breaking the glass in the first place. Just gather the appropriate materials and tools and follow the steps for the type of window you're repairing.

You need the following materials to replace a broken pane:

- **Replacement glass:** Ask a salesperson at a hardware store or home center to cut a piece of glass exactly to size. Follow the steps later in this section to make sure that your measurements are accurate.

- **Latex glazing putty:** This material, available by the can in the glass and painting departments, forms an airtight, watertight seal while allowing the pane to expand and contract in changing temperatures.

- **A box of metal glazing points:** Sometimes called *glazier's points,* these tiny T-shaped metal pieces have pointed ends that you force into the frame and two small flaps that hold the pane of glass in place.

You also need the following tools:

- Heat gun (available from rental outlets) to soften the old glazing if it's still intact and as tough as cement

- Flexible putty knife

- 1- or 2-inch stiff steel putty knife

- Flat-head screwdriver

When you work with broken glass, wear safety goggles to protect your eyes and gloves to cover your hands.

Wood-frame window

To replace a broken glass pane in a wood window, first measure the size of the pane. Measure the exact length and width of the grooves in which the pane will fit and then have a new piece of glass cut so that it measures ⅛ inch short of the exact dimensions in both the length and width, leaving a ¹⁄₁₆-inch gap on all four sides between the edges of the pane and the rabbet groove cut into the edge of the wood where the glass pane rests. This gap between the wood sash and glass is necessary because it allows room for the glass to expand when the weather changes.

When you have your tools and supplies ready, follow these steps, illustrated in Figure 2-4:

1. **Remove any remaining glass shards.**

2. **Use a heat gun to soften the old glazing putty.**

   Heat the glazing putty and try to scrape it away with a putty knife; if it doesn't lift off easily, apply more heat and try again. You may find that the putty around really old windows is as hard as concrete. Be patient — the heat will eventually soften all putty. Don't be tempted to chisel out the old putty unless you don't mind wrecking the window and creating even more work for yourself!

   As you remove the old glazing putty, you can see small triangular metal *glazing points,* which hold the glass in position until you apply the glazing putty.

3. **Use a putty knife or the tip of a screwdriver to remove the old glazing points.**

4. **Clean and inspect the rabbet groove to ensure that no glazing putty, glass shards, or glazing points remain.**

   Wear safety goggles as well as gloves; small chips of glass can cause permanent eye damage.

5. **Squeeze out a ¹⁄₁₆-inch bead of putty on the glass side of the rabbet groove between the edge of the glass and the window frame.**

6. **Press the glass down gently at the edges to bed the glass into the putty.**

   Allow the putty bed to spread out and form a moisture seal on the inside of the window between the glass and sash.

Book II

Basic Home Maintenance and Improvement

7. **Position the new pane in the rabbets so that a ¹⁄₁₆-inch gap remains between pane and sash on all four sides.**

8. **Place at least two new glazing points in each section of the window sash surrounding the new glass.**

    Space the points evenly around the perimeter, about 6 inches apart.

A. Wear heavy gloves when removing broken glass from the sash. (Step 1)

B. Hold the glass in place with glazing points. Push the glazing points into place with a putty knife or screwdriver. (Step 9)

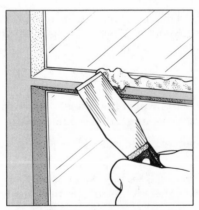

C. Drag the putty knife blade over the glazing putty at a 45 degree angle to smooth the putty. (Step 11)

Figure 2-4:
Replacing
a broken
window
pane.

9. Using the flat side of a putty knife or a screwdriver blade, push one corner of each triangular glazing point into the wood sash.

10. Roll a glob of putty between your bare hands to form a ½-inch-thick rope and then press the length of putty along all four sides of the glass.

11. Holding the putty knife at a 45-degree angle, press and smooth the glazing putty against the glass and sash.

12. Allow the putty to dry and then repaint the putty and repair area.

Don't use masking tape on the glass before painting because you want the paint to form a moisture seal between the glass pane and the sash. Allow the paint to overlap about ⅛ inch onto the glass.

Metal frame window

Some steel or aluminum window frames, such as those that you find in many basements, are welded together in one piece at the factory. The other common type of metal frame windows is storm windows. Glazing putty or some sort of gasket holds the glass in place. Except for some minor points, which we explain, replacing a broken pane of glass in either type of metal frame window is basically the same as for wood windows.

To replace the pane in a one-piece steel window, follow the instructions for replacing glass in a wood window with the exception of glazing points. The glass pane in steel casement windows is held in place with glazing putty and spring clips rather than glazing points. When you remove the broken glass from the metal frame, save these clips so that you can reinstall them later.

On some one-piece aluminum windows, such as metal storm windows, the glass is held in place by a vinyl strip called a *spline*. The spline acts as a seal between the metal and the glass, eliminating the need for glazing putty. Use a screwdriver or putty knife to pry out the spline. Carefully remove any broken pieces of glass from the frame and then replace the pane with new glass. Reverse the process and push the spline back into the frame with a putty knife or screwdriver.

Some metal window frames, including sliding sashes, are held together by screws placed at each corner of the frame. Remove the screws, slide out the broken pane, slide in a new pane, and redrive the corner screws.

Other metal frames are held together by L-brackets placed at the four corners. The faces of these frames are dimpled over the L-brackets. To take these frames apart, you have to remove only one side. To do so, follow these steps:

1. **Drill a hole in the depression at both ends of one side of the frame.**

   Use a bit slightly larger than the diameter of the depression.

2. **Pull the sides of the frame apart and carefully remove any broken glass from the frame.**

3. **Replace the pane, making sure that the new glass is fully seated into the gasket surrounding the glass.**

4. **Push the corners together so that the L-brackets are in place and the joint is tight.**

5. **Use a small nail set or a punch and hammer to dimple the metal back over the L-brackets and lock the frame together.**

Repairing a Rotted Windowsill

Windowsills are sloped outward so that water can run off the sill. Brilliant, huh? Still, if the paint is peeling and the sill is left unprotected, the wood may rot. Although moisture causes this condition, it's called *dry rot.* Go figure.

If you have a windowsill that's rotted, probe the wood with an ice pick or carpenter's awl. Wherever the awl penetrates easily, the wood is rotted. When you hit a point where the wood is difficult to penetrate, you've reached solid wood. If the wood is completely rotted, you'll have to replace the entire sill with a new piece of wood — a job probably best left to a skilled carpenter. If the rot is limited to a small area, you can make repairs by following these steps (illustrated in Figure 2-5):

1. **Using a wood chisel or sharp knife, cut away any soft wood.**

   Remove all the damaged wood down to the rot-free portion.

2. **Fill the damaged area with epoxy or polyester wood filler.**

   Filler bonds to sound wood and is very durable.

3. **Use a putty knife or small broad knife to shape the wood filler so that it matches the contours of the old sill.**

4. **Wait for the filler to set and then sand it smooth.**

   Follow the directions on the container; you want the filler to be rock-hard to the touch before sanding. Sand the repair area so that the new surface is smooth and level with the adjoining surface.

5. **Apply wood primer and paint to the repair area to match the existing finish.**

A. Chisel away all soft, rotten wood. (Step 1)

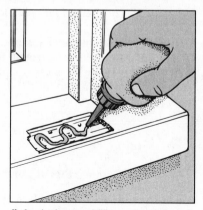

B. Apply the wood filler to the damaged area. (Step 2)

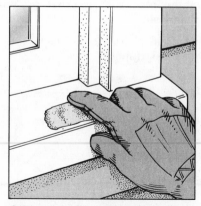

Figure 2-5: Use wood filler to repair small patches of rotted wood on the windowsill.

C. Smooth the filler and allow it to harden before sanding. (Steps 3-4)

Replacing Window Channels

If your sashes let in drafts and rattle in their channels, you may want to consider replacing windows. However, a less expensive solution is available: You can install replacement channels in your double-hung windows.

Replacing window channels is no walk on the beach, but it does give you an opportunity to clean and repair the windows while they're apart. (Okay, so these jobs are no picnic, either.) By replacing the channels, you can have windows that operate more freely and waste less energy, and you save hundreds or thousands of dollars compared to the cost of buying new windows. A typical size channel kit costs less than $50.

Buy new channels at a home center or glass company. They're sold in kits that range in sizes from 3 to 5 feet long, so they fit most sizes of windows. Measure the window opening from the top of the upper sash to the bottom of the lower sash for the correct dimension. Then choose a channel kit that's slightly larger.

The following steps walk you through installing new window channels. Consult Figure 2-6 if you are unsure about what some of the terms mean.

1. **Remove the window stops.**

   If the window stops are painted, use a razor knife to cut through the paint film along the line where the stops meet the jambs. To avoid breaking the stops, use a thin pry bar, pry only at nail locations, and work carefully.

2. **Pull out the lower sash and then pry out the parting strip to remove the upper sash.**

   Set the sash aside for later, when you can clean it, repaint it, or install new weather-stripping.

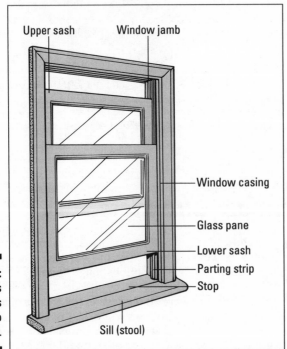

Figure 2-6:
All the bits and pieces that go into a window.

Upper sash Window jamb

Window casing

Glass pane

Lower sash

Parting strip

Stop

Sill (stool)

3. Release the sash cords from the slots in the sash.

Pull the sash cord out of the groove in the edge of the sash. Sometimes, the knotted end is held in place by a small nail. If this is the case, pull out the nail to remove the sash cord.

If you're replacing the channels in a double-hung window, this is a good time to replace the sash cords, as well. (See "Replacing the sash cords," earlier in this chapter.) If your replacement channels are spring-loaded, the sash weights are no longer necessary. In this case, remove and discard the old sash weights and cord and stuff fiberglass insulation loosely into the cavities.

4. If necessary, cut the new channels to length with a hacksaw.

Remember: Old windows may not be square. Carefully measure each side of the window jamb and cut the channels to fit. Note that the bottom of the channel is cut at a slight angle to match the slope of the sill. If the precut angle matches the slope of your windowsill, trim the top of the channel; if the angle is different, cut the bottom of the channel to the same angle as your sill.

5. Inspect and clean the sash and stops.

If paint is peeling, now is the time to repaint the windows, while they're out of the frame. To prevent paint runs, lay the sash flat on a workbench or across two sawhorses. Sand the sash carefully to remove any dried paint runs or other roughness from the frames and stops. You want to apply only a thin film of paint on the sash, so thin the paint a bit by adding a small amount of water (to latex paint) or mineral spirits (to alkyd paint).

Painted surfaces do not slide easily against each other. For this reason, some parts of the window sash, such as the backside of the meeting rails and the inside edges of the stops, are left unpainted. Because painting channels or the edges of the sash may cause them to stick, don't paint any exposed bare wood.

6. Reassemble the window, as shown in Figure 2-7.

Replace the upper sash first — it goes in the outside channel — and then place the lower sash in the inside channel. Hold the channels against the sashes and place the bottom of the channels into the window jamb. Then push the assembly into the jamb so that the channels rest against the outside window stop. The unit will stay in place while you install the inside stops.

Before you nail the stops permanently in place, test to make sure that the windows operate freely. Don't push the stops too tight against the channels, or the windows will be hard to open.

Book II

Basic Home Maintenance and Improvement

Figure 2-7:
Place the window sashes in the replace-ment channels and then slide the assembly into the jamb.

Energy-Saving Projects

Two of the easiest projects that you can do around the house happen to shave your heating and cooling bills. Weather-stripping and caulking fill in gaps and holes around the doors, windows, and other places that leak air. Buttoning up the holes and plugging the leaks are must-do projects that couldn't be easier.

Weather-stripping, step by step

Weather-stripping is material that seals the cracks between moving compo-nents, such as the crack where a window sash meets the frame or stop. In addition to saving energy, weather-stripping blocks drafts and keeps out dust and insects. The thin barrier also blocks outside noise.

Weather-stripping comes in many shapes. It's available with a felt, vinyl, or foam-rubber edge on a wood or plastic strip that you attach to the edge of a door or window with small brads. Some versions have an adhesive back so that you can install them without nails.

The easiest type of weather-stripping to install is the adhesive-backed V-seal type, available in a peel-and-stick roll. This type of weather-stripping is inex-pensive and easy to install. To apply adhesive-backed weather-stripping to a double-hung window, follow these steps (illustrated in Figure 2-8):

1. **With a damp rag, clean the window jamb or other surface where you plan to apply the weather-stripping and let dry completely.**

2. **Cut the strip to the length you want.**

   Use a measuring tape to find the length you need, or place the weather-stripping in position and cut a piece slightly longer. To fully seal the window, you need strips for each side of the inner and outer sash, the bottom of the inner sash, the top of the outer sash, and the outer meeting rail.

A. Raise the inside window sash and apply the weather stripping with the V facing towards the inside of the jamb.

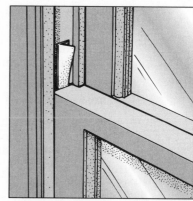

B. Lower the sash and remove the backing from the top inch or so of the weather stripping and press it in place.

C. Lower the outer sash and install the weather stripping in the jamb with the V facing inside.

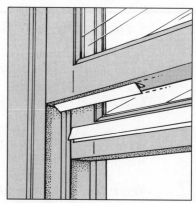

D. Install weather stripping on the bottom of the inner sash, the top of the outer sash, and the inside face of the lower portion of the outer sash.

Figure 2-8: Installing adhesive-backed V-seal weather-stripping.

3. **Raise the inner sash as far as it will go.**

4. **Peel away the backing of the strip, except for an inch or so at the top.**

    Later, you have to push this part of the strip up between the sash and jamb, which is easier to do if you leave the backing in place.

5. **Press the strip in place with the V facing inside.**

6. **Install the strip on the opposite side of the jamb in the same way and then close the window.**

7. **Remove the backing from the top of the weather-stripping that protrudes above the sash and press it in place.**

8. **Lower the outer sash as far as it will go and install the weather-stripping in this sash the same way that you did on the inner sash.**

    The only difference here is that you should leave the backing at the bottom of the strip in place until you raise the window.

9. **Raise the inner sash and apply a strip of weather-stripping to the bottom of the sash; then lower the outer sash and put a strip on top.**

10. **Lower the outer sash far enough to expose the inside face of the bottom of the sash; clean this surface and then apply a strip of weather-stripping with the V facing down.**

Modern windows often have a *kerf* — a slot into which the weather-stripping fits. The weather-stripping for these windows has a tubular edge on one side, with a felt or vinyl lip on the opposite side that closes and seals any crack. To replace this weather-stripping, pull or pry the tubular retaining edge from the slot in the window and then press the new weather-stripping into the slot.

Caulking, step by step

Caulk is a filler material that seals a crack where two nonmoving components meet, such as where a house's siding meets the exterior window trim. Caulk seals the crack against air infiltration, prevents drafts, and keeps moisture from entering the crack and causes paint to peel or wood to rot.

Caulk is available in many formulations, including latex, acrylic latex, and silicone. Unlike traditional oil-based caulks that are known to crack and fail within a very short time, modern caulks are warranted for 25 or more years. To avoid having to recaulk each summer, choose a quality paintable silicone or acrylic latex caulk product. These caulks are *elastomeric,* which is a fancy word meaning that they remain flexible after drying and don't crack when weather changes, which causes either of the two joined components to expand and contract.

Caulk is available in 10-ounce tubes, enough to caulk around the average door or window. At one end of the tube is a cone-shaped plastic nozzle. Because the nozzle gradually decreases in size from its base to the tip, you can squeeze out a bigger bead of caulk by cutting the nozzle shorter. How much coverage you get from a tube of caulk depends on the size of the caulk bead.

The caulk tube fits into a caulk gun. The gun has a trigger handle that you squeeze to apply pressure to the tube, forcing the caulk out the nozzle. Caulk guns are available at home centers, hardware stores, and paint outlets.

To seal the exterior of a window with caulk, follow these steps:

1. **Use a putty knife or scraper to clean away any old caulk remaining on the outside of the window.**

2. **Cut the tip off the caulk tube nozzle at a point where it produces a bead large enough to fill the crack.**

   A ¼-inch bead is large enough for most cracks. To avoid too large a bead, cut the nozzle tip near the end, test the bead for size, and then cut off more if you need a larger bead.

   After you cut the tip, you have to puncture the seal in the end of the caulk tube before any caulk will flow. To puncture this seal, insert a stiff wire, such as a piece of metal clothes hanger or a long nail, into the nozzle and push it into the caulk tube until you feel it puncture the seal.

3. **Apply a bead of caulk, moving the caulk gun at a measured pace along the crack and using continuous light pressure on the gun trigger.**

   Caulk on all four sides of the window trim to seal the crack between the trim and the siding.

4. **Smooth the caulk.**

   You can use a Popsicle stick, plastic spoon, or wet finger to create a smooth surface.

5. **Wash away caulk remaining on the gun, your hands, or other unwanted spots before it dries.**

Window Enhancements and Add-ons

To avoid living in the proverbial fish bowl, most people want some kind of covering for their windows. For rooms where privacy is a prime concern, such as a bathroom or bedroom, window coverings are more important. In other rooms, you may need them mostly for protection from bright sunlight. Whatever the motivation, basic window coverings are easy to install, even for the not-so-handy.

Installing a window shade

Window shades are spring-loaded so that they roll up or down and lock in the chosen position. The hardware consists of round support brackets at either end of the shade, as shown in Figure 2-9. You mount the brackets on the inside of the window stops. One bracket has a hole into which a round shade support is inserted; the opposite bracket has a slot to receive the flat support on the other end of the shade. Shades are so easy to install and remove that even a child can do the job; the problem is, a child is never around when you need one.

If you're replacing an old shade, measure the width of the old roller from end to end, including the metal tips, and then measure the length of the shade fully extended. Order a new shade of the same width and length.

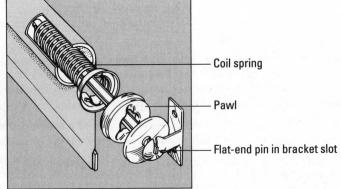

Figure 2-9:
The mechanics of a window shade roller.

Coil spring

Pawl

Flat-end pin in bracket slot

To measure for a new shade, hold a rigid measuring stick across the top of the window. Place one end on the inside upper window stop and carefully extend the rule across to the stop on the other side. Order a shade ⅛ inch smaller than the measurement.

Measure the inside of the jamb and then subtract ⅛ inch to find the proper length. You can purchase shades that are easy to cut to the exact length that you need.

To install a shade, follow these simple steps:

1. **Position the metal support brackets on the two window stops at opposite sides of the window. Mark the brad hole positions on the stops with a sharp pencil.**

   Allow enough room between the top of the window jamb and the shade for the roller to turn freely, remembering that when the shade is fully rolled up, it grows in diameter. Hold the shade up where you plan to install it. When you find the correct position for the first bracket position, make a pencil mark for the location of the brad hole. Measure the distance from the top and sides of the window frame and then use that measurement to locate the bracket on the opposite side.

2. **Secure the shade brackets to the window stops with small brads.**

   With a carpenter's awl or an ice pick and hammer, make starting holes in the stops. Hold the shade bracket in position with a tack hammer to drive in the brads.

3. **Slide the ends of the shade into the slots in the brackets.**

   Make sure that the shade is fully wound up when you install it, or it may not retract properly. If you pull the shade down and it doesn't fully roll up by itself, pull the shade down a foot or so and take it off the bracket. Rewind the shade on the shade roller and then reinstall it in the bracket.

To remove the shade, just push upward on the slotted end of the shade to free it from its bracket and then pull the round support from the hole in the opposite bracket.

Book II

Basic Home Mainte-nance and Improvement

Trim-to-fit shades

Many large retailers sell inexpensive window shades that you can cut to fit almost any window. These shades are lightweight and flimsy (what do you expect for about $8?), but they may be just right for a quick fix or when you're on a tight budget.

You can't do anything about the length of these shades, but you can custom-cut the width by using the score lines on the shade as guidelines. The steel shade roller slides together to fit the new width.

Install the brackets as we describe for regular shades. (See the "Installing a window shade" section in this chapter.) Insert the shade in the left bracket. Remove the plastic hem slat from the pocket and notice its score lines that match up with the score lines running the length of the shade. Hold the shade level under the right bracket, so you can determine the correct width. Then mark the width with a light pencil mark at the closest score line on the shade. Carefully begin to tear the length of the shade at its score line until the entire shade is done. Adjust the shade roller to fit the new width by pushing the end plug until it reaches the end of the shade. Then snap off the plastic hem slat to the same width and install it.

Installing a miniblind

Miniblinds are mounted in U-shaped brackets that have snap-on covers to provide a finished look. They're a mainstream decorating choice for a window treatment because they coordinate with just about any decor. Use them alone or with a fabric valance or cornice board covering the top of the window.

You can mount most miniblinds outside the window frame (on the outer trim of the window), on the wall (so that they cover the window trim), or on the inside of the frame between the window stops. Because you have all these options, most mounting brackets have pre-drilled holes on both the ends and the backs of the mounting brackets. You use only one set of holes, depending on how you mount the miniblinds.

Before you purchase miniblinds, decide whether you want to mount the blind inside or outside the window frame and then measure your windows using a folding wooden measuring rule or wooden measuring stick. Manufacturers have specific directions for measuring on their packaging or brochures, but the general procedure is to measure the width at the top, middle, and bottom of the window and use the smallest dimension for its width. Measure the length of the window to get the correct extension of the blind.

If you order custom blinds, you can indicate the length you want the blinds to be. If you buy blinds off the rack, you have to cut the blind cords to the proper length; usually, you want the bottom edge of the blind to rest on or slightly above the windowsill. Directions for cutting the blind cords for length are included in the miniblind package.

You can install small clips on both sides of the window to act as hold-down brackets to secure the bottom of the blinds so that they don't sway freely. These clips, secured with a small brad or finishing nail, are easy to reach but not noticeable.

To install a blind on the inside of the jamb, follow these steps:

1. **Measure and mark the locations for the U-shaped mounting brackets.**

   Position the mounting brackets at the top corner of the window jamb. Hold the brackets in place (paying attention to which is the right and which is the left bracket) and use them as a template to mark the location of the mounting screws with a pencil.

2. **Drill pilot holes for the mounting screws through the pencil marks on the window jamb.**

   Use a 1/16-inch drill or carpenter's awl to make starter holes for the screws.

3. **Use a screwdriver to install the mounting brackets with the screws provided.**

4. **Push the blind's header bar into the brackets, as shown in Figure 2-10, and secure it by closing each bracket.**

   Some designs simply slide into the bracket.

5. **If necessary, cut the blind cords to length.**

Figure 2-10: To install miniblinds inside the jamb, screw the brackets to the top or side of the jamb.

Book II

Basic Home Maintenance and Improvement

Driving small screws while reaching upward is an awkward and frustrating job that may introduce new and colorful words into your vocabulary. To make the job easier, use a cordless screwdriver, which is small and light-weight. You can use the toggle switch on a cordless to provide drive or reverse power.

Installing curtain rods and hardware

Rod-mounting brackets are often nailed to the window trim or stops to hold the rods for lightweight curtains. To install curtain rods, refer to the "Installing a window shade" section for directions, earlier in this chapter.

Installing rods to support heavy curtains or drapes can be a horse of a different color. If you're mounting drapery hardware on the window trim or on the wall at the window edge, you can drive the hardware screws into wood. But you may encounter difficulties mounting rods that extend onto the walls if the @*!%&* builder failed to install nailing blocks beyond the header to provide something into which you can screw the rod brackets. In this case, you must install hollow-wall fasteners like Molly bolts in the walls and then secure the drapery hardware with the fasteners.

If the wall is plastered over a wood lath base (rock lath became standard for plaster in 1950), you can drive screws through the plaster and into the wood lath. Pre-drill the screw holes. To be sure that you drill into the wood lath and not through the gaps or key strips between the laths, check the drill bit as it penetrates the plaster. If you penetrate the wood lath, you'll see wood chips in the plaster dust as the bit bores into the wood. If you don't see wood chips, plan on using a Molly bolt. If you see water, call a plumber.

Molly bolts include a metal shaft or sleeve into which you can insert a small machine screw, as shown in Figure 2-11. As the machine screw turns in the Molly shaft, the shaft collapses against the back side of the plaster or wallboard, providing a secure support for the weight of the rods and the drapes. Other types of fasteners are available for this purpose: Ask your hardware or home center clerk to suggest a fastener for your project.

Figure 2-11: Molly bolts expand behind the wall and are a good choice for holding curtain rods securely in place.

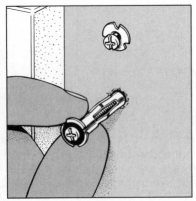

To install a Molly bolt, drill a hole at the rod hardware location through the wallboard or plaster. Insert the Molly screw into the hole and tap it lightly to seat it against the wall. Place the rod mounting bracket in position so that the screw holes line up with the Molly bolt(s) and use a screwdriver to drive the screw home. To test the installation, pull firmly on the mounting bracket. If the bracket moves, tighten the screw a bit more until you're sure that the screw is securely anchored.

Chapter 3

Doors: An Open-and-Shut Case

In This Chapter

▶ Caring for door hinges and locks

▶ Unsticking bifold doors

▶ Juggling panels in combination screen/storm doors

▶ Keeping sliding storm and closet doors on track

▶ Installing and replacing door locks

▶ Keeping garage doors in tiptop shape

They swing open; they slide shut — simple acts you probably take for granted. But when they squeak or refuse to budge, you start to notice the doors in and around your house. To keep everything in good working order, perform the typical door maintenance and repair jobs in this chapter. They may be all you need to keep your home safe and secure.

Maintaining Locks and Hinges

You probably don't spend much time thinking about your doors — and if you do, you may want to seek professional help — but consider that a family may open and close entry doors thousands of times each year. The hinges and locks on the doors can take a real pounding, so lubricate them at least once a year. To lubricate door hardware, you need a can of aerosol lubricant such as WD-40, paper towels, slot and Phillips-head screwdrivers, and a hammer.

Lubricating hinges

Interior doors typically have two or three hinges. Exterior doors are heavier than interior doors, so they have three or four hinges. To lubricate door hinges, first remove one hinge pin. Some hinge pins extend through the hinges, so you can use a large nail to tap them up from the bottom, as shown in Figure 3-1. Other hinges may require you to insert the blade of a slot screwdriver under the head of the hinge pin and then tap the handle of the screwdriver with a hammer to drive the pin up and out of the hinge.

Figure 3-1: Hinges with an open bottom have hinge pins that you can remove by tapping a large nail into the bottom of the hinge, driving the pin up and out.

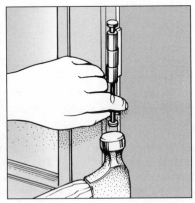

After you remove one hinge pin, drop a large nail in the hinge to temporarily replace the removed pin and prevent the door from sagging off its hinges. Lay the hinge pin on paper towels and remove any dirt. Then spray the pin with a light coating of lubricant and replace the pin in the hinge. Repeat this procedure for all the hinges, one at a time.

Lubricating door locks

Many people put up with the aggravation of a sticking door lock for years — an annoyance that would try the patience even of Harry Houdini. Ironically, you can fix most stubborn locks in a matter of minutes.

First, clean the keyhole with a penetrating lubricant like WD-40. (Don't apply household oil to the key or cylinder because it attracts dirt and eventually would gum up the lock.) Spray the lubricant into the keyhole itself and then spray it on the key. Slide the key in and out of the lock several times to spread the lubricant.

If this superficial cleaning doesn't free the lock, eliminate the aggravation altogether: Take about ten minutes to disassemble, clean, and reassemble the entire door lock. Here's how to remove and clean the most common type of door lock:

1. **With the door open, use a Phillips screwdriver to take out the two connecting screws that are located by the doorknob on the inside of the lock.**

2. **Remove the two screws that hold the lock faceplate on the edge of the door.**

3. **Slide the doorknob off the spindle, pull out the lock mechanism, and remove the latchbolt from its hole in the edge of the door, as shown in Figure 3-2.**

Book II

Basic Home Maintenance and Improvement

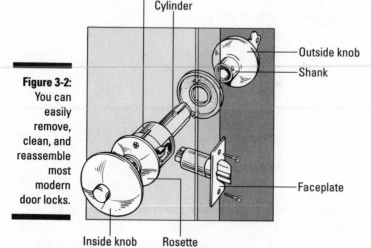

Cylinder case

Cylinder

Outside knob

Shank

Figure 3-2: You can easily remove, clean, and reassemble most modern door locks.

Faceplate

Inside knob   Rosette

4. **Lay the disassembled lock parts on layers of newspaper or paper towels.**

5. **Spray a light all-purpose household lubricant or silicone lubricant on all moving parts of the lock, flushing out the latchbolt. Use powdered graphite to lubricate the lock cylinder.**

Spray until all the dirt is flushed from the assembly and then let the latchbolt assembly lie on the newspaper or towels until all the excess lubricant has dripped off.

To reassemble the door lock after cleaning and lubricating it, follow these steps:

1. **Insert the latchbolt assembly into its hole in the edge of the door.**

2. **Insert the exterior doorknob and spindle into its hole, aligning it so that the spindles and connecting screws pass through the holes in the latchbolt assembly, as shown in Figure 3-3.**

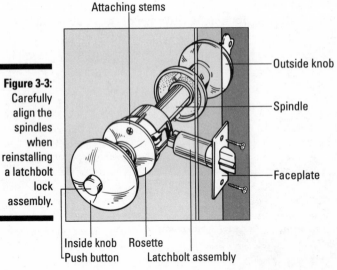

Figure 3-3: Carefully align the spindles when reinstalling a latchbolt lock assembly.

Attaching stems

Outside knob

Spindle

Faceplate

Inside knob   Rosette

Push button   Latchbolt assembly

3. **Drive in the latchbolt screws, but don't tighten them until the lock is completely assembled.**

4. **Slide the interior doorknob onto the shaft, aligning the screw holes, and then drive in the screws.**

Turn the doorknob back and forth to check that the cylinder and latchbolt are engaged and in proper alignment.

5. **Tighten the screws on the latchbolt and recheck the alignment by turning the knob.**

   If you have any parts left over, guess what? You goofed. Disassemble the lock and replace all the pieces.

6. **Test the lock by turning the knob and locking the lock.**

   If the lock doesn't work smoothly, loosen the screws, realign the cylinder and latchbolt, and try again.

You can lubricate deadbolts the same way. Remove the connecting screws, the faceplate screws, and then the knobs. Next, pull out the latchbolt assembly and clean and lubricate the lock as just described. To reassemble the lock, reverse the procedure.

Tightening loose hinges

Loose hinges can cause a door to stick, bind, or scrape the floor. Lucky for you, this is another common, easy-to-solve problem. First, check that the hinge screws are tight. Open the door, grasp it by the lock edge, and move it up and down. If you encounter movement at the hinge screws, they need to be retightened.

If the hinge screws have been loose for only a short time, you may only need to tighten them with a screwdriver. But when hinge screws are left loose for a long time, the constant movement of the hinge plate and screws enlarges the screw holes. Eventually, the holes become so large that the screws can't stay tight. The result: stripped screws that are completely useless!

If the door still moves even a tiny bit after you tighten its hinge screws, you have to repair the enlarged screw holes. Repair one screw hole at a time so that you don't have to remove the door. Here's how:

1. **Remove the loose screw.**

2. **Dip the bare end of a wooden match in some carpenter's glue and tap it with a hammer as far into the screw hole as it will go, as shown in Figure 3-4.**

   If the screw is large, you may have to put several glue-coated matches in the hole.

3. **Break or cut off the match(es) flush with the hinge plate and discard the heads.**

4. **After you've filled the void in the screw hole with the wooden match(es), drive the screw into the hole with a screwdriver.**

5. **Remove the next screw and repair its hole, continuing until you have fixed all the enlarged screw holes.**

In place of a match, you can use wooden golf tees coated with glue to plug a stripped screw hole. Golf tees are tapered, so they fit easily into the screw hole. Let the glue dry and then cut off the protruding part of the tee.

Figure 3-4:
Tighten a loose hinge screw by driving a glue-coated wooden match or small dowel into the screw hole and then reinstalling the screw.

Fixing Bifold Doors

Bifold doors suffer from another chronic condition; they tend to jump off their tracks or become misaligned and, consequently, don't open or open only partially.

Bifold doors are arranged in hinged pairs that fold like an accordion toward both sides of the *doorjamb* or frame when opened. Because bifold doors permit you to open the doors fully and provide access to all storage, they're often used on closets. They move via nylon rollers or pins mounted on the tops of the doors and travel on a track mounted at the top of the door jamb, as shown in Figure 3-5. The doors nearest the side jambs swing on pivot blocks installed at the top and, on some models, at the floor to keep the bottoms of the doors from swinging outward. To keep bifold doors operating smoothly, clean and lubricate the track, rollers, and pivot blocks at least once a year.

To tune up bifold doors and lubricate the top track, open the doors. Wipe the track with a clean cloth to remove dust. Use an aerosol lubricant to spray the track and rollers or pins. Apply the lubricant sparingly and be careful not to spray any clothes hanging in the closet. Leave only a light film of lubricant on the parts; use paper towels to wipe away any excess lubricant.

Rollers   Track

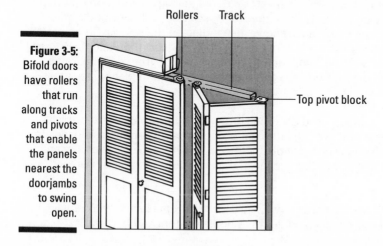

Figure 3-5: Bifold doors have rollers that run along tracks and pivots that enable the panels nearest the doorjambs to swing open.

Top pivot block

Book II

Basic Home Mainte-nance and Improvement

If your bifold doors *bind* (don't open or slide on their tracks easily), first check to see whether all the hardware is secure and working properly. If the parts are broken, replacement hardware is available at home centers. Check the hinges between each pair of doors. If the hinge screws are loose, use a screwdriver to tighten them. If the screw holes are stripped so that you can't tighten the hinge screws, remove the hinges and plug the screw holes following the steps we suggested for door hinges earlier in this chapter.

Working on bifold doors may be easier if you remove them from the doorframe first. To do so, unfold the doors and carefully lift them up and out of the frame. You may find this easier to do if you stand inside, not outside, the door. For example, to remove a bifold closet door, you may have to take some items out of the closet so that you can stand inside and see how the door sits in its track and lift it out.

If, when you rehang the doors, the gap between the door and jamb is uneven, use a screwdriver or wrench to adjust the top pivot blocks and even the gap. Some bifold doors have adjustable pivot blocks at the bottom corner.

Maintaining Combination Storm/Screen Doors

Combination storm/screen doors relieve you of the seasonal hassle of taking down screen doors and putting up storm doors, taking down storm doors and putting up screen doors. These units come with both a screen and a storm insert that you can install and remove, depending on the season. Combination doors can have any variety of screw-in or bolt-in systems that hold the screen or storm panes in place. Some newer versions have a groove in the frame that the screen or glass fits into and a gasket to hold it in place. The doors themselves may be made of wood or metal, usually aluminum.

To keep these doors in good condition, provide maintenance service at least once a year. Spray an aerosol lubricant on the door lock, hinges, and closer mechanism. Also lubricate the push buttons that hold the glass or screen units in place. These buttons are located on the bottom edge, at both sides of the unit.

If the lock isn't working properly, the easiest solution is usually to replace it. You can purchase replacement locks at home centers and hardware stores.

Replacing the screen

If you have a door with a loose or damaged screen (a given if you have kids or pets), don't fret. Replacing screens is relatively easy, and it's a useful skill to have, considering that you're likely to be doing it for many years to come.

Both aluminum and fiberglass screening is available at home centers and hardware stores. The screening fabric comes in prepackaged sizes of 25 inches wide x 32, 36, and 48 inches long; and 84 inches long x 32, 36, and 48 inches wide. It's also sold by the foot from bolts in the following widths: 24, 36, 48, 60, and 72 inches.

Measure your window before shopping for a replacement screen. Gauge the length and the width of the window opening and add a few extra inches to both dimensions to be safe.

If solar heat or bright light is a problem, consider using a special screen material like Phifer's Sunscreen to block out the sun. Black and dark-colored screens are easier to see through than bright reflective aluminum.

The screen is held in a frame by a rubber or neoprene *spline,* which looks like a thin cord pressed into grooves. To replace an aluminum screen, you use a *screen-installation splining tool.* The tool looks like a pastry cutter with a convex roller on one end and a concave roller on the opposite end.

Installation steps are basically the same for an aluminum or fiberglass screen, with slight variations.

Aluminum screens

To replace an aluminum screen, follow these steps:

1. **Remove the screen in its frame from the door and lay it flat on a workbench or a set of sawhorses.**

2. **Use small pliers or a carpenter's awl to pry the spline out of the groove and then lift out the screen.**

   To navigate around tight corners, use a screwdriver to ease the spline out of the frame, as shown in Figure 3-6. If the spline appears to be in good shape, set it aside for use with the new screen. If the spline is brittle or cracked, replace it with a new spline (available at hardware stores).

Book II

Basic Home Mainte-nance and Improvement

Figure 3-6: Pry out the old spline from the groove in the frame of the aluminum screen. Work carefully, and you can reuse the spline.

3. **Wipe the spline groove clean, making sure to remove the tiniest grit.**

4. **Lay a new aluminum screen over the frame so that it overlaps the groove by at least ⅛ inch on all four sides.**

5. **Cut off the corners of the screen at a 45-degree angle, just inside the outer edge of the spline groove.**

6. **Use the convex end of the splining tool to press the screen into the groove of the frame.**

   Hold the roller at a 45-degree angle toward the inside edge of the groove and then roll downward to press the screen into the groove. Hold the screen taut across the frame as you roll it into place. Sags and wrinkles are about as attractive on screen doors as they are on people.

7. **Use the concave end of the roller to press the spline into the groove.**

   Don't cut the spline at the corners: Instead, bend the spline around the corners and install it in one continuous piece. When you position it tightly in the groove, the spline holds the screen in place.

8. **Use a sharp knife to trim away any excess screen.**

   Place the tip of the knife between the spline and the outside edge of the spline groove and pull the knife slowly along the entire groove perimeter.

Fiberglass screens

To replace a fiberglass screen, first remove the old spline and clean the spline groove. Lay the fiberglass screen over the frame so that it overlaps about ½ inch on all four sides. Now use the concave end of the roller to roll both the screen and the spline into the groove at the same time, as shown in Figure 3-7. Be careful to hold the screen straight while you work on the first two sides and then roll in the last two sides. To cut away excess screen, position the knife tip between the spline and the exterior side of the spline groove.

Figure 3-7: Installing a new fiberglass screen.

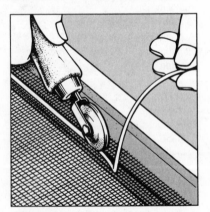

A. Lay the fiberglass screen over the frame so that it overlaps about 1/2-inch on all four sides.

B. Using the concave end of the roller, roll both the screen and spline into the groove at the same time.

Tightening loose storm door panels

You want your storm door panels to sit firmly in their channels, secured against air infiltration by weather stripping that's tucked into the grooves on all sides of the panel. When panels become loose from wear or weathering and begin to rattle in your door, it's time for new weather stripping.

The weather stripping in your storm door may be felt strips (common on older models) or rubber or vinyl gaskets. Replacement weather stripping, especially the felt kind, may be difficult to find. Look in large home centers for storm window or storm door repair kits or check out the weather stripping department. Chances are, you'll find something that comes close to the original.

Follow these steps to replace worn-out weather stripping:

1. **Remove the panels.**

   Most panels slide into channels in the frame and are held in place by thumb screws. Loosen these screws, turn the brackets that hold the panel in place, and lift out the panel.

2. **Remove the old weather stripping.**

   Pull up the weather stripping at one end and work it out of its groove. You may need to use a standard screwdriver to begin the job if the material is stuck in place.

3. **Press the new weather stripping into the groove at one corner and slide it down the groove.**

   Depending on the type of weather stripping, you may have to use a screwdriver to push it into place.

4. **Replace the panel by reversing the actions in Step 1.**

Sliding By with Sliding Doors

The two types of doors that are easiest to open don't have hinges at all; instead, they slide on tracks. Sliding-glass doors are a popular feature in rooms with decks or patios because their full-length glass panels open the room visually to the great outdoors while providing easy access to the outside. Interior sliding doors are frequently used for closets and pantries, and sometimes to conceal water heaters and furnaces. You can remove sliding-door panels easily to gain complete access to what's behind them. Follow simple repairs and maintenance procedures to keep your sliding doors on track.

Book II

Basic Home Maintenance and Improvement

Getting your patio door to slide better

Patio doors slide horizontally — or at least they're supposed to. All too often, these big, pesky contraptions stubbornly resist opening, and getting outside becomes about as easy as dragging a refrigerator through a sandbox.

The most common cause of a sticking patio door is debris in the lower track. This channel easily becomes clogged with dirt, leaves, and such because people and pets walk over it whenever they go in or out. Each time you vacuum your floors, use a small brush attachment or cordless vacuum to clean the sliding-door tracks. Apply a lubricant to both upper and lower tracks to keep the door hardware clean and operating freely.

In addition to cleaning and lubricating sliding-door tracks, you want to lubricate the door lock. The best way to lubricate any lock is to disassemble it and use an aerosol lubricant to flush away grime and coat the moving parts of the lock.

Sometimes, patio doors become hard to open even when the track is clean. In these cases, the problem is usually that the rollers at the bottom of the door have started to rub against the track. The rollers at the top can also wear down, lowering the bottom of the door so that it rubs on the track.

Most sliding doors have a mechanism called an *adjusting screw* located at the bottom of the door ends. Turning this screw raises or lowers the roller, as shown in Figure 3-8. Give the screw a clockwise turn and test to see whether the door slides easier. If the door becomes even harder to open, turn the screw in the opposite direction. After a bit of adjustment, the door should roll easily without rubbing on the bottom track.

Figure 3-8:
A screw at the base of the door controls the clearance between the bottom of a sliding door and the track.

Maintaining sliding closet doors

Sliding closet doors operate on rollers that are positioned in tracks at the top jamb and floor, allowing the doors to bypass each other in the tracks (see Figure 3-9). Because sliding doors don't fold out the way bifold doors do, they allow access to only half the width of the opening at a time.

To clean and lubricate the hardware of a sliding closet door, use a stiff brush, a toothbrush, or a hand vacuum to clean dust from the tracks. Use an aerosol lubricant to lubricate all the door rollers. If the rollers are damaged, install replacement rollers (available at home centers).

Book II

Basic Home Maintenance and Improvement

A simple roller-and-track assembly.

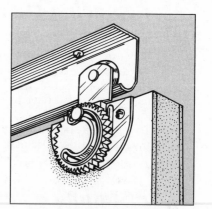

A roller with adjustable clearance.

Figure 3-9: Periodically clean and lubricate the tracks and roller assembly of a sliding closet door.

A two-track sliding door.

Removing a sliding door by lifting it up out of its tracks.

If the door doesn't hang level, leaving an uneven gap between the door and door frame, look for an adjustable mounting screw at the inside top of each door. Use a screwdriver to adjust the mounting screw and even out the door.

Locking Up

If a door in your house looks good, but its lock wobbles or shows signs of wear, consider replacing the lock. Standard interior locks come in a variety of styles and finishes that can improve the look of the door as well as provide security.

Replacing standard door locks

If your locks are becoming worn or damaged, replace them with new units. Because door locks vary somewhat in design, remove the lock and measure the diameter of the opening and the distance from the center of the hole to the edge of the door, which is either 2⅜- or 2¾-inches. If you find an exact match, you won't have to redrill the lock holes.

To replace a standard door lock, see the directions earlier in this chapter in the section titled "Maintaining Locks and Hinges."

Installing a deadbolt

Many exterior doors are fitted with an ordinary cylinder lock that has a keyhole in the doorknob. This type of lock offers little resistance to a determined burglar (and what other kind of burglar is there?). The latchbolt of most standard locks extends only into the doorframe and a stiff kick from a booted foot can splinter most doorframes. And thieves can wrench out the exterior knobs of passage locks by using a pipe wrench. For added security, install a deadbolt lock on every exterior door.

Deadbolt locks have latchbolts that extend through the doorframe and into the wall stud next to the frame. A deadbolt lock has no exterior knob, so it's impossible to wrench the lock from its hole in the door. From the inside, you operate a deadbolt lock by turning either a thumb-turn lever (if you have a single-cylinder lock) or a key (for a double-cylinder lock). If you have small children in the home who may not be able to find the key in an emergency, choose a thumb-turn lock. Keep in mind, though, that if your exterior door contains glass panels, a burglar can break the glass, reach inside, and unlock a thumb-turn lock.

Deadbolt locks are relatively inexpensive, and most come complete with a cardboard template that shows where to drill the cylinder and latchbolt holes. Follow these general steps, illustrated in Figure 3-10, to install a deadbolt lock:

A. Drive a nail through the template layout marks to indicate the position for the lock-set holes. (Step 3)

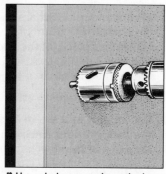

B. Use a hole saw to bore the large hole for the lock cylinder in the side of the door. (Step 4)

C. Use a wood-boring spade bit to drill the latchbolt hole in the edge of the door. (Step 5)

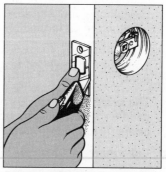

D. Use a utiltity knife to mark the outline of the faceplate on the edge of the door and then make the shallow mortise to recess the plate. (Step 6)

E. Insert the keyed portion of the lock into the hole in the latchbolt. (Step 9)

Figure 3-10: Installing a deadbolt lock for extra security.

1. **Choose a position on the door for the lock.**

   Most standard locks are set at or near 36 inches from the bottom of the door. Install the deadbolt lock above the standard lock or about 44 inches above the bottom of the door. If you have a combination storm door, position the deadbolt lock so that it doesn't interfere with the operation of the storm doorknob or lock.

2. **Use masking tape to affix the template to the door edge and face.**

3. **Use an awl, nail set, or large nail to mark the centers of the holes for the lock cylinder (through the face of the door) and the latchbolt (into the edge of the door).**

4. **Use the proper size of hole saw to bore the hole for the lock cylinder.**

   Some manufacturers offer a kit that includes a hole saw with the lock set. Drilling the hole from both sides helps prevent the door from splintering. The hole saw has a center pilot bit to guide the saw through the door. From one side of the door, drill until the tip of the pilot point pokes through the opposite side of the door, and then pull the hole saw out, position the bit in the hole, and finish boring the hole from the opposite side of the door.

5. **Use a 1-inch spade bit to drill the latchbolt hole into the edge of the door.**

   The *spade bit* is an inexpensive wood-boring instrument that looks like a paddle with a triangular point on the end. Attach it to your drill to cut a perfectly round hole into the wood.

6. **Cut a mortise, or recess, in the wood for the latchbolt faceplate.**

   The latchbolt faceplate must fit into a shallow mortise in the edge of the door. Cutting out this mortise isn't nearly as difficult as it sounds. All you need is a sharp 1-inch chisel and a hammer.

   To cut the latchbolt mortise, place the latchbolt in the hole and mark around the faceplate with a knife to indicate its outline on the end of the door. Use the chisel to deepen the marks about ⅛ inch. Then, starting at the top of the faceplate outline, make a series of closely spaced chisel cuts inside the marks. A 1-inch-wide chisel blade will fit inside the outline. Tap the chisel with a hammer so that it makes ⅛-inch-deep cuts.

   Remove the resulting wood chips with the chisel blade. Then use the chisel to smooth the bottom of the mortise. Place the latchbolt in the door and check the fit of the mortise. If the faceplate is not flush with the door edge, chisel away a bit more wood.

7. **When the faceplate fits flush with the door edge, hold it in place and use it as a template for installing the two mounting screws.**

8. **Before installing the lock, apply a thin film of aerosol lubricant to all the moving parts.**

9. Place the latchbolt in its hole and then insert the keyed portion of the lock so that the tailpiece extends through the hole in the latchbolt.

10. From the inside of the door, fit the inside cylinder so that the holes for the retaining screws are aligned with the exterior portion of the lock.

11. Use the two retaining screws to secure the two sides of the lock together.

12. Shut the door and use a pencil to mark the spot on the doorjamb where the latchbolt meets the jamb.

13. Using the strikeplate as a template, trace and cut a mortise on the doorjamb; then dig out the mortise with a sharp chisel.

14. Use a spade bit to bore a latchbolt hole in the center of the mortise.

15. Use the screws provided to install the strike plate into the mortise.

16. Shut the door and test the fit by operating the deadbolt lock. If necessary, you can loosen the screws and adjust the lock set slightly so that the latchbolt passes easily into its hole.

If you replace entry door locks on several doors, buy locks that are keyed alike so that you can use one key to open both or all entry doors. If you're replacing only one lock, ask the dealer to rekey the existing lock so that one key can open both back and front doors. If you use separate keys for your home's entry locks, you can have a locksmith rekey the locks so that one key fits all.

Securing the patio door

Because they're large and easy to force open, patio doors are common targets for intruders. Safeguard your residence by buying a locking device that blocks the track, preventing outsiders from forcing the door to slide open. Or create your own device by cutting a length of wood (such as a broomstick or a 2-x-2-inch board) to fit snugly between the doorframe and the stile of the operable door.

You can enhance this safety feature by drilling a hole through one door and into the other and then inserting a long nail or bolt through the holes: This setup prevents intruders from prying the door up and swinging out its bottom to gain entry. If the existing lock doesn't work, check home centers for replacement locks.

To prevent a break-in through the door pane, install a tough window film (sold at local glass installers) that prevents the glass from shattering and resists forced entry.

Book II

Basic Home Maintenance and Improvement

Maintaining Garage Doors

Because garage doors are especially exposed to weather extremes, you should inspect and service them at least once each year. Most modern garage doors consist of four or more panels that are hinged so that they can travel in a pair of tracks, as shown in Figure 3-11.

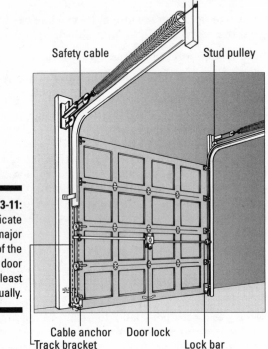

Safety cable   Stud pulley

Figure 3-11: Lubricate the major parts of the garage door at least annually.

Cable anchor   Door lock
Track bracket   Lock bar

Use an aerosol spray lubricant and wand to clean and lubricate all these moving pieces:

- ✔ **Combination hinge and rollers:** These gizmos are located at either side of the door, between each pair of panels. Apply lubricant to the roller and the hinge to which the roller is attached. Use lubricant sparingly; too much doesn't make the door work better, it just attracts dirt that will eventually gum up the works.

- ✔ **Hinges in the field or center of the door panels:** The hinges that hold the center of the door panels together don't have a roller. Apply lubricant to these hinges and then operate the door several times to distribute the lubricant to all moving surfaces of the hardware.

✔ **Lock mechanism on the door:** Spray lubricant into the keyhole and work the key several times to distribute the lubricant to the lock's moving parts. If your door is manually operated, lubricate the pair of locking latches at each side of the door.

If your garage door operates with an automatic opener, be sure that it's equipped with a safety-stop feature that prevents damage to the door and protects young children from being trapped and injured under the door. The safety-stop mechanism on an older door causes the door to reverse direction if it meets any resistance as it closes. Newer models have a safety-stop mechanism that causes the door to stop closing if anything interrupts a beam of light directed across the door threshold.

Book II

Basic Home Mainte-nance and Improvement

Chapter 4

Heating, Ventilating, and Cooling Systems

*I*t hides in a dark corner of the basement, amid a tangle of pipes and ducts. It roars, is silent, and then roars again. You can see flames burning brightly inside, behind its door. Is it the entrance to hell? Heck, no. It's your furnace (or boiler).

Most grown-ups would never admit it, but their furnaces frighten them. A furnace is a big, mysterious piece of machinery. Plus, as every kid knows, monsters live behind it.

We're here to tell you that a furnace is nothing to be afraid of. A furnace is less mysterious than you think. And according to our 5-year-old nephew, you can keep the monsters away by turning on all the lights and loudly humming the theme from *The Lion King*.

Your heating system simply heats up air or water and then moves that heated air or steam around the house. It's really that simple. However, the technology behind this process is pretty complicated, which means that a professional must perform most of the maintenance tasks that are associated with your heating system.

The maintenance that a do-it-yourselfer can do is easy and nonthreatening — we're confident that you can do it without difficulty (or monster trouble).

If you ask ten people what that thing in their basement is that heats the house, most say "a furnace." The truth is, it may not be. If your home is heated by air, it's a furnace. If your home is heated by water, it's a boiler.

Making Friends with the Heat Monster in the Basement

Because most people don't know diddly about their heating systems, here's a quick look at the most common types:

- ✔ **Forced air systems** heat air as it passes through the furnace. A blower and a system of ducts take the warm air throughout the house and then back to the furnace.

- ✔ **Hot water (hydronic) systems** heat water in the boiler and then circulate it through pipes to radiators or convectors. The water then returns to the boiler to be reheated and begins the journey again. The water can be circulated either mechanically through the use of circulator motors (pumps) or via gravity, as is common in older homes.

- ✔ **Steam systems** resemble hot water systems, except that the water in the boiler is heated until it becomes steam and can travel under its own pressure through pipes to radiators. Steam radiators get much hotter than water radiators and therefore are smaller. They should be covered to prevent burn injuries.

- ✔ **Electric systems** use electrical resistance to generate radiant heat in baseboard units or in cables embedded in the ceiling or floor.

Forced air systems

Have a qualified, licensed heating contractor inspect and service your forced air system every year before the heating season begins. This is not optional. Sure, you could save $75 by not doing it. But a dirty, inefficient furnace costs you ten times that much in wasted fuel. Even more important, a cracked heat exchanger or dislodged flue could fill your house with deadly carbon monoxide gas. You and your family are worth more than what it costs to make sure the furnace is functional and safe.

During an annual service, the furnace serviceperson performs dozens of maintenance tasks (lubrication, burner adjustment, and so on) to help maintain — and even improve — your furnace's efficiency and keep it running year after year. Frankly, these aren't the kinds of things that the typical homeowner can do, so we think it's best to let a pro do the job.

If you do decide to do your own maintenance, take heed. Certain parts of your furnace may be difficult to locate. They don't all look like the illustrations in this book. For specifics, refer to your owner's manual. In some instances, the local public utility or building department offers no-charge assistance in these matters.

Replacing the furnace filter

Of the maintenance tasks that you can do yourself, the easiest is replacing the furnace filter. Replace it every month during the heating season. If an air conditioning system is part of the same system, change the filter every month year-round.

The filter takes dust, dirt, pollen, carpet fibers, and pet dander out of the air, which keeps the house cleaner and helps keep allergies at bay. Without all that stuff in the airflow, the blower motor lasts longer, too. The filter also prevents compressor coils (hidden within the system) from becoming clogged.

It may seem silly to replace the filter so often, but you'd be surprised by how much airborne crud gets into your house. As a result, the filter gets clogged quickly, which makes the furnace work harder; it's like trying to breathe through a straw. Anyway, filters cost only a couple of bucks apiece.

Don't buy filters one at a time — get a case. They're cheaper by the dozen. What's more, the box reminds you to make a change, you see when you've missed a change, and you never skip a change because you don't have a filter on hand. As soon as you get home with the filters, open the box and label each one with the date that you intend to install it.

You usually find the filter near where the cool air enters the furnace — in the cold-air return duct or at the entrance to the blower chamber, or sometimes, in both locations (see Figure 4-1).

After you find the filter, slide it out and replace it with a new one. Make sure the airflow arrows on the side are pointing the right way (toward the blower and away from the cold air).

Cleaning the blower compartment

Before you put in a new filter, take a minute to clean the blower compartment. (Refer to Figure 4-1.) First, turn off the power to the furnace at the emergency switch. The switch may be mounted on or near the furnace itself. If you can't find the switch, turn the power off at the circuit breaker or fuse box before sticking your hands anywhere near the inside of the unit.

Next, open the hatch on the front (if it isn't already open to change the filter) and use a vacuum cleaner with an upholstery brush attachment to remove any dirt, lint, and dust bunnies you find.

Book II

Basic Home Mainte- nance and Improvement

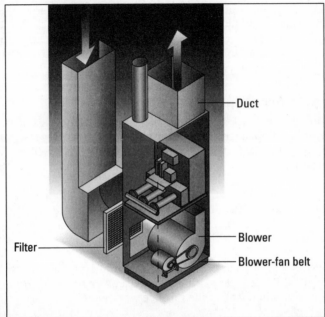

Figure 4-1:
The inside
of your
furnace.

Duct

Filter

Blower

Blower-fan belt

If you're feeling extra handy, you can clean the burner compartment, too. Moisture from the air can cause the burners to rust. Use a wire brush to clean them. Then use your vacuum's small snoot or the end of the hose. Don't get too ambitious — just carefully suck up the loosened rust, lint, and debris lying around in the compartment and on the burner elements. Make sure that the furnace is turned off and has had a chance to cool down before you start.

Be careful not to disturb any of the small wires inside the furnace. Most heating systems have low voltage controls, and if you were to inadvertently disturb a control wire, the system might not come back on.

Checking on the blower-fan belt

As long as you have the hatch off, check the condition and adjustment of the blower-fan belt (if you have one). A worn, wimpy belt isn't dangerous, but it makes a squealing noise that may drive you crazy and, more important, costs you money. If the belt isn't tight enough, it slips, and the fan won't turn like it should. You get less hot air for your money.

If the belt is frayed or looks worn, replace it. Loosen the adjusting bolt on the motor enough to get some slack and then slip the belt off the pulleys. Take the old belt with you when you go to the store to ensure that you end up with the right one. When you get back home (about four hours later), put the belt back on the pulleys and then tighten the adjustment bolt until you have a ½ inch or so of give when you press on the belt with your finger.

When you buy a new blower-fan belt, buy two. Keep the extra one in a plastic bag on a nail by the furnace. That way, you have an extra on hand when you have a middle-of-the-night, all-the-stores-are-closed, the-house-is-freezing, blown-fan-belt emergency.

If the belt looks fine but seems to have more than ½ inch of give either way (1 inch total), tighten it by taking up the extra slack using the motor adjusting bolt. Don't go too far — a too-tight belt damages the motor and fan bearings and makes a big, expensive mess of things.

While you're in there fooling with the belt, check the pulley alignment by placing a ruler against the pulley faces. The pulleys should line up perfectly, and the belt should travel between them without twisting even a little. If that isn't what you see, loosen the motor pulley mounting bolts and make an adjustment.

Put the hatch back on before you decide to try to fix or adjust anything else!

Checking the ducts for leaks

Take a step back from your furnace and check the ducts for leaks. The ducts are used to distribute warmed air to various locations throughout the house. A furnace with ducting is known as a *central heating system*.

If you see fuzz or feel warm air coming out through the joints between duct segments, seal them with metal tape (a new type of duct tape). For once, you'll be using duct tape on ducts!

If you don't already have a carbon monoxide detector, you need to install one. It could give you an important early warning of a potentially deadly leak.

Hot water systems

As with forced air systems, routine annual inspection and cleaning by a qualified, licensed heating contractor keeps your hot water system running for many years without trouble. Don't be a penny wise and a pound foolish. A dirty, inefficient boiler costs you far more than a service call. The service-person will catch little problems before they become big trouble. And a neglected system fails years sooner than a well-maintained one will.

Annual service keeps the system running properly and heads off most problems. You should also keep an eye on the system to make sure that all is well between inspections.

Gauging the pressure

Most hot water systems have a single gauge that measures three things: pressure, temperature, and *altitude* (the height of the water in the system).

Monitoring the pressure is important. Most boilers run with only 12 to 15 pounds of pressure. The boiler can become seriously damaged and even dangerous if the pressure exceeds 30 pounds.

Monitoring the pressure on a regular basis is probably all you ever need to do to maintain your system. The majority of the maintenance tasks should be left to a heating professional. However, if the pressure is abnormally high, you may have a waterlogged expansion tank that can be drained. Before calling in a repairperson, attempt to resolve the problem yourself by draining the expansion tank.

Located overhead near the boiler, a conventional expansion tank is cylindrical and has a drain valve at one end. To drain the excess water, turn off the power, turn off the water supply to the boiler, and let the tank cool. Attach a garden hose to the valve, open it, and let water out until the levels of the pressure gauges on the boiler and the expansion tank match. Don't forget to close the valve, turn the power back on, and reopen the water supply.

If you have a diaphragm expansion tank, the pressure problem is not too much water — it's too little air. You need to recharge the expansion tank. Use an ordinary tire pressure gauge to check the air pressure. If it's lower than the recommended psi, or pounds per square inch (look on the tank for the correct reading), use a bicycle pump to juice it back up.

Check with a representative from your local building department or public utility to determine which type of expansion tank you have.

After the expansion tank has been drained or the diaphragm tank has been refilled, restart the system and monitor it carefully. If the pressure goes back up, turn the system off and call a professional. You've done all you can do!

Boilers must have a proper pressure-relief valve, located at the top, which opens when the pressure reaches 30 pounds to prevent the boiler from exploding. If you ever see water draining out of the relief valve, chances are that the system is operating under excessively high pressure and should be checked by a professional.

Bleeding the radiators

Bleeding a radiator is sometimes necessary in even the best of systems. If you have a radiator in your system that just won't heat, chances are it's air-logged. Bleeding the air out of the radiator relieves the pressure and enables the system to fill normally.

To bleed the radiator, turn the bleed valve about a quarter-turn counterclockwise and keep the screwdriver or radiator key in the valve. If you hear a hissing sound, that's good — it's air escaping. As soon as the hissing stops and you see a dribble of water come out, close the valve.

Don't open the valve more than necessary; hot water will come rushing out before you can close it. At the very least, you'll make a wet mess. At worst, you could be scalded.

Steam systems

As with forced air and hot water systems, it pays to have a professional, licensed heating contractor check your steam system every year. Not only will you save money in the long run through greater efficiency, but you'll also have peace of mind knowing that your system is operating safely. We can't emphasize this point enough.

Most adjustments to your steam boiler should be performed by a pro. But you can do three important things yourself:

✔ **Check the steam gauge on a regular basis.** Make sure that it's within the normal range. If it isn't, shut the system down immediately and call for service.

✔ **Check the safety valve every month.** Located on the top of the boiler, this important valve vents excess pressure if the boiler goes crazy and exceeds safe levels. When the system is hot, push down on the handle to see if steam comes out. Stand away from the outlet — the steam is boiling hot. If no steam comes out, call a serviceperson to replace the valve immediately.

✔ **Check the water level once a month.** The water-level gauge has valves on each side. Open them both and make sure that the water level is in the middle, and then close the valves. If you didn't see any water, shut off the boiler, let it cool down, and then add water.

Because steam systems occasionally need water added, it's better and more convenient to have an automatic water valve added to the system. The valve monitors water levels and adds water ever so slowly to avoid damaging the boiler if the system needs it.

You also can do a few things to keep your radiators working well:

- ✔ **Make sure that every radiator slopes slightly toward the steam inlet pipe (which comes out of the wall or floor).** If one doesn't, slip a ¼-inch-thick rectangle of wood under the feet at the vent end. Doing so prevents those irritating knocking and clanging noises.

- ✔ **Check the vents to make sure that they aren't blocked.** Corrosion and paint can keep the vent from venting and then air trapped in the radiator prevents steam from entering the radiator. If your vent is blocked, replace it. Your local hardware store probably carries them (yours is not the only house in the area with steam heat), and they simply screw off and on.

- ✔ **Check the position of the inlet valves.** They should be either all the way closed or all the way open. A partially open or shut valve does nothing to regulate heat and causes knocking and clanging.

Got an inlet valve that's leaking? Chances are it's actually leaking at the *capnuts* (the big nuts at the vertical and horizontal connections). Luckily, a leak there can be cured with a little retightening. Get two wrenches — use one to hold the valve and the other to tighten the capnut. If the leak seems to be coming from under the valve handle, take off the valve head and tighten the topmost nut, which is called the *gland nut.*

If neither of those solutions fixes the leak, the *valve adapter* — the double-ended/double-threaded clunk of brass that connects the valve to the radiator — is probably the culprit. Once again, you need two wrenches to remove the valve, remove the adapter, and install a replacement. After you refill the system, check for leaks and tighten everything again.

Electric systems

Installations of electric heating systems hit their peak in the 1960s when electric rates were low. But now, at least in areas of the country not adjacent to a hydroelectric dam, the cost of electricity makes these systems very, very expensive to operate. If you have one, you're probably paying twice as much to heat your house as a neighbor with a gas-fired furnace or boiler.

A sad story about radiator valve connections

A Chicago friend of ours bought a newly rehabbed condo in an old building with steam heat. He moved into it in June, and everything was fine until the first cold night in October; a deafening hiss awakened him at 4:00 a.m. Finding his bedroom filled with a warm fog, he stumbled through his foggy hallway and living room toward the source of the noise and steam: his home office.

When he flipped on the light, he saw a jet of steam roaring out of the radiator's valve/valve adapter connection. The room was filled with steam, and big drops of condensation fell like rain from the ceiling. Rivulets of water were running down the freshly painted plaster walls, across the vintage moldings, and onto the refinished oak floor. Drops of condensation fell from the wood sash windows and pooled on the inside sills. The desk chair and area rug were soaking wet, his computer monitor and keyboard were filled with water (the CPU and laser printer were beneath the desk, luckily), and everything on the desktop was sopping wet.

After he closed the inlet valve, he discovered that the valve adapter capnut was screwed on but had not engaged the threads of the valve. And because the contractor hadn't fired up the system and checked all the newly installed radiators for leaks, the misconnection went unnoticed until the first time the heat came on, with terrible results.

Our friend mopped up the best he could, but everything was ruined. The walls, ceiling, windows, and doors had to be repainted (after being washed to remove mineral deposits left by the steam). And all the office furnishings and wet computer equipment had to be replaced. What a mess! But at least he had his contractor to blame — and pay for the damage. You won't have that opportunity if you fail to check your own connections.

That's the bad news. The good news is that electric heating, whether delivered via baseboard convectors or radiant floor or ceiling systems, requires you to do virtually nothing to maintain it. The only two things you have to do are

- Vacuum the convectors once a month (if you have them)
- Pay the electricity bill

Big or Small, an Air Conditioner Cools Y'all

Window units (which also can be installed through the wall) are refrigeration-type air conditioners. Central systems typically are refrigeration units too, but in hot/dry areas, evaporation units (sometimes informally called "swamp coolers") are popular.

Window units: Buy smart and live in cool comfort

Got a ten-year-old window air conditioner? Throw it out! A new unit will be 25 percent more energy efficient. But don't buy just any air conditioner; get one that works efficiently and does all it can to help you keep your electric bill reasonable:

- ✔ Measure the room you want to cool and bring the width, length, and height measurements to the store so that the salesperson can help you choose a unit that's efficient for the space.

- ✔ Get a unit with an energy-saving thermostat that cycles the unit on and off.

- ✔ Get a three-speed fan (high to cool the room quickly and medium or low to maintain the temperature).

- ✔ Choose a model with a timer to turn the unit on before you get home.

As for maintenance, you don't have to do much:

- ✔ **Clean the filter on the interior face every month.** To do so, unplug the unit. Pull off the front panel and remove the filter or slide the filter out the side. Then wash the filter gently in mild detergent, rinse, and dry.

- ✔ **Clean the condenser coil fins on the exterior face at least once a year.** Gently vacuum or brush the fins and then straighten any bent fins with a comb.

Never remove the cover and clean inside the unit. You could get a shock (even when it's unplugged), and all you can do is bend or break something. If you goof up something inside, all you'll have is an ugly doorstop.

Central systems: Let an A/C pro handle maintenance

If you have a central air conditioning system, just change the furnace filters monthly, hose off the exterior unit periodically to remove dust and debris, and most important, call a licensed heating/cooling contractor every spring for a thorough inspection and comprehensive maintenance. Refer to the section, "Replacing the furnace filter," earlier in this chapter.

If your air conditioner seems dead, or if it's blowing only hot air, check the circuit breakers before you call for service. Nothing makes you feel stupider than paying a serviceperson $75 to flip the breaker back on.

Ventilation: Letting You and Your House Breathe

When we talk about ventilation, we're actually talking about two different things: *interior* ventilation and *structural* ventilation. Proper interior ventilation is vital to your family's health and comfort. It helps your home rid itself of moisture, smoke, cooking odors, and indoor pollutants. Structural ventilation controls heat levels in the attic, moderates dampness in the crawlspace and basement, and keeps moisture out of uninsulated walls.

Interior ventilation

Kitchens, bathrooms, and laundries are the biggest sources of moisture and odors. The secret to having a nonstinky home is to have three key exhaust units: an exterior-venting range hood and bathroom and laundry exhaust fans.

Many kitchens have a range hood that doesn't actually vent anything — it just "filters" and recycles stovetop air. It's much better to get rid of the greasy, smoky, steamy air, and that requires ductwork to an exterior vent.

If your kitchen is perpetually stinky and the walls are covered with a thin film of grease, you need to stop eating so much fried food, and you need an exterior-venting exhaust fan. Your favorite appliance retailer can make it happen for you.

Airborne grease makes exhaust fans sticky, which in turn attracts dirt and dust. Clean the grill and fan blades twice a year, or whenever they start to look bad. The filters in recycling range hoods need cleaning every couple of months or so (depending on how and what you cook), and the fan and housing need a good cleaning every six months. If the filters have charcoal pellets inside, they need to be replaced annually. We clean our range hood filter in the dishwasher. Works great. For the grill and fan blades, use a spray-on degreaser. (Test the degreaser first to make sure that it won't remove paint.) Follow with a mild soap and water wash. Finally, flush with fresh water and towel-dry.

Bathrooms generate huge amounts of moisture and some unpleasant odors — especially at our brother's house. If you have incurable mildew in the shower, paint peeling off the walls, or a lingering funky smell, you need to install an exhaust fan or get a bigger, higher-capacity fan. Exhaust fans can vent the bad air through the wall or through the ceiling and attic. Call an electrical contractor, not your brother-in-law, to do the work.

Steam, hairspray, and other grooming products create a tacky surface that attracts dust, dirt, and fuzz at an alarming rate. Clean the housing, grill, and fan at least twice a year. Use the same techniques for cleaning that we suggest in the preceding section.

Structural ventilation

To keep heat and moisture from roasting and rotting your home over time, having adequate ventilation in the attic and the crawlspace (and the basement, if it's unfinished) is important.

In the attic, the idea is to create an upward flow of air. Cool air flows in through vents in the eaves and out through vent(s) nearer to, or at the peak of, the roof. In the crawlspace, cross-ventilation is utilized.

If insulation, crud, or dead squirrels block the vents, or if there aren't enough vents, the attic and subarea can become tropical. Rot can develop. Condensed water can soak insulation, making it ineffective. Condensation from above and below can make its way into the house, ruining ceiling, floor, and wall finishes and short-circuiting electrical wiring. If you notice that your vents are clogged, clear them immediately.

Building codes specify how much ventilation you need. As a general rule, have 1 square foot of vent area for every 150 square feet of attic area or crawlspace. We think more is better.

Roof ventilation

If your attic is hot and humid in the summer, you may need to install additional vents at the eaves and at the ridge of the roof. Assuming you're not a trained carpenter, we think it's best to leave this kind of work to a professional, someone who knows his way around the roof structure and knows how to install leak-free roof penetrations.

Yep, even venting must be maintained. Make sure that each vent and screen is painted (to prevent deterioration) and that the screens are secured to the frame of the vent. Animals, baseballs, and other common household missiles have a way of dislodging vent screens. Badly damaged vents should be replaced. Solid vent screens prevent varmints of all sorts from settling in your attic.

You can staple cardboard baffles to the rafters inside the attic adjacent to the vents. The baffles prevent insulation from being blown into piles, leaving bare spots.

Moist air can cause rot in the crawlspace, too, attacking your home from below. Just like an attic, a crawlspace needs a good flow of fresh air. If your crawlspace is always overly damp, or if you see mildew on the walls or structure, you may need better ventilation.

Extra vents are difficult to install and require special tools to cut through lumber, concrete block, concrete, and brick. Don't go poking holes in your foundation on your own — call a carpenter or masonry contractor to do the work. They have the know-how, tools, and experience to do the job right.

Foundation ventilation

Foundation vents can be damaged in the same way as eave vents. In fact, because they're closer to the ground, the potential for damage is greater. Critters that can't get into your attic will settle for the area beneath the floor. Establish a no-holes policy. Maintain foundation vents in the same way that we suggest for eave vents.

Book II

Basic Home Mainte-nance and Improvement

Chapter 5

Attending to Appliances

There's something warm and magical about a home's kitchen that inevitably and unquestionably seems to draw people to it. It is, for all intents and purposes, the entertainment hub of most homes. If you doubt this fact, just throw (or go to) a party and watch where everyone congregates. The kitchen becomes a warm and cozy gathering place, and the nicer and more inviting the kitchen, the more crowded it is.

The wonderful appliances that you find in a kitchen certainly add to this attraction. In this chapter, we offer tips and ideas for the safe operation and maintenance of the incredible array of ingenious life conveniences that make the kitchen the heart of the modern 21st-century home.

Although most home appliances are found in the kitchen, some are found in other parts of a home. For example, a washer and dryer can be located in the laundry room, mudroom, basement, porch, or garage. A secondary refrigerator or freezer may also be found in any of these locations. Thus, as we discuss appliances throughout this chapter, we invite you to use the information to care for your appliances wherever they may be — hopefully not in the repair shop.

For some parts of this chapter, we sought the sage advice of one of our all-time favorite appliance gurus, Otto "Butch" Gross of Middletown, Maryland, who often consults as the Carey Brothers' appliance expert in our newspaper columns. He also visits our radio broadcasts from time to time and is thus nationally known as the lovable, all-knowing "Appliance MD."

Making Cleaning Job One

You can severely shorten the life span of most major household appliances by neglect — and often greatly prolong it with simple care and basic preventive maintenance that centers mostly on — you guessed it — cleaning.

Cleaning appliances doesn't have to be complicated or expensive. You don't need a cabinet full of the latest high-tech cleaners and commercial products. Rather, a few simple household ingredients and a little elbow grease from time to time keeps appliances sparkling, operating efficiently, and often one step ahead of the repairman.

Many of our favorite cleaning formulas have simple, recurring components. Here's what they are and what they do:

- **Baking soda:** This is sodium bicarbonate, an alkaline substance in everything from fire extinguishers to sparkling water and antacids. It's produced naturally in mineral springs or made from another natural substance called sodium carbonate. Its mild abrasive and foaming action is a gentle but effective favorite.

- **White vinegar:** It's been around since ancient times and is used for everything imaginable. The acetic acid in vinegar gives it a tart taste — and great cleaning properties! When we say vinegar in the following sections, we mean distilled white household vinegar with a standard 5 percent acidity. For tough jobs, you can increase its acidity (and cleaning power) by boiling off some of the water content. Just remember: Higher acidity requires more careful handling.

- **Lemon juice:** Next to vinegar, lemons are the hands-down favorite for all-around cleaning and freshening. The secret ingredient of this wonder fruit is ascorbic acid — commonly known as vitamin C. It's a little more acidic than vinegar and often is a good substitute or an even better choice. By comparison, vinegar is inexpensive and has a sharp odor, while lemons cost a bit more and smell a heck of a lot better.

- **Salt:** There are almost 15,000 uses for this ancient natural food accent and preservative. Salt's mild abrasive and absorbent action makes it a cleaning natural.

Even though our homemade cleaning solutions are made with natural products, they still contain mild acids that can sting and burn both eyes and skin. Commercial products can be even more dangerous and highly volatile due to caustic components and chemical ingredients that can sting, burn, and give off vapors. Always wear rubber gloves, protect your eyes with goggles, and have plenty of ventilation when using any type of cleaner, whether store-bought or homemade.

In the following sections, we give recipes for our favorite cleaning solutions. We refer to these recipes frequently in the pages that follow.

All-Purpose, Handy Dandy Cleaner

You can use this solution to clean and freshen just about any surface. It works especially well for day-to-day cleaning of range tops and cooktops. Mix up the following ingredients:

- 1 teaspoon borax
- ½ teaspoon washing soda
- 2 teaspoons white vinegar
- ¼ teaspoon dishwashing liquid
- 2 cups hot water

You can replace the washing soda with baking soda and use lemon juice instead of white vinegar, depending on what you have lying around the house. The former is a bit stronger than the latter.

The secret to most cleaning formulas is hot water. It helps the various ingredients become a solution.

D-1-Y Cleanser Scrub

This cleaning formula is especially well suited for cleaning baked-on spills on glass or porcelain ranges and cooktops when you would normally pull out the cleanser. Start with the following ingredients:

- ¾ cup borax
- ¼ cup baking soda
- Dishwashing liquid to moisten

Combine the two powders and moisten them with just enough dishwashing liquid to create a gooey paste. You can use all borax or all baking soda if you wish. For a more pleasing and lingering aroma, add ¼ teaspoon lemon juice.

Gentle Glass Cleaner

The following solution works well for cleaning the glass shelving in your refrigerator, glass cooktops, and the windows in range and oven doors. You need the following materials:

- ✔ 2 tablespoons ammonia
- ✔ ¼ teaspoon dishwashing liquid
- ✔ ½ cup rubbing alcohol
- ✔ Hot water

Mix the ingredients and add enough hot water to make 1 quart of cleaner. If you prefer, you can avoid the smell of ammonia by using white vinegar or lemon juice. However, this substitution will make the formula less powerful.

For super-duper window cleaning — especially in cold weather — add 1 teaspoon of cornstarch to the formula.

People-Friendly Oven Cleaner

The following is a safe alternative to conventional caustic oven cleaners. It's also great for cleaning barbecue grills and grungy pots and pans.

- ✔ 2 teaspoons borax or baking soda
- ✔ 2 tablespoons dishwashing liquid
- ✔ 1¼ cups ammonia
- ✔ 1½ cups hot water

Mix the ingredients, apply generously to spills, and let soak for 30 minutes or as long as overnight. Loosen tough spills with a nylon scrubber and then wipe up with a damp sponge.

Super-Duper Disinfectant

This solution works well anywhere you would use a store-bought disinfectant, such as appliance pulls and handles, the inside face of the refrigerator where the gasket seats, the refrigerator drip pan, counters and cutting boards, and around the opening of your clothes washer. Mix the following ingredients and then scrub:

✔ 1 tablespoon borax or baking soda

✔ ¼ cup powdered laundry detergent

✔ ¼ cup pine-oil-based cleaner or pine oil

✔ ¾ cup hot water

For kitchen use, dilute with more hot water.

Easy Mildew Remover

Our mildew formula works great on painted and other washable surfaces.
Wear gloves and eye protection and have plenty of ventilation when working
with this solution:

✔ ⅓ cup powdered laundry detergent

✔ 1 quart household liquid chlorine bleach

✔ 3 quarts warm water

Book II

**Basic Home Mainte-
nance and Improvement**

Apply the remover by using a spray bottle, a sponge, or an old toothbrush.
Allow the solution to sit for five to ten minutes, but don't let it dry. You'll know
the solution is working when the black mildew stains turn white. Rinse all the
surfaces well with hot water and towel-dry.

Roaming the Range Top

Use our All-Purpose, Handy Dandy Cleaner for day-to-day surface cleaning
and our D-I-Y Cleanser Scrub for tougher cooked-on spills. Let the cleaner sit
for a longer time to soften really tough stains and hardened spills.

When food spills occur, immediately sprinkle them with table salt, which
absorbs moisture and makes the spill easy to clean up later when the stovetop cools. Cut and remove filmy grease with full-strength white vinegar or
lemon juice.

When cleaning a range top, pull off the upper and lower control knobs and
wash them separately in warm soapy water. Air-dry the knobs thoroughly
and completely before replacing them. Use a hair dryer to remove moisture
from nooks and crannies if necessary.

Electric range tops

Plug-in burners tend to collect grease and moisture down at the tips where they go into the power source receptacle. This leads to minor *arcing* (electrical shorting) that slowly builds and eventually ruins the burners. When you replace a burner, you must also replace the plug-in receptacle to prevent the arcing problem — not a cheap or convenient repair.

To prevent this problem, remove the plug-in burners and carefully clean the surfaces and tips with a damp rag or stiff nylon brush. You can use a soapy steel wool pad if plain water and a rag or nylon brush don't do the trick.

Never submerge plug-in burners in water. If you do, trace amounts of moisture usually remain on the plug-in tips and electric receptacles even if the metal prongs appear fully dry. The tips and receptacles contain porcelain, which is extremely porous and absorbs water. The result: You've brought water and electricity together for a potential electric shock.

Most ranges have two 6-inch and two 8-inch interchangeable plug-in burners. When removing them for cleaning, mark their origin so that you can put them back in exactly the same receptacle. If you don't, you switch one burner that may be corroded or dirty and starting to burn out to a nice, clean receptacle that's functioning okay. You cause cross-contamination that can make *both* burners fail.

Another kind of electric burner, the fixed unit, is hard-wired and generally lifts up for cleaning. The advantage of this type is that the tips never corrode or burn out from dripping grease. Euro-style solid cast-iron burners (also called *hobs*) have a coating that wears off with use. To prevent rusting, manufacturers and dealers offer a special cleaner/sealer that you apply to a cold burner; it burns off when the burner heats. You can also use a light coat of mineral or cooking oil to prevent rusting, but oil smokes a bit when the burner heats. Turn on the vent fan to remove any light residual smoking or burning odor.

Round cast-iron tops that cover elements to create a neat Euro-burner look distribute heat more evenly and prevent spills from dripping down into the drip pan and receptacle below — but they often cause undue heat stress and can shorten the life of a burner. It's a question of whether you want to trade a longer lifespan for a slicker image and ease of cleaning.

Always keep lightweight inexpensive aluminum drip pans under the heating elements to prevent grease and oils from entering the works of the range. Clean the drip pans with baking soda rather than soap to keep them shiny. Never line your drip pans with aluminum foil, which can create hot spots underneath a burner that can quickly end the useful life of an electric element.

Gas range tops

Take out removable gas burners periodically and clean them with a stiff nylon brush, cleaning the gas jet holes with baking soda and hot water. You can remove most burners by simply lifting them out of the opening in the cooktop, without the need for tools. If you aren't sure whether your burners are the removable type, refer to your owner's manual.

Between the burners is a connector tube (called a *flash tube*) with an opening and a pilot light or electric spark igniter. This is where the gas is ignited and carried or drawn to each burner by what's called a *venturi action.* In most cases, this configuration is part of the burner assembly and can be cleaned as described earlier. Cleaning is important since the flash tube can become clogged with grease.

Book II

Basic Home Mainte- nance and Improvement

Clean nonremovable sealed gas burners with a small brush and a solution of baking soda and water. You'll know for certain if you have a sealed gas burner — the drip pan that surrounds each burner is anchored securely to the cooktop and can't be removed. The only components that can be removed for cleaning are the *burner grate* (the part that rests above the flame, where you put the pots) and the *burner cap,* which distributes the flame evenly. Use an all-purpose cleaner or the D-I-Y Cleanser Scrub described earlier in this chapter to clean these components.

Never use soap to clean burners. The chemicals in soap trigger corrosion on burner housings, which are made of aluminum. Baking soda is noncorrosive and is not harmful to aluminum.

Make sure that you wipe the burner housings thoroughly clean and remove all water from the gas jet holes — first use a soft cloth and then use a hair dryer to remove any remaining moisture, if necessary.

Taking a look at your gas grill jets

Outdoor gas barbecues operate just like indoor gas ranges. Dripping food juices easily clog your grill's gas jet orifices, and nature's little critters (like spiders) like to deposit egg sacks in the jets for family breeding.

Before you fire up your grill, and especially after it's been sitting all winter, carefully inspect each opening and the tubes leading to it for obstructions. Sometimes, one side lights while the other spews unlit gas that quietly collects and ultimately goes kaboom when it reaches the other side.

If you notice that a flame jet shoots farther out than the others, then the opening is partially blocked and needs cleaning. Generally, if the flame burns yellow, it needs attention because it's starved for air or blocked at some point. A proper gas flame burns clear and blue.

Opening the Door and Rolling Up Your Sleeves: The Oven

Aside from saving you embarrassment when company calls, a clean oven operates more efficiently by providing even heating. A dirty oven can prevent the door from sealing properly, which allows heat and smoke to escape.

You can clean oven interiors with commercial cleansers, steel wool soap pads, or our cleaner described in the "People-Friendly Oven Cleaner" section, earlier in this chapter.

If a commercial cleaner says that you must wear rubber gloves and avoid breathing fumes, it's probably very caustic and possibly toxic. It may give off harmful gases even after the cleaning is complete and the oven is heated for use. Thus, we suggest that you avoid using them. If you must use a commercial cleaner, follow the label directions to the letter.

To loosen up tough, baked-on spills, preheat the oven to 200 degrees, turn off the heat, and then put a bowl of ammonia in your oven overnight. This technique works well as long as you don't mind the smell of ammonia in your kitchen the next day. Ammonia and commercial window cleaners that contain ammonia are also great for cleaning browned and discolored oven window glass. You can use mild abrasives and scouring pads for tough spots, too.

For wire oven racks that are severely caked with food spills, put them in a plastic trash bag, add some ammonia, and seal the bag well with a twist tie. Leave the bag outside overnight, and then either hose them off, hand-wash them, or put the racks in your dishwasher.

Speaking of spills, many people believe that they can simplify oven cleaning by lining the bottom of the oven with aluminum foil to catch spills. This is a no-no! A layer of foil causes the oven to heat unevenly and can shorten the life of the element by causing it to superheat in certain locations.

Checking the oven temperature control

You don't need to be in the same culinary league as Julia Child to know that the accuracy of an oven temperature control can make all the difference when it comes to producing a perfect meal. A poorly calibrated control can make it virtually impossible to conform to recipe heating instructions. Thus, you end up with a dish that's either undercooked or overcooked. Yuck!

To check the accuracy of your oven's temperature control, put an oven thermometer on the middle rack. Set the thermometer for 350 degrees and heat the oven for 20 minutes. Write down the temperature. Check three more times at ten-minute intervals, noting the temperatures. The average temperature should be within 25 degrees of 350.

If you find that the temperature is off, recalibrate the temperature control dial by removing the oven temperature knob and doing one of the following:

✔ Loosen the screws and turn the movable disk on the backside. One notch represents 10 degrees.

✔ Turn the adjustment screw inside the hollow shaft clockwise to lower the temperature or counterclockwise to raise it. If it requires more than an eighth of a turn or is off by 50 degrees or more, install a new temperature control.

If the temperature in your gas oven fluctuates, or if the oven bakes unevenly, chances are good that your thermostat is faulty. Your best bet is to leave the installation to a pro. The only tool you should pick up to make this repair is your telephone.

Book II

Basic Home Maintenance and Improvement

Cleaning an electric oven

In an electric oven, you find two heating elements: one for broiling (above) and one for baking (below). If possible, buy a model that allows you to lift the bottom bake element for easier cleaning of the bottom of the oven.

Open the oven door 8 to 10 inches and try lifting. Most ovens have special hinges that allow the door to lift right off. You can then easily clean deep in the oven's interior without stretching over the lowered open oven door. You also can clean the glass and the inside surface of the door on a towel at countertop level.

Replacing the oven light

When your oven light burns out, turn off the power at the main circuit, remove the glass shield, and, using gloves or a dry cloth, unscrew the old bulb. Replace it only with a special 40-watt appliance bulb that can stand extreme temperatures (or whatever the manufacturer recommends). If the light doesn't light, you may have a larger problem that needs professional attention.

Use our recommended oven cleaner in the "People-Friendly Oven Cleaner" section, discussed earlier in this chapter, to clean the interior of your oven.

Cleaning a gas oven

You can use our People-Friendly Oven Cleaner to make the inside of your gas oven sparkle. For baked-on spots, use our D-I-Y Cleanser Scrub. (You can find the recipes for both of these solutions in the "Making Cleaning Job One" section, earlier in this chapter.) If neither of these solutions does the trick, try a store-bought oven cleaner, following the label directions to the letter. Rubber gloves, eye protection, and plenty of ventilation are essential.

As with most ovens, the bottom of a gas oven is the object of most cleaning attention. You can remove the bottom panel simply by lifting it out or by removing a couple of screws that hold it in place. Doing so enables you to work on it in a deep sink or bathtub. Over time, the bottom panel can become corroded or broken. You can replace it by using the steps to remove and replace it for cleaning.

With the oven bottom out, you can inspect and clean the gas burner. Uneven heating, poor baking, or a gas odor when the oven is on are telltale signs of a clogged burner. Your best bet to determine how the burner is working is to turn it on with the bottom panel off. If the flame isn't continuous along both sides of the burner, some of its holes are probably clogged. To set your burner free, turn off the oven control and insert a wire — such as a coat hanger — into the clogged holes. Works every time!

After the gas burner is clean, check to make sure that it's burning efficiently — a steady blue 1-inch cone, with an inner cone of about ½ inch. The air shutter, which you can adjust, controls the air mixture and, in turn, the color of the flame. Consult your owner's manual for information about how to adjust the burner flame in your gas oven.

Cleaning a self-cleaning electric oven

Never use a commercial oven cleaner on a self-cleaning oven. These harsh cleaners can pit, burn, and eat into the porcelain surface. The result? When you reach the normal 850- to 900-degree level for self-cleaning, you can actually pop chunks of porcelain off the oven walls as large as 6 inches across.

Instead, let the intended high heat action turn food spills into carbon, which all but disappears with complete combustion, and then wipe up any minor dustlike ash residue with a damp cloth, paper towel, or sponge when the oven cools.

Don't open the oven door if you notice a flame-up or smell something burning. The oven is doing what it's supposed to do. If you're really worried, shut the oven off. The lack of oxygen in the closed and sealed oven and diminishing heat level will extinguish any burning in a matter of moments.

You can clean the area surrounding the oven door gasket with a mild abrasive, such as our D-I-Y Cleanser Scrub or a commercial silver polish. With a wide spatula or paint scraper, lift up the gasket edge to prevent rubbing against it and possible fraying.

Many heavier-weight porcelain-coated drip pans can be put in the oven during self-cleaning, making the cleanup of drips and spills a snap. Manufacturers recommend removing racks during the self-cleaning process to prevent the racks from turning brown. Instead, clean them by using the process mentioned earlier in this chapter in the "Opening the Door and Rolling Up Your Sleeves: The Oven" section. We strongly recommend that you consult your owner's manual for specific information about how to use your self-cleaning oven.

Cleaning a continuous-cleaning oven

Continuous-cleaning ovens have a special rough-texture porcelain interior. Spills gradually burn off as you use the oven. A speckled surface helps hide foods while they burn off, but these ovens may not always look clean in the process.

Combusted foods tend to remain on the oven walls. To prevent this problem, wipe up large spills as soon as the oven cools — especially sugary or starchy foods. These models work best on greasy spills.

Never use harsh abrasives, scouring pads, or commercial oven cleaners on continuous-cleaning ovens. These cleaners damage the special lining. Gentle cleaning by hand with baking soda and warm water works best.

Tidying up behind the range

Occasionally, you may want to clean and vacuum the back of your range and the area behind, to the sides, and below it. The back of a range consists of a metal panel that can be removed for service or repair. It's okay to clean dust and grime that collects on this panel, but otherwise it should not be removed.

To accomplish this task, you'll need to pull the range out of the opening. If the range is electric, the cord should be long enough for you to move the appliance out and then unplug it. Gas models should have a flexible gas line that allows you to pull the appliance out. Do not move a gas range that has a rigid gas pipe — call a service professional.

Be especially careful not to damage flooring in front of an appliance when moving it. An old piece of carpet turned upside down and placed under the appliance feet, an appliance dolly, or an appliance skid pad (available from an appliance service company) simplifies appliance moving and prevents torn vinyl, scratched hardwood, or chipped tile.

Hanging Out in the Range Hood

The range hood has an important job: It removes the excess moisture and smoke that are produced when cooking. The most important aspect of range hood maintenance is cleaning. Remove and clean the metal mesh filter(s) that keep grease from getting into the ductwork. Soak the filters in a sink full of hot water and liquid dish detergent. Then rinse them clean with very hot water.

Inspect the filters for grease buildup once a month or more, depending on how much you cook and operate the vent and fan. Worn or damaged filter screens should be replaced with new ones, which you can obtain from an appliance repair shop or through the manufacturer.

If you put mesh filters in the bottom rack of your dishwasher (as many amateur tipsters advise), they may leave a greasy residue behind that's hard to remove and can ultimately clog lines and affect your dishwasher's operation. It's okay to put them in the dishwasher after you've given them an initial once-over, though.

For nonvented hoods, remember to replace the disposable charcoal filter every year (or according to the manufacturer's directions).

With filters removed, wash the range hood interior with our All-Purpose, Handy Dandy Cleaner (see the "All-Purpose, Handy Dandy Cleaner" section earlier in this chapter) or with warm water and liquid dish detergent.

Microwave Maintenance Mania

Most kitchens today include a microwave oven, which saves cooking time and makes cleanup much easier. Following a few simple maintenance procedures can extend the life of your microwave and ensure that it operates safely and efficiently.

✔ **Check microwaves that are more than 15 years old for output efficiency and radiation leakage.** For a 600- to 1,000-watt microwave, place an 8-ounce cup of water in the oven and operate the unit on high for three minutes. The water should reach a rolling boil. If it doesn't, take the microwave to a service shop for inspection.

Have a professional appliance repair technician test for radiation leakage. In addition, the pro can check other aspects of operation to determine whether it should be repaired or replaced.

✔ **Never attempt to repair an ailing microwave yourself.** Besides the inherent dangers (the unit's capacitor holds up to 4,000 volts of electricity), unauthorized repairs by anyone other than an authorized service technician almost always void the manufacturer's warranty.

✔ **Provide a separate electrical circuit for the microwave whenever possible.** Poor heating in your microwave can result from an overworked electrical circuit. Operating a microwave on a circuit that's serving other appliances not only diminishes its effectiveness, but also could result in an electrical fire. If lights dim when you use the microwave, consult an electrician.

✔ **Wipe up spills promptly after use.** Keep the interior of the oven and the area surrounding the door clean, using a damp sponge to catch spills and splatters as they occur.

✔ **Remove stuck-on food particles with an all-purpose cleaning solution.** Food particles left over long periods eventually turn to carbon and cause arcing (electrical sparking), which can etch interior surfaces and can even compromise the seal around the door.

Book II

Basic Home Maintenance and Improvement

Appliance repair pros say that the most common problem they find is a simple microwave fuse that gets metal fatigue after three or four years' use. At that point, even a minor power surge can cause the fuse to burn out. If your microwave quits, don't panic: It may just be an interior fuse that needs replacing by a pro.

Dishwashers

The single most important aspect of dishwasher maintenance is to keep the interior clean. Doing so keeps all the hoses and passages clear, which, in turn, lets the machine operate freely and ultimately washes your dishes better. Check out these tips for keeping your dishwasher clean:

✔ Most people use far too much soap when they run the dishwasher. Any more than 1 tablespoon is too much, leading to a residue buildup that's hard to get rid of.

✔ Never wash anything other than dishes in your dishwasher. Tools, clothes, sneakers, greasy range hood filters, and so on can leave harmful grease and residue that clog the machine's works and inhibit proper operation.

✔ If you see interior staining or have soap residue buildup, your pump is working too hard to move water through the system. The best way to clean the interior is with citric acid. Use pure citric acid crystals, which you can find in grocery stores and drugstores. Fill your main soap cup and then run the dishwasher through a complete cycle with the dishwasher empty. Then, once a week, add 1 teaspoon of the acid crystals to your soap for general maintenance.

You can substitute Tang or a lemonade mix that contains vitamin C (citric acid) for the crystals. They work well, too, only with smaller amounts of citric acid per dose.

✔ Run your dishwasher at least once a week to keep the seals moist and to prevent leaks and eventual failure. Periodically wipe the area around the seals to prevent soap scum buildup, which can cause leaks.

Refrigerators and Freezers

The most important thing to remember for any refrigerator is to keep the condenser coils clean. These coils are usually located at the bottom of the refrigerator behind a removable grille. On some older models, they're located on the back. Air passing over these coils cools the refrigerator, and if the coils are dirty, the unit has to work harder to do its job.

To clean the coils, first unplug the refrigerator. Remove the grille by grabbing both ends and pulling gently. Use a vacuum cleaner with a brush or crevice attachment to get as far into and under the unit as possible, being careful not to force access, which can bend condenser tubing and the thin metal coil fins. While the grille is off, also remove and wash the refrigerator drain pan.

Use the power-saver switch (usually located inside your refrigerator). It controls small electric heaters that keep the outside of the cabinet from sweating. Turn the switch on only when it's humid and you see moisture beads. When both the weather and your refrigerator are dry, turn this function off to save energy costs. The power-saver switch also helps prevent rust and nasty mold buildups.

A refrigerator's chilly environment is kept that way primarily by a gasket at the perimeter of the door. It helps maintain an airtight seal. It's also a prime candidate for mold. To remove mold from around the gasket, clean it with a solution of liquid chlorine bleach and water (4 tablespoons in a quart of hot water), scrubbing well with an old toothbrush. Afterward, wipe off all residue with warm water and a mild liquid dish detergent.

Replace the rubber gasket's oils that you've removed by applying a light coat of lemon oil, mineral oil, or any type of body lotion with lanolin in it to keep the gasket soft and supple (just like your skin). Wipe off any food or liquid spills, drips, and runs from around the door and gaskets. If you don't, they'll dry and become sticky, possibly ripping away the gasket when you open the door.

Most people know that an open box of baking soda keeps the refrigerator or freezer smelling fresh. Did you know that you can also use a small bowl with a few tablespoons of instant freeze-dried coffee crystals in it? Believe it or not, granulated cat litter works, too. An added bonus: The litter eliminates food odors in ice cubes. Kill two birds with one stone by pouring the contents of a box of baking soda into the garbage disposal and filling the baking soda box with cat litter. The baking soda will freshen the garbage disposal, while the cat litter will keep the fridge odor free.

To clean the interior of the refrigerator, first turn off the refrigerator and remove all the food. Wash removable shelves and bins in the sink with liquid dish detergent and warm water. Wipe down the interior walls with our All-Purpose, Handy Dandy Cleaner or a solution of warm water and baking soda.

Book II

Basic Home Mainte-nance and Improvement

Defrosting the freezer

Defrost your freezer when ice begins to build up on the interior. Aside from diminishing usable freezer space, the ice can prevent the door from sealing properly. Most freezers need to be defrosted at least once and sometimes twice a year. Start by turning off the power to the freezer and removing all the contents. You can allow the ice to melt on its own or speed things up by placing a pot of hot water in the freezer and closing the door. Clean the interior by using the method for cleaning the interior of the fridge described in the preceding section.

Defrosting the freezer drain line

Defrost the freezer drain line leading to the drain pan at least once a year. Mold buildup starts to retain moisture, which, in turn, starts to freeze and ultimately blocks the line.

First, turn off the freezer so that you can melt the ice in the drain line. Then clear the line by putting very hot water into a turkey baster and inserting it into the ½-inch drain hole located at the back of the freezer floor. Release hot water into the line until it runs free, and then blast in more hot water to blow out any mold buildup. Finally, put 2 tablespoons of chlorine bleach in 1 cup of hot water and pour it down the drain to kill off any remaining mold spores.

Garbage Disposals

Clean your sink's garbage disposal by putting ice cubes and ¼ cup of white vinegar into the unit and operating it with no running water. As the blades grind up the ice, it removes food particles and gooey buildup. When it sounds like the cubes are all gone, start a slow trickle of cold water. You'll probably find that the disposal's drain openings are frozen and clogged with ice, and the water will start to back up — which is good, because the churning water also washes the sides before the ice melts, the drain clears, and everything drains away.

For a more thorough cleaning, sprinkle some baking soda on top of the ice cubes. To make the disposal smell fresh, add some citric acid crystals, Tang, a drink mix containing vitamin C, or half a lemon.

You can also use vinegar ice cubes as an easy means of cleaning your disposal and sharpening its blades. Pour 1 cup of vinegar into an empty ice cube tray and fill the balance of the tray with water. Put the tray in the freezer until you have solid vinegar ice cubes. Periodically pour an entire tray of ice cubes into the disposal while it's running. Just be sure to mark the tray with the vinegar ice cubes. Otherwise, your guests will have an unpleasant experience the next time that you serve them a cold beverage!

Washing Machines

To clean tub interiors, use the same citric acid cleaning procedure outlined for dishwashers earlier in this chapter. Doing so removes mineral deposits, lime, and soap buildup, all of which affect the pump's operation.

If you find rust stains inside the tub, try a professionally installed plastic tub liner before considering replacement. You can make temporary patch-ups on small nicks in the porcelain where rusting occurs with a dab or two of enamel paint or clear nail polish. A better solution is a porcelain repair kit made for bathtubs, available at your local hardware store. It lasts longer but not forever.

If your water outlet hose drains into a laundry basin rather than a stand pipe, cover the end with an old nylon stocking. Doing so collects 95 percent of all lint that otherwise would go into your sink's drain line. The nylon stocking filter also reduces splashing when the washer empties into the sink. When the stocking fills with lint, remove and replace it.

If your cold water is running slowly, turn off the water inlet valves, remove the water hoses, and clean the small screen filters, which are probably clogged with mineral buildup and debris. The fine mesh filters are usually at either end of the hose or on the back of the washing machine's water inlet port. If debris gets past these screen filters, it can damage the pump and lead to a costly repair.

Also consider switching from rubber water inlet hoses to long-lasting braided stainless steel hoses. They cost a little more, but they're good insurance against flooding caused by hose failure.

Clothes Dryers

Clean the lint screen in your clothes dryer thoroughly after every load. If it's clogged with lint, the air won't circulate, the clothes won't dry, and the dryer will run far longer, which wears it out faster and wastes plenty of energy in the process.

In addition to making the dryer work extra-hard, dryer lint is a big fire hazard. Therefore, you should clean the dryer duct at least twice a year. The easiest means of cleaning a short dryer duct is with a dryer duct cleaning brush, which looks like a miniature version of what a chimney sweep would use. A stiff-bristle circular brush is attached to a flexible handle, and you move the brush back and forth inside the duct to dislodge the lint. The brush and a vacuum is a winning combination for cleaning almost any dryer duct.

If you have an excessively long (20 feet or more) dryer vent leading outside or to the roof, make a vent-cleaning tool by fishing a nylon line from outside to the vent hose mounting inside (after removing the big, plastic, accordion-type flexible dryer vent exhaust hose). Then tie a nylon brush — one that's big enough to brush the vent walls — to the line, which can then be drawn up into the vent, leaving enough line on the other end to draw it back again. When you're finished, leave some line exposed outside and, pulling the inside line off to the side, reattach the accordion-type flexible vent hose and let the brush and excess line lay off to the side for the next vent-scrubbing episode.

To prevent damage due to excess moisture, a dryer duct should always termi-nate at the home's exterior — never in the attic, basement, or crawlspace. Most dryer ducts terminate at a hood mounted on an exterior wall. The hood contains a damper that's designed to open only when the dryer is blowing air through the duct. The damper prevents cold air and birds and rodents from nesting in the duct. However, crafty varmints often find a means of breaching the damper. If you experience such a problem, install a protective screen. If you already have such a device, make sure to patch any holes so that the screen can do its job.

Regardless of the length of your exterior vent, periodically remove the flexible accordion-type exhaust hose and vacuum it out. Lint buildup reduces efficiency, wastes energy, and can cause a fire by preventing superheated air from passing freely.

Better yet, replace a flexible accordion-type exhaust hose (especially if it's vinyl) with sheet metal ducting. It doesn't clog nearly as easily and is a more efficient vent, making your clothes dry faster.

Excess lint in a clothes dryer exhaust system is an accident waiting to happen. Aside from the lint screen and the dryer duct, lint can accumulate at the bottom of the housing that contains the lint screen. An easy means of removing this lint is to construct a custom vacuum hose attachment by using a short piece of rubber hose, the cap to an aerosol can, and some duct tape. The cap acts as an adapter that fits over the end of a wet/dry vacuum hose. Make a hole in the center of the cap the size of the outside diameter of the hose. Insert the hose snugly into the hole and attach the two with duct tape. Attach the cap to the end of a wet/dry vacuum and insert the hose into the filter housing until it reaches the bottom (see Figure 5-1).

Figure 5-1:
Removing lint from inside the machine.

If you have an electric dryer, never open the door mid-cycle without first turning the dial to the air-dry mode or advancing the timer to shut off the heater. Otherwise, the red-hot heaters allow heat to collect inside the unit until it triggers the thermal fuse. The fuse is a built-in safety mechanism that works only once; after it goes off, a service technician has to fix it before your dryer will operate again. If you want to interrupt a drying cycle, always let the heater cool off before stopping. If you don't, you may wind up line-drying your duds for a while.

Chapter 6

Foundation Fundamentals

. . . .

In This Chapter

▶ Laying down the basics on foundations

▶ Knowing the difference between fungus and efflorescence

▶ Keeping your basement dry

▶ Caring for brick and block foundations

. . . .

This chapter tells you how to care for one of the most important components of your home: the foundation. A sound foundation keeps the other parts of a home in good working order. Here, we show you how to keep cracks in concrete from spreading, maintain mortar that's surrounding brick, control excess water, and keep your basement or crawlspace dry.

A Little Foundation about the Foundation

The foundation is a home's infrastructure. It supports the floor, wall, and roof framing. Moreover, the foundation helps keep floors level, basements dry, and, believe it or not, windows and doors operating smoothly. The foundation is also an anchor of sorts, making it especially important if your home is built on anything other than flat ground or is in an area prone to earthquakes.

Interestingly, the origin of many leaks and squeaks can be traced to the foundation. A cracked or poorly waterproofed foundation, for example, can result in excess moisture in a crawlspace or basement. Without adequate ventilation, this moisture can condense and lead to, at best, musty odors, leaks, squeaks, and, at worst, rotted floor framing.

If your foundation is made of brick, be sure to read the sections of this chapter on dealing with efflorescence, moisture control, grading and drainage, and especially tuck-pointing.

If your brick foundation isn't reinforced with steel or is crumbling, consult a structural engineer immediately to determine what means can be used to improve the foundation's integrity. (Although this matter goes beyond the scope of home maintenance, be aware that an unreinforced brick foundation that's in good condition can be reinforced by capping the foundation with concrete reinforced with steel.)

If your home was built after the 1930s, chances are high that the foundation consists either of poured-in-place concrete (grade beam), concrete block, or a concrete slab (see Figure 6-1). The latter has become especially prevalent in the last couple of decades by builders seeking to cut costs and create more affordable housing.

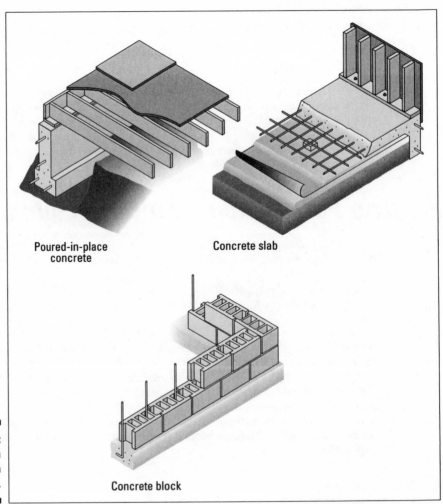

Poured-in-place concrete

Concrete slab

Figure 6-1:
Common
foundation
types.

Concrete block

Is There a Fungus Amongus?

One of the most common foundation ailments is a white powdery substance that appears on the ground under your home, on the floor framing, or on your foundation or basement walls. Although most people mistake the white powder for a fungus (fungus is typically green or black), it's really *efflorescence,* which is a growth of salt crystals caused by the evaporation of salt-laden water.

Efflorescence appears when mineral salts in the concrete or mortar leak to the surface. Although efflorescence isn't particularly destructive, it's unsightly and can result in splintering or minor deterioration of the surface on which it grows.

The area below the main floor and within the foundation walls can consist of a concrete slab, a crawlspace, or a basement. With each of these configurations comes a host of specific maintenance routines that can safeguard your home's integrity.

Book II

Basic Home Maintenance and Improvement

Cleaning up efflorescence

Applying a solution of 1 cup vinegar in 1 quart warm water with a nylon brush removes efflorescence in a jiffy. To clean stubborn areas, use a wire brush and a 10 percent solution of muriatic acid in water. (*Muriatic acid* is swimming pool acid. You find it in swimming pool supply stores as well as at many hardware stores and home centers.) After applying either the vinegar or the acid solution, rinse the area thoroughly with fresh water. More than one application may be required to achieve the desired result.

Working with acid can be dangerous. Always wear safety goggles, rubber gloves, and protective clothing, and have plenty of ventilation. Add the acid to the water in a plastic bucket. Adding the water to the acid can produce a dangerous reaction.

Preventing efflorescence

Often, you can prevent efflorescence from recurring by sealing the concrete, block, or brick with a high-quality silicone concrete and masonry sealer. These sealers are generally clear and last for six months to a year, depending on the climate.

We don't recommend using inexpensive "water seals" because they don't offer the high level of protection that better-quality, pricier products do. Keep in mind that you need to apply the cheaper stuff more frequently, which generally ends up costing more money in the long run.

You can apply concrete sealer with a brush, roller, or pump garden sprayer. It's imperative that the concrete be clean before you seal it. A good power washing with a pressure washer or water blaster prior to applying the sealer offers the greatest penetration and longevity.

Preventing Moisture from Building Up under Your Home

If you see efflorescence (discussed in the preceding section) on your basement walls and/or crawlspace and your crawlspace is perpetually damp and mildewy, you've got a moisture problem! A natural spring, a high water table, a broken water or sewer line, poor grading and drainage, excessive irrigation, and poor ventilation are some of the most common causes of this problem.

What's a little water under the house going to hurt, you ask? Lots! Aside from turning a trip into the crawlspace into a mud-wrestling match or your basement into a sauna, excess moisture can lead to a glut of problems, such as repulsive odors, rotted framing, structural pests, foundation movement, efflorescence, and allergy-irritating mold. We can't stress enough the importance of doing everything you can to keep excess moisture out of this area of your home.

Rooting out the cause of moisture

A musty or pungent odor usually accompanies efflorescence and excessive moisture. Accordingly, a good sniffer proves invaluable in investigating the problem.

Start by checking for leaks in water and sewer lines under your home. A failing plumbing fitting or corroded pipe is often the culprit. Fitting a replacement or installing a repair "sleeve" around the damaged section of pipe almost always does the trick.

Believe it or not, a wet basement may be the result of a leaking toilet, tub, or valve located in the walls above. When it comes to finding the cause of a damp basement or crawlspace, leave no stone unturned.

Overwatering planters surrounding the house is another common cause of water down under. Adjusting watering time, watering less often, installing an automatic timer, and adjusting sprinkler heads are the simplest means of solving this problem. Better yet, at planters next to the house, convert the traditional sprinkler system to a drip irrigation system. Doing so not only helps dry things out under the house, but it also makes for a healthier garden.

Using gutters to reduce moisture

Rain gutters are more than a decorative element to the roofline of a home. Their primary purpose is to capture the tremendous amount of rainfall that runs off of the average roof. Without gutters, rainwater collects at the foundation and eventually ends up in the crawlspace or basement. If you don't have gutters, install them. And if you do, keep them clean.

Make sure that your gutters and downspouts direct water a safe distance away from your house. Even worse than not having gutters and downspouts is having downspouts jettison water directly onto the foundation. We recommend piping the water 20 feet away from the foundation. You can use a length of rigid or flexible plastic drainpipe (without perforations) to carry water away from the downspout outlet to a safe location. Better yet, to avoid an eyesore and a potential tripping hazard, bury the drainpipe below the ground.

Draining water away from the house

Be sure that the soil around your home slopes away from the foundation. This setup helps divert most irrigation and rainwater away from the structure. The earth within 30 inches of the foundation should slope down and away at a rate of $\frac{1}{10}$ inch per foot. We think that $\frac{1}{4}$ inch per foot is better. A good general rule is "More slope equals less ponding." Keep in mind that grading should be built up with well-packed dirt and not loose topsoil, which erodes.

If you're having a difficult time determining the slope, use a measuring tape and a level. Rest one end of the level on the soil against the foundation and point the opposite end away in the direction the ground should slope. With the bubble centered between the level lines, use a measuring tape to measure the distance between the bottom of the level and the top of the soil. For example, if you're using a 3-foot level and establishing a grade of $\frac{1}{4}$ inch per foot, the distance between the level and the soil should be at least $\frac{3}{4}$ inch.

Generally speaking, grading requires a pick, a shovel, a steel rake, and a strong back. You also need a homemade tamp that consists of a block of wood attached to a wooden post that serves as a handle. Use the pick to loosen the soil and break large clumps into smaller, more manageable soil that you can grade with a rake. Remove rocks and large clumps and replace them with clean fill dirt that can be well packed.

After you complete your grading work, use a garden hose to wet the area, which further compacts the soil. Wetting the area also gives you an opportunity to test how the soil drains.

The same holds true for paths and patios. A patio or path that slopes toward the home discharges water into the basement or crawlspace, which in turn breeds foundation problems and structural rot. Unfortunately, the only sure way to correct this problem is to remove and replace the source, and replacing a path or patio can be pricey.

Giving the problem some air

Ventilation is another effective means of controlling moisture in a crawlspace or basement. Two types of ventilation exist:

- ✔ **Passive ventilation** is natural ventilation that doesn't use mechanical equipment. *Foundation vents* (metal screens or louvers) and daylight windows for basements are the best sources of passive ventilation.

- ✔ **Active ventilation** involves mechanical equipment, such as an exhaust fan.

Passive ventilation should be your first choice because it allows nature to be your workhorse and doesn't necessitate the use of energy to drive a mechanical device. You save on your utility bill and help the environment by not relying on fossil fuel. Having said that, don't hesitate to use active ventilation if your crawlspace or basement needs it.

If you use passive ventilation, you must keep vents clean to allow maximum airflow. Thinning shrubbery, vines, and ground cover may be necessary from time to time. If your vents are clear and moisture is still a problem, you may be able to add vents. Because adding vents can affect the aesthetic and structural elements of your home, consult a qualified engineer for this project.

All the passive ventilation in the world may not be enough to dry out some problem basements. In these cases, install an active source of ventilation, such as an exhaust fan.

Installing a vapor barrier

Excessive dampness in a crawlspace or basement can condense, causing floor framing to become damp, covered with fungus, efflorescence, and rot. To prevent this damage to the floor framing, install a vapor barrier consisting of one or more layers of sheet plastic (six mil visqueen) on top of the soil in the crawlspace or basement (see Figure 6-2).

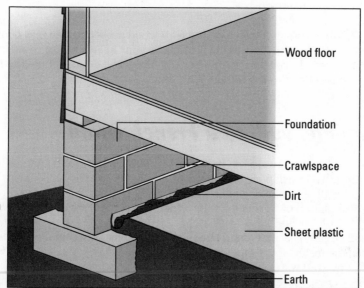

Wood floor

Foundation

Crawlspace

Dirt

Sheet plastic

Earth

Figure 6-2:
Installing
a vapor
barrier.

Book II

Basic Home Mainte-nance and Improvement

The plastic should be lapped a minimum of 6 inches and sealed with duct tape at the seams. Cut around piers and along the inside edge of the foundation. In severe cases, the plastic can run up the sides of piers and the foundation and be secured with duct tape or anchored with a line of soil at the perimeter.

Not so fast! Just because you installed a vapor barrier doesn't mean that your work under the house is done. With the plastic in place, you have a nice, dry surface on which to work to remove efflorescence or mold that has propagated on wood framing. Wearing safety goggles, use a wire brush and a putty knife or paint scraper to clean the affected areas. Also see the section "Cleaning up efflorescence" earlier in this chapter.

As you remove efflorescence or mold, have a blunt tool, such as a flat blade screwdriver, handy to test for evidence of rot. If you can insert the blade of the screwdriver into the wood fibers by using moderate pressure, it's time to call in a pest control specialist to make an inspection and suggest needed repairs.

Treat wood framing that was previously damp, but not severely damaged, with a wood preservative that contains a pesticide such as copper or zinc naphthenate. The wood preservative is a liquid that you can brush on with a throwaway paintbrush.

Use extreme caution when working with wood preservatives that contain pesticides because they can be hazardous to your health — not to mention the fact that they have a fierce odor for the first week or so. Follow the manufacturer's directions to the letter.

Saying "oui" to a French Drain

If the advice we gave in the previous sections doesn't help and you're still faced with a crawlspace or basement that looks like the La Brea Tar Pits, it's time to call in a soils engineer to determine whether the condition requires the installation of a French Drain, which is an elaborate drainage system.

If you already have a French Drain, even it needs occasional maintenance. Clean the inside of the pipe once a year by using a pressure cleaner, which is a high-powered water blaster with a hose and nozzle for use within drainpipes. You can rent this equipment from a tool rental company, or you can have a plumbing contractor or sewer and drain cleaning service clean a French Drain for you.

A Few Pointers on Brick and Block Foundations

Bricks were once used extensively to construct foundations. Today, however, if a foundation doesn't consist of concrete, it's probably constructed of concrete block. In either case, brick and block have one thing in common: They're joined together with *mortar,* a combination of sand and cement.

Unfortunately, over time, mortar tends to deteriorate. Cracked and deteriorating mortar joints aren't only unsightly, but they also diminish the integrity of the surface and can allow water to get behind the brick or block, causing major damage. You prevent this problem by *tuck-pointing* the brick or block foundation, which means removing and replacing cracked or missing mortar.

If the cracked or deteriorating mortar is extensive (an entire foundation, wall, or wainscot), tuck-pointing is a project that's best left to professionals.

If the area is manageable, a do-it-yourselfer can easily perform the task by following these steps (see Figure 6-3):

1. **Chip away cracked and loose mortar by using a slim cold chisel and a hammer. Remove the existing material to a depth of approximately ½ inch.**

   Wear safety goggles to avoid catching a piece of flying mortar in the eye. Use the cold chisel slowly and carefully to avoid damaging the surrounding brick. Use a brush to clean up all the loose material and dust after you finish chiseling.

2. **Prepare your mortar and allow the mix to set for about five minutes.**

   You can purchase premixed mortar, or you can create your own batch by using one part masonry cement to three parts fine sand. In either case, you want to add enough water to create a paste — about the consistency of oatmeal. It's best to keep the mix a touch on the dry side. If it's too runny, it'll be weak and will run down the wall, making it difficult to apply.

3. **Brush the joints with fresh water.**

   Doing so removes any remaining dust and prevents the existing mortar from drawing all the moisture out of the new mortar. Otherwise, the mortar can be difficult to apply and is likely to crack.

4. **Apply the mortar by using a pie-shaped trowel called a *pointing trowel*.**

   Force the mortar into the vertical joints first and remove the excess (to align with the existing adjacent mortar) by using a brick jointer. The brick jointer helps create a smooth, uniform finish. After you've filled in all the vertical joints, tackle the horizontal ones.

   Avoid applying mortar in extreme weather conditions; mortar doesn't set properly in such circumstances.

5. **A week or two after the mortar has set, apply a coat of high-quality acrylic or silicone masonry sealer.**

   Seal the entire surface — brick, block, and mortar. The sealer prevents water damage, which is especially important if you live in an area that gets particularly cold. Unsealed brick, block, and mortar absorb water that freezes in cold weather. The water turns to ice and causes the material to expand and crack. Periodic sealing prevents this problem from occurring.

Book II

Basic Home Maintenance and Improvement

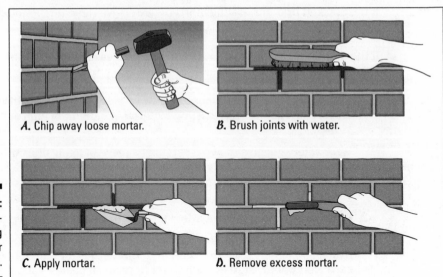

Figure: 6-3:
Tuck-
pointing
mortar
joints.

A. Chip away loose mortar.

B. Brush joints with water.

C. Apply mortar.

D. Remove excess mortar.

Chapter 7

Roofing and Siding

*Y*our home and its contents depend on the integrity of your roof and exterior walls in the same way that you depend on protective clothing to keep you dry in foul weather. Getting temporarily stuck in bad weather can make you uncomfortable and may even ruin your hairdo, but left unchecked, a roof leak — even a tiny one — can end up costing a fortune in damage to a home's interior and its precious contents. Damage to flooring, plaster, wallboard, furniture, important papers, and more is no small matter.

Your Roof: The Fifth Wall of Your Home

Most folks are pretty conscientious about maintaining the exterior walls of their homes. On just about any day during good weather, you can drive through a neighborhood and find the sides of at least one home under siege by painters. But rarely do you see anyone on the roof of a home unless the roof is being replaced. For some reason, people just don't pay as much attention to their roofs, which we think is a mistake.

The whole idea of maintenance is to ensure longevity, reduce costs, and improve value. We think this concept applies to the roof in the same way it applies to walls. In fact, we like to think of the roof as the fifth wall of a home that requires maintenance with the same regularity as the walls that support it require. With proper care and maintenance, a roof can outlast its warranty without leaking a drop or suffering ugly damage.

Staying safe on the roof

A pitched roof is an alien plane. We don't mean a spaceship from another planet, rather an unfamiliar surface to walk on. And for novices, an angled surface is often even more dangerous than the dastardly spaceships that tried to destroy the Earth in the movie *War of the Worlds*.

If you aren't agile or athletic, or if you have a fear of heights, think about hiring someone else to maintain your roof. If you do go up there, be sure to wear rubber-soled shoes. They grip better than leather. Never walk on a wet roof, and don't be afraid to wear a safety harness, too; it prevents broken bones and may even save your life.

Cleanliness is next to godliness

Streaks or discoloration can cause a perfectly good roof to look worn and tattered. And ugly isn't a good thing — remember curb appeal? So, for appearance's sake, use the following universal roof cleaning formula when your roof gets dirty. This concoction also gets rid of mildew or moss on your roof, which can cause extensive damage if left unattended.

You need these supplies:

- ✓ 1 cup liquid chlorine bleach
- ✓ 1 cup powdered laundry detergent
- ✓ 1 gallon hot water
- ✓ Bucket or large mixing bowl
- ✓ Garden hose
- ✓ Pump garden sprayer
- ✓ Safety glasses or goggles
- ✓ Stiff-bristle broom
- ✓ Stir stick (the kind for paint is okay)
- ✓ Tall ladder (the height you need depends on the height of your roof)

Do this project on a cool, humid, overcast day to ensure that the cleaner doesn't dry too fast on the roof. Wait until the weather's right and then follow these steps:

1. **Mix the hot water, bleach, and detergent until the soap granules dissolve and then pour the mixture into the garden sprayer.**

2. **On the roof, spray the cleaner on a strip about 3 feet high x 10 feet wide and let it sit for about 15 minutes.**

   Begin cleaning the lower portion of the roof, moving up as you clean each lower section. That way, you always stand on dry ground and reduce the chance of slipping.

3. **If the cleaner begins to dry out, spray on a bit more.**

4. **Use a broom to scrub the area as needed to get it clean.**

5. **Rinse the cleaned area with fresh water.**

   Repeat the process until the roof is clean.

A few uplifting words about ladders

You can choose from as many different ladders as there are tasks that require them. They range from the small two- and three-rung stepstool type to the common 6- and 8-foot folding models to the granddaddy of them all, the extension ladder. An extension ladder telescopes in length — you know, like the ones firefighters use.

If your home-maintenance budget can afford only one ladder, get a 6-foot stepladder, which gives you the length you need when tackling most home-maintenance and repair projects. You can change light bulbs at ceiling-mounted fixtures and paint ceilings and walls. However, if your ceilings are 10 feet or higher, you need an 8-foot ladder. If your project involves a multistory roof, you need an extension ladder.

Don't try to save money by purchasing a cheap ladder unless you intend to give it to someone you don't like. A cheap ladder falls apart in no time — usually with someone on it. When buying a ladder, look for secure connections, metal-supported wood steps, and superior hinges. As the ladder ages, keep an eye out for loose connections, splits, cracks, and missing rivets.

Follow these tips to avoid downward trips off your ladder:

✔ A sinking ladder can tilt and throw you to the ground. When working on dirt or turf, you may need to stabilize the ladder by placing the feet on boards or a sheet of plywood to prevent them from sinking into the earth. For added stability, place the bottom of the ladder away from the wall one-quarter of the ladder's length.

✔ When you're working on the roof, make sure the ladder extends a minimum of 2 feet above the edge of the roof. The extension provides support so that you can steady yourself as you traverse from ladder to roof and vice versa.

✔ Never climb onto a roof from the gable end where the roof crosses the ladder rungs at an angle. Instead, mount the roof from a horizontal side. Make sure the plane of the roof is parallel to the ladder rungs at the point where you leave the ladder to mount the roof.

✔ To maintain proper balance, keep your hips between the side rails when climbing the ladder or reaching out. Keep one hand on the ladder and the other free for work.

A wood shake or shingle roof covered with pine needles, leaves, moss, and other debris may retain water, causing the shingles to rot prematurely. An annual sweeping with a stiff-bristle broom cuts down on fungus damage by enhancing watershed. Cleaning to promote proper watershed is important with other types of roofs as well. Built-up debris can create a dam, which can cause a leak. However, never, ever walk on a wood shingle or shake roof! Hose off debris with a garden hose from a ladder or, if needed, a roof ladder.

The naked truth about flashing

Roof flashing creates a watertight connection where the roof is adjoined to a wall, as when a first-story roof connects to a second-story wall. Roof flashing also creates watertight connections between the roofing and items that penetrate it, including plumbing pipes, furnace flues, skylights, and chimneys.

All roofs have roof flashing. Although some flashings are made of lead, most are made of galvanized sheet metal or aluminum. And that means rust or corrosion. And rust or corrosion means leaks.

To prevent flashing from leaking, you need to keep it from rusting. Applying a good coat of paint every few years generally does the trick. After you apply the first coat of paint to your flashing, maintaining it is easy. You want to focus on removing any rust that appears and keeping the paint in good condition.

Follow these steps to remove rust from your flashing:

1. **Wash the surface with tri-sodium phosphate, or TSP, mixed to the manufacturer's specifications.**

   The TSP *etches* (chemically roughens) the painted surface.

2. **Use sandpaper or a wire brush to remove all rust.**

3. **Clean away the dust and use a paintbrush to apply the rust converter.**

   The rust converter acts as a primer while converting leftover rust to an inert material.

4. **Apply latex paint as a finish coat.**

   We like to paint our roof flashings, vent pipes, and flue caps the same color as the roofing material, making them less noticeable and more aesthetically appealing.

One type of flashing, called *vent flashing*, incorporates a rubber grommet that seals the connection between the centermost portion of the flashing and a plumbing vent pipe. Keep this rubber grommet in good condition with a shot of rubber preservative every year or two.

Wood shake and shingle roof preservation

No matter how clean you keep it, and no matter what condition the flashings are in, a wood shake or shingled roof usually starts looking a little worn out after a few years. The intense ultraviolet rays of good old Mr. Sun cause the majority of the damage, drying shingles out and causing them to split and literally burning holes in others. The shingles can lose virtually all their moisture (water and natural resins) in as little as five years, which can result in cupping, curling, splitting, and an almost certain early demise. However, with proper care and maintenance, you can double or even triple the life of a wood shake or shingle roof.

Want to inspect a roof and don't want to climb up there to do it? Get a good pair of binoculars. Then you can stand back and take a close look! Split shingles, shingles with holes, cupped and curling shingles, and other damaged shingles will be as easy to spot as if you were standing right there next to them.

Book II

Basic Home Maintenance and Improvement

Super-cleaning to open the pores

The roof preservation process begins with a much more thorough cleaning than the general roof-cleaning technique we described earlier in this chapter — roof preservation requires a super-cleaning that exposes all the pores of the wood. Then, later in the process, the preservative can easily penetrate deep and completely into each and every pore. This super-cleaning also cuts through the grime and makes your wood shake or shingled roof look almost as good as new.

We recommend a pressure washer for super-cleaning a roof. This small device converts water supplied from a garden hose to a high-pressure mix of forced air and water. This mixture comes through the hose with enough force to cut through soft wood. Talk about eliminating elbow grease! You can get a power washer from a tool rental place — and some paint stores — for $50 to $75 a day.

When using a pressure washer, hold the spray tip approximately 8 to 12 inches from the roof's surface while working backward from the lowest part of the roof up to the highest part.

Don't stand on a wood shake or shingle roof. The projects in this section should only be done from a roof ladder.

Paying special attention when mold exists

When mold is present, follow pressure washing with an application of mold-killing bleach (1 quart bleach to 1 gallon hot water) to eliminate any remaining spores that reside deep within the pores of the wood.

Place the mixture in a garden sprayer and thoroughly wet the entire roof. Keep it wet for at least 15 minutes and then rinse with fresh water. It's important to perform this process after pressure washing — after thorough cleaning has opened the pores of the wood.

Replacing damaged shingles

After super-cleaning the wood roof, wait until it dries, and then follow these steps to replace any damaged shingles (see Figure 7-1):

1. **With the blade of a hacksaw, cut the nails anchoring a damaged shingle and carefully slip it out.**

   Attempting to pry nails loose or pull a shingle out may damage surrounding shingles and make it more difficult to install the new one. Sometimes, you may have to split the shingle into numerous pieces to get it out.

2. **Use the shingle you just removed as a pattern to custom-cut a replacement.**

3. **Slip the new shingle up and under the building paper until the butt end (the fat end) is within 1 inch of the adjacent ends.**

4. *Toenail* **(nail at an angle) two barbed roofing nails as high up as possible without damaging the butt end of the overlapping shingle.**

5. **Finish the repair by placing a woodblock against the butt end of the new shingle and striking the block firmly with a hammer. Drive the shingle until it aligns with the surrounding shingles.**

   This process conceals the new nails, providing a more watertight installation.

Applying the preservative

The preservative restores the natural oils to the wood fibers, safeguards the roof from fungus and rot, and protects the roof from the harmful ultraviolet rays of the sun. You see both oil-based and water-based preservatives. We prefer the oil-based type because it penetrates deeper, combats weather stress better, and lasts longer.

Non-pigmented preservatives can have pigments added to improve ultraviolet protection. The pigment actually masks the sun's ultraviolet rays, preventing them from damaging the wood. The pigment also blends together, into one color, the older shingles and the new ones that you used to make patches.

Although you can apply preservative with a garden-type pump sprayer, you can do it more professionally and in less time by using an airless paint sprayer. You can rent one for about the same cost as a pressure washer. The process is simple: Just spray the oil onto the roof. When the surface becomes shiny, stop spraying in that area and move on.

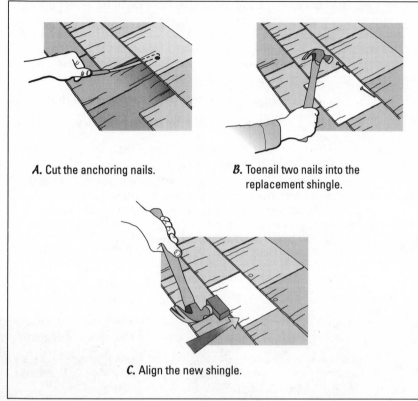

A. Cut the anchoring nails.

B. Toenail two nails into the replacement shingle.

C. Align the new shingle.

Figure 7-1:
Replacing
a wood
shingle.

Apply preservative when no breeze is blowing, ensuring that the majority of the product ends up on the roof and not on the neighbors' new car. Work backward from the low end to the high side, being careful not to walk on an already treated area, which may be slippery.

Most preservative applications last three to five years, depending on the climate. Keeping the roof clean and free of debris helps extend the lasting quality of the preservative and therefore the life of the roof.

Replacing a composition shingle

Replacing a damaged composition shingle is a little different from changing one made of wood. A composition shingle is more flexible and therefore somewhat more forgiving. Because composition shingles become more flexible when warm, this task is best saved for a sunny day. (But if the shingles are too hot, walking on them can destroy them, so you may not want to bother in the middle of the afternoon on a 90-degree day.) Here's what you do (see Figure 7-2):

1. **Fold back the shingle(s) above the one to be removed.**

2. **Use a flat pry bar to remove the nails that hold the damaged shingle in place.**

   First, pry under the damaged shingle at the nail location to raise it above the surface; then pry on top of it to pull out the nail.

3. **Slip a new shingle in position to replace the one that was removed.**

4. **Nail the new shingle in place by using a flat pry bar as a hammer extension.**

Using a flat pry bar as a hammer extension is a neat trick. This technique allows a nail to be driven in from beneath an overlapping shingle. First, you press the nail into the shingle by hand, which requires reasonably strong fingers and a bit of force. After the nail is in place, you position the bottom of the flat bar so that the straight end rests atop the nail head. As the hammer strikes the flat bar, the offset below drives the nail home.

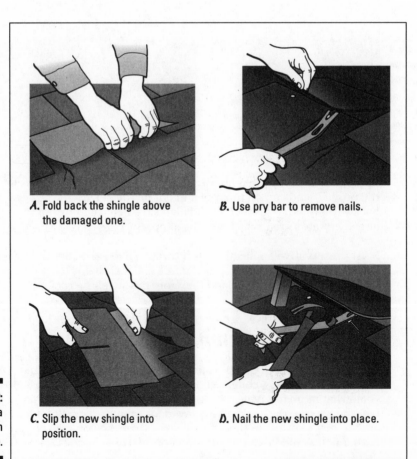

Figure 7-2:
Replacing a composition shingle.

A. Fold back the shingle above the damaged one.

B. Use pry bar to remove nails.

C. Slip the new shingle into position.

D. Nail the new shingle into place.

All That Dam Ice

Did you know that if you have icicles, you might have an ice dam, as well? And if you have an ice dam, you may soon be fighting a roof leak.

When snow falls on a roof, it seals the roof, which becomes almost airtight. As the house warms to a nice, toasty temperature, heated air escapes into the attic. As the attic gets warmer, it melts the snow atop the roof, and water rushes downward toward the overhangs. The moment the liquefied snow hits a cold overhang, it begins to freeze. The water that freezes after it rolls over the edge becomes icicles.

Water that freezes before it rolls over the edge builds up to create a barrier known as an *ice dam,* which becomes larger and larger as runoff continues to freeze. Finally, the ice on the overhang widens to the point where it reaches the edge of the attic. At this point, the water remains liquid and the ice dam causes it to back up over the attic, where it can leak into your home.

Having ice on your roof brings other negative consequences. Ice buildup can damage rain gutters, necessitating costly repairs. By preventing ice buildup, you may be able to save your house from being flooded during a freeze and add a little life to your gutters, as well.

To prevent an ice dam, you need to keep the attic cold. If the attic is cold, the snow on the roof won't melt, and ice dams won't form. Here's how to make that happen:

- **Don't close off eave and roof vents during the winter.** Doing so traps the warm air that melts snow on the roof.

- **Fill all penetrations between the living space and the attic area with foam sealant.** You can buy it in a spray can. Look for penetrations in the ceiling in the following places (many may be hidden beneath attic insulation): plumbing vents, ventilation ducts, heat registers, electric wiring, and ceiling light fixtures.

- **Don't caulk around furnace flues.** A flue that contains hot gases shouldn't come in contact with combustibles, such as wood or foam sealant. Contact your local heating or sheet metal contractor and have a metal draft stop installed. He or she can seal it to the pipe and the house frame without creating a fire hazard.

- **Check your attic insulation.** Be sure that your attic insulation is loose (as opposed to compacted) and that you have a sufficient amount up there. Check with your local utility company — most offer free energy audits. Your local building department is another inexpensive inspection alternative.

- ✔ **Consider installing an eave-heating device, such as heating tape or heating wire (see Figure 7-3).** These devices prevent water from freezing on your eaves. Eave heaters operate on extremely low voltage, making them inexpensive to operate.

- ✔ **Install special metal flashings at problem eaves.** Ice doesn't stick to metal as readily as it does to most types of roofing. The nice thing about metal flashings is that your local heating or sheet metal contractor can make them to order. You may be able to save money by looking for a product at your local home center known as "Ice and Water Shield."

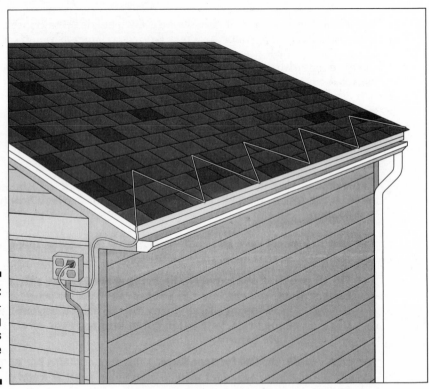

Figure 7-3:
An eave-heating device helps avoid ice dams.

Find That Leak!

The first step in repairing a leak is finding its point of origin. This task can be extremely difficult on a flat roof, so we recommend that you hire an industry professional to find and repair a leak in a flat roof. However, on a pitched roof, do-it-yourselfers can find the leak themselves. You still need to hire a contractor to repair the leak, but being able to tell the contractor where the leak is saves time and shows the contractor that he or she is dealing with an informed homeowner.

Although water testing a pitched roof isn't a difficult process, it's often time-consuming and tedious. Be prepared to exercise a bit of patience. The process requires two people, one on the roof and one in the attic (or living space below if no attic exists). Follow these steps (see Figure 7-4):

Book II

Basic Home Mainte-nance and Improvement

1. **Use a garden hose to run a modest amount of water over the roof at a point below the area where you suspect a leak.**

   Don't run the hose full blast. Don't use a spray nozzle, and don't force the water between the shingles. Doing so may force water into your home, creating the illusion that you've found a leak when, in fact, you did nothing more than create a temporary one.

   Work from the lowest point of the roof (near the eaves or gutters) in an area about 4 to 6 feet wide. Work your way up the roof a couple of feet at a time. Standing on dry roofing above the water helps prevent slips.

2. **Station your partner in the attic and tell him or her to holler at the first sign of water.**

   The moment your helper sees water, he or she should let you know. A wailing screech usually does the trick. An inexpensive pair of kids' walkie-talkies allows you to communicate clearly without yelling.

Figure 7-4:
Water
testing a
pitched roof.

It's Okay If Your Mind's in the Gutter

Gene Kelly probably wouldn't be remembered as well for his part in *Singin' in the Rain* if the movie set had been equipped with rain gutters. As a matter of fact, the producers probably would've changed the title of the film to something like *Stayin' Dry While Singin' near the Rain*. When it comes to your home, *singing* in the rain isn't what you'll be doing if you haven't maintained your gutters and downspouts properly.

Cleaning gutters and downspouts

Gutters and downspouts filled with debris can back up, causing roof leaks, rot at the overhang, and structural damage. Once a year, get up on a ladder and give those gutters and downspouts a good cleaning. Gutters that haven't been cleaned for a while may be filled with a mud-like substance, which you can scoop out with a small garden trowel or putty knife. You may even want to invest in a *gutter scoop* (a trowel-like plastic scoop made for cleaning gutters).

After you remove the majority of the debris, flush the rest away by using a garden hose with a spray nozzle.

Patching leaks

When galvanized sheet metal gutters aren't properly maintained (regularly cleaned and painted), they tend to rust. As we mention earlier in this chapter, unpainted metal rusts, and rust results in leaks. Use the same technique on gutters that you use to maintain roof flashings. (See the section, "The naked truth about flashing," earlier in this chapter.)

If the gutter is sagging, replace the mounting brackets before fixing leaks. You don't want the gutter shape to change after you've fixed the leak. Doing so may cause a patch to open.

When a rusty area turns into a leak, try this quick repair:

1. **Use a wire brush or the wire wheel on a drill to remove as much rust from the area as possible.**

2. **Apply a coat of rust converter over the repair area.**

   The converter renders remnants of rust inert. With rust, you can't be too careful. Allow the converter to dry completely.

3. **Apply a ⅛-inch-thick coat of roof cement around the leak.**

   Before the cement dries, add a strip of aluminum foil to the repair area (kind of like taping a Band-Aid to your arm). Use a putty knife to gently flatten the foil and squeeze out the excess cement.

   The total thickness of the repair shouldn't exceed ¹⁄₁₆ inch. You can create a dam if you use too much roof cement.

   For repairs that are larger than a pinhole, substitute a piece of sheet metal for the aluminum foil. Heating contractors typically have a trash can full of scraps that are perfect for this type of repair. Chances are that you can get the scrap you need for a handshake and a "Thank you." For badly damaged areas, sheet metal plates can be pop-riveted into place and sealed with liquid aluminum. However, you may want to leave this maintenance task to a sheet metal contractor.

4. **With the foil in place, use a putty knife to add another thin layer of roof cement to cover the patch.**

If the repair area is large, consider replacing the damaged sections. The style you have is probably still available. You'd be amazed at how little gutter shapes have changed over the years.

Occasionally, a gutter seam or joint opens, producing a leak. Catching this problem early on reduces the chance of rust and, possibly, a major repair. You can caulk seams in aluminum and galvanized sheet metal gutters with

Book II

Basic Home Maintenance and Improvement

liquid aluminum, and you can repair plastic gutters with polyurethane caulk. Be sure to clean the area thoroughly before applying the caulk.

Siding: A Raincoat for Your House

Water can attack and damage wood siding. Stucco walls crack when the house shifts as winter rains expand soil. Metal siding dents easily. Vinyl siding pits as it oxidizes. Even brick chips and cracks with winter freezes and summer ground settlement.

No surface is perfect; no material perfectly withstands the rigors of nature and the force of the elements. But you can take action to add life and beauty to your home's exterior.

Treating wood siding

Treat wood siding with an application of oil, stain, or paint to prevent rot. These materials act as a barrier, preventing water from coming into direct contact with the wood. Which finish you choose is mostly an aesthetic choice:

- **Oil,** a clear finish, is absorbed into the wood, filling all pores and voids, thereby displacing water that otherwise would be absorbed.
- **Oil stain** is the same as oil except that a pigment is mixed into the oil.
- **Paint** penetrates and protects in the same way that oil does. Additionally, paint coats the surface of the wood with a thin, durable, waterproof hide.

Oil is easier to apply than paint, and if the oil is clear (or almost clear), mistakes are nearly impossible to detect. If the oil contains stain, the added pigment makes application slightly more difficult, as mistakes show up more readily. But the added pigment helps filter out more of the sun's damaging ultraviolet rays. Unfortunately, oil has a tendency to evaporate and doesn't last as long as paint. However, unlike paint, oil and oil stain don't split, chip, or blister.

Everything's a trade-off. With oil, you never have to sand, scrape, or chisel the surface to prepare it for another application. But be ready to apply a new coat every several years. With an oil stain, expect three to five years of lasting quality. A good grade of paint, applied to a properly cleaned surface, lasts seven to ten years or more.

Paint experts agree that 80 percent of a good oil, stain, or paint job is in the preparation. But the exterior of your home is no small area. And when it comes to preparation (removing old layers of loose paint, a tattered layer of stain, a discolored layer of wood, or just plain dirt), you can expect to do some major work. Fortunately, tools are available at home centers, paint stores, and rental outlets that help make cleanup and removal almost a fun job. Sand blasters, soda washers, and pressure washers involve some degree of work on your part, but they're a breeze to use compared to hand scrapers, hand chippers, or blowtorches. We recommend a pressure washer.

Painted surfaces

Prepare for repainting by ensuring that all old loose paint has been removed. A new coat of paint won't stick any better than the old paint below it.

Whether you hand scrape or pressure wash, be sure to sand spots where a painted surface meets a bare spot. Feathering these transition points makes them less visible and guarantees a nicer-looking finished product.

Prime all bare spots with a high-grade oil-based primer. Then caulk all joints with a high-grade 50-year, paintable silicone or polyurethane product to prevent water from getting behind the siding. Caulk any joint that allows this to happen.

Tinting a standard white primer a shade or two lighter than the finish coat improves coverage. For example, a light brown finish coat covers a beige primer more effectively than it covers a white primer.

Oiled surfaces

With an oiled surface, clean the wood with a pressure washer, apply a coat of wood bleach, let it stand (per the manufacturer's instructions), and pressure wash again. At this point, you can apply a fresh coat of oil or oil stain. Your oiled siding will look so good that you won't believe you did it yourself.

Maintaining stucco

Stucco is really cool stuff. It doesn't rot, and compared to other types of siding, it's relatively easy to maintain. Stucco is very porous and holds on to paint better than most other kinds of siding. Also, it's one of the easiest surfaces to prepare and paint. If you have stucco, count your blessings.

Unfortunately, its brittle, damage-resistant surface can be a drawback. When the house shifts, stucco can crack.

Repairing cracks

For cracks up to ¼-inch wide, caulking solves the problem. Follow these simple steps:

1. **Clean all loose debris from the crack.**

   A can opener and a vacuum cleaner work wonders here.

2. **Use a paintable 50-year silicone caulk — and your finger — to make an invisible repair.**

   Don't use a putty knife. Doing so prevents you from matching the existing texture. With your finger, you can force the caulk in the crack to align with the irregular surface of the stucco.

Repair wider cracks and gouges with a latex patching compound. Follow the manufacturer's mixing instructions carefully because the amount of water you use changes the properties of the patching compound, which may lessen its ability to hold. Then, follow these steps:

1. **Clean all loose debris from the crack or gouge.**

2. **Use a latex patching product and a putty knife or trowel to fill the area.**

3. **Apply a second coat to match the surface texture.**

   Thin the patching compound to pancake batter consistency. Dip the end of a paintbrush into the mixture. Holding your hand between the wall and the paintbrush, slap the handle of the brush against your hand. The patching compound splatters onto the surface, matching the texture of the stucco. If the texture is flat, wait for the splattering to become slightly firm and then wipe it to the desired flatness with a putty knife or trowel.

Painting stucco

Really porous stucco absorbs gallons of paint, causing you to use a great deal more paint than you really need to. If you're painting stucco for the first time, save paint by using a water hose to wet the surface of the stucco before applying paint. The water fills the pores in the stucco, preventing excess amounts of paint from absorbing deep into the stucco. Wait for surface water to evaporate first, and then begin painting.

Cleaning vinyl siding

Vinyl siding is a great-looking product. It doesn't warp, split, or buckle, and, according to several manufacturers, you never need to paint it.

This fact wouldn't be important except that, like all types of exterior siding, vinyl does have its shortcomings. The surface of vinyl siding etches in time.

As the surface deteriorates, the pitting causes the material to become dull and prone to stain.

Several brands of exterior paint are now available that are designed for use on vinyl siding. Check with your local paint shop or hardware store for the lowdown.

To prevent the need to repaint your siding, clean it regularly. Twice a year is good — once in the spring and then again in the fall. Use a pressure washer with laundry detergent to get the surface sparkling clean. Most pressure washers have a plastic dip tube that you can use to blend in agents like detergents. Keeping the surface of the vinyl clean won't prevent it from oxidizing, but it will prevent corrosive chemicals in the air from attacking the surface, slowing the process of deterioration.

Maintaining aluminum siding

Aluminum is a beautiful siding that man has created in an attempt to outdo nature. They said it wouldn't rust like steel, that it would never have to be painted, and that it would simply last forever. Well, the truth is that it probably will last forever. But by then, it won't look new at all.

Think of aluminum siding in the same way that you think about a car body. It's a smooth metal surface covered with paint that needs to be cleaned, polished, and waxed regularly. Think about it: Aluminum siding is metal that's formed, polished, and given a factory paint job just like a car body. So what automobile paint job do you know of that lasts forever?

If you want to see a good case of *chalked* (oxidized) paint, look closely at a 20-year-old home sided with aluminum that's never been cleaned or painted. So how do you prevent chalking? You don't prevent it (in fact, chalking is the paint's way of self-cleaning), but you can make light work of getting it to disappear. All you have to do is attend to your siding. Pressure wash once or twice a year, making sure to fill the plastic dip tube on the pressure washer with laundry detergent. Your aluminum siding will remain bright and shiny for years, and the task won't seem overwhelming.

When the time comes to paint your aluminum siding, keep these tips in mind:

- Never scrape aluminum siding. Aluminum has a smooth surface; sand it with 400- to 600-grit sandpaper.
- A zinc oxide primer (metal primer) is best for bare aluminum.
- Because an aluminum surface is smooth, spray-paint it for best results.
- Always patch an aluminum surface with a filler made especially for metal — like Bondo, used for cars.

Chapter 8

Light Up Your Life with Electrical Repairs and Replacements

● ●

In This Chapter

▶ Dealing with blown fuses and short circuits

▶ Wiring light switches and electrical outlets

▶ Bringing a broken lamp back to life

▶ Replacing a ceiling fixture

▶ Adding a phone extension

▶ Installing a security light in place of your porch light

▶ Adding low-voltage outdoor track lighting

● ●

Ever since that grand moment when Ben Franklin decided to go fly a kite in an electrical storm, civilization has had a curious fascination with and an addictive dependence on electricity. But what happens if you're suddenly thrown into darkness by interrupted electrical service? What do you do then? Going to a friend's house to watch TV isn't the response we're looking for. This chapter explains how to make all sorts of minor electrical repairs and improvements to your home.

Replacing a Fuse and Resetting a Circuit Breaker

You plug in the rockin' new stereo, flip the switch, and suddenly the whole house goes dark. Sure, you've *heard* of blown fuses and short circuits, but how do you fix them? The first step is to locate your electrical panel and open it. (See the sidebar "When it comes to electricity, always be prepared" for tips on finding and labeling your electrical panel.)

Electricity flows through a pair of wires called a *circuit*. Electrical energy flows out one wire (the *hot* wire) through the light, stereo, or whatever you're running and then returns to the main power panel through the other wire (the *neutral* wire). These wires are sized to carry a certain amount of electrical energy without overheating. But if you plug too many appliances into a circuit, the wires supplying this energy get very hot. And if the wires supplying the energy touch each other, they create a *short circuit* — a shortcut for the electrical power to flow — and the wires begin to glow in a matter of seconds.

Each circuit is protected by either a fuse or a circuit breaker, both of which you can see in Figure 8-1. If a short circuit occurs anywhere in the wiring, if the wires overheat, or if an appliance malfunctions or catches fire, the fuse or circuit breaker shuts down power to that circuit. Additionally, the entire panel is protected with a *master* or *main* fuse or breaker.

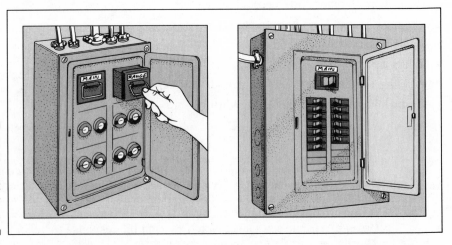

Figure 8-1:
A fuse box panel (left) and a circuit breaker panel (right).

✔ **Fuses:** Houses that are more than about 30 years old often have fuses rather than circuit breakers to protect the wire circuits. To shut down a circuit in these homes, you have to remove the fuse. Shut off the power to the electrical panel before replacing fuses. Look for a fuse labeled *Master* or *Main* (usually located at the top of the electrical panel); pull this handle and remove the rectangular block containing the main fuses to shut down the power to the entire house. Make sure you have a working flashlight on hand!

If the fuses aren't labeled, look into the glass window of each fuse to determine which one is blown. A good fuse shows a solid metal bar; a bad one usually has either a broken bar or a discolored glass window. Unscrew the blown fuse and replace it with one of equal amperage. Restore the power by replacing the main fuse.

Have replacement fuses on hand at all times.

✔ **Circuit breakers:** Newer homes have *circuit breakers* — protective switches that enable you to fix short circuits without turning off the power. Circuit breakers simply switch off when they become overloaded, but the breaker doesn't flip fully to the Off position. To reset a circuit breaker, flip it fully to the Off position and then fully in the opposite direction, to the On position. If the breaker shuts off again, you have a short or some other problem that needs to be fixed before you attempt to switch it on again.

Working with live wires is never a good idea, and sometimes wires from more than one circuit may be present in a single outlet. So to ensure that the electricity is turned off on every circuit you come in contact with, purchase an inexpensive neon voltage circuit tester. This little device lets you know whether a circuit has power running to it. The tester's not a loud, dust-spewing, macho tool, but it could save your life.

Book II

Basic Home Maintenance and Improvement

When it comes to electricity, always be prepared

To prepare for electrical emergencies, familiarize yourself with the *electrical entrance panel*— the circuit breaker box usually found in the utility room or basement. Have a flashlight with good batteries somewhere near the electrical panel to give you good light for looking inside the panel — remember, the overhead light may not be working when you need to change a fuse.

The electrician who wired your house should have marked each circuit on the panel with a label telling which lights or appliances it controls. But things don't always happen the way they should, and you may find yourself with a panel of unlabeled breakers. Before a short circuit leaves you in the dark trying to guess which

fuse or breaker controls what, get down to business and label those breakers yourself.

To label the breakers, plug a lamp into each receptacle and turn on all the lights in your house. Then go to your electrical panel and turn off each circuit breaker, one at a time. Have a helper call out which lights or appliances shut down and are, therefore, on that circuit. Label all the breakers with lists of what they control.

Labeling the circuits can be a one-person job. Plug a radio into the outlet you're testing and turn up the volume so that you can hear it from the electrical panel. When the radio stops playing, you know that you've found the circuit that connects to that fuse or circuit breaker.

Wiring Switches and Receptacles

If a switch fails to function or a receptacle (commonly called an outlet) no longer holds a plug securely, it should be replaced, but often people just want to upgrade, change style, or modify the configuration of outlets to meet changing styles or needs. Most modern switches and receptacles have screw terminals on each side and may also have holes in the back to accept the end of the wire, as shown in Figure 8-2. Although plug-in connections may be more convenient, they are less reliable than those at screw terminals, so don't use them!

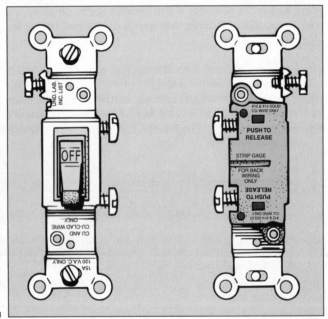

Figure 8-2: Single-pole switches have two screw terminals on the side and a possible third green terminal for the ground wire. The backside of the switch has holes for back-wiring the device.

You can easily loosen the screws on the side of the device with a standard screwdriver (turning counterclockwise), but you may find getting the wires out of the back of the device tricky. To remove these wires, insert the blade of a small screwdriver into the slot under the hole into which the wire is inserted and push in as you pull the wire loose. Pushing the blade of the screwdriver into the slot releases the grip on the inserted wire. Here are descriptions of the wires and where they go:

  ✔ The white *(neutral)* wire connects to the silver screw, or you place it in the back wire hole on the same side of the device as the silver screw.

✔ The black *(hot)* wire goes to the brass screw or into the hole in the back of the device on the same side as the brass screw. This wire is sometimes red.

✔ The green or bare copper *(ground)* wire, if the device has one, attaches to the green screw terminal on the switch or to the electrical box.

Swapping a light switch

Most kitchen and bedroom switches are the single-pole type and are designed to control a light or receptacle from a single location. Hallways, on the other hand, usually have three-way switches that are designed to control a light or receptacle from two locations. Sometimes, an electrician places a four-way switch between three-way switches to allow control of lights or receptacles from three separate locations.

TIP

Book II

Basic Home Maintenance and Improvement

Making a wire-to-wire splice

You sometimes find that the existing wires are very short and difficult to work with. You can make the job easier by splicing on an additional length of wire.

You may also have to join the ground wire of an appliance (ground wires are usually bare copper or green) with other ground wires in the electrical box. You can do that most easily with a twist-on wire connector called a *wire nut*. Strip off about 1 inch of insulation from the end of the wires and use pliers to twist their bare ends together with electrician's pliers. Then screw the wire nut down over the twisted wires until it's tight.

Wire nuts come in many sizes, and using the proper size is important. If the nut is too small, you can't screw it down over the wires and provide an insulated shield. If the nut's too large, it screws down over the wires but may shake

loose. Look on the wire nut package for the number of wires of a given size that this wire nut can join. For example, a wire nut could join four #14 wires but only three #12 wires. (The number refers to the gauge of the wire — the smaller the number, the thicker the wire.)

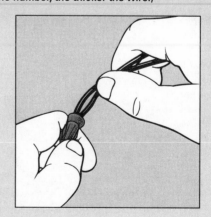

Turn off the circuit breaker or fuse to a light receptacle before you unscrew the switch plate. Then test the wires with a voltage circuit tester to make sure that power isn't flowing to them.

Replacing a single-pole switch

If the switch has *On* and *Off* embossed on its body and it's the only switch that controls lights or receptacles, it's a single-pole switch. To replace this kind of switch, follow these steps:

1. **Turn off the power to the switch at the main circuit breaker or fuse panel.**

2. **Unscrew and remove the switch plate; then use a voltage tester to make sure that the circuit is dead.**

3. **Unscrew the switch from the electrical box and pull it out with the wires still attached, as shown in Figure 8-3.**

   Two or three wires will be attached to the switch: an incoming hot wire, which is black, and a *return* wire, which carries the load to the fixture. It may be black, red, or any other color except green, and sometimes a grounding wire, which is green or bare copper. There may be other wires in the box, but you are only dealing with the ones connected directly to the switch.

   You may find a white wire that has black tape on it connected to the switch, as in Figure 8-3. This tape indicates that the white wire is being used as a black or colored wire in the switch leg, so it's not neutral.

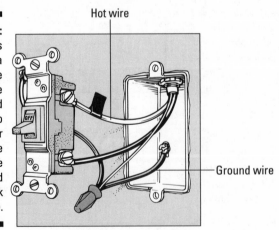

Hot wire

Ground wire

Figure 8-3: Both wires leading to a single-pole switch are hot. If wired with two conductor cables, the white wire is marked with black tape.

4. **Compare your new switch with the one you're replacing to find the corresponding locations for the electrical screw connectors.**

Because the power is off, you can match up the connectors the easy way: Instead of disconnecting all the wires at once and possibly getting confused, unscrew and connect one wire at a time.

5. **Attach the first wire you unscrew to the same-colored screw on the new switch as it was on the old; do the same with the second.**

To connect a wire to a terminal, strip off about ½ inch of insulation, using a wire stripper, and twist the end into a clockwise loop with long-nose pliers. The loop must wrap at least two-thirds but no more than three-quarters of the way around the terminal screw. Hook the wire clockwise around the screw so when you tighten the screw with a screwdriver, the clockwise force of the tightening screw makes the loop wrap tighter around the screw.

6. **Gently push the new, wired switch back into the electrical box and screw it in place.**

7. **Screw on the switch plate and turn on the power.**

Replacing a three-way switch

A three-way switch is a handy convenience to control a light from two locations, such as at the top and bottom of a staircase. If the words *On* and *Off* aren't embossed on the switch and it's one of two switches that control a single light or receptacle, you have a three-way switch. Seems like it should be called a two-way switch, right? The name refers to the fact that these switches have three terminal screws.

To replace a three-way switch, follow these steps:

1. **Turn off the power to the switch at the circuit or fuse panel.**

2. **Unscrew and remove the switch plate; then use a voltage tester to make sure that the circuit is dead.**

3. **Unscrew the switch from the electrical box and pull it out with the wires still attached, as shown in Figure 8-4.**

A three-way switch has at least three wires and possibly four, depending on whether it has a ground wire. Two wires attach to brass screw terminals, which are usually at the top of the switch, and an additional wire attaches to a dark-colored (not green) screw terminal, which is usually at the bottom of the switch. Mark this third wire with a piece of tape and mark the wire on the same side of the switch directly above it with a piece of different-colored tape.

The new switch may have the electrical screw connectors in slightly different locations than the switch you're replacing. Most switches have a pair of terminals on opposite sides of the switch top and a single terminal at the bottom.

Book II

Basic Home Maintenance and Improvement

Figure 8-4:
A three-way
switch
controls
a light
from two
locations.
The
common
screw
terminal is
wired to the
light or to
the source
of power.

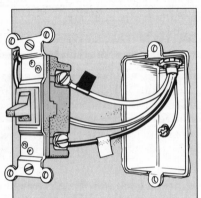

4. **Remove the wires from the switch.**

5. **Attach the tagged wires to the corresponding terminals of the new switch.**

   Alternatively, you may choose to transfer one wire at a time from the old switch to the new switch.

6. **If the existing switch has a green ground wire, attach the wire to the green screw terminal on the new switch or to the electrical box.**

7. **Push the new, wired switch back into the electrical box and screw it in place.**

8. **Screw on the switch plate and turn on the power.**

Replacing a four-way switch

If the switch doesn't have the words *On* and *Off* embossed on its body and it's the center switch of three switches that control a single light or receptacle, it's a four-way switch. Figure 8-5 shows a typical four-way switch.

To replace a four-way switch, follow these steps:

1. **Turn off the power to the switch at the circuit panel or fuse box.**

2. **Unscrew and remove the switch plate; then use a voltage tester to make sure that the circuit is dead.**

3. **Unscrew the switch from the electrical box and pull it out with the wires still attached.**

   This switch has at least four screw terminals. It may also have a fifth ground terminal (green).

4. **Mark the location of the four wires with tape so that you can replace them on the new switch; then remove the wires from the switch.**

   Alternatively, you may choose to transfer one wire at a time from the old switch to the new switch.

5. **Attach the wires to the corresponding terminals of the new switch.**

   If the existing switch has a green ground wire, attach it to the green terminal on the new switch or to the electrical box.

6. **Push the new, wired switch back into the electrical box and screw it in place.**

7. **Screw on the switch plate and turn on the power.**

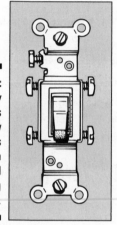

Figure 8-5: A four-way switch has four screw terminals plus an optional grounding screw.

Replacing a standard switch with a dimmer switch

Replacing a standard single-pole or three-way switch with a dimmer switch is no different than replacing a standard switch. ***Remember:*** Dimmer switches don't work on most fluorescent fixtures, and low-voltage lighting requires special low-voltage dimmers.

Check the rating of the dimmer switch you purchase. Most dimmer switches can handle 600 watts of power. Count the number of light bulbs that the switch controls and add up the maximum wattage bulb allowed for the fixture. For example, if the switch controls a light fixture which accommodates up to two 100-watt bulbs (200 watts total) a 600-watt dimmer will have no problem, but a string of seven recessed lights could overload the dimmer.

To replace a standard switch with a dimmer switch, follow these steps:

1. **Turn off the power to the switch at the circuit or fuse panel.**

2. **Unscrew and remove the switch plate; then use a voltage tester to make sure that the circuit is dead.**

3. **Unscrew the switch from the electrical box and pull it out with the wires still attached.**

4. **Remove the wires from the old switch.**

   Dimmer switches are usually connected to the house wiring by short lengths of wire coming out of the switch body rather than by screw terminals.

5. **Use the connectors *(wire nuts)* supplied with the fixture to attach the black wires coming out of the dimmer switch to the colored wires that were attached to the terminals on the old switch, as shown in Figure 8-6.**

   First, twist the wires together, and then screw on the wire nut.

6. **Push the new switch back into the electrical box and screw it in place.**

   The body of a dimmer is larger than the switch being replaced. Don't just force it in. Often, you need to reposition or better organize the wires first to make room for it.

7. **Screw on the switch plate.**

8. **Push the control knob, if there is one, onto the shaft protruding from the switch.**

9. **Turn on the power.**

Figure 8-6:
Some dimmer switches have screw terminals and are wired like a single-pole switch; others have wire pigtails that are spliced with wire nuts.

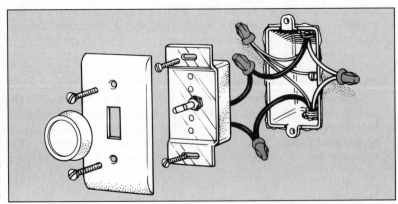

Replacing duplex receptacles

The procedure for replacing a *duplex* (two-outlet) wall receptacle is the same as for replacing a switch. The only difference is that, depending on where the receptacle is located in the wiring scheme of your house, it may have more wires attached to it than you find attached to a light switch.

Look closely at the terminal screws of the new duplex receptacle. On each side of the receptacle is a pair of terminal screws. The upper screw is connected to the upper outlet, and the lower screw services the lower outlet. A thin metal break-off tab connects these screws. This tab enables you to attach a single wire to either screw and feed electricity to both outlets of the receptacle. If the tab is broken off, you can connect the upper and lower outlets to separate wires and control them independently.

If the receptacle is wired to the end of a series of receptacles, it usually has only two wires, and possibly a third ground wire. If it isn't the last receptacle, two additional wires may be connected to it in order to carry current to the next receptacle. Just rewire the new receptacle the same way the old one was wired. (See Figure 8-7.)

Book II

Basic Home Maintenance and Improvement

Figure 8-7: A receptacle in the middle of a series (left) and at the end of a series (right).

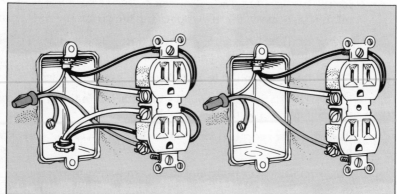

You may also wire the receptacle so that a switch controls the upper outlet and the lower outlet is on, or *hot,* all the time. In this case, you need to remove the break-off tab connecting the two sets of like-colored terminals on each side of the receptacle. Otherwise, the tab remains intact, and you can see a metal bridge connecting the terminals.

The important point to keep in mind is that hot (black or colored) wires attach to brass screws and neutral (white) wires attach to silver screws. If the unit is back-wired, the colored wires are located in the holes behind the brass screws and the white wires in the holes behind the silver screws. If you attach a white wire to a brass screw or a colored wire to a silver screw, you may see fireworks.

Replacing a standard receptacle

To replace a standard duplex receptacle, follow these steps:

1. **Turn off the power to the receptacle from the main fuse or circuit panel.**

2. **Unscrew and remove the cover plate; then use a voltage tester to make sure that the circuit is dead.**

3. **Unscrew the receptacle from the electrical box and pull it out with the wires still attached.**

   Note where the white and black wires are attached to the old receptacle.

4. **Remove the wires.**

5. **Carefully inspect the old receptacle to see if the break-off tab connecting the two sets of terminals on each side of the receptacle is broken off. If it is, remove the corresponding tabs from the new receptacle.**

   To break off the tab, grip it with long-nose pliers and bend it back and forth until it breaks off.

6. **Attach the wires to the terminals of the new receptacle.**

   If the wiring has a green ground wire, attach it to the green terminal on the receptacle or to the electrical box.

7. **Push the new receptacle back into the electrical box and screw it in place.**

8. **Screw on the cover plate and then turn on the power.**

Replacing a receptacle with a GFCI

A GFCI (*ground fault circuit interrupter*) receptacle is the same as an ordinary receptacle, except that it has a sensitive built-in circuit breaker and reset switch. Building codes require that you install this device in outlets located in areas prone to dampness, such as bathrooms, kitchens, basements, garages, and outdoors.

Normally, the amount of current flowing in an electrical circuit is the same in all the wires. For example, if your hair dryer takes 10 *amps* (a measure of the amount of electricity flowing in a circuit) to run, then 10 amps of current flow into the dryer through the hot (black) wire and 10 amps flow out of the dryer through the neutral (white) wire. If the dryer experiences a short, current could flow through your wet hand to, say, the faucet handle as you turn off the water. If this happens, the amount of current going into the dryer exceeds the amount coming out because some of the electricity is going through *you*. The GFCI senses this discrepancy and trips open to stop everything before you turn into a French fry.

We're sure that you don't have any crash-test dummies in your household foolish enough to volunteer to stick a finger in a receptacle to test the GFCI. Fortunately, these devices have a Test button on them so that you can check that they're functioning properly instead of finding out the hard way. Press the Test button, and the device trips and shuts everything down. To reset the device, press the Reset button.

Book II

Basic Home Mainte-nance and Improvement

You can install a GFCI receptacle the same way you install an ordinary receptacle. To replace a standard duplex receptacle with a GFCI receptacle, follow these steps and refer to Figure 8-8:

1. **Turn off the power to the receptacle from the fuse or circuit panel.**

2. **Unscrew and remove the cover plate; then use a voltage tester to make sure that the circuit is dead.**

3. **Unscrew the receptacle from the electrical box and pull it out with the wires still attached.**

4. **Note where the white and black wires are attached to the old receptacle and then remove the wires.**

5. **Transfer the wires from the old receptacle to the GFCI.**

   GFCI receptacles are connected to house wiring either by short lengths of wire coming out of the receptacle body or by screw terminals.

   If the GFCI receptacle has wires, use the wire connectors (wire nuts) supplied with the fixture to attach the black wires coming out of the GFCI receptacle to the colored wires that were attached to the terminals on the old receptacle. Twist the wires together first and then screw on the wire nut.

   If the GFCI receptacle uses screw terminals, attach the colored wires to the terminals of the new receptacle. If wiring includes a green ground wire, attach it to the green terminal on the receptacle or to the electrical box.

6. **Push the new receptacle back into the electrical box and screw it in place.**

7. **Screw on the cover plate and turn on the power.**

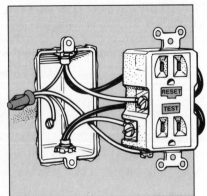

Figure 8-8:
A ground fault circuit interrupter (GFCI) is wired like a standard receptacle.

Repairing a Faulty Lamp

As electrical appliances go, lamps are very reliable. But after a while, the socket may act up and cause the lamp to flicker, to be difficult to turn on, or to just flat out refuse to light. If this sudden disobedience gives you the perfect excuse to get the hideous thing out of your living room, do it. But if you aren't ready to part with the little feller, you can replace the socket and give the lamp a new life. You can replace a socket so easily that, even if it's not your favorite lamp, you may want to fix it and give it to someone else, like your nosy neighbor.

You can purchase replacement lamp parts at any hardware store or home center. These parts are standard; you can buy lamp cord by the foot, and you can use just about any type of plug to replace the one on your old lamp.

You can find several varieties of lamp socket switches. You control some by pushing a short shaft on the side of the switch, others by turning a knob, and still others with a pull chain. You also need to consider whether your present lamp has a three-way bulb in it. If you could turn the lamp on to several degrees of brightness, be sure to purchase a socket switch that's designed to control a three-way bulb.

You can probably get the right replacement parts most easily by taking the lamp apart (according to the following directions) and bringing the bad parts to the store so that you can find matching replacements.

To replace a lamp socket, follow these steps:

1. **Unplug the lamp.**

2. **Remove the shade, bulb, and *harp* (the wired shape that holds the shade).**

3. **Snap off the socket shell from the socket shell cap, as shown in Figure 8-9.**

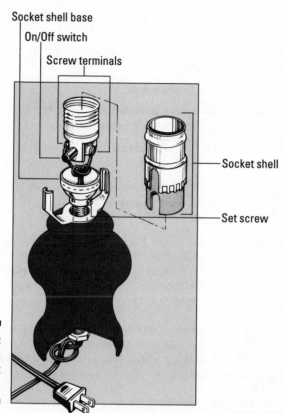

Socket shell base

On/Off switch

Screw terminals

Socket shell

Set screw

Figure 8-9:
Removing the socket shell.

Most sockets have the word *Press* stamped in two places on the shell. Squeeze the shell at those points and pull up to remove it. If the shell doesn't budge, push the end of a screwdriver between the base of the socket and the side of the shell and then pull the shell up and off the socket base.

4. **Pull the socket switch up out of the shell base to expose enough of the switch to reveal the two wires attached to it.**

   If the screws are loose, tighten them and reassemble the lamp. Loose screws may have been the lamp's only problem. If the lamp works after you tighten up the screws, great! If not, take it apart again and proceed with the following steps.

5. **Unscrew the wires.**

   A lamp switch has a brass screw to which the hot (black) wire is attached and a silver screw to which the neutral (white) wire is attached. Lamp cords, however, don't have colored wires in them. So, before you remove the wires from the old switch, note which color screw each wire is connected to.

6. **Loosen the socket cap set screw and then unscrew and discard it along with the old socket shell and socket.**

7. **Screw the wire leads to the new socket.**

8. **Place the new socket shell over the socket and push the cover down until it snaps into the new socket shell cap.**

9. **Replace the harp, light bulb, and shade.**

Replacing a Ceiling Fixture

Residential ceiling fixtures come in many different shapes, and people have devised many ways to attach them to the ceiling. (See Figure 8-10.) Most of the time, a central threaded hollow rod holds a chandelier in place. Ceiling fixtures hang by two screws that attach the fixture base to the outlet box or to a mounting strap in the outlet box.

No matter how you suspend a fixture from the ceiling, the wiring is simple. Other wires may pass through the box, but you have to deal with only three wires: a colored wire (usually black), a white wire, and a green ground wire. These three wires are joined together with twist-on wire connectors.

Get someone to help you replace a ceiling fixture. After you loosen the screws that hold the existing fixture to the ceiling box, you have your hands full holding the fixture and trying to work on the wires. You may be able to pull off this juggling act with a light fixture, but if you're messing with a chandelier, you need another pair of hands to help.

To replace a ceiling fixture, follow these steps:

1. **Turn off the power.**

   You may find several pairs of wires in the ceiling box. Some of these wires may be wired to different circuits than the fixture you're working on. Be safe: Use a circuit tester or turn off the power to the whole house to ensure that all the wires in the box are dead.

2. **Remove the light bulb cover and bulbs from the fixture.**

3. **Unscrew the screws or nuts holding the fixture base to the ceiling box.**

4. **Lower the fixture base and remove the electrical tape or wire nuts from the black (hot) wire, white (neutral) wire, and, if present, green (ground) wire.**

5. **Attach the wires from the new fixture with wire nuts to the corresponding wires in the electrical box.**

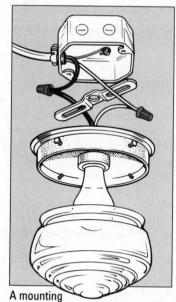

A mounting strap can hold a fixture to the ceiling.

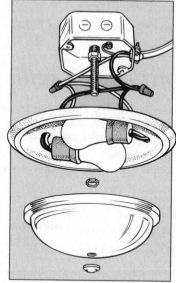

Screws and nuts often hold a fixture to the base.

Book II

Basic Home Maintenance and Improvement

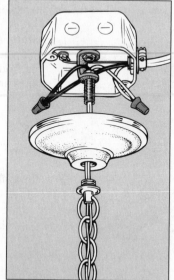

Figure 8-10: Ceiling fixtures stay secure with different mounting hardware.

A threaded hollow rod serves as a ceiling attachment.

6. **Raise and position the new base plate so that you can screw the new bolts through it to attach it to the mounting strap.**

7. **Screw in new light bulbs, install the cover, and turn on the power.**

Installing a ceiling fan

A ceiling fan is a stylish and functional addition to any room. If the room already has a ceiling outlet, wiring a ceiling fan is the same as wiring any ceiling fixture. If the room doesn't have an overhead box, hire an electrician to install the box and fish the wires through the walls and across the ceiling. Save the fun of installing the actual fan for yourself.

Because ceiling fans are so heavy, the National Electrical Code (NEC) prohibits attaching a ceiling fan to a standard ceiling box. Before you purchase the fan, check the manufacturer's installation instructions and purchase an approved electrical ceiling box.

If you can access the ceiling on which you want to attach the fan from the attic or from an overhead area, you have several choices in the type of box you install (see Figure 8-11). If you can't get to the area above the box, you have to use an adjustable hanger bar designed for installation through the hole left by the existing ceiling box. If you have no idea whether your house has an attic, maybe you shouldn't be playing with wires.

Figure 8-11: Attic access allows options in electrical boxes for attaching your ceiling fan.

To replace a ceiling fixture, follow these steps:

1. **Turn off the power at the fuse or circuit panel.**

   You may find several pairs of wires in the ceiling box. Some may be wired to circuits other than the one that the fixture you're working on uses. Be safe: Use a circuit tester or turn off the power to the whole house before attempting to install a ceiling fan. That's the only way to be sure that all wires in the box are dead.

2. **Remove any light bulb cover (such as a globe) and bulbs from the fixture.**

3. **Unscrew the screws or nuts holding the fixture base to the ceiling box.**

4. **Lower the fixture base and remove the electrical tape or wire nuts from the black (hot), white (neutral), and, if present, green (ground) wires.**

5. **Disconnect the wires to the existing ceiling box and remove it.**

    First, loosen the cable clamp screw that secures the incoming cable to the box. Then remove the box, working from above, if possible. Otherwise, remove any accessible fasteners (nails or screws) that attach it to the framing or push it up into the cavity to pry it from the framing or bend its hanger bar, depending on how it is attached.

6. **Follow the manufacturer's directions to install the adjustable hanger bar and ceiling box.**

    You install most hanger bars by pushing them through the hole in the ceiling left by the old electrical box. When you have the hanger bar completely through the hole, rotate it until it's perpendicular to the ceiling joists. The bar expands until it engages the ceiling joists. The ends of the hanger bar are equipped with sharp steel pins that dig into the wood joists when the hanger bar is expanded, as shown in Figure 8-12. You then attach the special ceiling box to the hanger bar, locking it in place to provide a secure base for the fan.

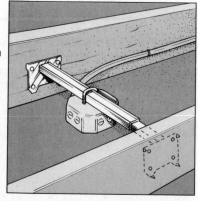

Figure 8-12:
The hanger bar holds the fan firmly within the framing of the ceiling.

7. **Assemble the fan according to the manufacturer's instructions.**

    A fan kit contains a ceiling hanger bracket designed for that particular model. Follow the directions and bolt the bracket to the ceiling box. The installation kit for the fan should provide all the necessary hardware.

Ceiling fans are heavy, so they require support while you attach the wires. Most models provide a way for you to suspend them below the ceiling box while you attach the wires. If yours doesn't, get a helper to support the fan assembly while you attach the wires.

Wiring schemes differ slightly from fan to fan, depending on whether they're equipped with a light or speed control. The basic installation of a ceiling fan is no different from that of a standard light fixture. Use wire nuts to attach the fan's black or colored wire and white wire to matching wires in the ceiling box. If the wiring has a green ground wire, attach it to the green or bare wire in the box.

8. **Complete the attachment of the fan assembly to the ceiling box.**

9. **Install the trim and fan blades according to the manufacturer's directions.**

10. **Turn on the power and test the installation.**

Installing track lighting

From its theatrical roots onstage, track lighting has evolved into individual fixtures along a track mounted on a wall or ceiling. Because you can place the light fixtures anywhere on the track and adjust their direction, a track lighting system is a good choice when you want to direct light to a specific area, like a wall of artwork or down a long hallway, or when you want to accommodate changing lighting needs.

An advantage of track lighting is that the track can be powered by a single source, usually a ceiling box. Because track systems vary, become familiar with the assembly before you begin following the instructions to install it.

One end of the track is designed to accept wiring from the ceiling outlet and connect it to the rest of the track. This end is attached to a plate that screws to the ceiling box. The wiring scheme is exactly the same as for any fixture. You connect like-colored wires together, and the green or bare ground wire attaches to the grounding terminal on the track or cover plate.

Follow these basic steps to install a track lighting system in an existing ceiling box:

1. **Turn off the power from the fuse or circuit panel.**

You may find several pairs of wires in the ceiling box. Some of these wires may be controlled by different circuits than the fixture you're working on. Be safe: Use a circuit tester or turn off the power to the whole house to be sure that all wires in the box are dead.

2. **Remove the old fixture as described earlier in this section.**

3. **Pull the existing black or colored wire, white wire, and green or bare wire that were connected to the old fixture through the opening in the new cover plate.**

4. **Attach the plate to the ceiling box with the screws provided.**

5. **Use the lighting track as a template to locate the position of the mounting screws on the ceiling.**

   Have a helper hold the track in place while you use a pencil to transfer the location of the mounting holes in the track to the ceiling.

6. **Drill a hole for the mounting toggle bolts in the ceiling.**

   Depending on the weight of the track, manufacturers specify different types of fasteners for holding the track system to the ceiling. Most even supply the fasteners. In some cases, you only need plastic plug-type anchors, but to be on the safe side, we recommend installing toggle bolts. This type of anchor holds the most weight and isn't difficult to install. It requires a hole in the ceiling the same diameter as the folded toggle.

7. **Follow the manufacturer's instructions for securing the track to the ceiling.**

   If toggle bolts hold up the track, you have to preassemble them on the track and then hold the whole assembly in place while you push the individual toggles through the predrilled ceiling holes, as shown in Figure 8-13. Thread the screw through the mounting hole in the track and then reinstall the toggle on the screw. After you push the folded toggle through the hole in the ceiling, it unfolds inside the ceiling and provides a secure grip. Tighten the screw to pull the track tight to the ceiling.

8. **Pull the wires through the end of the track and attach them to the screw terminals, as shown in Figure 8-13.**

   The black or colored wire goes on the brass-colored screw and the white wire on the silver screw. Attach the bare or green grounding wire to the green screw.

9. **Install the cover plate on the end of the track to hide the wiring.**

10. **Follow the manufacturer's directions for mounting the light fixtures.**

    You attach most track fixtures by slipping a mounting flange into the center channel of the track and then turning the fixture to force the flange under the track so that it contacts the internal wiring.

Book II

Basic Home Maintenance and Improvement

 Like other electrical devices, track lights have a specific current rating. Before you install more than five or six fixtures, check the system's amperage rating. Most can carry 15 amps. Overload the circuit and the breakers will pop so much that you'll think Orville Redenbacher is living in your basement.

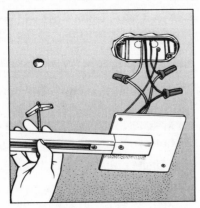

Figure 8-13:
Track
lighting can
provide
focused
illumination
within your
home.

A. A mounting flange fixes the light to the ceiling. (Step 7)

B. Wires are color-coded for coordination with screw terminals. (Step 8)

Adding a receptacle or switch by using surface wiring

If you don't mind the industrial look of surface wiring, the easiest solution may be to add an outlet or switched ceiling fixture. It's a great solution for wiring on concrete walls, such as in a basement. With surface wiring, you eliminate the hassle of running wires through walls. If you already have an outlet in the room, you can use a surface wiring system to expand it.

A protective system called a *raceway* contains the wiring like a hard-covered extension cord. Raceway systems vary by manufacturer, but you install all of them in basically the same way.

Check with your local building department before you purchase surface-wiring components. Electrical codes vary, and some local codes restrict the use of certain surface-wiring systems.

Here are the basic steps for extending a circuit from an existing wall outlet to an overhead light fixture controlled by a single pole switch:

1. Turn off the power at the fuse or circuit panel.

You may find several pairs of wires in the ceiling or wall box. Some of these wires may be connected to different circuits than the fixture you're working on. To be safe, use a circuit tester or turn off the power to the whole house so that you can be sure that all the wires in the box are dead.

2. **Decide on a source of power.**

   An existing receptacle is your best choice. Otherwise, you'd have to run a new circuit — clearly a job for an electrician.

3. **Sketch out the system.**

   You need an extension frame to fit over the existing outlet box to start the extension and enough raceway and fittings to connect the outlet to the new ceiling fixture. You also need a surface-mounted ceiling fixture box and a surface-mounted light fixture box. You can find all these components and the wires at most home centers.

4. **Work from the ceiling fixture back to the outlet and install the fixture to the ceiling with the hardware provided.**

   Secure the box base to the ceiling at a joist, or use hollow-wall fasteners.

5. **Mount the light switchbox in a convenient location on the wall.**

6. **Install the raceway between the ceiling fixture and the switchbox.**

   The raceway channels that hold the wires running from box to box attach to the walls with special hardware supplied by the manufacturer. Some styles use plastic wall anchors, and some use toggle bolts, but all are easy to install. These systems provide junction fittings for rounding corners, T-fittings for joining two raceways, and connectors for joining the raceways to the switchbox (see Figure 8-14).

7. **Install the raceway between the switchbox and the outlet.**

8. **Run the wires in the raceway.**

   To wire the fixture, you need a black wire, a white wire, and a green ground wire. Feed these wires into the raceway between the wall outlet and the switchbox. Leave a loop a foot or so long at each end so that you can wire up the switch and fixture. Similarly, run the wires from the switch to the ceiling fixture, as shown in Figure 8-14.

9. **After the wires are in place inside the raceway, snap on the cover and junction fittings.**

10. **Install the ceiling fixture while there's no power in the circuit.**

    Electrical power doesn't flow to the ceiling fixture until after you connect it to the wall receptacle, so now is the safest time to install the light fixture or new receptacle.

11. **Install the single-pole switch.**

    Refer to the section "Replacing a single-pole switch," earlier in this chapter, for instructions on replacing a switch. Basically, you have three wires running through the wall switchbox to the ceiling box. Tuck the white wire into the back of the box. Cut the black wire in the middle of

Book II

Basic Home Maintenance and Improvement

the loop you made when you installed the wires in Step 8. Strip off about 1 inch of insulation from the end of these wires and then attach the black wires to the screw terminals on the side of the switch.

12. **If the switch has a green screw terminal, attach the ground wire to the switch.**

    Cut the green ground wire and strip off the insulation from each end. Then take a 6-inch piece of green wire and strip off the insulation from each end. Twist one end of the pigtail together with the other two ground wires. Complete the splice by twisting a wire nut onto this bundle. Attach the other end of the pigtail to the green screw on the switch. Then push the switch into the box, secure it with the mounting screws, and install the switch plate.

13. **Check that the electrical power is off at the existing wall outlet and then connect the new circuit to the wall receptacle to energize the circuit.**

    Connect the black wire to the copper-colored screw and the white wire to the silver screw. The green goes to the bare or green wire in the box.

Figure 8-14:
Ideal for basements and storage rooms, surface wiring is more functional than attractive.

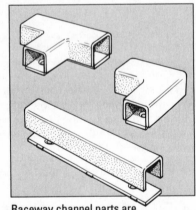

Raceway channel parts are designed for easy assembly and installation.

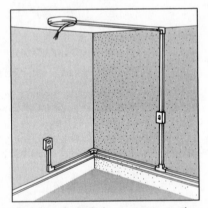

Wires run through the raceway, starting at the wall outlet.

Wiring a Telephone Extension

Adding a phone extension to an existing jack has become embarrassingly easy. You have only four wires to deal with, and they're all color coded. So as long as you aren't color blind, installing an extension phone is goof proof.

And because phone systems are low-voltage devices, you have little chance of getting shocked.

You can buy everything you need for this project at a home center. Buy a surface-mount modular phone jack and enough round (not flat, modular) four-conductor phone wire to reach from the existing phone jack to the location where you want to install the new wall jack. You can usually buy the wire in 50- and 100-foot spools.

Here are the basic steps involved in wiring a phone extension:

Book II

Basic Home Maintenance and Improvement

1. **Locate the working phone jack most convenient to the new jack you want to install.**

   Remember that the nearest jack may be in an adjacent room. Running the phone wire from an existing jack to the new location is your biggest challenge, so use your imagination. You can leave the wire exposed because it carries low voltage. You can hide it along the baseboard, tuck it between the baseboard and carpet, or fish it through walls — it'll be your secret.

2. **Decide where you want the new jack to be and mount the base on the wall or baseboard with the hardware provided.**

3. **Strip 6 inches of the outer insulation off the round telephone wire to expose the red, green, yellow, and black wires inside.**

4. **Strip 1 inch of the colored insulation off each exposed wire.**

5. **Loosen the terminal screws on the new wall jack and wrap the wires clockwise around the matching colored terminals, as shown in Figure 8-15.**

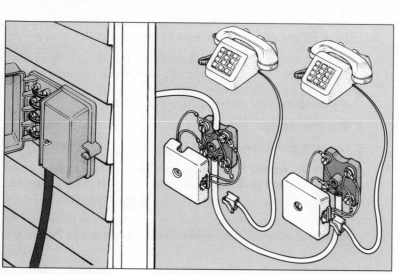

Figure 8-15: Make a telephone extension connection by matching wire colors with terminals and then wrapping the wires clockwise around the screw.

6. Tighten the screw terminals, making sure that the bare ends of the wires do not touch.

7. Replace the cover of the new wall jack.

8. Strip the insulation off the end of the phone wire at the existing wall jack.

9. Remove the cover from the existing wall jack that you're tapping into.

10. Loosen the screw terminals and wind each wire around the terminal of the same color.

11. Tighten the screws and replace the existing wall jack cover.

12. Plug the phone line back into the existing jack and test for a dial tone; then take a phone to the new jack and test for a dial tone.

   If you hear a dial tone, sign up for a job at the phone company. If not, keep your day job and recheck your wiring.

Replacing a Porch Light with a Security Light

Outdoor security lights use infrared or microwave sensors to light up whenever someone or something passes within a certain range. Use them to safeguard your house without the expense and inconvenience of leaving a harsh light glaring all night. You wire a security light just like an indoor ceiling or wall fixture. To replace an outdoor light fixture with a security light, follow these steps:

1. **Turn off the power at the fuse or circuit panel.**

   You may find several pairs of wires in the wall box. Some of these wires may be wired to different circuits than the fixture you're working on. Be safe: Use a circuit tester or turn off the power to the whole house to ensure that all the wires in the box are dead.

2. **Remove the light bulb cover and bulb from the fixture.**

3. **Unscrew the screws or nuts holding the fixture base to the wall box.**

4. **Lower the fixture base and remove the electrical tape or wire nuts from the black (hot), white (neutral), and, if present, green (ground) wires.**

5. **Use wire nuts to attach the wires from the new fixture to the corresponding wires in the electrical box, as shown in Figure 8-16.**

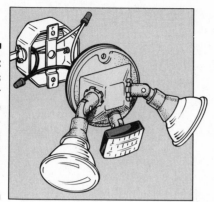

Figure 8-16:
Wire nuts attach your new fixture to the like-colored wires in the electrical box.

6. **Raise and position the new base plate so that you can screw the new bolts through it to attach to the mounting strap.**

   An outdoor fixture has a weather gasket that's inserted between the utility box and the cover plate of the fixture. The gasket helps prevent water from getting into the box. Use the gasket, even if you install the light in a weather-protected outdoor area.

7. **Screw in the bulb and replace the bulb cover (if any).**

8. **Turn on the power and try out your toy.**

   Most units have a sensitivity adjustment. You may have to do a bit of experimenting with this setting to prevent the light from turning on when a bird flies by or the neighbor's cat strolls into your yard at 3 a.m. Have a helper walk into the sensor's field of view. If the unit doesn't light up, increase the sensitivity until it does.

Adding a Low-Voltage Outdoor Light

Low-voltage lighting is an ideal choice for outdoor illumination because it's safe to work with and easy to install. Low-voltage systems, like the one shown in Figure 8-17, are engineered to be modular with easy-to-assemble components. Most systems are powered by a 24-volt transformer attached to a single multiconductor cable, onto which you clamp light modules.

The wiring comes easy. The most time-consuming part is positioning and running the lines, especially if you're digging up the ground to bury the lines and then covering them again. You can also lay the cable directly on the ground and cover it with mulch. If there's any chance that the cable can come in contact with your lawnmower or other garden tools, bury the cable by at least 12 inches.

Figure 8-17:
Low-voltage outdoor lighting comes in modular systems that you can customize to features of your yard.

Here are the basic steps to installing a low-voltage lighting system:

1. **Install the transformer close to a grounded outlet.**

   You should mount the *transformer,* which converts standard 120-line voltage to 24-volt current, close to an exterior outlet. You can mount a transformer that has a timer inside, but you have to install one with a photoelectric sensor outside so that the sensor is exposed to daylight. For obvious reasons, light-sensitive sensors don't work in the shade.

2. **Lay the cable on the ground according to your plan.**

3. **Attach the lighting modules to the cable.**

   Different systems have different connecting schemes, but the general procedure is to position the cable in a slot in the base of the light and then close the clamping mechanism that pierces the low-voltage wire to draw power.

    Extract your finger before closing the clamp!

4. **When you have all the lights in place, plug the wall-mounted transformer into the exterior outlet and test the lights.**

   You need to make all permanently plugged-in connections to an exterior outlet weather protected. You can find special outlet covers for this purpose at your local home improvement center.

5. **Conceal the cable with mulch or bury it in a shallow trench.**

 Even though you're working with low voltage, it's a good idea not to plug the transformer into the external outlet until you're done with the wiring. When you're working outside in a moist environment, it's nice to know that absolutely no current is flowing through the system.

Book III
Painting and Wallpapering

The 5th Wave   By Rich Tennant

In this book . . .

You probably don't need a market survey to tell you that the "I'd rather be painting (or wallpapering) my house" bumper stickers aren't breaking any sales records — except perhaps for the fewest ever sold. Yet more people probably tackle painting, finishing, and wallpapering than any other type of home improvement project. If you think about it, it's no real mystery why people paint and wallpaper their houses. Applying a fresh coat of paint or hanging wallpaper is the easiest and most economical way to transform a room or a home's exterior and to make it uniquely your own.

Here are the contents of Book III at a glance.

Book III
Painting and Wallpapering

The 5th Wave   By Rich Tennant

Seriously—why always a black Bat Cave? Why not a mauve Bat Cave? Or an eggshell Bat Cave? We could do a wallpaper wainscotting in contrasting stripes, ...

Why am I even trying?

COLOR CHART

In this book . . .

Y ou probably don't need a market survey to tell you that the "I'd rather be painting (or wallpapering) my house" bumper stickers aren't breaking any sales records — except perhaps for the fewest ever sold. Yet more people probably tackle painting, finishing, and wallpapering than any other type of home improvement project. If you think about it, it's no real mystery why people paint and wallpaper their houses. Applying a fresh coat of paint or hanging wallpaper is the easiest and most economical way to transform a room or a home's exterior and to make it uniquely your own.

Here are the contents of Book III at a glance.

Chapter 1

Planning Your Project

. . . .

In This Chapter

▶ Choosing the right finish for the job

▶ Playing it safe with lead paint

▶ Estimating how much paint you need

▶ Selecting the right applicators

▶ Using the proper brushing, rolling, and spraying techniques

. . . .

*W*ith good preparation and planning, any job — big or small — will go smoothly, and you'll reap the rewards of an attractive, long-lasting finish. This chapter walks you through the stages of planning a painting project, from selecting a finish to buying the right amount of paint to finding the best technique for the surface you're painting.

A Primer on Finishes

The greatest hurdle you're likely to face isn't on your walls or ceilings; it's in the aisles of your home center. Faced with mile-long shelves stacked to the ceiling with paints, stains, and other finishing products, you may stand there musing, "How the heck do I know what kind to buy?"

Beyond the ornamental purposes that paint, varnish, and other finishes provide, they bond with wood or other materials to protect the surface from heat, moisture, sunlight, chemicals, dirt, stains, and even fire. Depending on the formula and the application, a finish prevents (or slows) degradation caused by weathering and sunlight, wood rot, mildew growth, and rust. It also limits expansion and contraction due to changing moisture content and temperatures. It keeps surfaces cleaner and, when they get dirty, makes them easier to clean.

Water-based or oil-based?

When you reach the paint department, you face a choice between the two major types of paints, stains, varnishes, and other clear coatings: *alkyd* (oil-based) and *latex* (water-based). Alkyd paint produces more durable and washable surfaces, but because cleaning up afterwards involves using paint thinner (or *mineral spirits*), it isn't as user-friendly. Some professional painters insist on using alkyd paint, however, claiming that it's more durable in demanding situations.

Latex paint is the more popular choice because it's much easier to work with and cleans up with soap and water. For first-time painters, latex is the better choice because you get a professional-looking job with a durable finish. Plus, latex paint dries quickly and produces fewer odors.

One approach is to use alkyd paint on woodwork and trim, where a hard, durable finish can be washed frequently, and latex paint on the walls.

First things first: Primers and sealers

Base coats include primers, sealers, and combination primer-sealers. You apply a base coat under a *topcoat* (a finish that protects and sometimes colors the surface) to provide better adhesion and/or to seal the surface for a more even application of the finish, or in some cases to prevent stains from bleeding through the topcoat.

Certain topcoats don't require a primer when used on certain surfaces. For example, you don't need to prime when you're recoating well-adhered paint with an identical paint (latex semi-gloss over latex semi-gloss, for example) and you're not making a significant color change. Fortunately, you don't need to remember these rules — just read the label on the can of topcoat paint. It will specify primer requirements, if any, for various surfaces.

Primers

Primers are formulated to adhere well to bare surfaces and provide the best base for other paint to stick to. Water- and oil-based primers are available for virtually all interior and exterior surfaces. Before you paint, you need to prime all unpainted surfaces, patched areas, and spots that you make bare in the preparation stages.

If you're painting with a color that's significantly darker or lighter than the existing finish, use a tinted primer and a topcoat. Ask your paint supplier to tint an interior primer to the approximate color of the planned topcoat. Primer is less expensive because as an undercoat it doesn't need the expensive ingredients that make topcoats washable.

Most primers (also called *undercoaters*) contain little pigment and none of the ingredients that give topcoats shine, durability, and washability. Apply topcoats as soon as possible after the primer dries. (Primer generally dries fast.) Some primers can be top-coated after as little as an hour.

Sealers and primer-sealers

You should use a *sealer* or *primer-sealer* if you're painting a material that varies in porosity, such as newly installed drywall or a wood such as fir. The seal prevents the topcoat from being absorbed unevenly, which would give the finish a blotchy appearance or an uneven texture. Sealers also block stains. If you have kids, for example, you may have marker or crayon stains on your walls. To prevent bleed-through, apply a stain blocker, stain-killing sealer, or white-pigmented shellac. These primer-sealers are available in spray cans for small spots and in quart and gallon containers for large stained areas. Also use them to prevent the wood knots' resin from bleeding through the topcoat.

Having had mixed results with the stain-sealing effectiveness of these products, especially when it comes to knots, we recommend that you apply two or three coats.

Categorizing finishes

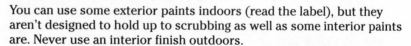

Sorting through the myriad choices of topcoats — one manufacturer's catalog we looked at listed hundreds of finishes in 90 categories — isn't as difficult as it may seem at first. You see, for example, that most fall into one of the following categories:

✔ **Exterior paints** are formulated to withstand the effects of weather, damaging ultraviolet radiation, air pollution, extremes in heat and cold, expansion, and contraction. They include house paints (intended for the body of the house but may be used for trim), trim paints, and a variety of specialty paints, such as those for metal roofs, barns, aluminum or vinyl siding, and masonry surfaces.

You can use some exterior paints indoors (read the label), but they aren't designed to hold up to scrubbing as well as some interior paints are. Never use an interior finish outdoors.

✔ **Interior paints** include flat ceiling paints, wall and ceiling paints in a range of sheens from flat to gloss, trim paints, and enamels in higher gloss ranges. Consider using special interior paints that contain fungicides for high-humidity areas such as kitchens, bathrooms, and laundry rooms. Interior textured paints, intended for use on ceilings and walls,

Book III

Painting and Wallpapering

contain sand or other texturing materials. Use vapor-retarding paint on interior walls in homes that have had thermal insulation blown into wall cavities without the required vapor retarder.

✔ **Interior/exterior paints** can be used indoors or out. Some alkyd, urethane, and water-based floor, deck, and patio enamels fall into this category.

✔ **Interior and exterior stains** are formulated for interior, exterior, or interior/exterior use. Although people associate stains primarily with wood, stains are also available for concrete. Stains intended for interior applications offer little or no protection and must be top-coated with a protective, film-forming sealer finish such as varnish, or with a separate sealer and a wax or polish. Exterior stains have water-repellent and UV-reflecting qualities.

✔ **Transparent finishes** are just that: *transparent,* not colorless. Alkyd and polyurethane varnishes are amber colored and will yellow further with time. Polyurethane varnish has largely replaced alkyd varnish because it's more moisture and stain resistant.

Water-based clear finishes dry three to six times faster than alkyds. Milky, water-borne polyurethane varnish and water-borne acrylic finish dry clear and remain clear, so they're excellent choices for use over pickled, pastel-stained, or painted surfaces. On the downside, they lie on the surface rather than penetrate, so they don't enhance or bring out the beauty of the natural wood as well as penetrating finishes do. Nor do they offer the stain and water resistance of oil-based finishes.

✔ **One-step stain-varnish combos** stain, seal, and protect in one coat. They don't penetrate wood well and are hard to maintain, so we recommend that you stick with the two-step approach.

A varnish offers more protection than other sealer/finish approaches, such as shellacs, oils, and polishes. However, varnish masks the beauty of the wood more than these alternatives do, so it isn't often used on fine furniture. Furniture oils, such as tung oil, boiled linseed oil, and Danish oil, are penetrating, wipe-on finishes with an amber color and a satin luster. Oils offer little moisture or stain resistance, but you can easily conceal scratches by recoating. This quality makes oils a good choice for wood that takes a beating — but only if stains and water aren't big concerns.

✔ **Specialty finishes,** including some primers, sealers, and topcoats, are formulated for specific and usually demanding applications. Whenever a project seems to go beyond the basics, look for specialty products. Primers are made for galvanized metal and mill-finish aluminum. Masonry sealers prevent dusting or leaching of alkalis. Two-part epoxy and two-part urethane paints are used when a particularly strong bond is required or when a finish must stand up to extreme abuse, such as on countertops or garage floors.

Lead, the Environment, and You

Lead, an extremely toxic substance, was present in most paints produced before the late 1970s, when its use was banned. An estimated 75 percent of homes built before 1978 contain lead-based paint. If your home has lead-based paint, exercise caution whenever you make repairs around the house.

If you're planning to paint, refinish, or wallpaper, and any of the repair or prep work will remove or disturb lead paint or create dust, the best advice is: Don't do it yourself. Don't allow an uncertified painting contractor to do the work, either. In addition to posing safety risks, hiring uncertified contractors may be illegal.

We have no doubt that this advice is sound for most people and a virtual no-brainer for large projects, such as stripping all the paint off your exterior siding or interior trim. On the other hand, we recognize — as does the U.S. Environmental Protection Agency — that it's neither practical nor realistic to expect homeowners not to work on certain smaller projects just because they involve lead paint. In fact, two EPA booklets describe how to go about it: *Protect Your Family in Your Home* and *Reducing Lead Hazards When Remodeling Your Home*. Call 1-800-424-LEAD to have the material mailed or download materials directly from the NLIC Web site: leadctr@nsc.org.

When you do prep work involving lead finishes, never dry-sand or dry-scrape (that is, without wetting the surface as you sand or scrape), and never use propane torches or heat guns to remove lead-based paint.

Book III

Painting and Wall-papering

Choosing an Exterior Finish

Unless you're building a new home or re-siding an existing one, your choices for what finish to use are dictated to a degree by your siding and the type and condition of any existing finish. For example, some finishes work better on smooth, painted wood, and others work better on rough, stained wood. So the first step is to narrow the options to the appropriate finishes. Next, choose the ones that offer you the right combination of qualities. Finally, choose a color.

Paint versus stain

If you have new siding or siding that has been treated only with a semitransparent stain, your options are wide open. However, you can't stain over previously painted surfaces.

As a general rule, paint is the preferred finish for smooth siding, trim, and metal siding like steel or aluminum. It offers maximum protection from UV radiation and moisture. Stains are commonly used on natural wood siding, especially rough-sawn boards, and on other exterior wood surfaces, such as decks and fences.

Although paint lasts longer than stain, paint finish builds up and may peel or otherwise fail. If it does, you're in for a lot of work. Stains, on the other hand, may not last as long, but thanks to the penetration, they just weather away. Over the long haul, less cost and work may be involved if you choose stain. It's easier to apply, and preparation is usually limited to simple power washing.

Exterior latex paint

Latex is the hands-down favorite for most painted exterior surfaces. It's popular because it's easier to use and more environmentally friendly than oil-based paint. Latex paint is more elastic and remains flexible, so it won't crack as the materials to which it's applied expand and contract. Oil-based paint, on the other hand, becomes brittle with age. Latex paint has superior color retention over most oil-based paint — it doesn't fade as much. The paint film also permits interior moisture vapor to pass through, so latex paint is less likely to peel due to moisture problems. You can apply a latex topcoat over either latex or oil-based primer.

Exterior alkyd paint

On a few surfaces, *alkyd* (oil-based) paint may be a better choice than latex. For example, if a house has numerous coats of alkyd paint, it's generally best to stick with alkyd. Believing that alkyd-painted surfaces are generally easier to clean and have more sheen than latex paints, some professionals use latex on the body of the house but prefer to use an alkyd finish on trim or other high-contact areas, such as doors. We think that the advantages of latex outweigh the purported advantages of alkyd-based paint in the vast majority of applications. We're inclined to agree with the professionals, however, who say that alkyd paints, especially primers, are better to use on problem areas.

Don't use alkyd paint over a latex topcoat. It's likely to peel off even a well-prepared latex finish because the latex expands and contracts too much for the relatively rigid alkyd film.

Exterior stains and clear coatings

Stains and clear coatings are the most natural-looking protective finishes for wood. Exterior stains and varnishes have fungicides, offer greater ultraviolet (UV) protection than interior versions, and may have more water-repellent qualities, too. Stains are available in both oil- and water-based versions and are colored with dye and pigment. A semitransparent stain uses more dye for deep penetration but allows the wood grain to show. A solid-color stain uses more pigment to cover all existing color and grain but retains some textures and contains a sealer, such as urethane or varnish. A solid-color stain offers better UV protection and hiding characteristics than semitransparent stain or transparent finishes, such as varnish. Solid-color stain penetrates more than paint and produces a thinner film, so it isn't as likely to peel.

You can only apply stains over new or previously stained surfaces — not painted ones. Oil-based semitransparent stains are a good choice for new wood siding, decks, and fences. These stains have a linseed-oil base, which offers good penetration of new wood (especially rough-sawn surfaces) while revealing the wood's grain and texture. For best protection, use two coats of semitransparent stain on new wood surfaces.

If your goal is to conceal discoloration, solid-color stains have more pigment than semitransparent stains and tend to hide the wood grain. This characteristic makes solid-color stains a better choice to finish pressure-treated wood that has a pronounced green or brown tint, which semitransparent stains may not cover.

Typically, the only treatment used for redwood is clear water repellent. Semitransparent stains won't cover the red. Tannin bleed is a problem with redwood, so if you want to change its color, you can use an oil-based solid stain, but only on rough-sawn redwood. For smooth redwood, you should prime and paint. When working with redwood, use a stain-blocking latex primer on air-dried siding or an alkyd primer on kiln-dried siding, regardless of the type of topcoat.

> **Book III**
>
> **Painting and Wallpapering**

Choosing the Right Interior Paint

Interior paints come in different gloss ranges, or sheens. In the past, only three were standard: flat, semi-gloss, and gloss. Today, you may be able to choose from up to seven gloss ranges, depending on the manufacturer and the type of paint. Keep in mind that these ranges may vary from one product to another. Some manufacturers get a bit more creative in naming sheens, but the most common are

- ✔ **Flat:** This paint is at the low (dull) end of the sheen spectrum. It's often used on walls and ceilings because it reflects a minimum of light off the surface, reducing glare and helping to hide small surface imperfections. It's generally not considered washable.

- ✔ **Eggshell, lo-luster, and satin:** These paints have increasing amounts of sheen, making them a little more dirt-resistant than flat paints, and washable. The slight sheen is generally noticeable only when the surface is lighted from the side. It's a good choice for walls in hallways, children's bedrooms, playrooms, and other high-traffic areas.

- ✔ **Semi-gloss:** This paint has still more sheen, making it even more washable. Walls in kitchens, bathrooms, mud rooms, and children's rooms are good candidates for semi-gloss paints. Semi-gloss is perhaps the most widely used latex paint for trim.

- ✔ **Gloss and high-gloss:** These paints dry to a durable and shiny surface. High-gloss paint has an almost mirrorlike sheen. Gloss paints are the most dirt-resistant and scrubbable choice for interior trim and most woodwork. Gloss enamels are particularly hard and are an excellent choice for doors, furniture, and cabinets because the surface can withstand heavy cleaning. Some gloss enamels, called deck or floor enamels, are specifically designed for wearing surfaces, such as floors.

Finding the Perfect Interior Stain

If you think that variety is the spice of life, you're going to love shopping for wood stains. Stains are available in a wide variety of wood tones, as well as pastels. Your paint dealer probably has samples so that you can see how various stains look on real wood.

Let your decor and tastes determine which is best for you. For nicely grained wood, such as oak, a penetrating stain that enhances the grain pattern is a good choice. For furniture, cabinets, or moldings made of less attractive wood, or for mismatched pieces of wood, consider using a *pigmented* stain (a colored "wiping" stain) or a pastel stain; they conceal more.

Can't find the perfect color? Play chemist and mix together different stains from the same manufacturer to make your own unique stain or a stain that matches the stain on existing wood. If you decide to experiment, be sure to mix enough stain to do the entire job. Measure and record the proportions carefully because if you run out of stain in the middle of a project or if you need to mix up a batch for a future repair, matching the tone without a formula is difficult.

You can also make your own pigmented stain by thinning alkyd paint with mineral spirits. For example, for a deep black stain, thin flat black alkyd paint with mineral spirits. Start with a 50-50 mix and add mineral spirits, testing often on a scrap of wood until you get just the result you want.

Estimating How Much Paint to Buy

To estimate the amount of paint you need for a project, first consider how much surface area you want to cover. Dust off a math formula that you probably learned in the fourth grade: length (in feet) × width (in feet) = area (in square feet).

The second factor in determining your paint needs is coverage. Virtually all paints and other coatings describe coverage in terms of the number of square feet (area) that 1 gallon covers. The coverage varies by product and is printed on the label. When estimating a smaller project, remember that there are 4 quarts in a gallon and 2 pints in a quart.

The third factor to consider is the condition of the surface. A rough, porous, unpainted surface absorbs much more paint than a primed or topcoated surface. Similarly, a six-panel door requires more paint than a smooth, flat door.

Estimating isn't an exact science. Keep in mind that you can usually return standard colors, but not custom ones, so it's more important to be accurate when using custom colors. Although you don't want to waste paint, a reasonable amount of leftover paint is handy for touch-ups. If you're like most people who fail to record custom paint colors in a safe place, keeping some extra paint is also the only way to know what color you used when you need to repaint!

Follow this process to figure out how much paint to buy:

1. **Find the total area of the surface you want to paint.**

    For walls, just add together the length of all the walls and multiply the result by the height of the room, measured from the floor to a level ceiling. The number you get equals the total area.

    Ceiling measurements are usually fairly straightforward — just multiply the room's width by its length. Add this number to the area of the walls or leave it separate, depending on whether you're planning to use different-colored paints for the ceiling and the walls.

Book III

Painting and Wall-papering

If the room has a cathedral ceiling, it has some triangular wall sections (usually two identical ones on opposite walls). Dust off one more math formula: area (of a triangle) = ½ base × height. Measure from the top of the wall (usually 8 feet above the floor) to the peak of the triangle. Multiply that number (the height) by ½ the width of the wall (the base) to get the square footage of the triangle. If your room has two identical triangles, either double the number or multiply the height by the entire width.

Measuring a home's exterior is more complex, but the procedure is basically the same. Just break up the surface into rectangles, multiply length by width for each rectangular area, and total them up.

Don't bother to climb a ladder to measure the height of a triangular gable wall section; count the rows, called *courses,* of siding from the ground. Measure the *exposure* (the distance from the bottom of one course of siding to the bottom of the next course) on siding that you can reach easily, and then multiply that number by the number of courses to come up with the height measurement.

2. **Account for windows and doors.**

   To figure how much of the total area is paintable area, you need to deduct for the openings — windows and doors. Unless you have unusually large or small windows or doors, you can allow 20 square feet for each door and 15 square feet for each window. Add up the areas of the openings and subtract that total from the total area.

   On the exterior, however, don't make any deductions unless an opening is larger than 100 square feet. This general rule helps to account for some of the typical exterior conditions described in Step 5.

   If you plan to paint the doors, use the following rules. Allow 20 square feet for each door (just the door, not the trim); double that if you're finishing both sides.

3. **Calculate the total area of the trim.**

   This measurement is a little trickier because widths are usually measured in inches, and lengths are measured in feet. In many cases, you can add up a number of widths and round off the total to feet. For example, take door trim. The 3-inch inside casing + 6-inch jamb + 3-inch outside casing = 12 inches (1 foot) total width. The two sides and the head add up to roughly 17 feet in length. So 1 foot × 17 feet = 17 square feet.

   Generally speaking, you can figure about 8 square feet to paint the sash and trim of a standard-sized window.

4. **Make a preliminary calculation of gallons required.**

   Knowing the area to be covered, divide the total square footage of paintable area by the coverage per gallon, which is stated on the label. For example, if you're painting walls with a paint that covers 350 square feet per gallon, you divide the paintable wall area by 350 to find the number of gallons of paint you need for the walls.

If you get a remainder of less than 0.5, order a couple of quarts to go with the gallons; if the remainder is more than 0.5, order an extra gallon.

5. **Factor in surface conditions.**

Out go the formulas for this final step. The coverage stated on the label applies under typical (if not ideal) circumstances. A quality latex top-coat applied over a primed or painted, smooth surface, for example, covers about 350 square feet. Just like get-rich-quick schemes or lose-weight-fast diets, though, results will vary. You rarely get as much coverage as the label claims.

Wood shingles and rough-sawn cedar siding require more than the stated coverage, in part because the surface is rough and loaded with joints and cracks. There's also more area than first meets the eye. On lap or bevel siding (where horizontal boards overlap each other), you must factor in the underside. On a house with board-and-batten siding, you have many edges to paint in addition to the rough faces of the boards. That's why you don't deduct for doors and windows on exterior wall calculations.

Similarly, you use more paint if you're painting interior walls or ceilings that are unfinished, heavily patched, or dark in color. Plan to apply a primer and a topcoat or two. Oddly enough, you may get better cover-age with a cheap paint, but the finish won't be as durable or washable, so pass up bargain paint.

You must make still further allowances for the following conditions:

- Weathered or dry surfaces
- Porous material
- Unprimed, unsealed, or unfinished surfaces
- Rough surfaces
- Molding with a complex or detailed profile
- Cornices or other trims that are assembled by using numerous pieces of lumber or molding
- Raised-panel doors
- Overlapping surfaces
- High contrast between base color and topcoat

Even the type of applicator and your skills can affect the amount of paint you use. A paint sprayer, for example, can waste 10 to 25 percent on sur-faces other than the one you're trying to paint, depending on the type of sprayer and the wind conditions.

Book III

Painting and Wall-papering

If you're painting problem surfaces, allow 25 to 50 percent extra in most cases. To allow 50 percent more paint, multiply your total painted area by 1.5. To allow 25 percent more paint, multiply the painted area by 1.25. On a large project, like painting or staining an entire house, seek the advice of experienced paint store personnel. If you're using custom colors, which usually can't be returned, be conservative and plan a second trip if you need more.

The cost of paint or other finish typically makes up 10 to 15 percent of the total cost of a professional paint job. Although a dollar-to-dollar comparison is impossible with a do-it-yourself job, you'll probably have a similarly high investment in labor as compared to the cost of paint. So buy the very best paint you can afford. Any difference in cost usually isn't worth the reduction in quality. To ensure that you're using quality paint, stick with well-known brands.

The Workhorses of Painting: Brushes and Rollers

Indoors or out, most painting tasks call for one or more of the big three applicators — brushes, rollers, and pads. (Actually, painting has four workhorses, but the fourth, the paint sprayer, is out in its own pasture. See the section, "Spraying Inside and Out," later in this chapter.) You can use all three applicators with oil- or water-based finishes, so the surface you plan on painting is the primary determining factor. These applicators produce slightly different textures, which can be a second reason for choosing one type over another.

Brushes

After fingers, the brush is the world's oldest painting tool. Brushes are made for every application, from the tiniest artist's brush to super-wide wall brushes. Many brushes are intended for specialized tasks, such as decorative painting techniques.

A good brush gives you the desired result with the least amount of work. Price and feel are the best indicators of quality, and you need to consider the size, texture, and shape of the surface you're finishing. Keep these points in mind:

✔ Check to see that the *ferrule,* or the metal band that binds the brush fill to the handle, is made of noncorrosive metal; otherwise, rust may develop and contaminate the finish. The ferrule should be nailed to the handle.

✔ Be sure the handle is made of unvarnished wood or a nonglossy material. The handle should feel comfortable in your hand.

Brush fill, as the brushing material on a paintbrush is called, is very important and falls into two main categories:

- **Natural bristle brushes,** sometimes called *hog bristle* or *China* brushes (the hogs are from China), are the best, but you can use them only for oil-based paints because the bristles soak up water and get ruined. Hog bristle has a rough texture that picks up and holds a lot of paint, and the ends are naturally split, or *flagged.* A flagged brush, which looks a bit fuzzy at the tip, allows each individual bristle or filament to hold more paint without dripping and to apply paint more smoothly.

- **Synthetic brushes** are made of nylon, polyester, or a combination of synthetic filaments. Nylon bristles are more abrasion-resistant than natural bristles, hold up to water-based paints, and apply a very smooth finish. Although you can use nylon brushes with oil-based paints, polyester brushes hold up much better to solvents, heat, and moisture and as such are better all-purpose brushes. The best synthetic brushes blend nylon and polyester filaments and are an acceptable compromise for use with exterior oil-based painting.

Regardless of which type of brush you choose, look for a mix of short and long bristles with flagged tips. As the flagging on longer bristles wears, the shorter bristles take over. Pass up brushes whose bristles are all cut to the same length. Bristles should feel full, thick, and resilient. If you fan the brush and tug lightly on the bristles, no bristles should fall out. Also, choose brushes with bristles that are contoured or chiseled to an oval or rounded edge. A chiseled-tip brush cuts in better around trim, ceilings, and other transitions.

After you know what type of brush fill you want, you need to choose the right style. Brush width, the shape of the brush fill (angled or square), and the shape and size of the handle are the most obvious elements. Brush fill quality also varies. As fill qualities are less obvious, some brushes, such as the enamel/varnish brush and the stain brush, are simply named according to their intended use.

Book III

Painting and Wallpapering

Here are the four standard brush styles:

- **Enamel (varnish) brushes** are generally available from 1 to 3 inches wide. The brush fill is designed to have superior paint-carrying capacity and has a chiseled tip for smooth application. Use these brushes for trim and woodwork.

- **Sash brushes** look like enamel brushes. They, too, are available in 1- to 3-inch widths, but the handle is long and thin for better control. Although laying paint on flat surfaces may be easier with a *flat* sash brush, an *angular* sash brush is okay for flat surfaces and is much better for cutting in (carefully painting up to an edge) and getting into corners.

✔ **Wall brushes** are designed for painting large areas, including exterior siding. Select a brush according to the size of the surface you're painting, but avoid brushes over 4 inches wide. They can get awfully heavy by the end of the day.

✔ **Stain brushes** are similar to wall brushes, but they're shorter and designed to control dripping of watery stains.

Rollers

A paint roller is great for most large, flat surfaces and is the runaway favorite for painting walls and ceilings. A roller holds a large amount of paint, which saves you time and the effort of bending and dipping. (The only bending and dipping we like to do while painting involves a bag of chips and a bowl of salsa.)

When you buy a roller, choose one made with a heavy wire frame and a comfortable handle that has an open end to accept an extension pole. This isn't the time to be frugal. Don't buy economy-grade rollers that tend to flex when you apply pressure and result in an uneven coat of paint. Choose a heavy, stiff roller that doesn't flex and enables you to apply constant pressure.

A 9-inch roller is the standard size, but you can buy smaller sizes for smaller or hard-to-access surfaces. If you're painting the town, you can find an 18-inch length.

The soft painting surface of a roller is called a *sleeve* or *cover*. It slides off the roller cage for cleaning and storage. Used properly, a quality roller sleeve leaves a nondirectional paint film that looks the same on an upstroke as it does on a downstroke. Clean a sleeve thoroughly after every job, and it'll last for years.

Look for rollers with beveled edges. These rollers are less likely to leave *tracks* — lines or beads of paint that form on the surface at the edges of the roller. Don't cut corners here, either; a cheap roller sleeve sheds fibers, and you'll spend more time picking fibers out of wet paint than you will actually applying the paint. Wrap masking tape around a new roller and then peel it off along with lots of loose fibers that otherwise would end up on your wall or ceiling.

You can buy two kinds of sleeves:

✔ **Natural sleeves,** made of lambswool, are preferred for oils because they hold more paint.

Lambswool shouldn't be used with water-based paints because the alkali in water-based paints detans the sheep leather and makes it vulnerable to rot.

✔ **Synthetic sleeves,** usually made of polyester, can be used for both oil- and water-based paints.

The nap length for the sleeve you choose depends on the type of job you're undertaking. Check out Table 1-1 for pointers.

Table 1-1	Picking a Nap Length to Suit Your Job
Nap Length	*Job*
¼ inch	For very smooth surfaces like flat doors, plastered walls, and wide trim
⅜ or ½ inch	For slightly irregular surfaces like drywall and exterior siding
¾ inch or longer	For semi-rough surfaces like wood shingles
1 or 1¼ inch	For rough surfaces like concrete block and stucco

Foam painting pads

Painting pads are rectangular or brush-shaped foam applicators, with or without fiber painting surfaces. Some people find them easier to use than brushes. They paint a nice, smooth coat on trim and leave no brush marks, and the larger pads work well on wood shingles. We especially like one that has rollers on the edge to guide the pad when cutting in ceilings and interior trim.

On the downside, pads tend to put paint on too thin. They don't hold as much paint as rollers or brushes and aren't as versatile. Using a pad makes it harder to control drips and to apply an even coat on a large surface. Given the time most people need to develop techniques, it may be better to stick with a brush and/or roller for most applications.

Book III

Painting and Wall-papering

Considering Power-Painting Systems

If you plan to do a big painting job, you may want to check out the power-painting systems: power rollers (some include brush and pad accessories) or power brushes. Spray systems are fast, too, and they have several advantages unrelated to speed that make them desirable for many painting and fine finishing projects. (We discuss spray-painting later in this chapter.)

The advantage of power-painting gear is that, after you're set up and properly adjusted, you can paint like crazy, putting on a lot of paint in record time. If you're facing a major interior paint job, like when you move into an empty house, or if you plan to paint the exterior of your home with a roller, power rolling is definitely worthwhile. You may also get better results. Most people tend to brush or roll out paint too thin, perhaps to make the most of each time they load the applicator with paint. You're less inclined to do so with a power-painting system.

Some power rollers have an electric pump that draws paint directly from the can. Others are hand-pumped and use air pressure to push the paint from a reservoir to the roller, where it seeps out of little holes in the roller-sleeve core and saturates the fabric. The techniques for a power roller and a manual one are the same except that you don't have to reload a power roller. You just roll away and occasionally push a button or pull a trigger to feed more paint to the applicator. Instead of filling a roller tray with paint, you either fill a reservoir or pump directly from the can.

Other than cost, the principal downside of this equipment is the increased setup and cleanup time. You also end up with a fair amount of waste every time you clean. Unlike a brush, roller, or rolling pan that you can scrape to remove most of the paint, you have to wash the paint out of much of this equipment.

Brushing Up on Techniques

Knowing how to use a paintbrush is largely intuitive. Even someone who's never seen a paintbrush and a can of paint can figure out how to get the desired results, namely to get the paint on the right surface. In this section, we show you a few techniques and tricks that can help you get better results with less fatigue.

It's all in the wrist

Painting can feel awkward at first, but if you use the techniques we describe in this section, you can look like a pro even if you feel kind of weird.

To hold and load your brush:

1. **Hold the brush near the base of the handle with your forefingers just barely extending over the *ferrule* (the metal band that binds the brush fill to the handle).**

   For detail work, you probably want to use your good hand; but otherwise swap hands often. Alternating hands takes a little getting used to, but the more you do it, the less fatigued your muscles become and the faster you paint. Changing bodies works well, too.

2. **Dip your brush about a third of the way into the paint and tap it (don't wipe it) on the side of the bucket to shake off excess.**

   To get the most bang for the buck, fully load your brush. Don't overload it, but don't shake off any more paint than necessary to get the brush to the surface without dripping. This brush-loading technique enables you to paint a larger area without having to move your setup.

To lay on an even coat of paint with a paintbrush:

1. **Unload the paint from one side of the brush with a long stroke in one direction.**

2. **At the end of the first stroke, unload the paint from the other side of the brush.**

   Start in a dry area about a foot away from the first stroke and brush toward the end of the first stroke.

3. **Keep the brush moving, varying the pressure of your stroke to adjust the amount of paint being delivered to the surface.**

   The more pressure you apply, the more paint flows out of the brush, so start with a fairly light touch and gradually increase the pressure as you move along. If you must press hard to spread paint, you're probably applying it too thin.

4. **Brush out the area as needed to spread the paint evenly.**

   Oil-based paint requires more brushing out than latex, but don't over-work the finish, especially when using varnish.

Minimize brush marks and bubbles with a *finishing stroke* — a light stroke, as long as possible, in one direction and feathered at the end. To feather an edge with a brush:

1. **Start your brush moving in the air, lightly touch down, and continue the stroke.**

2. **Slow down near the end of the stroke and, with a slight twisting motion, lift the brush from the surface.**

3. **Continue in the same fashion in an adjacent area.**

4. **Immediately brush the paint *toward* the previous wet feathered edge to blend those two surfaces.**

5. **Spread and level the paint with additional strokes and feather a new wet edge.**

   You can't maintain a wet edge everywhere if you're painting a large area, so start and finish at corners, edges, or anywhere other than the middle of a surface so that the transition won't be noticeable. To slow drying, avoid painting in direct sunlight or on very windy days.

Book III

Painting and Wall-papering

Secret weapon: Backbrushing

For some applications, you can take advantage of a roller's speed, but you should follow up with a brush — a technique called *backbrushing*. Backbrushing smoothes out roller stipple, pushes out air bubbles, and works the paint into the surface for a better bond. These examples show you when to use this technique.

✔ Rollers leave a slightly stippled paint film that's fine for walls and siding, but you may not like it on a door or cabinet. A short-fiber pad or wide brush levels the finish on a door or trim nicely.

✔ On exterior surfaces, where a good paint bond to the surface is important, a roller doesn't do as good a job as a brush. Nothing works paint into a surface quite like a brush.

We recommend backbrushing to work spray-applied penetrating and solid-color stains into exterior surfaces.

Backbrush immediately after you apply the finish and while it's still wet. Dip your brush in the finish just once to condition it, but wipe it against the side of the can to remove the excess. You don't need to add finish; just work what's already there.

One final tip: When a project calls for backbrushing, use a team approach — one person with a roller and another with a brush. You'll fly through the job. Don't forget to swap tasks on big jobs to avoid the fatigue associated with each task.

On a large project, check whether you're applying the correct amount of paint by measuring the area covered with about a quart of paint. The painted area should equal about one-fourth the coverage per gallon that's described on the paint label. In other words, if you paint your entire house with half a gallon of paint, you're spreading it too thin.

May I cut in?

Cutting in describes two quite different painting techniques. In one sense, cutting in refers to the process of carefully painting up to an unpainted edge or an edge of a different color or sheen, such as the joint between trim and siding or between a wall and a ceiling.

Cutting in also refers to using a brush or other applicator to get into corners that a roller or larger applicator can't get into, such as where the ceiling and wall meet. Accuracy isn't an issue, so work quickly. Just remember to feather the edges and to paint to the feathered wet edges as soon as possible, especially when applying oil-based paint (see the preceding section).

When cutting in carefully up to an edge, remember that you have the best control if you use an angled sash brush. Use the edge of the brush, not the face, and follow these steps:

1. **Lay the paint on close to, but not right on, the edge that you want to cut in.**

   Keep in mind that more paint is on your brush when you start a stroke, so apply less pressure and/or stay a little farther away at the outset. For the same reason, apply more pressure and move closer to the edge you want to cut in as you lay on the paint with a long stroke or two. Lay on the paint evenly and uniformly close.

2. **Start a finishing stroke, varying the pressure to push the paint that you left on the surface in the first pass right up to the edge.**

   It may take a couple of passes, but with practice, you'll be able to apply a finishing stroke in one long stroke.

You may need to reshape a brush that has lost its shape from being used on edge this way. Just dip it in paint and wipe both brush faces several times against the edge of your paint bucket.

Roller Techniques

The goal — getting paint from the can to the surface — is the same for a roller as for a brush. You just get done faster with a roller. The most important thing to remember is that a roller spreads paint so efficiently and easily that the tendency is to spread it far too thin.

The best way to ensure that you don't spread the paint too thin is to use a methodical approach:

1. **Load a roller fully by dipping it about halfway into your paint reservoir.**

   Roll the roller very lightly on either the sloped portion of your roller tray or the roller screen, depending on your setup. This technique coats the roller surface more evenly while removing excess that would otherwise drip on the way to the surface.

2. **Unload and spread the paint in an area of about 10 square feet.**

   On large surfaces, especially rough ones, unload the paint in an N or other three- or four-leg zigzag pattern; then spread the paint horizontally and make your light finishing strokes vertically. Figure 1-1 shows this three-step zigzag process. Alternatively, you can roll out the paint in one straight line (or two straight lines next to each other), covering about the same area.

3. **Reload the roller and unload another pattern that overlaps the just-painted area.**

   Spread the new paint, blend the two areas, and wind up with finishing strokes.

Book III

Painting and Wall-papering

Figure 1-1:
Lay on a zigzag pattern, roll it out horizontally, and finish with light vertical strokes.

Normally, you don't need to feather the wet edge when you're rolling on paint because you overlap and blend each section before the paint dries. However, a few exceptions exist:

✔ If you're unable to start or finish an edge at a natural breaking point, such as a corner or the bottom edge of a course of siding, you may need to feather the edge.

✔ When you roll paint onto large surfaces where one painted area must sit while you're working your way back to it, you may have difficulty blending if you don't feather the edge.

✔ Although oil paint takes longer to dry than latex, blending one area with another is harder with oil paint unless you do it almost immediately.

To roll a feathered edge:

1. **Start the motion in the air, lowering the roller to the surface.**

2. **Roll with light pressure until you near the edge.**

3. **Gradually reduce pressure and lift the roller off the surface as you pass into the unpainted area.**

Feather when touching up with a roller. Doing so blends in the newly painted area, which almost always has a slightly different tone than the surrounding area. In fact, feather more than usual: After you feather an edge as just described, use a nearly dry roller to make a few very light passes over the touched-up area, extending at least a foot into the unpainted area.

Indispensable painting accessories

You need more than a brush or roller to paint. You need to accessorize. We've found the painting accessories listed here to be particularly helpful.

✔ **Swivel/pot hooks:** A must for exterior house painting, a pot hook lets you securely hang a paint can or bucket on your ladder, and it swivels to allow you to rotate the can for convenient access.

✔ **Extension poles:** Spend a couple of bucks for an inexpensive handle extension that screws into the end of a roller handle. You can roll from floor to ceiling without bending and with less exertion, and you avoid constant trips up and down a ladder. Some poles have adjustable heads to which you can attach a paintbrush for hard-to-reach spots or a pole sander for sanding ceilings and walls.

✔ **5-gallon bucket with roller screen:** An alternative to a roller tray is a 5-gallon bucket with a *roller screen,* a metal grate designed to fit inside the bucket. The rig is ideal for large jobs because it saves you the time you'd spend refilling the paint tray. The bucket is easier to move around and not as easy to step into. At break time, drop the screen in the bucket and snap on the lid.

✔ **Trim guard:** This edging tool is very useful for painting around windows, doors, and floor moldings. Press the metal or plastic blade of the guard against the surface you want to shield from fresh paint. Don't forget to wipe the edges clean frequently to avoid leaving smears of paint.

✔ **Aerosol spray-can handle/trigger:** This inexpensive handle/trigger snaps onto any aerosol can. The comfort is astonishing, especially if you have a lot to do, but the device's other value is that it makes it easier to hold the can at the proper angle.

✔ **Clamp lamp:** These inexpensive lamps let you direct light where you need it.

✔ **5-in-1 tool:** The Swiss Army knife of painting tools, it can scrape loose paint, score paint lines for trim removal, loosen or tighten a screw, hammer in a popped nail or other protrusion prior to spackling, and scrape paint out of a roller sleeve.

✔ **Paint mixer:** This inexpensive drill attachment does a faster and more effective job than a paint stirring stick. It's so easy that you'll actually take the time to stir as often as the instructions say to!

Book III

Painting and Wall-papering

Spraying Inside and Out

If you love toys — oops, we mean tools — you're going to love paint sprayers. They apply paint, and more of it, many times faster than brushes, rollers, and power rollers do. They're also excellent for working on difficult or complex surfaces, such as rough-hewn cedar, concrete, shutters, fences, detailed roof trim, and wicker furniture. Painting or staining exterior siding usually involves applying the same color of paint to large areas, which makes siding a perfect candidate for spray-painting. In this section, we explain what you need to know to choose the right spray equipment, prepare the paint, and use a sprayer safely and effectively.

Spray equipment requires meticulous cleaning. For a detailed description of that process, see Chapter 3.

Keeping an eye on safety

Compressor-driven and airless sprayers *atomize* paint, which means that the paint breaks up into many tiny particles. These particles float in the air and can be carried for long distances on a breeze, polluting the air that other people breathe and landing on their property. Before you begin, make sure that municipal ordinances permit the use of spray equipment on exterior projects, and never spray on a breezy day or when parked cars or other buildings are nearby.

Personal and environmental risks also vary according to the type of sprayer and tip you use. Of the three types of power sprayers that we recommend for homeowners, only the airless system creates significant overspray. You must take precautions to reduce the risk of overspray, or it becomes a health and/or environmental risk.

Paints, stains, and related products, such as solvents and cleaners, are chemicals. They shouldn't be ingested. Heed the label warnings. Remember that the fumes of poisonous chemicals are poisonous, and the fumes of flammable chemicals are flammable or explosive. Always work in cross-ventilated areas. To protect yourself, take the following precautions:

✔ Always wear a tight-fitting, organic vapor respirator when spraying solvent-based coatings indoors or outdoors and when spraying water-based coatings indoors. Masks note what they're safe for — read the packaging to determine whether a mask is appropriate for the job you plan to do. Dust masks don't offer adequate protection for most spray-painting applications.

✔ Wear splash goggles (preferably a pair with interchangeable lenses), gloves, a hat, and clothing that covers your skin no matter what type of paint you're using or what the ventilation conditions are.

✔ Wear a painter's hood to cover your head and neck.

✔ Apply protective lotion or petroleum jelly to exposed skin.

✔ Never point a sprayer at anyone in jest, and keep your own fingers away from the tip. The pressure of the spray is so great within a few inches of the tip that you may accidentally inject paint deep into your skin.

Without ventilation, you need a controlled environment with special lighting, switching, and ventilation equipment that doesn't spark. If you can't ventilate, don't spray. To minimize the risk of fire or explosion, heed these safety tips:

- ✔ Never spray flammable products in a hot room or near any source of ignition, such as a spark or standing gas pilot light.

- ✔ Don't smoke.

- ✔ Turn off or unplug all sources of ignition, including appliances such as refrigerators, coffee pots, and automatic fans.

- ✔ Turn lights on or off and put tape over the switches.

- ✔ Don't activate any electrical switch until the vapors have cleared.

The spray-painting process

You can't just hook the sprayer up to the paint and start painting. Well, you can, but you won't like the results. Spray-painting really involves four steps: preparing the work area, preparing the paint, practicing your technique, and, finally, painting the object, all the while adjusting your technique to fit your sprayer.

Don't spray-paint when the air temperature is below 45 degrees or above 75 degrees. Don't spray-paint in direct sunlight, either. Too much heat dries the paint too fast, and it won't bond well. If it's too cold, the paint dries too slowly, attracting bugs and dirt, and the gun is more likely to clog.

Book III

Painting and Wall-papering

Prepare the work area

If you're renting a sprayer, plan to do all your preparation work (covered in the following bullets) before you pick up the sprayer. Don't forget that the clock starts ticking — and the cost starts adding up — the instant you walk out of the rental shop. Prepare as follows:

- ✔ Make sure that the work area is clear and free of tripping hazards or objects that may snag the sprayer hoses.

- ✔ Protect nearby surfaces, such as windows, trim, and floors. In most cases, you want to mask off or cover these areas with dropcloths.

Stir and strain the paint or stain

Always stir paint well and then strain it to prevent clogs in the tip or at any internal filters. Clogging is the number-one complaint about spray-painting, but you can prevent nearly all clogs by straining the paint first. Paint suppliers carry a variety of strainers appropriate for different spray equipment. Figure 1-2 shows a typical setup.

Figure 1-2:
Strain paint before spraying to prevent time-consuming clogs.

Some paints must be thinned for use with most sprayers. Know what your particular situation requires. Paint that's sprayed on too thick leaves a textured finish that looks like an orange peel, and paint that's sprayed on too thin doesn't cover well and tends to sag or run. To be sure that the paint is the right *viscosity* (thickness), you can buy a *viscometer.* This small cup has a calibrated hole in the bottom (or a similar device) that you fill with paint and time how long the paint takes to drain out.

Practice basic techniques

Painting practice makes perfect. Sharpen your spraying skills with the following techniques:

- ✔ **Start moving the gun before you start spraying and keep the gun moving in long, straight strokes.** (See Figure 1-3.) Sprayers apply paint quickly, so you must use this technique to get an even coat that doesn't run. Move as fast as you would brush out a stroke, or 2 to 3 feet per second.

- ✔ **Hold the paint gun nozzle perpendicular to and 10 to 12 inches away from the surface.** Even a slight change in this distance significantly affects the amount of paint being applied: If you hold the nozzle twice as close to the surface, you apply four times as much paint. Avoid tilting the sprayer downward or upward, which causes spitting and results in an uneven application.

- ✔ Keep the nozzle perpendicular to the surface as you move it back and forth. The natural tendency is to swing the gun in an arc, which results in an uneven "bowtie" application.

- ✔ Overlap each pass half the width of the spray coverage area to avoid leaving light areas or creating stripes.

- ✔ Test and adjust the spray equipment until you produce the pattern you want. If the pattern is too narrow, you could apply too much paint to the area, resulting in runs. With a pattern that's too wide, you have to make more than two passes to get good coverage. A pattern that's 8 to 12 inches wide is adequate for most large surfaces.

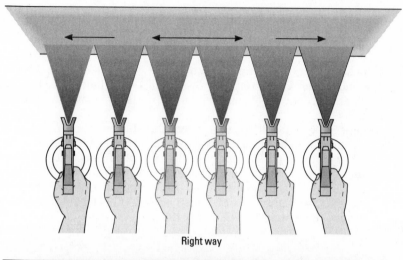

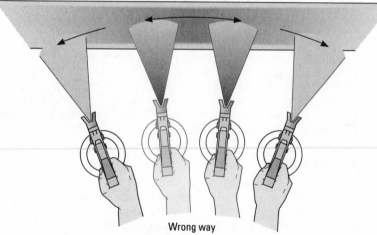

Book III

Painting and Wall-papering

Figure 1-3:
Use long, sweeping strokes and maintain a constant distance from the surface.

Right way

Wrong way

It's better to put on the paint a little light and go back and apply a little more than to load the surface with a coat of paint that's too heavy and may sag and dry unevenly. In time, a heavy coat may peel.

Start painting

When you're comfortable and getting the results you want on cardboard, move on to the real thing. Do the corners and any protrusions first and finish up with the large, flat areas. Indoors, for example, paint the two inside corners of one wall and then spray the wall between those two corners before moving on.

Spray corners with a vertical stroke aimed directly at the corner. Move a little quicker than usual, especially on outside corners, to avoid overloading the edges.

After you complete each area, or about every five minutes, stand back and look for light spots or missed areas. Touch up, making sure that you move the gun before spraying. Keep a brush or roller handy for touch-ups.

Most sprayers have a tip guard to protect you from injecting yourself with paint. Remove your finger from the trigger and wipe off the guards occasionally — with a rag, not your finger. Paint buildup at the tip may affect the spray pattern.

Some spray applications require backbrushing or back-rolling — that is, brushing or rolling in the sprayed-on finish to get a more even coat and better penetration. The sprayer, then, is just a fast way to get the paint to the surface. In particular, you should backbrush stain applications on unfinished or previously stained wood. Backbrushing is strongly recommended when applying primers and sealers as well. (Check out the sidebar, "Secret weapon: Backbrushing," earlier in this chapter.)

The tools of the trade

In the power arena, we recommend three types of sprayers for do-it-yourselfers: the tank sprayer, the airless sprayer, and the newer, HVLP (high-volume, low-pressure) sprayer. Figure 1-4 illustrates these types of sprayers. Learning to operate them takes just a few minutes. Conventional sprayers, which are powered by compressed air, require considerably more skill and training. They also create excessive overspray. For these reasons, conventional sprayers are best left to the pros.

Airless sprayers

Handheld airless sprayers won't win any National Noise Pollution Control awards — they're noisy little devils — but they're popular with do-it-yourselfers because of their versatility and moderate price, which ranges from about $50 to $175. The higher-priced units have more power, more features and controls, and more tip options. With a high-powered unit, you can paint everything from a radiator to the entire exterior of your house.

With most models, you draw the paint from a paint cup attached at the base of the sprayer for small projects. On larger projects, you can draw paint from a backpack tank or directly from the can.

Pump airless sprayers are priced from about $250 for do-it-yourself models to as high as $900 for professional models. These sprayers draw paint from 1- or 5-gallon containers to a spray gun through a long hose. Although you can paint a house exterior with a handheld model, a high-productivity pump sprayer is a better choice. These units pump paint much faster, and the gun is much lighter to hold because no cup full of paint is attached to it.

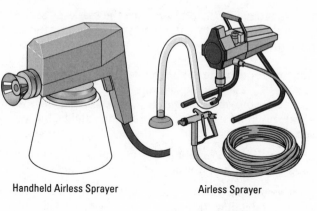

Figure 1-4:
Good spray-
painters for
the do-it-
yourself
painter
include a
handheld
airless
sprayer,
a pump
airless
sprayer,
an HVLP
sprayer,
and a tank
sprayer.

Handheld Airless Sprayer   Airless Sprayer

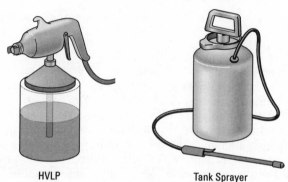

HVLP   Tank Sprayer

Book III

Painting
and Wall-
papering

Operating an airless sprayer isn't difficult, but you do need a bit of practice to be able to apply an even coat. Here are some tips on using an airless sprayer:

✔ Keep your finger on the trigger, but snap your wrist as you reverse the direction to avoid overloading at the end of each stroke.

✔ When using a handheld airless unit drawing paint from a cup, keep one hand on the trigger and the other hand under the cup to support the weight.

✔ When using a gun, use your second hand to manage the hose, which is sometimes more difficult than handling the spray gun.

✔ When buying or renting, ask for a reversible, self-cleaning tip, which flips open to clear a clog without having to be removed.

Tank sprayers

Tank sprayers are available in manual pump and battery-powered models. You can use this multipurpose sprayer to apply oil-based stain to wood decks, fences, and even wood siding. Although you usually need to brush in spray-applied stain (called *backbrushing;* see the sidebar, "Secret weapon: Backbrushing"), the sprayer does the hard part — getting the otherwise drippy finish onto the surface.

Here are some tips for using tank sprayers:

- ✔ Never use tank sprayers to spray any liquid thicker than water, which means you shouldn't use them to spray latex stains, but you can spray oil-based stains.

- ✔ Adjust any available speed control — faster for large surfaces and slower for greater control when working on smaller surfaces.

- ✔ Adjust the spray tip to change the spray pattern — wide for large surfaces and narrow for detail work.

- ✔ Backbrush as required to smooth drips or work the finish into the surface.

HVLP sprayers

An HVLP sprayer doesn't atomize paint. Instead, it uses a high volume of air at very low pressure to propel paint onto the surface. As a result, you have virtually no overspray and no risk of explosion. You can produce a very narrow spray pattern, and you don't need to cover and mask everything in the room or get dressed up like an astronaut — unless, of course, you're into that sort of thing. Minimum personal protection — splash goggles, protective clothing, and gloves — is usually all that's required, but use a respirator when using solvent paints or when ventilation is questionable.

HVLP sprayers, priced from $200 to $400 and up, are great for small projects and trim painting, indoors or out. They're best used with low- to medium-viscosity finishes, such as lacquers, varnishes/enamels, oils, and stains. On models that claim to handle heavier-bodied finishes, such as acrylic latex, you usually must thin the paint. This requirement, combined with the low pressure and relatively small paint cup, makes the HVLP sprayer unsuitable for large projects, such as exterior house painting — unless it's a doghouse.

Here are some tips on using HVLP sprayers:

- ✔ Stop spraying momentarily at the end of every pass.

- ✔ Control the size of the pattern by moving the gun closer to or farther from the surface and vary the amount of trigger pressure.

Aerosol paint

Aerosol spraying (with a spray-paint can) is by far the most expensive approach to spray-painting on a per-square-foot basis, but it's worth every penny on the right job. Aerosol paints dry very fast and are great for small, irregularly shaped objects that are difficult to brush, such as some furniture, iron railings, and exterior light fixtures.

A stain-killing primer in an aerosol can is great for touching up water-stained textured ceilings. Brushing or rolling paint on these surfaces can quickly turn some textures to mush.

Paint as wide an area as you can reach by using side-to-side strokes, starting closest to you and moving away. As you begin each stroke, point the nozzle to the side of the object you're painting and start moving toward it. Just before you reach the object, start spraying. Stop spraying as you pass off the other side. Then spray the area again by using top-to-bottom strokes. Several light coats applied this way give uniform coverage without puddling or sagging.

Here are some tips on using aerosol cans:

✔ Before you start painting, shake the can for a full two minutes after you hear the *agitator* (a little steel ball) rattling in the can. Spray only at room temperature — roughly 65 to 75 degrees. Avoid spraying continuously; use short bursts instead.

✔ Frequently wipe the tip clean to prevent spitting. When you've finished painting, turn the can upside down and spray-paint against a piece of cardboard until only clear propellant comes out. Then remove the tip and soak it in lacquer thinner.

✔ A spray handle tool that snaps onto an aerosol can makes it easier to control and easier on your finger, too.

✔ Remove the tip from the aerosol can before you attempt to clear a clog.

Handy accessories

Quite a few different accessories can help make your painting project a little easier. Here are several that we recommend for spray-painting:

✔ **Filters:** Set yourself up with a couple of extra paint buckets and paint screens or filters, available at paint outlet stores.

✔ **Spouts:** With all the pouring back and forth, you'll find a couple of inexpensive pouring spouts that snap into gallon-can rims and prevent dripping to be quite useful. Cans that have a pouring spout built right in are terrific for this job.

✔ **Earplugs:** Airless sprayers are noisy, especially indoors. Protect your ears with inexpensive earplugs that conform to your ear canal.

✔ **Spray shields:** Use a spray shield on virtually every spray job. Pros use aluminum ones with handles. You can buy inexpensive disposable ones made from plastic or cardboard at paint stores (see Figure 1-5). You also can make your own with sheet aluminum, acrylic sheeting, or any other semirigid, lightweight material and a handle fashioned from a piece of wood. Old slats from a Venetian blind work well, too.

Book III

Painting and Wallpapering

✔ **Spray pole extension:** It can get pretty foggy when you're using an air-less sprayer indoors. Use a spray pole extension to move the working end of the tool away from your face. Extensions are available in sizes from 12 inches to 4 feet. By extending your reach, this accessory may also eliminate the need for constant up-and-down movement on a ladder.

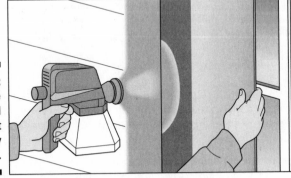

Figure 1-5:
A large
spray shield
keeps paint
off nearby
surfaces.

Should you buy or rent?

Now the money question: Should you buy or rent your spray-painting equip-ment? Well, it depends.

If you expect to spray-paint only occasionally, consider renting — especially if you're doing a major interior or exterior job where a good spray unit may save you many hours of work. By renting, you can also step up to a professional-quality unit that applies paint faster and better than a do-it-yourself model that you can afford to buy.

Go where the pros go — to a paint store — to get the right equipment and expert advice on using the equipment. Ask to speak to the person who's best informed about spray-painting. Describe what you want to paint and what type of finish you're using so that the employee can recommend the best unit and appropriate spray tips for the job. Get a crash course in how to operate a rental unit and ask for any written material on using or cleaning the equipment. Cleaning is complex and important, so a checklist can come in handy. Also, if you don't own or want to buy the necessary respirator, rent it.

Chapter 2

Preparing Surfaces for Painting

- -

In This Chapter

▶ Starting with a clean surface

▶ Tackling problems associated with specific types of surfaces

▶ Repairing and prepping walls, textured surfaces, and woodwork

▶ Priming, sealing, and caulking

- -

We're not going to beat around the bush: Properly preparing the surface for a finish is often the most time-consuming, difficult, and least rewarding part of a painting job. If you're thinking, "Fine. Let's skip this part of the work and the book," think again. Any painter worth his colors will tell you that the key to a successful painting job is preparation. This chapter describes what you need to do and how to get it done in the most efficient way possible. The rest is up to you.

Preparing Exterior Surfaces

Although good-quality paint and proper application techniques are important, surface preparation is usually the most important factor in determining the success of a painting job. This section is devoted primarily to the process of preparing the exterior of a house and a few additional preparations to make before you pick up a paintbrush.

Here's an overview of the proper sequence for preparing a house for repainting:

1. **Correct problems that may be causing premature paint failure.**

2. **Repair or replace any loose, missing, rotten, or damaged siding or trim.**

3. **Remove any peeling or loose paint.**

   Hand-scraping and power-sanding are the usual ways to do this job, but sometimes you need to use power-washing, chemicals, or heat.

4. **Treat any mildew problem with either a bleach-detergent solution or a commercial house cleaner that contains a mildewcide.**

5. **Prime bare wood or other problem surfaces that require primer.**

6. **Patch nail holes and seal gaps and cracks with paintable caulk.**

7. **Pressure-wash the entire exterior to remove sanding dust, dirt, and grime.**

Proper preparation varies according to the type and condition of the exterior surface, as well as the type of finish you intend to apply. Some tips for dealing with the problems associated with typical exterior surfaces are

✔ **New wood siding:** Make sure to brush the wood clean, working from the top down. Caulk after you stain or prime. If you plan to paint or use a solid-color stain, set any nails that the carpenters missed below the surface and fill the nail holes with caulk.

✔ **Weathered wood siding:** Stain bonds well to unpainted wood that has weathered. If you plan to paint, then sand or power-wash the wood to remove any gray, weathered surface and to smooth siding that has been exposed to the weather for more than a few weeks. (See the section "Saving time by power-washing," later in this chapter.) You may have to remove as much as ⅛ inch of the gray, weathered surface to get to the *bright wood* (nonweathered, natural-colored wood). If you're staining, use a wood restorer or power-wash the wood to bring it back to its natural color so that staining produces the desired color.

✔ **Old painted siding:** Scrape off loose paint, using any of a variety of scrapers. Then power-sand to feather the hard edges left by scraping (as shown in Figure 2-1), prime any wood made bare in the process, and caulk all joints. Also, set any popped nails, fill the holes with caulk, and spot-prime the siding.

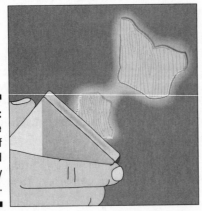

Figure 2-1:
Feather the edges of scraped areas by sanding.

✔ **Hardboard siding:** Because hardboard siding is vulnerable to weather-related failures, you must carefully maintain a sound protective paint barrier. You can easily ruin hardboard siding by neglecting maintenance or by doing the work incorrectly. Follow the procedures recommended in "Maintenance for Hardboard Siding," a free booklet available from the American Hardboard Association, 1210 W. Northwest Highway, Palatine, IL 60067; phone 847-934-8800. Some of the preparation guidelines include

- Use a 300-degree steam cleaner (a rental item) or scrub the siding with a very hot detergent solution if the normal siding cleaning process fails to remove a waxy coating or oily grime.

- Lightly sand glossy finishes to remove the sheen (called *scuff sanding*), but sand, scrape, or cut into the surface only as much as is necessary to correct problems. Replace or fill badly damaged areas.

- Don't set nails or you'll break the factory-applied protective coating.

✔ **New cedar and redwood:** New cedar and redwood bleed tannin. Wash them with a general cleaning detergent and water solution (see the following section) before priming them with a stain-blocking alkyd primer.

✔ **Concrete and masonry:** Unfinished, fully cured concrete can be finished with concrete stain or paint after being cleaned with a power-washer to remove dirt, stains, and any residue from old sealers. If you're repainting, use the same type of paint: latex or oil. Although you can scrape or sand small areas of peeling paint off concrete or masonry surfaces, doing so dulls scrapers and chews up sandpaper very quickly. If you're working on a large area, consider sandblasting or stripping with a chemical remover.

Clean out cracks with a wet-dry vacuum or blow out dust with compressed air before caulking the cracks. Do the same when using a concrete patch and mist the surface before applying the patch.

✔ **Stucco:** In many cases, a masonry cleaner — available at any janitorial supply store — is all you need to renew a stucco surface. Hose off the loose dirt and, while the surface is still wet, apply the cleaner to lift the remaining dirt. Then scrub with a stiff brush. If the stucco still looks dingy, consider having a stucco contractor *redash* the finish, a process in which a new cement surface is either sprayed or brushed onto the stucco. For information about patching, repairing cracks, and caulking joints on stucco, check out *Home Improvement For Dummies* (Wiley).

Power-washing stucco, especially old stucco, is risky. The force of the water can blast the finish off, turning a simple cleaning job into a major repair.

Book III

Painting and Wallpapering

✔ **Glossy finishes:** Paint doesn't bond well to glossy surfaces, including painted ones. If a cleaned painted surface still shines, you must dull it. Sanding is a surefire approach, but it's time-consuming and especially difficult on detailed areas of trim, windows, and doors. Brush-on deglosser, available for both oil- and latex-based paints, is a much easier way to dull the surface.

✔ **Iron railings, siding, and so on:** Clean the metal to remove dirt, grime, and oil before priming with a rust-inhibiting (direct-to-metal) primer. Follow the paint manufacturer's cleaning guidelines. Generally, you can use a 50-50 vinegar and water solution for all metal except galvanized steel. Clean new galvanized metal with mineral spirits before priming with special galvanized metal primer.

Rust often occurs under the paint on these surfaces, causing stains and a bumpy finish. Eventually, the corrosion flakes off with the finish. There are two basic approaches to preparing rusty metal for paint: You can eliminate rust by sanding, grinding, or sandblasting. Or, when removing every last spot of rust is impractical, you can use a wire brush to scrape off only the loose, flaking rust and then treat the metal with a chemical to neutralize the corrosion. Results with chemical neutralizing will vary, so always apply rust-inhibiting or rusty metal primer on bare metal. You also can apply a paint conditioner, such as Penetrol, to rusty areas before you apply paint. The conditioner seals the rusty areas and provides a better paint bond.

✔ **Aluminum or vinyl gutters:** Avoid painting aluminum and especially vinyl gutters, if at all possible. If you do paint, scuff-sand for better bonding.

✔ **Mill-finish aluminum storm and screen windows and doors:** You can topcoat the exterior face of mill-finish aluminum storm and screen windows and doors with 100 percent acrylic-latex paint to match trim colors. However, you must remove corrosion with sandpaper or a wire brush and apply a primer made specifically for aluminum or galvanized metal. Don't get paint into the tracks or on the glass or screen sash.

✔ **Aluminum siding:** A good cleaning is generally all aluminum siding needs before you paint.

Scrubbing the house down

The secret to a long-lasting paint job is cleanliness. The ideal time to clean is after you finish scraping, sanding, spot-priming, and caulking — and take a long nap. Allow two to three days for drying before you paint.

In addition to the many commercial cleaners available, you can make two widely recommended homemade cleaning solutions:

- ✔ For general cleaning, mix ½ cup laundry detergent or trisodium phosphate (TSP) in 1 gallon water. Scrub with a stiff brush and rinse thoroughly with water.

- ✔ To remove mold, mildew, algae, and lichen, mix 1 quart household bleach and 2 ounces TSP detergent, or a phosphate-free substitute, with 3 quarts water. Spray on with a garden sprayer. If necessary, cover the area for about an hour to prevent it from drying out. Rinse well with water and repeat as necessary.

Saving time by power-washing

Washing your house may seem like an insurmountable job, but an electric or gas-powered washer is one of the most useful and labor-saving machines homeowners can get their hands on. Plus, they're just plain fun to use.

Small electric power-washers (or *pressure-washers,* as they're also called) sell for as little as $150. Gutsy gas models cost two to four times as much. You can also rent a killer unit for about $65 a day. If you rent, you may want to share the rental cost with a neighbor — cleaning the exterior of two houses in a day is entirely possible.

Virtually risk-free uses of a power-washer include preparing concrete and asphalt surfaces for protective coatings and restoring a slimy green or severely weathered wood deck to its original beauty. Other applications may present risks both to you and to your house. For example, if you have an old house with little or no insulation, loose-fitting windows, or very old siding, especially wood shingles, you may want to skip the power-washer and wash the house by hand, instead.

Handling a power-washer

Power-washers usually have a control to vary the pressure of the water stream. For most cleaning projects, especially on wood, 800 to 1000 psi (pounds per square inch) is adequate. On less vulnerable surfaces, you can go up to a maximum of 1,500 psi. Read the power-washer's operating instructions or request a demonstration of a rental unit.

The jet of water spraying from a power-washer can be lethal. Exercise good judgment when using a power-washer, and most important, never use it around other people or pets. If you're on a ladder, keep one hand on the ladder and be prepared for the considerable kick that occurs when you pull or release the trigger.

Depending on the application, some products may be used with power-washers that meter chemicals into the water stream from a detergent bottle or through a siphon hose. Be sure to read the label. Many solutions contain chemicals that can damage the washer and/or put your health at risk when used with a power-washer.

Preparing the site and using safety precautions

High-pressure water finds its way into any unsealed opening in its path, so make sure to protect everything you don't want to spray. No matter what you're washing — siding or deck — follow these basic guidelines:

- Wear rain gear, boots, and safety goggles.

- Use drop cloths or large sheets of cardboard to catch paint chips.

- Test pressure adjustment, spray pattern, and working distance on an inconspicuous area.

- Practice your spray angle by holding the sprayer to the surface until you get the even results you want. Overlap passes for even cleaning.

- Don't swing the wand in an arc; you'll get uneven results because you're closer to the surface in the center of the arc.

Battling mildew stains

A brown, gray, or black stain on siding or trim may be simple grime, or it may be mildew. To test whether a stain is grime or mildew, try washing the stain away with water and a detergent like Spic and Span. If the stain doesn't wash away with water and detergent, it's probably mildew.

Because mildew is a fungus growth, it thrives on moisture and dirt, so keep the siding open to the sun and air. Don't store firewood or other materials close to the house. Prune tree branches that shade the house. If you have recurring mildew problems, power-wash the house's exterior once a year and apply a mildewcide solution every two to three years.

Handle bleach and mildewcide solutions with care. Read label warnings, and always wear protective clothing, especially neoprene gloves and goggles. Protect shrubs and other plantings by watering them down well and covering them before you power-wash the house. Water them well again after.

Cleaning chalking surfaces

Some exterior paints, such as those used on aluminum siding, intentionally chalk for self-cleaning. Wipe the surface with the palm of your hand. If the paint color comes off on your hand, the paint is chalking. Scrub off the chalk with a strong solution of water and Spic and Span or TSP detergent (or a non-phosphate TSP alternative). You can also use a commercial wood cleaner to remove chalked paint. Water pressure alone doesn't do the trick.

As you scrub the surface, work from the bottom up to avoid streaking. Rinse frequently with clear water, and allow the surface to dry before painting.

Cleaning stucco and other masonry

Efflorescence, mold and algae, lichen, and stains from chalking paint or rusting metal are problems that you should attend to before painting masonry, which includes surfaces such as stucco, brick, and concrete block.

First, eliminate the sources of the problems. Overhanging trees can cause mold and algae; a deteriorating chimney cap can allow water to penetrate behind the brick and cause efflorescence. Rusting may result from the use of various metals reinforcing materials in masonry construction, such as wire mesh or steel structural materials over windows and doors. Even if the metal isn't visible, the rust stains may bleed through to the surface. If the paint on siding above masonry is chalking, it washes down onto the masonry and stains the surface.

In most cases, you need to scrub the surface with a chemical cleaner. See the introduction to this "Scrubbing the house down" section for cleaning solutions to use for general cleaning and for removing mildew, mold, and lichen. For efflorescence and other stubborn stains, mix 1 cup of 10 percent muriatic acid in 1 gallon of water. (Muriatic acid is available at your local hardware store.) Heavy stains may require up to a 1:1 solution, but the risk of damage to the surface increases. Scrub the surface with a stiff brush and rinse thoroughly with water. Strong acid solutions must be neutralized with a 1:10 ammonia-water solution to stop the etching.

Book III

Painting and Wall-papering

Add the acid to the water or it will spatter. Because the acid vapors can burn your lungs, keep your distance from the acid by using a long-handled brush to scrub the surface. Wear protective gear, including a respirator, heavy neoprene gloves, and splash-proof goggles, and read the label for additional handling instructions.

Sealing cracks and holes with caulk

Filling cracks and holes in your home's trim and siding before painting not only makes the paint job look better, but also makes the paint last longer. Cracks and holes in any surface collect water, which eventually causes paint to peel.

Caulk is a substance designed to seal a joint between two surfaces and to fill small holes. Use top-quality caulk outdoors, where it needs to withstand extreme temperature changes and remain flexible for 30 to 50 years. Before caulking joints between dissimilar materials, make sure that the manufacturer recommends the caulk for both materials. If you're going to paint the area, the caulk must be paintable. If you're unsure whether a caulk is suitable for a particular application, contact the manufacturer's customer service department.

The best time to caulk is after you scrape, sand, and prime. Caulk adheres better to primed surfaces, and the gaps, cracks, and holes are more evident.

Scrape away any peeling paint adjacent to the caulked areas. If doing so exposes any bare wood, recaulk all cracks between any two nonmoving materials. Let the caulk cure for a few days before power-washing the exterior.

Don't caulk the horizontal joints on siding where the siding courses overlap. The cracks between two courses of siding provide ventilation points to let moisture escape from the siding and from inside the wall. In fact, one of the often-recommended cures for a moisture problem involves inserting numerous wedges between siding courses to create a larger gap through which moisture can escape. For the same reason, don't try to fill the joints between courses with paint.

Patching surface cavities before painting

Fix small holes in siding with an exterior patching compound, available in a premixed form (much like interior spackling compound) and in a dry powder form that you mix with water. Just make sure the package states that the patching compound is for outdoor use.

To patch holes and depressions in siding of any kind, follow these steps:

1. **Clean the hole or depression you plan to fill.**

   Roughen the area you want to patch with 80-grit sandpaper for a better bond.

2. **Fill the area with patching compound.**

   Apply the compound to the hole or depression in one direction and then smooth it in a perpendicular direction so that it's level with the original surface.

3. **Allow the compound to harden and then sand it smooth.**

   Compound shrinks, so a second coat may be necessary. Be sure to remove the dust from sanding the compound before you apply a second coat.

To repair large cracks and damaged trim, remove any rotten wood with a chisel. Use a two-part polyester-based compound, similar to auto-body filler, to make the repair. Two-part fillers come with a thick paste base and a small tube of hardener. Mix the hardener with the paste according to the manufacturer's directions. The filler sets up within three to five minutes, so mix only as much as you can use right away, and clean your tools immediately after use.

Use a putty knife to apply the compound to the damaged area and level it with the surface. This filler doesn't shrink as much as premixed exterior fillers do, but you still may need to apply several coats to fill a large hole. When the filler hardens, it's suitable for rasping, sanding, or drilling.

When the compound has set firm but isn't completely dry, you can easily shape or smooth it with a Surform tool or rasp.

Use auto-body fillers or two-part polyester-resin fillers for aluminum siding in a similar way. But before you apply the filler, drill numerous ⅛-inch-diameter holes in the patch area. When you apply the compound, it locks into the holes for a better bond. You can also cover damage with a new piece of siding. Just cut the top flange off so that the patch fits under the course above and embed it in adhesive caulk along the top and sides.

Although you can use the same procedure for repairing vinyl siding, replacing a course of damaged vinyl siding is easy. For more information about these and other siding and stucco repair or replacement procedures, check out *Home Improvement For Dummies* (Wiley).

Book III

Painting and Wallpapering

Preparing Interior Surfaces

Most interiors will look better if you just slap on a fresh coat of paint. However, you'll get results that are even more striking, and a longer-lasting paint job to boot, if you take special care in cleaning and preparing the surfaces. Preparation includes making minor repairs to the walls, ceilings, and woodwork and scraping and sanding to remove any loose paint.

Cleaning a room for painting

Unless you know that you'll be undertaking messy repairs or surface preparation work, start work with a thorough cleaning. The goal is to strip the room of all dirt and cobwebs and to clean the baseboards, windows, and door casings. A vacuum with a crevice tool can catch the cobwebs and dust. While you're at it, vacuum up dust and dirt around radiators and heating ducts. Open the windows to remove all dirt and debris from inside the sill, and clean any closets.

If walls and woodwork have dirt or grease on them, wash them with a sponge and a phosphate-free household cleaner. Then rinse the surfaces with clear water and let them dry.

Solving kitchen and bath problems

Paint's number-one enemy in a kitchen is grease, which clings to walls, ceilings, cabinets, and other woodwork. Use your favorite household cleaner to remove grease. Keep in mind that wood cabinets don't like harsh detergents or water, so work quickly and dry the surface immediately. If you intend to paint cabinets, they need special attention; see the section, "Repairing and preparing to recoat painted wood," later in this chapter.

In addition to dust and dirt, bathrooms often have mold or mildew stains. These living critters thrive on warm, moist surfaces. Give the bathroom the same general cleaning that you would any other room, but know that if you just wash away mildew stains, they'll return. To kill mildew, try a solution of 1 part household bleach and 3 parts water. Sponge or spray on the solution and let it sit for at least 15 minutes. Repeat the process if necessary until the stains are gone.

Bleach isn't good for painted surfaces. After it does the deed on the mildew, stop the bleaching action by rinsing the surface well with a neutralizer, such as clean water or a vinegar-water solution. Also, bleach is caustic and splashes easily, especially when you're working overhead. Wear goggles, rubber gloves, and your spouse's clothes.

Clearing the way

As you empty a room for painting, the idea is to clear the room as much as possible so that you have free and easy access. Move out as much furniture as you can. You may want to leave that tank of a sleeper sofa or other large pieces that may ding your walls or woodwork when you move items out or, worse, back in after you paint. Just make sure that everything remaining is in the center of the room and out of the way. You need room to move a ladder around and enough floor space for your paint setup — and make sure that you can reach the entire ceiling.

Go through the following checklist to get your room ready for the big makeover:

- ✔ Take down pictures and other wallhangings. If you plan to return them to the same locations after you paint, leave the picture hooks in place. If it's time for a change, carefully pull the nails straight out. If you have plaster walls, twist them out with a pair of pliers to avoid chipping out the plaster.

- ✔ If the room is very large, stack the furniture in two areas with space between them. In a smaller room, pile everything in the center, at least 3 feet away from the walls. Cover all furniture with plastic drop cloths.

- ✔ Remove any area rugs. Put plastic drop cloths under your paint supply and mixing area, but cover the floor with quality canvas drop cloths, which are less slippery to walk on than plastic ones. Use two layers on carpeting for added protection.

- ✔ Minimize the amount of tedious work painting around electrical switch plates and receptacle covers. Remove them and place a strip of wide masking tape over the switches and receptacles to protect them. Also remove or lower light fixtures. Keep all the small parts together in a shoebox or similar container.

- ✔ If you're painting doors, mask the hardware or remove it. Removing and replacing hardware takes less time than painting around it, and you eliminate unsightly goofs and don't waste time cleaning paint off hardware later. See the section, "Making final preparations," later in this chapter to find out the best ways to mask hardware.

- ✔ Even if you're painting during the day, you need good electric lighting, and you may need power for tools. Plug an extension cord into a nearby room or hallway to bring power to the room.

Book III

Painting and Wall-papering

Before you remove outlet covers or light fixtures, shut off the power at the circuit breaker. Remember, wall receptacles and lights are usually on different circuits. Double-check that the power is off by using a neon circuit tester or plugging in a lamp or other electrical device that you know is working. Place tape over the breaker as a reminder to others that the power is off.

Smoothing the walls

After you take down all the pictures and remove or cover the furniture, it's time to repair damage to the walls. The best way to spot all the problems is to shine a bright light across the wall at a sharp angle and to circle areas that need attention with a light pencil mark.

Making minor drywall repairs

You probably have a few minor dings or nail holes to repair. Buy a small container of spackling compound and apply it with a putty knife. When it's dry, sand the patch smooth with fine sandpaper on a rubber or padded sanding block. Because spackling compound tends to shrink, you may need to add another coat to fill the remaining indentation.

Popped nails are an all-too-common problem with drywall installation. The nails, which were originally set below the surface and concealed with joint compound, pop out enough to make a bump or even break the surface. Use this four-step solution to correct this problem:

1. **Secure the drywall tightly to the framing with new nails or, better yet, drywall screws, one on either side of the popped nail, as shown in Figure 2-2.**

   On walls, studs are vertical, so drive fasteners above and below the popped nail. On a ceiling, you can usually tell which way the framing is running by the line of popped nails or by tapping lightly. A tap sounds hollow between framing and more solid on the framing.

Figure 2-2:
Press drywall against the framing as you drive a fastener on either side of the popped nail.

2. **Drive the popped nail back where it belongs.**

   Because the new fasteners are doing all the work, the popped nail should stay put this time. Drive both the new fasteners and the popped nail so that they're just below the surface but don't break the paper facing of the drywall.

3. **Apply two or three coats of joint compound to conceal the fasteners and dimpled areas around them, as shown in Figure 2-3.**

Scoop a glob of compound onto a 5- or 6-inch taping knife. Apply it to the wall with the knife held at about a 45-degree angle to the surface. Then draw a clean knife across the patch in a direction perpendicular to the first pass and with the knife nearly flat against the wall. Allow the compound to dry (anywhere from a few hours to overnight, depending on the humidity) and apply another coat.

4. **After the compound dries, sand the area smooth with fine sandpaper on a sanding block.**

Figure 2-3:
Apply two or three coats of joint compound with two strokes perpendicular to each other.

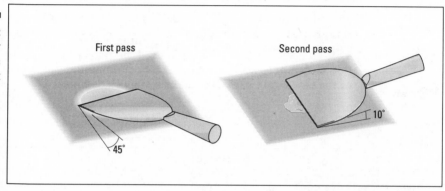

First pass

Second pass

45°

10°

Book III

Painting and Wallpapering

TIP

Surface cracks at the joints of corners may be due to the buildup of taping compound or paint. These hairline cracks are in the excessively thick material and don't extend through the reinforcing tape itself. To repair these cracks, fold a piece of sandpaper over the blade of a 6-inch taping knife or over the corner of a block of wood and carefully sand away the excess material. Stop sanding as soon as you see the reinforcing tape.

Repairing cracks in plaster walls and ceilings

Back in the years B.D. (before drywall), a common way to form walls was to put plaster directly onto wooden slats or a wire mesh, called *lath backing*. If you have an older home with plaster walls, you can apply spackling compound over small holes with the technique described in the preceding section. For minor cracks, which have the nasty habit of reappearing in a year or two, try the following method, which we picked up from the nation's leading plaster and drywall manufacturer.

For starters, use *paper* reinforcing tape and *dry* joint compound — the kind you mix with water, not the premixed stuff. This combination, the manufacturer says, offers the greatest strength and surface bonding. We tried it on a ceiling that had cracked repeatedly, and to date, no cracks have reappeared. We make no such guarantees for your cracks, but here's what we did:

1. **Scrape out any loose or protruding materials by dragging a can opener or old screwdriver along the crack; then blow out or vacuum the dust and mist the crack with water.**

   Misting helps prevent the dry plaster from sucking all the moisture out of the patching material and may improve the bond. It may not be necessary, but it's easy to do . . . and every little bit helps!

2. **Mix Durabond 90 or a similar dry joint compound in a large plastic bucket with water according to package instructions.**

3. **Use a 6-inch taping knife to apply a bed of compound along the crack.**

4. **Embed perforated paper reinforcing tape into the wet compound and scrape the taping knife along the tape to level the material and squeeze out the excess, as shown in Figure 2-4.**

   Don't attempt to scrape out every bit of compound from under the tape or the tape won't stick. Just make it smooth and level.

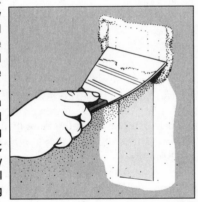 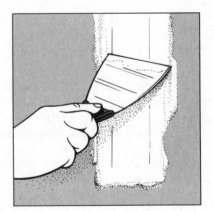

Figure 2-4: Apply compound over the crack and embed the paper tape. Apply a second smoothing coat (left); then apply a final smoothing coat (right).

5. **When the first application is dry, scrape off any loose bits of dried compound with your taping knife. Then apply another smoothing coat of compound over the tape.**

   If you have a 10-inch knife, use it; otherwise, use the 6-inch knife to smooth on a thin, 10-inch-wide coat.

6. **After the second coat of compound dries, scrape off any loose bits of compound and sand lightly with a pole sander.**

TIP

Be careful not to sand into the reinforcing tape or you'll make it fuzzy.

When sanding, put a fan in an open window. Open another window in a nearby room. Set the fan to exhaust, and dust won't migrate to other parts of the house.

7. **Repeat Steps 3 through 6 for a third, and we hope final, coat that's a few inches wider than the second.**

Dry compound dries faster and harder than the ready-mix variety. When you use dry compound, cleaning tools is easier if you wash them off while the material is still wet.

You can't expect to cover a patched area with a single topcoat of paint. Your best bet is to prime the patched area with the finish paint and, when that's dry, apply a topcoat over the entire surface.

Repairing and preparing to recoat painted wood

Woodwork is one of those details that make a difference, as designers describe what distinguishes an ordinary room from an extraordinary one. If it doesn't look good, the whole room can look shabby, even if the walls and ceiling are perfect. In this section, we describe how to make your woodwork look new again.

Patching chipped or gouged wood before painting

If the wood is chipped, gouged, or otherwise damaged, and you plan to paint, you can make an easy, invisible repair by using a two-part polyester resin compound:

1. **Clean out any loose material and scrape off any finish so that the patching material will bond better.**

2. **Mix the hardener (part one) with the filler (part two) as directed and apply it with a putty knife.**

   Generally, you want to overfill the hole.

3. **Use a rasp or Surform tool to shape or level the material as soon as it sets up hard but before it *cures* (dries) completely.**

4. **When the material is fully cured, sand the patch to smooth and blend it in with the surrounding area.**

5. **Apply a primer to the patch and any bare wood before you paint.**

Book III

Painting and Wallpapering

Making paint stick to paneling and cabinets

Getting rid of dark paneling is complicated by the fact that when you pull it off, you find the adhesive has ruined the drywall underneath. For this reason, many folks turn to paint instead.

Factory-finished wood cabinets and paneling require special preparation for painting. To ensure that the paint adheres properly to factory-finished panels or to waxed or varnished board paneling, follow these steps:

1. **Clean the wood especially well to remove dirt, grease, and wax.**

   For paneling, use a solution made of equal parts of household ammonia and water. For cabinets and paneling that are beyond cleaning with a mild detergent solution, try a solvent, such as mineral spirits.

2. **Take the shine off the surface by sanding lightly or with a chemical deglosser, especially on irregular or molded surfaces.**

   If you sand the wood, put an exhaust fan in the window of the work area and open a nearby window outside the room. The fan prevents sanding dust from going anywhere but outdoors.

   If you use a chemical deglosser, remember to apply paint within a half-hour or the deglosser loses its effectiveness. Apply a thorough coat of deglosser on varnish or polyurethane finishes.

3. **Wipe the surface well with a *tack cloth,* a sticky cheesecloth for removing sanding dust.**

   The oil in a store-bought tack cloth may interfere with the proper adhesion of latex finishes. If you plan to use latex, just use a cloth dampened with mineral spirits or water.

4. **Prime the wood.**

   Mix a bonding additive with your primer or use an alcohol-based primer-sealer or other special bonding primer tinted to the approximate color of the topcoat. See Chapter 1 for advice on choosing the primer and topcoat.

If you're painting cabinets, remove the handles and drawer pulls so that you don't have to paint around them.

Toiling with wooden windows

The amount of work required to prepare windows for painting can vary from a good cleaning to everything short of replacement. This section looks at the most common problems and their solutions.

One problem you may encounter is a sash in a double-hung window that has become stuck. You can solve this problem by using a *paint zipper,* a serrated tool designed to cut a paint film between the formerly movable sash and its channel.

Improper painting technique contributes to another common window problem — peeling paint where the wood meets the glass. Failure to create a paint seal between the glass and the wood allows condensation and window-cleaning chemicals to seep into the joint. To remove loose paint, follow these steps:

1. **Scrape or sand the area to remove loose paint.**

   Wrapping sandpaper over the edge of a putty knife makes it easier to sand close to the glass without scratching it.

2. **Apply a stain-killing primer to water-stained wood before applying a topcoat.**

   Avoid this problem in the future by using proper window-painting techniques, which we describe in Chapter 3.

When old-fashioned double-hung windows need painting, you should also replace the cords (or replace an old-fashioned rope-and-pulley system with a more modern counterbalance mechanism). To do so, you must remove the sash. This and other window repairs are covered in greater detail in Book II, Chapter 2.

Book III

Painting and Wall-papering

Making final preparations

If you've read the other sections in this chapter, you're probably getting anxious to paint. However, don't make the mistake of thinking that skipping things like priming and sealing, caulking cracks, back-prepping, and masking saves time and work. On the contrary, in the long run, you're just creating more work for yourself.

Priming and sealing

Spot-priming improves the bond of the topcoat to surfaces such as bare wood and metal. It also seals the surface of unfinished or patched areas so that they absorb topcoats to the same degree that surrounding areas do. If you try to just topcoat, the patch area will have less sheen than the area around it, making the patch more noticeable. This advice applies to patches and repairs to drywall, plaster, and trim. Therefore, spot-prime these areas, being careful to feather the edges of the paint into the surrounding areas.

See Chapters 1 and 3 for feathering and other painting techniques. For information on how to prepare previously wallpapered surfaces for paint or wallpaper, see Chapter 5.

Sealing cracks with caulk

Caulk covers a multitude of sins and prevents many problems from occurring. It has a consistency like thick toothpaste, which makes it easy to spread and fill small holes and narrow cracks. When it dries, it becomes firm but remains flexible and can tolerate movement between materials that expand, contract, or otherwise move in relation to one another. If you're painting, choose a quality paintable acrylic latex caulk or a siliconized acrylic latex caulk. Buy it in cartridge form to fit a caulking gun.

Cracks show up better after priming, and caulk adheres better to primed wood, so complete any priming before you caulk. For a neat job, caulk all joints. Caulk all the joints between trim and wall surfaces to prevent penetration of moisture vapor into walls.

Cut the tips of two tubes of caulk. Cut a very small opening in one tube and use it for narrow cracks at nearly all joints between the woodwork and walls or between different trim members, such as window stops and frame joints. Cut the tip of the second tube with a larger opening for caulking wider cracks.

Apply caulk by squeezing the trigger as you either push or pull the tip along the joint. Use as little caulk as needed to fill the crack, or the excess will spread out onto the surface and be visible. Use a wet fingertip to fill very small holes and smooth the caulk. Allow adequate curing time (read the label instructions) before you paint.

Masking

Take a little time to mask areas that you don't want to paint. We especially like these materials:

- ✔ **Painter's tape:** This tape, available in various degrees of tackiness and width, is designed for masking. It seals well but comes off much easier than regular masking tape does. Read the label to choose the correct type for your situation.

- ✔ **Pretaped masking paper or plastic:** The self-stick edges adhere to surfaces such as the tops of window and door trim for a straight painting edge. The paper or plastic, which ranges in width from a couple of inches to many feet, drapes the surface. The seal isn't as reliable as that of painter's tape.

Don't use regular masking tape. It has too much adhesive, making it harder to remove; plus, paint bleeds under regular masking tape more easily, creating a rougher edge.

After you apply painter's tape or other masking systems, keep these tips in mind:

- ✔ Press the edge with a putty knife, a block of wood, or another hard material to seal it. Doing so prevents paint from bleeding under the tape.

- ✔ Remove the tape as soon as the paint has dried to the touch. Generally, you should wait three to four hours but not more than 24 hours. It's especially important not to leave the tape on for longer than 24 hours if the sun might bake the tape on or if the tape might get wet.

- ✔ When you remove the tape, slowly peel it back at an angle away from the painted surface to avoid peeling off the freshly applied paint.

When you plan to paint walls and ceilings, consider masking the following areas:

- ✔ The tops of base moldings

- ✔ The tops of windows and door casings

- ✔ The tops of chair rail moldings

- ✔ The tops of baseboard heating trim

- ✔ Heating or air conditioning grilles that you can't remove

- ✔ The base of wall- or ceiling-mounted light fixtures

Pretaped paper or plastic systems are handy when it comes to protecting the area below a chair rail molding if you're not painting it the same color as the wall above, or for covering the face of baseboard heaters.

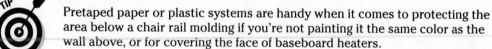

When painting or finishing the following areas, follow these recommendations:

- ✔ When painting baseboards, mask hardwood flooring at the baseboards.

- ✔ When finishing or painting flooring, mask the baseboards.

- ✔ When painting doors and windows, mask all hinges and other hardware.

- ✔ When painting baseboard heating trim, mask the walls.

Sanding stripped or unfinished wood

Sanding is no one's idea of fun, but you must smooth new wood or wood that has been stripped of its finish before you can apply a stain or finish. Sand out imperfections, such as deep scratches, tooling marks, or an overall rough or fuzzy surface. In addition to removing imperfections and making the wood look and feel smooth, sanding takes off a thin top layer of wood, enabling stains and other finishes to penetrate evenly.

Book III

Painting and Wall-papering

If you need to remove deep scratches, start with 80-grit (medium) or even 60-grit (coarse) sandpaper. Otherwise, start with 120-grit (fine) sandpaper. Work your way up to at least 150-grit, and preferably 220-grit, making sure that all scratches left by the coarser grit sandpaper are removed at each stage. Most do-it-yourselfers switch to the next finer grit paper or stop sanding long before a professional would.

Smoothing by hand or with a power sander

Whenever possible, use a sanding block or pad that conforms to the shape of the surface being sanded: flat for flat surfaces, concave for outwardly curving profiles, and so on. Holding the sandpaper in your hand usually produces uneven results because you exert more pressure in some places than you do in others. Just as foam sanding pads are available that conform to irregular surfaces for hand sanding, accessory pads are available that conform to gently curving surfaces for some finishing sanders. If you have a lot of detail work to do, such as when refinishing the moldings in many rooms, you may want to purchase a profile sander, which has a variety of rubber sanding block attachments to conform to irregular surfaces.

The *electric palm sander* and its more aggressive cousin, the *random orbit sander,* are finishing sanders that make wood smooth faster — a lot faster — than sanding by hand. These power sanders are ideal for smoothing flat surfaces such as wide baseboards and tabletops. A palm sander costs $30 or more but is well worth the investment. You not only save time and effort but also do a better job. Somehow, when you're hand-sanding, you usually decide a lot sooner that the surface is smooth enough.

Exercise extreme caution when sanding veneered furniture or cabinets, especially if you're power-sanding. Wood veneer is thin, sometimes very thin. You often don't have a clue that you're about to sand too far. Suddenly the material under the veneer, such as particleboard, appears. Staining doesn't help disguise the damage, and sometimes it makes the damage stand out like a sore thumb. Also keep in mind that sometimes what appears to be wood veneer is either a photographed plastic film or a convincing plastic laminate — and neither can be sanded unless you plan to paint them.

Knowing when enough is enough

To make sure you sand with a light hand, try these tips:

- ✔ Make a series of *light* pencil marks across the surface and sand the area until the pencil marks are all gone.
- ✔ Sidelight the surface to make imperfections more evident.
- ✔ Cover your hand with a sock or a pair of pantyhose and wipe it over the surface. The sock or hose will snag on rough spots.

The rule is to follow the grain of the wood as you sand. This means that you sand along the length of a board rather than across it so that you don't scratch the surface. However, if you must remove a lot of wood to get out deep scratches, start sanding on a diagonal to the grain until the imperfections are gone. Then sand with the grain until you remove all the diagonal sanding scratches.

Getting furniture-quality results

To achieve a super-smooth surface on a beautiful door, cabinet, or other piece of wood that's new or has been stripped of its finish, try the following furniture maker's method for final sanding:

1. **Wipe down the surface with water or denatured alcohol to intentionally raise the grain; it will feel peach-fuzzy.**

2. **Sand the fuzzy surface until it's smooth.**

3. **Repeat Steps 1 and 2 one or two more times. With most woods, the grain no longer rises after repeated sanding.**

Another trick that furniture makers use is to apply a liberal coat of a clear *sanding sealer,* a liquid product available at hardware stores and paint outlets that you brush or roll on before the final sanding.

Sanding to a super-smooth surface with open-grained woods, such as oak, is especially difficult. You need to fill the wood pores. Woodworking specialty shops and mail-order outlets sell special grain fillers in a variety of wood tones for the purpose. Apply the filler by rubbing it on with a rag across the grain. As it starts to dry, rub off the excess, at first across the grain and then with the grain. Press hard at each stage to force the filler into the open-grained surface. Filling the grain isn't necessary if you're planning a wax finish because the wax itself will do the job nicely.

Use sanding sealers and filler only *after* you apply stain.

Book III

Painting and Wall-papering

Chapter 3

Painting, Finishing, and Cleaning Up

*N*ow's the time to reap the rewards of all your preparation. Painting and finishing go fast, and with every brushstroke, your projects start looking more like they do in your mind's eye. This chapter walks you through the process of actually applying paint: on the outside, from siding to windows and doors; on the inside, from floor to ceiling and everything in between.

Painting the Exterior of Your Home

You did your homework and chose just the right finish and color for your house's exterior. You worked hard to repair and prepare the surfaces. But now you're having a hard time keeping up your enthusiasm. Your house, which didn't look all that bad to start, now looks terrible, stripped of shutters and other decorative touches and scraped and sanded everywhere.

Cheer up! Now comes the relatively easy part — applying the paint. The work goes quickly, and seeing the house transformed before your eyes is very satisfying.

Other safety precautions

✔ Use extreme caution around electrical service lines, especially if you're using an aluminum ladder. Don't forget to look for them when moving a ladder. Also, get help moving a heavy extension ladder so that you're in full control of it, and not the other way around.

✔ Expect bees, wasps, or bats to fly out of cracks in the roof soffits. Keep one hand on the ladder so that you're less likely to fall when you're startled. You can't run, so protect yourself with a long-sleeved shirt, long pants, and a hat or painter's hood. Tap suspicious areas with a broom handle before you get too close, and use wasp spray that you can aim from a safe distance.

✔ Don't assume that you have good ventilation just because you're outdoors. There may be little or no air movement on an inside corner of a house. If you're working in such areas with products that suggest application in a well-ventilated area, wear a respirator.

✔ Don't overdo it on a hot day. Drink plenty of water (or a sports drink) and take breaks to avoid heat exhaustion.

Using ladders safely outdoors

When painting a house's exterior, you can reach the top sections by using ladders of various heights. In addition to standard step and extension ladders, many special-purpose ladders are available. You can use some ladders both as stepladders and straight ladders, or even as scaffolds.

As tedious as it is to have to stop repeatedly to move the ladder, never overreach. When using a stepladder, the trunk of your body must remain entirely within the ladder's rails. If you use an extension ladder, a good practice is to crook the elbow of your free arm around the rail of the ladder (for example, your left arm around the left rail) and reach out with your free arm only as far as this grip allows.

Always open a stepladder fully and lock the braces in place before climbing on it. Don't lean an unopened stepladder against a wall and try to climb on it.

Set up your extension ladder so that the bottom is the proper distance away from the house wall — approximately one-fourth the working length of the ladder. Ladder rungs are spaced 1 foot apart, so just count the number of rungs from the bottom to the point where the ladder rests against the house to determine its working length. Divide that number by four to determine how far (in feet) from the wall that you should position the bottom.

Before you start a big job, take time to make sure that your ladders are in good condition. In most cases, if a ladder is bent, cracked, or otherwise damaged, you should discard it. Use a spray lubricant, such as WD-40, on all moving, metal-to-metal parts, taking care to wipe off any lubricant that gets on the rungs.

Several ladder accessories make your work easier and safer. Although an accessory from one manufacturer may work for a ladder made by another, your best bet is to buy ladders and accessories from the same manufacturer. You may find the following accessories helpful:

- ✔ A *stabilizer* (or *stand off*), shown in Figure 3-1, gives the ladder more lateral stability and allows you to center a ladder over a window so that you can paint the entire window without moving the ladder. In addition, if your house has roof overhangs, it stands the ladder off the wall so that you can safely paint the overhang without bending backward.

- ✔ *Scaffolding* allows you access to a wider area. You can use two ladders to support a scaffold plank (see Figure 3-1). The equipment is available at tool rental outlets. A wood or aluminum plank sits on a pair of *ladder jacks,* which hook onto the rungs of each ladder. Although this setup is relatively safe at low to moderate heights, we don't recommend it for second-story work. Without guardrails or fall-arrest protection, such as a safety harness, you could fall. These protections just aren't feasible for do-it-yourselfers.

- ✔ *Automatic levelers* let you quickly set an extension ladder with secure footing on uneven surfaces. Without them, you need to dig out the area under a rail or build it up with lumber. Avoid unsafe jury-rigged setups, such as stones or too-small wood blocks.

Book III

Painting and Wall-papering

Figure 3-1:
A stabilizer spans windows and positions you to paint roof overhangs safely, and a ladder jack scaffold lets you paint a wide area.

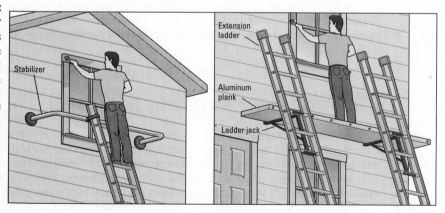

Consulting the weather forecast

Coordinating an exterior paint job with the weather and your schedule can be quite difficult in some parts of the country. First, you must wait for warm weather to allow a house to dry out after winter and early spring. Most paints and other finishes require that the temperature be at least 50 degrees and preferably above 60 degrees Fahrenheit. Next, you need at least a couple of days of sunny weather to dry the house after rain or power-washing. You need another good day if you're priming. Finally, you need a nice day to apply the topcoat; an ideal day sees temperatures between 60 and 85 degrees Fahrenheit and no wind.

Differences between latex and *alkyd* (oil-based) finishes may affect your decision of when to paint. Although you can apply most alkyd finishes even if you expect rain within a few hours, don't try it with latex finishes. On the contrary, you can apply latex on a slightly damp surface, but you're asking for paint blisters if you try it with an alkyd.

Whatever type of paint you use, allow the specified drying time between coats — or more if the weather is cool or humid. If you apply the topcoat over a primer too soon, paint failures such as alligatoring and blistering occur.

The best time to paint a surface is after the sun has warmed it but when it's no longer in direct sunlight. If you paint a hot surface, the paint dries too quickly. Then, as you go back to adjacent areas, you end up brushing over paint that has begun to dry. The result is distinct brush marks. Painting in the direct sun also may cause a variety of more serious failures, including cracking, flaking, blistering, and wrinkling — and that's just on the back of your neck.

Avoid painting or applying any surface coating outdoors on a breezy day. Windborne mold spores, pollen, dirt, bugs, and other debris lodge in the wet paint. The wind may also dry latex paint too fast, causing the finish to crack or flake.

Planning your painting sequence

In most cases, you should paint the body of the house first and then paint the trim, windows, and doors. (As you paint the trim, you automatically cover any areas on the trim that were inadvertently painted with siding paint.) Use a large brush, roller, or sprayer on the body of the house. For the trim, use a smaller brush, such as an angled sash brush, which helps you paint with more precision. Paint from the top down to minimize touch-ups for those inevitable drips.

Time is money to the pros, so they plan their ladder moves carefully. They plan their work by painting everything within reach at one time: siding, trim, gutters, and all, even if they're using different colors or types of paint. The harder the setup, the more advisable this approach may be. This technique is a no-brainer if you're using scaffolds or trying to maneuver around shrubs and have to level the ground to set up a 30-foot extension ladder so that you can access a roof peak. But at lower heights with less setup, follow the siding-first rule.

Making last-minute preparations

After you get the brush out, you don't want to stop to remove light fixtures or hardware or take time to tie back a bush that's in the way. Before you start to paint, make sure that your path is clear and that you've removed everything in the way. See Chapter 2 for more preparation steps.

To avoid paint drips on storm-window screens, remove them or slide them in their tracks so that they're concealed. If your home has a screened porch, take out the screens that are removable and drape plastic drop cloths over those that aren't.

Always place drop cloths below the area you're painting. This step takes only a moment and saves a great deal of cleanup time later. Use canvas drop cloths or buy heavy paper drop cloths to cover walks, drives, porches, and patios that abut the house. Plastic drop cloths are slippery to walk on, especially when they're wet, so only use them under your painting tools.

Be sure to mix paint well before you use it. It's difficult to do so in a full container even if you use a paint-mixing drill accessory. There may also be slight differences in color between the paint in one can and another, which won't be noticeable until it's too late. To overcome this problem, use a mixing process called *boxing.* Mix at least 2 gallons together in a large container; then, when you've used about a gallon, add a new gallon, and so on.

Before you carry that large can of paint up a ladder, think about the mess it will make if it falls. You're better off pouring about a quart of paint — or just enough to cover the area within reach of the ladder — into a smaller can.

Tooling up for the job

To apply paint or stain to a house's exterior, choose from any of the paint application tools, including brushes, pads, and rollers. Refer to Chapter 1 for descriptions of the applicators and tips on buying and using them.

Book III

Painting and Wall-papering

Which applicator you need often depends on what you're painting and the type of finish you're using. A paint pad, for example, is especially appropriate for painting siding because the top edge of the pad paints the bottom edges of the siding while the face of the pad paints the face of the siding. A stain brush holds watery stain better than a paintbrush. If a roller cover is sized to suit the siding, laying on the paint will go much faster. If you use a roller, go back with a brush to get the undersides and to remove the stippled texture left by the roller.

Carry sandpaper, a scraper, a wire brush, wood putty, a putty knife, and caulk so that you can clean and patch any defects you missed during preparation. Don't forget painter's rags to wipe off spatters and other goofs.

Priming the surface

On most unpainted exterior surfaces, the standard procedure calls for a primer coat followed by two topcoats of paint. (See Chapter 1 for information about choosing these finishes.) We recommend this procedure for any painted surface that requires significant scraping and repairs. However, you may be topcoating only because the surface is dull or because you want a new color. If that's the case and the existing paint is sound, a single coat of "one-coat" acrylic latex paint applied properly offers adequate protection and coverage in lieu of the two topcoats.

You can apply quality latex paint over any oil- or latex-painted surface that's in good shape. If the paint is sound, you generally need to prime only scraped or repaired areas. You can also use a stain-blocking primer in lieu of regular primer to seal knots in board siding or trim and to cover stains that you can't remove, such as rust.

The solution for rusty nailheads isn't difficult, but it sure is tedious. You'll be tempted to just set and fill the holes, paint over them, and hope for the best. Unfortunately, the corrosion continues, and rust stains will probably bleed through the topcoat. The right way to correct this problem is to use an awl or other pick to remove any caulk or glazing compound wherever rust stains are visible and set any nails that are exposed. Then use a stiff-bristled artist's brush to coat nailheads with stain-blocking, rust-inhibiting metal primer before covering them with caulk or exterior spackling compound.

If you're applying latex paint over a glossy paint, play it safe and prime the entire house, even if you've sanded or treated the existing finish with a deglosser. Hardboard siding may also require a primer (see Chapter 2 and the section "Painting hardboard siding," later in this chapter). As a general rule, use an alkyd primer and a latex topcoat when repainting.

Be sure that your primer is appropriate for the surface you're painting. Cedar and redwood, for example, usually require an oil-based primer to seal the surface so that tannin stains don't bleed through the topcoat. Also make sure that the primer and topcoat are compatible. How do you know? By telling your supplier what you're painting, reading the label, and (though not always necessary) using the same brand of primer and topcoat. To make it easier for a colored topcoat to cover primer, have your paint dealer tint the primer to the approximate color of the finish coat.

If you already have three or more coats of oil-based paint on the house, use oil-based house paint. Using latex may cause the old paint to lift off the substrate.

Painting your (house) body

Although siding is certainly the largest area to paint, the work goes surprisingly fast, even if you're using a brush. And with a sprayer, you move so fast that you have to be careful not to bump into yourself! This is your reward for doing such a good prep job.

Painting wood siding

Consider a few tips for painting wood siding:

- **New or untreated wood siding:** Coat new wood siding as soon after installation as possible. Untreated wood requires a primer and two topcoats, if painting, or two coats of stain. Previously untreated or bare redwood and cedar may bleed tannin through a paint finish unless you seal the surface with an alkyd primer-sealer (preferably two coats) before applying a 100 percent latex topcoat.

- **Rough lumber:** Airless spraying works best for painting or staining rough surfaces, but be sure to brush the finish as you apply it. *Backbrushing,* as this technique is called, gets paint into areas that the roller or sprayer misses and works the finish into the surface. Brushing also results in a more uniformly stained surface and gives you the chance to brush out drips and runs. New rough-sawn wood may snag roller and pad fabrics, but if the wood is already painted, use a roller followed by a brush. This technique is called *backbrushing.*

- **New, smooth wood:** Some new siding that's installed with the smooth side out doesn't accept stain well and sometimes is even too shiny for paint or solid-color stain, which is like thin paint. If you plan to use stain, you can have professionals install the wood siding with the rough side out. The smooth, sometimes shiny, planed surface (called *mill glaze*) doesn't provide enough "tooth" for paint or solid-color stain to grab onto. Sand off the mill glaze with 100-grit paper and then stain or paint. If you plan to use a penetrating stain, you can let the siding weather for six months to a year and save yourself the sanding work.

Choosing finishes for decks

Unfinished decks usually require annual applications of a protective coating. A clear water repellent (also called a *water sealer*) prevents the problems associated with the constant wetting and drying of wood by helping it maintain a more even moisture content. Some water repellents contain mildewcides; none block damaging ultraviolet (UV) rays. Semitransparent stains with UV protection limit the effects of UV radiation to a small degree. Some clear wood finishes also contain UV-blocking particles. Solid-color stains and paints offer the greatest UV protection, but solid-color stain wears on walking surfaces, and paint is likely to peel.

Renew stained and painted areas every two to three years. You can apply clear water repellent or, even better, a water repellent with UV blockers over a semitransparent stain as a maintenance coating between stain applications.

Decking, railings, and steps may call for different finishing. You should annually coat stained or natural wood with a water repellent and restain it as necessary. Decking needs abrasion-resistant stain; don't paint it. Even railings are easier to maintain if stained rather than painted. Some woods accept paint better than others do. Redwood, for example, is better than pressure-treated Southern pine.

You can treat the largest deck in a matter of minutes using a low-pressure garden sprayer or similar tool. For best results, follow up with a bristle-type pad on a long handle.

Painting hardboard siding

You can topcoat previously painted hardboard siding if the finish is clean and in excellent condition. The American Hardboard Association recommends using an alkyd primer if you're painting over the original factory finish or if you're unable to determine when the existing finish was applied. After cleaning and making any repairs (see Chapter 2), use an alkyd primer to spot-prime any areas where you removed the existing finish.

Apply quality latex paint approved for hardboard siding, paying special attention to grooves and drip edges. A brush gives the best results. If you use another applicator to lay on the paint, we recommend backbrushing (see Chapter 2). We recommend always using two topcoats, but two coats are required for satisfactory spray applications.

Painting aluminum siding (and gutters)

People usually think of aluminum siding as maintenance-free, but the finish eventually fades and ages. If you're happy with the color but the finish looks dull, try cleaning the siding with a wood-cleaning product designed to renew wood decks. Another approach that works wonders is to apply a coat of Penetrol, a paint conditioner. Buy a pint and test it in an inconspicuous spot.

Often, it will renew the luster so that you don't need to repaint. If Penetrol does the trick, apply it with a sponge or paint pad over the entire surface. If you decide to paint after all, Penetrol provides an excellent base.

Some painting experts say that you need only to apply a good-quality, light-colored, acrylic latex paint. Perhaps that's true, but you can improve your chances of success by first applying a high-quality primer-sealer, such as those used for hardboard siding. Or, if you want, you can skip the primer but mix a bonding additive, such as Emulsa-Bond, with the first topcoat of paint to improve paint adhesion to the existing paint. (Add 1 quart of bonding additive to 1 gallon of paint.) Don't add Emulsa-Bond to the final coat. It just isn't necessary, and it can cause variations in the amount of sheen.

If you've made repairs that expose bare metal, you must spot-prime those areas with a primer formulated for aluminum or galvanized metal. Despite claims to the contrary, our experience is that if you try to topcoat bare aluminum without this primer, the paint peels off.

Painting vinyl siding

Vinyl siding doesn't have a surface coating of paint. The color is continuous through the material. Painting eliminates one of the primary advantages of this siding material, namely that it is maintenance free. Nevertheless, if you can't stand the color or it has become dull with age, painting is an option.

Use a light color when painting vinyl siding. Dark colors cause excessive expansion and contraction, resulting in paint failure and buckled siding. Use a high-quality primer-sealer or a bonding additive, as recommended for aluminum siding.

Painting concrete, brick, or stucco

Generally speaking, you can paint brick, stucco, concrete, or concrete block with exterior latex paint after you clean the surface to remove accumulated grime. (See Chapter 2 for information about cleaning these surfaces.) Use a finish with a satin sheen to make cleaning easier the next time.

Think twice before you tamper with unpainted brick, because removing paint from brick is nearly impossible. Instead, use a water-repellent sealer or stain, both of which offer some weather protection but don't peel.

Ask a paint dealer or stucco contractor about painting stucco in your area. Typically, you can paint stucco with an acrylic latex product. You need to seal some masonry, especially highly alkaline surfaces such as stucco, with an alkali-resistant masonry primer. Moisture from the ground and from the house's interior rises to the exposed portion of the foundation and escapes

Book III

Painting and Wall-papering

harmlessly when the foundation is unpainted. If you paint it, make sure that you use a water-based product that allows moisture vapor to pass through. Use a sprayer, long-nap roller, or rough-surface painting pad/brush to paint a masonry surface.

Seal the joint between the foundation and the house with caulk. Uncaulked, this area is a major source of energy loss and cold drafts.

Painting trim, windows, and doors

Although it's important for the body of a house to look nice, pay special attention to the trim, windows, and doors. These elements attract the most attention and are the most vulnerable to paint failure because of all the joints where water can enter if the seal fails.

Roof and wall trim

After you prime bare wood, apply caulk along all open seams between trim-boards. Allow the caulk to dry for the amount of time specified on the label before applying a topcoat.

Brushes are best for applying paint to most trim. A 2½- to 3-inch angled sash brush is generally all you need, but if you have a lot of wide trim, you may want a 4-inch square brush, a pad, or even a mini-roller.

Windows

The outer surface of a window is painted to provide weather protection. Some double-hung windows have removable *sashes* — the operable part of the window. If you're painting with a removable sash, remove the sash by following the same procedure that you use for cleaning the windows, or consult the owners' manual — if you can find it. Lay the sash flat on sawhorses or a workbench to paint it.

Begin in the center and work out. This approach ensures a wet edge on all the surfaces so that you have a smooth transition and no lap marks. The problem with painting the window trim and frame first is that those areas will be tacky by the time you finish painting the sash. Here's the sequence to follow:

1. **Begin painting the wood next to the glass, using an angled sash brush.**

2. **Paint the stiles and rails of the sash.**

3. **Paint the window frame and *casing,* or trim.**

4. **Open the lower sash to paint the exterior windowsill.**

Don't paint the edges of the sash. When these surfaces are painted, they tend to stick to the frame. This advice is especially important when you're painting a window with a sash that slides in vinyl channels. Even a little paint on the edge of the sash can make it stick shut. Instead, seal these areas with a clear penetrating wood sealer to prevent moisture from entering the sash.

If you're painting a window sash while it's in the frame, use a brush that has very little paint on it to coat the outside edge of the sash. The dry-brush method prevents paint from running into the crack between the sash and the exterior stops, where it may cause the window to stick. Also, move the window sash frequently as it dries to prevent the window from sticking. If the window does stick, try using a butter knife to cut through the paint that glues the sash to the exterior stop. Years of paint buildup may require a more aggressive tool, such as a serrated paint zipper.

To form a moisture shield between the glass and the sash, overlap the paint by about $\frac{1}{16}$ inch onto the glass. If you have a steady hand and a quality angled sash brush, apply the paint freehand and wrap a clean cloth over the tip of a putty knife to clean off any mistakes. For the mere mortals, mask the glass before you paint or use reasonable care and plan to use a razor scraper after the paint has dried. If you decide not to mask, you can use a trim guard to protect the glass, but don't push too tightly against the glass or you won't get the desired overlap.

If you leave masking tape in place and it gets wet or the sun bakes it on, it's nearly impossible to remove. Apply painter's tape when you're ready to paint, not before, and remove the tape before you move on to the next window.

Entry doors

Choose a semigloss or high-gloss alkyd-based paint for doors, which get a lot of use and abuse. Latex enamel also holds up well. If the door was previously painted with a high-gloss paint, use a deglosser to dull the finish and clean the surface. If a wood or metal door has never been painted, or if you expose bare wood or metal by sanding, apply the appropriate primer.

You're much less likely to have drips and runs if you take a few moments to remove the door and lay it flat on sawhorses. Use a shoebox or similar container to keep all the parts together.

Make sure that you paint the bottom and top of a wooden door. If you don't, moisture may enter the door and cause it to swell or warp. A convenient mini-pad paint applicator lets you paint the bottom edge without removing the door.

Book III

Painting and Wallpapering

If the door has a flat surface, paint it with a 2- or 3-inch-wide brush, pad, roller, or sprayer. A roller typically leaves a stippled finish that may not be acceptable on surfaces when viewed up close. If you use a roller for speed, plan to backbrush with a brush or pad. (See Chapter 1 for more on backbrushing.)

If the door is paneled, use a brush and paint the panels first. Then paint the horizontal cross pieces (the *rails*), and finally paint the vertical pieces (the *stiles*). Paint with the grain as you do when sanding. To avoid applying too much paint in a corner, brush out of a corner rather than toward it. As you paint, check often for drips and excess paint in inside corners and brush out the excess paint before moving on. Refer to Chapter 1 for information about paint applicators and techniques for using them.

Garage doors

Paint failure is common on wooden garage doors, especially raised-panel ones, which have many joints where water can enter. Of course, run-ins with bicycles, basketballs, and Buicks don't help. After you remove all the loose paint and degloss the surface with deglosser or by scuff-sanding, prime any bare wood or hardboard panels. You must use an alkyd primer on hardboard panels, so plan to use it on the whole door. After priming, carefully apply a thin bead of paintable caulk to the sides and bottom of each panel where it meets the door's stiles and rails (the vertical and horizontal members of the frame). For extra protection and better bonding, mix Emulsa-Bond into the first topcoat. If the existing finish is in good condition, you can apply one topcoat to the cleaned and caulked door. If the door needs scraping, repairs, and sanding, finish the primed door with two topcoats.

Shutters

If the weather is iffy and you don't want to risk painting the siding or trim, and if you've removed your shutters and put them in a garage or other protected area, now's the time to paint them. Before you do, however, make sure that you won't obscure any label or other identification. Hardware stores sell tack-like numbers, which you can apply to the shutter, that correspond to numbers on the window frames to help you put shutters back in the right place.

After you've made any necessary repairs, scrape off loose paint, feather-sand your shutters, and then prime any bare spots. If you have a paint sprayer, there's no better time to pull it out. Spray the louvers first at a slight upward angle so that you can paint the upper portion of each slat. Then spray the entire face, including the frame. Two or three light coats are better than a single heavy coat, which can drip and run. Do the back first. Check both sides frequently for drips and runs, both as you paint and as the shutters begin to dry. Brush out drips with a dry paintbrush.

If the shutters are held in place with metal hinges or other brackets, paint the fasteners, too.

Winding things up

Before you store painting tools and equipment, make one final inspection, making sure that you didn't miss spots or overlook drips. Be sure to remove all masking tape. If it bakes on or gets wet and dries, it can be nearly impossible to get off.

Cleaning up the yard

Yard cleanup is minimal if you're careful to use drop cloths during preparation and painting. Be careful not to contaminate the ground with paint chips, especially if they contain lead.

We've found it helpful to use a wet/dry vacuum to pick up paint chips that escaped our drop cloths. If you're careful and hold the nozzle just above the ground, you can pick up paint chips and sanding dust without sucking up too much soil or an occasional chipmunk.

Removing drips and spills

While drips and spills are fresh, wipe them up with water (for latex) or mineral spirits (for alkyd paints). Use denatured alcohol to clean up alcohol-based coatings, such as some fast-drying primers.

If the paint has dried but not fully cured, use denatured alcohol on latex paints or mineral spirits on alkyd paints. Several commercial products, such as Goof-off, are available to soften latex paints. You may need an abrasive pad, but be careful: Abrasives can dull a glossy finish.

On glass and other relatively nonporous surfaces, you're often better off letting the spatter dry and scraping it off with a fingernail or a razor scraping tool. Use caution to avoid scratching the surface. A little paint spatter is much better than a ruined pane of insulated glass.

For fresh spatters and spills on masonry and other porous surfaces, flood the surface with water or thinner and scrub, scrub, scrub. Repeat the process as needed, using clean thinner each time. If the paint has dried, try a paint-and-varnish remover.

Book III

Painting and Wallpapering

Painting the Interior of Your Home

After you finish all the heavy and dirty prep work described in Chapter 2, you're ready for the fun part: the room transformation. So put on your painting duds, dust off the top of the paint can before you open it, and get to work.

When painting a room, the usual top-down sequence works best: ceiling, walls, woodwork (including windows, doors, and moldings), and then the floor. Of course, it's common to paint only the walls and the ceiling and just give the trim a good washing, thanks to the durability and scrubability of trim paint. However, you do have room for some flexibility in determining the sequence for painting walls and woodwork.

The argument for painting walls before trim is that you're likely to spatter wall paint onto the trim while rolling paint on the walls. But if you want to paint the trim first, go for it! Painting walls without messing up the trim is relatively easy to do. If you get wall paint on the trim while rolling or cutting in the walls (refer to Chapter 1), it's relatively easy to wipe off, and gloss trim paint covers flat wall paint much better than the other way around. You may also find that cutting in around already painted trim by using a brush or edging pad on the wide wall surface is easier than brushing the narrow edge of the trim — we do.

If you're planning to put two coats on the trim, you may want to paint the first coat before you paint the walls so that it's dry by the time you apply the second coat. If you have a lot of trim to paint, you may want to paint the windows right after you roll the ceiling. Then break from that meticulous small-motor-skill work for some big moves with a roller on the walls before going back to finish the doors and baseboard.

Painting ceilings and walls

Interior ceiling and wall painting is a project that's best divided into two: cutting in and rolling. (Having two people do the work is nice — especially if you're not one of them!) One person uses a brush to cut in, or outline, all the areas that a paint roller can't cover without getting paint on an adjacent surface. The other member of the team spreads paint on the ceiling and walls with a roller. If the ceiling and walls are the same color, you can cut in both at the same time. Otherwise, work on the ceiling first. (For a detailed description of these techniques, see Chapter 1.)

If you're painting with a partner, have the person with the brush, who we'll call the *outliner,* start by spreading a 2-inch band of paint on the ceiling, all around its perimeter. Lap marks result if the cut-in paint dries before you blend in the rolled area with the cut-in area, so don't let the outliner get too far ahead of the roller. You also want the roller to roll over as much of the cut-in band of paint as possible. The textures that a brush and a roller leave are quite different.

Both the outliner and the roller must observe the top-down rule and paint in the following sequence:

1. **The outliner paints the ceiling molding, if any, and then cuts in a band of paint on the ceiling along the short wall.**

2. **The roller follows the outliner, rolling the ceiling as soon as it's cut in along one wall.**

3. **The outliner cuts in a band of paint on one wall at the ceiling and down the wall in the corners and then across the bottom at the baseboard; the roller is then free to begin that wall.**

4. **The outliner cuts in around any windows and doors on that wall and then any other areas the roller can't do, such as around light fixtures or behind radiators.**

5. **The outliner completes the wall by cutting in the wall at the baseboards.**

6. **The roller follows along, usually at a pace that makes the outliner feel as if she is being pushed along.**

   (So the outliner says, "You missed a spot," but refuses to say where.)

7. **The process continues in this manner until all the walls are done.**

For a perfect paint job, follow the brush and roller techniques described in Chapter 1. To apply paint to broad, flat surfaces, such as walls and ceilings, use a 9-inch roller and either a shallow roller pan or the bucket-and-grid setup, also in Chapter 1.

Book III

Painting and Wall-papering

Before you use a new roller, wrap it in masking tape and then peel off the tape. Taping the roller gets rid of new-roller fuzzies that can drive you crazy if they get onto a newly painted wall.

Start painting by *carefully* rolling a band of paint to smooth and blend in the cut-in areas while you still have a wet edge. Now you have a nice, wide band, so you won't spatter the adjacent surface as you roll the rest of the ceiling. Then work your way across the narrow dimension of the room in 3- or 4-foot-square patches. By working across the narrow dimension and starting each row at the same wall, you maintain a wet edge and spread the paint into new areas without creating noticeable lap marks.

Attach a *pole extension* to your roller. This device enables you to do the work with less neck strain, with less bending, and without the need for ladders, staging, stilts, or platform shoes.

When rolling walls, keep these tips in mind:

✔ **Begin in a corner.** For ceilings, lay down a big "W" pattern about 3-feet wide. For walls, lay down a roller-width coat of paint from top to bottom. Then smooth out your work by rolling lightly a 3-foot-square area on the ceiling or from ceiling to floor on walls with a dry roller. Continue to work your way across the ceiling or along the wall in this fashion.

✔ **Don't skimp on paint.** By applying a single ceiling-to-floor vertical stripe or "W" pattern of paint per roller of paint, and then smoothing only that area you will assure adequate coverage.

✔ **Frequently step back and observe your work from several angles, checking for lap marks and missed spots.** Adequate lighting is important here. As long as the paint is wet, you can go back over an area without creating noticeable lap marks.

Painting woodwork

When painting wood windows, doors, and moldings, make sure that you keep your work area clean and free of drafts and airborne dirt to prevent dust and lint from settling on the wet paint. Turn down the thermostat to prevent the furnace from cycling on, which causes dust-laden drafts.

Getting professional results depends on good prep work as described in Chapter 2. If the wood is bare, apply a primer. (For information on choosing a primer, refer to Chapter 1.)

If you're painting over already painted or varnished woodwork, prepare the surface as described in Chapter 2 and apply one or two coats of paint, always sanding between coats. If the finish has a glossy sheen, sand it or use a deglosser.

If enamel is too thick, it sags and leaves brush marks. We like to use Penetrol for thinning alkyd enamels and Floetrol for thinning latex enamels. Don't add the thinner to the paint can. Instead, pour the paint (in the amount the directions suggest) into a new container and then add the thinner until you get the right consistency. Thicken the mixture with more paint or thin it with more Penetrol or Floetrol.

Working on windows

You want to paint windows from the inside out. That means that you paint the operational part of the window, the *sash,* first. Then you paint the frame and the casing. (*Casing* is the molding or trim on the top and sides of a window frame.) Paint the interior windowsill (called the *stool*) last. While you're working on the sash, paint any interior horizontal and vertical dividers (called *muntins*) before you paint the *stiles* and *rails* that make up the frame of the sash.

The two most common window styles are *double-hung,* in which two sashes slide vertically in channels, and *casement,* in which the sash has hinges on the side and cranks open outward. In many modern double-hung windows, you can easily remove the sash. Do so for painting so that you don't get paint in the channels. Even the slightest bit of paint on plastic channels can make the sash difficult to slide — or even inoperable. For the same reason, don't paint previously unpainted surfaces. Instead, coat these surfaces with a clear, penetrating wood sealer to prevent moisture from entering the sash. Set the sash on a surface at a comfortable working height. (About 36 inches high works for most adults.) Because most tables are 30 inches tall or lower, you need to prop up the table or the window to avoid back strain.

Taking an orderly approach to double-hung windows

Paint older double-hung windows in place. If someone's painted the upper sash shut or the pulley/counterweight system needs repair, consider correcting the problem before you start painting. Inevitably, these repairs will damage the finish, so now is the best time to take care of the situation. When you're ready to paint, follow these steps:

1. **Reverse the positions of the lower, inner sash and the upper sash, leaving both slightly open, as shown in Figure 3-2.**

2. **Using an angled 1½-inch sash brush, paint the lower exposed portion of the outer sash.**

Book III

Painting and Wall-papering

Figure 3-2:
Reverse the sash on a double-hung window to paint the lower half of the outer sash first.

3. **After the paint dries, return the upper and lower sashes to their normal positions, but don't close them completely.**

4. **Paint the remaining portion of the outer sash and the entire inner sash.**

   Don't paint the outside sloped portion of the window (the *sill*). This area is an exterior surface, and you must paint it with an exterior paint, typically while painting window exteriors.

5. **Switch to a wider 2½-inch angled sash brush to paint the casing.**

6. **Cut in the casing where it meets the wall. Then do the stops, which form the inner edge of the channel for the inner sash, finishing with the face of the casing.**

7. **Paint the stool.**

8. **After the sash has dried, paint the channels.**

   Slide the sash all the way up to paint the bottom half of the channels and, when the paint dries, slide the sash all the way down to paint the upper half. If unpainted metal weather-stripping lines the channels, don't paint the stripping.

To save all the waiting, we often paint the lower half of the window channels before we start painting the walls and ceilings so that it can dry while we cut and roll. As soon as the channels are dry, we stop rolling and do the upper half of the channels.

As you're painting around the glass, lay the paint on in the middle of the area you're painting rather than starting in a corner. Then, with less paint on the brush, work from the corners out, dipping your brush into the paint you initially laid down as necessary.

Use a brush with very little paint on it to coat the vertical, outside edges of the sash. The dry-brush technique prevents paint from running into the crack between the sash and the stops, where it may cause the window to stick. Move the sash as soon as possible to break any paint bond in these cracks before it dries completely. If, despite your best efforts, the sash sticks, use a serrated tool known as a *paint zipper* or the tip of a utility knife to cut through the paint that binds the stop to the sash.

Working on casements from the inside out

Follow the same inside-out procedure for casement windows, with one exception — paint the outer edges of the sash first so that they start drying ASAP. Don't close the window until it's completely dry. If you close a casement window before the paint dries, you need a jackhammer to open it.

Start by opening the window partway so that you can remove the operating mechanism from the sash. After you paint the outer edges of the sash, cut in the glass perimeter and then paint the face of the sash. Next, crank the window wide open to access and paint the frame. Finish by cutting in the casing and painting the frame and the face of the casing.

You need to overlap paint onto the glass slightly, especially on the lower third of each pane, to prevent water that condenses on cold glass from soaking into the wood behind the paint. This process causes the paint to peel and eventually leads to wood rot.

Doing doors

Doors take a lot of use and abuse, so for best results, choose a durable finish that has a semigloss or gloss sheen. Semigloss or gloss makes cleaning easier and holds up to frequent cleaning. You need to lay down at least two topcoats to get a uniform appearance. If the current finish on the door is a glossy paint, use a deglosser to dull the finish.

Leave doors hanging on their hinges while you paint them so that you can paint both sides at the same time. You can remove most modern lock sets in less than a minute (and replace them in under two), so removing them for painting is easier than masking. Make sure that you do one or the other.

You must seal all surfaces of new doors to prevent moisture from entering the door and causing it to warp. This step is critical for a solid-wood door or a solid-core veneered door. We even recommend sealing for hollow-core doors (the most common lightweight interior door), which aren't as prone to warping. If you don't plan to take the door off, slip a mirror under it to see if the bottom edge has been painted. If not, either use a mini-painting pad that enables you to paint the bottom edge or remove the door from its hinges, apply a sealer to the bottom edge, and rehang the door to paint the rest of it.

Rolling a flush (flat) door

Paint a flat door with a brush, pad, or roller (with a ¼-inch nap or foam sleeve). If you use a roller, backbrush immediately with a wide brush or pad to smooth the roller stipple. The texture that rollers impart works well for walls and ceilings but isn't attractive on doors or wood trim. (Refer to Chapter 1 for more on backbrushing.)

Doors with a luan mahogany veneer have a rougher texture than those with a birch veneer. Although you'll never get a mahogany door as smooth as you can a birch door, sanding between coats helps, especially if you're priming and painting a new door. After painting the door itself, paint the doorjamb and casing, beginning at the doorstop and working out.

Painting raised-panel doors

Paint a raised-panel door, shown in Figure 3-3, with a brush and paint with the natural grain of the wood. Painting around the panels is time-consuming, making it difficult to keep a wet edge.

Figure 3-3:
Paint a pair
of door
panels
at a time,
starting
with the
detailed
frame
around
each panel.

One commonly recommended approach is to paint all the panels first. But this approach works only if you cut in carefully and avoid getting paint on the faces of the stiles, muntins, and rails that frame the panels. If you get paint on a stile while painting the first couple of panels, for example, the paint may set up before you're ready to paint the rest of the stile.

For most painters, the best approach is to paint the top pair of panels and the stiles, muntins, and rails around them. Then move to the next lower pair of panels, and so on. Using a paint conditioner keeps a wet edge longer, makes the paint go on more easily, and improves its bond, which are all important qualities for door painting.

Making transitions

When painting a door frame that's a different color on each side, apply one color up to, but not including, the face of the stop on the in-swinging side of the door. Paint the same color on the in-swinging face of the door but not on any edges. Make the final cut along the outside edge of the casing and wall and then finish painting the face of the molding.

Getting up close to baseboards and other molding

Put away the roller, hotshot — it's time for precise paintbrushing. Choose a sash brush or brushes that match the dimensions of the woodwork you're painting. An angled brush that's comfortable to hold at various angles works best because painting trim, balusters, or a fireplace mantle sometimes requires the flexibility of a contortionist. Get up close to whatever you're painting, whether doing so means lying on the floor to paint baseboards or climbing a ladder to reach areas higher than shoulder height.

When painting woodwork, use a box with the sides folded down to hold the can of paint and a couple of rags, one which you dampen with water (for latex) or paint thinner (for alkyd) to wipe up drips or splatters.

Putting on the finishing touches

Before you pack away the paint and equipment, remove any masking tape and check carefully for spots that need a touchup. Look for paint drips, too. Drips and runs take time to form, and despite your best efforts to keep checking just-painted surfaces, you may find some. You must wait until they dry completely before you scrape, sand, and retouch them with paint.

If you find paint on the glass in windows or doors (and you probably will), use a single-edge razor or a razor scraping tool to scrape it off. Before you scrape the paint off the glass, score the paint with the point of a utility knife and then scrape up to the scored line. Doing so prevents you from accidentally peeling paint off the wood. If you're trying to maintain a $\frac{1}{16}$-inch overlap on the glass (see the "Painting windows" section, earlier in this chapter), hold a wide taping knife against the wood as you score, as shown in Figure 3-4.

Book III

Painting and Wallpapering

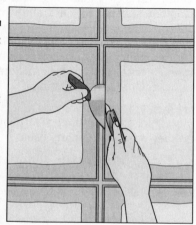

Figure 3-4: Score a paint line before you scrape paint off glass. The taping-knife guide reserves the $\frac{1}{16}$-inch overlap on the glass.

Be careful while scraping glass. Hold the razor at a low angle with its entire edge on the glass and work slowly to avoid scratching the glass.

Next, reinstall hardware, fixtures, and outlet covers that you removed when preparing the room. If you haven't done so already, clean, polish, lubricate, or otherwise spruce up these items before reinstalling them. You may want to invest in replacements. Inexpensive finishing touches, such as new cover plates, can really make a difference.

Finally, move the furnishings back in, and please, *watch out for the trim!*

Cleaning Up the Mess

With a little planning, cleanup is relatively simple. Walking away from a clean work area at the end of a day feels good. You'll appreciate that spic-and-span condition even more the next day. And if you've invested money in good painting tools and applicators and you clean and store them properly, they last for many years.

Assembling cleanup tools and supplies

Post-painting cleanup shouldn't be as big a chore as painting itself. Gathering some basic cleaning items will help make cleanup a breeze and extend the life of your painting tools. To make the task easier, set up a shop with the following items:

- **Solvents:** The proper solvent for cleaning up latex paint is warm, soapy water. The best solvent for cleaning up alkyd paints, enamels, and oil-based varnishes and stains is mineral spirits, or paint thinner. Use denatured alcohol to clean up shellac or other alcohol-based coatings, such as some fast-drying, stain-killing primers. These solvents won't work on brushes that have a buildup of dried paint. For them, you need a special brush cleaner solvent or paint remover (or a garbage can). Some paints require special solvents. Always check the label directions.

- **Painter's rags:** If you have a medium to large painting or refinishing task, buy a quantity of absorbent rags. Paint stores usually sell them by the box or loose by the pound, and they have many, many uses.

- **Small containers:** Use coffee cans and jars (some with lids); clean, empty quart paint cans; plastic paint buckets; and other similar containers to store solvents and paints and to clean brushes.

✔ **Brush/roller spinner:** Buy a brush/roller spinner — a must-have tool for pros who use it to clean their brushes and rollers. A brush/roller spinner works like an old-fashioned spinning top with a centrifugal action that forces excess paint out of the brush or roller. First, clean most of the paint out of your applicator with water or mineral sprits and then put it on the spinner. If it's a brush, force the handle into the spinner clamp, and if it's a roller, slide it over the clamp. Then spin the liquid out into a 5-gallon bucket or an empty garbage can and voilà — a spray of the excess appears on the sides of the container. Without removing the applicator, dip the applicator back in clean solvent or water and spin again. Repeat this process once or twice more until the spray is color-less and the bristles or nap are dry.

✔ **Brush comb and wire brush:** To get a brush really clean, open up the bristles with a brush comb to allow the solvent to get into the heel of the brush, where paint tends to hide. Lay the brush on a flat surface and brush the bristles from the heel toward the tip. These tools are indispensable when trying to restore an old brush with dried paint in it.

✔ **5-gallon buckets with lids:** Keep one bucket nearby half full of water to rinse out paint rags. Use a bucket instead of your kitchen sink to wash out painting tools. Spin roller covers and brushes inside a bucket to contain the spray. Buckets have plenty of other uses, too, especially if you wipe them out well after each use.

✔ **5-in-1 tool:** The curved side of this multipurpose tool scrapes paint off roller covers before you clean them or dispose of them. Paint-stirring sticks have a similar curve.

✔ **Heavy-duty rubber gloves:** An essential cleanup accessory. You need to use your hands to work the paint out of a brush, and you don't want to get any more paint or solvent on your hands than is absolutely necessary.

Book III

Painting and Wall-papering

Using the three-container approach

Basically, cleaning an applicator involves these three steps:

1. **Scrape as much paint out of the applicator and into the original paint can as possible.**

2. **Brush or roll out as much paint as you can onto newspaper.**

3. **Clean the applicator in the appropriate solvent (water or mineral spirits).** Clean latex applicators under running water, but to conserve thinner — and limit environmental problems — use the three-container approach for cleaning up applicators used with alkyd paint.

The basic idea behind using three containers is that you wash out as much paint as possible in each container before moving on to the next. At each step, the brush gets cleaner, and by the time you get to container number three, nearly all the paint is out of the applicator, so the solvent in the third container stays relatively clean and is used as a final solvent rinse. Used thinner, after the paint has settled out, can be recycled.

Follow this simple step-by-step process:

1. **Wash the applicator in container 1, taking time to work the applicator with your fingers (don't forget your gloves) or by brushing the applicator back and forth on the bottom of the container.**

   This step gets the solvent deep into the applicator, such as the heel of a brush or the foam backing of a pad.

2. **Remove all excess liquid before moving on to the next container.**

   With brushes and rollers, the most effective approach is to use a brush spinner. With pads, draw the applicator firmly across a straightedge, such as a paint stick that's held over the container.

3. **Repeat Steps 1 and 2 using container 2 and then container 3.**

   Blot a pad on an absorbent towel.

4. **When the applicators are completely dry, store them properly.**

   See the section "Finishing up: End-of-project procedures," later in this chapter.

5. **Recycle chemical solvents.**

   Pour all the solvent from container 2 into container 1. Then rinse out container 2 with solvent from container 3, and pour that into container 1. Wipe the two empty containers clean with rags or paper towels. Put a lid on container 1 and let it sit for a few days, or until all the paint has settled to the bottom of the container. Pour off the now-clean solvent into the original solvent container by using a funnel. Scrape the settled paint onto a newspaper and allow it to dry before disposing of it properly.

Although warm, soapy water removes most latex paint from brushes and rollers, some paint residue is often left behind. Rinse the tool with a brush cleaner and spin it dry before hanging it up for storage.

Stopping for a while

When you complete the last brushstroke for the day, resist the temptation to drop everything and rush out for a cold beverage. First, do the following:

1. **Remove any masking.**

2. **Check carefully for spatters or drips that you missed and remove them.**

   If latex spatters haven't fully cured, dampen a cloth with denatured alcohol and rub off the paint. Use mineral spirits (and elbow grease) to remove semidry oil-based paints. On hard, slick surfaces, such as glass and glazed tile, use a single-edge razor blade to scrap off dried paint.

   Porous surfaces are the most difficult to clean because spills get below the surface, so make every effort to protect these surfaces from spills in the first place. Even fresh spills are nearly impossible to clean unless you can flood the surface with solvent under pressure. You may need to employ paint remover, sandblasting, power-sanding, or other drastic measures to remove dried paint from porous surfaces.

3. **Pour paint from trays or paint buckets back into their containers, using a paintbrush to wipe out as much paint as possible.**

4. **Scrape as much paint as you can from the applicators back into the paint can.**

   Use the rim of the paint can to scrape brushes and a 5-in-1 tool or the curved part of a paint stick to scrape roller covers.

5. **Wrap the applicators in plastic and stick them in the refrigerator until an hour or so before you're ready to paint again.**

   You can also leave a brush in solvent. If you do so, keep the bristles off the bottom by attaching a paint stick to the handle with a rubber band so that the stick extends below the bristles.

   If a brush is overloaded and messy, clean it a little before either wrapping and refrigerating it or suspending it in solvent. Scrape out excess paint, rinse the brush in solvent, and spin out the excess liquid with a brush spinner.

6. **Replace the lids on paint cans and solvent containers.**

   Drape a rag over paint cans to absorb any paint in the rim and prevent it from spurting out as you tap the lids on.

7. **Clean the work area by picking up trash and dirty rags and taking ladders down or putting them away.**

Book III

Painting and Wallpapering

Finishing up: End-of-project procedures

At the end of a project, break down your temporary shop and store things in their proper places. Dispose of trash and properly store or dispose of leftover paints and solvents. (See the "Disposing of paint and solvent safely" section, later in this chapter.)

Cleaning oil-based paint from your skin and hair

The only way to get dry oil-based paint off your skin and out of your hair is with solvents. Solvents are toxic and absorb quickly into the skin, so try to remove paint from your skin before it dries. At that point, the friendlier, natural citrus-based cleaners are effective. Some are general cleaners, and others are made specifically for cleaning hands and skin. If you do use solvent, follow up with a mild grease-cutting dish soap and rinse well. Use hand lotion or hair conditioner to restore the moisture robbed by the cleaning process.

Cleaning and storing applicators

Thoroughly clean your brushes and other applicators by following the three-container method described earlier in this chapter. Plain water is fine for end-of-session cleanup of latex brushes, but at the end of a project, use soapy water and a brush comb to get solvent deep into the brushes and a wire brush to clean and straighten out the bristles. Then fan the brushes to inspect for hidden paint. Give the brushes a final rinse in mineral spirits or brush cleaner to remove any residue. When the brushes are clean and dry, put them back in their original sleeve or wrap them in heavy paper secured with string. If possible, hang brushes for long-term storage or make sure that they're flat.

Use the full three-container approach for cleaning rollers and paint pads. Place these tools on their edges to dry on an absorbent towel and then store them in a plastic bag.

Cleaning and storing power rollers, brushes, and sprayers

Power painting is fast; cleaning the equipment usually isn't. Each unit has specific end-of-session and end-of-project cleanup procedures. If you own the unit, read the instructions for cleanup before you use the tool. If you rent a piece of equipment, such as a paint sprayer, go over the cleaning procedure with the salesperson and ask for a detailed cleaning checklist. Returning it clogged with paint can cost you a bundle.

In general, you want to empty any paint reservoirs and clean them with solvent (water or mineral spirits, according to the type of paint you're using). Then run solvent through the unit. At first, only paint comes out, and you can put that paint into the paint can. When the liquid starts to run clear, direct it back into the solvent container that's feeding the process until the solvent runs clear.

If you used the system for a water-based finish, run a gallon of mineral spirits or a water-based solvent made specifically for this purpose through the system before storing it. Because mineral spirits are petroleum based, they don't cause rust to develop inside the system the way water can. Recycle solvents as described in the section "Using the three-container approach," earlier in this chapter.

When the inside of the unit is clean, wash down the outside, especially the spray gun and the hose near the gun where paint tends to build up. Doing a thorough job requires some disassembly. Don't take a rented spray gun apart unless directed to do so. Soak the parts in the appropriate solvent and scrub them clean with a toothbrush. When the parts are dry, reassemble the unit for storage. If you end up with extra parts, disassemble the unit and start over.

Don't use needles or anything that might scratch or otherwise damage an expensive spray tip on a power painter. Use soft copper wire or a brush bristle to clear a clog.

Cutting down on waste

Avoid waste by storing finishes properly and by recycling applicators, solvents, containers, and drop cloths. Save a little paint for touch-ups, but get rid of larger quantities. Return any unopened cans of non-custom-mixed finish. Pass unwanted paint or solvent on to others who can make good use of it. Try churches, community organizations concerned with housing, schools, theater groups, or community swap shops at waste disposal facilities.

Seal leftover paint in the smallest can possible so that it takes up less room and the finish doesn't dry out. (Buy small, empty paint cans or use ones that you've recycled.) Label unmarked containers with relevant information, such as color, sheen, room/location used, solvent, and any special instructions for use. For a better seal, lay plastic wrap across the top of the can before you put the lid on. Tip a paint can upside down momentarily before storing it right side up or store it upside down for an airtight seal.

Solvents have a low *flash point* — the lowest temperature at which a volatile vapor of the solvent ignites when exposed momentarily to a spark or other source of ignition — especially when mixed with some finishes, such as spar varnish. For that reason, store solvents and paint in a locked metal cabinet, away from excessive heat or sources of combustion. Also, be sure to protect paint from freezing temperatures.

Disposing of paint and solvent safely

Oil-based paint and solvent and sludge from chemical removal of oil-based paints (especially lead-based finishes) are hazardous wastes. Never pour these materials onto the ground or into a sewer system. State and municipal governments typically regulate disposal of paints and solvents. Some communities accept oil-based paint in the regular trash collection, but only after it has been allowed to dry. Other communities have special collection sites or collection days.

Book III

Painting and Wall-papering

Municipalities may also regulate disposal of less toxic water-based paints. You can often pour small quantities of such paint into an absorbent material, such as shredded newspapers or cat litter, allow it to dry, and toss it into the trash. Treat larger quantities of paint as hazardous waste.

If you've used a chemical solvent to remove lead-based paint, you may be required to have the material tested and to have even relatively small quantities hauled away by a licensed toxic-waste hauler.

Chapter 4

Wallpapering Basics

· ·

In This Chapter

▶ Deciding what wallcovering to buy

▶ Estimating your needs and buying wallcoverings

▶ Gathering the right tools and supplies

▶ Buying the right adhesive

· ·

Wallcovering adds rich texture and interest to walls and other surfaces in your home that paint alone doesn't. You can choose from a virtually unlimited variety of patterns and styles in fabric, foil, natural grasses, papers, wet-look vinyls, and dozens of other materials. A room papered with your favorite pattern is a welcome sight that draws you inside; wallpaper is one of those little things that make a big difference. In this chapter, you explore your options.

Selecting the Perfect Wallpaper

Yes, the choice of wallpapers can be daunting, but allow yourself time to peruse as many wallpaper books as you can find. This undertaking sometimes involves a whole lot of time, but being thorough gives you a good idea of the styles and designs you like — *really* like. And you really want to like the wallpaper you choose because you'll be looking at it for quite some time.

Locate and take full advantage of a knowledgeable wallpaper supplier (flip to the section, "Buying Wallcoverings," later in this chapter). You need professional expertise to help you choose a paper that's appropriate for your skills and experience and to calculate how much paper you need. A wallpaper expert can suggest the necessary wall preparations and materials (such as primer/sealer and liner paper) and offer advice on using the right adhesive according to the type of wall surface and wallcovering. A professional also can help you plan proper seam placement, which not only improves the appearance of the finished product, but also substantially simplifies the work (music to a do-it-yourselfer's ears!).

Determining how much work you can handle

Wallpapering sometimes requires the skills and experience of a lifelong professional and the eye of a true artist. Yet a first-time do-it-yourselfer can also do the job perfectly. The chosen wallcovering, the condition of the surface, the complexity of the room, and how many thumbs you have all determine the degree of difficulty.

To help you identify wallcoverings that are appropriate for you, ask yourself the following questions:

- **Am I choosing a wallcovering suited to my skill level?** Describe your experience and level of comfort to your wallpaper salesperson, who can suggest professional installation for wallcoverings that demand greater skill or at least caution you about the potential difficulties or quirks of a wallcovering that you're unfamiliar with. Take a trip to the library to find out more about hanging the particular type of wallcovering you're considering.

- **Are my walls and ceilings reasonably straight, level, and truly vertical? (If they are, alert the media.)** Even the easiest-to-hang self-adhesive wallpaper can be a bear to hang when nothing is that perfection called *true*. If you're working with less-than-perfect walls but still want to do the job yourself, look for patterns that are more forgiving (see "Selecting a pattern that suits the room," later in this chapter) and use some of the tricks of the trade (check out Chapter 6) that disguise rather than emphasize problems.

- **Will I hang my wallcovering on a standard, easy-to-paper surface, such as plaster or drywall, or will I cover a problem surface, such as concrete block or wall paneling?** It's true that you can wallpaper just about anything, but only when the surface is properly prepared. Work with your salesperson to determine what work and skills are necessary, and then decide whether you have the skills and inclination to do the work yourself.

Many types of wallcoverings are available. Each requires slightly different preparation, application, and finishing work according to its characteristics. Check out the following section for the lowdown on the most popular wallcoverings and some key things you should know when you buy wallcovering. Ask your dealer whether the wallcovering material or its pattern will complicate hanging. Also, find out any special instructions for the wallcovering you select. For example, make sure that you know how to position and match the pattern. With some papers, pattern matching is pretty confusing. If window treatments are in your decorating plan, don't forget to ask to see sample books of wallcoverings that have coordinated fabrics.

Choosing a workable material

In spite of its name, wallpaper isn't always made of paper. The material and coatings used to make and color the wallcovering determine its appearance (natural, shiny, metallic, or wet, for example) and greatly affect how easy or difficult the covering is to hang. For example, with some coverings, you must be very careful not to get *any* paste on the decorative surface. We don't know how you work, but we can't even imagine doing that!

The material and coatings also determine how durable, stain resistant, and easy to clean the wallcovering will be. A paper may be washable or scrubbable (or neither), which is usually determined by how much cleaning the paper or color can handle. You can occasionally sponge a *washable* wallcovering with warm, soapy water. *Scrubbable* coverings are made of tougher stuff and can take more frequent washes. Scrubbable papers are ideal for hallways, stairways, and toddlers' rooms, where smudges (and worse) are inevitable, in addition to kitchens, where spills and grease tend to build up on the walls. Choose a paper that's suitable for the planned location, considering both the type and amount of abuse you expect the wall to take. Like in choosing a spouse, you may have to compromise, but you shouldn't go so far as to disregard either appearance or practicality. Here's how your choices stack up:

✔ **Standard papers** are inexpensive and generally easy to hang. Just be careful not to tug on the paper too hard as you position and reposition the sheets on the wall. Standard papers tear quite easily, soil easily, and are relatively difficult to clean because they lack a protective coating. However, if money is an obstacle, you'll be thrilled to hear that these papers are relatively cheap.

✔ **Vinyl-coated papers** have a paper backing and a paper surface that's sealed with a liquid vinyl. This seal makes the wallcovering washable, meaning that you can safely sponge it off with soapy water.

✔ **Solid sheet vinyl wallcoverings** consist of vinyl bound to a cloth or paper backing. These wallcoverings are the most rugged, stain resistant, and scrubbable and make an excellent choice for kitchens.

Vinyls are the best choice for a beginning wallpaper hanger. Not only are they the easiest type of wallcovering to hang, but they're also easy to live with — they're durable, soil resistant, and easy to clean. They're even easy to remove.

✔ **Foils and Mylars,** which have a thin, shiny metal coating, reflect a great deal of light. This feature makes them a good choice for small rooms with little or no natural light, such as an interior powder room. The wall surface must be in nearly perfect condition, however, because the wallpaper's shiny surfaces accentuate any imperfections.

Book III

Painting and Wallpapering

Even though hanging reflective wallpaper on walls with imperfections isn't a good idea, you can improve the results by first covering the walls with a heavy liner paper, which is designed to bridge small cracks and imperfections. Foil and Mylar papers are expensive, and liner paper installation can be a bit advanced for the everyday do-it-yourselfer, so we recommend that you call a pro for this job.

✓ **Grasscloth, hemp, and other cloths-on-paper** are richly textured, woven coverings with laminated paper backings. Although grasscloth is traditionally made of a vine, many modern synthetic versions are available. All are good choices to cover less-than-perfect walls, but they are expensive and relatively difficult to hang. If you are experienced and want to try one of these natural-looking coverings, discuss the installation requirements in detail with your wallpaper dealer.

✓ **Flocked papers** have raised, velvety patterns and are good choices for covering walls that have minor surface imperfections. Washable flocks are easier to install than nonwashable ones, but both are expensive, and installation generally requires a pro. If you're experienced and want to step up to a more advanced project, discuss the installation requirements in detail with your wallpaper dealer.

Knowing what's on the backside

Your primary concern is rightly focused on the front side of the wallcovering. After all, that's the side that shows. However, what's on the backside counts, too. In particular, the back may or may not be prepasted, and the type of backing determines how you will eventually remove it.

The two primary differences on the backsides of wallcoverings and what they may mean to you are

✓ **Prepasted or unpasted:** Perhaps the most obvious difference on the backside of wallpaper is the presence or lack of paste. The vast majority of in-stock wallcoverings are prepasted. You activate this factory-applied adhesive by applying a pre-paste activator or by dipping the paper in a water tray, as you find out how to do in Chapter 5.

✓ **Dry-strippable or peelable:** This feature will be a greater concern down the road when you, or the next occupant of your home or apartment, want to remove the paper. *Dry-strippable* paper peels off in its entirety. *Peelable* paper peels off but leaves behind its paper backing. This backing can be papered over (assuming that it's in good shape) or removed with a wallpaper remover solution before painting. Keep in mind that strippable wallpaper or the paper backing of peelable wallpaper is easily removable only if the substrate was properly sealed before installation. See Chapter 1 for additional information about primers.

Selecting a pattern that suits the room

Without a doubt, the most important factor in choosing wallpaper is choosing a pattern you like. You also must make sure that the pattern works in the particular room that you plan to paper — it should achieve your design goals. Because patterns often affect the degree of installation difficulty, you also want to choose one that's appropriate for your skills if you plan to hang it yourself.

Some basic aesthetic guidelines to consider when you're selecting a pattern are

✔ Vertical stripes or patterns make the ceiling appear higher.

✔ Horizontal stripes or patterns seem to widen a room and bring ceilings down.

✔ Large patterns generally don't look good in a small room because they tend to overpower the space and make it seem smaller. A large, open pattern looks best in a larger space.

✔ A mini-print or a paper with a small pattern or geometric design suits smaller dimensions.

✔ Dark colors make a room seem smaller.

✔ Wallpaper with a light background makes a room look larger.

✔ A pattern of ducks ice-skating makes any room look silly.

Book III

Painting and Wall-papering

Matching repeating patterns

If you look at a roll of wallpaper, you see that patterns repeat themselves every so many inches or feet along the length of the roll. This is called a _vertical repeat._ The pattern on one strip may align with another adjacent pattern horizontally or at an angle. How the designs on one strip are positioned in relation to the same designs on adjacent strips is called the _pattern match._

Pattern matches come in five types: random match, random texture, straight-across, half-drop, and multiple drops. (The term _drop,_ in this sense, refers to how much the pattern drops to match the adjacent strip.) Ask your dealer about the implications of the pattern for your particular project and about any special cutting and installation requirements.

The following list describes the five types of pattern matches shown in Figure 4-1.

Random match

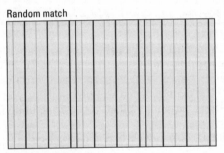

Random texture

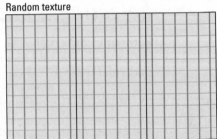

Straight-across

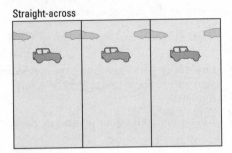

Conventional half-drop

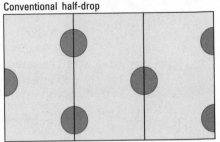

Multiple drop

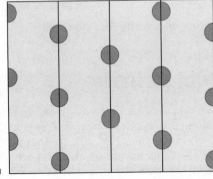

Figure 4-1:
The types of
wallpaper
patterns.

✔ In a **random match,** such as a vertical stripe, you don't need to match
patterns, but you do need to install each drop with the same edge
always on the left.

✔ **Random texture** wallcoverings, such as grasscloth, don't have a pattern;
therefore, matching is not necessary. However, the left and right sides
of a roll often have shading differences that can cause problems. Installing
the paper as it comes off the roll juxtaposes a light edge with a darker

one, making the shading difference more obvious. To overcome this problem, manufacturers often recommend flipping every other drop.

- ✔ **Straight-across** patterns line up and match horizontally but may also be laid diagonally on a wall. The pattern always looks the same on every drop from the ceiling or other horizontal elements, such as chair molding and the tops of windows.

- ✔ **Half-drop** patterns line up or match on a 45-degree diagonal line rather than a horizontal one. Each strip is positioned so that it's above or below the adjoining strips at a distance equal to one-half the vertical repeat. Every other drop looks the same at the ceiling.

- ✔ A **multiple drop** (called ⅓ multiple drop, ¼ multiple drop, ⅕ multiple drop, and so on) is similar to a half-drop; the difference is that the amount you offset on each strip varies. The higher the multiple (3, 4, 5, and so on), the less often a design repeats itself at the ceiling line. This type of pattern is great for out-of-level ceilings but can be very confusing.

Hanging wallpaper with a low vertical pattern repeat (a few inches versus a foot or more) is easier and wastes less paper.

Buying Wallcoverings

In many cases, calculating how many rolls of wallpaper you need is very straightforward. Just figure the area you need to cover and divide that number by the area that each roll covers. However, many times you're better off letting the dealer figure out your needs. In either case, get out your tape measure and a pad of paper.

Sketching the layout

Make a simple sketch of each wall in the room, including any doors, windows, or other openings. Get out your tape measure and grab a helper; measure the dimensions (the width and height) of each wall and opening. Then calculate the area of each by multiplying width times height. Add up all the wall areas and then add up all the opening areas separately. For the total area to cover, subtract the total area of the openings from the total area of the walls and multiply that number by 115 percent to allow for waste.

Book III

Painting and Wallpapering

Estimating the number of rolls to buy

For random texture, random, or straight-across patterns in a typical room, you can handle the figuring. For example, for a bedroom with two doors and two windows, simply divide the total square footage you need to cover (refer to the preceding section, "Sketching the layout") by the total coverage of the roll of wallpaper you're buying to determine the number of rolls you need. Most likely, the answer isn't an even number of rolls, so round up to the next highest number to determine the number of rolls you need to buy or order.

If your project is complex and involves lots of cutting, irregular openings, or an out-of-square room, or if your wallcovering has a tricky pattern or is otherwise a difficult type to hang, we strongly recommend that you let an experienced salesperson estimate your needs. The dealer can evaluate the pattern repeat, the pattern match, the length and width of the wallpaper, the complexity of the job, how the covering is sold (in single, double, or triple rolls), the size of the rolls, and other factors to determine the amount of wallcovering you should buy.

When you buy wallpaper off the shelf, or when you receive paper that you preordered, make sure that the pattern numbers on all the rolls are the same and that the pattern is what you ordered. Also verify that the *dye lot* (or *run*) of all the rolls is the same. Each time the factory does a new run of the paper, changes can occur in the coloring, quality, or appearance of the coating. Keep a permanent record of this information. If you have to order additional paper, be sure to request the same pattern number and dye lot.

Tracking down the right paper

You can purchase your wallpaper from a number of sources:

- **Wallpaper outlets:** These stores offer the largest selection of carryout paper and have a library of manufacturers' books on hand to order from.

- **Home centers and paint stores:** Most of these retailers offer a modest selection of wallpaper-to-go and keep a large library of manufacturers' books on hand to order from.

- **Mail-order catalogs:** Some manufacturers publish catalogs with pages of actual wallcoverings that you can order by phone. Look through the advertisements in decorating magazines for information about obtaining these catalogs.

Tooling Up for the Task

After you determine what you need to do to prepare the surface (see Chapter 5), it's time for a trip to a home center, paint store, or hardware store. The tools you need for wallpapering may vary from our suggested list. For example, even if we suggest a breakaway razor knife, your utility knife with a sharp blade may work just fine.

This list and Figure 4-2 show you the tools, supplies, and other items that a do-it-yourself paperhanger typically needs:

- ✔ 2-foot level
- ✔ Adhesives, activators, or water tray (as required)
- ✔ Breakaway razor knife
- ✔ Bucket, sponges, and clean rags
- ✔ Canvas drop cloth (for areas you'll be walking on)
- ✔ Flat, hard work table (a half sheet of plywood on sawhorses will do just fine)
- ✔ Metal straightedge (such as a 6-inch taping knife or a painter's trim guard)
- ✔ Paint roller and tray (for prepasted activator or unpasted paper)
- ✔ Pencil
- ✔ Plastic drop cloth (to cover everything that's not covered by your canvas drop cloth)
- ✔ Plumb and chalk line
- ✔ Seam roller
- ✔ Sharp scissors
- ✔ Smoothing brush or plastic wallpaper smoother
- ✔ Spackling compound, primer/sealer, sizing, and liner paper, all as needed for preparing the walls
- ✔ Stepstool or ladder
- ✔ Tape measure
- ✔ Work lights and extension cords

Book III

Painting and Wall-papering

Plumb and
chalk line

Break-away razor knife

Seam
roller

Figure 4-2:
Wall-
papering
tools, equip-
ment, and
supplies.

Smoothing brush

Choosing Your Wallpaper Adhesive

If you choose to use unpasted wallpaper, it goes without saying that you need to apply wallpaper adhesive to get the paper to stick to the wall. Wallpaper adhesive is generally available premixed in standard and heavy-duty versions. Standard is fine for most wallcoverings, but some types — heavy grasscloths, for example — require greater holding power. Tell your wallcovering dealer the type of paper and the surface you will apply it to, and he or she will tell you whether the wallpaper requires a heavy-duty adhesive.

If you're applying vinyl over vinyl or intend to put a border on top of vinyl paper (see Chapter 6 for more information about borders), you need vinyl-to-vinyl adhesives, which bond to just about any surface without priming.

Chapter 5

Preparing Surfaces for Wallpapering

In This Chapter

▶ Cleaning and setting up the room

▶ Repairing and preparing wall surfaces for wallcoverings

▶ Removing old wallpaper

Many of the preparations you need to make before hanging wallpaper are the same steps you take in preparation for interior painting. You want to set up a clear, well-lighted, and safe work area and then take the necessary steps to ensure that surfaces are smooth and in good condition. In most cases, you need to prime and seal the existing wall surface to ensure that the wallpaper adheres properly and that it can later be removed without damaging the wall.

Clearing and Cleaning the Room

To get the room ready for work, remove as much furniture as possible. Ideally, you want a completely empty room, but you can get by with a good 3 feet of work area in front of the walls. In addition, you need a work area where you can set up a table to roll out, measure, and cut wallpaper into strips.

Remove the covers on electrical receptacles and light switches and cover the face of each fixture with masking tape. Also, remove any heating grates or wall-mounted light fixtures.

Before you remove a light fixture, shut off the power to the room from the electrical panel. Put a piece of tape over the circuit breaker as a reminder to others to leave the power off. Then verify that the power is truly off by using a circuit tester. Cover any exposed wires with electrical tape. If you don't have a circuit tester, you can plug a radio (that works!) into the outlet and turn it on. If you hear music, the electricity is still on.

A primer on primers

The key to good wallpaper adhesion is the proper condition of wall surfaces. If you start with a perfectly clean, painted wall, you're likely to get good results with any prepasted wallpaper. However, you're *guaranteed* to get good results if you first apply an acrylic wallpaper primer/sealer to the wall. A primer/sealer not only promotes adhesion but also makes it easier to strip the paper off when you get tired of it or when the next owner prefers another wall finish. Primer/sealer makes it easier to position the wallpaper without stretching it, and that means fewer seams opening up when the paper dries.

If you're papering over new drywall, applying a coat of primer/sealer is a must. If you don't start with a primer/sealer, which soaks into and seals the paper surface of the drywall, you'll never be able to remove the wallpaper without doing serious damage to the drywall. If your walls have ink, lipstick, crayon, nicotine, or other stains on them, seal the stains or they will bleed through both the primer/sealer and the wallpaper itself. For this task, you need an acrylic pigmented stain-killing primer/sealer. However, stain-killers are not wallpapering primer/sealers, so you must follow up with a primer/sealer made for wallcoverings.

Acrylic all-surface wallcovering primer/sealer goes on white but dries clear. *Pigmented acrylic all-surface wallcovering primer/sealer* is more expensive than the clear stuff, but it helps cover dark or patterned surfaces and helps prevent the color or pattern from showing through the paper. It's a good idea to tint a primer to the approximate color and shade of the wallpaper background so that the wall color doesn't show as much if the seams open slightly. Both primers perform equally well on porous and nonporous surfaces.

A coat of wallcovering primer/sealer takes two to four hours to dry, so paint it the day before papering or at least a few hours before you hang the paper. Be sure to read the instructions from the wallcovering and paste manufacturer and consult your wallpaper dealer regarding priming/sealing requirements for your project.

Next, dust and clean the walls and woodwork. Remove any fuzzy-wuzzies and cobwebs from corners and, if the woodwork is dirty or greasy, wash it with a phosphate-free household cleaner according to the directions. Avoid using cleaners that contain phosphates such as TSP (trisodium phosphate); they're bad for the environment and leave a residue on walls that prevents primer/sealers from bonding properly.

If you see any mildew, eliminate the source of the problem, such as moisture within a wall or a lack of proper ventilation. Then kill the mildew spores and remove the stain. To do this, use a solution of one part household bleach and three parts water with a little nonphosphate cleaner or detergent. Sponge or spray-mist the stains with the solution and let it sit for at least 15 minutes. Bleach is not good for painted surfaces, so after it has done the deed on the mildew, stop the bleaching action by rinsing well with a neutralizer, such as clean water or a vinegar-and-water solution. Repeat the bleaching and neutralizing processes, if necessary, until the stain is gone.

Never mix bleach with ammonia; it produces a lethal gas.

Remove other stains the best you can and seal any that remain by following the advice in the sidebar "A primer on primers."

If you're planning to paint the woodwork in the room to match the new wall-covering, or if your ceiling could stand a fresh coat of paint, paint before you hang. Then you don't have to be so concerned about protecting the walls or spend so much time carefully cutting in. In addition, getting wallpaper adhesive off a painted surface is no problem, but removing paint spatters or drips from wallpaper can be tough.

Preparing Wall Surfaces

You can apply wallpaper successfully to a variety of surfaces if you take the necessary steps to prepare the surface. You want smooth walls without any holes, cracks, popped nails, or other bumps that would show through the paper. In addition to following the surface preparation work described in that chapter, you need to be aware of some special preparation considerations for wallpaper.

In most cases, you apply wallpaper over painted drywall or plaster walls or over existing wallpaper on these same surfaces. But occasionally, you may want to apply wallpaper over problem surfaces, such as plywood, metal, prefinished paneling, concrete block, and ceramic tile. If you want to install wallpaper on these surfaces, we suggest that you get detailed instructions from your wallpaper dealer. In some cases, the task calls for hanging a liner paper to level the playing field. In other cases, covering the surface with drywall may be easier.

Book III

Painting and Wall-papering

Smoothing painted walls

To guarantee good wallpaper bond and future removability, coat all painted walls with an acrylic wallpaper primer/sealer (see the sidebar "A primer on primers," earlier in this chapter). Use 80- to 100-grit sandpaper to machine-sand oil-painted and glossy surfaces before sealing them, but be careful to not sand into the drywall paper covering. If you do, it gets fuzzy. If latex paint comes off when you rub it with a wet cloth, it is of poor quality, and you should use the pigmented variety. You must either machine-sand painted walls until they're smooth or have them professionally skim-coated with joint compound and then prime them.

Sealing new drywall before papering

New drywall (including patched areas on existing walls) must be well sealed before you hang wallpaper over it. Apply a coat of oil or latex drywall primer/sealer and then follow up with a pigmented wallpaper primer/sealer (see the sidebar, "A primer on primers," earlier in this chapter).

Removing Wallpaper

If you want to feel a sense of power, stand in a large room with the world's ugliest wallpaper and imagine that you can change the destiny of that room. (Dynamite is not an option.) In a perfect world, you could gently pull at a loose seam and the old paper would miraculously peel off the wall, leaving no residue or adhesive — just a nice, clean surface.

In the real world, that scenario is very unlikely. But you don't have to dread the task of removing wallpaper. Although taking down wallpaper isn't fun, it's a good example of grunt work that any do-it-yourselfer can accomplish. The downside is that it's a messy and time-consuming job.

Knowing what you're up against

Before you can determine the best approach, you need to know the type of wallcovering and the type of wall surface that's under the wallpaper. In most cases, walls are either drywall (gypsum sandwiched between layers of paper) or plaster smoothed over lath (either strips of wood or metal mesh). You can usually tell what you have by the feel (plaster is harder, colder, and smoother than drywall) or by tapping on it (drywall sounds hollow, and plaster doesn't). When in doubt, remove an outlet cover to see the exposed edges.

Remember that drywall is more vulnerable to water damage; you must avoid overwetting it. And use care when you're scraping because drywall gouges more easily than plaster.

What about the wallpaper? Be optimistic — assume that the paper is dry-strippable. Lift a corner of the paper from the wall with a putty knife. Grasp the paper with both hands and slowly attempt to peel it back at a very low angle. If it all peels off, you're home free.

If the wallpaper doesn't peel off, or if only the decorative surface layer peels off, you must saturate the wallpaper or the remaining backing with water and wallpaper remover solvent and then scrape it off.

Some papers, such as foils or those coated with a vinyl or acrylic finish, are not porous. If you're removing such wallpapers, you must scratch, perforate, or roughen the entire surface to permit the solution to penetrate below the nonporous surface to the adhesive layer (see "Choosing a removal technique," later in this chapter). You can test for porosity by spraying a small area with hot water and wallpaper remover. If the paper is porous, you should see the paper absorb the water immediately. After the paper is wetted, you can scrape it off.

Now that you know what you're dealing with, you can choose an appropriate removal technique for the entire surface. Depending on your situation, choose one of three wallpaper-removal approaches: dry-stripping, wallpaper remover, or steam. Read the how-to for each approach later in this chapter in the section "Choosing a removal technique."

Preparing for the mess

All wallpaper removal approaches are messy, so take the necessary precautions to protect your floors. For all removals except dry-stripping, we recommend that you lay down a 3-foot-wide waterproof barrier around the perimeter of the room.

You may find pretaped plastic drop cloths, such as adhesive polyethylene sheeting, convenient and reliable. To prevent the watery mess from getting on your floor, tape the plastic to the top edge of the baseboard or, even better, to the wall just above the baseboard, which prevents water from seeping behind the trim. (You can remove the tape when working on the bottom inch of the wall.) Cover the outer 2 feet of plastic with canvas drop cloths or a few old absorbent towels in the area where you're working. Be careful where you step; the plastic sheeting is slippery.

Water will probably end up dripping down the walls and under your feet. For that reason, you need to tape over switch and receptacle covers or shut off the circuit breaker at the electric panel. Use an extension cord to bring power from another room for work lights and for the steamer, if you choose to go that route.

Tape down two layers of plastic on the floor. That way, you can roll up the top layer with all the paper goo, and the second layer will protect the floor while you sponge the adhesive residue off the wall. Also, keep plenty of old dry towels or rags around to mop up in case (or should we say *when*) your protective measures fail.

Gathering tools and supplies for removing wallpaper

You need only a few basic tools and supplies for wallpaper removal. The following list describes the various tools that are available; see the following section for the specific tools you need based on the removal technique you plan to use.

- ✔ **Razor scraper:** This push-type wallpaper-scraping tool (about 3 to 4 inches wide) looks like a putty knife but has a slot for replaceable blades so that you always have a sharp edge.

- ✔ **Paper scraper:** This nifty gadget can scrape and perforate wallpaper applied on drywall. It has a round, knoblike handle attached to a scraping blade that cuts the paper. Solvents or steam can then penetrate to the adhesive layer but can't damage the drywall's paper facing.

- ✔ **Wallpaper remover:** Although warm water may do the trick (and is certainly priced right), you can turn to commercial wallpaper removal solvents if you need to.

- ✔ **Spray bottle or paint roller:** Use one or both of these tools to get the water/remover solution onto the wall.

- ✔ **Wallpaper steamer:** Rent one (or buy a do-it-yourself model if you've just bought a fixer-upper!) to steam the wallpaper off of your walls.

- ✔ **Plastic and canvas drop cloths:** You need both types to adequately protect your floors from the watery mess.

- ✔ **Wide masking tape:** Tape the plastic drop cloths to the base molding to avoid ruining your floors.

- ✔ **Water bucket, towels, rags, and wall sponges:** After removing the old wallpaper, wash down the walls well.

Choosing a removal technique

The technique you use for removing the old wallpaper depends on what kind of paper you're taking down and what kind of surface is underneath (refer to "Knowing what you're up against," earlier in this chapter). The following sections outline the steps involved in the different approaches.

Dry-stripping

If a wallpaper is dry-strippable, you just need to loosen each strip at the corners with a putty knife and slowly peel it back at a 10- to 15-degree angle, as shown in Figure 5-1.

Book III

Painting and Wallpapering

Figure 5-1:
Starting from a corner, pull off strippable and peelable papers at a very low angle.

Don't pull the wallpaper straight out or you may damage the underlying surface, especially if it's drywall.

After you remove all the paper, follow the adhesive removal procedures the next section describes. If only the top, decorative layer peels off, leaving a paper backing behind, it's a peelable paper. Dry-strip the entire top layer and then follow the steps in the next section to take off the backing and adhesive.

If you plan to repaper and the old backing is secure and in good condition, you may be able to hang the new wallcovering right on top of it. Discuss this option with your wallpaper dealer.

Soaking and scraping it off

To remove nonstrippable paper or any paper backing that remains after dry-stripping a peelable paper's decorative layer, turn first to warm water and wallpaper removal solvent. Soak the surface with a wallpaper remover solution. Although a spray bottle works, the most effective way to get the solution on the wall and not all over the floor is to use a paint roller or a spray bottle. Then scrape the sodden paper off with a wide taping knife or a wallpaper scraper.

Don't wet a larger area than you can scrape off within about 15 minutes. You shouldn't let water soak into drywall for longer than that, or it may cause unnecessary damage. Usually, you can wet about a 3-foot-wide, floor-to-ceiling section at a time.

Scrape off the wet wallpaper and let it fall to the floor. The canvas drop cloth or towels that you put down absorbs most of the dripping solution and keeps your shoe soles a little cleaner.

If the wallpaper is nonporous, you must roughen or perforate the surface so that the remover solution can penetrate and dissolve the adhesive. To roughen the surface, use coarse sandpaper on either a pad sander or a hand-sanding block. You can also use a neat gizmo called a Paper Tiger or another perforating tool devised for use on wallpaper applied over drywall. Rounded edges on these tools help ensure that you don't cause damage that may require subsequent repair. Don't use the scraper after the wallpaper is wet, though; you may damage the drywall.

If you're successful in using the soak-and-scrape approach, skip to the "Winding up" section. If not, it's time to pull out the big gun: a wallpaper steamer.

Giving it a steam bath

You're talking major work if you must remove more than one layer of wallpaper or remove wallpaper that has been painted over. And if the wallpaper was not applied to a properly sealed surface, removing it without damaging the wall can be next to impossible. For these tough jobs, you may have to rent a wallpaper steamer (about $15 for a half-day) or buy a do-it-yourself model (about $50). A wallpaper steamer is a hotplate attached to a hose extending from a hot water reservoir that heats the water and directs steam to the hotplate, as shown in Figure 5-2.

Figure 5-2:
Use a wallpaper steamer to steam and scrape away old paper.

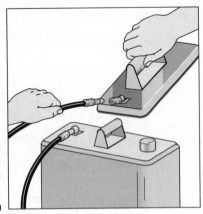

Although you can use a steamer and wallpaper scraper with relative confidence on plaster walls, use caution on drywall, which is much more vulnerable to water damage and is more easily gouged.

Before you start steaming, prepare the room (refer to "Preparing for the mess" earlier in this chapter) to protect the floor. Fill the steamer with water and let it heat up.

Keep a baking pan handy to put the hotplate in when you're not using it.

Starting at the top of the wall, hold the hotplate against the wall in one area until the wallpaper softens. Move the hotplate to an adjacent area as you scrape the softened wallpaper with a wallpaper razor scraper and let it fall onto the plastic as described in the preceding section. When you're through scraping one area, the steamer usually has softened the next area, depending on the porosity of the paper.

Both steam and the water that condenses from it can drip off the hotplate and burn you. To prevent hot water from dripping down your arm, stand on a stepstool when you're working above chest height. Wear rubber gloves and a long-sleeved shirt, too.

Winding up

After you remove all the wallpaper and any backing, the walls are usually still quite a mess, with bits of backing and adhesive residue still clinging to them. Wash off any remaining adhesive residue with remover solution or with a nonphosphate cleaner in water, using a large sponge or sponge mop. You can use an abrasive pad or steel wool on plaster, but use caution on drywall. Avoid overwetting or abrading the paper facing.

Rinse your sponge often in a separate bucket of water, squeeze it out, and rewet it in the removal or cleaning solution. Continue washing this way until the walls are clean.

When the walls are completely dry, make any necessary repairs and do surface preparation work as we describe in the section "Preparing Wall Surfaces," earlier in this chapter.

Book III

Painting and Wall-papering

Chapter 6

Hanging Wallpaper

· ·

· ·

Hanging wallpaper is usually a relatively simple process. Just follow the steps — measure, cut, apply paste (or activate prepasted wallcoverings), and smooth it on the surface. It's also a Dummies-approved project for first-timers, provided that you start with relatively simple projects and standard papers. (For more on choosing wallcoverings and factors that may complicate wallpapering, see Chapters 4 and 5.)

If you're hanging wallpaper for the first time, start in a bedroom and tackle a kitchen or bath when you have more experience. You say that a kitchen or a bathroom is the only room that you want to paper? Then by all means start there, but be prepared for a challenging job.

Plan Before You Hang

A famous baseball player once claimed, "Ninety percent of this game is half-mental." We're not sure about his math skills, but we are sure that two of the most important parts of wallpapering are half-mental — visualizing exactly where you want your seams to fall and then determining where to hang the first strip (called a *drop*).

Locating seams

To avoid unpleasant surprises that result from poor seam placement or having patterns cut off in awkward places, plan before you start hanging wallpaper. Take a few minutes to evaluate the room to determine where you want each seam to fall and where the patterns will begin relative to the ceiling or the corners of a room. Ask yourself:

- ✔ **Which is the dominant wall?** That wall is your showpiece and the one that your guests look at most closely. Plan to lay seams where they'll be the least noticeable. Although seam planning should start on the dominant wall, it's not the place you want to start papering.

- ✔ **How are windows, doors, or focal points (such as a fireplace) spaced on the wall?** Try to minimize the impact that any one special feature has on the wallpaper layout. For example, if the wall has two windows, a symmetrical approach works best. Simply start by centering a seam or strip on the wall between the two windows and work your way out to the corners.

- ✔ **Where do you want the kill point?** The *kill point* is the final seam. Because you'll be working around to the kill point from two directions, you need to cut one or both of the last two strips to fit the remaining unpapered space. This means that the pattern probably won't match at the final seam. A good inconspicuous place for the kill point is usually anywhere over an entry door, where the eye isn't usually drawn. The vertical mismatch is limited to about a foot.

- ✔ **Are the ceilings and walls reasonably level and plumb?** Ceilings that aren't level and walls that aren't plumb present a problem when you're wallpapering. Because the patterns on the paper are truly horizontal and vertical, they make out-of-whack walls and ceilings even more noticeable.

- ✔ **Does the wallpaper pattern create a special need?** With a large pattern, cutting the paper vertically at a corner of a room may cause a noticeable break in the pattern. To overcome that problem, start working from the center of the wall or from another spot.

In cases where precise placement of seams is important, you must know the *expanded width* of the paper. Most papers expand a percent or two — as much as an inch — after the paste is wetted or applied, while some papers don't expand at all. Paste and book a foot-long, full-width cutoff for the specified time. (To find out how to do this, you have to read ahead in this chapter to "Pasting the wallpaper — and relaxing with a good book.") Then measure the width and use that figure, not the dry width, for laying out your seams.

Working around unlevel ceilings and out-of-plumb walls

If you have ceilings that are badly out-of-level, avoid a straight-across pattern (one in which the pattern placement is the same distance from the ceiling for every strip), which would emphasize the out-of-level ceiling. Instead, consider a vertical pattern, such as stripes, or *drop-match* pattern (one where every other strip starts with the same pattern). The larger the drop, the less evident any horizontal pattern elements are. Similarly, if you have out-of-plumb walls, avoid vertical patterns because a vertical pattern may start on one wall and cross over to the other at inside and outside corners.

You may be able to further minimize such problems, at least on the most noticeable wall, by adjusting the position of the paper to avoid having pattern elements close to the edges of ceilings or outside corners. The more space that you have between your design elements, such as sheep, the easier it is to adjust the position so that the sheep don't lose their heads.

No hard-and-fast rule exists about pattern placement. Do whatever you think looks best in the most noticeable areas. Follow a truly plumb guideline or one that's not plumb but perpendicular to the ceiling, described in the following section, "Finding a starting point." You can even compromise between the two guidelines.

Sometimes, evaluating a situation and imagining the results are very difficult. Undoubtedly, pattern placement is one area where experience pays and when a professional installer earns his money.

Finding a starting point

If you plan seam placement, then start wallpapering wherever you want, with one exception — avoid starting with either of the two strips that lie on either side of the final seam (the kill point). You want these two drops to be the last ones you do because both drops may have to be cut simultaneously, which requires that they both be wet enough to peel back and reposition.

Keep in mind, however, that it's usually easier for a right-handed individual to work counterclockwise around a room and a left-handed person to work clockwise.

Wherever you start, don't rely on a corner of the wall or the edge of a door and window trim to guide the first piece. Instead, use a plumb and chalk line (or a carpenter's level and pencil) to create a straight, vertical (plumb) guideline (see Figure 6-1). Position the plumb or level at the desired location. Install the first drop about ⅛ inch from the guideline.

If an out-of-level ceiling calls for it, you can establish an out-of-plumb vertical guideline by taking the following steps and checking out Figure 6-1:

1. **Measure about 4 feet down from the ceiling at each corner and snap a chalk line between the two points.**

2. **Use a framing square (or any object that you know has a square corner, such as a plywood scrap) to draw a line perpendicular to the chalk line.**

3. **Extend the out-of-plumb line by using a pencil and a straightedge until the line runs from floor to ceiling.**

Book III

Painting and Wall-papering

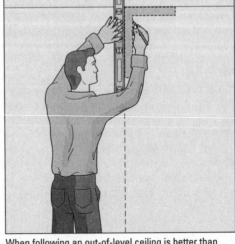

If ceilings are fairly level, use a plumb and a chalk line to establish a plumb line.

When following an out-of-level ceiling is better than hanging paper plumb, make a guideline that is perpendicular to the ceiling.

At Last You're Ready to Paper

With the planning complete and your first guideline established, it's time to hang the paper. Well, almost time. First, make sure that your spouse is out of the house (or at least make arrangements to minimize household traffic) and that your tools, work area, and hands are all as clean as a whistle. Then reverse-roll every roll of wallcovering.

To *reverse-roll,* place a roll in an empty water box or cardboard box positioned on the floor at the end of your cutting table. Draw one end up onto and down the length of the table, pattern side up. (You may have to flip the roll end-for-end in the tray to make this possible.) Then reroll the paper so that the pattern faces in. After it's fully rolled, roll the entire roll back and forth under the pressure of outstretched hands. Then unroll the entire roll in back-and-forth folds at the base of the table so that the top end of the pattern is on the top of the pile. Now, you're ready to cut.

Reverse-rolling enables you to inspect every roll for imperfections and lessens the paper's tendency to curl or roll up during the soaking or pasting process. If you find flaws, you have two options: You can return the roll immediately (you can't return a cut roll), or you can keep it if you determine that you have enough paper to cut out the defect.

Cutting strips of wallpaper

Cutting wallpaper involves two steps: First, you rough-cut the wallpaper and then trim the wallpaper in place for a precise fit.

When you rough-cut, first draw the paper, design side up, onto your table. Then cut a strip to size with a pair of large scissors. Always pull the top of the strip up to the same end of the table for cutting and leave a 2- to 3-inch allowance at the top and bottom of each strip. Keep these other points in mind, too:

- ✔ **For papers without a vertical pattern repeat, such as woven coverings and those with vertical stripes, or for papers with a vertical repeat of less than 3 inches,** just measure the height of the wall and add about 5 inches (total) for top and bottom allowances. For example, cut 101-inch strips for a 96-inch wall.

  When installing every other strip upside down is called for (such as for grasscloths and other woven wallcoverings), clip the upper-right corner of every top as you cut it so that you know which way is up (or down) when you hang it.

- ✔ **For papers with a vertical pattern repeat of more than 3 inches,** place the paper on the floor at the base of the wall and, while holding the paper against the wall, carefully pull up enough paper to reach the ceiling. Move the paper up and down to adjust the position of the most dominant pattern, such as the largest flowers in a floral pattern. Then mark the paper at the intersection of the ceiling. Take it down for cutting. First, cut the top 2 to 3 inches above your mark. Then measure and cut the bottom so that the full strip is 5 to 6 inches longer than the height of the wall.

  If the vertical pattern repeat is more than 3 inches, always use the pattern as your guide instead of just cutting a measured amount from the end of the roll. You'll be less likely to make errors or generate unnecessary waste.

- ✔ **For a straight-across pattern** (one in which the pattern placement is the same distance from the ceiling for every strip), cut all full-length strips so that they're identical to the first — that is, the same length and always starting at the same point on the pattern.

- ✔ **For paper with a half-drop pattern** (see Chapter 4 for a description), every other strip (strips 1, 3, 5, and so on) are cut at one point on the pattern. To determine where to cut the alternating strips (strips 2, 4, 6, and so on), roll out the paper side by side with the first strip and align the patterns correctly, making sure that the top of the uncut paper extends above the top of the odd strip. Then mark and cut the top and bottom of the even strip in line with the odd strip. Measure and cut all future even-numbered strips from this point above the dominant pattern.

  When you're cutting alternating strips at different points on the pattern, as you do for drop patterns, keep the different strips that have been cut in separate piles, all oriented the same way.

Book III

Painting and Wallpapering

When Henry Ford wallpapered his house, you can bet that to maximize efficiency, he cut nearly all the full-length strips that he needed in advance. To minimize waste, he then would have used any shorter cutoffs above and below windows or above doors. But if *you* take this approach and cut the first one or two drops (strips) wrong, you've cut them *all* wrong. To avoid a scenario where you're wondering whether perhaps it would be cheaper to lower the ceiling than to buy new paper, we suggest a more cautious approach. Cut only the first two strips; use them to mark the next two as a pattern for future strips, but don't do any more cutting until you've hung the first two strips successfully. Even then, don't cut all the strips. Instead, do enough for one wall at a time.

Pasting the wallpaper — and relaxing with a good book

After you cut the first drop, it's time to activate the paste on a prepasted wallcovering or apply paste to an unpasted wallcovering. The procedures are generally quite straightforward, but be sure to follow the manufacturer's instructions for the particular wallcovering that you're hanging. For example, the instructions may tell you to gently fold over the paper (without creasing it) and let it relax for a time before you hang it — a process called *booking*.

During the time that wallpaper relaxes, it may expand as much as ½ inch or more. After the paper is hung and it dries on the wall, it tends to pull itself nice and tight on the wall, but the adhesive causes it to hold its expanded size. Booking the paper keeps the paper moist during this relaxing time.

The success of your project depends on the proper application of the right adhesive. For example, if you apply too much adhesive on grasscloth or fabric coverings, the paste seeps through the backing and onto the decorative surface. Too much adhesive can also cause excessive shrinking or slow drying, which can create mildew problems. Too thin and — you guessed it — it won't stick or the edges will curl. The backing of the wallcovering and the type of wall surface determine the type of adhesive you should use, how thick it needs to be, and how much you should apply, but you need to consider other factors, too.

Activating prepasted wallcoverings

The dry paste on the back of a prepasted wallcovering must be *activated* (liquefied) by soaking the wallcovering in water or by brushing on a prepaste activator, which is like a thinned wallpaper paste. If you're using a prepaste activator, follow the same procedure as described in the "Doing it the old-fashioned way" section, later in this chapter.

If you're using the water-soak method, follow the manufacturer's guidelines:

✔ **If the instructions say to go directly from bath to wall,** place the water box in position at the base of the wall. Submerge the loosely rolled strip in the water bath for the specified time and then hang it as described in the "Hanging the wallcovering" section, later in this chapter.

✔ **If the instructions say to book the wallcovering,** loosely fold the back-sides of the strip together so that the pasted sides are over each other as follows:

   1. Fold the bottom end to about one-half or two-thirds of the way up the paper.

   2. Fold the top down just to meet that point. Be careful not to crease the paper at the folds.

   3. With the pasted sides together, fold the strip in half or roll it up loosely and set it aside to relax for five to ten minutes, as suggested by the manufacturer.

The following tips help you lessen the chances of making an error when you hang the booked strip on the wall:

✔ Follow the same sequence and procedure every time you book and fold or roll a strip.

✔ When you book, fold, or roll a pasted strip, make sure that the end that will hang up to the ceiling is on the top of a fold or the outside of the roll.

✔ Lay a booked strip down to relax facing the same direction every time.

Doing it the old-fashioned way

Use a *standard* premixed wallpaper paste for unpasted wallcoverings unless the manufacturer (or dealer) recommends a *heavy-duty* paste for the particular wallcovering you've chosen. Then follow these steps:

1. **Lay one or more cut strips on your pasting table.**

   Make sure that all the strips are oriented in the same direction and that the pattern side is facing down.

2. **Position the top of the first strip at one end of the table and apply the paste to at least the top half of the paper.**

   Use a short-nap paint roller or pasting brush to spread the adhesive as uniformly and smoothly as possible.

3. **Book the top half of the strip by folding the pasted surfaces together.**

Book III

Painting and Wall-papering

4. **Slide the booked end down the table so that you can paste and book the rest of the strip.**

5. **Loosely fold or roll the booked strip if the manufacturer recommends resting time before hanging.**

Don't paste more than one strip at a time or one may dry prematurely while you're hanging another.

Hanging the wallcovering

To hang the drop, follow these steps:

1. **Grasp the top edge and peel open the fold that you made when booking the paper.**

   Leave the other half booked for the time being.

2. **With one hand on each edge a few inches down from the top, hold the drop in place on the wall.**

   Align the edge about ⅛ inch away from the vertical guideline and locate the top with the dominant pattern at the planned distance from the ceiling. This procedure automatically leaves a 2- to 3-inch allowance at the top and bottom.

   You don't want the edge right on the guideline because the chalk or pencil line may show through the seam. If the edge is not a uniform ⅛ inch from the guideline, peel the paper back as needed to reposition it; do the same to remove any large folds or air bubbles. Do not force badly misaligned paper into position by pushing it. Doing so stretches and may tear the paper and may also result in an open seam when the paper dries. If the paper needs only a slight adjustment, push carefully with two outstretched hands, or three if you have them.

3. **Smooth the upper half of the strip as shown in Figure 6-2.**

   Make your first strokes vertical ones, up and down, along the guideline. Then brush horizontally from the guideline toward the opposite side and finish with diagonal strokes.

4. **Grasp the bottom end and peel it apart until it hangs straight.**

   Smooth it as shown in Figure 6-2. (On subsequent strips, you'll work from the seam as you now work from the guideline.)

Continue with the remaining drops — paste-book-hang, paste-book-hang — one next to the other. As you get the "hang" of it, a helper can paste, book, and then relax while you hang.

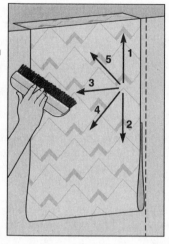
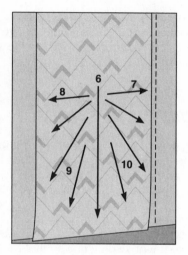

Figure 6-2:
Use a smoothing brush or plastic smoother to smooth the wall-covering onto the wall.

Trimming the paper

Trim the allowance at the ceiling and baseboard (see Figure 6-3) by using a breakaway razor knife guided by a metal straightedge, such as a taping knife or painter's trim guide. Change blades often to ensure that you're using only the sharpest blade, or you may tear the paper. Alternatively, you can crease the paper at the ceiling-wall corner, peel it back to cut along the crease with shears and then smooth it back onto the wall.

If your walls are drywall, paper reinforcing tape and joint compound cover this ceiling-wall joint. Use just enough pressure to cut the wallcovering in a single pass but not enough to cut into the drywall or the paper tape. Oddly enough, the sharper your knife is, the easier this will be.

Book III

Painting and Wall-papering

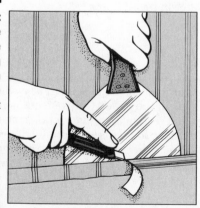

Figure 6-3:
Trim the allowance by using just enough pressure to cut through the wall-paper cleanly in a single stroke.

Before you move on to the next drop, remove any adhesive from the face of the wallcovering with a damp sponge. Wiping up wet paste is easier than getting it off after it dries. Also, wipe adhesive off the ceiling, baseboard, and other trim.

Smoothing seams

For a perfect seam, start with proper wall preparation (priming/sealing), proper choice and application of the adhesive, adequate booking/relaxing time, and proper hanging techniques. The seaming method you choose depends in part on the location — midwall or at the corners.

By far the most common type of midwall seam is the *butt seam,* where the two edges touch but don't overlap. As you hang each drop, position it right next to the preceding one so that the edges just touch. If you don't get it quite right, just peel it back as needed to reposition it. If the paper still needs a slight adjustment, push carefully with two outstretched hands. Do not force badly misaligned paper into position by pushing it. Overworking the paper stretches it, and when the paper returns to its normal expanded size, the seam will open. This is the numero uno cause of open seams. You may also tear the wallcovering.

Use a seam roller to seal the seam. Be firm but don't press so hard that you roll out all the adhesive. As you finish hanging each drop, always make a point to check the previous seam. If the edge has lifted, lightly reroll it. If it has pulled apart slightly, smooth the paper toward the seam or give it a little tap toward the seam with the smoothing brush.

At inside corners (and sometimes at badly out-of-plumb outside corners), use a *wrap-and-overlap seam,* in which one drop wraps the corner about ½ inch and the other drop overlaps the first drop and ends right in the corner. For details on how to make this seam, see the sections "Papering inside corners" and "Papering outside corners," later in this chapter.

Getting some relief

Anytime you turn a corner or paper around an obstacle, such as a window, you need to make what's called a *relief cut* in the paper. Only one cut is required at right angles. When papering around rectangular obstructions, such as electrical outlets, however, you need to make four cuts; one cut must originate from each corner, and the cuts should connect to form an X. You need to make many closely spaced relief cuts around a curve, such as an archway or the base of a round light fixture.

To make a relief cut, smooth the paper as close to the obstacle as possible. Then make the cut in place with a razor knife or crease the paper at the edge of the obstacle and peel it back to make the cut.

The following situations call for relief cuts:

- **Inside and outside wall corners:** Smooth the wallcovering up to the corner. Make a relief cut out from the corner. Start the cut precisely at the ceiling-wall-corner intersection and extend it to the edge of the paper. Then you can wrap the corner.

- **Electrical switch and receptacle boxes:** Paper over the outlet. Starting at each corner, make a diagonal cut so that all cuts connect to form an X. Then trim the flaps by making cuts from corner to corner around the perimeter.

  In the preparation stages for wallpapering (see Chapter 5), you should have shut the power off, removed cover plates, and taped over the face of the receptacles or switches. These steps are necessary to eliminate any electrical hazard associated with wet adhesive, cutting, and damp sponging around electrical outlets. These precautions also keep the devices adhesive-free. Otherwise, the next time that you plug in a lamp, you won't be able to unplug it.

- **Window and door trim:** Cut the paper, leaving a 2-inch allowance at the trim. Smooth the paper up to the side of the trim and crease it into the corner formed by the trim and the wall. Make a diagonal relief cut starting precisely at the 90-degree corner of the trim and extending out to the edge of the paper. You can then smooth the paper over the window and door. After you smooth the paper and roll the seam, trim the flaps with a razor knife and straightedge as described in the "Trimming the paper" section, earlier in this chapter (see Figure 6-4).

  Book III

  Painting and Wallpapering

- **Round or curved obstacles:** Smooth the paper up to the closest edge of the obstacle and make a relief cut up to that edge. Smooth a little more and make one relief cut on each side of the first cut. Continue smoothing and cutting.

- **Handrail or pipe:** Assuming that you can't simply remove an obstacle that you can't go around, such as a handrail or a pipe penetrating a wall, you must make a single cut from the obstacle to the nearest edge of the paper. Then you can proceed with the multiple relief cuts as described for round or curved obstacles. As you complete the circle, smooth and seam the long cut as you would any butt seam. (Refer to the section "Smoothing seams," earlier in this chapter.)

  Sometimes, the pattern itself suggests where a cut can be least conspicuously located — along the stem of a flower or the edge of a line in a geometric pattern, for example.

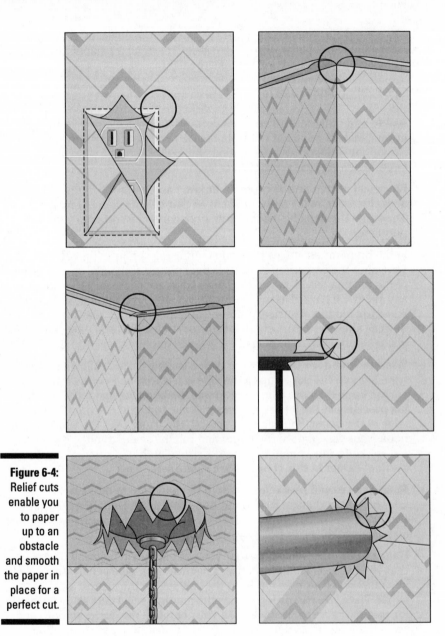

Figure 6-4:
Relief cuts
enable you
to paper
up to an
obstacle
and smooth
the paper in
place for a
perfect cut.

Papering inside corners

Never wrap wallpaper more than ½ inch around an inside corner with a drop. Even if the walls are perfectly plumb, the paper will pull away from the corner as it dries, making it vulnerable to tearing or wrinkling. Instead, make a wrap-and-overlap seam. Use the wrap-and-overlap seam for out-of-plumb outside corners, too, as shown in Figure 6-5 and in the following steps:

Figure 6-5:
Use a wrap-and-overlap seam at inside and out-of-plumb outside corners.

Book III

Painting and Wall-papering

1. **As you reach the last strip before a corner, measure and cut the strip lengthwise so that it will wrap the corner about ½ inch.**

2. **Hang the strip but peel it back from the corner a few inches.**

3. **Using a vertical guideline that's about ⅛ inch farther from the corner than the narrowest width of the cutoff, apply the next drop on the adjacent wall, allowing it to wrap the corner.**

4. **After you smooth the second drop into place, trim it at the corner with a breakaway razor knife guided by a metal straightedge.**

5. **Toss the trimmed paper and peel the paper back from the corner enough to enable you to reposition the first drop.**

6. **With the first drop wrapping the corner and smoothed into place, smooth the second drop over the first.**

   Smooth the paper with a side-arm seam roller, which has no frame on one side of the roller so that you can get into corners with it.

Papering outside corners

Outside corners present two problems. First, because they physically stand out, people often brush against or bang into them. And second, because outside corners stand out in the sense that they're eye-catching, you want things in such a position to look as nice as possible. For these reasons, avoid placing a seam right at the corner where it may be brushed apart or may be more noticeable.

If the corner is perfectly plumb, you can just round it. If it's out-of-plumb, you can use the wrap-and-overlap technique as described in the preceding "Papering inside corners" section, but with two differences. First, instead of wrapping the first drop about ½ inch (Step 1), wrap the corner at least 3 inches to ensure that it stays put. Second, instead of having the second drop end right at the corner (Step 4), measure, cut, and position it so that it stops about ¼ inch shy of the corner. (See Figure 6-5.) Both cuts are located by measurement and made on the cutting table, not in place.

Making cuts along the length of wallpaper is usually done with a special (read: expensive) 6-foot-long magnesium-alloy straightedge. As a substitute, you can use a 4-inch-wide strip of ¼-inch plywood. If you don't own a table saw, ask your lumber store to cut the plywood for you.

Cutting wallcovering dulls blades really quickly. Snap off dull blades on a breakaway razor or change blades often on another type of cutter.

Applying the final strip

As you close in on the kill point — the location you planned for the final seam (see "Locating seams" at the beginning of this chapter) — stop when you've done all but the drop on either side of the last seam. At that point, the unpapered gap on the wall measures something less than the width of two rolls. When applied, therefore, one drop will overlap the other, and you must double-cut to make the final seam. Plan this cut at a location where the pattern mismatch will be the least noticeable. For example, if there's open background on both drops at any point where they overlap, make the cut there, as shown in Figure 6-6.

Planning this double-cut is easier when the paper is dry. Place two strips on your worktable so that, together, the width is equal to the width of the unpapered wall area. Tape them in position with a low-tack (easy-to-remove) tape, such as painter's masking tape. Then lift and reposition the top layer so that you can locate the best place for a seam. Mark or measure the location and make the cut after you hang both strips.

Figure 6-6:
Use the double-cut method to make the final seam.

A. Overlap the first drop and cut through both pieces using a knife guided by a metal straightedge or level.

B. Peel off the cut-away pieces of both drops.

C. Gently but firmly seal the seam with a seam roller.

Quick Fixes for Wallpaper

Two of the most typical repairs for wallpaper are fixing seams that lift off the wall and pull away and patching torn or stained areas. The fixes are surprisingly easy — after you know how.

Loosey-goosey seams

To reglue the edges of wallpaper that have pulled away from the wall, use wallcovering *seam sealer*. It comes in a small, squeezable tube with an applicator at the tip, so it's easy to apply. The best part is that the sealer dries clear, leaving no telltale signs of the repair work.

Work through these simple steps to bond those loose edges of wallpaper:

1. **Gently peel back the loose wallpaper without stretching or tearing it.**

2. **Sponge to soften the old glue with a clean wet rag.**

   Wipe away as much of the old paste as you can reach on the back of the paper and the wall.

3. **Carefully put the nozzle of the opened tube of seam sealer behind the paper and squeeze the seam sealer onto the wall.**

4. **Gently smooth the edge of the wallpaper against the wall, removing any excess sealer with a damp rag or sponge.**

   Hold the paper carefully and firmly in place for several seconds.

5. **Seal the edges with a seam roller to apply *light* pressure.**

   If more sealer oozes out of the seam, wipe it with a damp rag or sponge.

Repairing a tear or stained area

Things may look bad, but you can easily patch a torn or stained area of wallpaper — easily, that is, if you have extra wallpaper to cut a patch the size of the damaged area. For a problem area — larger than about a foot square — you're better off replacing the whole strip (which we talk about in Chapter 5).

For small patches or stains, begin by assessing the pattern and how it relates to the damaged area so that you can cut a patch piece that will blend in. Follow these steps, which are illustrated in Figure 6-7, to correct the damage:

1. **To make a patch piece, unroll a piece of matching wallpaper on a flat surface and cut an area large enough to cover the damage.**

2. **Hold the patch piece over the damaged area and secure it with masking tape or drafting tape, which doesn't stick as tightly as other tapes.**

   Carefully align the pattern on the patch with the damaged area.

3. **Use a razor to cut through both the patch piece and the paper underneath.**

   It's important to cut through both layers in a single pass for a clean cut with sharp edges.

4. **Untape the patch piece, remove the damaged wallpaper, and clean the area so that it's free of old wallpaper paste.**

   Check out Chapter 5 for tips on doing so.

5. **Coat the back of the patch with wallcovering adhesive (or seam sealer for a small patch) and position it carefully.**

6. **Hold the patch in place until it feels secure and then use a damp sponge to smooth the paper and wipe away any excess adhesive.**

7. **Seal the edges of the patch with a seam roller.**

   Roll it gently so that you don't squeeze out the adhesive or seam sealer. When the patch dries, you won't be able to find it.

A. Cover the damaged area with a
large scrap of wallpaper, lining
up the patterns, and affix it with
drafter's tape. (Steps 1 and 2)

B. Cut around the damage with a razor
cutter, pressing through both sheets.
(Step 3)

Figure 6-7:
Patching
damaged
wallpaper
is easy.

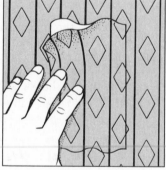

C. Remove the damaged piece, and
replace it with the new cutout.
(Steps 4 to 7)

Border Incidents

We don't know of a faster way to change the look of a room than to add a
wallpaper border. You can use borders in all kinds of ways. Apply a border at
the ceiling, as a chair rail, or as a detail around windows or doors. Wherever
you hang a border, it's sure to enhance the room. And talk about easy.

Sizewise, a border can be a few inches or a foot wide, and the patterns and
styles are almost as bountiful as those of wallcoverings. You'll find them
coordinated with wallcoverings and fabrics, but you can also find a huge

variety of patterns just waiting to bring a splash of color and pizzazz to plain walls. Most are prepasted and strippable and sold in rolls of 5 or 7 yards in length.

Here's how to determine how many spools you need:

1. **Measure the length of the area you intend to border.**

2. **To determine the number of spools without a waste factor, divide that figure by the length of the spool you're buying.**

3. **Add about ½ yard for every spool to allow for matching and an additional ½ yard for every corner or miter, such as when you border windows.**

You can apply a border to any painted wall or on top of wallpaper that has been up for at least two days. Generally, borders look best on neutral backgrounds, but many patterned papers have borders with coordinating colors or patterns.

In a small room, a border at the ceiling level makes the space look larger. But don't assume that a border has to go at the ceiling-to-wall joint, which can be rough. For a different look, you can place a border a couple of inches below the ceiling. Placed at chair-rail height (24 to 36 inches from the floor), a border tends to make a room look smaller because it divides the walls. If you have a really large room, though, that may be just the effect that you're looking for.

Making your borders straight as an arrow

Even some newly built homes have walls and ceilings that are not *true* (level, plumb, and square), but you can establish a horizontal guideline with a carpenter's level and measuring tape to act as a guide for hanging a wallpaper border.

To establish a level line below the ceiling, use a measuring tape and a carpenter's level to establish guidelines on the walls around the room as follows:

1. **Use masking tape as an experiment to help decide where you want to position the border.**

   Affix the tape lightly at different heights to see the different effects the border will have on the room.

2. **After you decide where you want the border, mark the location on one wall at a corner.**

Measure down from the ceiling or up from the floor — whichever is shorter.

3. **Hold the level flat against the wall at the point you marked and adjust the level until the bubble is centered.**

4. **Draw a light pencil line on the wall at that mark.**

5. **Work your way around the room, using the level in the same manner to create a line on all the walls.**

Hanging borders

Before you hang the border, make sure that the walls are clean and remove electrical outlet covers if you're installing the border over them. Plan the job to begin and end in the least conspicuous point of the room so the joint of the two end pieces are less noticeable, which in many rooms is a corner behind a door.

To hang a border, follow these steps:

1. **Get the adhesive working by activating it.**

   Read the directions for prepasted borders, which usually involves soaking them in water.

2. **To hang a border that's not prepasted on painted walls, use a pre-mixed wallpaper adhesive.**

   For hanging a prepasted or non-prepasted border on top of a wallcovering, use a vinyl-to-vinyl adhesive for better adhesion. Apply with a wallpaper brush, paint roller, or clean paintbrush (foam or man-made bristle), spreading the adhesive on the back of the border. Make sure to coat it evenly, especially on the edges.

3. **Fold the wet pasted sides together accordion-style to keep the adhesive moist.**

   This is called *booking*.

4. **Carefully align the top or bottom edge of the border just on top of the guideline to conceal it, unfolding the booked strip as you work along the wall.**

5. **Gently but firmly, smooth the border onto the wall with a smoothing brush or a large, damp sponge.**

Book III

Painting and Wall-papering

6. **As you continue to hang the rolls of the border, butt the joints together so that they're smooth and evenly aligned.**

   If the pattern doesn't match exactly, overlap the new roll over the previous one until the pattern aligns. Then cut through both layers with a sharp razor, guided by a ruler or other metal straightedge. This process, called *double cutting,* ensures a perfect match every time. (Refer to Figure 6-6.) Then peel back the border to remove the cutoffs and press the ends back into place.

7. **When you get back to the point where you started, overlap the end of the border onto the beginning for cutting.**

   Peel it back and overlap it again as needed to find the least conspicuous spot to double-cut the border. Usually (but not always), you want to cut at a point where there is little to no pattern.

8. **Lightly roll any seams with a seam roller.**

Using corner miter cuts on borders

Use a *miter cut* — cutting two pieces at a 45-degree angle so that, when joined, they meet at a right angle — where a horizontal border joins a vertical one. A miter cut is a *double cut* because you cut two overlapping pieces at once. In an outside-corner miter cut, a border outlines a door or window; in an inside-corner miter cut, a border turns and runs up the side of a window or door. Follow these steps, as shown in Figure 6-8:

1. **Cut the horizontal border to extend at least a couple of inches beyond the corner of the window or door casing.**

   Don't press down firmly, because you will trim and peel back the border.

2. **Cut the vertical border and hold it so that it overlaps and covers the horizontal border, forming a small cross.**

   Cut both strips long so that you can match up the pattern by moving the vertical strip up and down or the horizontal strip back and forth. Although you can certainly get a perfect match on one side of a door, you just as certainly won't get a perfect match on the other side. As you move the one horizontal and two vertical pieces, you strike a compromise that looks best at both corners. Although borders are often placed up against the casing, no rule says that you must position them this way. You can also space the borders an equal distance from all sides of the casing.

3. **Use a taping knife or ruler to lay a straightedge on a diagonal line from the corner at the trim to the opposite corner.**

4. **With the straightedge to guide you, carefully cut through both layers of the border with a sharp razor.**

5. **Remove the bottom horizontal cutaway piece by lifting the vertical border and then carefully removing it.**

6. **Reapply the vertical border so that it forms a perfect mitered joint with the horizontal border.**

7. **Carefully press the two joining edges together and seal them with a seam roller.**

   The seam roller presses the edges tight against the wall.

8. **Let the joint dry and then use a damp sponge to lightly remove any adhesive that may have oozed out from the seam.**

A. Apply a horizontal border and lay a vertical border over it. (Steps 1 and 2)

B. Align a straight edge diagonally across the intersection. (Step 3)

C. Cut through both layers with a razor knife. (Step 4)

Book III

Painting and Wall-papering

Figure 6-8:
Use a double-cut miter cut for a border that outlines a window or door.

D. Remove the cut-away pieces and apply the vertical border. (Steps 5 and 6)

E. Seal the edges with a seam roller. (Step 7)

Book IV

Bathroom and Kitchen Remodeling

The 5th Wave

By Rich Tennant

@RICHTENNANT

"What if we put the solid granite Jacuzzi on the first floor?"

In this book . . .

We're a nation of countless bathrooms and kitchens on the brink of being torn apart, redesigned, and remodeled. You may be asking yourself, "Can I remodel without spending every penny I have, destroying the harmony of my household, and breaking the spirit of everyone involved?" The answer is yes, but it's a qualified yes that hinges on how you plan the project and prepare for the inconvenience.

This book tells you how to transform these important rooms from blah to beautiful. We explain how to manage the remodeling process, how to do certain jobs yourself, and when to hire a professional. We also guide you through the maze of decisions and options. Undoubtedly, you'll enjoy immediate payback and pleasure, but you'll also raise the resale value of your house. Even a modest bathroom or kitchen makeover adds value, but an honest-to-goodness remodel is an investment worth making.

Here are the contents of Book IV at a glance.

Chapter 1

An Overview of the Remodeling Process

In This Chapter

▶ Going through the stages of a remodeling project

▶ Mentally and physically gearing up for the work

All remodeling projects have key elements or processes, and knowing what they are prepares you for the adventure. That's a good way to look at remodeling. The experience consumes your life for a period of time, but when it's over, you've created a new and improved home and learned something along the way. Maybe you decide that you never want to do it again, but maybe it entices you to remodel another part of your house.

The old saying "a little knowledge goes a long way" certainly applies to a bathroom or kitchen remodeling project. You can't be too informed about what to expect and how to plan and carry out the work. Understanding the process is important because, although you can perform some phases of a job independently of the others, many depend on other tasks being completed first.

Think of these stages like dominos: They're all related. Every kitchen and bathroom is different, but we include just about every scenario we can imagine. Making a list of the elements of your own bathroom or kitchen — for example, what you're going to replace and anything you plan to reposition — helps you create a custom list of phases for your particular project. The more time you spend noodling the process, the less time you waste after you begin the actual remodeling.

Walking through the Stages of a Typical Remodeling Project

Remodeling any room involves a lot of individual processes and projects that you have to complete in sequential and workmanlike order. When you understand the process of remodeling, you're better prepared to know what to anticipate. From start to finish, the following sections give you a breakdown of the ten stages of remodeling a bathroom or kitchen.

Getting the permit

So you have your plan, got bids for the project, and selected a contractor or are confident that you can handle the project yourself. You're ready to roll. Stop! Don't even think about lifting a hammer until you have a building permit in hand. And don't contemplate doing the job without one, or some bright, sunny day (building inspectors don't go out in the rain), someone may knock on your door and ask to see the permit. If you think a building inspector can be cranky on a good day, just try to deal with one after you're caught red-handed without a permit.

Most building departments are helpful and can make suggestions to get the plan approved. If you're hiring a contractor to do the work, he deals with getting the permit, but you should insist on seeing it before the work starts. In most towns, you have to display the permit before the job gets underway.

Creating the work zone

When a bathroom or kitchen is the construction site, you must remove all furnishings and personal belongings so that work can proceed. Don't underestimate the time it takes to do this removal. You're going to be amazed at all the stuff you find stashed away behind the towels.

All construction creates dust, and now's the time to take preventive action. You may think that you won't notice drywall dust in your cornflakes, but you will — and the rest of the family will, too. You can contain most dust by taping heavy plastic dropcloths to the doors. Cut two plastic sheets several feet larger than the door opening. Tape the first to the top of the door molding and to the left jamb molding. Then tape the other sheet to the top and right molding. The overlap seals the door but enables you to enter the room. You can also find commercial door seals complete with zipper doors.

Don't forget to seal the furnace ducts, too — especially the cold air returns. The furnace blower can spread dust throughout the house if you don't seal the ducts carefully.

Finally, place a box fan in a window so that it blows air out of the work area. The fan creates negative pressure in the room and helps keep the dust at bay. The air moves into the room and carries the dust out the window. During the winter or a hot summer, you can run the fan during the worst of the demolition.

Tearing out the old stuff and taking it away

The size and scope of the project determine how much demolition you need. For a swap job that involves simply replacing fixtures, cabinetry, and flooring, you basically have to remove, replace, and redecorate. But if your project involves replacing windows, framing in a new door, bumping out a wall, or combining two rooms, the job can be much more complicated.

You may need a dumpster to haul away the old materials. This large box is delivered on the back of a truck and dropped in place. After it's full, the truck picks the box up and takes it to a landfill. Schedule a delivery date that gives you enough time to fill it up, but not so much time that the dumpster becomes a permanent fixture in the neighborhood. You can find companies that rent dumpsters listed in the Yellow Pages under "Rubbish & Garbage Removal." If you're having your regular trash collector remove materials, check to see whether you need to make special arrangements, pay a fee for pickup, or secure a permit to leave the container on the street if you can't store it on your property.

If you're enlarging a bathroom, obviously you must remove the adjacent walls. This step, of course, affects the room that shares the common wall with the bathroom. A closet that shares a common wall is a natural place to borrow space for a larger bathroom; if that's the case, you must empty the closet.

Removing cabinets and fixtures requires turning off and disrupting water and electrical services. Careful planning of this phase ensures that you have the utilities off for the shortest time possible. You can cap water lines temporarily as you remove fixtures and then easily turn the water back on. The same is true for electricity. Remove the electrical fixtures and install wire nuts on the ends of the wires and tape the ends. Push the wires back into the electrical boxes so that they're out of the way.

Book IV

Bathroom and Kitchen Remodeling

Let your family know as far in advance as possible when the water and electricity may be shut off. Everyone needs to know when they can't flush the toilet or how long the furnace won't be cranking out heat.

Framing and making structural changes

In this phase of the project, the bathroom or kitchen is empty, the walls and floor are pocked with holes, and the room is ugly. During this period, you or your contractor frame the new walls in to create the floor plan. You install rough framing outlining the new walls and build partitions around tubs and showers in a bathroom. Unless you're making major structural changes to the floor or other parts of the room, this phase of the project goes surprisingly fast. The old bathroom or kitchen begins to transform with the smell of lumber outlining new walls, windows, or skylights.

Laying out and roughing in plumbing lines and electrical wires

This phase changes the room with new plumbing supply lines for all the water fixtures (sink, toilet, shower, and tub). If you have to move the drain pipes to accommodate a new location for a fixture, you or your contractor may have to cut up the floor and then reinforce it after you install the piping.

The electrician arrives and *roughs in* (does all the behind-the-walls work) new electrical boxes for switches, outlets, light fixtures, venting, and heating and cooling lines. Then the electrician runs wiring to the boxes and back to the power panel but doesn't turn on the power just yet.

Getting code work approved

While the walls are still open and you can see the new plumbing and electrical rough-ins and the wall framing, local building inspectors must visit the work site and inspect the job. The inspector may require leak testing of the drainage system if you've made major alterations. Many jurisdictions require you to bring whatever you can access up to current code. If all the work meets the local building codes, the inspector approves the work, and the next phase of the project can begin. Any exterior walls must then be insulated and inspected. Until the inspection is complete, you can't close up the walls, so scheduling the inspection is key to keeping the remodel on schedule.

Finishing wall, ceiling, and floor surfaces

After the rough-in plumbing, electrical, and framing work passes code inspection, workers can close up the walls. They apply standard drywall in adjacent areas and moisture-resistant drywall (called *green board*) to interior bathroom walls. Waterproof cement board goes on tub and bath enclosures. Workers tape and finish the walls with several coats of drywall compound to conceal the joints between panels. This phase of the job produces a lot of dust, but the bathroom or kitchen is taking shape. Next, workers install the flooring and wall tile, paint, and add wallcoverings.

Setting fixtures and furnishings

The room begins to take on its new life when you put the fixtures in position. This process involves setting the toilet, tub, and shower in place and hooking up and testing plumbing lines. You may want to place large one-piece showers and whirlpools in the bathroom before you complete the wall framing. Carpentry work includes installing cabinetry, open or linen closet shelving, and any other built-in furnishings.

Finishing up the electrical and mechanical work

Workers hook up new receptacles and outlets, along with heating and cooling lines and lighting and venting systems. Everything is in place, so you should have a good idea what the room will look like when it's complete. Now's the time to go over the original plan and check that all the fixtures, lights, outlets, and heating and cooling ducts are in place and that nothing is damaged.

Start a notebook and write down any problems that you discover and the date. The building trades call this notebook a *punch list*. At this stage of the project, you need to meet with the builder and work through any problems.

Book IV

Bathroom and Kitchen Remodeling

Getting final code approval

The local building department makes a final inspection and signs off on the job. This sign-off usually comes in the form of an *occupancy certificate*. The inspector checks that you have installed the wiring correctly and that all the plumbing fixtures work. He notes any problems, which you have to correct before the inspector issues the final approval. Because the inspector has already been on the job for the initial inspection and knows that everyone is aware of the code requirements, this step is only a formality, in most cases.

Bracing Yourself for the Destruction

The kitchen or bathroom is only one room, but you'll be amazed at how much material goes into making it fully function as the room of your dreams. So where does all the stuff get stashed when it's delivered prior to installation? You guessed it — wherever you can find space in and around your house. Some folks feel that living around large boxes and building materials is the worst part of remodeling because those annoyances discombobulate daily life. But if you can mentally prepare yourself for being displaced for a while, it's not so bad.

Watching your house turn into a mini-warehouse

Any remodeling project creates stress. To make it go as smoothly as possible, think about the process and how it may affect family members. Also take into account that the house will become a mini-warehouse of materials to be used in the new room. This storage issue may not be much of a problem in a large home, but it can be a challenge in a smaller house that's already packed full.

Plan a staging area for the new materials. Make space for all the components of the new room. It's a good bet that they're delivered at different times, and often the first items to arrive will be the last things that you install, so be sure not to block access to anything. Most of the elements are large and bulky. Framing lumber, whirlpool tubs, and cabinets take up a lot of floor space, and you need to provide a clean, dry storage area. An enclosed garage offers the best protection; a porch or breezeway is another possible location. You should protect any wood products stored outside, such as flooring, from the rain and bring them inside for several days before installation to allow them to adjust to the indoor environment.

As materials and fixtures arrive, open the containers and check to see that what's delivered is what you ordered, that all the parts are included, and that the parts aren't damaged. Check fixtures for the correct color, style, and size. Make sure that the flooring is the correct style and amount, and check the wallcovering to see that it's the correct pattern and that all the rolls came from the same dye lot or run.

Making it easy on yourself

During any major remodeling project, the contractors you hire become part of your family, whether you like it or not. To make it as stress-free as possible, take preventive steps to prepare for the increased activity.

Decluttering

Get ready for the invasion — not of body snatchers, but of contractors, plumbers, carpenters, and electricians. Before they arrive and during the remodel, your house becomes an open door to tradespeople and inspectors, who are all focused on the kitchen or bath. They want to get in, do their job, and get out, so make it easy for them to do so. Unclutter the hall or area leading to the room by removing any furniture. Lay down a heavy-duty dropcloth to protect the floor or carpeting from foot traffic.

Creating a tool zone

Designate a space near the kitchen or bath where workers can put their tools or gear — or where you can store yours if you're doing the work yourself. Some workers store their tools in their truck, and others leave their large, heavy tools at the job site (your house). If you do the work, you want to designate a place *near* the room to keep your tools so that you don't clutter up the small confines of the work area.

Surrendering to dust

If you're hanging new wallboard, prepare for drywall dust — not just once, but several times as installers sand and then resand the seams. Even when contractors hang protective plastic sheeting at the door to seal off the rest of the house, the sanding produces clouds of fine dust throughout the house. Until workers paint or finish the walls, get used to a fine white haze that covers every conceivable surface of your house.

Purchase a shop vac that's designed to pick up dust and debris. A standard vacuum isn't designed to pick up this type of material. The fine dust eventually damages the motor, and the vacuum just spreads the dust around the house. Most shop vacs have an optional bag that fits over the standard filter that's designed to contain fine particles, such as drywall dust.

To prevent a nervous breakdown, take major cleaning chores off your schedule during remodeling. Admit that you can't contain the dirt and dust. Concentrate instead on keeping the job site clean, which reduces the possibility of accidents. This attitude also sends a message to the workers that you expect them to maintain a clean, professional work site.

Book IV

Bathroom and Kitchen Remodeling

Avoiding entertaining

Remodeling a bathroom or kitchen is stressful enough. Don't plan other major events while you're living through it. Unless you're Martha Stewart, don't think about entertaining or having a houseguest. If you wait until the room is remodeled, you can enjoy your guests *and* show off your new kitchen or bath.

Being there 24/7

You may be tempted to avoid the project and take off on a vacation during the remodel, but doing so is a bad idea. You gotta be there. First, someone has to be home to accept deliveries of materials, which come at different times before the project begins. Second, you have to be available in case a snafu occurs. Despite the best-laid plans, remodeling often involves on-the-spot decisions and improvisations. When a plumber discovers a water line that can't be rerouted, which affects the position of a sink, you have to be there to consider the options and make a decision. If you're not available 24/7, you can't expect the workers to make the right call for you.

Chapter 2

Installing Cabinets

In This Chapter

▶ Getting your tools together

▶ Figuring out where to put your cabinets

▶ Installing wall cabinets

▶ Fitting base cabinets to the wall

*C*abinets are expensive. You'll probably spend the biggest chunk of your remodeling budget on them, so you want to install them correctly.

Have your cabinet supplier assume the responsibility for measuring up your kitchen to determine the proper cabinets sizes and include in the order any prefinished *filler strips* that might be required. These narrow boards are installed between stock-size cabinets to make them fit a space, provide necessary clearance around appliances and sometimes to fill a gap between a cabinet that abuts a wall that is badly out of level.

Installing basic kitchen cabinets — those without a lot of prefinished molding — is a project that most intermediately skilled DIYers can handle. If you decide to tackle this project yourself, make sure that you allow yourself enough time — and don't rush through any of the steps. Rushing leads to mistakes, and mistakes lead to frustration and dissatisfaction. Remember, these cabinets may be in your home for many, many years. And if you're not happy with the installation or the cabinets' operation, you're reminded of your dissatisfaction every time you reach inside.

Plan your work schedule before you begin the installation. Set aside the better part of a weekend to install cabinets for a small kitchen and a week or more for a larger kitchen or more complex installation.

Gathering the Right Tools

Gather all the tools that you need before you start a project. You need them at various stages of the project; but it's better and faster to be able to walk (or send a helper) to your tool area and grab what you need to keep the job moving. If you're not familiar with a tool mentioned in this chapter, flip back to Chapter 2 in Book I for a quick review. Here's a list of the tools you need to install new cabinets:

- One 2-foot and one 4-foot level (the 2-footer is good for checking level and plumb in tight areas; use the 4-foot level for checking level and plumb and to determine the high point of your floor)

- Straight, 6- or 8-foot 2 x 4 (used with the level for checking the floor's level and high point)

- 8-foot 1 x 4 pine board (used as a ledger support board when installing wall cabinets)

- Chalk line

- Tape measure (25 foot minimum)

- Stud finder

- 6-foot stepladder (a 4- or 5-foot ladder works, but I prefer a 6-footer)

- Variety of clamps — squeeze, wooden screw, and spring clamps of various sizes

- $3/16$-inch-diameter countersink drill bit

- 3-inch #10 cabinet screws

- Several No. 2 Phillips screw bits

- $3/8$-inch drill/driver (corded or cordless)

- Hammer

- One or two packages of wood shims

- Jigsaw

- Heavy-duty extension cord for a corded drill or jigsaw (a 25-foot cord is best, especially if you need to draw power from another room)

Marking Reference Lines and Mounting Locations

Marking reference lines is the first and most crucial step in installing cabinets. If you don't have accurate reference lines, your cabinets likely become misaligned, which affects their operation and appearance.

Adding cabinets before flooring is the way to go

A lot of people ask, "Should I run my new floor from wall to wall and then install the cabinets on the new floor, or should I install the cabinets first and butt the new floor up to it?" Either method works, but installing new cabinets before new flooring is better. (See Book V, Chapter 1 for more on flooring.)

If you choose to install the cabinets first and then lay the floor, you save money by using less flooring material. Plus, you can work on the sub-floor and not have to worry about damaging a new floor when you're installing cabinets. And if you're even moderately skilled, you can make your flooring cuts close enough to the cabinet so that you can cover any small gap by a toe-kick trim strip.

Checking your floor for level

Don't assume that your floor is level. Most floors are off by a little bit, but not so much that cabinet installation is impossible for a DIYer. To check your floor for level, follow these steps:

1. **Lay a long 2 x 4 on edge against a wall where you will install the base cabinets and set a 4-foot level on it as shown in Figure 2-1.**

   The long 2 x 4 spans a greater distance of the floor, giving you a more accurate reading with the level. To determine if it is straight sight down one edge and the other, looking for any bends.

2. **Determine the first high point. Lift one end or the board or the other as needed to center the bubble between the lines in the level's vial.**

   If the vial already indicates level, there is no high point in this floor section. If an adjustment is needed, then the point where the level contacts the floor is your first high point.

3. **Use the level/straightedge to determine if there is any point higher along that wall or an adjacent wall where base cabinets are to be installed.**

   Place an end of the board on the first high point and extend the board further along the wall or to any adjacent walls, checking for level as you did in Step 2. To make sure that the highest point along the wall is not lower than a point 2 feet off the wall (rare), check with a 2-foot level perpendicular to the wall. If it is you need to add the difference to the height of your reference line (see next section).

Book IV

Bathroom and Kitchen Remodeling

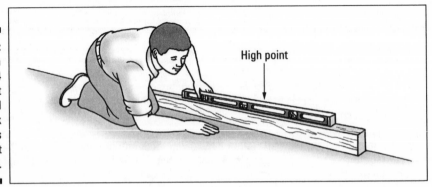

Figure 2-1:
Use a
straight 2 x 4
and a 4-foot
level to find
and mark
the floor's
high point
on the wall.

High point

Measuring cabinet heights

When you have your measurements marked on the wall, have a helper assist you and snap chalk lines at the top of your base cabinets and the bottom of your wall cabinets (see Figure 2-2). These lines give you your reference lines for installation. Perform this procedure on each wall where you plan to install cabinets. Be careful as you chalk the lines — make sure that your lines stay level around the entire room.

1. **Measure up 34½ inches from the highest point and mark the wall. Using a level, pencil a level reference line on the wall to represent the top of the base cabinets.**

2. **Measure up 49½ inches from the reference line at both ends and mark the wall to represent the top of tall cabinets and wall cabinets.**

3. **Measure up 19½ inches from the reference line at both ends to represent the bottom of 30 inch wall cabinets.**

When you have your measurements marked on the wall, have a helper assist you and snap chalk lines that represent the bottom and top of your wall cabinets. If you have shorter wall cabinets, such as those over a range or refrigerator, measure down from the top line a distance equal to the height of the cabinet to determine the bottom edge. These lines are your reference lines for installation. Perform this procedure on each wall where cabinets will be installed. Be careful as you chalk the lines — make sure that your lines stay level around the entire room.

Standard height cabinets installed in a room with standard 8-foot ceiling leaves you approximately 12 inches of space above the cabinet for open storage or for a *soffit* — a nearly square, boxed-in shape that's found above many kitchen cabinet installations.

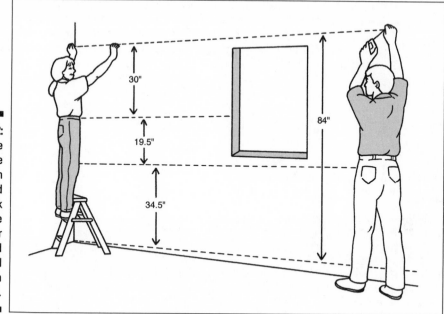

Locating the wall studs for mounting

You must secure wall cabinets to the walls with screws that you drive into wall studs. Hanging cabinets with hollow wall anchors is asking for a disaster! Even the most heavy-duty hollow wall anchor can't support the weight of a cabinet plus the weight of all the items stored inside.

Use a stud finder to locate each wall stud. In most construction, especially in homes built after the 1960s, the wall studs are spaced every 16 inches or 16-inches-on-center (16-o.c.). In older homes, spacing can vary. Mark each wall stud along the three level lines wherever cabinets will be installed. You will use these marks to guide where you drive screws that secure the base cabinet, the ledger, and the top and bottom of the wall cabinets to the wall.

A slick way to verify your marks and ensure that you have indeed located the wall studs is to pound a finish nail in an area hidden by the cabinets. If you've found the stud, you'll have trouble driving the nail after it has penetrated the drywall.

After you've marked the wall stud locations, attach a temporary ledger board to help support the wall cabinets during installation. I suggest using a long 1 x 4 pine board. Secure the ledger board along and below the line that marks the bottom of your wall cabinets. Drive a 2½-inch-long drywall screw into every other stud to secure the ledger board to the wall (see Figure 2-3). Cut the

Book IV

**Bathroom
and Kitchen
Remodeling**

ledger board to length as needed, depending on the length, or *run,* of your wall cabinet sections. After the wall cabinets are up and secured to the wall with #10 coarse thread cabinet screws at every stud location, and to each other, you remove the ledger board, patch the small screw holes, and paint the walls.

Figure 2-3: Attach a ledger board to support wall cabinets temporarily.

Checking your walls for plumb

You need to check to see if your walls are *plumb,* or vertically level. The best way to check is to place a 4-foot level vertically on adjacent walls at an inside corner. If the wall against which the cabinet end butts is either in or out of plumb (walls can go in either direction), you will need to shim the cabinets (both base and wall cabinets) as you install them to make them plumb. Cabinets that butt an out-of-plumb wall will leave a tapered gap you will need to address. If the gap is not more than ¼-inch wide and you are installing face-frame cabinets, you can plane the edge of the stile (the vertical member of the frame) as needed to close the gap. Larger gaps require that you install a tapered filler strip. Such a strip is best cut on a table saw so you may want help for this. Cabinets must be installed truly vertically and typically base cabinets must line up exactly with wall cabinets. To ensure that will be the case, especially when walls are out of plumb, it is essential to lay out cabinet positions on the wall before you start the installation.

Noting cabinet position

Just as you establish a level horizontal reference line to determine cabinet heights, you must also establish a plumb vertical reference line to locate the cabinet sides. Walls are rarely perfectly plumb. Starting at an inside corner like the one shown in Figure 2-4, (assuming there is one), use a 4-foot level to check for plumb. If the top of a wall that the end of a cabinet butts into leans in, measure along the wall it will be installed on and mark a point that is equal to the width of the first cabinet. You can find this dimension on your cabinet order or by measuring the width at the front face of the cabinet. Then using your level, pencil a plumb line from that point to the floor. If the wall leans out, then measure out from the bottom of the wall to locate the reference line; and if it bows out at the middle, measure from the middle.

Repeat the procedure on the adjacent wall so in the end you have a line on each wall indicating the location of the first cabinet.

If you have face-framed cabinets, the frames or faces extend ¼ inch beyond either side of each cabinet. Since the initial plumb reference line and the other plumb lines measured from it, represent the full width of the cabinet, the back edges of an installed cabinet will be ¼ inch away from its the line on the wall. If you have frameless cabinets (often referred to as European-style cabinets), the front and rear width dimensions will be the same, so the edge of a cabinet will fall on its line.

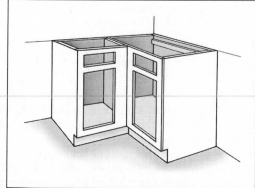

Figure 2-4:
A blind
inside
corner
cabinet unit.

Hanging Wall Cabinets

We recommend installing wall cabinets first because you don't have to work above the base cabinets. The open area of the floor allows you, your helper, and your stepladder clear access.

Before you mount the wall cabinets, get organized. Uncrate each cabinet and remove the doors. Mark each door and cabinet so that the door that came off a specific cabinet goes back on the same cabinet. They may look the same, but each door and cabinet box was matched, drilled, and attached to fit only the cabinet it came with. Mix them up and you're in for misalignment, poor operation, and less-than-desirable appearance. Identify each cabinet and door with a piece of masking tape. We start with a corner cabinet as No. 1 and then work out in each direction, using the No. 1 cabinet as our starting point.

Note: This section describes installing framed cabinets. Installation instructions for frameless cabinets are similar except when connecting adjoining cabinets, as explained in the next section.

It's time to install the first wall cabinet. Once you start, you'll be amazed at the quick progress you'll make by following these steps:

1. **Transfer stud locations from the wall to the inside of each cabinet before you lift it into place; and drill clearance holes for the mounting screws.**

   Measure carefully and measure twice. Drill the holes in the upper and lower *hanging rails* of the cabinets (the two horizontal pieces of lumber along the top and bottom of the back of the cabinet). Clearance holes, which are the same diameter as the screw, ensure that the cabinet will be drawn tight to the wall by the head of the screw.

2. **Set the first wall cabinet on the ledger strip and ¼-inch away from its reference line on the wall; secure the top and bottom of the cabinet to the wall with 3-inch-long #10 cabinet screws, as shown in Figure 2-5.**

   Go ahead and snug up the screws as you go, but don't tighten them completely. You'll go back later for a final tightening of all the screws after cabinets are aligned with each other, joined together with screws and plumbed.

   If you have a helper, have her hold the unit in place while you secure it with screws. If you're working alone, cut some lengths of lumber and make a V-shaped notch in one end. Use these pieces as braces by placing the notch against the bottom of the cabinet and wedging the lumber up to hold the cabinet in place (see Figure 2-6). Put a rag or piece of cardboard over the cabinet where the notched lumber will go to protect the cabinet's finish.

3. **Position the second cabinet on the ledger and next to the installed cabinet. Attach it with screws as you did the first one.**

4. **Join the two cabinets with two clamps, located about ¼ the distance from the top and bottom.** Use wooden screw clamps or short bar clamps with padded jaws that won't mar the cabinets. Don't position clamps at hinge locations because this is where you will join the cabinets with screws. As you tighten the clamp ensure that the face, top, and bottom of the two frames are all perfectly flush.

5. **Drill clearance holes through the face frame, countersinks so that the screwheads will be flush with or below the surface, and pilot holes in the adjoining cabinet.**

Figure 2-5:
Position the wall cabinet on the ledger board and drive 3-inch-long cabinet screws through the top and bottom hanging rails and into wall studs.

Figure 2-6:
Use shims to make a cabinet plumb.

Locate the holes at the hinge positions so when the hinges are installed, the screwheads will be concealed. The easiest way to drill these holes is all at once, using an adjustable combination bit.

6. **Drive 2¼-inch drywall screws into each hole and remove the clamps.**

   If the holes are not properly sized or if you overdrive the screws, they can easily snap off. Use the proper bits and adjust the clutch on your drill/driver to limit the torque to only what is necessary to drive the screws.

7. **Install the remaining wall cabinets along this wall in the same manner and then remove the ledger.**

8. **If the plan calls for a filler strip at a particular location clamp it to the face frame and attach it as you would attach two cabinets together.**

   Often a filler strip must be *ripped* (cut to width along its length) to suit a particular space, and sometimes it must be tapered as well. As this task should be done on a table saw you may want to hire a carpenter to help with fillers.

9. **Starting at the corner plumb the cabinets using the reference line on the adjacent wall and a 2-foot level, and insert shims as required.**

   Install shims behind the cabinet at the bottom or top as indicated until the cabinet is plumb and the proper distance from the reference line. Back out an installation screw, insert the shim until the cabinet is plumb and drive in the screw. When all cabinets are plumb, trim off the shims. Make numerous passes with a very sharp utility knife until it is scored enough to snap off or until you cut entirely through the shim.

10. **Similarly complete the installation of cabinets first on adjoining walls and then other walls.**

    Clamp the filler strip in place and drill ³⁄₁₆-inch pilot holes through the cabinet face frame and filler strip, using a countersink bit to recess the screw head into the face frame. Secure the strip with 3-inch drywall screws.

11. **Reinstall the doors and check each one for smooth operation.**

    Doors have a tendency to misalign after they've been removed. However, many styles of hinges allow you to make minor adjustments to get doors operating smoothly. Be careful when redriving the screws for the hinges. The screws are generally made from a fairly soft metal, which makes the heads easy to strip and the shafts easy to snap off. A stripped screw can be replaced. A snapped off screw will need to be extracted, because you need to use the same hole that has the broken screw in it. To remove a broken screw, use a screw extractor. Extractor kits are available at home centers and hardware stores for less than $20.

Before moving on to the base cabinets, install a decorative valance over the sink, if your design includes one. You need to position the valance between the two cabinets that flank the sink, secure the valance temporarily with clamps, drill countersink, clearance and pilot holes through the adjacent cabinet stile into the ends of the valance, and then secure it with 2¼-inch screws.

The installation steps in this section and those that follow are for face-framed cabinets. Frameless cabinets are installed in much the same manner except when connecting adjoining cabinets. To join frameless cabinets, use wood screws that are just shorter than the thickness of the two cabinet sides.

Secure each cabinet with four screws placed about 1 inch in from the front edge of the cabinet. If you drill pilot holes, be very careful not to drill completely through both cabinets.

Adding the Lower Level: Base Cabinets

Now you get to fill in the bottom half and install the base cabinets. You start the same way you did with the wall cabinets — unbox each cabinet and remove all doors and drawers, marking each one as you go, to make sure that you return the right door or drawer to its intended spot.

Installing the corner cabinet (s)

Start on the same wall and corner where you installed the wall cabinets. There are three ways to handle corners. You made this choice at the time you ordered your cabinets.

In the first option, a *blind base* installation, the cabinet on one wall (the blind base) extends almost to the corner, and then a standard base cabinet installed on the adjacent wall butts into it. Install these cabinets as a team and clamp them together as you level, plumb and attach them to the wall.

A corner base, often equipped with revolving "Lazy Susan" trays, is a single cabinet that extends 36-inches along adjacent walls. You must align it to reference lines on both walls as you level, plumb, and attach it to the wall.

In the third option, two standard base cabinets meet at their front corners creating a 2x2-foot dead (inaccessible) space in the corner. Install these cabinets in pairs to ensure that they meet precisely.

The steps that follow describe an installation that starts with a blind base:

1. **Position the blind base cabinet and then the standard base cabinet on the adjacent wall that butts into it, as shown in Figure 2-4.**

2. **Working on both cabinets, insert shims under the exposed ends and front edges until each cabinet is flush with the horizontal line and ¼-inch away from the plumb reference line on its wall.**

   Use a level across the top, from front to back and on the face of the cabinet, while inserting tapered shims. Shim under exposed edges to raise the back to the line; shim under the front to level the front from side to side and back to front.

Book IV

Bathroom and Kitchen Remodeling

3. **Clamp the top edges of the cabinets together.**

   Because the face frame overhangs the base cabinet by ¼-inch, insert a ¼-inch shim between the cabinets near the back edge to maintain that ¼-inch space.

4. **Attach the cabinets to the wall with 3-inch screws through the mounting rail at each wall stud location.**

   Drill clearance holes in the rails first and don't drive the screw tight just yet. Chances are you'll still need to spend time shimming the cabinets until they are just right.

5. **Check the cabinets again to make sure that they are plumb and level in all directions, and that they still align properly with the two reference lines and with each other.**

   Back out an installation screw to insert a permanent shim behind the cabinet at each stud location as needed (see Figure 2-7). Reinstall the screw to secure the cabinet and keep the shim in place. Spend lots of time getting this corner perfect. Proper installation of the remaining cabinets all depend on it.

Figure 2-7: Use shims as needed to level the blind base cabinet.

Finishing the base cabinet run

Finishing the base cabinet runs is less strenuous than hanging the wall cabinets because the cabinets rest on the floor and don't need to be supported while you secure them to the wall. However, it's still a good idea to have someone nearby to help make adjustments.

Before you install your sink-base cabinet, you may need to make cutouts for the plumbing pipes if the cabinet has a back (see Figure 2-8). Measure from the side of the adjacent cabinet to the center of each plumbing supply or pipe (drain line and water supply lines). Transfer those measurements to the back of the cabinet and use a hole saw or jigsaw to cut out openings for your plumbing pipes to fit through. Make sure that the measurements are accurate — you'll make an expensive mistake if you have to replace the sink base cabinet. Remember the old rule: "Measure twice, cut once." If you do happen to screw up big-time, you can cut a piece of ⅛-inch-thick Masonite plywood/paneling, adhere it to the messed-up panel and cut new holes. No one will know that you goofed!

Figure 2-8:
Cut openings in the back panel of the sink base cabinet for the drain line and water supply lines.

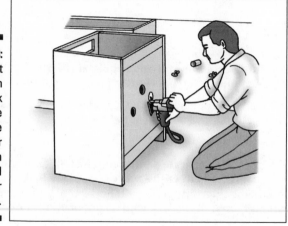

Follow these steps to finish the base cabinet run:

1. **Place the second cabinet in position and check it for plumb and level.**

2. **If shims are needed, gently tap them into place with a hammer.**

   Don't trust your eye to check for level. Just because the two cabinets are flush along the top edge doesn't mean that they're both level and plumb. Check it and adjust as necessary. You may need to place shims under the front or exposed side of the cabinet and between the back of the cabinet and the wall.

3. **Attach the cabinets together as you did the wall cabinets. (See the "Hanging Wall Cabinets" section, Steps 4, 5 and 6, earlier in this chapter, and check out Figure 2-9.)**

Book IV

Bathroom and Kitchen Remodeling

Figure 2-9:
Connect
the base
cabinets
with
2¼-inch
screws.

4. **Install the remaining cabinets and any required filler strips the same way, attaching each one to the previously installed cabinet.**

Complete the installation of each cabinet and then check all installed cabinets for level, plumb, and alignment before moving on to the next cabinet.

If your new cabinets include a separate pantry unit, install it the same way you installed the first cabinet of either the wall or base run: Make sure that it's level, plumb and that it aligns properly with horizontal and plumb reference lines before you secure it to the wall with 3-inch drywall screws.

After the cabinets are secured, score and break off all protruding portions of shims as you did for wall cabinets. You may find that you have a gap along an end panel and the wall or along the floor where shims may have been needed. Use a decorative trim molding to cover the gap between the end panel and the wall, as with the wall cabinets. To cover the gap at the floor along the area called the toe-kick, install a strip of matching hardwood or vinyl base molding, which can be cut with a utility knife and is adhered with special mastic.

If a wall or base cabinet run has an exposed end panel, you may want to use trim molding to cover any gaps between the cabinets and the wall. Sometimes a wall is just too wavy or weird to get an end panel to fit snugly, and a piece of trim molding not only looks nice but also covers up the imperfection.

Don't reinstall the doors and drawers on the base cabinets until after you've installed the countertop (see Chapter 3). They are safer out of the way, and you need to have access to the underside of the countertop to secure it to the cabinets.

If the corner where the countertops fit is out of square even by as little as ½ to ¾ inch, you're likely to damage the countertop by trying to make it fit. If you find that your walls aren't close to square, hire a contractor to do the installation.

To shape the edges of your countertop, you need to transfer the contour of the wall onto the countertop's edge surface. Use a compass to *scribe,* or transfer, the wall's contour onto the laminate.

1. **Set the countertop in place where you plan to install it.**

   When installing any section of countertop, check that it's level. Use a 2- or 4-foot level. If the countertop isn't level, slide shims between the countertop and the support struts of the cabinet frame to level the countertop. The shims will remain in place and won't move after you secure the countertop to the cabinets.

2. **Set your compass to fit the tip in the widest gap between the countertop and the wall.**

3. **Move the compass along the wall to draw a pencil line on the countertop's surface that matches the wall contour (see Figure 3-1).**

   Do so for both the backsplash and for any edge that's against a wall.

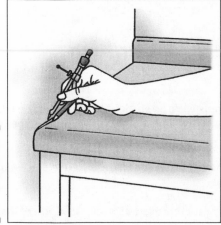

Figure 3-1:
scribe a line on the countertop surface.

4. **Remove the countertop and set it on a pair of sawhorses.**

5. **Secure the countertop to the sawhorses with squeeze clamps.**

   Place a rag or piece of cardboard between the clamp jaws and the countertop's surface to protect the surface.

Chapter 3

Installing Countertops and Sinks

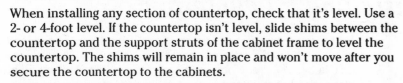

In This Chapter

▶ Getting your tools together

▶ Attaching a post-formed countertop

▶ Installing a sink and faucet

▶ Installing tile

A new countertop can add a finishing touch to a total kitchen remodel or stand alone as an upgrade that makes an outdated kitchen look like a million bucks. A new countertop doesn't cost that much, either. Stock countertops cost as little as $3 to $4 per linear foot. Even custom-made and ceramic tile countertops and backsplashes aren't that expensive — at least when compared to the cost of remodeling an entire kitchen.

A moderately skilled DIYer can handle the installation of a *post-formed countertop,* which is a seamless piece of laminate with a particleboard *substrate* (base) that covers the entire backsplash, flat surface, and front edge. A ceramic tile countertop isn't too far beyond the skill level of most average to experienced DIYers, either, if you take your time and have some patience. However, leave installing solid-surface, granite, and concrete countertops to a pro.

The main focus of this chapter is on installing a post-formed countertop. We also show the basic steps for installing a ceramic tile countertop and backsplash. We don't get into every possible problem or situation, but we do give you a solid primer on what to expect and where to go for assistance if you decide that installing a tile countertop is a project you want to tackle.

Gathering the Right Tools

We can't stress enough how much easier you make your task by getting all the tools together for the entire project before you start. Set up a pair of sawhorses and a half sheet (4 x 4 feet) of plywood to act as a staging area for tools. With that setup, you have all the tools laid out so that they're easy to grab when you need them. A well-laid-out staging area also makes your helper's job easier if you send him off to get tools.

Here are the tools you need for installing countertops:

- ½-inch open-end wrench
- ⅜-inch corded or cordless drill
- ¾-inch spade bit
- ¾-inch thick wood strip for support behind the laminate end cap
- Belt sander (an 18-, 21-, or 24-inch model)
- Carpenter's wood glue or liquid hide glue
- C-clamps
- Clothes iron (for applying end caps to post-formed countertops)
- Compass (Check your kid's geometry gear before you run out and buy one!)
- Drywall screws (1-, 1¼ and 1½-inch)
- End-cap kit (for finishing ends)
- Fine-tooth steel plywood blade
- Hand file
- Heavy-duty extension cord
- Heavy-duty work gloves and eye protection
- Household iron
- Levels (both 2-foot and 4-foot)
- Masking tape
- Package of wood shims
- Phillips screwdrivers (medium-sized, straight-tip, and No. 2)
- Portable circular saw
- Powered jigsaw
- Pressure sticks (short lengths of 1 x 1 or 1 x 2 board or trim)
- Rags or cardboard (to protect your countertop's surface when you use squeeze clamps)
- Sanding belts, sized for your belt sander (coarse, 60 grit; medium, 100 grit)
- Sawhorses (two)

- Scrap 1 x 4 board of short length (a 4-footer works)
- Squeeze clamps (at least one pair)
- Tube of construction adhesive
- Tube of silicone caulk and a caulk gun
- Utility knife

Installing a Countertop

Post-formed countertops are great for DIYers because the lam eliminated and the mitered corners are precut. Stock countert able in 2-foot increments, so to complete an installation you h work ahead of you. First, you need to *scribe* it to fit against any then cut it to length; if it turns a corner, you'll join the precut 4 mitered ends. After you've installed the countertop, you follow lation by cutting out a hole for your sink (if your countertop w precut for a sink — certainly enough sawing and drilling to giv DIYer's high!

Before you begin, remove the cabinet doors as well as the draw base cabinets. Clear access makes countertop installation easi

Ensuring a perfect fit: Scribing and trimming

Wouldn't it be great if your walls were as straight and true as the countertop? Well, we haven't seen a house in all our years of exp where this is the case.

The best way to check whether a corner is square is to use the 3 It's a simple geometric formula:

1. **Start in a 90-degree corner, measure out 3 feet, and mark**

2. **From the same corner, measure out 4 feet in the opposite and mark that spot.**

3. **Using a tape rule, measure the distance from the end mar 3- and 4-foot marks.**

   If the walls are square, the distance between the marks will l

6. **Remove the excess countertop (up to the pencil line) with a belt sander and a coarse (60-grit) sanding belt (see Figure 3-2).**

   A coarse belt works best because it removes laminate and the substrate quickly yet neatly. If you have a lot of excess countertop, say ⅛ inch or more, cut off most of it with a jigsaw and then use a belt sander to finish up to the pencil line.

   Hold the sander as shown in Figure 3-2. Avoid an upward cut, which might chip or lift the plastic laminate.

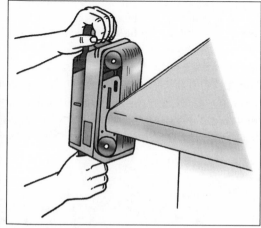

Figure 3-2:
Sand off
excess
laminate
and
substrate
up to the
scribed line.

7. **Reposition the countertop and check for any tight spots.**

8. **Touch up any tight spots with the sander and recheck the fit again before cutting it to length (as described in the following section).**

   You want the countertop to fit, especially if you're installing it during the humid summer months when the wall is fatter with humidity. If you're installing the countertop in the drier winter months, leave a gap of about 1⁄16 inch along the wall to allow for movement due to changes in temperature and humidity. Fill the gap with a bead of silicone caulk as one of the final steps in the remodel.

Sizing and finishing your countertop

Stock countertops are sold in 2-foot increments, so most folks have excess to cut off. Because most situations call for cutting, post-formed countertops are generally manufactured without end caps, which you need to apply.

Cutting off excess

The easiest way to cut off any extra length of a post-formed countertop is with a circular saw and fine-tooth steel plywood blade. Don't use a carbide-tipped blade — those blades have larger teeth, which increase your chances of chipping the laminate. Just follow these steps:

1. **Place the countertop upside down on a pair of 2 x 4s on sawhorses.**

   Be sure to extend the 2 x 4s under the entire countertop so that the cutoff is fully supported. You may want to clamp the countertop to the sawhorses for extra security; however, the weight of the countertop should be enough to keep it from moving.

2. **Measure the length of countertop that you need and mark a cutting line on the substrate.**

3. **Cut and clamp scraps of 1 x 4 to the backsplash and to the underside of the counter to guide your cuts (see Figure 3-3).**

   The distance between the guide and the cut line varies according to the saw and blade that you use. Measure the distance from the edge of the saw shoe (base) to the inside edge of the blade to determine proper spacing.

Figure 3-3:
Cut the countertop along your cutting guide.

4. **Make your vertical cut through the backsplash first and then cut from the rear of the countertop toward the front.**

   Support the cutoff end or have a helper hold it while you cut. Failure to do so will cause the piece to fall away before it's completely cut and will break the laminate unevenly, ruining the countertop. If you have trouble finishing the cut with the circular saw, stop about 1 inch from the end and finish with a jigsaw or handsaw.

Applying end caps

If your countertop has an exposed end that doesn't butt against a wall or into a corner, you need to finish it by applying a laminate *end cap* — a piece of the laminate surface that covers the exposed end of the countertop substrate.

Laminate end caps are designed to cover either left- or right-hand counter ends. Kits usually come with one of each. End caps are precut to fit the counter profile but oversized at the back edge to allow for a scribed fit, so you need to do some trimming with a hand file. End caps also come coated with heat-activated adhesive, which makes installation a snap. Follow these steps:

1. **Attach the provided wood strips to the bottom and back edges of the countertop with wood glue and brads, which the kit may also provide.**

   These strips support the end cap because the substrate alone isn't thick enough. Make sure that the strips are flush with the outer edge.

2. **Position the end cap on the cut end of the countertop and align the angle and corner with the contour of the countertop's surface.**

3. **Maintain that alignment as you run a hot clothes iron over the end cap to activate the adhesive.**

4. **After the glue and end cap have cooled, finish the edges.**

   File off excess material that extends past the backing strips. Also, lightly file the top edge so it isn't quite as sharp. A hand file works best. Push the file simultaneously toward the countertop and along its length.

   Never remove excess by pulling the file — always push! Pulling breaks the glue bond, and the end cap will come off and may even break.

5. **Reinstall the cabinet doors, put the drawers back in place, and you're set.**

Installing a mitered corner

If your countertop turns a corner, it probably has two pieces, each with a 45-degree angle, or *miter cut.* These cuts meet to form the 90-degree corner. Chances are good that you have to do some scribing and trimming of the backsplash to get it to fit against the wall without leaving gaps and to make the front edges of the two pieces meet without any of the substrate showing. Follow these steps:

1. **Place the countertop pieces in the corner to assess the fit.**

   Align the two pieces so the mitered edges meet properly. Push the counters against the wall and into the corner as far as possible without misaligning them. At the same time, adjust them until the overhang at the cabinet face is exactly the same along the entire length of both tops.

Book IV

Bathroom and Kitchen Remodeling

2. **Scribe and trim the back edges of each piece (as described in the "Ensuring a Perfect Fit: Scribing and Trimming" section) so that the rear mitered points fit exactly in the corner of the wall.**

   Typically, excess joint compound in the corners requires you to trim some material from this area. Additional trimming may be required to compensate for other wall irregularities.

3. **Before you join the pieces, mark the ends where you need to cut them to length (as described in the preceding section).**

4. **After cutting the tops to length and applying the laminate ends, apply yellow carpenter's glue or liquid hide glue to both edges of the mitered joint and reposition the two sections.**

   Either glue works well; however, carpenter's glue sets up more quickly. If you use it, you need to work faster.

5. **Connect the two pieces from the underside with the toggle bolts that came with the countertop.**

   Position the wings of the bolt into the slots on each piece. Tighten the bolt with an open-end wrench. As you do so, check the joint on the surface to make sure that the seam is perfectly flush. If it isn't, adjust the countertop position and retighten the toggle bolts.

6. **To ensure that the joint stays flush while it dries, place a C-clamp on the front edge joint and place pressure sticks on either side of the joint, as shown in Figure 3-4.**

   Pressure sticks are simply two equal lengths of board (usually 1 square inch in thickness) that are slightly longer than the distance between the countertop and the bottom of the wall cabinets. They need to be longer than that distance so you can wedge them in place to force pressure onto the countertop.

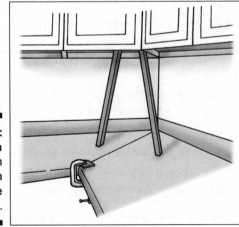

Figure 3-4:
Create a
smooth
seam with
pressure
sticks.

Cutting a hole for the sink

In some cases, the backsplash interferes with making the rear cut for a sink cutout. In that case, you must make the cut with the countertop upside down, so make the sink cutout after testing the fit but before joining any miter joints or attaching the countertop.

You can order your countertops pre-cut, including a hole for the sink, but do so only if you know that all your measurements are absolutely, positively dead-on, with no chance of being off by even a little bit. And if you're like us, that's very unlikely. Cutting a hole in a post-formed countertop isn't difficult. Just follow these steps and take your time for professional-looking results.

Using a template

Most sinks come with a paper or cardboard template to help outline the area you're going to cut out. Quite often, the cardboard template is part of the shipping box for the sink. Use a utility knife to cut the template from the box. Just be careful not to cut yourself, and be sure to follow the line so that the template is as straight as possible.

If your sink doesn't come with a template, or if you bought a good-looking closeout-sale sink without a box, you can make your own template:

1. **Lay the sink upside down on the countertop where you're going to install it.**

2. **Measure from the back edge of the sink to the backsplash to make sure that the sink is evenly positioned.**

   Make sure that the sink is back far enough — typically very close to the backsplash — so that when you install the sink, it will fit behind the cabinets with room for the mounting clips.

3. **Trace around the outer edge of the sink with a pencil.**

   Have a helper hold the sink in place or tape it to ensure that it doesn't shift while you're tracing.

4. **Measure the lip on the underside of the sink.**

5. **Mark the dimension of the lip in from the line you traced around the sink.**

   Mark it on the counter at several points inside the traced line and then draw straight lines connecting the marks. You can freehand the corners — just follow the same shape as the corners you traced by using the sink.

   The distance between the two lines forms the lip on the countertop to support your sink. The inner line is the cutting line.

Book IV

Bathroom and Kitchen Remodeling

Making the sink cutout

To cut a hole for a sink, we always use a jigsaw, which allows for great control. (*Note:* Always, always, always use a new jigsaw blade. An old or dull blade can chip the laminate along the cutting line.) Some people use a circular saw; however, doing so involves making a plunge-cut with the blade because you don't have a starter hole to work with. Most folks find that a jigsaw is the easiest, most reliable, and safest saw to use. Wear heavy gloves and eye protection when making this cut.

1. **Drill two starter holes in opposite corners just inside the cutting line. Use a ¾-inch spade bit and drill through the laminate and substrate.**

   Don't worry if the cut edge is rough. The rim of the sink will cover it. You're cutting into sections that you'll eventually cut out and toss (in the garbage; not just up in the air).

2. **Place the blade of the jigsaw in the starter hole and line up the blade exactly on the cutting line (see Figure 3-5).**

3. **Cut slowly along the line.**

   Don't be in a rush — let the saw do the work. Again, don't worry about any little chips that may occur. The sink lip will cover them.

Figure 3-5:
Insert the jigsaw blade in the starter hole and cut around the entire inner (or cutting) line.

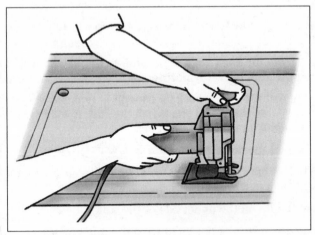

If the backsplash interferes with the saw shoe and prevents making the cut, turn the countertop over to complete the cut from the underside. If you choose this method, make this cut first.

To make a clean, safe cut, ask a helper to support the cutout area so that the piece doesn't drop and cause the saw blade to bind. Make sure your helper wears heavy gloves and eye protection.

When it's time to install the sink and faucet, move on to the "Installing a Sink and Faucet" section for all the information you need. You'll find it easier to drill for and even install the faucet before you attach the countertop.

Attaching countertops other than corners

After you've scribed, trimmed, test fit and applied any end caps to the countertops and the glue has set at any mitered corners, you can begin the job of securing them to the base cabinets.

Don't start securing the countertop to the cabinets until the mitered joint has dried. Allow the glue to dry for at least four hours, or overnight if the weather is humid. It's better to wait a little longer than to rush the job and have the seam break because the glue hasn't set up. If the seam does break, you need to remove the old glue — a very difficult task — and start over.

Follow these steps to attach a countertop to the base cabinets:

1. **Position the countertop pieces on the cabinets.**

2. **Apply a bead of silicone caulk or construction adhesive along the top edge of all the cabinet parts that support the countertop.**

   Tip up a straight countertop to apply the adhesive. Insert shims under a mitered countertop rather than trying to tip it up — doing so is easier and is less likely to break the glue joint. The caulk or adhesive will hold all the parts in place after it dries.

3. **Lower the countertop back into place or remove the shims.**

4. **Place pressure sticks every 12 to 18 inches to help the adhesive bond the countertop to the cabinets at the back edge and apply clamps to the front edge.**

   Be sure to place pressure sticks along the back corners (where the corner blocks are located) to get the countertop down tight.

5. **Seal any gap between the backsplash and the wall or along the edges and the wall with a clear silicone acrylic caulk.**

6. **Reinstall the cabinet doors, put the drawers back in place, and go have another beer.**

If you're going to paint the walls and you want to paint the clear caulk, make sure the label says that it can be painted! Most silicone acrylic caulk is paintable, whereas regular silicone caulk isn't.

Book IV

Bathroom and Kitchen Remodeling

Installing a Sink and Faucet

Installing a sink and faucet in your kitchen is easy whether you're doing a complete kitchen remodel or simply upgrading the look of your kitchen. The information in this chapter, coupled with the manufacturer's instructions for both the sink and the faucet, will help you through the steps.

Gathering the right tools

The fewer trips you make to get tools and materials, the less time you waste and the faster you finish your project. Here are the tools you need to gather for installing your sink and faucet:

- Groove-joint pliers
- Adjustable wrench
- No. 2 Phillips screwdriver
- Medium-sized slotted (straight tip) screwdriver
- Caulk gun
- A tube of silicone caulk/adhesive
- A small container of plumber's putty
- Spud wrench
- Bucket and rags

Of these tools, the spud wrench is the one you are least likely to own, but it's one that will make the job easier. The spud wrench is engineered to fit the locknut that is used to secure the sink basket to the sink. A spud wrench costs under $10 and is available wherever plumbing tools are sold.

Setting the stage: Preparing to install your sink

Much of the work of sink installation actually takes place before you set the sink into the countertop. Taking your time with the preliminary work ensures a smooth installation.

If you don't install your sink and faucet according to the instructions, you'll have to foot the bill for the replacement even if the product is defective. If the manufacturer sees signs of abuse or misuse or an improper installation, they're off the hook. And I know from my years in the home center business that the first thing a manufacturer checks is how a product was used or installed.

Taking the measurements

In most cases, the old plumbing configuration will work with your new sink. But if you're making a major change in the design of the new sink, be sure that the old plumbing fits the new sink's requirements. So, before you buy or order a sink, take a few measurements.

Establishing the drain height

Make sure to measure the distance from the underside of the countertop to the center of the drain line that comes out of the wall. This distance is usually between 16 and 18 inches, which allows adequate space for the water to drop into the trap and still leaves enough space below the trap for storing items underneath the sink in the cabinet.

The drain height is usually not an issue unless you're going from a very shallow sink to one that has very deep bowls (9 to 12 inches deep). Even if you do switch to deeper bowls, it may only be a problem if your old setup had a shallow bowl coupled with a high drain exit position. This may sound like a less than likely setup but it does happen.

If you do find that you only have a few inches of space between the bottom of the bowl and the center of the drainpipe, contact a licensed plumber to assess the situation and determine if the drainpipe needs to be lowered.

Determining the shut-off valve heights

You should also measure the height of the shut-off valves. Measure from the floor of the sink base cabinet to the center of the valve.

Remember, though, that houses built before roughly 1980 were not required to have shut-offs on every sink supply line, so you may not have any at all. If your sink doesn't have shut-off valves, install them now while you're working on the system. If your kitchen didn't have shut-offs when you tore out the old sink and faucet and you've been working on the sink installation for a few days, you better have installed individual shut-off valves by now or your family won't be speaking with you. Where there are no shut-off valves and there are open pipes or lines, the only way to keep the water from running out is to shut down the entire water supply. Not a good idea when your daughter is getting ready for a big date.

Book IV

Bathroom and Kitchen Remodeling

Making sure to attach the faucet before installing the sink

Yes, the heading is correct. The easiest and best way to install a faucet is before the sink is in place. If you install the faucet before installing the sink, you won't have to strain or reach because everything is completely open.

Getting to know your sink

Most sinks come with factory-drilled holes along the back edge or lip. The number of holes should be equivalent to the number of holes needed for your faucet, so pay close attention when buying your faucet and sink. If you have a single-lever faucet, you'll want a single- or two-hole sink, depending on if your faucet needs a separate sprayer hose hole or if you want a soap dispenser on the sink.

Many sink and faucet combinations use four holes. In most cases, the first three holes from the left (as you face the front of the sink) are for the faucet. The hole furthest to the right is for a spray hose, separate water dispenser tap, or soap dispenser. Some newer sink designs have the holes positioned so that the dispenser hole is the one on the left, but this would be clearly marked on the carton or explained in the instructions. The first hole from the left and the third hole from the left are spaced 8-inches-on-center, which is commonly shown as 8-inches o.c.

Securing the faucet to the sink

Before you begin, create a stable workspace where you can safely position the sink. You can simply set the sink on a solid work surface, such as a work-bench. Just remember to clean off the surface or put down some cardboard to prevent accidentally scratching the sink surface when it's time to flip the sink over to tighten the faucet nuts. Or, if you want to avoid flipping your sink over, place it on a set of sawhorses. Just rest the side ends on the horses and you're ready to have at it. Make sure that the sawhorses are stable and can't slip or move. If a sawhorse moves, chances are good that the sink will fall.

Well, it's time to begin the assembly process.

1. **Place the faucet over the three holes on the left with the faucet's water supply *tailpieces* (threaded pieces located directly beneath the faucet handles) going into the two outside holes.**

2. **Screw the plastic nuts onto the threaded tailpieces (which will later connect to the supply lines) and hand-tighten until snug.**

3. **Use groove-joint pliers to finish tightening the nuts.**

   Be careful not to over tighten the nuts. Plastic nuts are easy to strip or ruin with pliers.

4. **Seal the area where the faucet meets the sink, according to the manufacturer's instructions.**

   Some faucets come with a rubber gasket that goes on the bottom of the faucet body between it and the sink. Other faucet manufacturers recommend applying a bead of silicone tub-and-tile caulk on the bottom of the faucet body before positioning the faucet on the sink. Both methods keep water from getting underneath the faucet where it could run down the factory-drilled holes and drip onto the sink base cabinet floor.

At this point, you may want to install the sink *baskets* in the sink, but don't do it just yet. (The baskets are the stainless steel strainer-like baskets used in kitchen sinks to let water run out but catch food scraps and other sink debris.) Leaving the baskets out keeps the holes open and these holes are the perfect handholds for lifting and lowering the sink. Having these holes available also reduces the chance that you'll grab the neck of the faucet and lift the sink. We know of several folks who ruined a brand new faucet because they used it as the holding point to lift a cast-iron sink! One of the faucet necks simply snapped off, not only ruining the faucet but also causing a huge ding in the countertop when the sink dropped well before it was in position.

Attaching water supply lines to the faucet

After the faucet is secured to the sink, you can attach the water supply lines that will eventually be connected to the shut-off valves on the main water supply pipes. Regardless of what your supply line is made of, it probably uses a coupling nut to secure it to the faucet tailpiece. Simply screw the coupling nut onto the tailpiece until it's snug and then give it a couple of final snugs with groove-joint pliers.

Don't rush when attaching the supply lines. Faucet tailpieces are usually either brass or plastic, depending on the quality and the manufacturer. But no matter which material is used, the threads can be easily stripped if the coupling nut is started unevenly. Finger-tightening the nut onto the tailpiece helps ensure that it's going on straight. Eyeball it to make sure it looks straight; if it doesn't, back off the nut and start over.

Dealing with factory-attached tubes

Some faucets come with factory-attached soft-copper supply lines on both the hot- and cold-water tailpieces, which means the only attaching will be directly to the shut-off valves. You should, however, do a little preshaping of the soft-copper before setting the sink into position in the countertop.

Measure the distance between the water supplies under the sink and then gently bend the soft-copper supply tubes until they're about the same distance apart as the water supply. They don't have to be exact, just close.

Be very, very careful when shaping the soft copper. Notice we said *shaping* and not *bending* the pipe. When people hear or read the work "bend" they think they need to be forceful with the copper. But soft copper is very fragile and kinks relatively easily. And after it's kinked, you won't be able to get rid of the kink, which restricts water flow and will eventually begin to leak.

The best way to shape the copper into position is to gently slide it through your hands as you gradually move it into position. Don't try to shape it in one shot. Make two or three passes through your hands for best results.

Installing flexible copper supply tubes

Flexible copper supply tubes are similar to, if not the same as, the factory-attached soft-copper supply tubes found on some faucets. The same care is needed to bend and shape the copper tubes that you install. Try to shape the tube into position before attaching it to the sink's tailpieces. After the tube has been shaped, secure it to the tailpiece with the coupling nut.

Although these copper supply tubes are somewhat flexible, they can't be looped or twisted around if they're too long for your supply setup. You need to cut them to length to fit into the open end of the shut-off valve. Determining how much to cut off is easy:

1. **Position the tube between the tailpiece and the shut-off valve and mark the tube so that it will fit down into the valve after it has been cut.**

2. **Use a tubing cutter to cut off the excess.**

3. **Attach the tube to the tailpiece with a coupling nut and use the compression nut and ring to secure the other end of the tube to the shut-off valve.**

Installing the newest tubes — Braided!

One of the best new plumbing products to come along is the line of braided steel supply lines. They're constructed of a rubber supply (like a hose) wrapped in a steel-braided outer jacket. And what's really great about them is their flexibility. You can take the excess length and simply put a loop in it and then connect it to the shut-off valve.

Because this product is fairly new, you should check with your plumbing inspector to make sure that they meet your local plumbing code. They're not accepted in all regions — yet!

After you've attached the supply tubes, attach the spray hose if you have one. Slide the coupling nut end of the hose through the mounting ring and hole in the sink. The sprayer head rests in the mounting ring when not in use. Attach the coupling nut on the sprayer hose to the threaded outlet on the underside of the faucet, usually located under the center of the faucet body.

Other sink extras, such as a soap dispenser or hot water spigot, should be installed now. Follow the manufacturer's installation instructions.

Putting things in position: Finishing your installation

Now that the plumbing supply stuff is in place, it's finally time to put the sink in place and see how it looks. After the sink is in place, you can make the supply line and drain line connections that will transform the gaping hole in your countertop into a working sink.

Setting in your sink

If you're installing a stainless steel sink, you can probably handle the lifting and positioning yourself. However, if your new sink is cast iron or cast enamel, get a helper. These sinks weigh 80 pounds or more and are awkward to handle.

1. **First, dry-fit the sink to determine exactly the right spot.**

   Set the sink into the opening in the countertop. Remember to use the basket holes to grip the sink, not the faucet. Center the sink in the opening and then draw a light pencil line on both sides and along the front edge of the sink.

2. **Lift out the sink and flip it over.**

   You don't need to take the sink back to your shop to do this, either. Lay a piece of cardboard on the countertop to protect it (and the sink) from scratching and then flip the sink over so that the faucet handles and neck hang over the edge of the countertop.

3. **Apply a bead of silicone caulk (about ¼-inch wide) around the edge.**

   The caulk prevents water from getting between the sink and the counter, and it also holds the sink in place. Use a silicone-based tub-and-tile caulk, which usually contain mildew killers and stand up against the dirt, soap scum, and crud that you're sure to find around the kitchen sink. Silicone caulks also remain somewhat flexible, which is helpful because the sink will actually drop very slightly when it's filled with water and then lift when the water is drained. The movement is very slight, but over time this movement would cause a regular latex-based caulk to crack.

   After the caulk has been applied, you need to keep the installation moving so the caulk doesn't dry before you get the sink in place.

4. **Lower the sink into position using the pencil lines to get it in the same location.**

5. **Let the sink rest for about 30 to 45 minutes before you install the sink baskets so that the caulk has time to set up or *cure*.**

Book IV

Bathroom and Kitchen Remodeling

Installing the sink baskets

After the caulk has cured, install the sink baskets (the stainless steel catcher/strainers we mentioned earlier).

1. **Start by applying a ¼-inch thick rope of plumber's putty around the entire underside lip of the basket.**

   The putty seals the gap between the lip and the groove of the sink basket hole. Don't put the putty on the groove — it's too easy for it to get shifted out of position and then the basket will leak.

2. **Now fit the baskets into the holes in the sink bowls and secure them to the sink using the rubber washer, cardboard gasket, and metal locknut that are supplied with the basket.**

   Make sure you install the rubber washer first, the cardboard gasket second, and the locknut last. If you don't, water will leak under the basket lip.

3. **After you've hand-tightened the locknut, use the spud wrench to finish securing the locknuts.**

4. **Finally, remove the excess putty that is forced out between the sink basket and the sink and beneath the sink.**

Always follow the manufacturer's instructions and use the right materials. Don't substitute a bead of silicone caulk for the rope of plumber's putty when installing the baskets. The caulk will be very difficult to remove if you need to remove the basket. Plus, it won't fill the gap as evenly as the plumber's putty. This putty has been used by professionals for decades and is the only way to go.

Connecting the supply lines

No matter what type of material you use for your water supply lines, you want leak-free connections. The fastest connection to use is the screw-on nut and washer that's on the ends of a steel-braided supply line. Simply tighten the nut onto the threaded outlet on the faucet tailpiece and the shut-off valve and you're set to go.

Another commonly used type of connection is called a *compression fitting.* It consists of a *coupling nut,* which secures the fitting to the faucet tailpiece and the shut-off valve, and a brass *compression ring,* which forms the sealed connection between the supply line and the fitting it's attached to. Compression fittings are a tighter connection than a screw-on nut and washer fitting. Here's how to properly install a compression fitting:

1. **Start by sliding the compression nut onto the supply line with the nut threads facing the valve.**

2. **Now slide the compression ring onto the supply line.**

3. **Place the end of the supply tube into the appropriate valve, making sure that it fits squarely in the valve opening.**

   If the supply line end doesn't go in straight, the connection will leak, because the angle of the end of the supply line won't allow the compression ring to sit or "seat" properly between the supply line and the valve fitting.

4. **Reshape the tube until it fits squarely.**

5. **Once the tube is in place, pull the compression ring and nut onto the valve and screw it tight.**

6. **Open the shut-off valve to check the connection for leaks.**

   Keep some rags handy, just in case.

Hooking up the drain line

Drain kits come in different materials and configurations, but installing them is a snap. Choose the kit with the configuration for your sink type, and you're halfway home!

Choosing the right kit

You have a couple of choices for drain kits: chromed metal kits and PVC drain kits. Both work well and are about equally easy to use. The main factor on deciding which one to use is cosmetic — will the drain line be visible? If it will be visible, you'll want to use the chromed kit. If it's out of sight in the sink base cabinet, which most kitchen drains are, then the good-old white plastic PVC kit is the way to go; PVC is cheaper.

Kitchen sink drain kits, whether they're chromed or PVC, use nut and washer screw-together connections. Besides being easy to install, they also let you easily disconnect the assembly when it's time to unclog a drain or quickly rescue that wedding ring that fell down the drain. A basic, single-bowl kit includes

 ✔ A **tailpiece,** which connects to the bottom of the sink strainer

 ✔ A **trap bend** (or P-trap), which forms a water-filled block to prevent sewer gas from coming up through the sink drain

 ✔ A **trap arm,** which is connected to the downstream end of the P-trap and then to the drain line that leads to the main drainage line

Book IV

Bathroom and Kitchen Remodeling

A double-bowl drain kit will have everything the single-bowl kit has along with a waste-Tee connection and additional length of drain line to connect both bowls to a single P-trap.

If your sink has a garbage disposer, you need an additional longer section of drainpipe to connect the disposer's drain line to the bowl drain line. The crosspiece that comes in the kit may or may not be long enough to make the connection between the disposer and other sink bowl drain pieces. You have to check yours out to be sure. Follow your disposer's installation instructions.

If your sink is a triple-bowl, you need a third set of pieces for the third bowl. Individual traps, bends, tailpieces, and pipe sections, as well as slip nuts and washers, are sold separately, so finding the extra pieces is no problem. Availability of individual parts is also especially nice for occasions when, for example, you accidentally cut off too much of the tailpiece and it doesn't reach the connecting waste-Tee. (Gee, does it sound like we may have some personal experience here?)

You probably won't find glue-together drain kits, but if you do, replace it with a nut and washer setup. (A glue-together kit uses liquid adhesive to secure the pieces of drain line pipe instead of a slip nut and washer, making it impossible to take apart and clean.)

Making the connection

Assembling and connecting the drain kit is fairly simple.

The great thing about drain line kits is that the pieces are really quite easy to move and maneuver, so you can adjust them to fit almost any setup. Don't expect the horizontal pieces to be in super-straight alignment with the tailpieces or the drainpipe. The only thing that matters is that they all eventually get connected together. Take a look at your old sink drain setup and you'll see what we mean.

1. **Start by attaching the tailpiece to the sink drain and tightening the slip nut and washer by hand.**

   If you have a multiple bowl sink, all of the drain tailpieces should be the same length for an easier installation.

2. **Next, slip the trap onto the tailpiece and then position the trap's horizontal piece next to the drain line coming out of the wall.**

   The horizontal piece must fit inside the end of the drain line. Remove the trap and cut the horizontal section to fit.

3. **Reattach the trap to the tailpiece and into the drain line and tighten the slip nuts and washers.**

Checking for leaks (Put on your raincoat first)

Before you do anything else, get the bucket and rags ready. Lay some rags directly below each connection so that, if there is a leak, the towels will immediately soak up the water. And leave the rags there for a couple of days, just in case a leak develops over time.

Have your helper turn on the water while you begin inspecting for leaks. Don't open up the shut-off valve just yet. Let the water pressure build up to the shut-off valve so that there's time for any slow-leak drips to occur. Leaving the valves closed for a few minutes should be long enough to know whether any water is leaking. Once you know the shut-off valve connection isn't leaking, open the valve so that the water goes into the supply lines. Again, let the water pressure build in the supply lines for a few minutes and then inspect the supply connections at the faucet tailpieces.

Don't be alarmed (or upset) if you have a joint that leaks. We've done a lot of plumbing projects and we still get the occasional leaky joint. Just shut off the water, take a deep breath, disassemble and reassemble the connection, and check again for leaks. No sense crying over spilled milk — or, in this case, a drippy plumbing joint.

Installing a Ceramic Tile Countertop

Another type of countertop that is quite popular and is a manageable DIY project for most homeowners is ceramic tile. Ceramic tile is not only attractive, but also very durable and resistant to spills and stains. Tile is available in a wide range of colors, sizes, and styles. A ceramic tile countertop is more expensive than a post-formed top and involves considerably more work, but the beauty of ceramic tile is usually enough to offset the extra cost and labor.

Gathering additional tools for tile

In addition to the tools listed at the beginning of this chapter, here's what you need to install a tile countertop:

- ¾-inch AC-grade plywood
- 1 x 2 board (used for front edge build-up)
- Framing square

✔ Grout and grout sealer

✔ Latex underlayment filler

✔ Notched trowel

✔ Plastic tile spacers

✔ Rubber grout float

✔ Tile adhesive (mastic) or thinset

✔ Tile backer board

✔ Tile cutter (available at rental stores)

✔ Tile nipper (special pliers used for cutting/nipping small pieces)

✔ Tiles, straight and bull-nose (or countertop edge trim)

Sheet-mounted field tiles can speed installation significantly, but if you use this approach, you may still need to adjust the spacing between tiles before the adhesive sets. You do this by twisting them or, if necessary, cutting the mesh.

Constructing your ceramic countertop

A ceramic tile countertop is made up of ¾-inch exterior plywood and *tile backer board* (a cement or special gypsum panel) cut to the same size as the tops of the cabinets. You then edge the edges of the plywood and backer board sandwich with 1 x 2 strips of wood. You apply the tiles directly to the backer board and secure them with mastic or thinset mortar. Finally, you fill the gaps between the tiles with grout; you must seal these gaps to prevent moisture from getting under the tiles and loosening them.

You need two styles of tile for a countertop: straight-edged, or *field tiles,* and *bull-nose tiles.* Bull-nose tiles come in two styles: a single rounded edge for use along a straight edge, and a *double bull-nose* (two adjacent rounded edges) for use on outside corners. Alternatively, you can use *countertop edge trim tiles* instead of bull-nose tiles. Using a wet saw, you must cut them to length and miter them to fit inside and outside corners. (Your tile dealer can usually make wet-saw cuts for you.) The backsplash on a ceramic tile top can be installed over a separate particleboard core (backerboard isn't needed) or directly on the wall. The top of the backsplash can end with a bull-nose tile or extend to the underside of wall cabinets. Figure 3-6 shows how a ceramic tile countertop fits together.

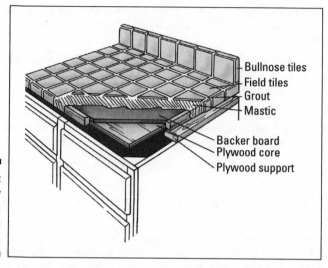

Figure 3-6:
The many
layers of a
ceramic tile
countertop.

Bullnose tiles
Field tiles
Grout
Mastic
Backer board
Plywood core
Plywood support

Here's a quick look at the basic steps for building a ceramic tile countertop:

1. **Cut and position the plywood core so it fits against the wall flush with the face of the cabinets. Secure it to the cabinets with drywall screws.**

   Drill pilot holes through the plywood into the top edges of the cabinets. Measure carefully and pencil a line to guide (center) pilot hole placement. Lift the top to apply construction adhesive, and replace it to drive the screws.

2. **Cut tile backer board, such as cement board, and test its fit.**

   To cut cement board, score the surface with a utility knife guided by a metal or wood straightedge; snap to break in along the scored line; and complete the cut of the reinforcing material with your utility knife.

3. **Attach the backer board cement board screws or exterior-rated drywall screws, as suggested by the manufacturer.**

   For a more rigid installation, use a notched trowel to apply mastic or thinset mortar (available where tile is sold) over the plywood before attaching the backer board.

4. **Apply self-adhering fiberglass mesh tape over any joints and fill in the screw-head holes with a latex underlayment filler or thinset.**

   Allow the filler to dry and then sand it smooth.

5. **Attach a 1 x 2 board to the front edge, making sure it's flush with the top of the backer board.**

   Nail and glue the board to the plywood with 4d finishing nails.

Book IV

**Bathroom
and Kitchen
Remodeling**

6. **Determine the position of the first course and draw a line parallel to the front of the countertop to indicate where the back edge of the tiles will align.**

   Position bull-nose tile (or countertop edge trim tile) on the front edge and a field tile on the top separated by a tile spacer. Add more spacers on the back edge and place a board against it. Then trace a line along the board to mark the edge of the first course of field tiles.

7. **Measure the length of the countertop and mark the centerline perpendicular to the line you just drew, as shown in Figure 3-7.**

   Align one leg of the square with the line and the other with the mark you made to indicate the centerline.

8. **Dry-fit rows of tile along the lines using tile spacers, as shown in Figure 3-7.**

   On a straight counter, determine whether it's best to center a tile on the centerline or align an edge with it. Choose whichever leaves you with the widest tile at the ends. If you have a countertop that turns a corner, lay out the tiles starting at the corner. On a countertop that wraps two corners, lay out tiles starting at the corners and plan the last (cut) tile to fall in the center of the sink.

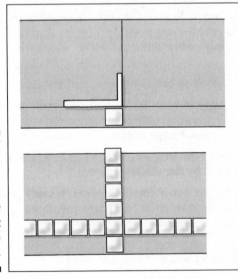

Figure 3-7:
Dry-fit rows
of tile along
the lines.
Mark any
tiles that
need to be
trimmed.

9. **Use a tile cutter to make straight cuts on field and bull-nose tiles (see Figure 3-8). If you have a countertop edge trim, have your supplier cut it with a wet saw after all tiles are in place.**

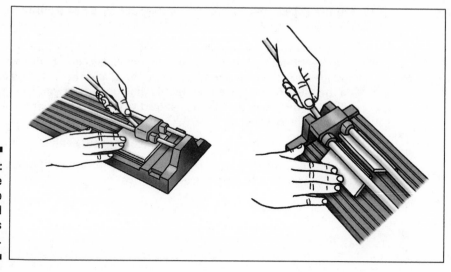

Figure 3-8:
Use a tile
cutter to
score and
cut the tiles
to fit.

10. **To make curved cuts, freehand score the area on the tile to be removed with a glass cutter. Then use a tile nipper to break off numerous small pieces until the cutout is complete (see Figure 3-9).**

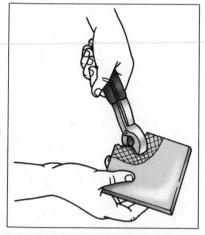

Figure 3-9:
Remove
small pieces
of tile with a
tile nipper.

Book IV

**Bathroom
and Kitchen
Remodeling**

11. **After you've dry-fit and cut all the tiles, secure them to the substrate with mastic or thinset mortar, as advised by your tile supplier.**

Apply the mastic or thinset with a notched trowel to ensure a uniform coat and use plastic tile spacers between tiles to ensure even spacing. Allow the mastic or thinset to set up for at least 24 hours.

12. **Fill the gaps between the tiles with grout by using a rubber grout float.**

    Hold the float at a 45-degree angle to the tiles and use a sweeping motion to force grout into the gaps. Wipe off any excess grout with a damp sponge. Let the grout dry for about an hour and then wipe off any haze on the tile. Don't let grout on the tile dry too long or you'll never get it off! After you clean the surface, allow the grout to dry per the instructions on the package.

13. **Seal the grout with a penetrating silicone grout sealer.**

    Although sealing the grout seems like a tedious job (and it is!), it's critical that you do it to keep the grout from staining and to extend its useful life.

Chapter 4

Fridges, Ranges, Disposals, and More: Installing Appliances

In This Chapter

▶ Putting in a range, cooktop, or oven

▶ Installing a fridge

▶ Looking into installing a few other appliances

*I*f you've decided that you'd like to include new appliances in your kitchen remodel, do your homework to make sure that the new units will fit properly. If you're simply replacing your old range with a new one, chances are good that the new one will fit in the old space. But if you're replacing the old range with one that's larger or uses a different fuel source, you need to make some adjustments. You're in luck! This chapter explains how to handle the situation should you need to make adjustments so that your new appliances fit in your remodeled kitchen. It also covers how to convert from gas appliances to electric and vice versa.

We're not going to go into great detail with regard to running a gas line to the kitchen for a new gas range or running a new circuit to the kitchen for an electric range. Both of these tasks involve making some tricky connections that are better left to a licensed plumber and electrician. (See Chapter 2 in Book I for advice on hiring a pro.) We will, however, give a broad explanation of each process so that you'll have an understanding of how they work. After reading this chapter, you'll be a smarter shopper and homeowner when it's time to get bids on the work.

Installing Ranges, Ovens, and Cooktops

The two major questions to answer for this part of the remodel are

- ✔ What is the fuel source: gas or electric?
- ✔ Where is the appliance going to be installed? In a row of base cabinets, in an island, or freestanding?

This section takes a look at installing a new cooking unit as well as converting your fuel source from gas to electric, including the basic installation steps for ranges, cooktops, and ovens. You don't need many tools, because this job is best left to a pro.

Changing the power/fuel source

The most common fuel-source change is going from gas to electric. However, the last house we purchased came set up for an electric range and clothes dryer. We were raised using gas-fired appliances and, in our opinion, once a gas appliance user, always a gas appliance user. So we decided to run gas lines to both.

Running a new power or fuel source to the kitchen isn't as messy as you may think, especially if you (or the pro you hire) do the work before the cabinets and new floor are installed. Doing the work when the kitchen is torn apart means that walls and floor areas are easier to access, which is important if you have to pull a new circuit through the wall for an electric range/oven.

Gaining space in your electric service panel before converting to electrical appliances

Just because you want electric-powered appliances doesn't always mean that your home's electrical service can handle it. The best way to figure out whether your system can handle adding electric-powered appliances is to have an electrician or your electric service provider come out and inspect your main panel.

If your home has fuses, either the screw-in plug type or fuse blocks, you probably won't be able to add electric appliances without upgrading to circuit breakers. If your home has circuit breakers, you may be able to add electric appliances without increasing the amperage to the house. However, just because the service panel has unused slots doesn't mean that you can simply knock them out and add a few breakers. Homes with circuit breaker panels have at least 100 amps of power *(100-amp service)*, which is considered the minimum standard for a medium-size home with no more than three major electric appliances, including central air conditioning. So, for example, if your home has 100-amp service, and it has central air, an electric water heater, and an electric clothes dryer, you probably won't be able to add an electric range without upgrading your system. Many new homes have 150- or 200-amp service or more.

Upgrading an electrical system should be left to a licensed electrician. Cities are (rightly) very picky when it comes to who can make what changes to a home's electrical system and will be almost overly picky if you attempt a complete service upgrade as a DIYer. A complete system upgrade should cost between $1,500 and $3,000, depending on material and labor costs. Just remember to build the costs of a system upgrade into your budget if you're considering electric appliances. You don't want a three-grand surprise just because you fell in love with an electric cooktop, and you didn't budget for it!

Making the move from gas to electric

A first-time electric range installation needs a dedicated 240-volt circuit for the range and oven. This process involves installing and attaching the correct size cable to your home's main electrical service panel. Unless you're skilled at working with electricity, hire an electrician to handle this job.

Electric codes require an electric range and/or oven to be on a dedicated 40- or 50-amp circuit. Check with your electrical inspector as to which is required in your area. To do this job, you (or your contractor) need

- ✔ Enough 6/3 cable to run from the service panel to the new receptacle in the kitchen. (See the sidebar "Wiring ID: It's all in the numbers" for more on wire numbers.)

- ✔ A 240-volt appliance receptacle, which has three plug prong holes and a ground prong hole. As you can see in Figure 4-1, the orientation of the prong holes is different than on a standard 120-volt receptacle.

- ✔ A double-pole, 40- or 50-amp breaker. A *double-pole breaker* consists of two individual breakers joined together to form a single unit and used on 240-volt circuits.

  Make sure the new breaker is the same brand as your service panel. In most cases, brands are not interchangeable, and you could create a fire hazard by installing the wrong brand.

After the new circuit cable is run to the kitchen, it needs to be connected to the receptacle. And new ranges don't come with plugs, so you'll need to install one. Make sure to buy a four-wire appliance plug. Most ranges or the plug packaging have instructions for making the right connections.

Book IV

Bathroom and Kitchen Remodeling

Wiring ID: It's all in the numbers!

Understanding electric wire numbers isn't difficult. For example, a 6/3 cable means that the wire thickness of all the individual wires is a #6 wire and that there are three individual wires (not including the ground wire) within the cable's sheathing. Therefore, a 6/3 cable uses a #6 wire and has one black, one white, and one red wire, plus a bare or green wire for the ground. Some regions may require only an 8/3

cable for an electric range. The only difference is that the wires used are slightly thinner than the #6 wire, but three individual wires plus the ground wire are still there.

Just remember that as the first number of the wire designation gets bigger, the wire thickness or gauge gets smaller. The second number indicates the number of individual wires within the cable, excluding the ground wire.

If you're replacing an existing electric range, it may have a three-wire setup; however, the current electrical code requires a four-wire setup. You can't use a four-wire plug with a three-wire receptacle, so the old setup must be replaced.

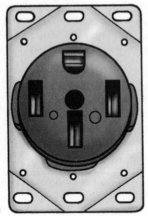

Figure 4-1: A 240-volt receptacle has three prong holes and one ground prong hole.

Converting from electric to gas: Running a new gas line

If your home has one gas-fired appliance, you can add as many as you like. The only thing that you need is a gas line to each of the new gas appliances. For this job, you need

✔ A roll (coil) of ½-inch outside diameter (O.D.) soft copper pipe (tubing). The beauty of running a gas line from an existing line is that most codes allow the use of soft copper from the main gas line pipe (which is usually black threaded pipe) to the appliance.

✔ Assorted short lengths of threaded black pipe, usually from 3 to 8 inches long (in 1-inch increments). These short lengths are called *nipples.*

✔ *Union fittings,* which connect the nipples to the main pipe.

✔ A Tee fitting for the nipple that will have the flexible copper line attached to it.

✔ A separate shut-off valve for the range gas line supply. You must have this valve so that you can shut off the gas to the range without having to shut off the gas to other appliances.

✔ Pipe joint compound, often called *pipe dope,* for coating all threaded connections (required by code).

Flexible copper pipe uses flare fittings to connect to the gas pipe. What makes this type of fitting so good is that it's easy to disassemble if you need to move the range for service or any other reason. You need a flaring tool kit to hold and form the flared end on the copper. The pipe is secured in the flaring tool base while you use a flaring tool to form the small lip or flare on the copper. If you work with flare fittings and don't form the lip properly the first time, don't try to reuse or reshape the lip. Cut off the flared lip by using a copper tube cutter and start over. After a lip is out of shape, it's unsafe to use. The lip must be round to seal properly inside the flare nut and against the flare union.

After reading all that's required for tapping into a gas line, you probably want to hire a professional to handle the job. Most plumbers can do this task. Permits and inspections are often required.

If you do install a gas line yourself, be sure to check it for gas leaks. Here's what to do:

1. **Apply a soap-and-water solution to each connection. Never use a match!**

   Pros use much more reliable but very expensive electronic sensors.

2. **Turn on the gas and look for bubbles.**

3. **If bubbles form, tighten the fitting slightly with a pipe wrench and recheck.**

   Be sure to wipe off the old solution and apply a new round of the mixture.

4. **If you still see leaks, disassemble the fitting and check the flare shape.**

   You may need to redo the flare end of the copper pipe.

If you smell any gas odor, shut off the gas immediately! Open a window to help move the gas fumes out of the room. Don't turn on a light or start an electric fan, either. Both have been known to cause a spark and ignite the gas fumes, causing a devastating and sometimes fatal explosion.

When working with flexible copper, be sure to leave two or three extra loops of copper behind the range before you attach it to the range and shut-off valve. The loops allow you to move the range in and out without putting stress on the connections. Repeated movement on the connections can cause them to leak. We've seen too many gas-fired ranges and clothes dryers with a straight line of soft copper pipe leading directly to the connection. The first time the owner moves the appliance, it puts a kink in the pipe, which then needs to be replaced.

If you kink soft copper tubing, cut off the kinked section and redo the fitting. This may mean replacing the entire length of pipe. Kinked soft copper tubing usually has a split in the side wall that's sometimes almost invisible. When you have a split, you also have a gas leak — a dangerous and possibly life-threatening situation.

Wrangling with a range

Assuming you purchased a *range* (a cooktop and oven combination unit) that uses the same fuel source as your old range, installing the new appliance should be as easy as sliding in or dropping in the unit. (You can also choose a freestanding range, but it's the same as a slide-in model — only not surrounded by cabinets.)

A slide-in range is the easiest to install regardless of the fuel source. After the fuel source connection is made, you simply push or slide the range into position — hence the name "slide-in."

The main thing to avoid in this installation is damaging the floor. Plastic appliance mover strips that you position under the legs of the range enable you to slide the range into place easily without scratching, or even contacting, the floor. You can also use part of the cardboard carton that the appliance was shipped in; however, be careful not to rip the cardboard while sliding the range. We've seen floors get damaged, and it really sours the mood of the project and its participants when it happens.

Electrically powered slide-in ranges use either a heavy cord that's plugged into a dedicated 240-volt/50-amp circuit or a length of flexible metal cable with individual wires inside, which is connected to an electrical box located behind the range. Gas-fired slide-in ranges use a flexible gas line that's attached to the gas supply line's shut-off valve, or *gas cock,* on one end and to the range's gas connection on the other. Gas connections use *flare nut fittings* to attach the gas supply line to the main gas line. When installed properly, they provide the best seal for preventing gas leaks, and they can be taken apart easily if, for example, you need to move the range out to work on the area behind it.

Making a gas connection to an appliance isn't difficult, but it must be done correctly to prevent a gas leak. Flare nut fittings are used on both ends of the flexible gas line. After the connections are made, check for leaks, as we explain in the "Converting from electric to gas: Running a new gas line" section, earlier in this chapter. If you detect a gas leak after testing and refitting the connection a couple of times, you may want to call a plumber to handle the hookup.

Both electric and gas ranges usually have a clock and other cooking accessories that run off of electrical power, but only 120 volts or a standard circuit is required. The ranges have a standard 120-volt power cord that's plugged into a 120-volt receptacle located on the wall behind the range. An electric range needs two outlets behind it — a 240-volt for powering the cooking components and a 120-volt for the clock and timer(s).

A drop-in range requires a cutout cabinet and countertop area so that the range drops into the cabinet. This type of range often has a flange around the edge of the cooktop surface. The flange rests on the countertop and supports the entire range. Then the range itself is screwed to the cabinet. The fuel-source hookups are the same for a drop-in range as they are for a slide-in type.

Installing a cooktop

Cooktops come in either gas or electric models and are installed in a cutout area of the countertop or in an island. Fuel-source connections are the same as for a range. The main difference is in how each type is installed in the countertop.

- ✔ **Electric models** typically have a flange around the cooktop (similar to a drop-in range) that supports the unit in the countertop. The weight of the cooktop is enough to keep it from shifting.

- ✔ **Gas-fueled units** are installed a little differently than their electric-powered counterparts. Gas cooktops do not have a flange around the edge for supporting the unit. Instead, they need to fit into a cutout or *dropped* section of the countertop and actually sit on the top of the cabinet frame. You (or your cabinet and countertop designer) should have figured this drop section into the plans so that the correct cabinets and countertop are ordered.

Built-in baking: Installing a built-in oven

A built-in oven is installed in a similar manner to a slide-in range except that it slides into a cabinet or, in some upscale installations, into an opening in the wall. Built-in ovens come in gas and electric versions, so hookups are the same as for slide-in units.

If your built-in oven is going into a cabinet, be sure that the oven dimensions fit in the cabinet opening. Most use industry standard dimensions, but double-check when ordering your cabinets to be sure that your new oven will fit.

Installing a New Fridge Complete with Dispenser Unit

The refrigerator is the easiest of all appliances to install. In many cases, when there's no in-the-door water and ice dispenser, it's as easy as sliding it into its designated space and plugging it in.

However, fridges today often come with popular extras that require more from you in the way of installation. The most popular of these extras is the in-the-door icemaker/water dispenser unit. For this feature, you need to run a water supply line to the back of the fridge. Fortunately, even the greenest of DIYers can handle this easy job.

You need the following tools:

- Two adjustable wrenches
- A ⅜-inch power drill (electric or cordless)
- A ½- to ¾-inch diameter spade bit
- An icemaker water supply kit (which usually includes a saddle Tee for tapping into the cold water supply line)
- A compression-fitting Tee kit (if a saddle Tee is not code-approved in your area)

Here's how the installation is done

1. **Determine which of the water supply pipes is the cold.**

    To find the cold water supply pipe, simply follow the two pipes that supply water to your kitchen sink. They should run parallel and be fairly close together. If the hookup is done correctly, the pipe on the right (as you're looking at them and as they're going to the sink) should be the cold. Believe it or not, we've been in a few houses where the hookups are backwards — hot on the left and cold on the right. If you're still not sure which is which, turn on the hot water tap at the kitchen sink and grab the pipes. Whichever pipe turns warm is the hot water supply pipe, so you know the other pipe supplies cold water.

If you have a basement, tap into the cold water pipe down there. Doing so gives you easy access to the pipe and from the pipe to the floor area just behind the refrigerator. Also, it doesn't take up space under the sink with another valve and the necessary supply pipe to the refrigerator. If your home doesn't have a basement, tap into the cold water supply line that goes to the faucet.

2. **Determine whether you can use a saddle valve in your area of the country.**

   Most icemaker kits come with a length of copper tubing and a saddle valve; however, in many areas a saddle valve doesn't meet code.

3. **If you can't use a saddle valve, you need to install a compression-fitting connected valve (see Figure 4-2). Simply cut out a short section of copper and install the compression-fitting valve.**

   Turn off the water before cutting into the water supply pipe!

   If you can use a saddle valve, follow these steps:

   a. **Attach the two straps (saddles) over the cold water pipe and secure them with the supplied bolts and nuts.**

      The shaft or spike of the valve is hollow and pointed so that when you tighten or close the handle of the valve completely, the tip of the shaft pierces the copper pipe and water then flows through the hollow center.

   b. **Open the valve completely to allow water to flow through the tubing to the fridge.**

      The copper tubing uses a compression fitting to connect it to the tapping valve's threaded end. Use an adjustable wrench to tighten the nut to the fitting.

   Don't reopen the saddle valve or the compression-fitting valve until you've attached the tubing to the refrigerator, or you'll have a big, wet mess!

4. **Drill a hole through the floor (if you're coming up from the basement) so that you can feed the copper tubing up to the refrigerator.**

   Use a spade bit to drill up through the flooring. Remember to wear eye protection, as you'll be drilling overhead, and it's easy for something to fall in your eye.

   If you're working in your basement, a quick way to spot the hole location from below is to drive a nail through the kitchen floor from above. Then simply go in the basement and look for the tip of the nail — that's where you drill the hole.

Book IV

Bathroom and Kitchen Remodeling

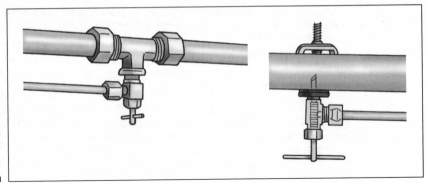

Figure 4-2:
Compression-fitting valve (left) and saddle valve (right).

5. **After the hole is drilled, feed the tubing up into the kitchen.**

   Don't cut off any extra tubing; instead, bend two or three large coils behind the fridge so that you can move the fridge in and out for cleaning without putting any stress on the tubing or the connections.

6. **Use a compression fitting to connect the kitchen end of the tubing to the back of the refrigerator's water fill valve, usually located in the lower left corner.**

7. **After all the connections are made, open the water supply and check for leaks.**

Make your icemaker work better and last longer

For pure, clean ice and better-tasting water, install an in-line water filter on the icemaker's water supply tube. Adding a filter increases your icemaker's life, because it removes particles and sediment from the water that would otherwise end up on the moving components of the icemaker and water dispenser. These hot dog-shaped filters get rid of particles and contaminants that can eventually clog the water inlet valve, the dispensing spout of the water dispenser, and the fill spout for the icemaker. Install the filter unit where you can access it easily. Otherwise, you may be discouraged from changing it because it's a hassle to reach. I've seen them installed behind the refrigerator in the coiled tube section and in the basement, too, before the tubing goes up to the kitchen. Either place works fine. You'll need to change the filter about every six months. (The actual length of time depends on your family's water usage habits.) Adding a water filter costs less than $20, including the fittings. Replacement filters cost between $10 and $15, depending on whether you replace just the filtering material or the entire cartridge. All the materials are sold at appliance parts stores and at most home centers.

You shouldn't have a leak at the refrigerator unless you didn't connect the threaded fitting on the water inlet valve properly. If it leaks there, carefully remove the fitting and reconnect it, keeping the fitting straight with the threads. If the compression-fitting valve leaks, turn off the water and redo the compression fittings.

Doing the Dishes — Automatic Style

For most families, an automatic dishwasher is a must-have appliance. It not only cleans the dishes, glasses, silverware, and cookware, but it also keeps your counters cleaner and neater by preventing dirty dishes from piling up.

Try to install a dishwasher next to the kitchen sink, because then the connections and drain lines are shorter. Shorter connections ensure that you get hotter water to the dishwasher and that dirty water gets into the drain lines sooner. Plus, loading dishes is easier when the dishwasher is right next to the sink.

Gathering the right tools

Installing a dishwasher is pretty straightforward, and you don't need much fancy tools and equipment. Simply gather the following common tools:

- A power drill
- A bit for drilling a hole in the cabinet side wall (the correct size bit will be listed in your dishwasher's installation instructions)
- A straight-tip screwdriver
- A 6-inch adjustable wrench

You'll also need a hot water supply connection (which you get by tapping into the hot water supply line of your kitchen sink faucet), a drain connection, and a 120-volt receptacle or electrical box. Check with your city's electrical inspector to find out which type of power hookup is allowed in your area. A dishwasher can drain directly into the sink's drain line or into a food (garbage) disposer.

Some cities require that an air gap be installed if you drain the dishwasher directly into the disposal. The air gap prevents a clogged drain from backing up into the dishwasher by actually causing a break in the direction of the water flow. An *air gap* is a piece of plastic pipe with a V-shaped split at one

Book IV

Bathroom and Kitchen Remodeling

end; the split ends are called *nipples*. This setup allows you to attach the dishwasher drain hose to the smaller straight nipple and a second, shorter length of pipe to the other air gap nipple and to the nipple on the disposer. Check with your city plumbing inspector to see what's required for your installation.

If you do drain your dishwasher through your food disposer, be sure to remove the plug or knockout in the dishwasher nipple on the disposer before attaching the drain hose from the dishwasher or air gap, depending on your situation. If you don't remove the plug, the dishwasher won't drain, and you'll be bathed in dirty, soapy water when you open the dishwasher door!

Installing the dishwasher unit

The basic steps for installing a dishwasher are listed as follows. Be sure to follow the manufacturer's instructions as steps may vary slightly among brands.

1. **If an air gap is required, mount it in one of your sink's predrilled openings.**

   If you don't have enough openings in your sink, drill a hole in the sink or in the countertop next to the sink.

2. **Cut a hole in the side of the sink base cabinet right next to where the dishwasher will be installed.**

   This hole is for the dishwasher drain hose and the water supply line. Consult the manufacturer's instructions for the exact size and location of the hole.

3. **Remove the lower access panel from the front of the dishwasher.**

   This is where you'll make the water and electrical connections to the dishwasher.

4. **Attach a brass L-fitting to the water inlet valve.**

   This fitting is threaded and simply screwed on. Apply some pipe dope on the threads of the fitting that go into the inlet valve to make a leak-free connection. Consult the installation instructions for the location of the water inlet valve — it varies between manufacturers.

   Again, your machine may or may not come supplied with a brass L-fitting. Dishwasher installation kits that do and L-fittings are sold at home centers and hardware stores. Check this out when you buy your machine.

5. **Feed the drain line hose through the hole in the cabinet as you slide the dishwasher into place.**

6. **Level the dishwasher by following the installation instructions.**

   Most dishwashers have adjustable front feet that are threaded for easy adjustment. This is one time when it's okay to eyeball the unit for level.

7. **If your system has an air gap, attach the dishwasher drain hose to the smaller air gap nipple.**

8. **Attach a second hose to the other air gap nipple and then to the dishwasher nipple.**

9. **Secure all hose connections with screw hose clamps (often referred to as *radiator hose clamps*).**

   If your unit didn't supply clamps, you can find them at home centers or auto parts stores. Buy a 2-inch or 3-inch clamp.

10. **Connect the dishwasher water supply tube to the hot water shut-off valve and feed it through a hole in the cabinet to the underside of the dishwasher.**

    Get a supply tube that has a braided steel or nylon shell. This type of tube is very flexible, it doesn't have to be cut to the exact length, and it lasts for years. You need a shut-off valve that has two outlets — one for the dishwasher and one for the faucet — which means that you have to replace the shut-off valve if there's only one outlet for the faucet.

11. **Attach the other end of the water supply tube to the other threads on the L-fitting.**

12. **Open the water supply valves and check for leaks.**

13. **If you don't find any leaks, make the electric connections so that the unit will run, and reinstall the front panel.**

    Consult your owner's manual for step-by-step instructions for this process because the steps vary among brands.

    But one rule applies to all units: Turn off the power before making any electrical connections!

Taking Out the Trash — Sink Style

A food (garbage) disposer's main job is to grind food waste so that it can be flushed down the drain, which cuts down on the amount of bagged garbage that goes into the local landfill. Yes, it does create more wastewater to be treated, but at least it can be treated and reused.

A food disposer takes the place of a sink basket and drain piece on one of the kitchen sink bowls. To install this appliance, consult the installation instructions that come with the unit, because the steps vary among brands.

Here are the basic steps for installing any food disposer:

1. **Remove the sink basket (if one was installed).**

2. **Send the *sink sleeve* (which replaces the sink basket and secures the disposer to the sink bowl) through the hole in the sink bottom and secure the sleeve to the bowl by using the gasket and mounting rings, following the unit's installation instructions.**

   The gaskets and mounting rings keep the sink sleeve from leaking when you run water. There are two mounting rings: the upper mounting ring and a backup mounting ring. There's also a snap ring that goes into the groove on the backup mounting ring as extra security for keeping the unit in place.

3. **Lift the disposer and align the *mounting lugs* (small, rolled curls of metal attached to the mounting ring) and *mounting ears* (90-degree angled metal cliplike pieces also attached to the mounting ring near the lugs) with the mounting screws located between the upper and backup mounting rings.**

   The mounting screws are threaded. The lugs and ears are located on the lower mounting ring, which is attached to the *disposer housing* (the main body of the unit).

   Turn the disposer clockwise until it's supported on the mounting assembly (sleeve and mounting rings).

4. **Attach the *discharge tube* (a short, approximately 90-degree plastic elbow where the waste and water is discharged) to the *discharge opening* (the larger hole in the side of the housing) in the side of the disposer housing.**

   The tube uses a rubber gasket and metal flange to secure it and keep it from leaking.

5. **If you're draining your dishwasher through the disposer, remove the plug in the smaller dishwasher nipple and attach the dishwasher drain hose to the nipple with a hose clamp.**

   If you don't have a dishwasher, *do not* remove the plug! If you remove the plug but don't have a hose to connect to the nipple, the water will spew out the hole.

6. **Connect the drain line pipe from the sink drain setup to the disposer's discharge tube with a slip nut and washer.**

   You may need to cut either the discharge tube or the drain line pipe to fit.

7. **Lock the disposer in place by using the disposer wrench (included with the unit).**

   Insert the wrench into one of the mounting lugs on the lower mounting ring and turn it clockwise until it locks.

8. **Make the electrical connection.**

   A standard plug-end cord is the electrical power connection for most disposers. But you do need to connect the cord to the motor wires. Here's how:

   1. **Remove the disposer's bottom plate.**

   2. **Strip off about ½ inch of insulation from each wire of the power cord.**

   3. **Connect like color wires by using wire connectors.**

   4. **To ground the unit, attach the green ground wire from the power supply to the green ground screw that will be on the disposer housing.**

      The screw is easy to spot, because it's actually painted green.

   5. **Gently push all the wires in and reinstall the bottom plate.**

   6. **Plug in the cord and you're good to go!**

All disposers need a dedicated electrical circuit with an on-off switch on the wall near the sink and a receptacle in the sink cabinet. If you're replacing an existing disposer, use the existing circuit, as long as it meets current electrical codes. If you need to install a receptacle and switch, have an electrician install the circuit. Working with the combination of electricity and plumbing can be dangerous — let a pro do it!

Book IV

Bathroom and Kitchen Remodeling

Chapter 5

Go Flush! Selecting and Installing a Toilet

*I*f you always took toilets for granted, you're in for a big surprise when you find yourself in the toilet-buying market. Don't be overwhelmed by the fact that you have hundreds to choose from. Consider this chapter Toilets 101, where you'll find everything you need to know about choosing and installing the toilet that's right for your home.

When it comes to a toilet, function follows form, so begin by pinpointing who the primary users are and how often it will be used. A good choice for an infrequently used powder room is a distant cousin from one that's used in a family's one-and-only hall bathroom. If you have large family members, you may want to consider elongated toilets, which are larger and more comfortable. Also available are elevated toilets, which are convenient for anyone who is physically challenged or has difficulty sitting down or rising. A standard toilet has a 15-inch rim height, but many of today's toilet manufacturers are now offering 17-inch rim heights, which are more comfortable for most adults and meet the requirements of the Americans with Disabilities Act (ADA). Choose a toilet to fit the person who will use it.

You can buy a toilet for under $100 or over $1,000, and both of them can get the job done. But obviously, the durability, design, quality, and style are what account for the price difference. Figure an average price of $300 for a good-quality toilet that may outlive the people who installed it. Actually, the life expectancy of a toilet is 40-plus years. Set your budget first because it may limit the color selection, quality, quietness, flushing mechanism, water-conserving quality, and ease of cleaning.

Taking a Tour of Toilets

Most toilets are made of vitreous china, which means that they're impervious to water. It's a durable material that's easy to clean, making it the obvious choice for a bathroom. Toilets come in two basic designs:

- ✔ **One-piece:** This style is seamlessly molded together, has a streamlined look, and is, consequently, easy to clean.

- ✔ **Two-piece:** Less expensive than a one-piece unit but slightly more difficult to install, the more typical two-piece toilet has a separate water tank that hangs on the wall and rests on the toilet base or bowl.

Check out Figure 5-1 to see the differences between one-piece and two-piece toilets.

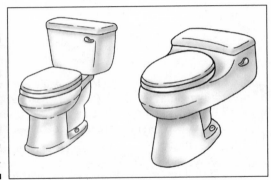

Figure 5-1:
Notice the differences between a two-piece toilet (L) and a one-piece toilet (R).

When you buy a two-piece toilet, you have to buy the toilet seat separately because the seat isn't sold as part of the toilet — strange but true.

Considering flushing mechanisms

The rush of the water moving through the toilet to remove the waste causes that whoosh that you hear when you press the flush lever. Good old gravity, water, or air pressure causes the water rush. Depending on where your toilet is located, one flushing method is better than the other. The types of flushing mechanisms are as follows:

- ✔ **Powered by gravity (the quiet flush):** Gravity toilets are a lesson in basic physics: Press the lever to release water in the tank into the bowl. The weight of the water, located above the toilet's drain, flushes the water and waste down the drain.

✔ **Pressure assisted (the big whoosh):** Pressure-assisted toilets (see Figure 5-2) use water pressure or compressed air to force water through the bowl and flush the water and waste down the drain. This type of toilet gets the job done, but because it's sometimes noisy, everyone in the house may know just what you're doing. The noise level also makes these toilets a bad choice near a bedroom or family room, but that may not be the case forever: Manufacturers are working on reducing the noise.

Figure 5-2: A pressure-assisted toilet.

Getting a good fit

The typical height of a toilet is 14 to 15 inches, a convenient and comfortable height for most people. For tall or large people, elevated toilets are available that are up to 18 inches high. These elevated toilets are also convenient for anyone who is physically challenged and has difficulty sitting down or rising. You'll also find ADA-compliant toilets that meet the standards of the Americans with Disabilities Act for wheelchair accessibility. And if parenthood is in your future, you may be interested to know that you can get a small toilet that's scaled down for a child and designed for potty training.

Book IV

Bathroom and Kitchen Remodeling

The lowdown on low-flow toilets

In the early 1990s, a national law was passed to conserve water. It mandated that all new toilets sold in the United States require a maximum of 1.6 gallons of water per flush. The thinking was that by reducing the water from 3.5 gallons used by the old-style tanks, a lot of water would be saved. However, these early low-flow toilets were flawed in design and required two or sometimes, three flushes to empty the bowl.

This, of course, gave credence to complaints of many homeowners, builders, and remodelers that low-flows nullify any water savings.

That's all an unpleasant part of our history, and if you had one of those early low-flows, we hope you've replaced it. If you haven't, do it now with one of today's new and improved low-flow models.

Considering features and comfort

When you begin your personal survey of toilets, you'll be amazed at the differences and nuances in comfort you'll discover. Here are some things to notice in your quest for the perfect toilet for your remodeled bathroom:

- **Comfortable size:** Is the toilet too small for a large person's use? Consider an elongated toilet, which is usually about 2 inches deeper than a standard toilet and has an oversized seat, making it more comfortable and convenient to use.

- **Elevated height:** For anyone who struggles while lowering and raising themselves, consider an elevated toilet, which is approximately two to four inches higher than a standard toilet.

- **Cleanability:** Some people consider the ease of cleaning a toilet the most important feature. For them, a one-piece toilet with a smooth-sided bowl is the best choice. Another option is a toilet seat that pulls off without tools, so it's easy to clean.

- **Quiet flush:** If your bathroom is next to living quarters, consider a toilet that offers a quiet flushing system. It's much like a dishwasher: You want it to work, but you don't want to hear it working.

- **Power flushing:** Many toilet manufacturers have their own patented flushing systems designed to exceed performance standards. Most of these designs use water pressure to compress air in a chamber. When the toilet is flushed, the air pushes the water out of the chamber at high velocity, flushing the toilet with less water.

- **Automatic seat closing:** Some toilets are designed with a slow-moving hinge that gradually lowers both the seat and lid. Doesn't this sound like the perfect solution for the lone woman in an all-male household?

- **Insulated water tank:** To prevent a build-up of moisture on the outside of the tank (a breeding ground for mold and mildew), many toilets have an insulated water tank. The insulation prevents condensation by keeping the cold water inside. This feature is popular in humid climates.

- **Two-lever flush lever:** To conserve water, many toilets offer a double-action flushing lever. You push the small lever to release less water for liquids or use the large lever to flush away solid waste.

Reinventing your bathroom with new fixtures

Decisions, decisions, decisions — that's what you'll face when you begin looking at toilets. Fortunately, the major manufacturers of plumbing fixtures have done some of the work for you by offering eye-catching suites or collections of fixture styles. You'll find toilets and bidets, sinks, tubs, and faucets in a variety of styles that include contemporary, traditional, country, Victorian, and retro, just to name some of them.

If you're remodeling a particularly small bathroom, you'll find compact-size toilets designed specifically to fit in small spaces.

Some manufacturers offer a special corner toilet when that's the only space available.

You can choose from a rainbow of colors for toilets and fixtures, as well as the more versatile white and off-white. If you're choosing a colored fixture, make sure that you see a life-size floor model first — not just on a sample board. This isn't wallpaper that you can just remove if you get tired of it. You can expect to live with a toilet, one of the more permanent fixtures in your home, for a long time.

Shopping for la toilette

Depending on where you live, you can shop for bathroom fixtures in several places. Many of the large home store chains have design centers within their stores, where a wide selection of toilets and related fixtures are installed in showroom settings. Kitchen and bathroom design centers feature extensive displays of bathrooms and a selection of fixtures and cabinetry. The more sources you can visit, the better. That way, you're able to preview different types, styles, and colors of toilets, along with their related fixtures.

You can also purchase toilets and other bathroom fixtures from several sources on the Internet. But if you decide to buy online, do so only after you've done the footwork and know the toilet style, model, and color you want. Before placing an order online, investigate the cost of shipping and handling, as well as the return policy.

Realtors tell us that brightly colored bathroom fixtures can be a real turnoff to prospective buyers. Your ultimate bathroom may have hot pink fixtures, but if you're not going to live there forever, be more subdued in your choice of toilet colors. Basic white may be boring to you, but it can be beautiful to others.

Book IV

Bathroom and Kitchen Remodeling

Roughing Dimension: Measuring Your Options

Installing pipes behind the walls or beneath the floor, called *roughing in,* is the first stage of a new plumbing job. In a remodeling project, the pipes are already there but may have to be altered. In either situation, the location of these pipes must match up with the fixtures that are installed later. To make sure that pipes and fixtures are properly aligned, manufacturers provide rough-in dimensions for each fixture. For a toilet, the important rough-in dimension is the distance from the wall to the center of the drainpipe in the floor and the height on the wall behind the toilet for the water supply line. If the drain isn't the proper distance from the wall, the toilet could sit far from the wall and look silly. Even worse, if the drain is too close to the wall, the base of the toilet can't be aligned over the drain. (See the section "Installing a New Toilet," later in this chapter.)

If you're replacing a really old toilet, measure the distance between the bolts that hold it to the floor and the wall. Prior to the mid-1930s, tanks were hung on the wall, and the bowl was attached to a sewer pipe with a mounting flange located either 10 inches or 14 inches from the wall. Today, toilets use a 12-inch roughing-in dimension, so if you're replacing one of these good ol' boys, you may have to hire a plumber to modify the drainpipe or install an offset toilet flange, which may give you the extra two inches that you need to install a 12-inch toilet on a 10-inch rough-in. Figure 5-3 illustrates a rough-in position for a toilet. Toilets are available on special order to fit the old dimensions, but the choice of styles is very limited.

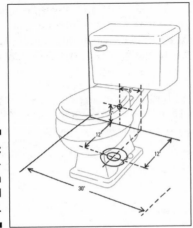

Figure 5-3: The rough-in position for a typical toilet.

To get a heads-up about what's involved before you buy and install a fixture, go to the manufacturer's Web site and find the product specifications, which usually include installation instructions and roughing-in information. Before buying and installing any fixture, read the instructions so that you have time to think it through and plan the job before actually doing it. Ain't the Internet great?

Dethroning the Throne

Disconnecting an old toilet to prepare for the installation of a new one is nothing regal. The steps to install a toilet are the reverse of removing one, so you get a practice run before connecting the new one. Clear the floor and lay an old blanket or newspaper nearby so that you can rest the parts of the toilet on the paper as you disassemble it. You'll also need a bucket, a large sponge, rags, rubber gloves, a wrench, and a scraper.

Don't worry about touching the water! The water in the tank is clean, and the water in the bowl is flushed out before you begin.

Follow these steps to remove an old toilet:

1. **Pour ¼ cup of toilet bowl cleaner or household bleach into the toilet and flush it a few times.**

2. **Turn off the water to the toilet and flush the toilet again, lift off the top of the tank, and set it aside so that it's out of the way.**

3. **Mop water out of the tank with a sponge and disconnect the supply line to it at the bottom of the toilet tank.**

   The toilet bowl will have a small amount of water at the bottom.

4. **Wearing rubber gloves to protect against bacteria, use a large sponge to soak up the water remaining in the bowl and squeeze it into a bucket. Continue until all the water is gone.**

   You can also use a wet-dry shop vacuum to remove the water left in the bottom of a toilet.

5. **Remove the gloves and wash your hands thoroughly.**

6. **Look on the underside of the toilet base where the tank rests to find the tank mounting nuts and bolts. Use a wrench to loosen and unscrew them.**

If the nuts and bolts are corroded and won't budge with a wrench, give them a shot of WD-40 or Liquid Wrench, a spray lubricating oil. If that doesn't loosen them, try a hacksaw, inserting the blade between the toilet base and the nut to cut through the bolts. Place masking tape on the surface of the toilet that's near the bolts to protect the base.

7. **Find the nuts and bolts on either side of the base of the toilet that hold the toilet to the floor. If they're covered with plastic caps, remove the caps and use a wrench to loosen and unscrew the nuts.**

   If the bolts are too corroded to unscrew, remove them with a hacksaw. (See Figure 5-4.) Keep a rag handy to wipe up any water that may seep out.

Figure 5-4:
Use a hacksaw to cut through badly corroded closet hold-down bolts.

8. **Standing over the toilet bowl, gently rock it from side to side to break the seal of the wax ring; then lift it straight up and keep it level.**

   Water is likely to be left in the trap, and you'll slosh it all over your feet and the floor if you tilt the toilet. Rest the toilet on an old blanket or newspapers.

9. **Stuff an old rag in the hole in the floor, called the *closet flange.***

   This hole is a direct path to the soil pipe that leads to the sewer or septic system. The rag prevents sewer gases from entering your home.

10. **Find the old wax ring that sticks the base of the toilet to the floor and remove it.**

11. **Use a scraper or putty knife to thoroughly clean the floor of all the residue.**

12. **Wipe down the flange and surrounding area with a mixture of household bleach and water or use a disinfectant cleaning solution.**

Preparing the Floor for a New Toilet

After you remove the toilet, inspect the underlayment for damage. The *underlayment* is a material that provides a flat, level surface for the finished flooring and toilet to rest on.

Look for telltale signs of moisture. Dark or discolored underlayment around a toilet indicates water damage. You can replace only the damaged sections, leaving in place what's in good condition (see Figure 5-5). To make the repairs, cut away the damaged underlayment with a circular saw, setting the saw blade depth to match the thickness of the underlayment. Cut through the underlayment with the saw and remove the bad section around the toilet. Then cut a piece of underlayment of the same thickness as the old and replace the damaged pieces.

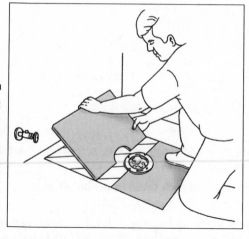

Figure 5-5: Before installing a new fixture, replace any damaged underlayment.

If you're installing a new floor over an existing one, plan to get an extension flange that raises the toilet up to align with the new flooring height.

Book IV

Bathroom and Kitchen Remodeling

Installing a New Toilet

You install a two-piece toilet in three phases: First, you secure the toilet base to the floor, then you fasten the tank to the base, and finally, you connect the water supply to fill the toilet with water.

A one-piece toilet is installed in the same way as a two-piece unit except that it's more cumbersome and heavier to handle. Because it's all in one piece, however, the installation goes faster, because you don't need to install pieces separately. Use the basic instructions later in this section to install both types of toilets.

To install a two-piece toilet, you need the following:

- Adjustable wrench
- Carpenter's level
- Plumber's putty
- Putty knife
- Scrap of carpeting or heavy blanket
- Screwdriver
- Toilet and its mounting nuts and bolts
- Wax ring or bowl gasket

Carefully read the installation instructions packaged with the toilet and identify the parts and then follow these steps to install a new toilet:

1. **Remove the rag in the flange hole in the floor.**

2. **Prepare the floor for a wax ring.**

    If you haven't already, scrape up any old wax and debris from the flange and surrounding area.

3. **Locate the closet bolts and attach them to the toilet flange.**

    Turn the T-shaped head of each bolt so that it slips into the slot in the flange. Push the bolt into the slot and slide it into position so it's parallel to the wall behind the toilet. Turn the bolt, so the head can't be pulled out of the flange. Slide the plastic retainer washers down the threads to hold the bolts in place.

4. **Turn the toilet upside down and rest it on a padded surface.**

5. **Locate the *toilet horn,* the short spout in the center of the toilet's base. Place the wax ring and its sleeve onto the toilet horn and press it down firmly, as shown in Figure 5-6.**

    This wax ring fits around the toilet horn and compresses against the drain flange as you press it to the floor and then bolt it into place. The plastic spout must face up. You have a one-time shot with a wax ring, because after the ring is compressed, it won't spring back. The key to a proper seal is to lower the toilet onto the flange without disturbing it.

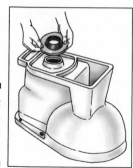

Figure 5-6:
Installing a
new wax
ring seal.

6. **Carefully lower the toilet base on the flange by lining up the closet bolts over the holes in the toilet base (see Figure 5-7).**

   It's helpful to have another person on hand to line up the bolts with the holes in the base as you lower the toilet onto the floor. Keep the base level as you lower it to the floor.

   Put plastic drinking straws over the bolts to lengthen them and act as guides as you lower the toilet onto the bolts.

7. **Gently but firmly press the base down on the wax ring.**

8. **Put a carpenter's level across the toilet base to assure that the bowl is level both side to side and front to back (see Figure 5-8), and then place the washers and nuts on the bolts, using an adjustable wrench to tighten them.**

   Alternate side to side as you tighten the nuts, checking that the bowl is still level side to side and front to back.

Figure 5-7:
Lower the
toilet bowl
onto the
bolts
installed in
the slots on
the side of
the toilet
flange.

Wax seal
Floor bolts
Toilet flange

Book IV

**Bathroom
and Kitchen
Remodeling**

Figure 5-8:
Use a
carpenter's
level to
ensure that
the bowl
is level.

Be careful not to overtighten the bolts. You don't want to tighten them so hard that they crack the base of the toilet.

9. **Cover the bolts with the trim caps.**

If the bolts are too long for the trim caps to cover them, shorten them with a hacksaw. Snap the plastic trim caps in place to cover the bolts.

10. **Install the flush mechanism (if necessary).**

The fill and flush mechanism in a toilet tank regulates the flow of water into the tank when you push the lever. It opens a valve so that clean water in the tank flows into the toilet bowl, flushing out its contents. Most toilets come with the mechanism installed, but if yours does not, follow the instructions included with the toilet to install it.

11. **Turn the tank upside down and attach the rubber seal, called the** *spud washer,* **to the pipe that protrudes from the bottom of the tank.**

12. **Carefully turn the tank right side up and center the spud washer over the water intake opening, which is at the back edge of the bowl in the toilet base.**

13. **Lower the tank to the back of the bowl, align the tank bolts and rubber washers with the holes in the tank, and insert the tank mounting bolts through the holes in the bowl.**

14. **On the toilet bowl's underside, thread on the washers and nuts, tightening by hand at first and then with a large screwdriver (see Figure 5-9).**

Do so carefully and don't overtighten. Be sure to turn the nut, not the bolt. Some toilet tanks have preinstalled mounting bolts, and others require that you preinstall the bolts. Follow the directions that come with the toilet.

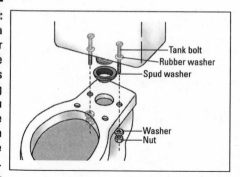

Figure 5-9:
Use a screwdriver to keep the tank bolts from turning while you tighten the nuts from below the tank.

Tank bolt
Rubber washer
Spud washer

Washer
Nut

15. **Connect the riser (supply) tube and shut-off valve by fastening the coupling nut to the tank fitting and the compression fitting to the shut-off valve, first by hand, and then with a wrench.**

    Reinforced flexible tubes available in various lengths in white or braided stainless steel are very reliable and easier to install than standard plastic or chromed brass tubes.

16. **Turn on the water supply at the stop valve to fill the tank and toilet with water, checking for any leaks and watching the toilet as it begins to fill with water.**

    The water flow should begin to slow and stop at the fill line marked inside the tank. Tighten connections only as needed to stop leaks. Don't overtighten.

17. **Follow the manufacturer's directions about adjusting the water level.**

    Some valves have a float arm that can be adjusted, and others have a setscrew to adjust.

18. **Install the toilet seat by pushing the seat bolts through the holes in the toilet base and then holding the nuts on below while you tigheten the bolts with a large screwdriver.**

That's it! Enjoy your new throne.

Book IV

Bathroom and Kitchen Remodeling

Chapter 6

Rub a Dub Dub! Replacing a Tub

In This Chapter

▶ Choosing and installing a new bathtub

▶ Removing the old tub

▶ Sprucing up an old tub that can't be removed

This is where remodeling a bathroom gets personal. Are you a tub person or a shower person — or both? Shrinks probably have theories about what people's personal bathing preferences disclose about their personalities, but we'd rather leave that one alone. We do know that most people have definite preferences. If you're a tub person who delights in soaking in bubbles or steaming in hot bathwater, you have a lot of options. Even if your space is limited or odd shaped, you can probably find a bathtub or whirlpool tub to fit your space and satisfy your desire for bathing luxury.

What if you have an old bathtub that can't be removed? Sure, with a sledge-hammer anything's possible, but we discuss when it makes sense to leave an old tub in place, give it a cover-up, and improve the room around it.

 In your quest for the perfect bathtub, visit the Web sites for Kohler (www. kohler.com) and American Standard (www.americanstandard-us.com), where you get an overview of the variety of tubs available — colors, finishes, sizes, prices, configurations, installation notes and specifications, and complementary products.

Selecting a Bathtub

Want to soak and simmer in hot, steamy water? How about easing your aches and pains with a soothing massage? Or maybe you're an in-and-out kind of bather who wants nothing more than hot water and plenty of it. Do some noodling about what you like and don't like about your current tub and make a list of your preferences. After you nail down your bathing priorities, you're in for a whole lot of choices. Options range from posh platform tubs to charming replica claw-foot tubs.

The typical bathtub is 5 feet long, 14 inches deep, and 32 inches wide, but there are variations on this theme. Longer, deeper tubs are available to accommodate different shapes and sizes of bathers. Many 6- and 7-foot tubs are sized for two bathers. Square or corner tubs range from 4 feet square and larger. Most tubs are configured with either a left- or right-hand outlet for the drain to accommodate different installations.

Try before you buy. You sat in your recliner before you bought it, didn't you? Why not a bathtub? Climb in when no one's looking and see how it fits. If you're buying a two-person bathtub, definitely try it on for size.

Bathtub manufacturers offer a rainbow of colorful shades, many of them coordinated with matching sinks and toilets. Whites and neutral shades are the least expensive and easiest to get. For resale purposes, real estate agents say that subtle neutrals are the best choice. But if your heart is set on taking a bubble bath in a navy blue bathtub, go for it.

Bathtubs are made from a variety of materials. Your budget will likely determine which material you choose:

- **Cast iron:** A cast-iron tub is the most expensive option. The heaviest material, cast iron offers deep, rich colors and a glossy surface that can't be matched. It's the best you can buy.

- **Steel:** Formed steel coated with enamel is a popular material for tubs. It's lighter than cast iron but not as durable.

- **Acrylic:** Acrylic tubs are molded and shaped in any number of configurations and feature a durable easy-care surface.

- **Fiberglass:** These lightweight tubs are easy to handle and are an economical alternative to acrylic.

Bidding Good Riddance to an Old Tub

Anyone who has remodeled a bathroom will tell you that the most difficult part of the project is removing the old tub. You have to remove all the plumbing fixtures, disconnect the plumbing lines — that's the easy part — and then dislodge, cajole, and finally lift out the monster. The finale involves manhandling the tub (in one piece or many pieces) out of the bathroom, through the house, and to the trash. Everyone should experience this act of skill and brute force. The sense of relief is sheer bliss.

Built-in, platform, and footed tubs offer unique challenges. An old built-in may have layers of wallboard, tile, or surround material holding the tub in place, so removing the walls is the first job. (See the section "Taking out the tub," later in this chapter, for those instructions.) That old charmer of a platform or footed tub is heavier than an elephant and just about as easy to move down a staircase. Sometimes the only way to get it out is to bust it up with a sledgehammer and remove it in pieces.

Before you take up a sledgehammer, check the Yellow Pages. A local architectural salvage outfit may be willing to remove the tub for you. You can also advertise it as a giveaway item in your local newspaper's classifieds. There's a good chance that a salvage dealer or contractor will be willing to remove it for you — or even pay for the tub.

After the old tub is gone, the bathroom will appear to have grown in size, and you'll probably discover (if you haven't already) the key to unlocking the inner workings of your bathroom's plumbing.

Gaining access to the plumbing

First, a word about working on the plumbing lines of a bathtub. If you're lucky, your bathtub plumbing lines are accessible through an *access panel,* a removable inspection panel that's often located in a hall or the closet of an adjoining room. The panel is a piece of plywood that's framed in and fastened by screws that probably have been painted over. If you have one of these inspection panels, working on the tub, faucet, and valve will be much easier, and you won't disturb the walls around the tub.

If you don't have an access panel, build one so that working on the pipes is convenient — now and in the future. Follow these easy steps:

1. **On the wall, mark off a 30-inch rectangle of wallboard that gives you full access to the tub's pipes and fittings.**

   Use a carpenter's level to mark off the rectangular outline so that the horizontal and vertical lines are square.

2. **Use a drywall saw to cut the wallboard, following the outline to make the opening.**

3. **Make the panel by cutting a piece of ¼-inch plywood a couple inches larger than the opening and sanding the edges.**

4. **Secure the corners of the panel with wood cleats or screws.**

5. **Paint your new access panel to match the wall.**

Disconnecting the plumbing lines

All tubs connect to the plumbing lines in the same way. Turn off your water supply and then follow these steps to disconnect your lines:

1. **Standing in the tub, unscrew the faucet handles from the valve body and remove the spout.**

   You may need a screwdriver or hex wrench if you find a hex nut under the spout.

2. **Remove the screws holding the overflow plate in position and remove the plate.**

   You may have to pull the drain linkage mechanism out of the overflow along with the cover.

3. **To loosen the tub drain, push the handles of a pair of slip-joint pliers into the tub drain, called the *spud*.**

4. **Put a large screwdriver between the handles of the pliers and turn the pliers counterclockwise to unscrew the drain from the pipe under the tub, called the *shoe*.**

Taking out the tub

Now's the time to bring in friends and neighbors with bulging biceps. Don't attempt to do this job alone. Get two strong helpers to assist with the pulling, lifting, and carrying.

If the tub surround has tiles, use a cold chisel to chip away the lowest course of tile around the tub's perimeter (see Figure 6-1). Remember to wear safety glasses. If the tub has a fiberglass enclosure, cut the enclosure 6 inches above the tub.

Figure 6-1:
When removing a tub, carefully chip out the first row of tile with a cold chisel.

To remove a built-in tub, follow these steps:

1. **Use a screwdriver or pry bar to remove the screws or nails that attach the tub flange to the wall studs.**

2. **When the tub is free from the walls, use a pry bar to loosen the front of the tub from the floor.**

   Place the end of the bar between the floor and the tub and pry up to raise the tub off the floor. If your floors are tile, you may need to break out a course or two of floor tiles as you did for the walls tiles.

3. **Insert several scraps of plywood or cardboard skid under the front edge of the tub.**

   The wood protects the floor and makes it easier to pull the tub out of its enclosure.

4. **Slide the tub onto the plywood and pull the tub away from the wall (see Figure 6-2).**

Figure 6-2:
Use a wood or cardboard skid when removing a tub.

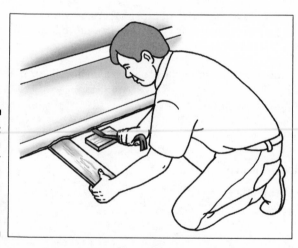

The challenge is to lift and move the tub safely down a steep staircase. Be careful — making turns can get dicey.

If the tub won't budge, you may have to cut it in pieces. A reciprocating saw with a metal cutting blade cuts through a steel or fiberglass tub. Use a sledge-hammer to break up a cast-iron tub, but cover it with an old dropcloth first. To protect yourself, wear long sleeves, long pants, and heavy leather work-gloves. And don't forget safety glasses to protect your eyes.

Putting In a New Tub

Installing a tub isn't an easy do-it-yourself project because it involves working with a large, heavy object in a small space. If you have any misgivings about doing it, hire a plumber who has the experience to install it and the license to hook up the fixtures.

If you want to do it yourself, inspect the new tub before you start the installation. Measure its dimensions and check them against the size of the opening. Make sure that the drain outlet is at the correct end of the tub. Look for signs of damage and then protect the tub surface with a dropcloth.

Before you get started on the installation, inspect the floor joists and look for joists that have been weakened by rot or were cut to remove pipes. Remove a rotten joist and replace it. Reinforce a bad joist by fastening a new joist to the existing one with machine bolts. Then install a new subfloor over the joists if necessary.

Such work is beyond the capabilities of most DIYers, so don't hesitate to hire a carpenter if you run into situations that seem like more than you can or want to handle.

Gather the following tools and materials to install an acrylic or platform tub.

- 1-inch galvanized roofing nails
- 2 x 4s
- Carpenter's level
- Construction adhesive
- Electric drill and bits
- Measuring tape
- Mortar mix
- Pipe wrench
- Plumber's putty
- Screwdriver
- Silicone caulk
- Trowel
- Wood shims
- Woodworking tools

Installing an acrylic tub

An acrylic tub is set in a bed of cement — check the manufacturer's recommendations. The sides are screwed or nailed through flanges into wall studs. The tub is supported on a 1-x-4-inch ledger nailed to the wall studs. In models with integral supports under the tub, you can shim under the supports to compensate for a slightly out-of-level floor. Then you connect the overflow assembly to the tub drain and main drain line, connect faucets to the water supply lines, and hook up plumbing pipes and drain lines.

Installing a ledger board

The first step in installing a tub is to set in place a ledger board that supports the edges of the tub that contact the walls of the tub enclosure. Follow these steps:

1. **Push the tub into the enclosure to mark the top of the flange on the wall studs with a pencil.**

2. **Measure and mark the location for the top of the ledger, usually about 1 inch below the first mark.**

   Use the manufacturer's specifications or measure the distance from the top of the flange to the underside of the tub; it's usually 1 inch.

3. **Use coarse drywall screws to fasten the ledger board horizontally and level across the back wall of the alcove (see Figure 6-3).**

Figure 6-3: Installing a ledger around the perimeter of the tub enclosure.

Book IV

Bathroom and Kitchen Remodeling

4. **Fasten shorter ledger boards to the ends of the enclosure, level with the board you install on the back wall.**

   Doing so creates a continuous ledge on the tub enclosure wall for the tub to rest on.

Hooking up the plumbing

It's easier to install the drain and overflow pipes on the tub before it's permanently installed in the enclosure. Turn the tub over or rest it on its side and then follow these steps:

1. **Follow the manufacturer's directions and assemble the shoe fitting, which is placed under the tub and the waste pipe.**

2. **Assemble the overflow fitting with the overflow pipe.**

   Insert the ends of the overflow pipe and waste pipe in the T-fitting (see Figure 6-4).

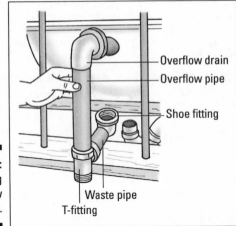

Overflow drain

Overflow pipe

Shoe fitting

Waste pipe

T-fitting

Figure 6-4:
Installing an overflow drain.

3. **Put this assembly in place to check that shoe and overflow align with the openings in the tub.**

4. **Place a bead of plumber's putty around the drain flange and wrap Teflon pipe tape around the threads on its body.**

5. **Place a rubber washer on the shoe and position the shoe under the tub in alignment with the drain flange.**

6. **Screw the drain flange into the shoe.**

7. **Tighten the drain flange.**

   Place the handles of a pair of pliers in the drain flange. Insert the blade of a large screwdriver between the handles of the pliers and use it as a lever to tighten the drain flange.

8. **Place a rubber washer on the overflow drain and install the overflow cover with the screws provided.**

   You may want to leave the drain linkage and pop-up assembly out of the tub until you set it in place.

Securing the tub

Follow these steps to apply mortar to the subfloor of the tub:

1. **Mix a batch of mortar according to the package directions.**

2. **With a notched trowel, spread a 2-inch layer of mortar on the subfloor where the tub will sit.**

3. **Lift the tub in place and position it so that it's tight against the walls.**

   Hold a carpenter's level on the tub and check that it's level. If not, adjust it by placing wood shims under the tub.

Finishing up

After the tub is level, you secure it to the enclosure to keep it that way. Secure the flange to the studs by driving 1-inch galvanized roofing nails through the holes in the flange (see Figure 6-5). If the tub is fiberglass, drill holes at each stud. If it's a steel or cast-iron tub and it has no holes, or they don't align with the studs, drive the nails above the top of the flange so that the head of each nail engages the flange. Hammer carefully so as not to damage the tub.

Figure 6-5:
Securing
the tub
flange to the
wall studs
with roofing
nails.

Installing a platform tub

When a tub becomes the centerpiece of a bathroom, it's often enclosed in a framed platform that's given a surface of tile, wood, or other finishing material. The project may require reinforcing existing floor framing in addition to the construction skills and tools to build the platform and plumbing know-how and tools to install the unit, its water and drain lines and faucets. If you are so gifted, follow the tub manufacturer's directions for the wiring and plumbing requirements and use these guidelines for building a platform. If you prefer to sit this one out, hire a contractor for all or part of the task. In either case, the following sections tell you what's involved.

Doing the prep work

Follow the tub manufacturer's suggestions and design a platform that's at least a foot wider and longer than the tub and high enough to support it above the existing floor. Build the framework for the platform from 2 x 4s and ¾-inch exterior grade plywood, using nails and deck screws to fasten them together. Keep in mind that the height of the platform should allow for the plywood decking plus the thickness of backerboard, thinset mortar, and tile and allow a ¼-inch expansion gap between the tub and the finish material. If you're installing a whirlpool tub, make an opening in the framework for an access panel for the pump and drain.

Constructing the platform for a tub isn't difficult, but it requires accurate measuring and cutting. This project is very straightforward for a carpenter, so you may be well served to hire out this phase.

1. **Check the height of the platform that your tub requires and calculate the height of the platform wall studs.**

   For example, if the tub requires a 36-inch-high platform, the studs should be cut to 31¾ inches. This length allows for the thickness of the top and bottom 2-x-4 plate, the ¾-inch plywood, backerboard, mortar, and tile.

2. **Nail the studs to the top and bottom plates to form the walls for the platform.**

3. **Secure the wall framework to the floor with nails, and use deck screws to cover the framework with plywood to make the deck.**

4. **Use a jigsaw to cut an opening in the deck for the tub, either by using the template provided by the manufacturer or after carefully marking the dimensions for the rough opening (see Figure 6-6).**

5. **Follow the faucet manufacturer's instructions for measuring and marking the rough-in locations for supply pipes.**

6. **Drill the holes in the deck and then rough in the water supply and drainpipes.**

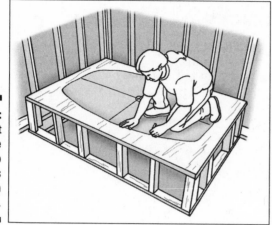

Figure 6-6:
Laying out
the outline
of the tub
so that it's
centered on
the deck.

Dropping in the tub

After the platform is built and the plumbing is roughed in, you place the tub in the platform. It's easier to install a whirlpool tub after you've installed the tile on the top surface of the platform, but you may not have enough room to move the large tub around the bathroom as you build the partitions. If that's the case, install the tub before the tile. Both options are discussed here.

Follow these steps to secure the tub in the platform:

1. **If the tub must be installed *before* the tile, place wood blocks on the platform along the perimeter of the cutout to support the tub at the correct height above the plywood deck.**

   The wood blocks should be the thickness of the thinset mortar, backer board, thinset mortar, and tile and be positioned as shown in Figure 6-7.

   If the tub can be installed after the tile is installed on the plywood deck, the blocks are not needed. The tub will rest directly on the tile.

2. **Apply a layer of mortar to the floor below the tub for additional support (following the manufacturer's directions).**

3. **Carefully lift the tub by its rim and set it in the cutout hole, with the help of at least one other person (see Figure 6-7).**

4. **After the mortar has set, install the drain assembly and connect the wiring to the motor and controls.**

5. **Complete the installation by finishing the surface of the deck and platform.**

   Install backerboard to the sides and top of the platform with backerboard screws (see Figure 6-8). Apply thinset mortar and install the tile or other surface material.

Book IV

**Bathroom
and Kitchen
Remodeling**

Figure 6-7:
Lifting the
tub very
carefully
into position
in the
opening.

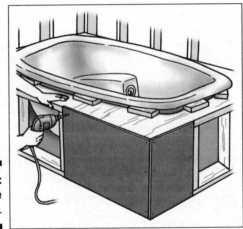

Figure 6-8:
Finishing the
platform.

6. **Install the faucet on the deck of the platform. Run the riser tubes from the faucet to the rough-in water supply pipes.**

7. **After the tiling work is completed apply caulk to fill the joints between the tub and the tile and between the tiled base of the platform and the finished floor.**

When Removing a Bathtub Is Mission Impossible

If you can't remove an unattractive tub, you have two options: refinishing the surface or having a liner made to go over it. These aren't do-it-yourself options. A new tub liner, which costs about $1,000, lasts longer than having a tub refinished, which costs anywhere from $200 to $500. To complete your tub's transformation, replace the old fixtures with new ones.

Reglazing

If the overall tub surface is worn or damaged, one option is having it refinished through a process called reglazing. First, the technician thoroughly scrapes the surface of the bathtub and then applies an etching solution to dull the old finish. Then the technician sands it thoroughly, finishing up the project by spraying the surface with a new polyurethane finish and polishing it. Because of the heavy-duty sanding, this can be a messy job that sends sanding dust throughout your house unless proper precautions are taken, such as using a window exhaust fan and closing of adjacent rooms.

Adding a tub liner

The second choice in covering up an old tub's surface is having a tub liner custom-made to fit over the surface of the old tub. An installer measures the old tub. Then a matching acrylic model is made, using the tub manufacturer's specifications for the contours and the exact location of plumbing cutouts. The liner is trimmed to fit, slipped over the old tub, and fastened with adhesive. You can also have matching wall panels made and installed at the same time.

Book IV

Bathroom and Kitchen Remodeling

Chapter 7

Showered with Possibilities

Are you a showerhead? You know what we mean. Nothing gives you greater pleasure than standing in a shower with an invigorating spray of water that lets you shut out the world. You can't find any other place where you have such profound thoughts and insights than when you're mesmerized by the steady stream of refreshing water. If that's you, get ready for some major life choices when selecting a shower for your bathroom. Sure, you find the basic enclosure in all shapes and sizes, but you also discover shower rooms and systems with body sprays and jets designed to pamper and massage, faucets and fixtures that range from simple showerheads to panels with body sprays and jets, and shower environments with lighting and audiovisual equipment. All these elements let you adjust water intensity and coverage, from relaxing to invigorating, to create a shower that's custom-made for you.

Creating a shower oasis is not as difficult as you may think. In this chapter, we show you how to choose a shower that meets your space requirements and offers the options you want, and we show you how to install it, too.

Standing Room Only: Selecting a Shower Unit

Today's showers range from basic enclosures to custom-designed systems that stand alone as the centerpiece of a bathroom. If you're interested in one of the custom units, you should probably have it installed by a bathroom design firm and their fabricators, who are familiar with installing those systems. If you want to install a shower unit yourself, consider a fiberglass or acrylic enclosure, designed for do-it-yourself installations.

The two things that determine the size and shape of the shower unit you want are the floor space where you plan to install it and the features you want it to have. In a large master bath, you may have plenty of room for a separate shower and tub, but in a small guest bathroom, a corner unit, called a *neo-angle unit,* may be the only thing that fits. Use your bathroom's dimensions as your guide.

Most manufacturers post sizes and specifications for their shower units on their Web sites, so the Internet is a good starting point. To test-drive a shower unit, go to a bathroom design showroom or home center where you can walk in, move around, and see how you fit in the space. You also have the option to check out showers when you spend the night with friends or relatives. If you find a shower you like, step inside to see if it feels right and then measure its size to determine whether it can fit in your bathroom. The more opportunities you have to test-fit showers, the more likely you are to choose a style and size that you'll enjoy for years to come.

Typical shower surrounds and enclosures are made of fiberglass and acrylic and come in one, three, or four pieces made up of wall surrounds, some of which include a receptor or floor pan that you stand on. Multipiece designs let one person bring the unit into a house in sections, so it's handy for a do-it-yourselfer. You install these units in place and then seal the joints with caulk. Other shower units have wall components with a tongue-and-groove interlocking system that eliminates the need for caulk.

The advantage of a one-piece unit is that you don't have to worry about joints — no caulking required — so no openings give mold a happy home. However, getting a large one-piecer into a house requires wide access or an open wall or window, so it isn't the unit of choice to transport into a tight space or up a narrow stairway.

You can use one of these enclosures as a standalone shower in a wall recess or as a freestanding unit. If the bathroom design includes both a tub and a shower, you often place the shower and tub back to back so that the plumbing lines can run next to each other.

Installing a Shower Enclosure

A shower enclosure makes good use of a small space because it takes up limited floor space. For a successful installation, spend some time upfront planning the project and assessing any groundwork that you need.

Laying the groundwork

Before you begin installing a shower enclosure, you need to address a couple of points. First, the shower requires wood framing to support the walls of the enclosure (see Figure 7-1). If you place the shower in a corner, you have to construct fewer walls. In any case, the manufacturer supplies a layout plan for the enclosure. Follow it carefully. You usually place the wall studs closer together than on a standard wall.

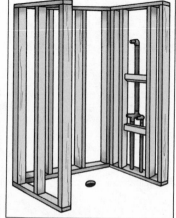

Figure 7-1:
Nonbearing partition walls support the shower stall wall panels.

One advantage to installing this type of shower enclosure is that you mount the wall panels directly to the wall studs, so you don't need drywall or backer-board. Before installing the shower stall, you can install wood backing for grab bars. Consult the manufacturer's installation instructions to find out what type of backing you need to support a grab bar. In most cases, you should have solid backing of 2 x 6s nailed between the wall studs.

You want to hire a plumber to install the rough-in plumbing. The shower enclosure requires a 2-inch drain centered in the enclosure. The rough-in dimensions give the exact measurements for its location. Unless you're experienced with plumbing, you should leave this part of the project to a professional. Have the plumber install the drain fittings in the shower receptor that meet local plumbing code requirements, too.

Book IV

Bathroom and Kitchen Remodeling

Installing a shower enclosure

To install a shower enclosure, you need these materials:

- 2 x 4s or 2 x 6s
- 2-inch masking tape
- Carpenter's square
- Dropcloth
- Electric drill
- Hammer
- Hole saw or jigsaw with fine-tooth blade (32 teeth per inch)
- Large-head nails
- Level
- Measuring tape
- Pliers
- Putty knife
- Safety glasses
- Screwdrivers
- Silicone sealant (for shower door installation)
- Utility knife
- Woodworking tools

Follow these instructions to install a shower enclosure:

1. **Open the packaging and identify all the components of the enclosure.**

2. **Place the shower receptor in the enclosure and check that it's level and doesn't rock back and forth.**

   You may have to install shims under the receptor to level it. Put the necessary shims in place and retest the level of the shower. When the surface is stable, remove the shims one at a time, apply construction adhesive to them, and replace them.

3. **Use galvanized roofing nails to secure the receptor to the wall framing (see Figure 7-2).**

   Follow the manufacturer's recommendations and drive the nails through the predrilled flange holes, or place the nail against the top of the flange so that the head of the nail catches the flange.

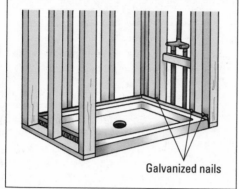

Figure 7-2:
Secure the
shower
receptor to
the framing
with
galvanized
nails.

Galvanized nails

4. **Position the panels in the enclosure.**

   Some kits have wall panels that interlock to form watertight seals. In this case, follow the manufacturer's directions and position the panels in the enclosure in the proper sequence so that they can interlock.

5. **Check that the panels fit snugly against the wall framing.**

   You can't place the panel at the shower valve end of the enclosure against the studs yet because of the rough-in plumbing.

6. **Mark the location of the shower valve and shower riser pipe by making a cardboard template of the location of the valve and shower head pipe.**

7. **Place the template on the shower enclosure panel and drill a pilot hole at the center of the cutout to guide the hole saw.**

   Use a hole saw or jigsaw with a fine-tooth blade to make the holes for the valve controls and the shower head pipe.

8. **Install the shower wall panel on which the valve is located.**

   Check that you have all panels properly aligned and square and that you have the shower valve and shower head pipe properly aligned.

9. **Fasten the panels to the wall framing with galvanized roofing nails (see Figure 7-3).**

   Wherever you find a gap between the wall stud and the shower wall panel, insert a wood shim before driving the nail.

10. **Apply silicone caulk to all joints in the enclosure.**

    Follow the manufacturer's instructions and use a top-quality caulk.

Book IV

Bathroom and Kitchen Remodeling

Making your shower accessible

Shower units that comply with the Americans with Disabilities Act (ADA) are designed for people with limited physical abilities or confined to a wheelchair. The key to their design is a low threshold so that you can enter them without an obstacle or you can roll a wheelchair in. These showers are usually one-piece units with integral grab bars and a built-in or fold-up seat. A person in a wheelchair should be able to roll up next to the shower unit, adjust the controls to the right water temperature from the outside, and then use grab bars to move to the seat inside the shower unit. The faucet control should be a single-lever handle and include a hand shower that someone sitting or standing can operate.

You don't find many examples of ADA-compliant shower units at retailers, but you can find them on manufacturers' Web sites, such as www.kohler.com. Use Kohler's search boxes to narrow the search by specifying "ADA compliant." Web sites also note the cost of each unit, the installation requirements, specifications and rough-in dimensions, and the actual installation manuals — valuable planning material.

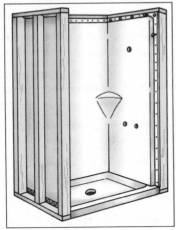

Figure 7-3: Fasten the wall to the wall studs with galvanized nails; shim where necessary.

Your next steps are to install the wall finish that covers the flange and complete the plumbing work before moving on to installing a shower door (often sold as part of an entire shower kit), which is covered in the next section

Installing a Shower (or Tub) Door

Don't stop now! Complete your shower installation with a glass door. (Many shower kits that include a base and a surround also include a door.) Same goes for those of you that are tired of dealing with a leaky mildew-stained shower curtain on an existing shower. The installation, which is essentially the same for a stall shower or tub/shower, is a no-brainer. It involves measuring and cutting the top and bottom horizontal tracks to the width of your shower (or tub) opening, fastening the tracks with screws or adhesive caulk, and attaching a door panel(s) to the side track or inserting sliding doors, between the horizontal tracks.

Getting started

Remove your toiletries from the shower and thoroughly clean the walls and surfaces around it.

Take a look at the parts of the door assembly and identify the frame and track and hardware. Set the door panels aside and lay out the parts as you read the installation instructions supplied by the manufacturer. Most of them are installed in the same way.

Gather up the following tools, and you'll be ready to go:

- Carpenter's level
- Caulking gun
- Center punch
- Electric drill and bit
- Fine file
- Hacksaw
- Miterbox
- Hammer
- Masking tape
- Masonry bit for ceramic tile
- Measuring tape
- Phillips screwdriver
- Pliers
- Safety glasses
- Silicone caulk
- Slotted screwdriver

Measuring and cutting the tracks

The top and bottom tracks supplied by the manufacturer is longer than needed for many applications to allow the door to be installed in a variety of enclosures. These tracks usually must be cut slightly shorter than the width of the opening. As always, read the manufacturer's installation instructions carefully before you do anything, and then follow these steps:

1. **Use a measuring tape to find the distance from wall to wall along the top edge of the shower base (or tub) and, for the top track, at 6-feet above it.**

2. **Follow the manufacturer's directions and subtract the required amount for each track from the total width of the opening.**

3. **Cut the both tracks to length and smooth any rough edges at the cut end with a fine file.**

   Use a hacksaw and a miter box to ensure a square cut. Putting a block of scrap wood in the track and clamping helps keep the track square and in place while you cut it.

Locating the bottom track

You install the bottom track on the top edge of the shower base or tub.

1. **Place the bottom track on the flattest part of the shower base or tub ledge, following the manufacturer's instructions to determine which side of the track faces out.**

   Make sure that the space between the wall and the ends of the track is the same on both ends.

2. **Temporarily secure the track to the ledge with masking tape.**

3. **Make a light pencil mark on the shower base of tub along the front edge of the track to guide caulk application.**

Locating the wall jambs

The wall jambs are fastened to the sidewalls and support the top track. Ideally, you will screw the wall jambs directly to the studs. You can also use sturdy metal anchors to secure the jambs.

1. **Place a wall jamb against the wall and push it down over the end of the bottom track so that it's fully engaged with the track.**

2. **Hold a carpenter's level next to the wall jamb and adjust it to plumb.**

3. **Mark in each mounting-hole location.**

4. **Remove the wall jamb and drill the holes for the mounting screws or wall anchors.**

   If you're drilling into ceramic tile, use a carbide-tipped masonry drill bit.

5. **Repeat the drilling in the opposite wall for the other wall jamb.**

   Install wall anchors according to instructions where there is no stud available.

On tile walls use a center punch and hammer to nick the surface glaze before drilling. This helps to prevent the drill bit from wandering off the mark. Not too hard or you may crack the tile! For another trick that uses masking tape see "Hanging a shower curtain rod on tile," later in this chapter.

Caulking the bottom track

Lift the bottom track and apply a bead of silicone caulk into the groove on the underside. Then erase your pencil marks and reposition the bottom track in its proper place.

Installing the wall jambs

Work on one wall jamb at a time and follow these steps:

1. **Place one wall jamb into or over the bottom track, depending on the design. Then align the holes in the wall jamb with the holes or screw anchors in the wall (see Figure 7-4).**

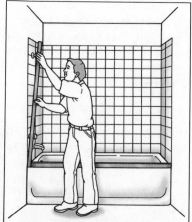

Figure 7-4:
Installing
the wall
jambs.

Book IV

**Bathroom
and Kitchen
Remodeling**

2. **Secure the jamb with the screws supplied by the manufacturer or the anchor.**

   Sliding door kits should include rubber bumpers. Install them over the screws at the top and bottom of the jamb.

3. **Repeat the installation on the other jamb.**

Installing sliding doors

Sliding doors hang from the top track so install it over the wall jambs as directed by the manufacturer. Prepare the doors by installing roller and, if applicable, handle/towel bar hardware. Place the rollers on the top frame flange of both door panels and secure them with lock washers and machine screws.

Hanging the door panels

Installing the door panels is easiest from outside the shower. Follow the installation instructions provided, as details may vary, but the following steps are typical:

1. **Install the inside panel first. Lift it up inside the top track and bring it back to vertical as you hang the rollers on the inside rail of the top track and lower it into the bottom track.**

2. **Install the outside panel by lifting it up inside the top track and hanging the rollers on the outside rail of the top track.**

Installing a hinged door

The bottom track and wall jambs for a hinged (pivoting) door are installed as described above, with small variations by maker or model. Usually there is no top track. With a hinged door you must determine the direction of swing. Typically the hinge is on the opposite side from the shower head, to make it easier to reach in and operate the controls.

1. **Prepare the door.**

   Following the manufacturer's instructions, install the seal, pivot pin or other connecting hardware, and attach the hinge expander jamb.

Hanging a shower curtain rod on tile

The biggest challenge to installing a shower door track, towel bar, or curtain rod in a bathroom with ceramic tile is making a hole in the tile without cracking it. If you have a masonry bit and a roll of masking tape, however, the job's easy.

Place the bracket in position and mark its general area on the tile. Then place a couple of strips of masking tape over the area. Place the bracket in the exact position and mark the location of the mounting screws on the tape with a felt pen. Then drill through the tape. The masking tape keeps the drill from moving off the mark until the bit starts to penetrate the tile.

---

2. **Lift the door into place and slide the hinge jamb over the wall jamb and strike expander over the other wall jamb.**

    Don't attempt this task working alone or you'll end up with some very expensive glass mosaic makings and a shower curtain.

3. **Adjust the two expanders as needed for a good fit, and so they extend the wall jambs about the same on each side. Secure them with self-drilling screws as directed.**

    Adjust the hinge jamb so the seal on the bottom of the door meets the bottom track evenly and makes the required seal; and secure it. Adjust the strike jamb so it is parallel to the door and spaced about ³⁄₁₆-inch apart; and secure it.

Some openings are too wide for a door to span so an additional glass panel is integrated into the design between the wall jamb and the strike jamb

Finishing up with caulk

Finish up any shower enclosure by applying beads of caulk in the specified locations on the exterior, and only those locations. Caulking on the inside, for example, may trap water that is otherwise intended to drain harmlessly into the tub or shower.

If like most folks you find it difficult to caulk neatly, try this: Apply masking tape on each side of the gap to be caulked. Immediately after you apply and smooth the caulk with a wet finger, peel off the tape. If necessary, wet your smoothing finger for another pass — clean it first unless you enjoy the taste!

Book IV

Bathroom and Kitchen Remodeling

Installing Grab Bars

Getting in and out of a shower isn't always easy even when you're fit and able. If you have a sore knee or a sprained ankle, you may find it nearly impossible to maneuver safely without a secure handle. For safe entry and exit, install a vertical grab bar inside your shower 18 to 24 inches from the shower head end. If you're installing a grab bar for someone with an injury or disability, have that person help you find the best location.

Inside a bathtub enclosure, position a grab bar horizontally, approximately 36 inches from the bottom of the tub, so that a bather can use the bar to help raise himself from a seated position. For stepping into and out of a tub, consider installing a vertical bar at the tub edge as a convenient handhold.

Grab bars have prevented accidents, but the early ones didn't do much for the aesthetics of a bathroom. Today's grab bars come in finishes and colors that make them much more appealing.

Don't be tempted to use any old towel bar. Get the best quality grab bar you can afford and install it either with a blind fastening system or with blocking in the wall. Do not rely on wall anchors.

You can use a new blind fastener, the WingIts system, directly on wallboard without an attachment to structural support. The anchors flare out behind the wall to hold firmly (see Figure 7-5). You should install the fastener on a sound wall made of ⅝-inch-thick wallboard or tile over plaster, cement board, or ½-inch wallboard. The system exceeds all building code and ADA (Americans with Disabilities Act) specifications. The directions that follow are for installing a grab bar on a tile shower wall.

Figure 7-5:
After it's behind the wall, the anchor expands and locks the mounting plate in position.

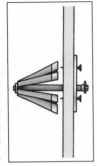

To install a grab bar with a WingIts grab bar system, you need the following tools:

- Electric drill with ⅛-inch masonry bit and 1¼-inch carbide-tipped hole saw
- Felt-tipped pen
- Measuring tape
- Rubber mallet or hammer
- Rubbing alcohol
- Screwdriver

Here's how to install the grab bar:

1. **Locate the 1¼-inch mounting holes so that the center of the grab bar fastener slides into the holes.**

2. **Measure from the inside of one bar flange to the outside of the other to find the center-to-center distance or the distance the 1¼-inch mounting holes should be spaced apart.**

3. **After making sure that the wall surface is clean, mark the location of the mounting holes with a felt-tipped pen.**

4. **Use a masonry bit to drill a ⅛-inch pilot hole through the surround, whether it be tile or another material, at each mark.**

5. **Hold the grab bar, with fasteners attached, to the wall to check that the pilot holes line up with the centers of the fasteners.**

6. **To cut holes in tile use a 1¼-inch diamond-tipped hole saw to enlarge the pilot holes (see Figure 7-6).**

   Diamond saws are very pricy for one-time use. Although you can use a less expensive carbide hole saw for plastic surrounds and some soft tiles, it may not cut through a hard tile.

   In lieu of using a holes saw in hard tile, you can drill a series of very closely spaced holes at the perimeter with a carbide masonry bit and use a cold chisel to carefully chip out the waste. A hammer-drill, which adds a high-speed hammering action to the turning drill bit, makes that job go very quickly.

   If you hit a wall stud while drilling a hole, you can mount the grab bar directly to the wall stud with 2½-inch-long #12 stainless steel screws rather than the fastener.

7. **Use a screwdriver to back the bolt out of the fastener until the end of it is flush with the nut at the opposite end of the fitting.**

TIP

Book IV

Bathroom and Kitchen Remodeling

Figure 7-6:
Use a carbide-tipped hole saw to bore the opening for a wall anchor.

8. **Temporarily install the fasteners to the ends of the grab bar with the stainless steel screws provided.**

9. **Wipe the wall surface around these holes with rubbing alcohol so that the tape sticks to it.**

10. **Remove the paper that covers the adhesive on the faceplate.**

11. **Insert the fasteners into the holes in the wall while they're attached to the grab bar.**

Maintaining water temperature

The best protection against scalding is a special valve called a pressure balance or anti-scald valve, which maintains a constant water temperature, even if someone in the house decides to do a super-sized load of laundry with a tub full of hot water while you are in the shower.

Some of these devices are valves that sense changes in the water pressure and adjust the mix of hot and cold water. Others are electronic systems that remember the temperature of the last shower and deliver the same level of hot water until you or someone else resets them. More elaborate systems allow you to program multiple water temperatures to suit the preferences of the different people using the shower. Whether you're doing the bathroom yourself or hiring a contractor, arrange for a licensed plumber to take care of this particular job.

If you want an easy, inexpensive (about $20) solution for your shower head, get a scald-guard device that shuts off the water if the temperature gets too high. You just have to remove the shower head, screw in the device, and replace the shower head. If you have a bit more money to spend but don't want to replace your existing shower valve, you can plumb a pressure-balancing valve into the supply line right before the shower valve, assuming that you have access from the back.

Incidentally, the Department of Energy suggests setting the temperature of your hot-water heater no higher than 115 degrees to provide a comfortable hot-water temperature for most uses. Dishwasher manufacturers, however, are looking for a minimum of 120 degrees, making this safety device all the more important.

12. **Press the grab bar tightly toward the wall for a moment so that the fasteners can adhere to the wall in the correct position.**

13. **Remove the grab bar from the fasteners and use a screwdriver to firmly and quickly punch the head of the bolt toward the faceplate.**

    You can also hit the screw gently but firmly with a rubber mallet or hammer.

14. **Simultaneously pull on the bolt and tighten it by hand.**

    Use a screwdriver to tighten the bolt very tight.

15. **Attach the grab bar to the fasteners with the stainless steel screws.**

Chapter 8

Bowled Over: Basins, Vanities, Medicine Cabinets, and Faucets

Depending on what dictionary you consult, a lavatory is either a built-in washbasin, a room having one or more toilets and washbasins, or both. So don't be confused when you order a sink and it comes in a box labeled "lavatory." What makes today's bathrooms interesting is the choices that you have when it comes to selecting a washbasin. Sure, you'll find the traditional sink sunk into a nice countertop and the old-style pedestal sink, but you can also get a whole new breed of basins today.

Looking at Types and Styles of Basins

Before you walk into a design center to look at basins and faucets, do some noodling about who uses the bathroom and how often, what your priorities are, what style you like, and how maintenance-friendly you want the room to be. Yes, a snappy red pedestal sink would be a knockout, but in a family bathroom, a better choice is a countertop sink with a vanity for storage in a light color that doesn't show soap scum and is easy to clean.

The range of basin styles is matched by the range in their prices. For example, a 19-inch-diameter sink made of *vitreous china* (which is fired to a hard, nonporous surface) sells for less than $100, and a cast-iron basin with a porcelain glaze goes for about $150. The price goes up to $1,000 if you want a fanciful pottery sink or a glass vessel that sits above a counter or in a metal bracket mounted on the wall. For a granite or marble bowl, the prices go into the $1,600 range.

Manufacturers sell both cast polymer and solid-surface sinks as one unit, called an *integral sink*, combining a sink and a countertop that you can install easily on top of a vanity base cabinet. They come in a range of sizes, from 25 to 49 inches wide, and are designed to fit the most popular vanity cabinets. The seamless design of these units makes them easy to clean and eliminates the need for caulk to seal a joint between the countertop and basin. A 36-inch-wide cast polymer countertop and sink, made of polyester resin and granite or crushed marble, costs less than $350. For under $700, you can get a solid-surface unit with color throughout its thickness, a popular choice for shaped and contoured edges.

If you choose a freestanding or wall-hung sink, make sure that you increase storage space in the bathroom because neither of these styles has any.

Putting In a Pedestal Sink

What it lacks in storage space, a pedestal sink makes up for in high style. A small-bowl pedestal is a good choice in a powder room because it takes up little floor space, and a wider console style with a basin ledge for toiletries makes a handsome addition to any bathroom. If you're replacing a wall-mounted sink, you can install a pedestal sink relatively easily. Just hook up the new sink to the old plumbing.

The old pipes that may be hidden inside a vanity are exposed under a pedestal sink, so if the pipes are rusty, consider replacing the short exposed sections with new chrome pipes and a new trap assembly. Or you can save money by cleaning up the pipes and painting them. At the same time, appraise the condition of the wall and make any necessary repairs because it becomes clearly visible, too, no longer hidden by the old sink.

Before you purchase a pedestal sink, remove the old sink and measure the location of the plumbing lines so that you can choose a new sink that matches up with them. To get these rough-in dimensions, make a sketch of the wall and note the following measurements:

- Distance from the floor (or wall) to where the drain enters the wall (or floor)
- Distance between the floor and the water supply pipes
- Distance right to left from each water supply pipe to the drain

Sit on the floor with the sketch in hand and visualize how the back of the pedestal sink will match up with the supply lines. Also, check the sink's specifications and rough-in dimensions. You can do this rough measuring by finding sinks that you like at a home center; note the manufacturer, style, and model number and then visit the manufacturer's Web site. Most manufacturers provide specifications and rough-in dimensions online, so deciding what fits and what doesn't is easy.

Of course, a plumber or knowledgeable salesperson in a home center can help you do the same thing, assuming that you have your sketch with you and your measurements are correct.

How you install a pedestal sink varies by style and manufacturer. Some use a wall bracket, although others are secured directly to the wall with lag screws or toggle bolts through holes in the back of the bowl. Most sinks rest on the pedestal but get major support from the wall mounting. The instructions in the following sections are for installing a pedestal sink with a mounting bracket. The project involves completing several individual tasks and then connecting everything. You purchase the faucet, drain, and pop-up assembly separately. Before you install the sink, install the drain, pop-up assembly, and faucet.

Installing the drain and pop-up assembly

This section contains generic directions for installing a typical assembly. Carefully read the directions that come with the unit that you buy to familiarize yourself with the parts and how they fit together. Figure 8-1 introduces the major players in this process.

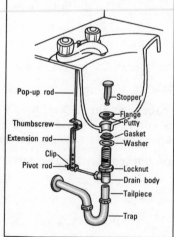

Figure 8-1: The main parts of a typical lavatory's drain assembly.

Pop-up rod
Stopper
Thumbscrew
Flange
Putty
Extension rod
Gasket
Washer
Clip
Pivot rod
Locknut
Drain body
Tailpiece
Trap

Book IV

Bathroom and Kitchen Remodeling

The drain consists of pipes that attach to the sink and lead to the trap. The following steps explain where the different metal and rubber washers go:

1. **Thread the large locknut onto the drain body.**

2. **Slip the flat washer and then the wedge-shaped rubber gasket onto the drain body.**

3. **Place a thin bead of plumber's putty around the underside of the drain flange.**

4. **Push the drain body up through the hole in the bottom of the sink.**

5. **Thread the drain flange into the body of the drain.**

6. **Turn the drain body so that the opening for the pivot rod mechanism faces the back of the sink.**

7. **Using groove-joint pliers, tighten the locknut on the drain from the underside of the sink until the plumber's putty is compressed and the flange looks and feels tight.**

The pivot rod operates the mechanism that opens and closes the drain. Most units have a rod with a ball on it that operates the drain plug. To assemble this mechanism, follow these steps:

1. **If the retaining nut is screwed onto the valve body, remove it and the washers. If not, skip this step.**

2. **Slide the washer seal over the short end of the pivot rod.**

3. **Insert the short end of the pivot rod into the drain body and thread on the nut.**

    Don't tighten it yet.

4. **Insert the pop-up rod through the hole in the faucet's body.**

5. **Push the pivot rod all the way down.**

6. **Connect the *extension rod* (the short arm through which the pivot rod extends) by placing the pivot rod in the first or second hole of the extension rod and sliding the pop-up rod into the extension rod.**

7. **Pull the rod all the way down and tighten the thumbscrew.**

Installing the sink

Before a pedestal sink takes its place, you need to shore up the wall behind it to hold its weight. After you do that, you can install the sink easily.

Shoring up the wall

To provide a solid surface for mounting the sink, reinforce the wall with wood blocking, which we describe in Steps 1 through 6 of the section "Installing a Cast-Iron Wall-Hung Sink," later in this chapter.

Mounting the sink to the wall

After reinforcing and repairing the wall, you can install the sink. Some sinks require you to install a separate bracket first, although others mount directly to the wall. The following directions are for a sink with a bracket, so you can skip them if the sink you're installing doesn't have a bracket. Figure 8-2 shows a typical installation.

Figure 8-2: You hang pedestal sinks on a wall bracket or secure them directly to the wall and support them with the pedestal.

1. **Position the bracket on the wall and use it as a template to mark the location for the _mounting lag bolts_ (large screws with a square or hex head).**

   To determine the exact location of the mounting bracket, consult the roughing-in dimensions provided by the manufacturer. Make sure that the bracket is level.

2. **Drill pilot holes through the layout marks on the wall into the wall reinforcement.**

   Make the holes about ⅛ inch smaller than the lag bolts that came with the sink.

3. **Install the bracket with the lag bolts.**

Book IV

Bathroom and Kitchen Remodeling

4. **Hang the basin on the wall bracket and then install the mounting screws to hold the sink to the bracket and wall.**

   If the sink doesn't have a mounting bracket, install it directly to the wall with the fasteners provided.

5. **Test-fit the pedestal, mark its location, and then move it safely out of the way.**

Installing the P-trap

With the sink on the wall, you can install the *P-trap,* the pipe that connects the sink to the house drain. The U-shape of this pipe is the trap that retains enough water to prevent sewer gases from entering the bathroom. You can adjust the P-trap, sliding it up and down on the pipe that leaves the sink drain. The other end of the P-trap can slide into and out of the fitting on the wall.

If the P-trap doesn't align with the drain that comes out of the wall, you may have to cut the tailpiece that protrudes from the pop-up assembly to install the P-trap.

Referring to Figure 8-3, follow these steps to install the P-trap:

1. **Slide the short side of the P-trap onto the tailpiece that drops down from the sink drain. Move the P-trap up or down to align the trap arm with the opening in the wall.**

   Use a hacksaw to cut the tailpiece if you can't move the P-trap higher up the tailpiece and the trap arm is below the wall drain fitting. Purchase a longer tailpiece if the P-trap lies above the wall drain fitting when attached to the end of the tailpiece.

2. **Take the lower part of the P-trap apart and insert the trap arm into the wall drain fitting as far as it will go.**

3. **Pull the trap arm out of the wall fitting until it lines up with the top U-shaped portion of the trap.**

   If the trap arm comes completely out of the wall before it can be attached to the trap, purchase a longer trap arm. If the trap arm is in the wall fitting as far as it will go and extends past the U-shaped part of the trap, cut it with a hacksaw.

4. **Insert the trap arm back into the wall drain, move it into alignment with the trap, and thread on (but don't tighten) the slip nut.**

5. **After you've joined the trap parts together, tighten the slip nuts on the tailpiece and the wall drain fittings.**

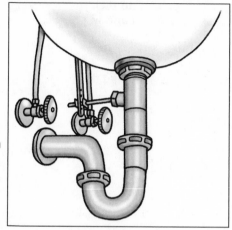

Figure 8-3:
The P-trap and riser tubes.

Attaching riser tubes to the faucet

After installing the P-trap, turn your attention to attaching the riser tubes (supply lines) to the faucet tailpieces, using the compression nuts that came with the faucet. The riser tubes connect the faucet to the stop valves. Here are a couple of pointers for attaching the tubes to the faucet:

- ✔ Snug up the nuts by hand.

- ✔ Bend or loop the riser tubes so that they fit between the stop valves and the wall before tightening them with a wrench.

Finishing up

The moment of truth has arrived: You have to turn on the water at the shut-off valves and the faucet and test for leaks in the supply lines and fittings leading to the faucet and in the drain lines and fittings. When everything is drip free, install the pedestal by positioning it properly beneath the sink and securing it to the floor with a wood screw (see Figure 8-4). If the floor is tile drill a clearance hole through the tile with a masonry bit first.

Don't overtighten the pedestal mounting screw — doing so may crack the pedestal base.

Lastly, caulk any gaps or voids between the wall and the basin, removing any excess caulk with a wet rag.

Book IV

Bathroom and Kitchen Remodeling

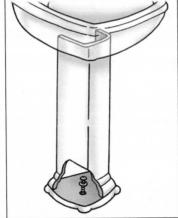

Figure 8-4:
The pedestal is held in place with a wood screw.

Installing a Cast-Iron Wall-Hung Sink

Wall-hung sinks that you mount on the wall can be customized to the user's height. It's a nice way to personalize a bathroom for someone who's particularly tall or short. A sink mounted on the wall is also ideal for a person in a wheelchair because the sink has access underneath it; however, be sure to slip an insulated cover over the trap so that the pipe (heated by hot water passing through) doesn't burn the person's legs. A wall-mounted sink also takes up less space in a small room than a traditional vanity with sink.

Cast-iron sinks are very heavy. Get help lifting the sink and follow wall reinforcement instructions to the letter.

Preparing the supporting wall

When you're going to install a sink in an existing bathroom, you have to remove the drywall in the area behind the sink to add blocking to provide the support needed for the sink. You have to open the wall to expose at least two studs, neither of which can be located directly behind the sink. If a wall stud happens to be centered directly behind the sink, you need to open the wall to three studs — the one behind the sink and the studs on either side of it. You have to support both ends of the blocking with a stud. Follow these steps to provide the necessary support:

1. **Cut a 2 x 4 into two 36-inch pieces.**

2. **Cut these two boards lengthwise to a 2¾-inch width.**

3. **In each board, cut a notch that's 1½ inches deep and 9¼ inches high.**

   Position the notches 23⅞ inches from the end of the board, as shown in Figure 8-5.

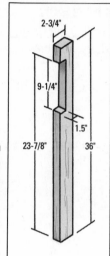

Figure 8-5:
The dimensions of the side braces cut from a 2 x 4.

4. **Nail or screw the boards to the studs.**

5. **Cut a piece of 2 x 10 to fit between the notches and studs, as shown in Figure 8-6.**

   If the 2 x 10 spans a center stud, you must notch the stud to accept the board.

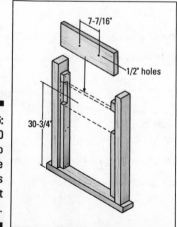

Figure 8-6:
Screw 2 x 10 blocking to the side braces to support the sink.

Setting the mounting bolts

Next, you need to set the mounting bolts into the support brace in the wall. Follow these steps:

1. **Mark the location of the mounting bolts on the 2 x 10.**

   The bolts are located 30¾ inches from the floor and 7⁷⁄₁₆ inches apart. You have to place the bolts behind the sink, but they can't line up exactly in the center of the 2 x 10 brace.

2. **Remove the 2 x 10 from the wall and drill ½-inch holes through the layout marks.**

3. **Insert the mounting bolts.**

4. **Install the threaded inserts to hold the bolts in place (see Figure 8-7).**

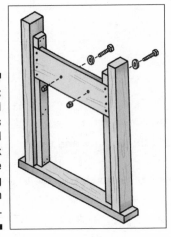

Figure 8-7:
Threaded inserts supplied with the sink hold the mounting bolts in place.

5. **Fasten the 2 x 10 brace to the wall studs by using 2½-inch screws.**

6. **Cut a piece of ¾-inch plywood to fit between the wall studs.**

   If the opening is three studs wide, you must remove ¾ inch from the front edge of the center stud so that you can install the plywood flush with the wall studs on the outer sides of the opening. In this case, make several ¾-inch-deep cuts in the edge of the center stud and use a wood chisel to knock off the wood between the cuts.

7. **Drill holes in the plywood for the mounting bolts and plumbing pipes.**

8. **Screw the plywood to the support boards (see Figure 8-8).**

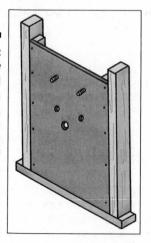

Figure 8-8:
Screw plywood filler to the side braces; it has to lie flush with the front of the studs so that you can cover it with drywall.

9. **Apply moisture-resistant drywall (green board) to cover the opening.**

10. **Tape and mud the joints between the existing wall and the new drywall with joint compound.**

11. **Sand the joints smooth and paint the wall.**

Bolting the sink to the wall

The last step is to mount the sink on the wall — it's heavy, so get help.

1. **Lift the sink onto the mounting bolts.**

2. **Slip on the washers and thread on the nuts (see Figure 8-9).**

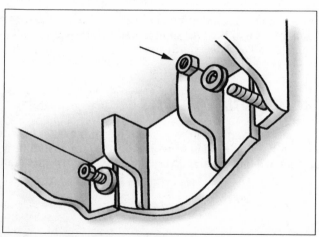

Figure 8-9:
Two large bolts hold a wall-mounted sink to the wall.

Book IV

Bathroom and Kitchen Remodeling

3. **Use a carpenter's level to position the sink so that it's level.**

4. **Tighten the bolts with a wrench.**

After you have the sink in place, see the earlier sections "Installing the drain and pop-up assembly" and "Installing the P-trap," earlier in this chapter, and the section "Getting a Handle on Faucets," later in this chapter.

You're So Vain: Vanity Cabinets

A vanity cabinet is like any piece of furniture: The price goes up as the quality improves. You can find in-stock factory-made vanities in a range of sizes and styles, meaning that you can walk into a store and leave with the vanity of your choice. Or you can order a semicustom vanity that's factory made and customized with specialty finishes and handy options like a pull-out tray, bins, and shelves. At the high end, you find a custom-made cabinet designed by you or a designer to specifications not available in stock or semicustom cabinets. Although a custom piece can be pricey, it can be a design solution that makes the most of a cut-up or tight floor plan. Remember to allow extra time if you purchase a vanity that's made to order.

You get what you pay for when it comes to the construction of a vanity. Better-quality pieces have backs made with tongue-and-groove construction, a solid face frame, full-depth drawers, and thick shelving. Doors have substantial hinges that open and close easily, and drawers glide on their tracks.

Vanities are shorter than kitchen cabinets, which may work for kids and shorter adults, but you may get tired of bending down to wash your face. Manufacturers now make taller vanity cabinets, or you can use a kitchen cabinet as a base to create a higher vanity and make a new *kickboard* (the board under the front of the cabinet that covers the platform).

If you have good cabinets but they're out of style, call a cabinet resurfacing company. For a fraction of the cost of replacement, these specialists can resurface cabinets and add new hardware for an updated look.

Looking at your options

You use the traditional vanity cabinet, which offers the most counter and storage space, with a single basin or pair of basins. You install it by fastening it to the wall. You can find several types of basins, and the installation methods vary:

- ✔ **A self-rimming sink** is dropped into a cutout in the countertop. Its rim overlaps the surface, forming a seal.

- ✔ **A flush-mount sink** is installed so that it's level with the surface of the countertop. It's also called a *tile-in installation* because the sink is designed to fit flush with a tiled countertop.

- ✔ **An above-counter basin,** also called a *vanity top installation,* is used for basins or vessels that are installed to rest on top of the counter.

- ✔ **An under-counter sink mount** is used with stone or solid-surface countertops. The rim slips beneath the countertop and creates a seamless appearance.

Every vanity needs a countertop. The following are the most common countertop materials:

- ✔ **Laminate:** This material comes in ready-made stock sizes or ordered in an endless number of colors and patterns.

- ✔ **Solid surface:** Like laminate, this man-made material is also available in a variety of colors and patterns. Pliability is its unique feature; you can configure it to be more versatile than laminate, particularly if you want edging details. It can also be ordered with an integral sink.

- ✔ **Ceramic, stone, slate, and marble tiles:** You install these materials over a base and then lay them in intricate patterns on a counter surface or as a solid design. Like solid surface, tile makes an ideal backsplash, wall covering, and countertop in a bathroom. When installed over a base cabinet, you place the tile on a base of plywood and backerboard with thinset mortar and then grout it.

Installing a vanity

Carefully unpack the vanity from its box, check that its measurements are correct, and move it into position. Use a carpenter's level to make sure that the floor is level so that the new vanity can rest on a sound, level surface.

TIP

When leveling and installing a vanity, removing the drawers and doors provides you with easier access and handling.

If you find that the floor isn't level, do the following:

1. **Find the high point of the floor using a carpenters level. Lift one end of the level or the other, as needed, to center the bubble in the vial. The point that touches the floor is the high point.**

Book IV

Bathroom and Kitchen Remodeling

2. **Measure the height of the cabinet.** Measuring up the wall from the high point on the floor, mark the height of the cabinet, and then draw a level line at that point.

3. **Use the level to draw a vertical line where one edge of the cabinet will be located.**

4. **Slide the vanity in place and align it with the horizontal and vertical reference line on the wall.**

   Drive tapered wood shims between the floor and the base as you need to adjust and level the vanity (see Figure 8-10).

Figure 8-10: Wood shims level the cabinet.

Finding wall studs behind your vanity is important. You can use an electronic stud finder to accomplish this task. The original builders probably used the studs to secure the old unit, so old screw holes may point to the studs.

If the wall behind the vanity isn't flat (plumb), you may need to insert shims in any gaps between the back of the vanity and the wall at each stud location. If you don't place shims here, the screws pull the vanity frame rail to the wall and rack the cabinet out of square. Here's how to finish the installation:

1. **Use long drywall screws to fasten the vanity to the studs through clearance holes drilled through the mounting board. (see Figure 8-11).**

2. **Use a utility knife to cut off any shims that stick out.**

3. **Caulk small gaps between the vanity and the floor and wall.**

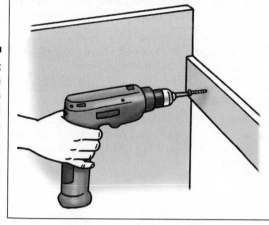

Figure 8-11:
Fasten the cabinet to the wall with screws driven through the back frame into the wall studs.

Topping your vanity with stone

One of the hottest looks in bathrooms is a granite countertop on a wood vanity. You often only need a rich-looking countertop of stone — a durable, high-style material — to update a cabinet. At home centers, you find a range of colors and sizes. Typically, stone countertops come in widths of 25, 31, 37, and 49 inches, with a separate backsplash and bowl that you glue to the underside of the countertop before fastening it to the vanity base. The countertop is conveniently predrilled with three holes on either 4-inch or 8-inch centers for a faucet.

Positioning the sink

A stone countertop comes ready for sink installation. Follow these steps:

1. **Lay the countertop polished side down on a work table or on 2 x 4s across a pair of sawhorses.**

2. **Unpack the sink and place it upside down over the sink hole in the countertop.**

3. **Line up the back edge of the sink so that it sits between the faucet holes and the inner edge of the sink hole in the top.**

   Make sure that the sink is centered over the sink hole. Feel around the edges underneath the countertop to ensure that the sink is centered.

4. **With a felt pen, draw a line all around the sink on the bottom of the countertop.**

Book IV

Bathroom and Kitchen Remodeling

5. Make alignment marks on the front and back of the sink and countertop.

Begin the line on the sink and continue it on the countertop. After removing the sink, you can replace it in the exact same position by matching the lines on the sink with those on the countertop.

Sticking the sink to the stone

The sink is attached to the underside of the stone countertop with epoxy (see Figure 8-12). This step isn't difficult, but you must set the sink in the right place. After the epoxy cures, you can't change your mind! Here's how you glue a sink to a countertop:

Figure 8-12: Apply epoxy around the perimeter of the sink opening.

1. Lift the sink off the vanity top and set it down within easy reach of the countertop.

You don't have much time to position the sink after you pour the epoxy.

2. Mix the epoxy by following the directions on the packet that came with the countertop.

To activate epoxy, you usually knead both sides of the packet together by hand or by sliding the packet up and down along the edge of the countertop to mix it thoroughly. Continue kneading the epoxy packet against the countertop edge until it begins to feel warm to the touch (about three minutes).

3. When the epoxy feels warm, immediately cut off one corner of the packet with scissors and squeeze the contents quickly and evenly onto the countertop around the inside of the line you drew.

Work quickly! After the epoxy begins to warm up, it continues to heat and hardens quickly. When finished (or if the epoxy gets too hot to handle), place the used epoxy packet in a metal can or on a nonflammable surface.

4. **Quickly place the sink back on the underside of the countertop inside the outline you drew, making sure to place the back of the sink toward the faucet holes and line it up exactly with the front and back alignment marks that you made.**

5. **Move the sink back and forth for about five seconds, making sure that it's within the layout circle.**

    Doing so ensures that you have the epoxy spread around as much as possible between the top and sink.

Before installing the countertop and sink on the vanity, install the faucet and drain body according to the manufacturer's directions while you have easy access.

Installing a sink and countertop on your vanity

After the epoxy has dried for about 45 to 60 minutes, check whether the sink has adhered to the countertop by carefully lifting up the sink a few inches by the bottom drain hole. If the vanity top lifts with the sink, you're ready to carry it into the bathroom and install it on the vanity.

Run a bead of silicone caulk around the top edge of the vanity, carefully lower the top in place, and center it over the vanity base. Clean up excess caulk with a damp rag.

To finish up, clean the surface of the stone countertop and sink thoroughly, let it dry, and then apply a stone sealer. Complete the supply and drain line connections as described for pedestal sinks earlier in this chapter.

Topping your vanity with tile

The selection of ceramic, slate, stone, and marble tile for bathroom countertops is vast, indeed. The choice of colors, textures, and patterns of ceramic tiles is awesome, and their hard finishes and durable quality make them good choices. Similarly, you may want to consider slate, stone, and marble tiles, which offer the same durability in more natural shades.

Tile comes in many shapes and sizes, but the specially shaped trim pieces are what make using tile so versatile. These preformed pieces make finishing off the edge of a counter or navigating an inside corner possible. Here's a short list of trim that you can find at most outlets:

Book IV

Bathroom and Kitchen Remodeling

✔ Edging or bullnose tiles with one rounded edge

✔ Inside-outside corners with four edges rounded

✔ Inside and outside corner caps

✔ V-cap for edging

✔ Bead for straight edges

You can transform a bathroom with a new tile countertop and add years of service to an existing vanity (or replace the vanity, too). The emphasis here is on the countertop, so choose tiles with that fact in mind. For inspiration, visit a tile retailer, where you can find the widest selection and most displays of tile countertops. Bring along a sketch of the vanity cabinet on graph paper with dimensions, including the backsplash on the wall behind it.

The old saying "Measure twice, cut once" certainly holds true for tile. Before ordering the tile or making your first cut, take these tips to heart:

✔ A self-rimming sink is the best type of sink for a tile countertop because you install it after the tile is set, and you can easily seal the joint between the sink and tile with caulk.

✔ Buy more tiles than you need, allowing yourself a few miscuts or tiles that break when you cut them.

✔ Double-check your measurements and ask the tile dealer to check your dimensions so that you order the correct amount of tile and material.

✔ Before beginning the job, open all the cartons and make sure that the tiles are the right size, color, and design.

Building the underlayer

The first stage in installing a tile countertop is preparing a sturdy, level surface to lay the tiles on. Before you can start, you need to measure the length and width of the vanity cabinet and build a backing made of ¾-inch AC grade plywood and tile backerboard, such as cement board. If you're replacing an old countertop, use it as a template to cut the backing and backerboard (see Figure 8-13). Otherwise, cut the plywood and cement board 1 to 2 inches larger than the cabinet (depending on how much overhang you want).

1. **With the template that came with the sink, trace an outline for the cutout where the sink will be located onto the plywood and cement board.**

2. **Drill a starter hole in the plywood so that you can use a jigsaw to cut the hole for the sink in the plywood.**

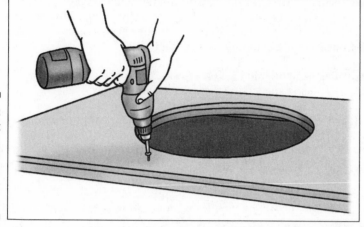

Figure 8-13:
Cement
board and
plywood
form a
sturdy base
for tiles.

3. **Using the plywood as a pattern, transfer the location of the sink to both sides of the backerboard in pencil.**

   Always flip the plywood when you mark the other side of the backerboard, even when the sink is centered.

4. **Score the marked cutout on both sides with a scoring tool and knock out the waste piece (where the sink goes) with a hammer.**

5. **Place the plywood on the cabinet and drive screws through the cabinet's corner blocks up into the plywood to secure it to the frame.**

6. **Mix and spread thinset adhesive on the plywood and comb with the notched edge of a trowel. Lay the backerboard in the thinset and secure with backerboard screws or roofing nails.**

7. **Fill joints between backerboard panels (if any) with thinset and fiberglass mesh tape.**

   The sink cutout should line up exactly on both pieces.

Placing the tile

Plan your layout with courses of full (uncut) tiles starting at the front edge; any rows of cut tiles will be at the ends and at the backsplash, where they will be less noticeable. To ensure that cut tiles at the ends are equal width and not too narrow, mark the left-to-right center of the counter and plan the first front-to-back row so it is either centered over this mark or a grout line between two rows of tiles will be. Choose whichever layout yields the largest cut tiles on the ends. Bend this rule on sink counters when the sink is not centered. Shift the layout so it is centered on the sink, which is typically a focal point.

Book IV

Bathroom and Kitchen Remodeling

If you plan to edge the front of the counter with trim tiles, dry-fit that trim and, if relevant, the tile that will face the countertop. Allowing for a grout line, pencil a layout line parallel to the front edge at this point to guide positioning the front edge of the first course of full tiles.

Many tiles have built-in lugs on the side for spacing. If your tiles don't have lugs, use plastic spacers so that they align properly.

Follow these steps to lay the tiles:

1. **Dry-fit the first course and the center row of tiles to verify your layout.**

2. **Using a framing square, mark a layout line perpendicular to the front edge along the edge of the row.**

   Your fits tile will be positioned adjacent to the two layout lines

3. **Mix a small batch of thinset mortar with latex bonding additive according to directions.**

4. **Apply thinset to the backerboard up to the layout lines with the smooth side of a trowel. Then use the notched side of the trowel, held at a 45-degee angle, to comb the thinset.**

   Combing assures that the correct amount is applied and that the application is uniform. This, in turn, ensures a flat tile surface.

5. **Continue to spread mortar and lay full tiles on one side of the layout line, using spacers between them if necessary.**

   Push each tile down to ensure full contact with the adhesive (see Figure 8-14), and lay a straight board across the set tiles to verify they are flat, check spacing and make needed adjustments as you go.

6. **After all the full tiles are in place, cut the border tiles and fit them into place before moving on to the next section of the counter and beginning the process again.**

   Depending on the type of tile you are using, use a manual tile cutter, which scores and snaps the tile to size, or a wet saw, which cuts the tile with a circular diamond abrasive blade. Both can be rented. Ask your tile dealer for a recommendation and the rental store for instructions on using the tool.

Grouting the tile

Read the grout manufacturer's instructions for an overview of applying grout. Then follow these easy steps:

1. **Spread the grout diagonally over area no more that 5 feet wide at a time Use a rubber float to push the grout into the spaces between the tiles (see Figure 8-15).**

   Start with the tool held at a 30-degree until joints are full then cut away the excess grout with the tool nearly perpendicular to the surface

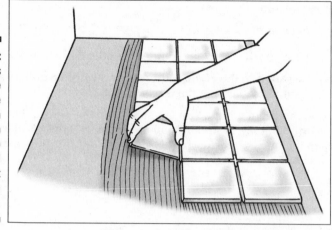

Figure 8-14:
Lay the tiles flat on the adhesive and then push them down to ensure full contact with the adhesive.

Figure 8-15:
Using a rubber float, push the grout between the tiles.

2. Wait a few minutes and use a damp grout sponge to remove excess grout off the face of the tiles before it dries, trying not to disturb the grout lines. Wait a few more minutes and repeat until the tiles are clean.

3. Use cheesecloth or a dry soft cloth to buff off any haze that may remain after 15 or 20 minutes.

4. Follow the tile dealers advice and manufacturer's instructions about whether, when and how to apply a sealer that will help prevent food stains.

Book IV

Bathroom and Kitchen Remodeling

Dropping in the sink

With the tile in place and grouted, the sink goes in next. Follow these steps:

1. **Place a bead of silicone caulk along the underside of the sink's rim.**

2. **Lower the sink into the cutout and secure it with the mounting hardware provided by the manufacturer.**

3. **Hook up the drain and pop-up assembly and the faucet. (See the sections "Installing the drain and pop-up assembly" and "Attaching riser tubes to the faucet," earlier in this chapter, and "Putting in an easy-install faucet," later in this chapter.)**

That's it!

Much Ado about Medicine Cabinets

You can't store medicines and toiletries in any better place than right where you need them — in a convenient cabinet in the bathroom. Yes, you find boring antiseptic metal boxes faced with mirrors, but you also see inspired and appealing designs with intricate beveled glass and mirrors and colorful, whimsical designs.

Hanging a surface-mounted medicine cabinet

Manufacturers sell medicine cabinets preassembled except for the doors, with drywall anchors to fasten them to walls. Because of its weight, the best location for this cabinet is on the wall with a wall stud behind it. You don't want it falling off the wall, so fasten it securely to the wall framing, which is much more secure than the wallboard alone. Because most wall studs are 16 inches on center, meaning that a space of 16 inches sits between the centers of two studs, and a cabinet is at least 15 inches wide, you should be able to adjust the position of the cabinet to center one of the mounting holes over the wall stud.

Follow these steps to hang a medicine cabinet:

1. **Locate at least one wall stud within the mounting area of the cabinet with a stud finder.**

2. **Level and mount the medicine cabinet to the wall by driving a screw through the back of the cabinet at the top and bottom into at least one wall stud.**

3. **Drill at least two additional holes through the cabinet into the wall. Remove the cabinet to install wall anchors and reposition the cabinet to drive in all screws.**

   If another stud is not located behind the cabinet, use a winged or coarse-threaded wall anchor. Follow the directions that come with the medicine cabinet to ensure that it doesn't require a different kind of mounting process.

Whenever you need to install a wall anchor, check the installation instructions. Depending on the type of anchor, you may need to drill a hole and install the anchor before you put the cabinet in position to hang it.

Replacing a recessed medicine cabinet

To replace a recessed medicine cabinet, choose a replacement cabinet that's the same or close to the same size as your original cabinet so that it fits in the existing wall cavity. Another good bet is to get a larger cabinet, which you can install after enlarging the opening. It's relatively easy to measure the additional space needed and enlarge the opening by cutting the wallboard with a drywall saw and modifying the wall framing.

If you have a large hole left from an old recessed cabinet and you choose a smaller cabinet, the job becomes more complicated. You have to apply new wallboard, tape, and compound; let it dry; and then finish the wall with another application, followed by sanding.

If you must cut a stud, install additional short pieces of 2 x 4 at the outside of the cutout to support the cabinet (see Figure 8-16).

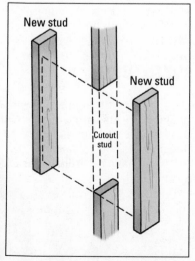

Figure 8-16: Adding support if you have to cut a stud.

New stud

New stud

Cutout stud

Book IV

Bathroom and Kitchen Remodeling

To replace a recessed medicine cabinet, you need a drywall saw, a recessed-mount medicine cabinet with fasteners, and shims. Follow these steps for a professional-looking installation:

1. **Empty the old cabinet, take out the shelves and, in some cases, remove the door.**

2. **Find the fasteners that hold the cabinet in the wall cavity, remove them and pull out the old cabinet.**

3. **If the new cabinet came with the door attached, remove it if possible, following the manufacturer's instructions.**

    Store the door carefully to prevent damaging it or any mirror.

4. **Test-fit the cabinet body in the wall cavity.**

    You should be able to adjust the cabinet to make it level and plumb.

5. **If necessary, remove the cabinet from the cavity and enlarge the opening by cutting the wallboard with a drywall saw.**

6. **Reinsert the cabinet into the wall opening and check again to ensure that the cabinet is level and plumb.**

7. **Insert the mounting screws in the mounting holes in the cabinet body, following the manufacturer's instructions, and tighten the screws to secure the cabinet in the opening.**

    If the cabinet comes with screw covers, snap them in place.

8. **Install the hinge mechanism for the door on the cabinet body and position the door so that it's properly aligned.**

9. **Position the shelf brackets where appropriate and set the shelves on top of the brackets.**

10. **Check the door for proper alignment and make any necessary adjustments.**

Getting a Handle on Faucets

When you're selecting a faucet, make sure that it's compatible with the sink you choose. Lavatory sinks are drilled for faucets with a distance of 4 inches (center set) or 8 inches (widespread) between the hot and cold faucet handles. A single hole accommodates most single-control faucets. Many sinks come with centered single holes, and some have no drillings for faucets mounted directly on the countertop or wall.

When it comes to faucet controls, some single-handle faucets have the handle mounted directly behind the spout, which can limit the space around the spout, making it challenging to keep clean. Short spouts don't take up much room, but they also don't always deliver water where you want it in the basin. The bottom line is to decide whether you're happy with the faucet control and handles of the faucet you have, and then choose a new one based on that decision.

Many people wouldn't consider a two-handle faucet because they enjoy the ease of operating a single-lever control, but many others love the two-handle look. Still other people swear that a pullout spout with a push-button spray in the bathroom is the handiest convenience because they like to wash their hair in the sink. Only you know what type of faucet and control gives you the convenience, comfort and look you want.

Finishes come in basic chrome and chrome brushed with polished brass and other finishes, including stainless steel, nickel, and accent colors and patterns. For design direction, consider choosing your bathroom fixtures and fittings from a manufacturer's collection of products, which are all coordinated, but from different price categories, and which you can use together stylishly.

Putting in an easy-install faucet

Many of today's faucet manufacturers have a line of easy-to-install single-control faucets designed for do-it-yourselfers. It's easy to install because it's accessible almost entirely above the countertop. No more lying on your back crammed into a dark cabinet. The manufacturers have figured out a way to preassemble the unit, which alone is revolutionary. Just knowing that you're not going to face a bag of strange-looking unfamiliar parts and the challenge of installing them correctly makes the unit a godsend for DIYers.

The nastiest part of this job is emptying the stuff under the cabinet so that you can reach inside to hold the faucet while you tighten it. You need only two tools to install the faucet: an adjustable wrench and a screwdriver. Follow these steps:

1. **Drop the flexible supply lines through the holes in the sink.**

2. **Align the center toggle with the center hole in the sink and push the valve body down to force the toggle through the hole.**

3. **Use a standard screwdriver to tighten the setscrew in the back of the faucet body (see Figure 8-17).**

   You may have to hold the toggle that's now underneath the sink to keep it from turning.

Book IV

Bathroom and Kitchen Remodeling

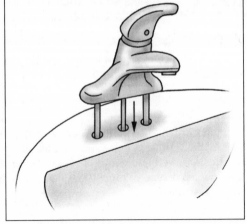

Figure 8-17:
This faucet has preinstalled supply lines and installs with a screwdriver.

4. **When the toggle reaches the underside of the sink, firmly tighten the screw to lock the faucet in place (see Figure 8-18).**

Figure 8-18:
Tightening the toggle.

5. **Thread the caps of the flexible supply lines onto the stop valves and tighten them with a wrench.**

Whenever you thread fittings on to a pipe, you should apply Teflon plumber's tape to male threads and pipe dope to female threads to help seal the joint and reduce the chance of leaks. Compression fittings used to connect riser tubes don't require tape or pipe dope.

Installing a two-handle faucet

A hardworking bathroom faucet doesn't have to be ordinary, but it does have to be installed properly. Some faucet designs use a rubber gasket to seal the joint between the base of the faucet and the sink. Others require that you place a bead of plumber's putty around the perimeter of the faucet's base. (See Figure 8-19.) Today's designs of these two-handle faucets make installing one easier than ever.

Figure 8-19: This two-handle faucet has a separate spout and valves handles.

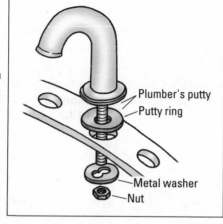

Plumber's putty
Putty ring
Metal washer
Nut

To keep the process simple, install the faucet before you put the sink in place so that it's easier to work on — especially if the sink or countertop will sit on a vanity cabinet. Working in a dark, tight spot makes installation difficult, not to mention uncomfortable.

You can find a wide selection of two-handle faucets on the market. You install them in basically the same way, but be sure to follow the instructions included with the unit. Generally, here's what's involved:

1. **Unpack the faucet and check that it's the model you want, fits the sink holes, and comes with all the parts needed for installation.**

2. **Follow the manufacturer's directions and install the gasket or apply the plumber's putty.**

   Many faucet designs have a rubber gasket that goes between the base of the valves and spout assembly and the countertop. Others require that you apply a bead of plumber's putty to the underside of the unit.

Book IV

Bathroom and Kitchen Remodeling

3. **Place the faucet spout on the sink or countertop.**

   If the spout has riser tubes already installed, align them with the hole in the sink and lower the spout body into place.

4. **Place the faucet valve assemblies (hot and cold) into the holes in the countertop.**

   If these valves have riser tubes already installed, thread them through the holes in the countertop.

   If the faucet isn't equipped with built-in riser tubes, thread them onto the valve tailpieces and then jump ahead to Step 8.

5. **From the underside of the sink, tighten the hold-down bolts.**

   Some models have large washers and nuts that screw on the valve tailpieces, although others are held in place with brackets that bolt to the underside of the valve body.

6. **From under the sink, connect the flexible hoses from the hot and cold valves with the spout (see Figure 8-20).**

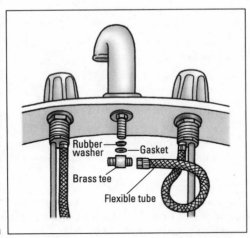

Figure 8-20:
Separate valves and spout allow this faucet to fit a wide variety of sinks. The valves are connected to the spout with flexible tubes.

7. **Connect the riser tubes from the hot and cold valves to the stop valves on the wall.**

8. **Turn on the water and check for leaks.**

9. **Remove the aerator screen from the spout and run water through the faucet to flush out any debris that may be in the pipes.**

10. **When the water runs clear, replace the aerator.**

Book V

Carpentry, Woodworking, and Flooring

In this book . . .

Over the years, the ability to handle small carpentry jobs can save you a great deal of money. Perhaps more important, you can make small repairs before they turn into big ones. In addition, you'll probably make a lot of little improvements that you might not have if you had to hire someone to do the work.

This book explains the basics of how to work with wood — drilling, fastening, finishing, and so on — and how to read diagrams if you'd like to create something yourself, such as a bookcase or a table. The book also contains a chapter on repairing and installing floors, which today's easy-to-work-with materials make doable for a typical do-it-yourselfer.

Here are the contents of Book V at a glance.

Chapter 1

Flooring: Keeping a Leg Up on Foot Traffic

The most used and abused interior surface of a home is the floor. No matter what type of flooring material your home has, it takes a beating every day. Whether it's hardwood or ceramic tile in the entryway, or sheet flooring or ceramic tile in the kitchen, the constant exposure to dirt, grease, and grime tests each type to the max. To get the most out of any flooring material, you need to select the correct type for the application. And, yes, some flooring materials are no-nos in certain areas of the home.

This chapter shows you how to refurbish, repair, replace, and install new flooring. We also discuss where to use and where not to use specific flooring types. From hardwood to carpet and from sheet flooring to ceramic and vinyl tile, this chapter's got you covered.

The Subfloor: A Solid Base

Whether you're installing flooring in a room for the first time or tearing out and replacing old flooring, a solid, smooth subfloor is critical for successful installation. So it all starts at the bottom: the subfloor.

The *subfloor* is the material — either wood or concrete, depending on where it's located in the house — that serves as the bottom layer of support for the flooring. In most cases, when you hear the term *subfloor,* it's in connection with wood, either plywood or boards. Homes built from the 1970s on generally have plywood subfloors. Older homes, say from the early 1960s and before, often have individual 1-x-8 boards as subflooring. Both form a solid base, and both can be damaged and require repair. The following sections take a look at the problems you might run into when inspecting and prepping a subfloor.

Fixing low spots

A new floor should be smooth and level. But over time, houses shift and settle, and low spots in the subfloor sometimes develop. The best way to check for low spots is twofold:

- ✔ Do a quick visual inspection — you can usually see any significant low spots.

- ✔ Lay a 4-foot level in various places over the entire floor, get down on your hands and knees, and look for spots where the subfloor and level don't touch. Light shining between the subfloor and level indicates a low spot.

To eliminate a low spot, fill the area with ready-mix latex underlayment. This stuff is easy to use because it's premixed; you simply spread it on the floor and smooth it with a floor trowel. Just be sure to feather the edges of the underlayment patch. *Feathering* an edge makes the material gradually thinner toward the edges until it forms a smooth joint and transition between the underlayment patch and the existing subfloor. After the patch dries, use a carpenter's level to make sure that you've leveled the low spot. If it's still off, fill in with additional latex underlayment until you get it right.

Making repairs to subflooring

You may find that the subfloor is damaged beyond repair with an underlayment patch material, especially if, for example, water has damaged a kitchen or bathroom floor. A water leak can wet the subfloor, causing it to rot or, in the case of plywood subflooring, delaminate. *Delamination* occurs when the individual layers of plywood separate. Water can also damage board subflooring. Individual boards can't delaminate because they're made of a single slab of wood and not three or four thin layers glued together. However, single-board subflooring can warp, which is just as bad.

A damaged subfloor will result in an uneven finished floor surface. If you find rot, delamination, or warping, you must replace the damaged areas.

To replace damaged single-board subflooring, remove the damaged section of the board. You may be able to get by with replacing a small length of the board, or you may have to replace the entire board. Replacing the entire board makes the repair easier because the joints at the end of the board will fall directly over the floor joists, and you can screw them (or nail them, although screwing them is easier) in place. If you're replacing only a section of the board, make sure to cut out the section so that the ends of the new board's length fall over the middle of floor joist. If they don't, the ends will be hanging free, and you won't be able to secure the joints to anything below. This setup creates weak spots in the subfloor.

Replacing damaged plywood subflooring is fairly easy. Most of the damage we've seen has required replacing an entire piece of plywood, although you can cut out a smaller section and replace it. When replacing an entire sheet of subfloor, you need to remove the nails or screws that secure it to the subfloor. If the fasteners are screws, you're in luck. Simply remove them with a powered drill/driver. If the subfloor is nailed down, a little more work is involved, but it's doable for most folks.

Use a hammer and cat's paw or similar nail puller to get under the head of the nail and loosen it slightly from the floor joist into which it's driven. You won't be able to pull it out completely by using the cat's paw. The nails used for securing subflooring, called *ring-shank or cement-coated nails,* are meant to be driven into wood but not to be removed easily. A ring-shank nail has a series of rings on the shaft or shank that hold the nail in the wood. To pull up these nails, you need a tool called — surprise! — a nail puller. Its design gives you enough leverage to pull out even ring-shank nails.

If you don't own either a cat's paw or a nail puller, you can rent them at a rental equipment store. Cat's paws aren't expensive, usually costing less than $10, and they're handy tools to own. A nail puller, on the other hand, is fairly expensive, and you won't use it often. We recommend that you buy a cat's paw and rent a nail puller.

Installing board or plywood subflooring is the same. Set the material into position and secure it with 3-inch-long drywall screws. We recommend using screws because doing so is easier and faster than using nails, and you can remove screws more quickly and easily, too.

Understanding underlayment

All types of flooring require an *underlayment* to be installed over the subfloor. The subfloor provides overall structural support and strength, and underlayment creates a level surface and helps prevent squeaks, prevent uneven wear on vinyl or sheet flooring, and even keep the finish on wood floors from cracking.

For most wood floors and vinyl or sheet flooring, a ⅛- or ¼-inch-thick plywood underlayment is adequate. Check your flooring's installation specs to see which thickness of underlayment it requires. If you use the wrong one, you void the warranty on the flooring.

Most plywood underlayment is conventional oak underlayment plywood or luan mahogany plywood. Both work fine, although luan is slightly softer than oak, and professionals usually recommend it for use under sheet flooring. Again, check the installation requirements for which underlayment material to use.

Underlayment for ceramic tile is completely different. Because of the weight of the tile, grout, and adhesive, a stronger, thicker underlayment is needed. For most installations, tile backerboard, most commonly cement board but also gypsum and other materials, are recommended. Cement boards are made of cement-based materials and are usually ½ inch thick. They come in 3-x-5-foot sheets, not 4-x-8-foot sheets like plywood does, so one person can handle them. However, even the 3 x 5 sheets are a handful, especially in tight quarters, such as a bathroom. Cement board is secured to the subfloor with cement board screws, roofing nails and ring-shank nails specifically made for use with cement board. Be sure to use the recommended nails.

If you plan to use an existing underlayment, make sure that it's in good shape — free of loose pieces, low spots, and damage. You inspect underlayment the same way you inspect subflooring, and make repairs the same way, too. Look for low spots and fill them with an underlayment patch. Secure any loose spots and get rid of those squeaks *now!*

It's also important to see what the flooring manufacturer's installation instructions say about how to deal with joints between pieces of underlayment. Most flooring companies recommend, and in some cases require, that you fill every joint with underlayment patch to eliminate gaps between pieces of underlayment, especially if you're installing sheet flooring. Filling the gaps creates a single, smooth, flat surface for the flooring and reduces the likelihood of high or low spots.

Hardwood Flooring

Something about the beauty and warmth of a hardwood floor just can't be topped. Whether it's a natural wood floor or one of the beautiful and real-looking synthetic wood floors, the rich color and grain of the wood really class up a room. And hardwood or synthetic wood flooring isn't limited to living rooms. You can use it in kitchens, family rooms, entryways, bedrooms, and dining rooms — wherever you want to add richness and style.

Refurbishing: When hardwood only needs a touchup

Regular dusting or vacuuming keeps most hardwood and synthetic wood floors looking good for years. Occasionally, however, the flooring needs an extra boost to gets its original look back. We're not talking about stripping and refinishing a wood floor or even a light sanding and recoating with finish; we're talking about simply using the cleaning product recommended for your flooring. Think of the way we used to take care of linoleum: A harder cleaning was all it took to make the floor shine again.

Before you delve into stripping your hardwood floor (covered in the next section), try this technique:

1. **Rub a small area with 0000-grade steel wool dipped in denatured alcohol.**

2. **Wipe it dry to remove any wax.**

3. **Damp-mop the area and apply a coat of paste wax.**

If this process brings the floor back to life, do the rest of the floor in the same manner. It may seem like a lot of work, and it does take time, but it's easier and neater than sanding and stripping and may make your floor look the way you want it to.

Don't try this method with synthetic wood flooring. The finishes on these products aren't designed for rubbing with an abrasive, such as steel wool, or cleaning with common cleaning products such as soap, floor polish, or scouring powder. Damp-mop the synthetic wood floor with a bit of ammonia or vinegar in water. Just be careful not to flood the floor. A wrung-out damp mop will do the trick.

Refinishing: Making your floor look new again

If you tried refurbishing and your floor still looks less than great, you probably need to refinish the floor. This process involves removing all the old finish (wax and stain). To do so, you need a walk-behind floor sander, which you can rent. You also want to rent a handheld power edge sander for sanding tight against walls and in corners and doorways. Both units have a vacuum and dust bag system to minimize the amount of sanding dust left behind.

A walk-behind sander has a large rotating drum that evenly removes the finish — if you use the correct series of sandpaper grades and operate the sander properly. Rental stores have the three grades of sandpaper you need for successful floor refinishing: coarse, medium, and fine. The large sheets are designed to fit tight against the drum. Some sanders have a slot into which you tuck in the sandpaper; other models have a screw-down bar that secures the paper. After the paper's in place, you tighten the drum with a wrench (supplied with the sander). For safety, wear a dust mask and eye and ear protection.

Some rooms may have a small piece of molding, called *base-shoe* or *shoe molding,* along the baseboards. For best results (and the least damage), we recommend removing the base-shoe. Doing so gives you maximum access when sanding and refinishing where the floor meets the wall.

Sanding off the old stuff

The most important idea to remember when sanding hardwood floors is to sand *with* the grain of the wood, maintaining an even pace. Sanding across the grain leaves gouges that not only look horrible but also are almost impossible to remove. Use the sandpaper in successively finer grades: Start with coarse to remove the toughest of the nasty finish and work your way to fine.

When operating the floor sander, lift the drum of the sander off of the floor and then turn on the power. If you start the sander with the drum resting on the floor, it's likely to damage the floor, and it could take off and shoot forward almost uncontrollably.

When you get to the end of the section you're sanding, or if you need to stop before that point, raise the drum and turn off the power. Make sure that the drum has stopped spinning before you set it down. Also, make sure that each sanding pass overlaps the adjacent pass. Doing so ensures that you don't miss any spots, plus it reduces the chance of gouging or leaving a ridge.

A floor sander can get only so close to the walls and into the corners. For these areas, we recommend an edge sander. These units use the same grades of sandpaper as floor units, but the sandpaper is disk shaped. Again, keep the unit off the floor and then start the motor. Gently lower the unit onto the floor and remove the finish. Sand with the grain and be sure to overlap the adjacent sanded area.

Corners can be especially tough to sand, and you may have to use a sanding block or paint scraper. A paint scraper works great for removing the finish in a corner. Follow that step by using a sanding block, again with the same succession of sandpaper grades. This way, you achieve a smooth, sanded surface from power-sanded to hand-sanded areas.

Book V

Carpentry,
Wood-
working,
and
Flooring

Filling nicks and gouges

Now is also the time to fill any nicks or gouges in the floor. Use wood putty and a broad knife to fill any spots. Let the wood putty dry according to package directions and then lightly sand the areas smooth by hand with medium or fine sandpaper.

Sucking it up

After you've completed all the sanding, you must remove all the dust from the floor, molding, and walls. Yes, dust will settle on the walls. A lot of dust. Wipe down the walls and moldings once to get the dust onto the floor, and then use a damp rag on the moldings to remove any residue. You don't want any dust falling onto the floor later, when the new finish is drying. Let the dust settle, and then vacuum.

A standard shop vacuum with a dust filter will do the trick. You can also rent a heavy-duty vacuum from where you rented the sanders. Use the vacuum's brush attachment to pick up all the dust and reduce the chance of blowing it around the room.

After you vacuum, wipe the entire floor surface with a *tack cloth,* a wax-impregnated piece of cheesecloth designed to pick up and hold dust residue. Plan to use several tack cloths — don't overextend the cloths' dust-holding capacity. Rotate the cloth, turn it inside out, and use all the surfaces, but don't be afraid to grab a new one if the old one looks too dirty. Tack cloths are inexpensive.

Selecting a finish

The type of finish you choose depends on the look you want for your floor. Durability is also an issue. Your choices are

- ✔ **Polyurethane,** either oil or water based, comes in various degrees of luster (shine). Polyurethane, or poly, has a sort of plastic look, which some people don't like at all. Both poly finish types darken or even yellow the wood's appearance, although some newer water-based products don't darken as much and leave the floor as close to natural as possible. Poly finishes are excellent for high-traffic and high-moisture areas, such as a kitchen or bathroom, because they resist water staining and abrasion. On the downside, if the finish gets nicked or gouged, it's extremely difficult to spot-repair. You'll need to resurface the entire floor to get an even appearance.

- ✔ **Varnish** comes in a variety of lusters, from matte to glossy. Varnish is very durable but is slightly softer than polyurethane. The higher the gloss, the more durable the surface. Varnish often darkens with age, so keep this fact in mind. On the up side, you can make spot-repairs to varnish.

✔ **Penetrating sealer** offers the most natural-looking finish. It brings out the grain in wood; however, it may darken over time. It's also available in various wood colors. Penetrating sealer offers good protection, especially when waxed. However, it's less durable than polyurethane or varnish. It's the easiest of the three to spot-repair, though, and you can usually buff out scratches. You should wax floors treated with penetrating sealer once a year.

Putting on a new face

Ideally, you want to seal the floor on the same day you finish sanding to prevent the open wood surface from absorbing moisture. For best results, apply the stain (if desired) and sealer with a sheepskin applicator. Be sure to apply the sealer evenly, and use enough to cover the surface. But be careful not to apply too much. Excess sealer doesn't soak into the wood — it pools on the surface. If you fail to remove it, it leaves an ugly, ugly spot.

After the sealer has dried, follow these steps:

1. **Buff the floor with No. 2 (fine) steel wool.**

2. **Vacuum and wipe the floor again with a tack cloth.**

   It's critical to remove all the dust between finish coats, or you'll have a rough and ugly floor.

3. **Apply the first of two coats of finish wax or other floor finish, such as polyurethane or varnish.**

   Follow the directions on the finish container for drying time between coats.

4. **Apply the final coat.**

   Wait at least 24 hours after the final coat dries before moving furniture into the room.

Repairing damaged hardwood flooring

Your floor may be in generally fine shape, with a damaged spot or two. If you find damage or stains, it may be easier and more effective to make small repairs than to refinish the entire floor. This section explains how to repair small areas of damage to hardwood flooring.

Replacing a strip or plank of flooring

If a strip or plank of flooring is damaged and is beyond being saved by sanding and filling, you have to replace it. Most floors use a tongue-and-groove design for connecting adjacent strips. This design makes replacing a single strip or plank challenging, but not impossible.

First, look for any nails in the damaged board and drive as far through the board as possible by using a hammer and *nail set,* a pointed tool that you place on the head of the nail and then strike with a hammer, driving the nail into the wood. Carpenters use nail sets to drive nails flush with trim without damaging the trim with a hammer. After you've cleared the nails, it's time to remove the damaged board and install a new one. Follow these steps:

1. **Use a carpenter's square to mark a perpendicular line across the section of the board to be removed.**

   If you're removing the entire strip, skip this step.

2. **Use a ½- or ⅜-inch-diameter spade bit and power drill to drill holes along the marks.**

3. **Use a wood chisel to split the damaged board into two pieces.**

   Doing so makes removal easier.

4. **Pry out the damaged board.**

   If you take a strip out of the middle you can pry the remaining pieces away from the adjacent boards before prying them up. Remove any additional boards the same way but cut them so the end joints are staggered.

5. **Square up the drilled ends with a very sharp wood chisel, and use a nail puller to remove any exposed nails or drive them in out of the way with a nail set.**

   You want the ends of the good sections smooth and square for easier installation.

6. **Cut a replacement strip to the same length as the one you removed. As needed, cut off the bottom side of the groove on the board.**

   Removing the bottom groove enables you to install a board between two others by inserting its tongue side first and then lowering its groove side into place. If you don't remove it, you won't be able to get the board past the tongue of the adjacent board.

7. **Test-fit the strip to make sure that it fits.**

   If it doesn't, recut the board.

8. **Remove the replacement strip and apply construction adhesive to the backside of the strip. Install the strip and gently tap it into place.**

   Use a scrap piece of wood to protect the strip's surface while tapping it into place. Nail the board with 2-inch-long ring-shank flooring nails and drive the heads just below the surface with a nail set.

Matching the finish of the new strip to the existing flooring may be difficult, but give it a shot before you refinish the entire floor. Apply stain and sealer or whatever finish the strip needs to match the existing floor.

Repairing a buckled board

Occasionally, a hardwood board buckles. When this happens, you need to fix it fast for two reasons:

- ✔ To avoid further damage to the floor
- ✔ More important, to get rid of a real tripping hazard

To fix a buckled floorboard, you need to be able to access the floor from below. The way to tackle this problem is to put weight on the buckled area from above — a cement block works well. Then install a 1¼-inch screw in the buckled flooring from below. Allow the screw to penetrate only halfway into the flooring, or it may come up through the finished surface. Driving the screw through the subfloor and into the flooring pulls the flooring down against the subfloor and gets rid of the buckled spot.

Dealing with stains

Stains are the toughest fix when it comes to hardwood floors. One stain or water ring can ruin the look of the whole floor. Unfortunately, refinishing the entire floor is sometimes the only way to get rid of a stain or ring. But before you rent a sander and start using language that would make a sailor blush, try to get rid of the stain. Doing so requires using a gentle touch and the right materials, but it's worth a shot.

Most stains on hardwood floors are very dark, even black. You don't need to try to get rid of the entire stain in one try. Getting rid of the blemish may take several attempts, but you may be successful.

Follow these steps to remove a stain:

1. **Sand off the old finish.**

2. **Mix oxalic acid crystals (sold at home centers and paint and hardware stores) in water, following the package directions.**

   Be sure to wear eye protection and acid-resistant rubber gloves.

3. **Soak a clean white cloth in the acid mixture. Then press the cloth on the stained area and let it set for about an hour.**

4. **Lift the cloth and check to see whether the stain has been bleached away. If it hasn't, repeat the process.**

   This may take several applications, but eventually the stain will be bleached away.

5. **After the stain is gone, rinse the area with household vinegar to neu-tralize the acid. Wipe away any excess moisture and allow the area to dry completely.**

6. **Apply a matching oil-based stain lightly to the bleached area.**

   Use several coats, if necessary, to match. Don't try to match the color with only one application. You can always darken the area with additional coats, but you can't lighten it after it's gotten too dark. If you think the stain is too dark, wipe the area immediately with a cloth dampened with mineral spirits. Doing so will remove some of the stain and lighten the area.

   After you've achieved the desired color, allow the area to dry overnight.

7. **Apply the topcoat finish and blend into the adjacent areas.**

   Once again, you may not get a perfect match; however, it may be good enough to avoid having to refinish the entire floor. If it doesn't match enough to suit you, refinish the floor.

Getting rid of nicks and scratches

You can usually cover up these little eyesores with color putty sticks. We know, it sounds like a Band-Aid repair, but it's the quickest and least involved way to handle these problems. Simply clean the nicked or scratched area thoroughly and rub the putty stick over the damaged spot. Let the color dry for a few minutes and then wipe it with a clean cloth. Most of the time, getting color into a nicked or scratched area is all you need to do to make the damage disappear — at least to those who don't know that the area was damaged before. Use the same stuff to fill nail holes in a patched floor after the top coat is applied.

If a nick or scratch is really a dig or gouge, you face a whole different type of repair. It involves using wood filler and stain and trying to match the existing floor color. If your floor is really showing its age, we recommend refinishing the entire surface instead of spending time and energy on smaller fixes that really are better handled by redoing the entire surface. You'll like the final results a lot more!

Transforming a room by replacing the floor

Wood flooring is nothing new. People have used it for hundreds of years. What hasn't been around is the wide selection of types, colors, and installa-tion methods. This section gives you a look at your choices and walks you through a typical hardwood floor installation.

Choosing the right flooring type for your project

Whether it's the front entry, dining room, living room, or kitchen, you can probably find wood flooring that meets your wants and needs. Whether it's all-wood strip or plank flooring or laminate (synthetic) wood flooring, it'll be beautiful and durable and should serve you for years.

Wood flooring is just that — all wood, either solid wood or laminated, like plywood. Most wood floors today are made of oak, which is strong and has an obvious grain. Other types of wood, such as ash and maple, are becoming popular; homeowners are even using exotic wood species, like mahogany, within oak floors as accents. (The cost of exotic woods is usually cost-prohibitive for an entire room's floor.) Softer woods, such as pine, fir, and cherry, aren't as common because they don't stand up to much wear.

Most wood flooring comes in 2¼-inch-wide strips, although wider and narrower sizes are available. If the flooring is 3 inches or wider, it's called *plank* or *board flooring. Parquet flooring,* which is made up of 9-inch to 19-inch squares of premade "tiles" of wood strips, is also quite popular.

Laminate or *synthetic wood flooring* is a combination of layers of material laminated together. The top layer is made of cellulose paper impregnated with clear melamine resins for durability. The second layer is a paper layer called the design layer, which has a pattern printed on it to give the appearance of wood. This layer is strengthened with resins. The third layer, the core, is made of engineered wood (particle board) or fiberboard. The bottom layer is made of paper or melamine (a plastic-like sheet material).

So which one is right for you? First, decide where you're going to use it. Is it a high-traffic area, like an entry or kitchen? Is it more for looks in an entertaining area, such as a dining room or living room? In a high-traffic area, laminate is a good choice because of its durability. But if you want the color, richness, and warmth of wood, a real wood floor is the right choice for you.

Installing a prefinished hardwood floor — the way the pros do it!

The most popular types of wood flooring use a tongue-and-groove system to connect adjacent boards. This arrangement allows for a solid connection between boards, sort of like locking the boards into each other. Many systems are nailed down too, but others use glue to secure strips together. The glue method is called a *floating* floor because the flooring literally lays or floats on a thin cushioned pad. You can find complete installation instructions for a floating floor at home centers and flooring stores. This section shows you the general steps for installing a nailed-down wood floor on a wood subfloor and underlayment.

Begin the installation at the longest wall and follow these steps:

Book V

Carpentry,
Wood-
working,
and
Flooring

1. **Place ½-inch temporary spacers between the first board and the wall to allow for seasonal expansion of the flooring.**

2. **Nail the first board to the underlayment at the wall by using 7d finish nails.**

3. **Continue installing boards, applying carpenter's glue to the grooved edge of each piece of flooring just before installing it onto the adjacent piece.**

4. **To mark the last plant or the first course for cutting, turn it so that the tongue along the edge of the board is against the wall.**

   You'll turn the plank to match the others after you cut it to length.

5. **Mark the turned board and cut it to length.**

   If you're cutting with a circular saw, turn the decorative face of the board down to avoid splintering.

6. **Turn the cut board into the correct installation position and install it at the end of the row.**

7. **Secure the tongue side of this row to the underlayment with 7d finish nails.**

   Drive the nails at a 45-degree angle through the tongue. Be careful not to split the tongue.

8. **Begin the next row with the leftover piece of the cut board.**

   Just make sure that the piece is at least 8 inches long. If it isn't, use another board, but make sure that the first joints of each row of boards are staggered for a good-looking appearance and to keep a minimum of 8 inches of plank length between the joints.

9. **Place a scrap piece of flooring against the tongue of the board to act as a buffer board and tap the boards together with a hammer before nailing.**

   The block keeps the hammer from damaging the tongue.

   The easiest and fastest way to nail wood flooring is with a *power flooring nailer,* an angled nailer that drives the size nail through the tongue at the correct angle and depth. Use one as soon as you are far enough away from the wall to fit it against the course being installed.

10. **Continue this process to complete the job.**

    You may need to cut the final row of boards lengthwise or rip them to fit because not every room's width exactly accommodates the various widths of flooring. Remember to leave a ½-inch expansion gap on this side of the room, too. It's best to rip a long board with a table saw, but you can use a circular saw. If you do use a circular saw, use a saw guide to keep your cut line straight. A length of 1 x 4 board clamped to the flooring works well as a cutting guide.

11. **Install base molding.**

When you must fit a board around a corner or an irregular shape, such as a doorway, you need to measure the length and depth of the obstruction that will protrude into the board. Use a combination square for accurate measurements. Then remove the marked area with a hand-powered coping saw or a jigsaw (motorized).

Doorways can be a problem because the door's jamb and casing (trim) extend to the underlayment. The best looking and easiest approach is to cut off the bottom of the jamb and trim by using a flush-cut saw or hand-saw. Place the saw on top of a scrap piece of flooring as you complete the cut. This spacer/template ensures a straight cut and one that removes just the right amount.

Ceramic Tile

Ceramic tile is one tough flooring product. In fact, it's the toughest of the bunch. It withstands stains, liquids, and high traffic. It's easy to take care of and comes in a variety of sizes, colors, and patterns. On the downside, drop a large pan or maybe the hammer that belongs in the kitchen tool drawer onto ceramic tile, and you could easily be faced with a cracked or broken tile that you need to replace. But don't let that deter you from choosing ceramic tile. It has its place, especially in entryways, bathrooms, and kitchens.

Replacing a damaged tile and cracked grout

Replace a cracked tile as soon as possible — not only for the appearance, but also to maintain the floor's integrity. Even one cracked or missing tile weakens the strength of the grout between the tiles, which can lead to adjacent tiles and grout becoming loose. This section looks at how to replace a broken tile and replace cracked or missing grout.

Replacing a broken tile

This project actually sounds harder than it really is, so don't be afraid to tackle it. You need specific tools, safety gear, and materials — we tell you what you need at each step.

1. **Wearing eye protection and heavy-duty work gloves, remove the damaged tile with a hammer and cold chisel.**

   Starting at the edge of the tile and grout, break the tile into smaller pieces during the removal rather than trying to take out the tile in one big chunk. After all, the tile's shot anyway. Just be careful not to chip the surrounding tiles.

2. **Use the cold chisel to scrape the old adhesive off the floor.**

   Remove as much as possible so that the new tile adheres properly.

3. **Apply *mortar* (tile adhesive) to the back of the new tile by using a wide-blade putty knife.**

   We use a 6-inch-wide knife. Be sure to spread the adhesive out to the edges for best adhesion. Use thin-set mortar for floor tiles.

4. **Set the tile firmly in position and level it with the surrounding tiles, and then tap it into place with a hammer and wood block.**

   You may need to apply more mortar if the tile isn't level. Use a short block of scrap wood to protect the tile when tapping with the hammer.

5. **After the tile adhesive has set up (usually a couple of hours), use a rubber grout float to spread the grout and fill the gaps between the tiles.**

   Hold the float at a 30-degree angle to the tile and work the grout into the gaps from all directions, and strike off the excess with the float nearly perpendicular.

6. **Wipe off any excess grout with a damp grout sponge.**

   Use as little water as possible and a light circular motion. Try not to rub or disturb the grout lines at this point. Just remove the grout on the face of the tile.

7. **After the grout has set up slightly (about 15–20 minutes), go back with the grout sponge and clean up the grout lines.**

   This time, wipe parallel to the grout lines. Rinse the sponge often and wring it out well for best results.

If you've done your job well, there will only be a light grout haze left when the grout is set. Buff this off with cheesecloth or a soft cloth.

Grout comes in different colors, so you should be able to match the existing grout. It's sold in powder form, which you mix with water or, better yet, grout additive. The additive helps the grout adhere.

Replacing cracked or missing grout

Cracked or missing grout looks bad, and it's a good way for otherwise solid tiles to become loose. So it's important to repair or replace grout that's bad. Don't fret, though — this job is more labor intensive than it is complicated.

Whether the grout is cracked or missing, you need to remove enough grout so that the new grout has solid grout to bond to. Follow these steps:

1. **Use a grout saw to scrape out the old grout.**

   A *grout saw* is a short-bladed hand tool that does a great job, although you will work up a sweat! Work the saw back and forth to loosen and cut out the old grout. The grout may come out in pieces, or it could turn into powder. Either way is okay — just get it all out.

2. **After the old grout is completely out or is back to solid material, vacuum out the joints.**

3. **Spread new grout into the joints by using a rubber grout float, as described in Steps 5 through 7 from the preceding section.**

Regrouting a tile floor with a different-colored grout also gives an old floor a new look. We've seen several kitchens where removing the old grout and replacing it with a new color of grout made the room look like it had been redone. Amazing!

Installing a ceramic tile floor

This project may appear to be beyond the abilities of most homeowners, but most DIYers can handle it. Just don't rush it — have a little patience! The materials are relatively easy to work with, and you can rent the tools, even the big ones.

Install ceramic tile over a subfloor that's no less than 1⅛ inches thick. A thinner subfloor will cause the floor to flex due to the weight of the tile. A flexing subfloor results in cracked tiles and grout — and a lot of headaches. Most tile manufacturers recommend installing a cement backer board instead of any other type of underlayment, such as plywood. The boards come in 3-x-5-foot sheets and are available where tile and grout are sold.

Getting down to business

Ever wonder how a tile layer always seems to get those tiles at a perfect 90- or 45-degree angle to the wall? They cheat! Not really, but they do use a pair of perpendicular *reference lines* for establishing a layout instead of relying on measurements from walls, which are neither straight not square to each other. To ensure the reference lines are square, they use a 3-4-5 triangle rule as follows:

1. **Establish your first reference line by measuring across opposite sides of the room. Mark the center of each side and then snap a chalk line between the two marks.**

2. **Measure and mark the center of that line. Then use a pencil, a framing square, and a straightedge held against its shorter leg — to mark a second 4-foot-long line perpendicular to the first line.**

   Before snapping a second line across the room, you want be sure the angle you formed is truly 90 degrees.

3. **Measure out 3 feet from the intersection and mark the penciled line. Then measure out 4 feet from the intersection and mark the spot on the chalk line. Measure the distance between the 3-foot and 4-foot marks.**

   The distance should be 5 feet — the 3-4-5 rule. If it isn't, make an adjustment and pencil a new line. Now snap a chalk line across the room that falls directly over the penciled line.

After you have reference lines, use them to establish *layout lines*, which actually guide tile placement. Dry-set two rows of tiles the extend from the center to adjacent walls. If the last tile in a row would be less that half a tile, plan to shift the first course to be centered on the reference line rather than next to it. Snap your layout line a half line away from the reference line. Repeat the procedure for the other row.

Laying out your tiles at 45-degree angles instead of 90 isn't that difficult. You need only a couple more layout lines. Mark the two layout lines as you would for a 90-degree job and then follow these steps:

1. **Measure out the same distance (for example, 4 feet) on the perpendicular lines.**

2. **From these points, make marks 4 feet out at right angles to the original lines.**

3. **Snap a chalk line through these new marks and through the intersection of the two original layout lines.**

   The two lines are now your layout lines for a 45-degree pattern.

After you establish your guidelines or layout lines, it's time to install the tile. Follow these steps and check out Figure 1-1:

1. **Before you think about setting the tile in place with mortar, make sure that the layout is even from side to side in both directions. To do so, dry-fit the tiles along the layout lines in both directions and make sure that the finished layout looks good to you.**

   One important measurement to note is the width of the tiles that meet the wall. Make sure you never have less than half of a tile's width at the wall. If you do, adjust the layout until you get an adequate end tile size. After you establish this, snap a new layout line to follow.

2. **Pick up the loose tiles and set them aside.**

3. **Use a notched trowel to spread thin-set mortar (used to secure floor tile) over a 3 x 3 section at the intersection of the layout lines.**

   Trowels come with different-sized notches, so check the tile manufacturer's recommendation for the correct size.

   Working in small, square sections — say 3 feet x 3 feet — is important. If you work with a larger section, the mortar may harden (known as *setting up*) before you put the tiles in place. Be careful not to cover the layout lines.

4. **Begin laying tiles at the center point of the two layout lines, setting each tile into the mortar by tapping it gently with a rubber mallet.**

   Use plastic spacers at each tile corner to maintain even grout lines between the tiles. Spacers are available where tile is sold.

5. **Continue laying tiles until you've covered the mortared area.**

6. **Continue the process by applying mortar to another section and then laying tiles.**

7. **Fit the last tile in the row at the wall.**

   This step usually requires that you measure and cut the tile. First, set a scrap tile against the wall — it allows space for grout. Next, place a loose tile directly over the last full tile you laid (this is the tile you'll cut to size). Then place another tile on the loose one and up against the tile on the wall. Mark the loose tile and cut it to fit along the edge. (We discuss cutting in just a bit.)

8. **After all the tiles are set in the mortar, mix the grout according to the manufacturer's instructions and install it by using the rubber grout float.**

   Use a sweeping motion, pressing the grout into the gaps.

9. **Wipe away the excess grout with a grout sponge. Let the grout dry slightly and then wipe off the haze that appears.**

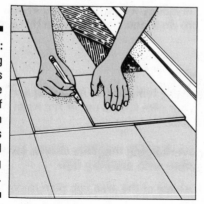

Figure 1-1:
Laying
border tiles
around the
edge of
a room
requires
careful
measuring
and cutting.

Book V

**Carpentry,
Wood-
working,
and
Flooring**

Cutting tiles

For most installations, you need a tile cutter, which you can rent. To make a straight cut with a tile cutter, simply place the tile face up in the cutter, adjust the cutter to the proper width, and score the tile by pulling the cutting wheel across the tile's face. Then snap the tile along the scored line.

If you need to make a cutout, say to go around a corner, mark the area you plan to cut out. Secure the tile in a vise or clamps — just be sure to cushion the vise jaws to protect the tile from scratches. Cut along the marks with a *tile saw,* which is a hand saw that's similar to a coping saw, except that it has a carbide saw blade designed for cutting ceramic tile.

If you need to make a round or circular cut, mark the area and then use a tile nipper to nip out small pieces of tile until you reach the line. A *tile nipper* is similar to a pair of pliers, but it has hardened cutting edges for cutting through ceramic tile.

Sheet Vinyl Flooring

Sheet vinyl is a popular flooring choice for bathrooms, kitchens, entryways, and laundry rooms. Sold in 6- and 12-foot widths, it's pretty durable, easy to maintain, and not too expensive.

Installing sheet flooring is a bit trickier than installing ceramic tile, and the flooring doesn't forgive you if you make a mistake. Cut the piece too short and you need to buy a new one. Make a cutout for a cabinet or plumbing fixture in the wrong spot and you're in the same boat. For that reason, having a professional install sheet flooring is money well spent. Whether you decide to tackle the job yourself or have a pro do it, the information in this section makes you a smarter consumer.

Using a template to cut your piece

Most manufacturers sell an inexpensive template kit for laying and cutting vinyl flooring. You can also make your own sheets out of red rosin paper. Follow these steps to use the template:

1. **Cover the entire floor with overlapping template sheets, large or small. Tape every piece together with masking tape.**

   The resulting template is the shape of the area you plan to cover.

2. **Carefully lift up the template, place it on the unrolled vinyl flooring, and trace the outline onto the flooring with a felt-tip pen.**

3. **Remove the template and cut the flooring with a utility knife with a new blade.**

   Change the blade often for smooth, even cuts.

4. **Place the vinyl flooring in position and slide the edges under the door casings.**

   Be careful when positioning the vinyl — you don't want to nick or tear it.

   It's helpful to cut off the door casings at the bottom by using the method described in the wood flooring section, earlier in this chapter.

Cutting a seam

Try to install your sheet flooring in one large piece. However, many areas are wider than 12 feet, which is the width that sheet flooring comes in. If you need to make a seam, plan to place it along a pattern line and not in a high-traffic area of the room. Follow these steps to cut a seam:

1. **Overlap the sheets by about 2 inches.**

2. **Match the pattern and tape the sheets together with masking tape.**

3. **Hold a straightedge tightly and make several passes with a utility knife to cut through both layers of flooring.**

Gluing it down

You need to glue down the flooring in an efficient yet unhurried manner. The adhesive begins to set up after a while, but you have plenty of time to do it right as long as you work in a logical order. Follow these steps:

1. **Pull up half of the sheet and roll it loosely.**

2. **Use a V-notched trowel to spread the recommended adhesive around the edge of the room and wherever a seam will lie.**

3. **Let the adhesive set up for about 10 to 15 minutes until it gets tacky.**

4. **Unroll the flooring over the adhesive.**

5. **Press the flooring against the underlayment with a rolling pin.**

   You can also rent a floor roller. Work around the entire area, including the edges and seams.

6. **Use a seam roller on each seam to ensure a solid bond of adhesive under both pieces of flooring.**

   A seam roller is slightly smaller than a floor roller. Roll it slowly along each seam to ensure that each seam is completely flat.

Repairing a damaged spot

To repair a damaged spot of sheet vinyl flooring, you need to have a scrap piece of the flooring available.

Don't plan on buying a small piece of the same style and having it match, especially if the vinyl is several years old. Different manufacturing runs have different dye lots, so you face a good chance that the new piece's color won't match your existing flooring.

If you do have a scrap piece, you're in luck. Try to make a patch repair along a pattern line, which does the best job of hiding the cut lines. Here's what to do:

1. **Determine the size and shape of the cutout you want to make.**

   For regular, straight patterns, size the patch so cuts are made along the "grout lines." For overall patterns, make a diamond-shape patch.

2. **Cut the patch material slightly larger, lay it over the damaged floor, align the pattern and tape it in place with masking tape on all sides.**

3. **Make a guided double-cut through the patch and the flooring and remove the damaged flooring.**

   If the floor is adhered in this location scrape all adhesive off the underlayment, being careful not to damage or lift the surrounding flooring.

4. **Brush adhesive on the back of the new piece and, if the surrounding flooring is not adhered, on the underlayment about 1 inch under the flooring edges.**

5. **Position the patch in the same orientation it had when it was cut and roll it with a rolling pin. Clean off any adhesive on the surface.**

6. **Press the seams together and hold them in place with masking tape.**

7. **Wait a half hour before removing tape and applying the recommended seam sealer according to directions.**

Carpet

Ah, the pleasure of digging your toes into rich, plush carpet. It's cushy, it's comfy, and it's neat. Carpet is still the most widely used floor covering in most homes. You have choices of color, texture, and style, all of which add to the overall look and feel of a room. The best carpets are made of wool or a mixture of wool and man-made fibers. Wool carpet is very expensive. However, blends of nylon, polypropylene, acrylic, rayon, and polyester help keep carpet prices reasonable. Plus, these blends are more durable and stain resistant.

Installing carpet isn't difficult, technically. It's challenging, however, because of the size of the rolls and the often-limited workspace. Carpet typically comes in 12-foot widths, which makes a roll of carpet heavy and hard to handle, even for an average-sized room of 12 feet x 12 feet.

If your carpet needs a seam, plan on having a pro install it. You'll be much happier in the long run.

Whether it's cushioned-back carpet for a basement or plush carpet and pad for a living room, this section gives you some general information to help you understand how to lay carpet in place.

Laying carpet with carpet pad

This type of installation requires no glue or adhesive to hold the carpet and pad to the floor. You do, however, need to secure it to the floor at the perimeter to prevent the carpet from moving and forming lumps or bumps.

The first thing that you install is a wooden tack strip, which runs around the perimeter of the room. It's nailed to the subfloor with its points angled toward the wall. The small points sticking up out of the wooden tack strip grab the carpet and hold it down once it's stretched over the tack strip. Tack strips should be spaced away from the wall at a distance equal to the thickness of the carpet being installed.

CALL A PRO

Installing carpet on stairs

We'd leave this task to the pros. If the carpet isn't tight on each step, someone may trip when going up or have his feet go out from under him when going down the stairs. The carpet needs to fit tight to the back (the riser) of each step, yet shouldn't look stretched or out of shape when pulled over the stair tread (the flat part you step on). Open sides on the stair treads can be very tricky to get carpet wrapped around, over, or under and still look good. Again, pay a pro for her time and experience. It's worth it!

Next, place the carpet pad within the tack strip layout and then staple it to the subfloor. The pad is easy to trim with a utility knife. You can seal the joints that form where two pieces meet with duct tape.

Loosely lay out the carpet in approximately the correct position. The less moving this monster of a piece, the better. An installer shifts and maneuvers the carpet a bit. Getting the carpet over the spikes of the tack strip requires the use of a carpet stretcher and carpet kicker. Again, these tools are easy for a professional to use but can be tricky for a novice to use correctly.

A competent installer will plan for seams to occur in low-traffic and low-visibility areas. All seams are cut using the double-cut method described in the previous section and the pieces are joined with seaming tape. The installer places the tape under the seam and then lifts the carpet to melt the adhesive on the tape with a seaming iron. Then he presses the carpet down onto the tape and pinches the pieces together before the adhesive cools.

Laying cushioned-backed carpet

This type of carpet is easy to install. It's a lot like sheet vinyl in that you lay the material out in the room, cut it to fit, and then glue it down. You can cut cushion-backed carpet easily with a utility knife. The adhesive is easy to spread with a trowel. It's also somewhat forgiving because you have a little time to reposition the carpet if it moves.

Patching a hole in carpeting

Cigarette burns and tough stains can cause permanent damage to carpeting. If the blemish is on the surface fiber only, use a nail clipper or small manicure scissors to clip away the damaged fiber. Remember to remove only a small amount of fiber at a time; unlike your hair, this stuff doesn't grow back if you cut it too short.

If the damage is deep or the carpet is torn, replace a section of the carpet as shown in Figure 1-2. Cut a replacement patch by using a straightedge and a utility knife to make a straight cutout around a damaged area. Then install a replacement patch cut to the same size, using double-stick cloth carpet tape to hold the patch in place.

The tape, sold in widths of 1½ inches and 2 inches, is available at home centers and hardware stores. Cut the tape to size to outline the perimeter of the patch area. Peel the protective paper from the face of the peel-and-stick tape and press the patch of carpeting into the repair area to ensure full contact between the carpet patch and the adhesive tape. Carefully separate the carpet fibers between the patch and the surrounding fibers. Give the adhesive time to set and then use a comb or brush to blend the carpet pile between the carpet and the patch.

Rather than cutting your own patch, take out the guesswork by using a doughnut. A *doughnut* is a circular cutting tool with a razor blade cutter fixed to the perimeter, and a center rotating pin to anchor the cutter in place. The tool cuts shapes that are 3 inches in diameter and it costs about $12.

Figure 1-2:
With careful measuring and cutting, you can replace a patch of damaged carpet without leaving a trace.

A. Use a framing square to guide the utility knife as you cut an area around the damaged carpeting and a patch from a matching piece of scrap carpet.

B. Outline the bare spot with double-stick cloth tape to hold the replacement patch securely in place.

Silencing Squeaks

Floors squeak. Period. Why? Because two pieces of wood construction materials are touching each other. But you can find ways to reduce, if not eliminate, these annoyances.

Locating a squeak is easy. In fact, doing so is one of the easiest parts of this project. The best way to pinpoint a squeak is simply to walk around the floor or up and down the stairs and listen. Pretty easy, huh?

Whenever possible, fix floor or stair squeaks from below. If, however, the bottom of the floor area or staircase is covered, you have to fix it from above.

Fixing a squeak from below

You have a few ways to eliminate squeaks from below. Which method you use depends on what the problem is. Take a look at each method (and see Figure 1-3):

- **Bridging:** Squeaking over a large area may indicate that the floor joists are shifting slightly and are not providing enough support to the subfloor. To solve or moderate this problem you can install bridging between the joists, which stabilizes them and stiffens the floor system. Typically, one centered row is used when joists span between 8 and 16 feet, and two equally spaced rows are used for longer spans.

  Before a subfloor is installed, you can install either metal or steel *cross bridging*, which is installed at a diagonal between two adjacent joists and holds them in place when weight is put on the floor. You nail steel bridging from the top of one joist, diagonally to the bottom of the adjacent joist. You wedge wood bridging between the two joists and then nail it to each joist.

  For existing floor systems, horizontal bridging, or *blocking* is more feasible.

- **Blocking:** Using this approach, you cut and nail short lengths of wood the same dimension as the floor joist (such as 2 x 8 or 2 x 10) to fit snugly between the joists in a perpendicular row. You nail through the joist into the ends of the block with 16d nails and block positions are staggered so that you have nailing access from both ends.

✔ **Shims:** Shims can be used to fill a small gap between the top of a joist and the subfloor. If the floor joist isn't tight against the subfloor, simply apply glue and tap tapered shims between the joist and subfloor until it is just snug. Do not overdrive the shims, which actually lifts the subfloor, causing more squeaking.

To stop a squeak, apply glue to a wood shim or shingle and drive it between the floor joist and subfloor.

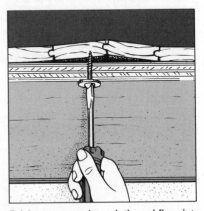

Driving a screw through the subfloor into the finished flooring can pull the boards together, stopping a squeak.

Figure 1-3:
Three ways
to squelch
a squeak.

If the underside of the floor is inaccessible, drive finish nails through the flooring at an angle to silence a squeak.

Fixing a squeak from above

Book V

**Carpentry,
Wood-
working,
and
Flooring**

If you can't access a squeak from below, you don't have much choice but to tackle it from above. Check out Figure 1-4 to see how these tricks work.

- ✓ **Squeaks in floor joists:** First, locate the floor joist so that you have something to nail into. Doing so involves drilling a small-diameter hole through the floor and then probing with a bent coat hanger. It's best to drill the probing hole near a wall or in another inconspicuous area. After you've located a joist, you can measure every 16 inches and you should find the next joist, then the next, and so on. After you've located the offending joist area, drill an angled hole from both sides through the flooring and subfloor and into the joist. This is a "by feel" type of job, but it should work. Drive screws into the joists in the pilot holes to silence the squeak.

- ✓ **Squeaks on stairs:** The most common squeaks on stairs occur where the front of the upper tread rests on the top of the riser just below the tread. The best way to silence this type of squeak and anchor the tread to the riser is to drive flooring nails at opposite angles through the tread and into the riser. If the treads are hardwood, drill pilot holes first, and then drive finish nails into the risers and use a nail set to recess the nails. Use wood putty to fill the nail heads.

Figure 1-4:
Methods
for fixing
squeaky
stairs.

Stop squeaking stairs by gluing and then screwing wood blocks between the risers and treads.

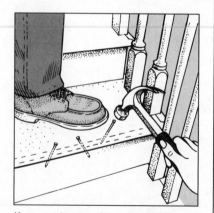

If you can't get to the underside of the staircase, drive finish nails into risers at an angle to help silence squeaks.

Chapter 2

Using Adhesives and Glues in Woodworking

*T*o make strong furniture, adhesives are essential. Only a few years ago, you didn't have many choices for adhesives, but nowadays the options are almost limitless. In this chapter, you discover the most commonly used adhesives for woodworking. The chapter also examines when and how to use each of them, as well as how to clean up when you're done.

Cluing In to Gluing: Understanding How Glue Works

Adhesives work one of two ways: mechanically or chemically. The type you choose depends on what material you glue and what type of joint you're gluing.

✔ **Chemical bonding:** For the most part, chemical bonding requires that the surfaces being glued together have even contact without gaps. They require undisturbed surface area in order to bond properly. That said, these glues *will* work with some voids, but not substantial voids. Chemical bonding adhesives include carpenter's glues (yellow and white) and hide glue.

✔ **Mechanical bonding:** If the items you want to glue together have large gaps, you're better off using an adhesive with mechanical bonding characteristics. These types of adhesives include epoxies and plastic resins. Their advantage is that they actually fill the voids between the joints and create a lasting bond when gluing less-than-perfect joints.

As for which type of adhesive to use on a specific joint, see the sections that follow.

Working with Carpenter's Glue

White carpenter's glue is the standard for gluing up wood. The stuff is inexpensive and easy to work with, and it creates a strong, lasting bond. Technically, white glue is a polyvinyl-acetate (PVA) adhesive and creates a chemical bond, but "white glue" is just so much easier to remember.

Yellow carpenter's glue is really just a newer version of white glue. Yellow glue is slightly thicker, dries quicker, and is more resistant to heat and moisture.

Knowing when to use carpenter's glue

White and yellow glues are chemical bonding glues, so they require joints with a substantial surface area and few voids. If you machine your joints with some degree of care and use the best joints for the job, you can use carpenter's glue without hesitation for nearly all your woodworking tasks.

If you intend to expose your finished project to moist conditions, choose a waterproof yellow glue.

Applying carpenter's glue for best results

To apply carpenter's glue, wipe or brush a thin, even coat on both surfaces of the joint. Don't put on so much that the glue drips out of the joint when you clamp the pieces together (a little oozing is good, though). Apply the glue and work fairly quickly because the glue will start to set in a few minutes. After you apply the glue, securely clamp the surfaces together for several hours (or preferably overnight).

When clamping a joint, apply enough pressure to pull the joint firmly together and hold the piece securely in place, but not so much that you squeeze all the glue out of the joint. If the joint starts to distort from the clamp pressure, you can be sure you're using too much.

Cleaning up

You can clean up both yellow and white glue with water when they're still wet. Use a damp rag or towel and wipe down the outside of the joint immediately after you've glued it. After the glue has dried, it's a pain to remove and will ruin the finish, so take some time before the glue dries to wipe all exposed surfaces free of extra glue. Doing so will save you tons of time and frustration later on.

If you miss some glue and it dries, you need to sand the glue off the wood or scrape it with a scraper or chisel. Unfortunately, you'll probably end up taking quite a bit of wood off in order to get all the glue because it soaks into the pores of the wood.

Choosing Contact Cement

Contact cement is a solvent, or water-based, adhesive that must be allowed to dry to tackiness before you put the pieces together. It's great for applying plastic laminates to wood or medium-density fiberboard (MDF). Contact cement is not all that good for wood-to-wood gluing.

To apply contact cement, coat both surfaces with a thin layer, using a rubber roller, and let it dry until tacky. Then carefully position one surface over the other before letting the surfaces touch. Try putting some scraps of wood, small-diameter dowels, or cardboard between the two surfaces and then removing the cardboard after you have everything where you want it.

The main drawback with contact cement is that after the coated surfaces touch one another, they're locked in place. Ordinarily, you can't adjust them. However, some newer versions of contact cement do allow some adjustment after contact.

Solvent-based contact cement is toxic, smells unpleasant, and is very flammable. Only use this stuff with adequate ventilation, and always wear a respirator. Solvent-based contact cement needs to be cleaned with a solvent-based cleaner such as paint thinner or acetone.

Relying on Resin Glues

Several types of resin glues are on the market, and all of them use a two-part system. The major types of resin glues are

- **Epoxy resin:** Epoxy resin adhesive consists of a two-part formula that you mix together to get it to harden. Many formulas are available, and they vary in their set time and strength.

- **Resorcinal-formaldehyde:** This formula consists of a powdered substance that you mix with a liquid hardener. To use this adhesive, you mix the two parts together in prescribed proportions and then apply the mixture to the workpiece. This type of adhesive is waterproof, so it's great for outdoor furniture and other projects that will be exposed to a lot of moisture. It is messier to work with, however, than waterproof yellow glue.

- **Urea-formaldehyde:** This type of epoxy has good gap-filling abilities. It comes in two parts, one powder and one liquid, and you mix the powder with water and apply it to one side of the joint. Then you apply the liquid part to the other side. This type of adhesive is water resistant, which makes it suitable for damp but not wet applications.

Knowing when to use resins

Resins aren't your everyday adhesives. They're most useful when you need gap-filling capabilities or when you need the ultimate in watertightness. The downside to these adhesives, however, is that they're

- A pain to mix
- Much more expensive than carpenter's glue
- Toxic

You need to work in a well-ventilated area and use gloves and lung protection when working with resin.

Applying resin for best results

Each brand and type of resin adhesive is a little different. Some require you to mix the two parts before applying it to your joints, and others need to be applied separately. Follow the instructions that come with the adhesive.

Cleaning up

Resin adhesives are toxic; you need to clean them with a solvent-based cleaner, such as acetone. Follow the guidelines on the adhesive's packaging to find out the best way to clean the particular formula you use.

Honing In on Hot Melt Glue

Hot melt glue comes in sticks that you melt in a glue gun and squeeze out onto your project. You can find a variety of glue formulas made for glue guns. You can also find veneer strips coated with heat-activated glue for quick and easy edge veneering.

Knowing when to use hot melt glue

Hot melt glue is fast and easy, but not the best solution for permanent projects. However, we highly recommend it for making mock-ups of cabinets because the glue dries quickly and holds well enough for that purpose. It's also good for gluing small, thin pieces that are too small to nail or difficult to clamp.

The hot melt glue used for edge veneers is good, but we still recommend that you use a good carpenter's glue if you want to edge veneer.

Applying hot melt glue for best results

Using a hot melt glue gun is easy: Just put the glue in the gun, wait a few minutes for the glue to melt, and squeeze the trigger to apply it. The only drawback is that it comes out as a thick droplet and tends to go on thick, as well.

To use hot melt veneer edging, all you have to do is put the edging where you want it and run a hot iron across it until it melts. Remove the iron and press the veneer down with a rubber roller until the glue hardens. Sand the edges and the joint is virtually invisible and less likely to be snagged and lifted accidentally. This step takes only a few seconds.

Cleaning up

Depending on the type of glue stick you use, you can clean up with a damp rag or a dull chisel, just like carpenter's glue (see the section "Working with Carpenter's Glue," earlier in the chapter, for more information).

Chapter 3

Drilling, Driving, and Fastening

· ·

In This Chapter

▶ Holding your work together before you commit to it

▶ Finding the best drill to buy . . . and some to rent

▶ Figuring out which hammer is right for the job

▶ Exploring basic wrenches, pliers, and other gripping tools

▶ Creating a tight hold with clamps and glue

▶ Looking down the barrels of stapling and caulking guns

· ·

Carpentry and related work, such as hardware installation, invariably involves assembly and, one way or another, attaching things together. In this chapter, you find out about the tools and techniques involved in this work — and how to use them safely without gluing your fingers together or nailing your shoes to the floor.

Trial Assembly Pays Off

You may have heard the old tip "Measure twice and cut once." The extra moment it takes to double-check your measurements often prevents disasters, or at least saves the time required to correct problems that arise from an error in measuring. The same principle applies to the assembly stage. Double-check your cut, positioning, or fit before final assembly. Make a habit of doing a *trial assembly* or *dry fit* before you nail, glue, or screw parts together.

If you're nailing, a dry fit can be as simple as holding the work, such as a piece of trim or length of siding, in place to make sure that it fits well before driving any nails. In other situations, you may need to *tack* the piece in place, which is what carpenters call it when they secure a workpiece with a minimum number of nails, driven just deep enough to hold the work in place but shallow enough that they can be removed easily if the piece must be repositioned or recut.

Trial fitting is especially important when glue and adhesive are involved. After you apply glue or adhesive, you're, well, stuck if the work doesn't fit. At best, you'd have glue all over a piece you need to recut. At worst, you'd be dripping glue all over the place and then tracking it through the house. Always trial fit before assembling with contact cement (which sets instantly) and other fast-drying glues. Disassembly without damaging the work is difficult or impossible.

Don't think you're home free just because you're using screws. Sure, you can easily remove them, but you've still got the holes you made in the process. Even if you can recut a too-long board or use a too-short board, the holes may not be where they need to be. Similarly, if the piece needs to be moved slightly, the holes in the base material may need to be plugged and redrilled. So hold, tack, brace, or clamp the work before you drill pilot holes or drive screws.

Drilling and Power Driving

Today's ⅜-inch variable-speed reversible drill/driver, available in plug-in and cordless models, uses steel screw-driving tips to drive in or remove screws and various bits and accessories to drill holes, sand wood, mix piña coladas, and other important carpentry tasks.

For decades, the electric drill has been the top-selling power tool and the first power tool that most people buy. A while after the drill's emergence, the makers added variable-speed triggers and reversing motors. This new tool, called a *drill/driver,* is more versatile. One tool performs both high-speed and low-speed drilling operations and, most significantly, drives and removes screws easily.

More recent improvements have put the drill/driver at the top of everyone's power tool wish list. Batteries replace cumbersome and inconvenient electrical cords, adjustable clutches let you control the *torque* (driving force), and with a keyless chuck, you can change bits or accessories in a flash. Simply grasp the keyless chuck with one hand and activate the tool with the other, in forward or reverse, depending on whether you're installing or removing a bit.

Having made driving screws almost as easy as pounding nails, the drill/driver brought on a parallel change in screw design and a dramatic reduction in swollen thumbs. Tapered, slotted-head wood screws have been widely replaced by straight-shank, Phillips-head screws. The changes also have spawned a line of screw-driving accessories, the most significant of which is the magnetic bit holder.

You may want or need to purchase or rent other drills for a particular task. A *hammer drill,* for example, adds a high-speed pounding force to the rotary action for drilling concrete, tile, your mother-in-law's meat loaf, and other hard materials. A *right-angle drill* fits in tight places that a standard drill won't because the shaft (and therefore the bit) is perpendicular to the body.

Accessorizing your drill/driver

Accessories turn this hole-drilling tool into a grinder, a sander, a carving tool, and even a fluids pump. Explore the possibilities, but start with these essentials:

- **An index of high-speed steel twist bits:** Buy a large *index* (a metal box with labeled slots for various size bits). Then, depending on your budget and the amount of use you anticipate, either buy a small set of bits and add to them as needed or bite the bullet and go for a full 64-bit set. If you own a ⅜-inch drill (the size we recommend) and buy twist bits that are over ⅜-inch diameter, make sure that the chucked portion of the shaft is ⅜ inch in diameter or smaller.

- **A set of spade bits:** These flat, wood-boring bits are required for deeper holes and holes with diameters larger than ½ inch. They work better at high speeds.

- **A set of multibore or screw pilot bits:** Although many situations allow you to drive screws without the necessity of drilling pilot holes, most often you try to avoid those loveliest of sounds — wood splitting and screw heads snapping off. These multi-duty combination drill bits eliminate the need to change bits because one bit bores the *clearance* (or *shank*) hole and the *pilot* (or *lead*) hole, and when called for, the *countersink* and *counterbore,* all in one easy step.

- **An assortment of Phillips and standard bits and a magnetic bit holder:** Start with the following five bits: Phillips (#1 and #2) and slotted (¼, ³⁄₁₆, and ⁷⁄₃₂). Buy bits for more exotic screws, such as the Pozidrive, square-drive, and Torx, as needed. The purpose of the magnet is to hold the screw and free up your other hand for more important things, such as holding the work, digging for the next screw, or scratching your nose.

- **A set of carbide-tipped masonry bits:** Buy bits ranging from ⅛ inch to at least ⅜ inch. These bits usually come in a handy plastic storage box. Use masonry bits for concrete, brick, other masonry products, plaster, and tile. (Never use steel twist bits, which quickly become dull and produce more smoke than a cheap cigar.)

The following are accessories that you may well need someday, but we suggest that you purchase them as the need arises:

- **Holesaw:** A holesaw is primarily for cutting large holes in metal or wood. (If you thought that a holesaw is twice as big as a "half saw," please put down this book before you hurt yourself.) One type has a cup-shaped cutter with teeth along the rim. Another has band-type blades. Each type of cutter fits on a spindle, called a *mandrel,* which also holds a pilot bit that enters the work and holds the holesaw in position as the large cutter enters the work. Holesaws come in several sizes, up to 5 inches or more, but the only application you're likely to need one for is to bore a 2⅛-inch-diameter hole in a door for a lockset. It's the only practical, affordable tool to make that size hole.

- **Doweling jig:** In many woodworking projects, wooden dowels reinforce joints. You drill holes in the mating pieces and insert a dowel. The doweling jig precisely locates the holes and sets the depth, so that when you join the pieces, they align perfectly. Today, professionals favor the *biscuit jointer.* It's worth the investment if you do a lot of woodworking, but doweling is fine for the occasional woodworker.

- **Sanding, grinding, and other abrading tools:** Take advantage of the drill's versatility with these accessories that enable you to shape and smooth wood, clean and debur metal, remove paint, and perform a host of other tasks.

- **Portable drill stand:** Precision or repetitive drilling is ideally done on a *drill press,* a heavy piece of stationary equipment that few remodeling professionals even own. If you don't have a drill press, lock your drill into one of these handy, portable stands for easier and more accurate drilling.

- **Bit-extension tool:** Lock a twist drill or spade bit into the end of an extension shaft to extend the reach or to drill very deep holes. This tool gets a lot of work when you rewire an old house. To fish wires from one place to another, you often need to drill holes at an angle through a wall, into a stud cavity, and through a floor or ceiling joist bay to the floor below or above — a distance of 12 inches or more.

- **Flexible shaft:** You can literally drill around corners by securing your drill bit in the end of a flexible shaft. It's not something you use every day, but it's still great to own.

Watch your speed!

After you determine the proper bit to use, it's time to put on safety goggles and, if required, a dust mask. Then figure out the speed that you want that bit to turn and the amount of pressure to exert (called *feed pressure*). We suppose you can memorize a chart full of specs on the optimal speed for drilling holes in dozens of common materials, but all you really need is one general rule, a little common sense, and some trial-and-error. In general, the larger the hole and the harder the material, the slower the speed you want to use; and if your drill doesn't spin as fast as it should, ease up on the feed pressure and take a little more time.

In some cases, you may find it easier to start slow and pick up speed after you establish the location. Similarly, stepping up from smaller-diameter bits until you reach the desired hole diameter is a useful trick when drilling in concrete, masonry, metal, and other hard materials. Lubrication — oil for metal drilling and water for concrete or masonry drilling — cools the bits and improves the efficiency of the cutter.

When drilling into masonry, always use a carbide-tipped masonry bit. Start with a ⅛-inch diameter bit and step up the bit size ⅛ inch at a time until the hole is the desired diameter. Your bits work more efficiently and more accurately and last longer with this method.

Assuming that you're using the proper bit/cutter and that it's sharp and properly secured in the tool, adjust your drilling speed and feed pressure if any of the following warning signs pop up:

- ✔ The bit or other cutter fails to do its job.
- ✔ The bit or cutter jams or turns too slowly.
- ✔ The bit or cutter overheats, as evidenced by smoke or blackening of the workpiece or bit.
- ✔ The drill motor strains or overheats.

As long as you can maintain control, you can often drive screws at a drill/driver's maximum speed. A screw gun, a single-purpose professional tool designed exclusively for driving screws, operates at speeds two or three times faster than the fastest drill/driver. However, if a screw is going in at a bazillion miles a second, you can't rely on the reaction of your trigger finger to stop the bit at just the right point. You'll likely drive the screw too deep, strip the screw head, snap the screw in half, or damage your workpiece — or all the above. Better drill/drivers have an adjustable clutch, which limits the torque. Basically, when the screw is seated, the bit stops turning.

Use your head. Slow down if you're not sure. Do you really want to drive a brass slotted screw into an expensive piece of hardware at high speed? Of course not. There are even occasions when it's best to pull out an old-fashioned screwdriver.

Drilling techniques

To accurately locate a hole, called *spotting,* it's often helpful to create a small indentation to guide the bit's initial cut and prevent it from spinning out of control like a drunken figure skater. The harder the surface and the greater the accuracy required, the more advisable it is to spot a hole before drilling. In soft wood, this step is as simple as pressing the bit or a sharp pencil point into the wood. In hard wood, you may want to use an awl. In metal, it's virtually required that you use a hammer and center punch. To further prevent the bit from wandering off course, hold the tool perpendicular to the surface. If you need to drill at an angle, tilt the drill after the bit has started to penetrate, or clamp an angle-guide block onto your work.

To make an angle-guide block, drill a hole through a block of wood with the bit you intend to use. Then cut the bottom of the block at an angle that equals the angle of the hole you want to drill. If, for example, you want a hole angled 30 degrees off vertical, then cut a 30-degree angle on the bottom of the block.

Grip the drill firmly, with two hands if possible, for better control. Heavy drills have higher torque and may even include a side handle so that you can control the tool if the bit jams in the work and the drill keeps turning. Whenever possible, clamp workpieces that may not be heavy enough to stay put under a drilling load.

A drill tends to splinter the exit hole. To prevent this splintering from happening, ease up on the pressure so that the drill is doing all the work. Or even better, take time to back up your workpiece with a piece of wood scrap before you start drilling. Any splintering will occur on the scrap, not the workpiece.

Driving Screws

Despite the overwhelming popularity of the drill/driver, screwdrivers are still an essential item for every homeowner. You've probably heard the saying "Use a tool only for its intended purpose." Very often, you can injure yourself, ruin a tool, or damage your work if you fail to heed that advice. However, if using a screwdriver for a task other than driving screws were a crime and the punishment were banishment from hardware stores, the aisles would be empty.

The first rule for driving screws is to use a driver that matches the type and size screw you're driving. The majority of screws are either *Phillips* screws, which have a cross-shaped recess in the head and require a Phillips screwdriver, or *slotted* screws, which have a single slot cut across the diameter of the screw head and require a standard driver.

You get the best deal and are prepared for most screwdriving situations if you buy an assortment of screwdrivers. At a minimum, you need two standard drivers, a ³⁄₁₆-inch cabinet and a ¼-inch mechanics, and two Phillips drivers, a 4-inch #2 and a 3-inch #1.

Alternately, you can buy a 4-in-1 or 6-in-1 driver. The 4-in-1 has a double-ended shaft, two ³⁄₁₆-inch and ⁹⁄₃₂-inch standard, and #1 and #2 Phillips interchangeable bits (tips). In the 6-in-1 model, the two ends of the shaft serve as a ¼-inch and ⁵⁄₁₆-inch nutdriver. Buy other size screwdrivers as needed. One advantage of these multidrivers is that they accommodate different bits; when you run across screws with square holes, star-shaped holes, or other tip configurations, you need to buy only the appropriate tip, not a whole other tool.

When it comes to screwdrivers, it's best to avoid the bargain racks. Shop for name brands and look for *tempered* (heat-treated) tips.

The way to use a screwdriver is essentially obvious, but we have a few points worth mentioning. First, don't hold the tool between your knees or teeth — you'll get lousy torque pressure. Always match the driver to the fastener. Failure to do so inevitably deforms the screwhead, sometimes to the point where you can no longer twist it out or in. This is particularly true with brass screws (which are easily damaged because brass is relatively soft) and when the screw is unusually tight or even stuck.

If you're trying to draw and fasten two things together with a flathead screw, for example two pieces of wood, join the two pieces together and use one of the following approaches:

- ✔ **Clamp the two pieces together and, using a bit that's a little smaller than the diameter of the screw, drill a pilot hole as deep as the screw is long.** Finish by using a countersink bit to bore a conical hole that suits the screwhead. Clamping is necessary because the screw tends to force the two pieces apart as it enters the second piece.

- ✔ **Alternately, bore the appropriate pilot, clearance, and countersink holes before driving the screw.** Using a bit that's a little smaller than the screw's diameter, bore a pilot hole that's equal to the screw's length through both pieces. Then, using a bit that equals the diameter of the screw, bore a clearance hole through the top piece only. A screw pilot or multibore accessory bit bores all three holes at once and is available in sets to suit various screw sizes.

Predrilling for screws is always best and makes driving screws by hand much easier. Predrilling is essential for most finish work (where neatness is important) and to prevent splitting when screwing into hardwoods, plywood, end grain, or near the ends of a board. On many occasions, however, you may not

Book V

Carpentry, Woodworking, and Flooring

need to drill pilot holes or countersinks, especially if you use a drill/driver. The best screws to use in wood without pilot holes have bugle heads (similar to flathead screws), straight shafts, and coarse threads.

Lubricate screws (especially brass ones) with wax to make them easier to drive. Don't use soap, as it tends to corrode screws.

Although you can buy a depth gauge for drill bits, a piece of tape (masking, electrical, duct, or whatever) wrapped around the shaft of a bit tells you when to stop drilling.

Sometimes, it's hard for beginners to drill holes at the desired angle — usually perpendicular to the surface. If accuracy is critical, hold a combination square (or a block of wood that you know is cut square) on the surface and against the top of the drill. As long as you keep the drill centered on your guide and in contact with it, the hole will be accurate.

Whenever you need to bore many holes in identical locations in more than one piece of wood, use a template. Take, for example, drilling screw holes to locate knobs on a number of cabinet doors, or drilling a series of holes in the side of a bookcase for plug-in shelf supports. For knobs, the template may be a board with a hole drilled in it that fits over the corner of a cabinet door so that the hole lies in precisely the same spot on each door it's placed on. For shelf supports, the template may be a 2-foot-long strip of ¼-inch hardboard with a series of holes so that you only need to align the template with the front or back edge of the bookcase side to drill holes in the exact same spots every time.

You must locate hinges accurately if one half is to mate well with the other, and to ensure that the door is located precisely in its opening. Pilot holes for hinge screws must be exactly centered, or they tend to push the hinge off mark or the screwhead won't sit flush with the hinge. Any irregularity in the wood grain can push an unguided drill or punch off the mark. A self-centering pilot drill or self-centering punch has tapered ends that fit into the countersink of a screw hole in the hinge, automatically centering the drill bit or punch. One size fits all for the punch, but the drill accessory comes in several sizes to suit #6, #8, and #10 screws.

The Nail Hammer: The Quintessential Carpentry Tool

Nail hammers come in two basic types: the one you bought and the one you borrowed from your neighbor three years ago. Just kidding. Actually, the

Book V

**Carpentry,
Wood-
working,
and
Flooring**

types include the *curved-claw hammer*, which has a curved nail-pulling claw, and the *ripping-claw hammer*, which has a straight claw.

For general use, we recommend a 16-ounce, curved-claw hammer with a fiberglass handle. Like wood, fiberglass cushions the vibrations to your hand and arm but has the added advantage that it won't break under tough nail-pulling conditions. The curved claw on this hammer gives you good nail-pulling leverage (see the section "Pulling nails," later in this chapter). It's also heavy enough for most nailing projects, including framing work, as long as the project is modest in scope — such as studding a basement wall.

For a big framing project, you want a heavier hammer. Although it's heavier to hold, the added weight (and usually a somewhat longer handle) of a 20-ounce ripping hammer does more of the work for you, whether you're driving large nails, banging things apart, or fine-tuning a dented fender. When a project involves demolition, you can easily force the claw of a ripping hammer between two materials that are fastened or glued together.

Taking precautions

When you want to bang on something other than a nail, think twice before reaching for your nail hammer. When you need to "persuade" something into position but might damage it by using a metal hammer, reach for a rubber mallet.

Never strike one hammer against another. The hardened steel can chip off a small piece of metal and send it flying at such great speed that the shard can embed itself deep into your body and presents a particularly great danger to your eyes. Plus, you'll never get through an airport metal detector without setting off the alarms.

For the same reason, don't use a nail hammer to strike cold chisels, masonry chisels, punches, or other hard metal objects, with the exception of nail sets, which are designed to be struck with a nail hammer. Avoid using a nail hammer on concrete, stone, or masonry, too. As a general rule, don't strike anything harder than a nail with a nail hammer.

Plus, such abuse ruins the face of a nail hammer. If you look closely at the face of a hammer, you see that it isn't flat. A quality nail hammer has a shiny, slightly convex face with beveled edges to minimize surface denting. Some ripping or framing hammers have a milled face (checkered or waffled), which makes it less likely that you'll slip off the head of a nail that you don't strike squarely.

For cold chisels and center punches, use an engineer's hammer (also called a *ball peen hammer*). For masonry chisels, concrete, and masonry, use a lump hammer (also called a *hand-drilling hammer* or simply a *mini-sledge*). See Figure 3-1.

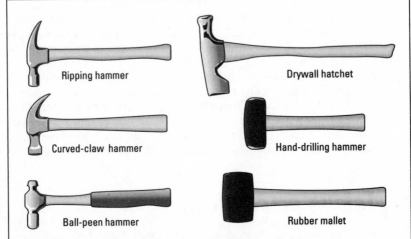

Figure 3-1: Use the right hammer for the job.

Ripping hammer

Drywall hatchet

Curved-claw hammer

Hand-drilling hammer

Ball-peen hammer

Rubber mallet

Driving nails (into wood, not from the store)

Like all carpenters, we've had our share of smashed fingers and bent nails. But you can avoid them most of the time by driving nails the right way. Whether you're nailing a hook for a picture or nailing a 2-x-4 to a garage wall, follow these basic steps for ouch-free installation:

1. **To have proper grip, grasp a claw hammer almost at the end of the handle and with your thumb wrapped around the handle.**

   Thinking that they'll gain more control, beginners often make the mistake of lining up their thumb on the handle. Not only does this grip fail to improve accuracy, but it's also inefficient and may cause injury to your thumb. The one exception to this rule is when you're nailing sideways across your body in a technique called *nailing out*.

2. **Start the nail by tilting it slightly away from you and giving it one or two light taps. Then, move your fingers out of harm's way and drive the nail with increasingly forceful blows.**

You want the handle to be parallel to the surface at the point that it strikes the nail. For rough work, drive the nail home — that is, until the nail draws the pieces tight and is set slightly below the surface. For finish work, stop when the nail is just above the surface. Finish the task with a *nail set* so that you don't risk damaging the wood. (See the section "Putting on the finishing touches," later in this chapter.)

The rules are a little different for a 20-ounce ripping or framing hammer. Unlike a claw hammer, you grasp the handle a little higher — about a quarter of the way up from the end — and keep a little looser grip. Also, take a bigger backswing and use a more forceful downswing. With the heavier hammer and the added driving force, it becomes imperative to keep your other hand well out of harm's way, preferably behind your back.

If a nail driven straight in would penetrate out from the backside of your workpiece and you don't want to use a shorter nail, you may be able to drive the nail in at an angle. Carpenters often use this technique when they nail up doubled wall studs or headers over framed door and window openings. Nailing at opposing angles improves the holding power significantly.

Because of their small size, brads and tacks are difficult to hold safely when starting the nail. If you have a tack hammer, use it, but if you must use a claw hammer, save your fingers by using long-nose pliers to grasp the nail while you give it the tap or two required to get it started.

Face-nailing and toenailing

Face-nailing and toenailing (shown in Figure 3-2) aren't horrible punishments that carpenters inflict on plumbers who cut too-big holes in their floor joists. Rather, they describe the two common ways of nailing objects together.

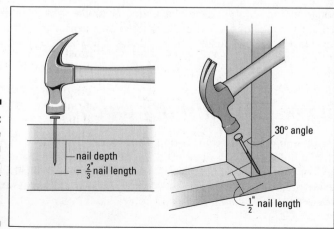

Figure 3-2: Most of the time, you either face-nail (left) or toenail (right).

nail depth = $\frac{2}{3}$ nail length

30° angle

$\frac{1}{2}$ nail length

Most often, you nail through the face of a board and into the backing material. This is called *face-nailing*. As a general rule, nail through the thinner member into the thicker one whenever possible. The deeper that nail goes into the backing, the more holding power it has.

Here's a good guideline to follow when you need to figure out the proper length of a nail: A nail should penetrate into solid backing material at a depth equal to twice the thickness of the member being attached. For example, if you're nailing a ¾-inch-thick furring strip on a drywall-covered wall, you want to use at least a 2-inch nail (2 × ¾ + ½ inch for the drywall).

When you want to secure one piece of lumber to another at a 90-degree angle, such as a wall stud to a sole plate or top plate, you have one or two nailing options, depending on whether you have access to the top of the T. Face-nailing through one board into the end of the mating board is typically the easiest and preferred technique. If you don't have access, or if the board is so thick that face-nailing through it would be impractical, you must *toenail* through the end of one board into the face of the other board.

Driving the first nail at such an angle tends to push the board off its mark, so as you drive the nail, you need to back up the board (typically with your foot). It also helps to drive the nail to where it just penetrates one board and then reposition it as necessary before driving one sharp blow. In fact, you may want to assume that driving will tend to push the board past its mark and compensate for that by positioning it a little to the opposite side of the marks.

Blind-nailing

Blind-nailing may sound dangerous, but it's nothing to worry about. The term describes any nailing technique in which the nail is hidden from sight without the use of putty or wood fillers. In its most common form, the technique is used to secure tongue-and-groove boards, such as solid wood paneling. Nail into the tongued-edge of the board at a 45-degree angle. When you install the next board, its groove conceals the nail, and so on across the wall or floor. The first and last boards typically must be face-nailed as described in the preceding section.

Putting on the finishing touches

In finish work, you generally want to sink the nail head slightly below the surface, as shown in Figure 3-3, and later fill the depression with putty, caulk, or wood filler. For this task, you need a nail set, which comes in sizes ranging from 1/32 to 3/16 inch in 1/32-inch increments to suit various nail head sizes. Buy a set of three and you're ready for any nail you're likely to encounter in home carpentry.

Book V

Carpentry, Wood-working, and Flooring

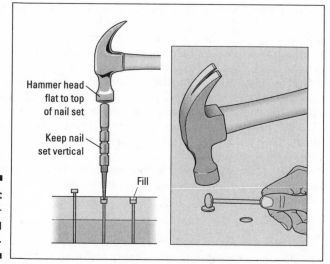

Figure 3-3: Two nail-setting approaches.

Anytime you need to hold one tool and strike it with another, your fingers are vulnerable. (Theoretically, you can ask for nail-holding volunteers, but you won't get much interest.) Generally, holding the nail as you hammer isn't a problem when setting finish nails because you need a relatively minor blow to drive the nail. Such light hammering is easy to control and does less damage if the blow is off the mark.

When nail-setting heavy common nails, such as you may need for face-nailed deck boards, a heavier blow is required. After mashing our fingers a number of times, we adopted an old carpenter's nail-setting trick, and it hasn't happened since. Lay a 16d common nail flat on the surface with its head over the center of the nail head to be countersunk. With your fingers holding the nail a safe couple of inches from the head, strike the edge of the nail head, and it will set the nail below. The process tends to mush the nail head, so after rotating the head a couple of times and setting a half-dozen nails or so, use a new nail.

Pulling nails

When it comes to pulling nails, you have many techniques and tools to choose from. The ones you choose will depend on whether you need to protect the surface, whether the situation allows you to pry the materials apart, whether you can talk someone else into doing this job, and several other factors. To be prepared for most situations, you need a nail hammer, one or two cat's paw–style nail pullers, and a couple of pry bars.

Try one or more of the following techniques, according to your needs:

✔ **Remove the board and then the nails.** Most often, the easiest way to take things apart is to either bang or pry them apart or give them to a two-year-old child. Take, for example, trim removal. To do this job while minimizing the damage to either the trim or the surface to which it's nailed requires a pry bar with a straight, wide blade that's thin enough to be driven between the materials — a *trim bar*. (You may want to grind the end of this tool to an even thinner taper to make it easier to insert.) Drive the tapered end of the trim bar behind the trim between two nailing locations. Pull gently toward you and work your way over toward the nailing locations. Then pry it still farther out, using the other end of the trim bar or a larger pry bar, working your way all along the board.

To protect the wall and increase leverage, insert a *shim* (shingle tip); a thin, stiff material, such as a stiff-blade putty knife; or a wood block between the pry bar and the wall, as shown in Figure 3-4.

Virtually all nailing, demolition, and nail-pulling operations require you to wear proper eye protection.

✔ **Pry nails from removed boards.** If you've pried a board off a surface and nails remain in the board, tap the pointed ends to drive the heads above the opposite surface, at least enough so that you can pull them from the face with a hammer claw or the bent end of a pry bar. If you're trying to avoid damaging the face of the board (as you might for trim that you've removed and plan to reuse), pull the nails through the backside. It's easy for finishing nails, and with enough force (and soft wood, such as pine), you can pull common nails out backwards, too.

To pull the nail, use a hammer as described in the section "Side-to-side technique," later in this chapter. Alternately, end-cutting pliers (sometimes called *nippers*) work well, especially with finishing nails. Grasp the nail shaft with the jaws of the pliers as close to the surface as possible. Roll the pliers over to one side, then the other, but don't grip too hard or you'll cut the nail.

✔ **Pry a little, then pull a little.** If you want to protect the surface and can pry a board a little above the surface, do so. Then drive the board back with a sharp hammer blow. The goal is for the board to go back in place and leave the nails standing proud (or humiliated). Protect the surface from the hammer blow with a scrap of wood. Then pull out the nails with a pry bar.

✔ **Pull nails from the face.** If you can't get behind a board to pry it free, you must attack the nails from the face of the board. For this task, you need a claw-type nail-puller. For rough work, where damage to the surface isn't a concern, a cat's paw, which has a relatively wide head, works well. But to minimize damage, you need a puller with a narrower head and sharper jaws that don't need to be driven so deeply into the wood in order to bite into the nail head. This style also has sharper claws that bite into the shaft of a nail; the wider paw generally needs a head to pull on. You can also find mini versions of these tools for small finish nails.

Position the puller with the points of the claw just behind the nail and drive it down into the wood and under the head of the nail. Pull back on the tool with a steady, controlled motion to pull it at least ½ inch above the surface. Then use one of the following approaches with a hammer or pry bar.

- **Standard approach:** After the nail's head is above the surface, hook onto it with a hammer claw (or with the V-notch on the bent end of a pry bar) and pull the handle of the tool toward you to pry out the nail.

  Don't jerk a hammer in an attempt to free a nail that's too stubborn to be pulled out with a steady, smooth motion. With the loss of control comes increased risk of injury. The sudden force may break a wooden hammer handle or snap the head off the nail, making it even harder to remove. (Try the next technique if you accidentally snap the head off.) Instead, use a pry bar or nail puller, which gives you the additional leverage required.

- **Side-to-side technique:** If the nail is long or if you need to protect the surface, slip a scrap of wood under the hammer, as shown in Figure 3-5, to add leverage and enable you to pull out a long nail entirely. To pull large or headless nails, carefully swing the claw into the nail with enough force to make it bite into the shaft as close to the surface as possible. Then push the hammer over side-ways, and the nail will come out about 1 inch. Reposition it and push sideways in the opposite direction to pull it another inch. If you have a good-quality hammer with a sharp claw, it won't slip off the nail's shaft. After you've sufficiently loosened the nail, use the standard pull-toward-you approach to pull it out the rest of the way.

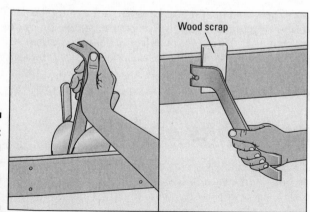

Figure 3-4: Minimizing damage to a board being removed.

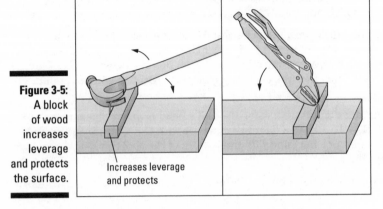

Figure 3-5:
A block
of wood
increases
leverage
and protects
the surface.

Increases leverage
and protects

Fastening with Staples

A staple gun is handy for many remodeling projects, such as securing insulation, ceiling tile, or plastic sheeting, as well as for such household repairs and projects as recovering a seat cushion or rescreening a porch. The tool is available in manual and electric models. Each has pros and cons, but given the typical limited use, it probably doesn't matter which you choose.

Most staple guns allow staples to be fired into the air, so you risk eye injury if you use them improperly or without care. Although an electric stapler may have a safety catch on the trigger, it's very easy to fire a staple accidentally — too easy, in our opinion. Make a habit of setting the safety lock after every series of shots and when you store the tool. The temptation to play "guns" with an electric model suggests that you keep it out of the hands of unsupervised children — better yet, keep it out of their hands, period.

A dial on the hand-powered model regulates the force of the blow. The harder the material you're stapling into and the longer the staple, the more force you need. To ensure that all the force that you set is delivered, press the stapler down firmly as you fire the staple. If an occasional staple stands proud, give it a tap with a hammer — not the stapler.

Getting Down to Nuts and Bolts

Product installations often involve nuts and bolts, and many carpentry projects make use of lag bolts and a variety of other metal anchors and fasteners that you can't grab with a screwdriver or nail hammer. In addition, you'll often find that you need a firm hold on a variety of nonfastener items such as pipes, product and machinery parts, wiring, hardware, and so on. These tasks all require one of the following gripping tools.

Pliers: Grippy, grabby, and pointy

Slip-joint pliers have toothed jaws that enable you to grip various-sized objects, like a water pipe, the top of a gallon of mineral spirits, or the tape measure you accidentally dropped into the toilet. Because its jaws are adjustable, slip-joint pliers give you leverage to grip the object firmly. This tool is on everyone's basic list of tools, but to be honest, few people use it very often. Instead, we prefer *locking pliers* (commonly known by one brand name, Vise-Grip). Locking pliers easily adjust to lock onto pipes, nuts, screws, and nails that have had their heads broken off and practically anything that needs to be held in place, twisted, clamped, or crushed.

For occasional minor electrical work and repairs, every tool kit needs a pair of *long-nose pliers* (often mistakenly called needle-nose pliers, which have a much longer, pointier nose). Long-nose pliers cut wire and cable, twist a loop on the end of a conductor to fit under a screw fitting, and, turned perpendicular to the wires, do a fair job twisting wires together. If you find yourself doing more than occasional electrical work, pick up a pair of *lineman's pliers,* too. This tool does a better job of twisting connections and cutting heavy cable. *End-cutting pliers* probably have some real electrical value that has eluded us for many years, but they're invaluable nail pullers and cutters.

Wrenches: A plethora of options

Carpentry work often involves minor plumbing work, primarily the temporary removal of piping connections for work such as installing cabinets and fishing Timmy's pet hamster out of the garbage disposal. And all sorts of projects involve nuts and bolts and similar fasteners. Wrenches are the primary tool for this work.

An *adjustable wrench* is included in most basic tool kits because it accommodates any size nut — metric or standard — and small to moderate-size pipe fittings. On the downside, they don't grip as well as fixed-sized wrenches. Even better quality ones are marginal, so don't waste your money on a cheap pair. Get a good automotive-quality tool.

For a better grip, choose a wrench that's sized for the fastener or fitting. *Combination wrenches,* which have one open and one closed (boxed) end, are sold in standard and metric sets and in sets that include both. Standard is still far more common in carpentry work, so buy a standard set first. For most carpentry work, you need only a small assortment (six to ten).

If you find that you run across metric bolts only a couple of times a year, save the cost of buying a set of metric wrenches by buying one of those self-sizing wrenches like the "Metwrench" sold at Sears stores and on TV infomercials.

For many projects, you can avoid the standard/metric debate altogether by purchasing a nice combination set of *socket wrenches*. Socket wrenches not only are sized for specific fasteners (which helps fight the age-old rounding-off-the-hex-head problem), but they also offer a ratcheted handle that enables you to tighten or loosen a nut without repositioning the tool every half-turn or so, as is required for combination wrenches.

Set screws, fittings, and other fasteners have hexagonal-shaped recesses that require an *Allen wrench* (also called a *hex key* or *hex wrench*). These metal bars come in several shapes — straight, L-shaped, and T-shaped (where the top of the T is a handle). Although you can buy Allen wrenches individually — they may even come with a product that requires one for assembly, adjustment, or maintenance — it's best to start with a matching set or two. On the rare occasion that you need one that's not included in a set, buy it separately. Straight-wrench sets fold into a handle like a pocketknife. L- and T-shaped sets come in a plastic case or little pouch. The L-shaped ones are more versatile because the shorter leg of the L gets into places that the longer straight or T-shaped ones can't.

Clamping and Gluing

Clamping is an essential part of many carpentry projects. Clamps hold your work in place while you tool the workpiece with saws, drills, sanders, and other tools. They also hold together two or more objects in precise alignment while you drill pilot holes and install fasteners. In the final stages, clamps hold things together while you wait for glue/adhesives to cure, in some cases reducing the number of fasteners required or eliminating the need for them altogether. The number of clamps a project requires varies widely, but typically, you need one every 8 inches or so along the joint.

Types of clamps

Because carpentry and woodworking projects assume an endless variety of shapes (flat, square, 90- and 45-degree corners, cylinders) and sizes (long, short, big, small), you need a variety of clamps and ones that offer versatility. Dozens of types exist, but a few basic clamps have proven their worth. (See Figure 3-6.)

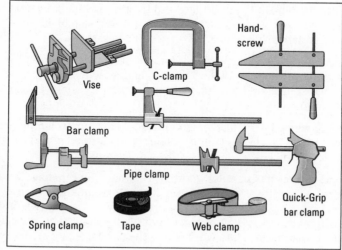

Figure 3-6: Get a grip with the right clamping tools.

✔ A **C-clamp,** named for its shape, comes in sizes that describe the maximum open capacity of the jaw, from ¾ inch to 12 inches. It's the primary clamp that woodworkers use. Most jobs require a minimum of two clamps, so make a practice of starting out with at least a pair of a particular size, and buy more as needed. C-clamps exert tremendous force: You never need to use anything other than your hand to tighten them. Prevent damage to your workpiece by placing a wood scrap between the clamp and the work. If they're heavy enough, such boards also serve to distribute the force more evenly.

✔ The **edge C-clamp** is a variation of the C-clamp. This clamp is designed to hold wood strips against the edge of another board, such as a plywood shelf or kitchen counter. To use it, lock the C onto the board and then tighten the edge screw against the edging strip.

✔ **Pipe clamps** consist of one fixed crank screw (head stock) and one movable jaw (tail stock) mounted on a pipe. The crank screw threads onto the end of the pipe, and the movable jaw slides over the pipe, locking onto the pipe when pressure is exerted. You can use any length pipe and easily move the clamps from one pipe to another to suit the project. *Bar clamps* work like pipe clamps, but the bars aren't interchangeable and therefore aren't as versatile. Both types may be equipped with rubber pads to prevent them from damaging the work.

If you put all the movable jaws on one side of the workpiece, they tend to make the work bow up at the middle. Counter this tendency by alternating the clamps from one side to the other. If that doesn't solve the problem, you can straighten a bowing surface by easing up on the clamp pressure just a bit, inserting a thick block of wood on the workpiece under the pipe at the midpoint, and tapping a shim between the block and the pipe. Check for straightness with the edge of a framing square or other straightedge.

If you need to use a pipe clamp for a nonrectangular workpiece, such as a round or triangular tabletop, cut a jig that, when clamped against the opposite edges of the work, yields a rectangular shape for the clamps to lock onto.

- **Spring clamps** work like giant clothespins for quick clamping and releasing of projects where clamping is near the outer edge and the boards aren't too thick.

- A **handscrew** has parallel wooden jaws that won't damage wood workpieces as readily as a steel clamp. It exerts tremendous power with little effort on your part, but most important, it won't apply twisting force, which tends to move your pieces out of alignment. The jaws also can adjust to accommodate work where the two faces are uneven or not parallel to each other.

- **Web clamps** wrap around irregular surfaces and exert inward pressure. Perhaps the most common application is gluing chair legs and the spindles that span between them. Loop the web around the work and thread it through a ratcheted metal fixture, much like you put a belt through its buckle. After you pull the band tight by hand, use a wrench or a large screwdriver to tighten the ratchet.

When clamping glued work, use just enough pressure to squeeze and hold the parts together. Too much pressure squeezes out too much of the glue, resulting in a weaker bond.

Real sticky stuff

If you're using contact cement, the bond between the surfaces occurs — as the name suggests — on contact. Because of this bond, you must perfectly align the mating surfaces before you bring them together. Depending on the size and shape of the objects, try one of the following tricks to ensure correct alignment:

Book V

**Carpentry,
Wood-
working,
and
Flooring**

✔ Rest the parts on a flat surface, with the bonding surfaces facing each other, and slide the pieces together. Doing so ensures that the bottom edges are in alignment. Tack a fence or guide to the worktable and keep the two pieces against both the guide and the tabletop as you slide. Then the two sides will be perfectly aligned.

✔ When the contact cement has dried sufficiently for bonding, lay dowels or other similar spacers on top of one piece. Then place the second piece on the dowels in proper alignment with the piece on the bottom. Then remove the dowels one at a time, allowing the glued faces to touch. With two boards, you may have just two or three dowels, depending on the length of the boards. For flexible material, such as plastic laminate or other veneers, you may need a dowel every 6 inches or so.

✔ Sometimes, you can glue two objects together and then cut, plane, or sand both pieces simultaneously. This approach may eliminate any need for special care during assembly because you can correct any misalignment.

For more info on glue, see Chapter 2.

Guns for Pacifists

Caulk, adhesive, and glue are messy materials; whenever possible, it's best that the containers that hold them also dispense them. Many such materials are available in squeezable containers, but sometimes dispensing tools (usually called guns of one sort or another) are required.

Hot-melt glue gun

No surprise here: A *hot-melt glue gun* does what its name suggests. Insert a stick of hard-cool glue in the back end, plug in the gun, wait for it to heat up, and squeeze the trigger. The trigger action forces the hard glue past the heating element, and out the nozzle comes burning-hot, melted glue.

The glue is not only very hot, but it also sticks to skin, so be careful! Arriving at work the next morning with a coffee table glued to your knees would be awfully embarrassing. The metal tip tends to ooze glue when the unit is hot, so protect whatever surface you rest it on. The metal tip remains very hot for a while after you unplug the tool, so use care in how and where you set it down. Use this type of glue gun when you need instant gratification or to hold something in place until you get a chance to install fasteners. It's really a lifesaver when you need to glue a very small or thin piece of wood in place that would crack if you attempted to use a fastener.

Flip to Chapter 2 to find out when to use hot-melt glue.

Caulking gun

A *caulking gun* dispenses caulk and adhesives that are packaged in cardboard or plastic cartridges. The open-frame-style dispenser is easy to clean, but the most important feature to look for is a quick-release button on the back end. Press it with your thumb as you near the end of an application. If you have to fumble with an inconvenient or unreliable release system, adhesive will ooze out all over the place before you relieve the pressure.

You usually apply adhesive from a cartridge in straight ribbons, such as when you apply it to floor joists before installing plywood subfloor or to studs before hanging drywall. When using it on larger surfaces, such as on interior paneling that you're installing over existing drywall, lay down squiggly lines. Just follow the installation instructions for the product.

Cut the tip of the cartridge at a 45-degree angle with a utility knife. How much you cut off depends on how wide a bead you want, but keep in mind that you can always cut off a little more if the bead is too small. You're stuck with wider beads if you cut off too much.

Chapter 4

Understanding the Building Process

A woodworking project involves a very definite process. From choosing the wood and milling it to size to assembling the piece, you need to do each step correctly, or your project won't be successful. In fact, it may not even go together at all.

This chapter guides you through the process of building a project and shows you how the various steps along the way lead to success. You explore all the details of a project plan — the diagrams, dimensions, and procedures. You get to know the best way to choose the part of the board from which to cut each piece, and you walk through the assembly process from dry-fitting to gluing in sections.

Following Plans: Making Sense of Diagrams, Dimensions, and Procedures

Unless you build on the fly and can visualize every step of the cutting and building process, you need plans from which to work. Plans make the building process easy because they spell out exactly how much, what kind, and what size of wood to cut for each part of the project. In addition, plans tell you how to put those parts together. If you can accurately follow a set of plans, you can make any project for which you have the skills and tools.

Checking out your material list

The *material list* gives you a rundown of all the wood, fasteners, and hardware you need to build a project. By glancing at this list, you can quickly determine what you need to buy before you get started. Figure 4-1 shows a typical material list for a table. It runs down the parts for the project, their quantity (bordered by parentheses), and their cut size in thickness (T), width (W), and length (L).

Figure 4-1:
A material list tells you what you need to make a project.

Material list

	Qty	T	W	L
1. Legs	(4)	2" x	2" x	29"
2. Short rail	(2)	3/4" x	3" x	35 1/4"
3. Long rail	(2)	3/4" x	3" x	71 1/4"
4. Top	(1)	1" x	36" x	72"
5. Cleats	(8)	3/4" x	1 1/2" x	2"
6. Screws	(8)	1 1/4" #8		

Numbers, give me numbers: Measured drawings

Measured drawings are the heart and soul of a project plan. A measured drawing details every board, screw, nail, and piece of hardware that goes into a project *and* where each object goes. With this drawing, you should be able to build a project even without the other two sections of a project plan.

You may need some time to get used to how a measured drawing organizes a project, but soon you'll be able to glance over a measured drawing and tell right away whether you want to tackle the project. And with a little experience, you'll likely be able to tell how much time you need to build it.

A measured drawing shows a project from several angles to give you a better idea of how the finished project looks. However, the level of detail varies depending on who created the drawing. Some designers detail everything and include full-size drawings of joints or unusually shaped parts (the back of a chair, for instance). Other designers provide simplistic drawings that show only the overall dimensions of a part, its position in the finished product, and an overall view of the project. Figures 4-2 and 4-3 show this kind of detail.

If you don't buy project plans, we highly recommend that you make your own drawings to work from. Creating the drawings alerts you to difficult sections in the project and helps you determine how much wood you need. You don't have to be elaborate; just draw something simple. If the project includes any tricky parts (curves, unusual angles, and so on), draw those sections full size so that you can see what you're up against.

We suggest that you make a *template*, a pattern for the part re-created in full size that you can use again and again. Templates are generally made out of ¼-inch plywood or Masonite. They're really handy if you need to make more than one copy of a particular part (chairs, for example, because many people make more than one chair at a time).

Book V

Carpentry, Woodworking, and Flooring

Top

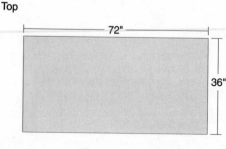

Figure 4-2: Measured drawings show the project from several angles and generally list the dimensions of each part.

Front

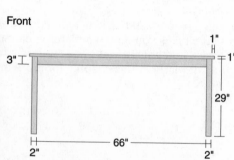

Side

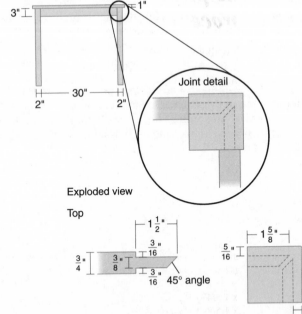

Joint detail

Exploded view

Top

45° angle

Side

$\frac{1}{4}$" groove $\frac{1}{4}$" deep

$\frac{1}{2}$" from edge

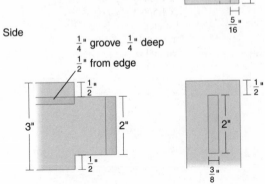

Figure 4-3:
More
detailed
drawings
for the
same
project
shown in
Figure 4-2.

Speaking of templates, we highly recommend making templates for any full-size drawings that are part of the plans you buy. Templates make milling the part to the right size much easier, and you'll always have them on hand. See the section titled "Making the Cut," later in this chapter, for more information about milling.

Putting the pieces together: Using a procedures list

A procedures list walks you through the process of assembling your project into its final form. Not all project plans include such a list because many people assume that you can figure out the best way to put a project together just by looking at the measured drawings. Procedures lists can be really helpful for beginning woodworkers, though, so we highly recommend that you find plans with detailed procedures lists when you first start out.

Figure 4-4 shows a typical procedures list. This one's pretty simple, but some plans have very detailed lists.

Figure 4-4: A procedures list helps you keep track of what you have to do.

Procedures

1. Choose, dimension, and assemble boards for top, leaving 1" extra in width and length.
2. Dimension legs and stretchers.
3. Cut groove in stretchers for cleats.
4. Cut 3/8" x 2" x 1 3/4" mortises in legs.
5. Cut 3/8" x 2" x 1 5/8" tenons in stretchers.
6. Sand legs and stretchers to 150 grit.
7. Assemble short stretcher to legs.
8. Assemble glued-up leg assemblies to long stretchers and check for square.
9. Cut tabletop to its final dimensions.
10. Sand top.
11. Finish sand leg/stretcher assembly.
12. Apply stain.
13. Apply top coat.
14. Attach top to leg assembly using cleats.

If you buy a set of plans that doesn't include a procedures list, make your own before you start to build. Create your procedures list by carefully looking over the material list and drawings. Then walk yourself through the building process, writing down the steps you need to take. When you start to build, you won't get confused and miss a joint or mill a part twice (which is really easy to do).

Creating a Cut List

Before you start building anything, take your measured drawing, pull out the wood you have on hand, and mark where each part of the project is coming from in pencil or chalk. Doing so minimizes waste and helps you plan the beauty of a project. For example, if you're making a dresser with four drawers, you want the wood you use for the drawer fronts and the face frame (if it has one) to match. You want the color and grain patterns to create a visually pleasing arrangement. The only way to ensure that you get this aesthetic appeal is to look at each board and carefully consider where it should go. This step takes some time, and you may end up rejecting a few boards in order to find a nice composition, which is why we always recommend buying more wood than you need for a given project.

Check out Figure 4-5 for a look at a cut list. The drawing on the left shows parts cut out of a solid board, and the drawing on the right shows how the parts of a *carcass* (the box for a cabinet) are cut out of a sheet of plywood.

Figure 4-5:
A cut list shows where you plan to cut your parts from a board (left) or sheet of plywood (right).

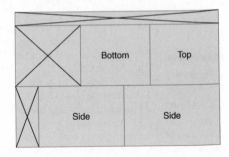

Selecting the best section of the board

Not only do you need to consider the look of the wood you use for a given part of a project, but you also need to think about how that wood behaves in response to moisture changes. Figure 4-6 shows how a board expands and contracts with changes in moisture. You want to make sure that any boards that meet expand and contract in such a way that they won't tear apart a joint or weaken your project.

Generally speaking, wood moves more against the grain than with it. So, as humidity changes, you see less change along its length and more along its width. Also, because plain-sawn boards have growth rings that run at a close angle to the face of the board, you may see more movement on one side of the board than another, which can cause warping, twisting, or cupping if the change in humidity is extreme.

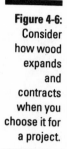

Figure 4-6:
Consider
how wood
expands
and
contracts
when you
choose it for
a project.

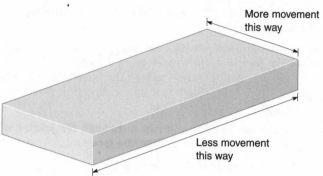

More movement
this way

Less movement
this way

Book V

**Carpentry,
Wood-
working,
and
Flooring**

Organizing your cut list

After you've chosen the wood from which to cut all the parts of your project, your next step is to decide in what order you want to cut the boards. We usually organize our boards according to the type of cuts they need and what tool we'll use to cut them. Start with the largest pieces, cut the pieces to size, and then work on the actual joints. Proceed in stages and, if you're working on a large project, work on one section at a time.

If you don't already have the wood, take your cut list with you to the lumberyard and mark off the parts of the cut list as you choose your wood. Doing so helps you choose the right boards for your project and ensures that you end up with the right amount of wood. In fact, we recommend that you mark the boards that you buy while you're still at the store, which saves you time when you get home.

Preparing the Board for Milling

Before you cut your wood down to size, do some preliminary cutting to prepare the wood for its final milling. This cutting is called (logically enough) *pre-milling.* Pre-milling means cutting the board to its near-final dimensions so that the wood can acclimate to its new size. We can't tell you how many times we've had a nice, straight board twist slightly when we cut it in half. This is the nature of wood: You can't predict what's going to happen after you change its shape. So cut the boards almost down to size and wait to see what happens.

Pre-mill a board to its final length and width plus an inch and to its final thickness plus ⅛ inch (if possible). Then let the board rest for a day or so before you do the final milling. After the board has rested, check to see that it's still flat and straight. If it isn't, you know that you need to flatten it out and square it by using a jointer and a planer. In that case, follow these steps:

1. **Run one of the faces of the board (the wide part) through the jointer until the board is flat.**

   This step may require a few light passes. Make sure that you run the stock over the jointer in the proper grain direction to avoid tear-out. If you don't know which direction to feed the board into the jointer, use a scrap piece and run it through first in one direction and then the other to see which provides a cleaner cut.

2. **Turn the board on its edge and run it through the jointer with the flat face (the one you just made) against the fence.**

3. **Flip the board over and do the other edge.**

   Again, make sure the freshly flattened face is against the fence.

4. **Run the board through your planer with the flat face against the bed until it's flat, too, paying attention to proper grain direction to avoid tear-out.**

   This step may take a few passes. At the end, you should have a flat, straight board.

Making the Cut

After the board is straight and flat, you can move on to the milling stage. *Milling,* simply an extension of the pre-milling stage, consists of doing the final cutting to the board to make the final part for your project. This process includes making all the joints, routing (like rounding over the edge of the board), and rough sanding all the parts so that they're all ready for assembly.

Follow this process when milling a board:

1. **Cut the board to width plus $\frac{1}{32}$ inch.**

2. **Run the freshly cut edge through the jointer until it's at its final width.**

   Set the jointer to take off $\frac{1}{32}$ inch or less and take only one or two passes off the edge to get your final width.

3. **Plane the board to its final thickness.**

4. **Crosscut a square edge on one end of the board.**

5. **Cut the board to length, measuring from the freshly squared end (the total length includes any tenons or other joints).**

6. **Cut out any mortises, tenons, or other joints.**

7. **Cut any curves or other shaping.**

   Do all shaping, such as rounding over the edge of a board, after all the joinery is done so that you don't lose any straight-line references that you need at various machines against fences, jigs, and so on.

After you mill all your parts, go over them with a random orbit sander and sand them smooth using 150-grit sandpaper. Doing so saves a ton of time later on and makes getting at inside corners easy — because they aren't inside corners yet. Be careful not to sand joint parts, such as tenons; doing so changes how well your joints fit.

Putting It All Together

You can approach the assembly and milling process in several ways. Some people mill everything and then assemble, whereas others prefer to mill a section of the project, assemble it, mill the next section and assemble it, and so on. We usually combine the two and mill according to cut type. Depending on the size of the overall project, we sometimes assemble in sections. As you do more projects, you find the method that works best for you.

Preparing for assembly

After you mill all the parts (or at least those parts for the section you're working on), the next step is to lay those parts out on your workbench. Doing so helps you confirm that you have all the parts that you need and visualize the assembly process. As you lay out the parts, double-check your material list and your measured drawing to see that you have everything and that all the parts are milled properly.

Next, get all your assembly materials ready:

- **Clamps:** Bring all the clamps you think you'll need (plus a couple extra, just in case) to your bench and put them within easy reach.

- **Damp rag and dull chisel:** You use these tools to remove any extra glue that squeezes out of the joints when you add the clamps.

- **Glue and glue brush:** You can't glue without glue! When you use carpenter's glue (see Chapter 2), always use an *acid brush* (a small, metal-handled brush) to apply it. The acid brush helps you achieve an even coat, and it's small enough to get into mortises and other joints.

- **Rubber mallet:** This tool enables you to tap any joint into place and to make adjustments to the square of the piece, if necessary.

- **Straightedge:** When you glue boards edge to edge (a tabletop, for example), a straightedge enables you to see whether your assembly is flat.

- **Tape measure:** This tool enables you to check that your work is square when it's glued.

Before you start, make sure that your work area is clean and free of clutter. Gluing a project is nerve-racking, and you don't want to trip over a tool or board while you're working. We also recommend keeping all other parts of the project away from your assembly area until you need them. Doing so eliminates any possible confusion as you work and keeps you from accidentally gluing up the wrong parts.

Dry-fitting

After you apply the glue to your parts, you have only a few minutes (about five to ten with white or yellow carpenter's glue) to get everything to fit properly. Because of this time limit and the stress that you'll undoubtedly feel as a result, we highly recommend that you do a *dry-fit* and run through the glue-up process before you break out the glue.

Walk yourself through the process of assembling the parts in front of you by putting each of the joints together, applying the clamps, and checking for square (follow the steps in the ensuing sections). Doing so ensures that all the parts fit like they're supposed to and that you have a clear idea of what steps are involved in putting the joints together.

Time yourself as you dry-fit the parts. If it takes you more than 10 or 15 minutes, consider breaking the assembly down into several smaller assemblies that you can glue together in stages. Or at least plan on applying the glue in stages so that each joint is put together before the glue starts to set.

When you're comfortable with the process, disassemble everything, take a few breaths, and break out the glue.

Applying the glue

If you've done a dry-fit of your parts, you just need to redo the process, this time using glue as you go. You shouldn't encounter any surprises along the way. Remember that when you work with the glue, you have only a little time to get everything to fit back together again. (For more on applying adhesives, see Chapter 2.)

Here are some other hints to consider when you glue up your parts:

 ✔ **Don't use too much glue.** People often use too much when they first start out. A thin coat is all you need on each part of a joint.

 ✔ **When gluing veneers, apply glue only to the backing material and not to the veneer itself, or the veneer will curl and become difficult to work with.**

✔ **After you assemble a joint, push (or tap with a mallet) or clamp the joint fully in place; otherwise, the joint may lock up partway.** This step is especially important with tight-fitting mortise-and-tenon joints. When joints are wet with glue, the wood swells and the joints require more clamp pressure to assemble.

✔ **Don't panic.** Yes, gluing can be nerve-racking, but if you panic, you end up with a partially assembled piece and likely have to start over (which is why dry-fitting is so important).

Clamping

The trick to clamping is to apply just enough pressure to pull the joints tightly together, but not so much that you squeeze all the glue out. Clamps hold the joints together until the glue has a chance to dry.

Here are some other things to consider when clamping:

✔ **Make sure that your clamps are perpendicular to the workpiece and not angling off one way or another.** This precaution is especially impor- tant when doing edge-to-edge joints because angled clamps pull the boards out of alignment.

✔ **Don't apply so much pressure that you warp the workpiece.**

✔ **Make sure that your clamps are centered on the board, applying even pressure.** If your clamps aren't centered, they may warp the workpiece. Ideally, clamp pressure should be applied down the centerline of the joint.

✔ **If you think that you need to use an additional clamp, use it.** You can never have too many clamps (within reason, of course).

Squaring up the parts and verifying flatness

After you've glued and clamped everything properly, you need to make sure that all your parts are flat and square.

When you edge-glue a bunch of boards into a tabletop, you want to make sure that those boards remain flat. If you did a good job creating perfectly straight and square edges on each board, the boards will want to lay flat. The only trou- ble you may have is with too much clamp pressure or an uneven benchtop.

To check for flatness, run your straightedge against the top of the boards. If you see light through the straightedge as it passes over the boards, they aren't flat. To straighten, adjust the clamps. If edges are sticking up, you may need to tap them down with a mallet.

To check that your assembled parts are *square* (they have 90-degree corners), you need a tape measure. This simple process involves the following steps:

1. **Measure diagonally from the upper right to the lower left corner and from the upper left to the lower right corner.**

   If these numbers match, you're square. If not, you need to square it up by moving on to Step 2.

2. **Gently push the upper corner of the measurement that was longer than the other toward that other corner.**

   If this maneuver doesn't work (it often doesn't), move on to Step 3.

3. **Take another clamp and run it diagonally from the corners that have the longer measurement and tighten the clamp until both diagonal measurements are equal.**

Cleaning up your mess

Cleaning up is our least favorite part of the assembly process — and we're sure we're not alone. After all the stress of getting everything to fit properly, all we want to do is sit back and admire our work . . . or break for a beer. But trust us when we say this: A little work now saves you tons of work later.

Glue is much easier to remove when wet. To clean up glue spills and seepage, follow these steps:

1. **Use a dull chisel or a scraper to gently scrape off the beads of glue that formed around the joints.**

   Go with the grain and be careful not to gouge the wood.

2. **Take a damp (not wet) cloth and rub around all the joints until you're down to bare wood.**

   Depending on how much glue spillage you have to deal with, you may need to rinse out your rag. We usually keep two rags available.

   Don't forget to clean up the bottoms of drawers and tabletops (or anywhere that can't be easily seen).

3. **Double-check that all the joints are completely clean before you quit.**

Letting it sit

We like to assemble at the end of the day so that we're not tempted to take the clamps off too soon. We always let the assembled parts sit in the clamps overnight before we try to remove them. Doing so minimizes any chance that the glue hasn't cured enough before we remove the pressure.

Chapter 5

Finishing Wood

A woodworking project isn't complete without the finish. This chapter helps you make this often-hated process (trust us, we're being nice here) of sanding and finishing into a chore that you'll love (well, maybe just *tolerate*). The chapter explores the frequently short-shrifted process of filling and sanding wood smooth, shows you how to add color to your projects, and demystifies the topcoat process. You discover the best type of finish for your project and go through the steps of applying it for best results.

Filling Holes and Cracks

Even though you may have tried to use wood without any cracks, splits, holes, or gouges, sometimes you end up with imperfections you didn't notice or couldn't avoid. And sometimes these imperfections result from a misplaced chisel or other accident while making the piece. For most types of furniture, you want to get rid of any problems before you do the final sanding. This section shows you how to fill both small and large defects as well as raise dents without hassle.

Fixing small imperfections

You can fill cracks, scratches, or even slightly mismatched joints with several different products, including wood putty, wax sticks, and shellac sticks. Each of these items has its strengths and weaknesses:

✔ **Wood putty:** Wood putty comes as a thick paste that you spread into the hole or crack with a putty knife and then let dry and sand flush. It's available in a variety of colors, so you're sure to find one to match the wood you're working with. If you can't find a match, either add some stain to the putty while it's still soft (before you apply it) or paint on some artist's paint to match the wood's surface after you sand it.

✔ **Wax sticks:** Wax sticks are like crayons, only harder. They come in various colors to match different woods. You have essentially two opportunities to use a wax stick: before you apply the final finish and afterward. If you use it before applying the final finish, you need to seal the wood with shellac first. This step isn't necessary when you use a wax stick after applying the final finish because the finish seals the wood.

To apply a wax stick, simply draw it on by pressing it into the defect with the tip of the wax stick, a putty knife, or your finger and then remove the excess with a putty knife or piece of plastic.

We don't use wax sticks unless we put a wax finish on the piece, which we don't do often. Find out why in the section "Protecting Your Work with a Topcoat," later in this chapter.

✔ **Shellac sticks:** Shellac sticks come in tons of colors, look good, and are easy to apply. Shellac is a natural, low-toxic product made from beetle excretions that you melt with a soldering iron and let drip into the surface imperfection. You then press it in with a putty knife or chisel and wait for it to harden. After the shellac is hard, you scrape it flush with a chisel or thin cabinet scraper and then sand it lightly with fine sandpaper.

✔ **Glue and sawdust:** On occasion, we've been known to use a mixture of wood glue and sawdust to fill a hole or crack in a project. Doing so allows us to match the wood we're working with exactly because we use sawdust that we created while milling the boards for the project. This low-tech solution requires just the right amount of glue and sawdust to get a filler that's both durable and stains well (not hard to do — it just takes some experimentation).

Dealing with big holes

If you have big holes — from using recycled wood or from a loose knot, for instance — you can fill them with another piece of wood, called a *dutchman*. This technique has been around as long as people have been working with wood. Some purists cringe at the thought of using wood that has a blemish large enough to require a dutchman, but in the American Southwest, where using recycled wood raises the value of furniture, dutchmans are common. Heck, many people here don't even bother to fill cracks or holes.

Book V

Carpentry,
Wood-
working,
and
Flooring

Whether or not you like the rustic look, you should know how to make a dutchman. The procedure is pretty simple, and it's made even simpler with a plunge router, a ⅛-inch straight-cutting bit, and two collars: one ⁵⁄₁₆-inch and the other ⁹⁄₁₆-inch. You can buy kits that contain these parts at most woodworking tool suppliers. They're called *inlay kits* or *inlay bushing bit with removable collar*. The process with this setup is as follows:

1. **Make a template of the dutchman out of ¼-inch plywood or Masonite.**

   Measure the size of the defect in your project and add a little extra around it — about ½ inch or so on all sides. Cut out a hole in the template material to this size. Be sure to use a large enough piece so that you can clamp this piece to the wood you want to work with and have enough room for the plunge router to move freely in the template. We recommend a piece at least 12 inches square.

2. **Attach the ⁵⁄₁₆-inch collar to the base of your plunge router, followed by the ⁹⁄₁₆-inch collar.**

3. **Insert the bit into the plunge router and set the depth of cut to ⅛ inch.**

4. **Clamp the template onto the board with the defect, making sure that the hole in the template is over the defect.**

5. **Run your plunge router clockwise along the inside edge of the template.**

6. **Carefully route or chisel out the remaining material in the center of the template.**

7. **Remove the outer collar (the ⁹⁄₁₆-inch one) and lower the depth of cut to ³⁄₁₆ inch.**

8. **Select a piece of wood that has a similar color and grain pattern to the wood where the defect was and clamp the template onto it.**

9. **Route around the edge of the template in a clockwise direction.**

   Be sure to keep tight to the edge of the template; otherwise, you'll cut into the dutchman itself.

10. **Remove the dutchman from the scrap wood by setting your table saw to cut ⅛ inch into the board.**

    If you use ¾-inch stock, set the rip fence ¹⁹⁄₃₂ inch from the side of the blade farthest from the rip fence (if your blade has a kerf of ⅛ inch, the rip fence is ¹⁵⁄₃₂ inch from the side of the blade closest to the rip fence).

11. **Set the depth of cut in the table saw so that it's higher than the dutchman on the board.**

12. **With the dutchman facing out, run the board through the saw.**

    The dutchman will fall out of the board as you run it through.

13. **Apply glue to the underside of the dutchman and a little to the receiving groove and then press it into place.**

    You may need to tap it lightly with a mallet. Use a scrap piece of wood of the same species to tap against. Doing so will keep you from damaging the wood. The dutchman will stick up $\frac{1}{32}$ inch from the surface of the wood.

14. **Sand the dutchman flush after the glue dries.**

Raising dents

If your unfinished wood has a dent, you don't need to fill it with putty or any other substance. All you have to do is place a damp cloth over the dent and cover it with a hot iron for a few seconds. The steam from the cloth will seep into the pores of the wood and lift the surface. Then all you have to do is sand the surface smooth. Pretty simple, huh?

Smoothing Out Wood

After you've removed the major defects from your wood project (see the prior "Filling Holes and Cracks" section for instructions), you need to smooth out the fillers and get rid of the minor scratches and milling marks. Then it's time to make the surface smooth enough for the finish you want to apply. This part of the process involves using sandpaper or a scraper. We cover both approaches in this section.

Sanding

Nearly all woodworkers sand to smooth the surfaces of their projects before finishing. This process isn't rocket science — all it takes are some simple steps and a ton of patience. If you don't get a finish you like, you simply didn't spend enough time sanding.

The process of sanding wood involves making progressively finer scratches in the surface. These scratches remove imperfections in the wood, such as visible scratches or uneven surfaces. Moving from one grit to the next finer one reduces the size of the scratches until they're so small that the wood seems smooth. Never skip a grit of paper when sanding — doing so makes it difficult to remove scratches that the previous grade of sandpaper would've removed easily, and you spend a lot more time trying to get a smooth finish.

Sandpaper comes in a variety of types, including glass, garnet, aluminum oxide, and silicon carbide. Each type has its benefits, but we generally use aluminum oxide, which is excellent for almost all woodworking tasks. It lasts a relatively long time and is able to sand all types of wood effectively. Steer clear of cheapie yellow glass paper, which breaks down too quickly. For sanding metal and for wet-sanding an oil finish (see the section "Protecting Your Work with a Topcoat," later in this chapter), look for black silicon carbide paper.

Getting into grits

Sandpaper comes in differing levels of abrasiveness, called *grit*. Grit refers to the number and size of the particles in the sandpaper. The fewer and larger the particles, the rougher the paper. Grits range from 40 to 600 — the lower numbers are for rougher papers. We generally use 80- to 320-grit papers unless we're doing wet-dry work with silicon carbide paper. In this case, we may go up to 600-grit for oil finishes.

Aside from the number rating of sandpaper grits, you have general categories:

- **Very coarse:** 40- and 60-grit papers.
- **Coarse:** 80- and 100-grit papers. This paper gets rid of scratches and other surface imperfections.
- **Medium:** 120-, 150-, and 180-grit papers. Medium is where you do most of your sanding.
- **Fine:** 220- to 280-grit papers. Fine paper is for final sanding.
- **Very fine:** From 320- to 600-grit papers. Only use this sandpaper occasionally.

Sand thoroughly with each grit of paper before moving on to the next finer grit. Determining when you've done enough sanding with one grit can be difficult until you gain some experience, so we recommend that you sand a few minutes longer than you think you need to with each grit of paper.

Trying your hand at sanding

Our regular sanding procedure consists of removing major surface defects with a belt sander, followed by smoothing with a random orbit sander, and then finishing off with a final hand sanding.

Follow these suggestions for a better and easier job of hand sanding:

- Wrap the paper around a block of wood to provide a flat, solid backing. If you hold the paper in your hand and press with your fingers, you don't get a flat, even surface, and your hand gets tired much faster.

✔ When sanding irregular-shaped surfaces, such as moldings, use a con-toured block in the same shape as the surface you're sanding. Make a block yourself by using a round dowel, for instance, on rounded sections or buy sanding blocks in a variety of shapes and sizes.

✔ Tear full sheets of sandpaper into halves or quarters to make working with it easier.

✔ Clean the sandpaper when it gets clogged. Simply tapping the paper with your hand removes some of the accumulated dust. Blowing on the paper or spraying it with compressed air also does the trick.

✔ If the paper remains clogged after you try to clean it, don't hesitate to get a new sheet. Sanding with dull or clogged paper is a recipe for frustration.

✔ Follow the sanding guidelines for the type of finish you intend to apply. Some finishes, such as oils, work best with a finely sanded finish (320-grit, for example), but others, such as polyurethanes, can handle a rougher finish (150-grit). Do your homework (the section "Protecting Your Work with a Topcoat" helps you out here) and decide what type of finish you want to use before doing any final sanding.

Scraping

Some woodworkers prefer a scraper to sandpaper. A *scraper* is simply a piece of metal with an edge on it that you scrape along the surface of the wood to smooth it out. When we use a scraper, we do the rough sanding work with a belt sander (if necessary) and random orbit sander up to about a 120-grit paper. From there, we use the scraper to smooth the wood.

Other people prefer to use a scraper instead of sanders. If you choose this route and your wood has major defects, you either need to use a hand plane or a *thick cabinet scraper* (heavy-duty scraper) to remove the defects before you move on to a *regular* (lighter-duty) scraper.

A scraper is a good choice for projects with oil finishes because it opens the pores of the wood and enables the oils to penetrate deeper. This gives the illusion of more depth to the final finish. A scraper isn't a good choice for fin-ishes that are designed to sit on the top of the wood, such as polyurethanes.

Adding Color with Stains and Paints

Most people think wood looks better after it develops a patina. *Patinas* develop through a process called oxidation, creating a color that's darker than the raw, freshly sanded wood that your project has right after you finish building it. Woodworkers often use stains to give the effect of an aged patina right from the start. They also use stains to give less expensive wood the look of a more expensive one. Sometimes, they use stains to even out color differences. Woodworkers use paints, on the other hand, to give color to less-than-beautiful wood.

This section goes over the ins and outs of adding color to your creations. From stains to paints, dyes to oxidizers, you find out how to choose the best approach for the type of wood you're working with. We also show you how to apply these different products for the best results.

Adding coloring agents such as stains, dyes, or paints requires you to sand the wood smooth and know in advance the type of topcoat you intend to use.

Wood stains come in several configurations, including pigments, dyes, and combinations of both. Likewise, you can find stains with an oil base, water base, or lacquer base. This section lays out all the options for you.

Pigment stains

Pigment stains use minerals to create color. They don't actually change the color of the wood; they simply add a color by distributing these minerals into the wood's pores. The minerals are suspended in mineral spirits, water, or lacquer thinner (called *carriers*), and a component called the *binder* seals them into the pores.

Pigment stains are good for wood that has consistent pores, such as oak or ash, where you want to accentuate the grain patterns. They aren't the best choice when you want to even out color changes, such as the contrast between the heartwood (the darker-colored stuff) and sapwood (the lighter-colored wood) in cherry. We also wouldn't use a pigment stain on a figured wood, such as curly maple, because it tends to look blotchy. Because of this tendency, many pigment stains contain dyes to even out the distribution of color and reduce blotchiness, making them useful for more types of wood.

Choosing stains

Pigment stains come in a large variety of colors, so you're sure to find one that fills your needs. After you pick the color, you need to decide what delivery medium to use: water, oil, or gel.

- ✔ **Water:** We really like water-based stains because they're nontoxic, easy to clean up, compatible with a variety of topcoats, and can be layered to get just the right amount of color.

The only real disadvantage to water-based stains is that they tend to raise the grain (meaning that the grain swells slightly from the water, creating a rough texture). You need to lightly sand the stained wood after the first coat. Just make sure not to sand too much. All you want to do is take the hairs off the wood.

✔ **Oil:** Oil-based stains were the old standby, but because of their toxicity and the improvements in water-based products, the days of oil-based stains are coming to an end. Oil-based stains have only one advantage over water-based ones: Because their drying time is longer, you have more time to work with the stain, which can be helpful for beginners. Nonetheless, we don't recommend oil-based stains unless you're restoring furniture and you need to match an existing oil-based finish.

✔ **Gel:** A gel stain is really an oil-based stain, but it acts so differently that we think it merits its own category. Gel stains are handy for non-horizontal surfaces and for tricky parts like turned legs because they're thicker than other stains, reducing the amount of dripping. Gel stains also tend to lessen the blotchy appearance of some woods because they don't soak into the wood.

Gel stains are relatively new on the market. The main drawback is that they're still somewhat expensive and you don't find quite as many color choices. They're oil-based, so they're smelly and messy compared to water-based varieties. Still, gel stains can be a good choice, especially for blotch-prone wood like birch.

Applying stains

You can apply stain with a brush, but we prefer to use a rag. A rag allows for better control of drips, and you get to feel the wood as you work, which helps you control the coverage. We always wear latex gloves when we use the rag approach because it can get pretty messy. Oil-based stains are toxic, so protecting your skin from contact with these finishes is important.

Before you put on a stain, seal the wood with a wood sealer or a diluted version of your topcoat. This seal keeps the stain from creating a blotchy appearance on the wood. Choose a sealer based on the stain and topcoat you intend to use. The manufacturer's recommendations are on the stain's label.

Putting stain on is pretty easy: Just wipe it on in the direction of the grain, wait a few minutes, and wipe off the excess. For a darker color, you may need to apply additional coats (we find that two coats are generally adequate). If you use more than one coat, wait until each coat is dry before you add another. The drying time depends on humidity, temperature, and the type of stain you use. Check your stain container to see what it recommends.

Book V

Carpentry,
Wood-
working,
and
Flooring

Cleaning up

Cleanup procedures vary depending on the type of stain you use. Take a look at the main differences:

- ✔ Water-based stains clean up with water. Easy cleanup is the main reason people prefer this type of stain. Just toss the rag you used to apply the stain in the wastebasket, wash your hands with soap and water, and wipe up any spills with a wet rag or towel.

- ✔ Oil-based stains require more work to clean up. You need to use mineral spirits to remove drips or spills and any stain that got on your hands. You need to dispose of the used rag carefully so that it doesn't become a fire hazard. We usually lay it out to dry on a brick or cement floor and then put it in a covered metal wastebasket.

Dyes

Dyes actually change the color of wood. One of the nice characteristics of dyes is that they go on more evenly than pigments. We really like to use dyes for cherry if we end up having to use a board with sapwood (lighter-colored wood) in it because the dye evens out the difference in color between the darker heartwood and the lighter sapwood.

Dyes stain whatever they touch. Soap and water don't remove dye — only time does. So we highly recommend that you wear latex gloves whenever you work with this stuff and wear clothes that you don't mind ruining. Also, some dye colors are toxic in powder or dissolved form. Read the product labels to determine what precautions you need to take.

Although dyes are available that dissolve in oil, lacquer thinner, and alcohol, we're big fans of water-soluble dyes for woodworking. You can usually buy these dyes as powder that you mix with hot water and stir until it dissolves. They come in a staggering variety of colors, and you can mix them as desired to get just the right color. You won't find powdered dyes at your local home center; get them from a specialty woodworking store.

You apply dyes with a rag, but unlike pigment stains, you don't need to wipe off the excess. Just wipe the dye on, being careful to apply it evenly with the grain and keep a wet edge (don't apply wet dye over a portion that has dried).

Dyes benefit from having a sanding sealer applied to the wood first. Wood sealed with sanding sealer takes dye more evenly and looks much better.

You can dispose of the rags you use to apply dye in the trash, and you don't have to worry about toxic smells or flammability issues. If you use a dye that dissolves in mineral spirits, lacquer thinner, or alcohol, you need to take the necessary precautions for these products. See the "Pigment stains" section earlier in this chapter.

Paints

Paint is a good choice if you want to hide a less-than-beautiful wood or you want the look of a solid color. Paints come in several varieties:

- **Oil-based:** Oil-based paints used to be the professional's choice because they go on smooth and flatten out well. Their main problem, however, is that they're toxic. Because of the vast improvements in water-based paints in the last few decades, we don't use oil-based paints any longer, and we don't know of anyone else who does, either.

- **Water-based (latex):** For brushed-on paint, latex is our choice. Water-based latex paint goes on almost as well as oil-based paint and is non-toxic. You won't have trouble finding just the right color.

- **Lacquer:** If you want a professional look, you can't go wrong with a lacquer. You spray lacquers on in thin coats, and they dry so fast that dust has no time to land on the wet finish. You can often spray the next coat as soon as you're done with the first.

  The main drawback to painting with lacquer is that you need special equipment, such as an air compressor and spray gun, and getting a feel for spraying the paint takes some time. After you have the stuff and figure out how to spray well, though, we're willing to bet that you won't touch a paintbrush again (at least, not for putting on paint).

Age, fast and easy

We don't usually mention products by name, but one stain is so unusual, effective, and easy to use that we just can't help ourselves. (We're not in any way affiliated with this company.) We like getting an antiqued look on our furniture and often use recycled wood when we can find (and afford) it. If we can't use old wood, we use a product called Old Growth, a two-part coloring product that speeds up the oxidizing effects on wood. The wood gets noticeably darker really fast. All you do is apply the activator solution, wait for it to dry, and then wipe on the catalyst solution. If the result is too dark for your tastes, dilute the activator solution before you apply it. This product is made by Old Growth Ltd., P.O. Box 1371, Santa Fe, NM 87504; phone 888-301-9663.

The number one tip to remember when applying paint is that you need a primer coat in order to get professional-looking results. Some people skip the primer and just put on two coats of paint, but please resist this temptation. You get a much better finish if you use primer. Make sure to choose one that's compatible with your paint. We usually choose primer from the same company that makes the paint we're using.

Book V

**Carpentry,
Wood-
working,
and
Flooring**

After you have a good (and dry) primer coat on your wood, brush on the paint. If you use a water-based primer, lightly sand the wood with 320-grit paper to smooth the grain. When brushing, use long, smooth strokes and don't put too much paint on the brush.

If you're using a paint sprayer, the key is to keep the sprayer moving parallel to the wood's surface and apply several thin coats rather than one thick one. Doing so reduces runs and drips.

Paint cleanup follows the same guidelines as any other finish material. Oil-based products need mineral spirits, lacquers need lacquer thinner, and water-based products clean up with water.

Brushes and sprayers need a good cleaning with the proper solvent followed by a soap and water wash to keep them in good condition. Make sure that you dispose of your rags properly. Oil-based products need to go into metal containers after you leave them out to dry in a safe, nonflammable place.

Protecting Your Work with a Topcoat

After all your hard work milling the wood, assembling the parts, repairing defects, smoothing the wood, and getting the color you want, you're finally ready to put on the protective layer. A topcoat is essential to maintain the piece's beauty and structure. It protects your work from spills and from natural seasonal moisture changes that cause wood to expand and contract. Without the protection of a topcoat, wood is more susceptible to warping and cracking. A topcoat also improves the look of the wood by adding depth and color.

This section goes over the most common topcoat options and weighs the pros and cons of each to help you make an informed choice about what to put on your work. We also walk you through the process of preparing your wood, applying the topcoat, and cleaning up the mess when you're done.

Shellac

Shellac is one of the oldest and most loved topcoats. It gives wood a rich, deep finish, is easy to apply and repair, and is nontoxic. Shellac is a natural product made from — get this — beetle secretions. Before you get grossed out, we have to tell you that you've probably encountered shellac many times before. In fact, we're sure you've probably even eaten it before. Shellac is used to coat pills and vegetables, among other things. We say this to let you know just how safe this stuff is. Shellac is our preferred finish for toys, for example.

Shellac's main drawback is that it doesn't hold up to liquids, heat, or scratches very well. (Some people consider these serious shortfalls.) You can minimize this problem by using a dewaxed shellac and putting a layer of varnish or wax over the top. Of course, doing so reduces your ability to repair the shellac surface easily.

You can buy shellac as flakes or premixed with alcohol. The premixed varieties have a shelf life of about six months (one company claims to make a premixed shellac that lasts years), but most flakes last indefinitely. We recommend that you buy flakes and mix it yourself. You not only get a longer shelf life, but you also can make the shellac the consistency you want.

Shellac comes in many varieties: blond, white, garnet, lemon, buttonlac, and orange, to name a few. Each has a different color, so you can often skip the stain when using shellac.

Preparing shellac

If you buy shellac already mixed, you don't have to do anything to prepare it. If you buy flakes, you need to mix it with denatured alcohol. The ratio of shellac to alcohol, called the *cut,* refers to how many pounds of flakes are mixed with gallons of alcohol. For most topcoats, a 2-pound mix is good (2 pounds of shellac flakes to 1 gallon of alcohol). For sealing wood, a ½- to 1-pound mix is good (the ½-pound mix goes on easier).

To prepare a wood surface for shellac, sand the project really well, going all the way up to 320-grit paper. Shellac sits on the surface of the wood and doesn't hide sanding scratches — in fact, it seems to accentuate them!

If you take your time and do a good job of sanding, you'll love the look you get from a few coats of shellac. If you skimp on the sanding, however, you're going to be disappointed with the final finish. After you finish sanding, remove all the dust from the surface by wiping with a cotton cloth dampened with mineral spirits and then wipe the surface with a lint-free rag dampened with alcohol.

Applying shellac

You can apply shellac in numerous ways: You can spray it on or apply it with a cloth, brush, or rubbing pad made up of a wad of wool wrapped in a linen cloth.

Shellac is somewhat tricky to apply because it dries so quickly. If you're new to using shellac, mix it in a 1½-pound cut (1½ pounds shellac flakes to 1 gallon alcohol). This cut makes the shellac easier to brush on and reduces brush marks. If your shellac dries too fast, you can add shellac retardant to slow the drying process.

To apply shellac with a brush, get the finest brush you can find. Use a natural bristle brush called a *fitch brush,* which is made with polecat or skunk hair. Apply the finish by following these steps:

1. **Dip the brush halfway into the shellac and lightly press it into the side of the container to remove excess finish.**

2. **Start an inch or two from the edge of the wood and lightly drag the brush to the edge, reverse directions, and go all the way to the other edge, gently lifting your brush as you reach the edge.**

3. **Make another stroke next to this one with a small overlap of about ¼ inch.**

4. **Repeat until you cover the entire surface.**

5. **Shellac the edges, repeating Steps 1 through 3.**

6. **Let the piece dry for at least an hour, and then lightly sand it with 320-grit paper.**

   Make sure to clean or change the paper when it gets clogged, which happens fairly quickly.

7. **Rub the finish with #0000 steel wool.**

8. **Wipe the surface clean with a lint-free rag.**

9. **Apply a second coat of shellac and let it dry overnight.**

10. **Start the next day by sanding this coat with 320-grit paper and follow it with the #0000 steel wool.**

11. **Wipe the piece clean with a lint-free rag.**

12. **Repeat Steps 9 through 11 until your piece has four or five coats of shellac.**

13. **Rub the piece with #0000 steel wool to get the sheen you want.**

Cleaning up

One of the great characteristics of shellac is ease of cleanup. Alcohol dissolves the shellac again, so if you find any misplaced shellac, use denatured alcohol on a rag to remove it. For cleaning brushes, regular household ammonia works well. We like to put ammonia in a small container and swish our brushes around in it until they're clean. Afterward, simply wash the brush with mild soap and water.

Oil

For a while, one of us used nothing but oil to finish our projects. Oil finishes, such as tung oil, Danish oil, teak oil, and linseed oil, are fast and easy to apply, but making them look really good takes time — and many coats. With the exception of Danish oil, which has some hardeners and varnishes in it, they don't protect very well against moisture.

Oils penetrate the pores of the wood. For this reason, oils don't give you the polished look that you can achieve with shellac or varnish. Also, you need to refresh oil finishes as the finish wears by adding additional coats. Oils do impart a rich, almost antiqued look to wood, though, which is why many people use them.

Because oils don't build up on the surface of wood, the wood itself must be perfect for oils to look great. This means that you need to sand meticulously with up to 320-grit sandpaper. You almost want the wood to shine on its own before you put the oil on. After you get the surface perfectly smooth, wipe it down with a rag dampened with mineral spirits to remove the dust and sanding residue.

Application is the easy part of oil finishes. Follow these simple steps:

1. **Put on a pair of latex gloves to protect your hands.**

2. **Using a lint-free cloth, generously wipe the oil onto the wood.**

3. **Let the piece stand for five or ten minutes.**

4. **Lightly sand with 600-grit wet/dry sandpaper.**

   This step isn't necessary for some oils, such as salad bowl oil. You need to do it only on the first one or two coats.

5. **Wipe off the excess and let it dry for 24 hours.**

6. **Buff the piece with a soft cloth.**

7. **Repeat these steps until you have four or five coats, skipping Step 4 after the second coat.**

8. **Buff the final coat with a soft cloth until you get the gloss you want.**

When using oil, watch the wood for *weeping* (releasing from the pores of the wood). Some woods, such as cherry, ooze out oil for a while. If you don't wipe it from the surface before it dries, you need to sand it off before adding another coat. This is a real pain. You may need to wipe the oozing oil a few times, so after applying the first coat, don't go anywhere until the wood is done weeping.

Cleaning up after using oil is as simple as disposing of the used rags and washing your hands. Use mineral spirits to get any oil off your hands. Follow it up with mild soap and water and hand lotion (the mineral spirits will dry your hands). If you spill or drip any oil, use mineral spirits to clean it up. Lay the rags flat until they dry completely and then put them in a metal container.

Oil-soaked rags are flammable — *very* flammable. In fact, they're so flamma- ble that they've been known to spontaneously combust. Don't put them in a wastebasket with other stuff until they're completely dry. One of us usually lays our rags flat on the brick patio outside the woodworking shop to dry them out. The only other safe way to deal with oil-soaked rags is to put them in a metal container filled with water until you can dispose of them properly.

Wax

Wax is another easy-to-use, age-old finish. Like shellac and varnish, it lies on top of the wood, and you can build it up by applying several thin layers. Wax adds a nice *patina* (wood's natural oxidation process that produces a darker, rich color) to wood and can be purchased with coloring agents to add more color to the piece.

We don't like to use wax as a primary finish; instead, we add it to varnished or shellacked wood. Wax is very delicate — just put a glass of water on it and you get an instant ring. To us, the beauty of wax is as a final topcoat buffed to a nice gloss. Don't let our lack of enthusiasm for wax deter you from using it, though. You have many good wax products to choose from. Check out your local woodworking store and we're sure you'll find a product that will provide the results you're looking for.

Most waxes are a blend of beeswax and carnauba wax. The more carnauba wax present, the more durable the finish, only it takes more effort to get it to shine.

Preparing for wax

Because wax is supposed to sit on the surface of the wood, we prefer to seal the wood first. Doing so protects the wood when the wax gets damaged and keeps any oils in the wax from penetrating the wood, which would make removing the wax very difficult. The wood surface under the wax doesn't need as diligent a sanding as it does if you use shellac or oil, but you do need to create a nice smooth surface. You really need to sand only to 220-grit to use wax successfully.

After sanding the wood and cleaning it with a rag dampened in mineral spirits, we recommend that you seal it with a ½-pound cut of shellac. Heck, we'd even apply two coats of shellac first. You'll get a better finish, and applying two coats doesn't take that long.

Applying wax

Applying wax is very easy — it's the same as waxing a car. Follow these steps:

1. **Put a liberal amount of wax on a cloth.**

2. **Wipe it on the wood using overlapping circular motions until you've covered the entire surface.**

3. **Let the wax dry until a whitish film appears.**

4. **Using a clean, dry cloth, buff the wax until the film disappears and a glossy shine replaces it.**

   Replace the cloths with clean ones as they get dirty.

5. **Keep buffing until you have a hard, shiny surface — you can't buff too much.**

   If you use a power buffer, make sure that you keep the polishing pad moving, or you may melt the wax.

6. **Let the wax dry for 24 hours.**

7. **Repeat these steps at least twice, for three coats minimum.**

Wax is easy to clean up. A little soap and water gets it off your hands and rags. If you use old cotton cloths to apply and buff wax, throwing them away is easier than cleaning them.

Varnish and oil-based polyurethane

Varnish, a common finish, comes in many varieties. Traditional varnishes are made of pine resins, but modern varnishes use a variety of solutions that produce a hard, durable surface. The most common type of varnish is polyurethane.

Varnish is the best topcoat for a project that will take a lot of abuse. However, varnish is toxic and hard to clean up, and because it can take a while to dry, you may end up with dust in your finish. However, these problems are becoming less of an issue as new formulas hit the market. Always wear gloves and a respirator when using an oil-based varnish.

Sanding to 150- to 220-grit works well for most varnishes. You don't need to go any smoother. Just make sure to do the best job you can, getting all the imperfections out of the wood. Varnish works best when you apply a sealer coat to the wood first. We don't recommend that you use a special wood sealer; instead, just thin the varnish down 10 or 20 percent with mineral spirits and apply it as you would a regular coat.

The surface of the piece should be clear of sanding residue and dust. Clean the surface by wiping a rag dampened with mineral spirits over all surfaces to be varnished.

Varnish goes on just like paint. Here are the basic steps:

1. **For the first coat, thin the varnish by adding 10 to 20 percent mineral spirits.**

2. **Dip the brush into the varnish about a third of the way and press the brush gently against the side of the container to remove excess finish.**

3. **Brush a thin layer on the surface.**

4. **Brush out any lap marks (overlapping brushstrokes) and drips by going over the finish with your slightly dampened brush.**

   Don't worry about getting rid of all the brush marks, only the big ones. The small brush marks will settle before the finish dries.

5. **Let the piece dry for 24 hours.**

6. **Sand it out with 400-grit wet/dry sandpaper.**

   You can use mineral spirits as a lubricant to make the process easier and to keep the paper from clogging as quickly.

7. **Repeat Steps 2 through 6 until you have four or five coats.**

8. **After the final coat, rub it out with #0000 steel wool to give it the gloss you want.**

Because varnish is solvent-based, you need to use mineral spirits to clean up. We keep a bucket of mineral spirits around to dip our brushes in. Swishing the brush around in the bucket removes the finish. We usually follow up with a mild soap and water rinse and wrap the brush in plastic until we need it again. Some people skip the soap and water and let the brush dry.

For washing hands, mineral spirits are the only way to go. To avoid the mess, we wear disposable gloves and throw them away after we're finished. Use a metal container with a lid on it to reduce the smell.

Water-based polyurethane

If you like the idea of varnish but don't want to put up with the smell and mess of a solvent-based product, a water-based polyurethane may be the solution. Water-based finishes are becoming very common, giving you the best attributes of varnish with the ease and low toxicity of water-based products. However, these finishes look less than sexy. (Okay, we'll admit it — they look like plastic.) They also raise the grain of the wood, so you have to add an extra step when using them.

You prepare for water-based polyurethanes in the same way you prepare for oil-based versions. Sand the surface well with 220-grit paper and wipe it clean. You can use a water-dampened rag to wipe off the sanding dust, but remember that it will raise the grain, which means that you have to sand it lightly again. This leaves some sanding dust, which leads to you wanting to wipe again, and so on. We usually wipe the final sanding with a tack cloth.

Because the grain is going to rise no matter what, we apply a sanding sealer and, after it dries, go over the surface with a 320-grit sandpaper to knock the grain down again. Then we wipe the surface with a dry cloth.

Apply water-based polyurethane by following the same procedure used for oil-based preparations. (See the section "Varnish and oil-based polyurethane" earlier in this chapter.) The only difference is that some water-based products dry pretty quickly, so you need to stop messing with the finish before it starts to get tacky. Also, we usually don't sand after the first grain-raising coat unless we need to get rid of brush marks or dust specks that have gotten in the finish. After the final coat (three or four is usually enough), you can either leave it alone or give a rubdown with #0000 steel wool wetted with water if you want less gloss.

Because this product is water-based, cleanup is easy. Just use soap and water.

Book VI
Plumbing

In this book . . .

*I*f you're like most people, a chill goes down your spine when you hear the word *plumbing*. The thought of fixing problems yourself — and preventing them from happening in the first place — is probably not one you entertain often, especially when everything's working well. Plumbing doesn't usually become a priority until you're standing in 6 inches of murky water wondering what to do next, and then most people's first thought is, "Where can I find a good plumber?"

This book takes the seemingly complicated world of plumbing and puts it in plain English. We make sense of the mess of pipes running into, out of, and throughout your house. And we give you the power to tackle plumbing problems yourself — as well as the insight to know when you need a plumber.

Here are the contents of Book VI at a glance.

Chapter 1

The Plumbing Do-It-Yourselfer

In This Chapter
▶ Doing plumbing tasks yourself
▶ Hiring a plumber when you need to
▶ Understanding building codes

Considering the range of plumbing-related replacements and repairs, a do-it-yourselfer can find plenty to do. Plumbing skills are sort of like computer skills: After you know how to format a proposal or generate a spreadsheet, you can do it again and again, although it may have seemed difficult at first. Well, after you unclog a kitchen drain, you can use that skill (and the tools you acquire in the process) many more times. You can then confidently tackle a stopped-up bathroom drain and, before long, become the neighborhood know-it-all for solving plumbing problems — all because you took the first step and plowed through the shreds of avocado in your kitchen sink's garbage disposal.

Figuring Out When to Do It Yourself

You can figure out how to do most plumbing jobs with a little know-how, an understanding of the rules (codes), and some spare time. Some of the easiest plumbing jobs to do yourself — mostly preventive maintenance — are the following:

✔ **Clearing slow-draining sinks and tubs:** This task usually involves using a plunger or opening a trap to remove hair, food, or paper. You may need to use a hand auger to get the proper flow of water through the drain. Tub drains are harder to clean than sink drains, and getting the pop-up drain stopper properly adjusted may take several tries, but you can do it yourself. (Chapters 4, 5, and 6 cover a variety of ways to unclog drains.)

✔ **Repairing or replacing leaky valves:** The steady drip-drip-drip of a faucet is certainly annoying, but it's a repair that can wait until the week-end so that you have time to get your hands on the correct repair parts before you begin work. (Chapter 8 shows you how.)

If you don't already have shutoff valves (covered in Chapter 2) on the water supply lines under your sink, this is a good time to add them. Future repairs will be much easier when you can shut off the water to individual sinks or appliances. You won't have any questions, such as "Dad, when can I wash my hair?" when the main water shutoff valve (also discussed in Chapter 2) is closed for plumbing repairs.

✔ **Solving toilet-tank problems:** Whether the problem is a valve that won't shut off or a tankball that won't seat properly, these repairs can wait until you have the time to work on them (see Chapters 6 and 7). But don't wait too long. A small leak can waste plenty of water.

✔ **Maintaining the washing machine:** Don't forget to check the hoses. If they've been in use for several years, change them. Purchase a set of replacement hoses that have a braided reinforced cover to prevent the hoses from bursting. The small extra cost is worth it; if one should burst, you'll be calling for help from more pros than just a plumber.

✔ **Preventing winter freezing:** You can prepare for winter by insulating water and drain lines that are subject to freezing or by wrapping them with automatic heat tape. (Don't use heat tape on plastic pipe, though — it will eventually deform the pipe.) Read the directions on the package: Suggested applications for the tape and its electrical requirements should be described clearly. This prep work may save you from a huge mess after a sudden subzero freeze.

Knowing When to Call a Pro

Don't lull yourself into believing that you'll never need a plumber. If you have a plumbing emergency, you and your family need to know two things:

✔ The location of the main water shutoff valve (see Chapter 2)

✔ The name and phone number of a reliable plumbing repair company

In addition to relying on your local plumber for occasional emergencies, the following situations are best left to professionals:

✔ **Low water pressure throughout the house:** Several factors can cause this problem: obstructions (rust or debris) in the water lines, which can start at the meter and run all the way to the faucet *aerators* (small strainers on the end of the spigot); low water pressure from the city supply or a well; or even poor supply-line design. A good plumber knows how to analyze the problem.

✔ **No hot water:** It's obvious *what* happened, but unless the hot water tank is leaking, it may take a while to find out *why.* If the tank is electric, it could be a bad heating element, a tripped circuit breaker or blown fuse, a faulty thermostat, or a bad overload switch. On gas heaters, thermo-couple burners and igniters can fail.

No one likes to be without hot water for long. Your grandmother may have heated bath water on the stove, but people don't do it that way today. Call a plumber for this one — he or she likely has loads of experi-ence and can tell you if you need a new heater or if the existing one can be repaired. If the heater needs to be replaced, your plumber can carry the new one to the basement, hook it up, make sure that it works prop-erly, and dispose of the old one.

✔ **Sewer line stoppage:** If you've tried all the tricks you know to get your sewer line to drain properly, yet backups continue, you probably have a bad plug in the line that runs out to the main sewer. (Tree roots are often the cause.) Rather than rent one of the big sewer rodding machines that you may break — or that may damage your sewer — call a plumber or drain-cleaning service. If they get in trouble, they'll make the repairs.

✔ **Frozen pipes:** If a pipe freezes, close the main water shutoff valve (see Chapter 2) before attempting to thaw the pipe and open a faucet nearby. Check carefully to see whether the pipe has already burst or cracked. If it's bad news, you may need a plumber. If not, hair dryers and heat guns are the safest ways to thaw a pipe. If you must use a propane torch, do so with great care — old, dry wood (which usually surrounds pipes) catches fire easily. Even if the pipe isn't burst or cracked, you still may want to call a plumber — some plumbers simply replace a section of frozen pipe rather than thaw it.

✔ **Extensive water line damage (usually caused by freezing):** Repairing the problem can take up much of your valuable time. It's better to pay a plumber so that you can earn money at your regular job.

Hiring a licensed plumber

Your local government wants to limit who can mess around with the public sewer and water lines, so they offer licenses to plumbing contractors who pass a rigorous test.

Find your plumber at a party

We find that the best place to locate any contractor — including a plumber — is at a neighborhood party. Why? Because word of mouth is still the best source for a referral that you can get. Who better to work on your house than someone who has worked in your neighborhood, where the houses are often of the same vintage? (Read that as "similar plumbing systems.")

All licensed plumbing contractors are plumbers, but not all plumbers are licensed. A plumbing contractor can have other (sometimes unlicensed) plumbers working under his or her license — the licensed plumbing contractor is responsible for the workers' workmanship. The government may revoke this license if the plumber has a history of doing shoddy work. Most professionals take pride in their work and value their licenses.

If you consider hiring a plumber, find one who is licensed. This is especially important if you're hiring an individual to do a side job for you or work on the weekends — you don't have much recourse with an unlicensed plumber if the work is unsatisfactory.

Working up a plumbing contract

Just as important as finding the right plumber to do the job is having a clear written agreement with the plumber before any work begins. The agreement doesn't have to be complicated, but it should contain some basic points. A contract with a plumber to repair, replace, or install a fixture should include the following:

- A description of the work to be completed
- A detailed list of the materials (brand name, style, color, or other specifications of the exact materials) to be used
- The cost of materials and a list of all warranties that the manufacturer provides for any fixtures
- The cost of labor
- The job installation date
- The amount of deposit, if required

Understanding Building Codes, Permits, and Inspections

Building codes are guidelines created to ensure the safety and building standards of new and remodeled buildings. They cover all the components of a building, including its plumbing lines, by specifying the minimum standards for materials and methods used. Codes work hand in hand with building permits and inspections to guarantee that good workmanship is performed and quality materials are used.

The most important thing for a do-it-yourselfer to know about building and plumbing codes is that they exist, that they're important, and they must be followed when repairing, remodeling, or building a home. It's impossible for a homeowner to know all the interpretations of these codes, but building inspectors and licensed plumbers can provide the answers.

Most of the United States is governed by rules made by one or a combination of three building code organizations: ICBO, SBCCI, and BOCA. (In the future, the International Building Code will be the only code.) Each community has the opportunity to modify these codes to suit its own special situations and idiosyncrasies. Unfortunately, though, the rules don't always seem so logical.

Don't count on the large home centers carrying the proper materials for your area. These chains order supplies for all their stores, and one store may carry materials that aren't acceptable in your community. Small hardware and plumbing supply stores are usually more knowledgeable about code issues. The final authority, though, is a city code official.

The right side of plumbing codes

We can't possibly include all the rules in this book, so it's up to you to find out what the rules are where you live so that you don't make any errors. Before you plan any plumbing job, first check the local building codes to make sure that you know the requirements. You can purchase a copy of your local building codes from your town government: Go to the town hall and find the building department. You may find that this document is filled with technical jargon, so consider having a discussion with the plumbing inspector in which you explain your project. In most cases, he or she will be able to give you the necessary advice to keep you on the right side of the codes.

Permits and inspections

When do you need a permit? That depends. In general, if you're replacing a plumbing fixture, faucet, or appliance, no permit is required. If you're relocating a fixture, faucet, or appliance, though, you may need a permit. If you're adding or extending new plumbing lines or installing a major appliance, such as a water heater, it's likely that you need a permit.

To obtain a permit, you fill out a simple form that describes the work and its estimated value. If you're doing the work yourself, you indicate this fact; otherwise, you supply the name(s) and license number(s) of the contractor(s) you plan to hire. On large jobs, the town may require that you or the contractor post a bond, which guarantees that the work meets the code. If it doesn't, the contractor or you may have to forfeit the bond money. In our town, a building permit and inspection goes for $35.

Your best bet is to get a copy of your local building codes (or just the plumbing part of the codes) from your local building department so that you have a clear-cut explanation of the requirements. You can find the building department under the local government listing in the phone book.

We've had our ups and downs with building inspectors, but in most cases, they're there to help, not to hinder or halt the work that you want to do. Depending on the extent of the project, you may have to have two inspections: one after you've worked on plumbing pipes and lines (behind the wall), and a second inspection when the wall is closed in. Keep this in mind when you're scheduling your work and the inspections.

Chapter 2

The Plumbing System in Your Home

*B*efore you begin fixing leaky faucets or unclogging drains, you need to know how water gets from one place to another in your house. This chapter covers the basic plumbing system of a home, introducing you to the water meter and the gate valve. You also get a grip on the drain-waste-vent (DWV) lines, so you can toss that acronym around among your buddies and feel like a real pro.

This chapter covers the location of the main shutoff valve and the many other valves that are a part of your home's plumbing system. These valves enable you to turn off the water supply to the particular fixture or appliance that you're working on or having problems with. If you want to replace a sink in the bathroom, for example, you don't have to shut off the water supply to your entire house while you do the repair. Almost all houses have a shutoff valve wherever the main water supply comes into the house, with individual shutoff valves at toilets, sinks, bathtubs, showers, and appliances, such as dishwashers and washing machines. If your house has outdoor spigots, you may need to locate the valves for those as well. Fear not — this chapter has all the information you need to locate the valves in your house before you make large or small repairs.

The Water Runs through It

You can easily understand the plumbing system of your house if you keep a few basic facts straight:

✔ The skinny pipes bring the water in, and the fat pipes carry it out.

✔ Leaks in the skinny pipes or in anything attached to a skinny pipe can flood a house.

✔ Leaks in the fat pipes cause your house to stink.

Okay. Plumbing is a little more involved than that, but if you think of your house as having two different water systems — one that brings fresh water in (see Figure 2-1) and another that takes waste water out to a sewer or septic system — the maze of pipes throughout your house may start to make some sense.

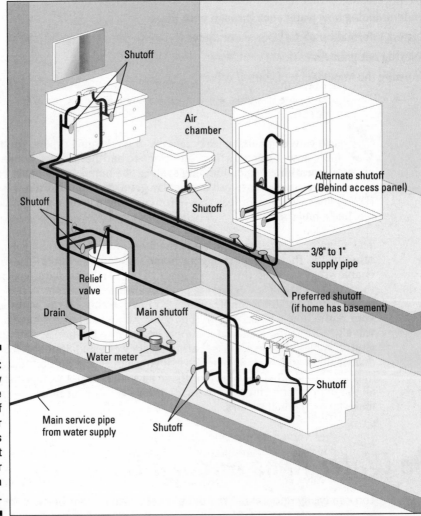

Figure 2-1: An overview of the network of the water supply pipes that are part of the water system in a house.

Plumbing really isn't complicated, and modern plumbing materials, such as plastic pipes and fittings (elbows and unions), enable you to tackle home plumbing projects that only a decade ago would have been considered too difficult for do-it-yourselfers. Recognizing the growth of the do-it-yourself market, manufacturers of plumbing tools, fixtures, and materials are constantly improving their packaging and instructions.

Most building departments now allow homeowners to do plumbing work on their own houses. Of course, regardless of who does the work, it still must meet the local building codes. So in Chapter 1, we provide important information about how to make sure that the work that you or the plumber that you hired does passes the code.

Book VI

Plumbing

Getting Water to Your House

Water running through the municipal water main is carried to your house by a smaller pipe that leads underground from the water main into your house. The water typically passes through three valves and a water meter on its trip to your house.

The three valves that help bring water to your house are the following:

- **Corporation stop:** The valve at the municipal water main that's buried underground, usually under the street, is used to turn off the water from the main to the curb stop. You'd have to dig a hole in the street to get to this valve, so you need to hire a professional if this is your plumbing problem.

- **Curb stop:** A valve that's somewhere between the corporation stop and your house is controlled by the municipality and is usually located close to the street. It may be in a chamber holding the water meter or in a cast-iron sleeve called a *buffalo box*. In northern locations, the curb stop is buried deep in the ground to prevent freezing — you need a special long-handled wrench to turn this valve on or off. In more temperate climates, this valve is located closer to the surface. Look around your property and find out where this valve is located. (The cast-iron head is a real lawnmower buster.) If you ever face a leak in the pipe between the street and your house, this is the valve to turn off. You may not be able to turn it off yourself, but you can call the city or show the plumber where it is.

- **Meter valve:** The third valve is inside your house. This valve is usually installed just before the water meter (so if the water meter is outside, this valve may be outside, too). Whoever installed the water meter installed the valve so that the meter can be removed for servicing should it fail.

The main shutoff valve

After the water passes through the three city-installed valves, it comes to what is known as the *main shutoff valve*. This valve is usually in the basement or on an outside wall in a utility area of the house. The main shutoff valve allows a full flow of water through the pipe when it's open. Turning off this valve (by turning it clockwise) cuts off the water supply to the entire house.

The main shutoff valve in your house probably has one of two designs:

- **Gate valve:** Gate valves are very reliable and last for years, but they become difficult to turn after not being turned for years. If you haven't closed the main shutoff valve since you moved into your house, do it now. Better to find out that you can't turn it with your bare hands now than to wait until you're standing in 6 inches of water.

- **Ball valve:** Houses with plastic or copper main water pipes leading into the house may have a full-flow ball valve. This valve is open when the handle is aligned with the pipe. To close it, turn the handle clockwise ¼ turn so that it's at a right angle to the pipe.

The main valve is the one to stop most plumbing catastrophes, such as a burst pipe. Make sure that everyone in the household knows where this valve is located and knows how to turn it off. Turning the handle clockwise closes the valve. You need to turn the handle several turns to fully close the valve.

After you've closed and opened the valve, it may start to leak a bit around the valve stem. The stem of the valve is held in place with a packing nut. Tighten this nut just enough to stop the leak. Don't overtighten it or the valve is difficult to turn again. (If you need a cheat sheet to remember which way to turn the control, use a label or tag with the simple reminder: "Right off" with an arrow pointing right, for example. See Figure 2-2.)

 Anytime you shut off the water and allow the pipes to drain, unscrew the *aerators* (small screens) on the ends of all faucets before you turn the water back on. Doing so keeps the small particles of scale that may shake loose from inside the pipes from clogging the small holes in these units. See Chapter 4 for more information about unclogging an aerator.

The water meter

If you wouldn't mind breaking any part of the water supply system, it's probably the water meter. Unfortunately, as water meters begin to fail, they usually run fast and record too much water usage, not the other way around. Besides, if your water meter stops, your local water company simply prorates your water usage to an average.

The meter is owned and monitored by the water company. Sometimes, the meter is buried in the ground and covered with a popup lid; it's usually located near the front of the house or on the side of the house near the street. In a cold climate, the meter may be located inside the house, but most municipal water companies have modified inside meters so that they can be read from the outside. By using plain old arithmetic, computing the difference between last month's reading and this month's reading, the utility company can figure out how much water your household has consumed. Sometimes, meter readings are done on an estimated basis; other times, meter-readers prowl through your neighborhood with handheld gizmos into which they input the readings on the meters.

By comparing the reading of the water meter over a very short time, you can spot a major leak. If you turn off all the faucets (indoor and outdoor), along with any appliances that may use water (such as a dishwasher or washing machine), no water should be flowing through the meter. To check for a major leak, make sure that everything is off and then record the meter reading. Check the meter in a few minutes, and it should read the same. If the dials have moved, you have a leak.

This technique isn't good for a minor leak, such as a dripping faucet. Eventually, the meter records the water used, but the amount is so small that it's difficult to notice any meter movement. Don't let the apparent lack of movement in the meter fool you, though. Over time, even a small drip, drip, drip wastes hundreds of gallons of water, which is why we devote later chapters in this book to fixing leaks.

Because you pay for water that passes through the meter, any leak past the water meter can cost you big bucks. If water leaks from the pipes that lead to your house, it doesn't pass through the meter and therefore can't be counted by the water company. Any leak, however, can cause damage to your house.

Book VI

Plumbing

Figure 2-2:
Label a tag on all shut-off valves showing an arrow pointing to the right (clockwise) to shut it off and to the left (counter-clockwise) to turn it on.

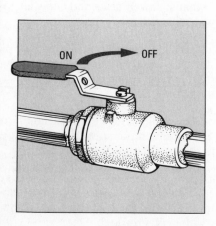

Reading a water meter

Most meters have a cover that opens when the hinged top is raised. The meter has a digital display or round dial that shows the number of gallons that have passed through the meter. The statement for a water bill reflects the total number or gallons used between the billing periods.

On the monthly or quarterly statement that comes from the water company, you can usually find an explanation of how to read the meter, so you can keep track of water usage yourself. Call your utility company and ask for directions if you're not sure how to read your own meter.

In most areas, sewer bills are based on water use. Some cities, however, give homeowners the option of installing two water meters: one for indoor household use, for which sewer rates are charged accordingly, and the other for a sprinkler meter that feeds outdoor hoses and lawn sprinkler systems, for which no sewer rate is charged. Not a bad idea, huh? Saves plenty of money!

Figuring Out Your Drain-Waste-Vent (DWV) Lines

The fat pipes in your house make up the *drain-waste-vent system* (also known as the DWV), carrying wastewater to a city sewer line or your private sewer treatment facility (called a *septic tank and field*).

- ✔ The *drainpipes* collect the water from sinks, showers, tubs, and appliances.

- ✔ The *waste pipes* remove water and material from the toilet.

- ✔ The *vent pipes* remove or exhaust sewer gases and allow air to enter the system so that the wastewater flows freely.

The drainpipes are made of cast iron, galvanized pipe, copper, or plastic (see Chapter 3 for more on materials). Local building codes that regulate the materials used in the DWV system have changed over the years, so most older homes have a combination of materials.

A typical bathroom sink is a good example of how all these components work together. You probably haven't spent much time observing the pipes beneath your vanity, but take a look and this is what you'll see:

- ✔ Water runs down the sink drain into a *p-trap* (so called because it's shaped like the letter), which fills up with water to prevent sewer gases and odors from getting into the house through the pipe. This water gets refreshed whenever more water runs through it.

✔ A drainpipe attached to the p-trap goes into an opening in the wall.

✔ Behind the wall (where you can't see), a vent line and drainpipe lead to a soil stack, which is the control center of the wastewater system. Drainpipes take the wastewater to the soil stack; through the stack, sewer gases are carried up to the roof through vent lines.

All the faucets and water appliances in a house use this same system of drains, pipes, and vents. All the waste lines have a cleanout, which is a Y-shaped fitting that's accessible so that you can clean out any serious obstructions within the system. Figure 2-3 shows a typical system, called a *plumbing tree*.

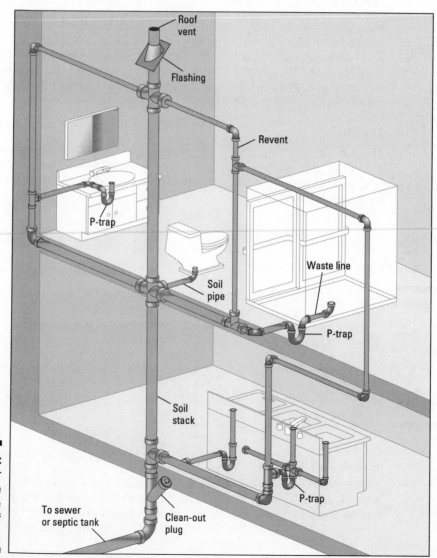

Figure 2-3: The major parts of the drainage system of a house.

Roof vent

Flashing

Revent

P-trap

Waste line

P-trap

Soil pipe

Soil stack

P-trap

To sewer or septic tank

Clean-out plug

Locating Shutoff Valves

The *shutoff valve* enables you to turn the water to a particular fixture or part of your house on and off. In general, shutoff valves are below or near the source of water. But unless you know where to look, the obvious isn't always so obvious. Take a tour of all these rooms and do some serious snooping around to find the valves in your house.

In the bathroom

Most bathrooms have shutoff valves that are designed to control the water flow to the toilet, sink, and bathtub or shower. These fixture shutoff valves are also called *stop valves,* because they stop the water from getting to the fixture. (Hey, some plumbing terms make sense!) Knowing where each of these valves is located can save you time and energy when you're doing plumbing repairs. We tell you just where to find them in the following sections.

The toilet

The shutoff valve beneath the toilet is one of the more accessible valves; it comes out of the wall or floor and is clearly visible (see Figure 2-4). In fact, you've probably seen it many times without noticing it. Just look for a handle behind your toilet.

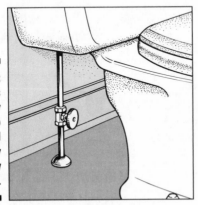

Figure 2-4:
Toilets usually have a stop located directly below the tank.

Sink or vanity basin

Your sink has two valves: one for hot water and one for cold (see Figure 2-5). A wall-hung or pedestal sink has shutoff valves that are clearly accessible, but the shutoff valves for a sink in a vanity cabinet aren't always easy to find or reach. So go on a cleaning binge, organize the bottles of shampoo and rolls of toilet paper in the cabinet under your sink, and find the shutoff valves. If you're lucky, the valves won't be tucked up high behind a cabinet partition. If they are, you may need to lie on your back and shine a flashlight to find them.

Figure 2-5:
Shutoff valves for both the hot and the cold water supply are usually located below the sink.

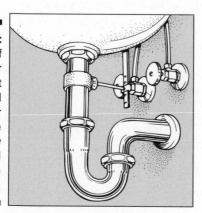

The bathtub or shower

Finding the shutoff valves for the bathtub or shower may take a little snooping. In most houses, one of the walls in a bathroom contains all the plumbing pipes. So look for the bathtub and shower shutoff valves on the opposite side of the wall that contains the plumbing pipes.

"How do I know which wall contains the plumbing pipes?" you may ask. The wall usually has a removable panel on the opposite side, which covers a recess in the wall and hides the pipes from view. The panel may be located in a closet, a bedroom, or a hall that's adjacent to the bathroom. So snoop around in your closets and look for a panel like the one shown in Figure 2-6. After you find it, remove the screws holding the panel in place, and you see the backside of the tub or shower. You may or may not find a set of shutoff valves in this wall recess.

If you can't find this panel, or you find the panel but then don't see any valves behind it, you haven't reached the end of your rope just yet. Many newer bathtubs and showers have shutoff valves installed behind the shower handle. Single-handle shower valves (in which you control the hot and cold water with one handle) have a cover plate sealing off a hole large enough that you can reach the shutoff valves from the bathroom side of the wall. If you remove the handle and cover, you may find shutoff valves (such as the ones shown in Figure 2-7) installed on the hot and cold lines just before they enter the valve body. If you have a double-handled shower valve, chances are that you don't have built-in shutoff valves.

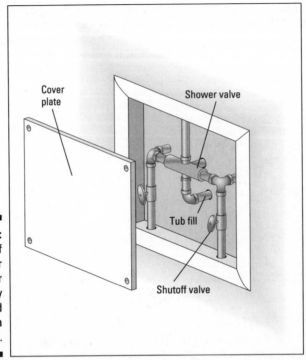

Figure 2-6:
Shutoff
valves for
the tub or
shower may
be located
behind a
panel.

Cover
plate

Shower valve

Tub fill

Shutoff valve

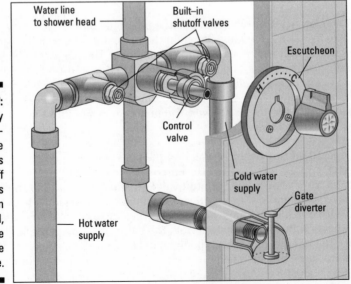

Figure 2-7:
Many
single-
handle
showers
have shutoff
valves
located in
the wall,
accessible
behind the
handle.

Water line
to shower head

Built–in
shutoff valves

Escutcheon

Control
valve

Cold water
supply

Gate
diverter

Hot water
supply

In the kitchen

The kitchen is another big place for water usage in a home. Depending on the appliances you have installed in your kitchen, you may have water running to one or two sinks, a dishwasher, and maybe an icemaker in your freezer. The following sections give you all the help you need to find the shutoff valves for these popular kitchen features so that you can get on with the task of repairing them.

The sink

The shutoff valves to the kitchen sink are located inside the base cabinet directly underneath the sink. The supply lines may either come out of the wall or emerge from the floor.

If the supply lines come out of the wall, you can find a shutoff valve on the hot line and the cold line. If the lines come out of the floor and you can't find shutoff valves on these lines, you may find a pair of valves in the basement, under a sink.

The dishwasher

If your dishwasher is next to the sink or in the same section of base cabinets as the sink, the shutoff valve is probably under the sink. Often, when a dishwasher is located near or next to the kitchen sink, the pipe leading to the dishwasher is connected to the pipe that supplies hot water to the sink. In this case, two shutoff valves control the hot water flow: One valve goes straight up to the hot water connection to the faucet, and the other goes off to the side of the dishwasher.

If the dishwasher isn't located next to the sink, the water supply comes out of the wall or the floor. The shutoff valve is located under the dishwasher. You can get to this area by removing the kickplate cover of the dishwasher, which should pull off easily. If you have trouble removing the kickplate cover, try lifting it slightly and then pulling it out. (See your owner's manual for specific instructions on how to remove this panel.) You should find the shutoff valve under the dishwasher, usually in the front, close to the water supply line running into the unit, as shown in Figure 2-8.

The icemaker

Your freezer's icemaker has its own water supply, which runs through a ¼-inch plastic or copper tube. In most cases, the tube leads to a larger pipe, where it's connected to a shutoff valve. Follow the tube to the larger pipe and look for the valve.

If you don't see the valve, your icemaker may work a little differently. The water supply still runs through a ¼-inch tube, but that tube may lead to a larger pipe that has a clamp-on device, called a *saddle,* that has a shutoff valve on it to control the supply of water.

Book VI

Plumbing

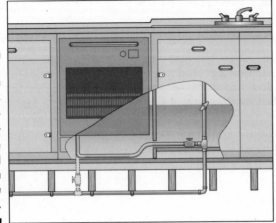

In the laundry area

The laundry area is another major place in your house where you use water. Your washing machine gets its water supply from something called a *hose bib,* which is hooked up inside a laundry box. This box contains the water supply and the drainpipe for the washer and is usually located in the wall just behind the washer. Instead of shutoff valves, you use the handles on the hot and cold hose bibs to turn the water on and off.

In a house without a laundry box, the hot and cold water lines are usually part of a laundry tub, and the faucets are used to connect the water supply pipes to the washing machine.

In the great outdoors

If your house has an outdoor faucet, called a *bib faucet* or *sillcock,* you can find the shutoff valve, called a *bib valve,* in your basement or crawlspace (located in the pipe leading to the faucet). Close the bib valve and then open the bib faucet to allow the water between the bib valve and the bib faucet to run out.

Letting the water run out of the pipes leading to your outdoor faucets prevents your pipes from freezing in low temperatures.

A valve that's designed to make draining the water out of the exterior portion of the pipe easier controls some bib faucets. This valve has a small, curled screw — called a *waste screw* — on its side. When you remove the screw, air can enter the pipe and speed the drainage. Turn the valve off, open the outside bib faucet, and then unscrew the cap on the side of the stop and waste valve. Doing so ensures that all the water drains out of the pipe. Then simply replace the cap.

Many houses have frost-proof bib faucets for which the actual shutoff valves are located well inside the house to prevent the faucets from freezing in the winter months. (See Figure 2-9.) If you have frost-proof bib faucets (also called *freezeless sillcocks*), you don't need to shut off the water at the valves inside the basement or crawlspace during the winter. Instead, these faucets have a thick pipe leading into the house. If you need to turn off the water supply for repair purposes, look for the shutoff valve at the inside end of the pipe, where it connects to the water supply pipe.

Never leave a hose attached to the frost-proof bib faucet during freezing weather.

Book VI

Plumbing

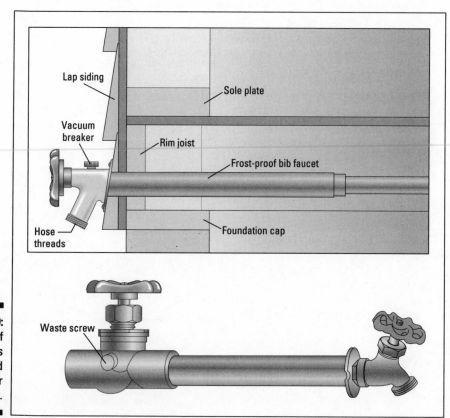

Figure 2-9: Frost-proof bib faucets withstand winter freezing.

Lap siding

Sole plate

Vacuum breaker

Rim joist

Frost-proof bib faucet

Hose threads

Foundation cap

Waste screw

Chapter 3

Materials and Tools

A hardware store clerk can always tell when a customer has a plumbing project to tackle. The first sign is the distraught look of someone carrying a rusted pipe or an odd-shaped piece of chrome. But the glazed-over look tells it all — the homeowner is clueless about what to buy to solve his or her plumbing problem.

You can avoid being that hopeless soul by taking a look at the materials and tools that we've gathered in this chapter. With a basic understanding of what this stuff is and what it does, you can walk down the hardware-store aisles with an air of confidence. You still may be clueless, but at least you'll be armed with the right vocabulary — and that's half the battle.

The larger the plumbing department, the more room for confusion. If you're lucky, you can find a hardware store, home center, or plumbing supply house that has plenty of in-store displays to demonstrate how plumbing parts and materials go together. If you're *really* lucky, you'll land in a store where the folks behind the counter or in the aisles have real-life plumbing expertise.

Finding Replacement Parts

Many times, you visit a plumbing department to find small replacement parts rather than large, new products. Take a look at these most popular replacement parts for plumbing appliances and fixtures so that, when the need arises, you know just what to ask for. This stuff may seem ho-hum, but knowing what you're looking for saves you countless return trips to the store.

- ✔ **Washers:** A variety of washers are used in plumbing applications. They generally help seal a temporary joint. Probably the most common washer is used inside the *female end* (the end that screws onto the faucet) of a garden hose. Washers are also used inside a faucet to seal the joint between the smooth valve seat that's inside the faucet and the valve stem, to prevent the flow of water. When you open a faucet, the washer rises above the valve seat, which allows the water to flow.

- ✔ **Aerator:** An *aerator* is a small system of screens and a baffle that's screwed into the end of many kitchen and bathroom faucets. Aerators introduce air into the flow of water and make it appear foamy. Aerators can become clogged with debris, so clean them regularly.

- ✔ **Valve seat:** A valve seat is present in the inside bottom of most faucets. These dime-sized, donut-shaped brass seals are threaded on the bottom and are screwed into place with a special seat-removing tool that's similar to a large Allen wrench — see Figure 3-1. Because they're made of brass, which is very soft, valve seats deteriorate over time, causing faucets to drip.

- ✔ **Valve stem:** A valve stem is located under the handle of both a hot- and a cold-water faucet. On the bottom of every valve stem is a washer that wears out over time. If your faucet is leaking, you want to replace this washer first. You can also find an o-ring or stem packing (which looks like string wrapped around the stem) designed to prevent water from leaking around the base of the handle (see Figure 3-1). Replace either the o-ring or the stem packing if water leaks from the faucet stem's base.

- ✔ **Washerless faucet parts:** Washerless faucets don't have valve seats, washers, or valve stems. Instead, they have a ball mechanism — the most common type being a kitchen faucet with a single lever handle. If this type of faucet starts to drip, the internal o-rings and/or ball mechanism need to be replaced. Replacement kits are widely available at home improvement and plumbing supply shops. Some washerless faucets have a cartridge-type mechanism that you can replace.

- ✔ **Toilet float:** A toilet float, shown in Figure 3-2, is a mechanism inside the toilet tank that turns on the water when you flush and turns off the water after the tank has refilled. Some toilets have a ball float — about the size of a softball — on the end of a metal rod; others use a can-shaped cylinder that moves up and down according to the water level in the tank. An overflow tube inside the tank prevents the tank from overfilling.

- ✔ **Toilet flapper:** A toilet flapper is located in the bottom of the toilet tank. When you push the flush lever down, a small chain lifts the flapper and allows the water in the tank to flow and flush the toilet.

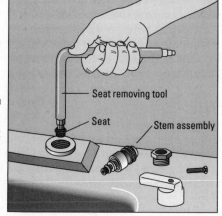

Figure 3-1:
A faucet showing the valve seats and stem assembly.

Seat removing tool

Seat

Stem assembly

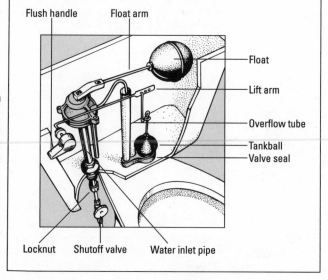

Figure 3-2:
The interior of a toilet tank showing the toilet float mechanism.

Flush handle   Float arm

Float

Lift arm

Overflow tube

Tankball
Valve seal

Locknut   Shutoff valve   Water inlet pipe

Common Plumbing Supplies

Just like a good cook has a kitchen full of supplies to create new and exciting entrees, a do-it-yourself plumber needs a stash of stuff to work with pipes and fixtures. Here's a rundown of the basic materials to have on hand:

✔ **Plumber's putty:** This material looks like modeling clay and is designed to stay soft and semi-flexible for years. Use it to make a seal between plumbing fixtures and in areas that have no water pressure. When you install a new faucet, for example, apply plumber's putty under the faucet where the faucet meets the top of the sink — this putty helps prevent water from seeping under the faucet and into the sink cabinet below. Other uses for plumber's putty include sealing drains in sinks, bathtubs, and shower stalls; sealing frames around sinks; and sealing other fixtures and bowls.

✔ **Pipe joint compound:** Pipe joint compound is sometimes referred to as *pipe dope.* It's used to seal the joint between a threaded fitting and steel pipe. Always use pipe joint compound when working with gas lines; many people also use it when working with galvanized steel water lines. Pipe joint compound is typically painted onto the threads cut into the end of the pipe that's called the *male end,* as shown in Figure 3-3.

✔ **Teflon tape:** You use this tape, a substitute for pipe joint compound, to seal the threads on steel pipe — see Figure 3-3. Use white Teflon tape for sealing pipe threads; use yellow Teflon tape, which is much thicker, for sealing pipe threads when working with gas lines.

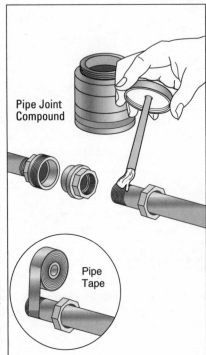

Pipe Joint Compound

Pipe Tape

Figure 3-3: A section of pipe with a union showing joint compound and Teflon tape.

- **CPVC cleaner:** You use CPVC cleaner to clean CPVC pipe prior to joining it with adhesive (see "Buying Drainage Pipes and Fittings," later in this chapter, for more on CPVC pipes). This purple liquid not only cleans PVC pipe, but it also softens the pipe slightly and makes the adhesive work better.

  Be careful when using CPVC cleaner — it stains whatever it lands on.

- **CPVC cement:** You use CPVC cement to fuse joints in CPVC pipe and fittings.

  Never use CPVC cement on ABS pipe.

- **ABS cement:** You use ABS cement to fuse joints on black ABS pipe and fittings (see "Buying Drainage Pipes and Fittings," later in this chapter, for more on ABS pipes and fittings). Using a cleaner prior to using ABS cement isn't required, but make sure you wipe the pipe and fittings with a clean cloth.

- **Solder:** You use solder (pronounced *sodd*-er) to seal joints when working with copper pipe. You heat the pipe and fitting with a propane torch until they're hot enough to melt the solder in a process called *soldering*. Solder is sold in rolls — usually 1 pound — and is made from various combinations of pure lead and tin. Look for 50/50 and 60/40 for plumbing joints. (The first number represents the percentage of lead; the second, tin.) The addition of tin helps the solder stick to the copper.

- **Leadless solder:** You use leadless solder to join water supply pipes. Many building codes require it because standard lead-based solder leaks lead into the water standing in the pipe. Your best bet is to use leadless solder for all plumbing projects.

- **Flux:** Flux cleans copper pipe and helps solder adhere better. It's available in paste or liquid form, but most plumbers prefer the paste type. You must use flux when soldering copper pipe; apply it with a small brush to both the end of the pipe and the inside of the fitting — see Figure 3-4.

Book VI

Plumbing

Figure 3-4:
Applying
flux.

Always wear inexpensive jersey gloves when working with solder and flux. The gloves eventually get eaten up (so use a cheap pair), but they protect your hands.

✔ **Steel wool:** You use steel wool to clean the ends of copper pipe and the insides of copper fittings prior to applying flux and soldering.

✔ **Emery cloth:** You use this cloth-backed sandpaper to clean the ends of copper pipe and the insides of copper fittings prior to applying flux and soldering.

✔ **Copper-cleaning brush:** You use this small wire brush to clean the insides of copper fittings — it cleans a fitting faster than an emery cloth does. Copper-cleaning brushes are sold in sizes to fit inside ½-inch and ¾-inch fittings.

✔ **Propane:** Propane is a liquid petroleum product that's used in a hand-held torch, which you use to heat copper pipe and fittings and to melt solder to seal a joint.

✔ **Wax bowl ring:** These large, inexpensive, donut-shaped rings are made from a special wax compound that seals out gases and water when you're installing a toilet.

Always install a new wax bowl ring when you're working with a toilet and the original seal has been disturbed.

✔ **Pipe thread cutting oil:** You use this light oil when threading the ends of steel pipe. Pipe thread cutting oil helps lubricate the thread cutter and wash away the steel particles that are created when the pipe threads are cut.

Finding the Right Water Supply Pipe

Water supply pipes are an important part of plumbing projects, and they're available in a variety of materials, including copper, iron, and plastic. The wide acceptance of plastic pipe by most building departments has been a boon to the do-it-yourself plumbing industry because plastic pipe is easy to cut and glue together. Most homes older than 20 years have pipes made of iron or copper.

Copper pipe

Copper pipe, used for water supply lines throughout most homes, is probably the most common type in use today. It's widely available in two basic types:

rigid and flexible. Both come in several wall thicknesses. This section gives you a basic rundown of copper pipe and its uses.

Rigid copper pipe

Rigid copper pipe is used extensively throughout modern homes for both hot and cold water supply lines. This pipe is widely sold in ½- and ¾-inch diameters and in lengths of 8 to 20 feet. Most suppliers carry several grades of rigid copper pipe, each having a different wall thickness — the most readily available are types L and M. Type K is a heavy-duty grade and is usually sold only in plumbing supply outlets.

Rigid copper pipe doesn't bend, so a variety of fittings are available to help you make the pipe go where you want it to go (see Figure 3-5):

- ✔ **Elbow:** Use an elbow to make copper pipe turn at an angle. Elbows (called *els* in the trade) come in 90-degree, 45-degree, and 22½-degree angles.

- ✔ **Tee:** A tee enables you to run another copper line off an existing line.

- ✔ **Straight connector or coupling:** Use these fittings when you want to continue a straight run of consecutive copper pipes.

- ✔ **Cap:** Use a copper cap to end a line of copper pipe.

All fittings for rigid copper pipe are soldered in place. (Refer to the section "Common Plumbing Supplies," earlier in this chapter, for an explanation of soldering.) Soldering involves the use of solder, flux (so that the solder sticks), and heat (usually from a propane torch).

Flexible copper pipe

Flexible copper pipe is sold in coils of various lengths and is available in two grades: K and L. Most stores stock the L grade. Common sizes of flexible copper piping include ⅜-inch, ½-inch, and ¾-inch diameters. The ⅜-inch size is commonly used for hooking up water supply lines to dishwashers and some icemakers. Flexible copper pipe and tubing are commonly joined with compression fittings rather than by soldering.

When you buy compression fittings for flexible copper pipe and tubing, the fitting comes with a single *compression ring.* When you tighten a compression fitting with a wrench, the compression ring seals the joint — but not always. If the joint leaks even after you tighten it, you may have damaged the compression ring when you tightened it. Purchase a few extra compression rings so that you can remove the damaged one and try again.

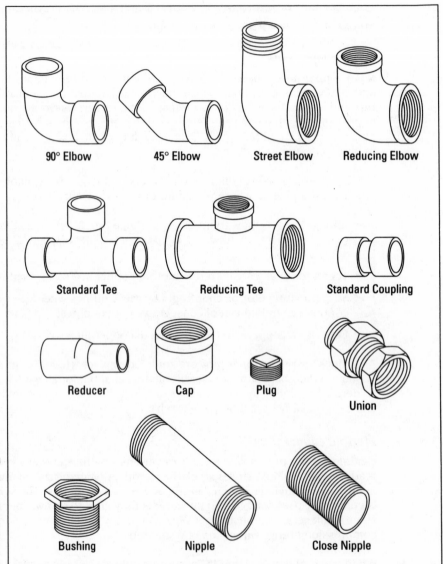

90° Elbow   45° Elbow   Street Elbow   Reducing Elbow

Standard Tee   Reducing Tee   Standard Coupling

Reducer   Cap   Plug   Union

Bushing   Nipple   Close Nipple

Figure 3-5:
Common
fittings used
to join iron,
copper, and
plastic pipe.

Galvanized iron pipe

Years ago, galvanized iron pipe was the only type of pipe that was widely
available for water supply lines. Today, other types of pipe, such as copper
and plastic, are beginning to replace galvanized iron because they require

less labor to install. Whether you have galvanized iron pipe depends on the age of your home and the part of the country you live in. If you have galvanized iron pipe, you'll find two basic sizes in your walls: ½-inch diameter and ¾-inch diameter.

If you aren't sure whether your pipes are made of copper or iron, try to stick a magnet to the pipe. If the magnet sticks, the pipe is iron; if it falls, it's copper.

Black iron pipe is used only for gas. Water heaters, furnaces, stoves, and other appliances that use gas are plumbed with black iron pipe. This pipe is available in the same sizes and has the same fitting configurations as galvanized iron pipe.

Book VI

Plumbing

When you need to join galvanized iron pipes together, you use the same kinds of fittings that you use for copper pipes — elbows, tees, straight connectors, and caps (see "Rigid copper pipe," earlier in this chapter, for more information about these fittings). In addition, you use a fitting called a *union,* which enables two sections of iron pipe to be joined or taken apart. Because iron pipe is threaded at both ends, you can thread only one end of the pipe into a fitting at a time. You thread pipes into fittings by turning them clockwise. As you thread the pipe into a fitting, the end that's going into the fitting is turning clockwise, but the other end of the pipe is turning counterclockwise. So you must thread pipe into fittings and fittings onto pipes in a sequential manner, which means that you have to plan ahead.

Plastic pipe

Plastic pipe is used in some parts of the United States for water supply lines, but many local building codes prohibit its use. The most common use for plastic pipe is in waste, vent, and drain lines (see Chapter 2). The second most common use is for underground sprinkling systems for lawn irrigation. Check with your local building department for specific requirements.

Two types of plastic water supply pipe are commonly used today: chlorinated polyvinyl chloride (CPVC) and polybutylene (PV) flexible tubing. Both kinds are available in ¼-inch, ½-inch, ¾-inch, and 1-inch diameters.

Plastic pipe is easy to work with because you can cut it to length with a fine-toothed saw. Joints for plastic pipes include elbows, tees, and caps (refer to Figure 3-5). Seal all the joints in plastic pipes with a liquid adhesive. Be sure to clean the joints for CPVC pipe with a special cleaner before applying a coat of adhesive.

Do it once — and do it right

If you're planning to replace old galvanized iron pipe with plastic, find out if plastic is allowed. You may think that it won't make any difference because the inspector will never know. He or she won't until you (or the person who inherits your house) sell the property. When the buyer has the house inspected and the inspector finds materials that aren't allowed, you have to replace those materials.

An old-time remodeler gave us some great advice the first time we added a new bathroom. He told us to get a building permit and then have the plumbing plan approved by the city inspector. The inspector changed a couple parts in the plan, but when he inspected the plumbing, it passed with no sweat. Getting prior approval is the best way to avoid problems.

PV tubing is joined with compression-type fittings or standard flared-type fittings that are used to join flexible copper pipe.

When you purchase any type of supply tube, always buy a longer tube than you need. You can cut copper and plastic tubes to the length you want.

Buying Drainage Pipes and Fittings

Pipes that carry water out of your home's drainage system look different from the water supply lines that bring water into the house. Fittings designed for drainage have to make gentle turns. Standard elbows used to join pressure pipes turn abruptly at 90 degrees, but a drainage elbow has a gradual bend. Drainage tee and wye fittings have 45-degree angles.

Cast iron pipes

Cast iron pipes, commonly used for drain lines in older homes, have largely been replaced by plastic drain lines. Joining cast-iron drain lines involves molten lead and plenty of mess. If you have to fool with cast-iron drainage pipes, we strongly recommend that you call in a pro. This pipe is heavy, is difficult to work with, and requires special tools.

Plastic pipes

Plastic drainage pipes and fittings have revolutionized the plumbing industry. They're much lighter than cast iron and are a lot easier to work with. Most building codes allow plastic drainage systems, but before you begin any plumbing project, check your local building codes to determine exactly which types of pipes are allowed in your area. (See Chapter 1 for more information about building codes and permits.)

Two basic kinds of drainage pipe are commonly used today: polyvinyl chloride (PVC) and acryaonitrile-butadiene-styrene (ABS). Both types are suitable for drainage. Plastic drainage pipe is available in several wall thicknesses; schedule 40 is the most widely available. Common diameters for these pipes include 1½ inches, 2 inches, 3 inches, and 4 inches. You can also find corresponding plastic fittings to match the pipes produced in cast iron, which are helpful if you want to replace iron with plastic in your home. (See Figure 3-6.)

When you're choosing fittings for pipes less than 2 inches in diameter, make sure to choose a drainage fitting and not one designed for supply piping.

When you're buying adhesive for ABS or PVC plastic pipe, always purchase the type of adhesive recommended by the pipe manufacturer. Although so-called universal adhesives are available, most local building codes require ABS adhesive for ABS pipe and PVC adhesive for joining PVC pipe.

Book VI

Plumbing

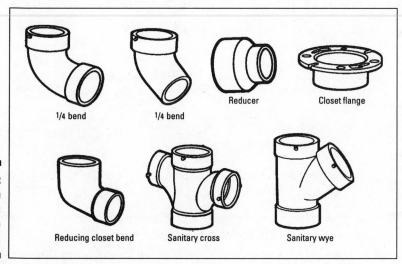

Figure 3-6: Common plastic drainage fittings.

1/4 bend 1/4 bend Reducer Closet flange

Reducing closet bend Sanitary cross Sanitary wye

Stocking Up on Valves

Valves control the flow of water in pipes. Your home has a valve on the incoming water line so that you can stop the inflow of water (see Chapter 2).

Some valves have a round knob on top that you turn to open or close the valve, but others have a single lever that you push or pull to open or close the valve. Valves are used for all types of plumbing pipe and are available with threaded ends (for use with galvanized steel pipe) and smooth ends (for use with soldered copper joints). You can also find valves with plastic bodies for use with adhesive in a plastic pipe application.

 When you're buying valves, be sure to buy the right kind. Some valves have threaded female ends that accept the threaded end of a pipe. Valves are also available to attach to copper and plastic piping — this kind features unthreaded female ends designed to be soldered or solvent-welded to the pipe. Still others have a compression-type female end that clamps down on the pipe when you tighten the compression nut.

Many different varieties of valves exist. In the following list, we introduce the kinds of valves that you're most likely to encounter. See Figure 3-7 for examples.

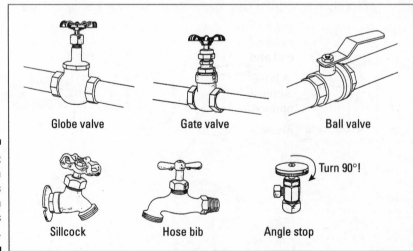

Figure 3-7: Common valves available in both brass and plastic.

Globe valve   Gate valve   Ball valve

Sillcock   Hose bib   Angle stop   Turn 90°!

✔ **Gate valve:** A gate valve allows the full flow of water through the valve and is the best kind of valve to use at the main shutoff and in pipes supplying cold water to a water heater or other device where water flow is important. Gate valves don't have rubber compression gaskets; instead, they rely on the close fit of the parts to stop the water. Turning the handle counterclockwise raises the wedge-shaped gate, allowing the water to flow.

✔ **Ball valve:** Ball valves can provide full flow of water. A lever opens and closes them. Inside the valve is a ball with a hole through it. When the hole in the ball is aligned parallel with the pipe, water flows through the valve. When the ball is turned with the hole across the pipe, the water is blocked. The lever is aligned with the hole in the ball. To close a ball valve, push the lever perpendicular to the pipe; to open it, push the lever parallel with the pipe.

✔ **Globe valve:** Globe valves, which are less expensive than gate valves, are a good choice for general water control where full flow is not necessary. These valves have a rubber compression washer that's pushed against a seat to squeeze the water flow.

✔ **Stop valve:** Stop valves are a variation of globe valves. They're designed to control water running to sinks and toilets. Stop valves come in two main varieties: angle and straight stops. *Angle stops* are designed to control the water flow and change the direction of the flow 90 degrees. They're mounted on the ends of pipes under sinks and toilets when the supply pipes come out of the wall. *Straight stops* are designed to be mounted on pipes that come out of the floor.

Choose a valve with the right kind of outlet. A valve is designed to attach to a pipe coming out of the wall or floor and to a riser tube going to the fixture. If, for example, you want a stop valve to attach to a ½-inch galvanized pipe and a ⅜-inch riser tube, purchase a valve with a ½-inch female threaded end and a ⅜-inch outlet to accept the tubing.

✔ **Hose bib:** A hose bib looks like a miniature faucet. It has a male-threaded end that's screwed into a coupling threaded to the end of a pipe. Hose bibs are commonly used to control water running to washing machines.

✔ **Sillcock valves:** Sillcock valves are used outside the house, on the faucets that you likely use with a garden hose (called a *bib faucet*). For houses located in cold climates, a freeze-proof version is available (see Chapter 2).

Using Plumbing Tools

When you're embarking on a new plumbing project, you have the upper hand if that hand is holding the tool designed for the job. Sure, a plain old screwdriver can tackle many of the jobs you need to do. We're not talking about pouring hundreds of dollars into outfitting your toolbox with tools. We do

Book VI

Plumbing

suggest that you begin to acquire tools as you need them, based on the suggestions we offer in this section. That way, you acquire the tools you need over time rather than forking over all your cash at once, and you have them for a lifetime.

Basic woodworking tools

As with any repair work you do around the house, you need a set of basic tools. Woodworking tools are a good place to start, because if you decide to replace a kitchen sink, for example, you'll be cutting and drilling holes in wood, driving screws, tightening bolts, and doing all kinds of jobs that at first glance seem unrelated to plumbing.

You should have these common woodworking tools in your toolbox:

- **Adjustable (crescent) wrench:** This wrench has a long steel handle and parallel jaws that open and close by adjusting a screw gear.

- **Allen wrenches:** A set will do.

- **Assorted screwdrivers.**

- **Carpenter's level.**

- **Claw hammer.**

- **Hacksaw.**

- **Locking pliers (also known as Vise-Grips):** Pliers with short jaws that you can open and set to a specific size by turning a jaw-adjustment screw in the back of the handle. When you squeeze the handles, the jaws clamp together.

- **Metal files:** You want to have both a flat and a half-round type with shallow grooves that form teeth.

- **Power drill:** ⅜-inch variable-speed, reversible drill with a variety of drill bits.

- **Retractable tape measure.**

- **Slip-joint pliers:** A tool with curved-toothed jaws and a hinge that adjusts or "slips," making the jaw opening wide or narrow.

- **Staple gun.**

- **Torpedo level:** This tool is a shorter, 8- to 10-inch version of a carpenter's level. It's useful for plumbing applications because it fits into restricted areas.

- **Utility knife.**

Tools for measuring

Accurate measuring is essential when you're installing new water or drain lines. As we point out in "Finding the Right Water Supply Pipe," earlier in this chapter, you need to know the diameter and length of the pipe you need. A retractable tape measure can do most of the measuring — the hook on the end of the retractable tape measure catches on the end of the pipe, making it easy for you to mark a cutting point.

For more precise measurements, use a measuring device called a *steel rule,* which has both English and metric graduations. Steel rules come in lengths of 12 to 48 inches. (The shorter length is easier to use for measuring plumbing-related pieces.) Place one end of the rule against an inside edge of the pipe and read the size at the opposite edge. This measurement may have little relationship to the pipe's *nominal size,* or outside diameter.

Wrenches and pliers

A number of tools have been designed to help you work efficiently with different kinds of pipe. Other special tools make it easier to remove and install plumbing fixtures and associated components, such as water supply lines and drain lines.

Some of these tools, like a pipe wrench, monkey wrench, basin wrench, and groove-joint pliers, are the minimum you need for basic plumbing repairs. If you have these tools on hand, you're ready if you ever experience a plumbing failure. Have them on hand even if you don't plan any big plumbing projects in the near future. Besides, you can use many of them for other jobs around the house. Here's a basic rundown of these handy-dandy tools:

✔ **Pipe wrench:** This wrench, shown in Figure 3-8, has serrated teeth on the jaws, which are designed to grip and turn metal pipe. One jaw is adjustable, with a knurled knob. This jaw is spring-loaded and angled slightly, which enables you to release the grip and reposition the wrench without changing the adjustment. Pulling the handle against the open side of the jaws causes them to tighten against the pipe. Pipe wrenches come in different sizes, with 8-inch, 10-inch, and 14-inch being the most useful.

Don't use pipe wrenches on copper or plastic pipe. You don't have to turn a copper or plastic pipe because it's soldered or solvent-welded (respectively) to the fitting. A pipe wrench can also crush the pipe if you apply a lot of pressure to the pipe with the wrench.

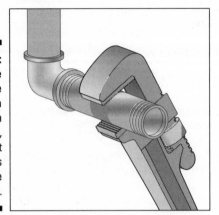

Figure 3-8:
After the teeth on the jaws of a pipe wrench grip a pipe, they won't let go unless you release the handle.

✔ **Monkey wrench:** The jaws of a monkey wrench are parallel to each other and set 90 degrees to the handle.

✔ **Spud or trap wrench:** This wrench is an adjustable one that's designed for handling drain trap and sink strainer fittings. The jaws are parallel and have a wide adjustment so they can grip the large-diameter lock ring that holds a sink strainer assembly in place. You set the jaws to size and then lock them in place by tightening a wing nut on the body of the wrench.

✔ **Strap wrench:** This tool has canvas webbing that wraps around pipes or plumbing fittings and enables you to tighten or loosen them without marring the finish.

✔ **Plastic nut basin wrench:** Many faucets have easy-to-tighten plastic mounting nuts, but they're still hard to reach. A plastic nut basin wrench (see Figure 3-9) is about 11 inches long and is designed to reach and tighten these nuts. This metal tool has notched ends that self-center on 2-, 3-, 4-, and 6-tab nuts and fit metal hex nuts.

✔ **Groove-joint pliers:** In larger sizes, these pliers are used for holding pipes. With the pliers' long-reaching parallel jaws, you can also tighten drains and use them for a multitude of other jobs.

✔ **Faucet spanner:** A faucet spanner is a flat wrench, usually stamped from heavy metal, used for installing faucets. You may get one when you buy a new faucet. These wrenches have a variety of hex or square holes punched in them, sized specifically to fit packing nuts and other fittings on faucets.

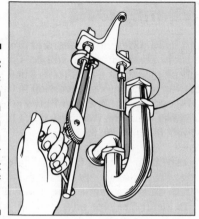

Figure 3-9:
A plastic nut basin wrench makes a tough job a little easier after you get the hang of using it.

You may need other specialty plumbing tools for one-time use. Don't go out and buy them unless the need arises. Better yet, you may be able to rent them.

Pipe clamps

Pipe clamps come in a variety of shapes and sizes. You use them to make temporary emergency repairs on a pipe that may have frozen and burst or sprung a pinhole leak due to corrosion. Place a rubber or plastic pad over the leak and then install the clamp over the pad and tighten — see Figure 3-10. Make sure the clamp extends at least 1 inch beyond the leak.

Figure 3-10:
After using a pipe clamp for emergency repairs, remember to make a permanent repair as soon as you can.

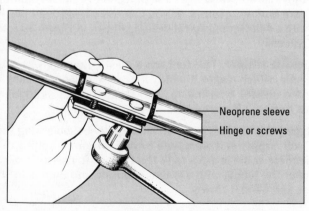

Neoprene sleeve

Hinge or screws

Pipe cutting and bending tools

Some tools are made specifically to bend pipes, cut pipes, and dress the cut end. When you need one of these tools, no substitution will do. Consider renting these tools if your pipe-cutting project is a small one. But if you'll be involved in more than one pipe-cutting job, consider investing in the tools. You'll enjoy a smug satisfaction when you can talk authoritatively to friends and co-workers about your pipe reamer, knowing that they don't have a clue about what you're saying. These tools include the following:

- ✔ **Tubing cutter:** Tube cutters come in sizes to fit tubing of different diameters. The most convenient size for homeowners is a model that cuts tubing from ³⁄₁₆-inch to 1⅛-inch in diameter. Some models are fitted with a built-in *reamer* to remove burrs inside the pipe after cutting. A *midget tube cutter* is designed for use in tight, tiny spaces. It doesn't have a handle, but large, knurled feed-screw knobs make it fairly easy to use.

- ✔ **Pipe cutter:** This large, heavy-duty cutter cuts iron pipe. It works similarly to a tubing cutter but has long handles for greater leverage.

- ✔ **Plastic tubing cutter:** This tool is designed for quick, clean cuts through plastic pipe and tubing. It features a compound leverage ratchet mechanism and a hardened steel blade and makes cutting pipe a one-handed operation.

- ✔ **Plastic-cutting saw:** This inexpensive saw is designed for cutting plastic pipe, plywood, and veneers. It has an aluminum or plastic handle and an 18-inch blade with replacements of either 12 or 18 inches long available.

- ✔ **Pipe reamer:** After cutting metal pipe, you find burrs or small ridges called *flanges* on the inside of the pipe. If you don't remove the burrs or flanges, they disrupt water flow, which leads to calcium buildup. Some cutters have built-in reamers, or you can use a half-round file. But a pipe reamer with a self-feeding spiral design, shown in Figure 3-11, makes the job fast and easy.

- ✔ **Inside/outside reamer:** This tool has a plastic housing with steel blades on the inside, which makes it handy for quick, clean, and easy inside reaming and outside beveling on ¼- to 1½-inch plastic, copper, or brass pipe. This tool isn't for use on iron pipe, however.

- ✔ **Spring-type tube bender:** This tool is a tightly coiled spring that aids in bending soft copper and aluminum tubing without crimping or flattening it. The benders come in sizes to fit the tubing. To use the tool, slip the bender over the tubing with a twisting motion and then place it over your knee and bend it slowly.

✔ **Flaring tool:** This tool is used for flaring soft copper pipe when used with flare nuts. You find this kind of pipe on icemakers and humidifiers. Place the flare nut on the pipe and then clamp the pipe in the proper size hole in the vise bar. Tighten the clamp to close the two halves of the vise bar tightly around the tubing. Slide the C-shaped die clamp over the vise bar and position the cone-shaped die over the mouth of the tubing. Tighten the large screw to which the die is attached, which pushes the die into the tubing and forces the edges of the tubing outward, thus creating the flare.

Figure 3-11: You can use a file or sandpaper to remove burrs, but a pipe reamer is helpful if you have several joints to repair.

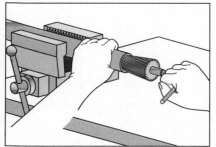

Plungers, snakes, and augers

A true tool geek wouldn't be without the special-use tools in this category. They give power to the weak when dislodging clogs in drains, drilling large holes, providing the oomph for bending pipes, and much more.

✔ **Toilet plunger:** Similar to old-fashioned sink plungers, the rubber cup on this type of plunger has an extension that fits tightly into the toilet bowl. You can fold back the extension when using the plunger for sinks. For the plunger to work properly, seat the ball in the bottom of the toilet, push down gently, and then pull up quickly.

✔ **Toilet (closet) auger:** When a plunger doesn't work, a toilet (or closet) auger, shown in Figure 3-12, is the next option. This tool is designed to fit a toilet bowl and clean out the trap. Fit the handle into the bowl and turn the crank while slowly pushing the flexible shaft through the hollow rod until it hits the blockage. (Chapter 6 offers more hints for unclogging a toilet.)

✔ **Powered closet auger:** Before you call a plumber, rent this tool to make sure that the toilet is really clean. Instead of cranking by hand, a drill-like driver powers the shaft.

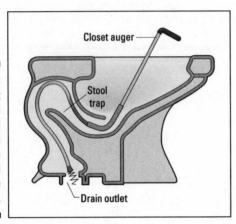

Figure 3-12:
A toilet auger is designed to reach into the trap and remove clogs.

Chapter 4

Unclogging a Kitchen Sink

In This Chapter

▶ Unclogging the kitchen sink and faucet aerator

▶ Clearing stuff out of the garbage disposal

Knowing how to unclog a sink drain is one of those life skills that no one teaches in any school or university. If you're lucky, when you were young and formidable, you watched your parent or a plumber perform this unpleasant task and paid close attention. If not, well, start reading. This chapter contains the best advice that we can give to help you dislodge the most stubborn clogs and get your sink drain flowing again. This chapter also includes tips for responding to the cry, "My ring just went down the drain!" and other drain dilemmas.

Unclogging a Sink Drain

With all the different kinds of food scraps that find their way down sink drains, it's not surprising that these drains get stopped up from time to time. Symptoms of a clog can range from water in the sink draining slower and slower to a stagnant pond in your sink.

The easiest solution for drain clogs (but not necessarily the environmentally safest) is to use any of a wide range of chemical drain uncloggers, available in solid and liquid forms at supermarkets, hardware stores, and plumbing-supply dealers. You pour the product in, wait for it to dissolve the blockage, and then flush the drain with running water.

Some chemicals can damage the plastic or rubber parts of a garbage disposal and can cause injury if the cleaner splashes into your eyes or onto your skin. If you decide to use chemicals, read the package directions and precautions carefully and follow them precisely; the directions vary by product. If the blockage doesn't clear after a couple of tries, you're ready for a more hands-on approach.

Finding lost treasure

It has happened to everyone: A treasured ring or favorite toy goes sailing down the drain, and you're desperate to retrieve it. The best rescue tactic is to remove the trap, hoping that the object is heavy enough to settle in the lower part of the trap. Don't run any water through the drain — water may flush it farther away.

Get a bucket and a wrench, and then follow the directions in the "Removing the trap" section. Keep the bucket under the trap to catch what's inside it when it's removed from the drainpipe.

Pouring a kettle full of hot boiling water down the drain is a nontoxic alternative that often eliminates clogs.

Removing the trap

To unclog your sink drain, remove and clean the *trap* (the U-shaped pipe located under the sink), as shown in Figure 4-1. Removing and cleaning the trap is easy. Wear rubber gloves and eye protection to shield yourself from the sharp pieces of debris or whatever has caused the blockage.

1. **Place a bucket under the trap (before taking it apart).**

   This way, you catch any debris or water that falls out when the trap is removed.

2. **Use a wrench or slip-joint pliers to unscrew the metal slip nuts a half turn or so, so that you can loosen them by hand.**

   Some traps have a clean-out plug instead of slip nuts. Simply remove the plug and allow the blockage to spill out.

   To protect the chrome finish on the slip nuts, wrap tape around the jaws of your wrench or pliers. Plastic traps have slip nuts that you can usually turn by hand.

3. **Scrape out any blockage from the trap.**

4. **Tighten the slip nuts with your hands to ensure that they're threaded on the trap correctly, and then tighten with a wrench or pliers.**

   Half a turn is usually all that's necessary to stop the trap from leaking; don't overtighten.

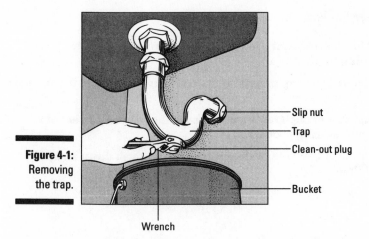

Figure 4-1:
Removing
the trap.

— Slip nut

— Trap

— Clean-out plug

— Bucket

Wrench

Some folks may advise you to try unclogging the sink drain with a plunger (covered in the following section, "Turning to a homeowner's best friend: A plunger") before you resort to removing the trap. We believe that cleaning the trap first is a better approach, because using a plunger can push the clogged material from the trap into the drainpipe, where it's more difficult to remove.

Turning to a homeowner's best friend: A plunger

A common plunger is capable of unclogging a drain that even the toughest chemicals can't budge. Unlike chemicals, a plunger uses suction to alternately push and pull the clog within the pipe until the force dislodges the blockage. If cleaning the trap doesn't clear the clog, try plunging the offending clog.

Don't confuse a common plunger that's used for drains with a toilet plunger, which has two cups, one inside the other. A *common plunger* has a wooden broomstick-like handle that attaches to a cup-shaped piece of rubber.

Before you start whaling away with a plunger, remove any standing water that may contain chemicals. Splashing diluted chemicals into your eyes can cause severe damage.

Here's the plunger procedure:

1. **If the sink has a stopper, try to remove the stopper first to give you a wider opening to the drain.**

2. **Pour a full kettle's worth of boiling water down the drain to break up the clog.**

3. **Fill the sink with enough tap water to cover the rubber portion of a plunger, thus assuring good suction.**

4. **Place the plunger over the drain and vigorously push down and pull up several times.**

If you're successful, you'll notice a sudden emptying of the sink.

Resorting to a snake

If neither cleaning the trap nor plunging clears the clog, your final weapon is a *drain auger* (also known as a *snake*). This tool, a coiled spiral snake that's usually about ¼ inch thick, with a handle on one end, works the opposite way that a plunger does: You push the snake into the clog and crank it to drive the snake farther into the obstruction, as shown in Figure 4-2. While parts of the clog break up and flush through the drain, the snake helps you gain access to the clog so that you can pull it out. Some snakes can fit as an attachment on an electric drill, giving it more power to force it through the clog. Snakes are especially handy because they're long enough to reach clogs that are deep within a drainpipe.

You can rent a manually operated or an electrical drain auger for a few bucks at a rental center. The equipment is easy to use, but ask the dealer for operating instructions.

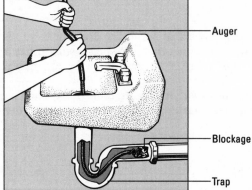

Figure 4-2: A snake and cable clear a drain.

Auger

Blockage

Trap

TIP

An ounce of prevention . . .

We may be too late with this information, but your best defense against clogs is to avoid them in the first place. The following are some common-sense practices to use:

✔ **Use a sink strainer.** A clogged kitchen sink is usually the result of garbage or foreign objects entering the drain. Use a sink strainer to prevent garbage and small items from entering the drainpipe.

✔ **Take care of your garbage disposer.** When using a garbage disposer, run cold water at full volume while the machine is chopping up the garbage; leave the water running for

a full minute after you shut off the disposer. This precaution flushes the garbage completely out of the small-diameter sink drainpipe and into the larger main drainpipe, where it's less likely to cause a clog.

✔ **Don't dump materials down your drain.** Do-it-yourselfers often flush building materials down the drain. The most common offender is plaster or wallboard compound, which seems innocent enough going down but can harden in the drainpipes and clog them. To prevent these clogs, never dispose of leftover building materials in sink drains.

Book VI

Plumbing

The basic process is as follows:

1. **Push the end of the snake into the drain opening and turn the handle on the drum that contains the coiled-up snake.**

   The auger begins its journey down the drain.

2. **Keep pushing more of the snake into the drain until you feel resistance.**

   You may have to apply pressure when cranking the handle to get it to bend around the tight curve in the trap under the sink. After turning the curve, the snake usually slides through easily until you hit the clog.

3. **Rotate the snake against the blockage until you feel it feed freely into the pipe.**

   The rotating action enables the tip of the snake to attach to the clog and spin it away or chop it up. If the clog is a solid object, the auger head entangles the object. If you don't feel the auger breaking through and twisting getting easier, pull the auger out of the drain — you'll likely pull the clog out with it.

4. **Run water full force for a few minutes to be sure that the drain is unclogged.**

   Sometimes, the clog flushes down the drain; at other times, the clog comes out attached to the snake.

If the snake doesn't fit down the drain or gets held up in the trap, you need to open the trap beneath the sink. Follow the instructions in the "Removing the trap" section, earlier in this chapter. Avoid contact with the water that comes out of the trap, because it may contain chemical drain opener. From the trap, insert the snake in either direction until you reach and clean out the clog.

Unclogging a Faucet Aerator

If a faucet seems to be running slower than usual, the aerator may be clogged with a build-up of mineral deposits. An *aerator* is a simple insert that fits inside a faucet spout's chrome cap — most faucets come with them — to conserve water and keep it from splashing all over the place, while still providing a steady stream and enough water pressure. Tiny holes in the aerator restrict water flow by mixing air bubbles into the water stream. The minuscule holes eventually become blocked by small particles in the water.

Follow these steps to clean and unclog an aerator:

1. **Place a towel or rag over the faucet cap or cover it with a bit of masking tape.**

   This protective barrier keeps the surface from being marred when you strong-arm the cap off.

2. **Using a wrench or pliers, turn the cap in a counterclockwise motion until it separates from the faucet.**

3. **When the cap is off, remove the screen and water restrictor.**

   Pay attention to the way these small internal parts are arranged. When the time comes to put the aerator back in place, you have to replace these parts in the same sequence and position. See Figure 4-3.

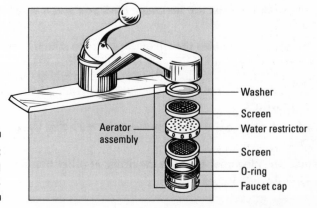

Figure 4-3:
Assembling
an aerator.

4. **Clean the screen by flushing it with water or using a brush. Push through the tiny holes with a needle or pin to unclog them.**

5. **Soak the aerator in a cup of vinegar overnight to clean out the small holes and flush it with clear water before reinstalling it.**

6. **Reassemble the aerator in the reverse order.**

You should notice a big difference in the water flow after cleaning the aerator — not gushing water but a nice, steady stream.

Unclogging a Garbage Disposal

Even a garbage disposal can be finicky, so don't expect it to devour and digest everything. For example, don't throw corncobs, artichokes, avocado pits, or fish and chicken bones down a disposal and expect it to continue working without a clog. Flip through the owner's manual to find out what your disposal's limitations are.

Clogs can and do occur, however. The following actions are what generally cause clogs in your disposal:

✔ Dropping a foreign object — usually a spoon or fork — into the disposal

✔ Feeding garbage in too rapidly

✔ Failing to run enough water (to completely flush out the drainpipes) while garbage is being processed

Never use chemical drain cleaners in a disposal. The chemicals are highly corrosive and may damage rubber or plastic parts.

Use Mother Nature's deodorizer for your disposal: Every few months, cut a lemon in half, throw one half in the disposal, turn on the unit, and let it run for a minute or two. The lemon removes the build-up of residue on the interior of the disposal and deodorizes the unit. You know it's working by the fresh lemony smell.

If the instructions in your user's manual are no help, follow these steps to unclog a disposal:

1. **Shut off the electrical power switch.**

   This switch is located under the cabinet, near the disposal, or on a wall nearby. If you don't find a switch, go to the main power panel and turn off the breaker or remove the fuse that powers the disposal.

Never put your hand in the disposal. Remember that the switch may be defective, so keep your hands out of the disposal even when power to the machine is turned off.

2. **Take a look in the disposal.**

A flashlight may shed some light on the problem — you may see a large object caught in the disposal.

3. **If an object caused the stoppage, use a pair of pliers to reach into the disposal and remove it.**

4. **Wait 15 minutes for the disposal motor to cool.**

5. **Turn on the power and push the reset or overload protector button.**

This button is located on the bottom side of the disposal.

If the disposal is still clogged, follow these steps:

1. **Turn off the power and insert a long dowel, a wooden spoon, or a broom handle — never your hand — into the drain opening.**

2. **Push the bottom end of the wooden probe against the *impeller* (the blades that grind up the garbage), as shown in Figure 4-4, and rock it back and forth to free it.**

3. **When the impeller moves freely, wait 15 minutes for the motor to cool, turn on the power, and push the reset button.**

Some disposal models come with a large L-shaped hex wrench. If you have such a model, turn off the power, insert the hex wrench into the opening in the center of the disposal's bottom, and turn the wrench back and forth until the impeller is freed. Again, wait until the motor has cooled, press the reset button, and then try operating the disposal.

Figure 4-4:
Inserting a wooden stick in the disposer.

Chapter 5

Unclogging a Tub or Shower Drain

In This Chapter

▶ Keeping your drains running freely

▶ Finding ways to unclog your shower or tub

▶ Cleaning and adjusting plunger-type and pop-up drains

A h, the luxury of taking a relaxing soak in the old bathtub or indulging in a long, hot, steamy shower — everyone has a preference, but when denied, it can be downright annoying. In most busy households, an out-of-commission tub or shower can throw a wrench in kids' and parents' schedules — a family nuisance to be sure.

A clog in a tub or shower drain usually doesn't come as a shock. The blockage comes on gradually. Take action as soon as you see that the water doesn't drain as fast as it usually does or when you find yourself standing up to your ankles in water that should have gone down the drain. This chapter shows you what to do.

Preventing tub and shower clogs

Tub and shower drains clog up with soap scum and hair — not a pleasant sight. As a defensive measure, fit a strainer over the drain to catch debris before it can enter and clog the drain. Keep the strainer in place and clean it after each bath or shower. If you get in this habit (and teach your kids to do the same), the nasty buildup just can't occur.

You can find replacement strainers in the plumbing section of your home center. Measure the diameter of the drain to find one that fits and then simply place it in the drain.

Clearing a Clogged Bathtub or Shower Drain

Sometimes, clearing a clogged drain is as simple as pouring a gallon of hot water down the drain to loosen the clog. If the water flows down the drain, repeat the process. That may be all that you need to do.

Some people rely on chemicals to open a clogged drain. It's as simple as pouring a chemical drain opener down the drain, waiting the specified amount of time, and then flushing the drain thoroughly with water. (Be sure to follow product directions carefully.) You may have to repeat this process a few times until the chemicals dissolve the blockage enough to dislodge it. With each application of chemicals, you may see incremental improvement in drainage. Chemicals are especially effective for clearing bathtub drains, because they contain protein-dissolving elements that can work wonders on the most common cause of bathtub clogs: masses of accumulated hair.

If neither hot water nor chemicals work, try using a plunger or snake. We describe how to use these tools in the following two sections.

Taking the plunge

A *common plunger,* also called a plumber's helper, has a wooden broomstick-like handle attached to a cup-shaped piece of rubber. (Don't confuse this piece of equipment with a *toilet plunger,* which has two cups, one inside the other.) Using a common plunger is simple. Just follow these steps:

1. **Remove the stopper if there is one.**

   The *stopper* is a pop-up plug that alternately seals the opening or opens the drain — see Figure 5-1. To remove it, push and pull it up and then down until it is released. Raise the *trip lever,* which lifts the stopper up, and remove the entire stopper assembly.

   If your drain doesn't have a stopper, remove the drain strainer by unscrewing it or prying it up around its edges.

2. **If you find an accumulation of hair and soap scum, clean the stopper by removing any debris and then flushing it in a stream of water. Reinstall the stopper assembly in the reverse order that you remove it.**

3. **Stuff a wet washcloth into the overflow holes to plug them up and improve suction.**

4. **Fill the tub with a couple inches of water, enough to partially submerge the plunger head, to assure airtight suction.**

5. **Push the plunger down and pull it up forcefully.**

   You know that the blockage has been dislodged when the water begins to drain much more quickly than it did before.

Putting a bit of petroleum jelly on the lip of the plunger helps form a tight seal, making the plunger more efficient.

Figure 5-1: Remove the pop-up assembly (or drain strainer) and any hair or soap scum from the drain.

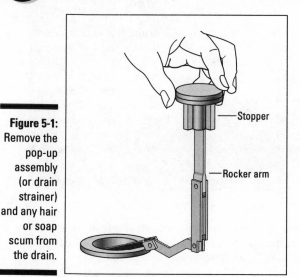

Stopper

Rocker arm

Charming your tub with a snake

If using a plunger doesn't work, try using a *drain auger,* or *snake,* to unclog the tub drain. (For more information about snakes, see Chapter 4.) Follow these steps:

1. **Remove the tub stopper or strainer.**

2. **Push the tip of the snake into the drain opening, continuing to feed the coil through until it meets an obstacle (see Figure 5-2).**

3. **Push the cable into the clog and crank it further to dislodge the obstruction.**

   Some snakes have an attachment for an electric drill, giving it more power to force through the clog. To remove a clog that's beyond the trap under the tub, rotate the snake while you push it into the pipe.

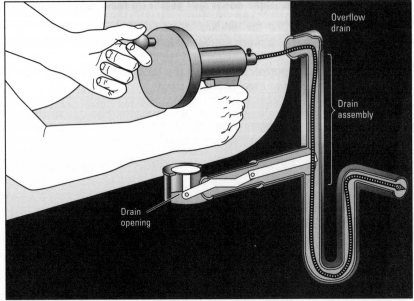

Overflow drain

Drain assembly

Drain opening

Figure 5-2:
Remove the overflow cover plate and feed the auger through this opening.

4. **If the snake continues to resist passing through the trap, remove the overflow cover plate, usually located at the end of the tub directly above the drain and below the faucet.**

   As you remove the screws that hold the cover in place, be careful not to drop the screws down the drain.

5. **If the drain-closing mechanism is attached to the cover, pull up on the cover; the linkage comes out of the overflow hole with the cover.**

6. **Push the snake directly down into the hole and through the trap.**

   Note that this approach doesn't enable you to get directly to any blockage that's stuck in the trap.

If the blockage is past the trap, somewhere down the drainpipe, reaching it may take you some time. The cable stops feeding in when it hits the blockage. You must work the snake against the blockage until the cable feeds freely into the drain — then you know that the clog is clear. Flush the drain with water to confirm that the blockage is gone.

Cleaning and Adjusting a Drain Stopper

Except for really old drains that rely on a rubber stopper to hold back the water, most sinks have a pop-up drain mechanism. Bathtubs have either the same type of pop-up stopper or a trip-lever (plunger-type) drain closure. When you're faced with a drain that won't hold water, you have to adjust the stopper. This section shows you how.

Trip-lever drain

A trip-lever drain system has a strainer over the drain opening and an internal plunger mechanism that closes the drain. The plug is operated by a lever located in the overflow plate at the front of the tub. Raise the lever and it lowers a plug into the pipe at the base of the tub, blocking the flow of water out of the tub. This plug may have a rubber seal on its base that can become old and cracked. Also, debris can get into the seat where the plunger rests, causing a slow leak.

Removing the plug, cleaning it, and adjusting the control mechanism cures most problems. Here's how:

1. **Remove the overflow cover plate.**

   The plate is held in place by a couple of screws. Remove the screws and pull out the linkage assembly, which is made up of the striker rod, middle link, and plug (see Figure 5-3).

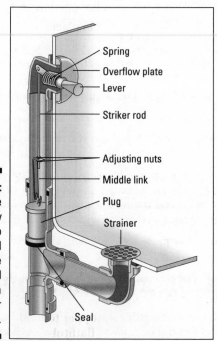

Figure 5-3: Remove the overflow plate to clean and adjust the internal parts of a trip-lever drain.

Spring
Overflow plate
Lever
Striker rod
Adjusting nuts
Middle link
Plug
Strainer
Seal

Book VI

Plumbing

2. **Clean any loose hair or buildup of soap scum from the linkage assembly.**

   This basic design has many different renditions. The drain in your tub may not be exactly like the one illustrated in Figure 5-3, but it'll be similar.

3. **Before you reinstall the plug, inspect the rubber seal (if there is one) at the bottom of the plug.** If it's cracked or broken, take the plunger assembly to a home center or plumbing supply house and get a replacement.

4. **Replace the linkage assembly.**

   You may have to wiggle the plunger a bit to get it to fall back into the drain.

5. **Run some water into the tub.**

   If the tub drains but doesn't hold water, adjust the plug so that it falls deeper into the overflow passage. Remove the assembly, loosen the adjustment nuts, and lengthen the linkage controls. A little adjustment — ⅛ inch or so — is all that's needed.

6. **Reassemble the assembly and test again.**

   Additional adjustments may be necessary.

Pop-up drain

The pop-up drain assembly has a drain stopper in the opening. A slow-running drain can be the result of a pop-up that isn't opening fully. A leaky drain may be the result of a bad rubber seal on the pop-up assembly or incorrect adjustment of the control mechanism that connects the pop-up to the lever at the end of your tub, which prevents the pop-up from closing fully.

Removing the pop-up assembly, cleaning it, and adjusting the control mechanism cures most problems. Here's how:

1. **Remove the pop-up drain assembly by pulling it out of the drain (see Figure 5-4).**

   Grasp the stopper and wiggle it around a bit to get it out. The stopper and the rocker arm it's attached to will come completely out of the drain. If you see a clog of hair or debris on the rocker arm, you may have to remove some of this goop before the stopper will come out of the drain.

2. **Remove the tub overflow cover plate by removing the screws and pulling out the assembly.**

   See the section "Charming your tub with a snake," earlier in this chapter, for more information about the tub overflow cover plate.

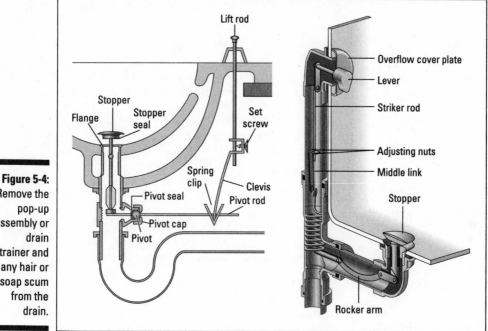

Figure 5-4: Remove the pop-up assembly or drain strainer and any hair or soap scum from the drain.

Labels on figure: Lift rod • Stopper • Flange • Stopper seal • Set screw • Spring clip • Clevis • Pivot seal • Pivot rod • Pivot cap • Pivot • Overflow cover plate • Lever • Striker rod • Adjusting nuts • Middle link • Stopper • Rocker arm

Book VI

Plumbing

3. **Clean the linkage assembly of any loose hair or buildup of soap scum.**

   This assembly is composed of the crank lever in the overflow cover plate, striker rod, middle link, and striker spring. The spring at the bottom of the control linkage is a magnet for hair buildup.

4. **Inspect the rubber seal (if there is one) on the pop-up. If it's cracked or broken, take the pop-up assembly to your home center and purchase a replacement.**

5. **Put the assembly back in its place.**

   You may have to wiggle the spring a bit to get it to fall back into the drain.

6. **Run some water into the tub.**

   If the tub doesn't hold water, adjust the pop-up so that it completely closes in the drain outlet. Remove the assembly, loosen the adjustment screw, and shorten the linkage controls. A little adjustment — ⅛ inch or so — is all that's needed.

7. **Reassemble the pop-up assembly and test again.**

   Additional adjustments may be necessary.

Chapter 6

Unclogging a Toilet

· ·

In This Chapter

▶ Diagnosing the cause of a toilet clog

▶ Unclogging your toilet in a variety of ways

▶ Unclogging the main line

▶ Knowing when to call for help

· ·

Although clearing a clogged toilet isn't the most pleasant plumbing chore around the house, no utility is used more often than *la toilette*. Getting it flushing — fast — is a top priority.

Diagnosing the Problem (Yuck!)

Sometimes, you can see what's clogging the toilet, but sometimes, the source of the clog remains a mystery. In either case, the chore at hand is getting the toilet flowing freely again, and for that, you need to do a bit of detective work.

When you flush the toilet, which of these results do you see?

✔ **The water isn't swirling down as usual.** Consider yourself lucky; this is a sign of an easy-to-fix problem. The mechanism inside the toilet tank may be clogged or stuck, so the tank isn't filling with water. See the section "Clearing the Main Line," later in this chapter, for a quick fix.

✔ **The water level goes down slowly and only weakly flushes the bowl.** This result usually indicates a partial block. Your toilet will probably clog completely the next time it's used, so get out the plunger.

✔ **The water level barely drops (if at all) and then begins to rise past the normal full bowl level.** This result is also an indicator of a partial block — one that may be located beyond the toilet.

✔ **The water continues to rise past the normal full bowl level until it overflows onto your bathroom floor.** To experience such an event is to understand the true meaning of the word *panic*. Your toilet is clogged. Follow the instructions in the next section to clear the clog.

Don't flush again if the bowl level rises past the normal height. You don't want to invite an overflow.

Clearing a Clogged Toilet

If your toilet plays any of the tricks mentioned in the preceding section, you have a clogged or partially clogged toilet bowl. Often, the clog is caused by a blockage in the *trap* — the curved passage inside the toilet bowl.

Don't attempt to unclog the toilet with a chemical drain cleaner. It usually doesn't work and you end up having to plunge or auger through water that contains a strong chemical. Even if you don't use a chemical drain cleaner, be careful when you handle toilet water and waste — it's laced with bacteria. Wash the area, your hands, and your clothing thoroughly with a disinfectant soap.

Partial or total blockage of a toilet requires one of three solutions, covered in the following three sections.

Using a plunger

A ball or cup-type plunger is designed specifically for unclogging toilets. The rounded lower surface nests tightly in the bowl, giving the plunger great suction action to dislodge the blockage. With the plunger in place, push down gently and then pull it up quickly to create suction that pulls the blockage back a bit and dislodges it (see Figure 6-1).

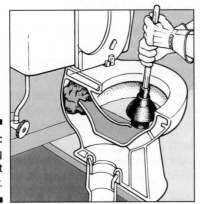

Figure 6-1:
Positioning
the toilet
plunger.

Using a toilet plunger (as opposed to a sink-type plunger) keeps you from splashing as much water around, because the ball of the plunger covers the entire hole. If all you have on hand is a small, sink-type plunger, try using it — it can't hurt.

Using a toilet auger

If using a plunger doesn't work, try using a toilet auger, which is different from a snake or hand auger (see the following section, "Using a snake"). A *toilet auger,* also called a *closet auger,* is a short, hollow clean-out rod with a spring coil snake inside that has a hooked end. Attached to the coil is a crank handle that you turn — it's designed to fit into a toilet bowl and clean out a clogged toilet trap. See Figure 6-2.

Follow these instructions:

1. **Pull the spring coil through the hollow handle until about a foot protrudes.**

2. **Insert the auger all the way in the bowl and push the spring coil back through the handle until it rounds the sharp bend in the base of the toilet trap.**

3. **Turn the crank while slowly pushing the flexible coil shaft through the hollow rod until it hits the blockage and pushes it through.**

Although the thought of renting or buying a toilet auger may not thrill you, the idea seems amazingly wise when you're faced with a clogged-up toilet. Toilet augers are inexpensive, and they're particularly handy, because most toilet clogs occur in the trap — exactly where this tool delivers its punch. Buy one *before* you experience a problem and have to explain to your dinner guests that the bathroom's temporarily closed for repairs.

Book VI

Plumbing

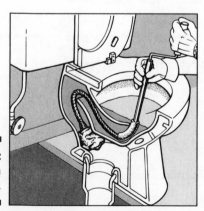

Figure 6-2:
Using a
toilet auger.

If you can't get the toilet running freely with a toilet auger, don't flush the toilet, even if it seems to run a little. The water may be backing up in the *soil pipe,* which is the large diameter pipe leading to the sewer or septic system (see the following section, "Using a snake," to find out how to handle this). If the water backs up there, it can start running out the basement sink or out of some of the first-floor fixtures. Not a pretty picture.

Using a snake

If the toilet auger doesn't do the trick, you probably have a blockage somewhere farther down the line — past the toilet trap and beyond the reach of the toilet auger's coil. It's time to rent a snake. (See Chapter 4 for details on this tool.)

Rent a snake that has a flexible shaft to bend past the tight curve in the toilet trap. The only thing worse than a clogged toilet is a clogged toilet with an auger stuck in the bowl; it's tough to explain to the guys at the rental shop why your toilet is stuck on the end of their snake.

After getting the snake home from the rental shop, follow these steps:

1. **Feed the flexible snake into the toilet until you feel it engage the clog.**

   You know you've hit the clog when the cable becomes harder to turn or refuses to move another inch into the toilet.

2. **Pull the snake back a bit to dislodge the clog.**

   The water level should go down, signaling that the clog is loose.

3. **Flush the toilet to push the clog down the drain line and, hopefully, out to the sewer or septic system.**

   If the clog is a diaper or rubber ducky, you may have to pull the offending item all the way out of the toilet to clear the line.

Singing the hard-water blues

Your toilet may flush slowly from a buildup of scale due to hard water in the high-pressure jet opening (hole) that's built into the trap of the bowl. This jet starts the siphoning action and swirling of water in the bowl, drawing waste down and out of the toilet. You can sometimes use a coat hanger to clear the hole, but if the toilet is too scaled or limed up, it's best to replace the toilet.

The snake is a powerful tool — use it cautiously so that you don't damage the toilet or drain line by using too much force. If the coil becomes really hard to turn, back off a bit and pull it out of the toilet a few inches before attacking again. If you turn the auger too hard, you can kink the wire coil.

Clearing the Main Line

The *main line* is the passageway for the waste that comes from the toilet and from the entire sink and tub traps. The line leads outside the house to the sanitary sewer or septic system. This section tells you how to clear a clog in that main line, which is also called the *sewer line*. Makes sense, right?

When the clog is beyond the fixture

Sometimes, the clog is so far from the toilet or sink drain that you can't reach it with a snake. If you've fed the snake through the toilet or sink drain to its full length and still haven't reached the clog, your last resort before calling in the pros is to feed the snake through the main clean-out in the sewer line that leads out of your house.

Removing the clean-out plug

The *sewer clean-out* is a fitting with a removable plug. It's usually located at the base of the *main soil pipe* (a large-diameter cast-iron, copper, or plastic pipe) where it enters the floor of the basement or takes a 90-degree turn to pass through the foundation wall. The clean-out may also be located in the basement floor.

To keep the waste inside the pipe, this fitting has a removable plug that's screwed into the clean-out fitting. Plastic clean-out plugs usually come out easily, but removing a clean-out plug from a cast-iron plumbing system can be a challenge.

To remove the clean-out plug, gather up the following tools:

- Large pipe wrench
- Small can of penetrating oil, such as Liquid Wrench or WD-40
- Hammer
- Cold chisel (a thick, short, hexagonal, steel bar tool)

✔ Bucket

✔ Work gloves

✔ Goggles or safety glasses

After you assemble your tools, follow these steps:

1. **Locate the clean-out plug.**

   Look for a round plug with a square lug on it.

2. **With your work gloves on, try to open the clean-out plug with a pipe wrench.**

   Place the wrench in the square tab located in the center of the clean-out plug and turn it counterclockwise.

3. **If using a pipe wrench doesn't work, apply oil to the joint between the soil pipe and plug.**

   Allow the oil to work its way into the joint for 10 or 15 minutes and then give the pipe wrench another try. Doing so usually loosens a brass plug.

If the plug isn't brass, it probably has rusted into place. To get it open, you have to break it into pieces. This is standard practice with plumbers but may seem a bit extreme to you. If you're not comfortable doing this, call a pro.

If you're up to the challenge of breaking up the clean-out plug, follow these steps:

1. **Purchase a new plastic plug so that you can close up the opening after you break up the old plug.**

2. **With your safety glasses on, place the point of a chisel on the outer edge of the clean-out plug and use a hammer to pound the chisel in a counterclockwise direction (see Figure 6-3).**

   Doing so usually loosens the plug. If it doesn't, proceed to Step 3.

3. **Break off the square tab in the center and then smash the plug into smaller parts with your hammer.**

   Keep in mind that water may be standing in the pipe, just waiting to come gushing out when you crack the plug. Use a bucket to catch any draining water.

Using a snake to clear the main line

After you get the clean-out open, you can push a snake into the line. Follow these steps:

1. **Push the snake into the clean-out and push it down into the pipe as far as it will go.**

2. **When you reach the clog, keep turning the snake, working it back and forth to loosen the clog (see Figure 6-4).**

   When you feel resistance, you know that you've reached the clog.

3. **Run some water through the pipe from a nearby sink.**

   If the water doesn't back up from the clean-out, you've cleared the clog. If the clog isn't clear, see the following section.

4. **Replace the clean-out plug and run hot water into the pipe from a nearby sink for several minutes.**

   When you flush the toilet, everything should run okay.

Book VI

Plumbing

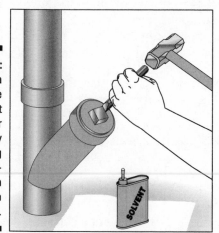

Figure 6-3: Clean out a blockage that's not at the toilet or fixture by removing the clean-out plug in the main sewer line.

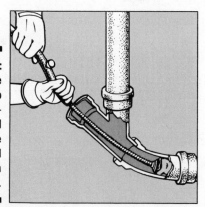

Figure 6-4: Insert the snake into the clean-out and feed it into the drain until you reach the clog.

Still clogged? Call a plumber

Some blockages are so far down the line that your snake can't reach them. If tree roots or some other tough object has caused the blockage, your little snake won't make a dent. In either case, you could rent a power auger from a rental center, but we don't recommend it. Power augers are difficult to operate and can be dangerous if the end of the steel coil gets lodged in the sewer. This type of machine has changeable cutter heads that are designed to cut roots or auger through tough clogs. If these heads jam and the steel coil kinks or breaks, you can get seriously hurt. You've done the hard part by removing the clean-out plug and identifying the problem, but it's time for you to call for help.

Chapter 7

Fixing a Leaky or Run-On Toilet

In This Chapter

▶ Recognizing toilet-tank anatomy

▶ Tackling a sticky tankball or flapper valve

▶ Fixing floatball and ballcock problems

A toilet is a pretty efficient appliance. Just push the lever and — almost magically — the toilet dispatches its contents in a few seconds with just a gurgle. Most toilets can get the job done with two or three gallons of water; newer models use only one and a half gallons. A leaking toilet, however, can waste hundreds of gallons of water a week. This chapter shows you how to stop the problem.

Getting Up Close and Personal with Your Toilet's Parts

If each flush doesn't end with a gurgle but instead continues with a hissing sound, with water running into the toilet bowl, you have a run-on toilet. You can fix this plumbing problem yourself. The mechanism inside the toilet bowl may seem complicated, but it really isn't.

The first thing that you need to do is scare up the courage to take the top off the toilet tank and familiarize yourself with the major parts, shown in Figure 7-1. As with almost every plumbing fixture, someone is always coming up with a better design, so, over time, many different types of valves and flushing mechanisms have developed. They all accomplish the same tasks, though.

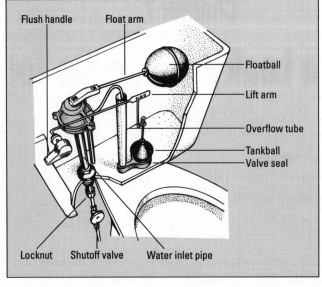

Flush handle   Float arm

Floatball

Lift arm

Overflow tube

Tankball
Valve seal

Locknut   Shutoff valve   Water inlet pipe

Figure 7-1:
The major
parts of the
mechanism
that fills the
toilet tank
with water.

Here's a rundown of what happens when you push that flush lever:

1. **The flush handle lifts a round rubber *tankball* (a rubber flapper) that's located in the base of the toilet tank.**

   When the tankball or flapper lifts, it opens the water passage between the tank and toilet bowl. As soon as this device lifts, water drains into the toilet.

2. **As the tank empties, the large ball attached to the end of a long rod, called a *floatball*, falls with the water level in the tank.**

   Some designs have a floatball that surrounds the intake valve, which is sometimes called a *ballcock*.

3. **At the other end of the floatball rod is the *ballcock*, which opens as the floatball moves down.**

   Water begins to flow into the tank as the ballcock opens.

4. **When the tank is almost empty, the tankball or flapper falls into the outlet, stopping the flow of water out of the tank.**

5. **When the drain is closed, the tank begins to fill.**

   The ballcock also directs water into an overflow tube that drains into the toilet bowl to ensure that the bowl fills with water.

6. **As the tank fills, the floatball rises with the water level until it gets to a predetermined position and closes the ballcock, stopping the inflow of water.**

   The toilet is now ready for another flush. As long as nothing is leaking, no more water is used until the flush lever is pushed again.

A run-on toilet is usually caused by a problem with the tankball, the ballcock or intake valve, or the floatball. To find the source of the trouble, remove the toilet tank top and place it in a safe location. Then push the flush lever and watch what happens. Don't worry about the water in the toilet tank — it's clean.

A Sticky Tankball or Flapper Valve

If, after you flush, the water keeps running until you wiggle the flush handle up and down, the problem is probably with the linkage between the flush handle and tankball. Or you could have a bad flapper valve or tankball. The following two sections can help you fix these problems.

Fixing or replacing a tankball

The tankball is screwed onto the end of a short rod that's held in place by an arm protruding from the overflow tube in the center of the toilet tank (refer to Figure 7-1). The flush lever attaches the tankball rod with another rod that slips over the end of the tankball rod. As you push the flush lever, the tankball is pulled up.

The tankball is hollow and filled with air, so as soon as it's pulled out of the drain in the bottom of the tank, it rises to the water level in the tank. When the drain opens, the tank empties and the tankball settles back into the ball seat, which is connected to the outlet pipe that leads to the toilet bowl.

To allow this open-close cycle to complete, the tankball rod and the flush lever rod need to be in alignment. If the tankball isn't falling into the drain properly, try bending the rods a bit until the tankball moves up and down without catching on anything.

To fix a sticking tankball, follow these steps:

1. **Reach into the tank and pull up on the tankball rod.**

   The rod and tankball should slide up and down easily and drop straight down into the outlet pipe. Note where the tankball hangs up.

2. **Bend the tankball rod and the flush lever rod until the tankball works freely, as shown in Figure 7-2.**

3. **If the tankball doesn't drop directly into the outlet pipe, use a screwdriver to loosen the setscrew that holds the guide arm.**

4. **Move the assembly back and forth until the tankball falls directly into the outlet pipe.**

   Check your work by flushing the toilet and making sure that the tank refills.

5. **If the tankball falls into the outlet pipe but doesn't stop the water flow, you may have to replace the tankball.**

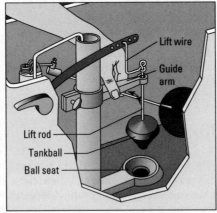

Figure 7-2: Adjust the lift rod and guide the arm so the tankball drops directly into the outlet pipe.

To replace the tankball, do the following:

1. **Check that the ball seat opening (which the flapper valve falls into) is clean.**

   If you see deposits on the seat, clean it with fine steel wool.

2. **Unscrew the tankball from the end of the tankball rod and get a replacement.**

   Take a close look at the tankball and flush lever rods. These inexpensive parts can corrode over time. Take the old tankball and rods with you to the store and get replacement parts that match.

If you can't get the tankball to fall into the outlet pipe and stop the water flow, buy a flapper-type tankball. Remove the old tankball by unscrewing it from the end of the brass rod (see Figure 7-3). Install the replacement by following the manufacturer's directions.

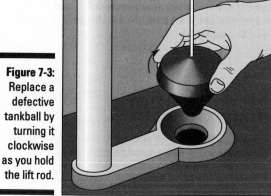

Figure 7-3:
Replace a
defective
tankball by
turning it
clockwise
as you hold
the lift rod.

Book VI

Plumbing

Adjusting or replacing a flapper valve

Some toilets have a flapper valve instead of a tankball. The flapper valve works the same as the tankball but is attached to the base of the overflow tube. A hinge allows the flapper to move up and down like a door. A chain is connected to the flapper and leads up to the flush lever.

Pushing the flush lever pulls on the chain and raises the flapper valve. This action allows the water to drain out. Like the tankball, the flapper is hollow and full of air, so it floats and stays in the raised, open position until the water level in the tank falls.

The following steps show how to adjust or replace the flapper valve:

1. **Make sure that the chain that connects the flush lever to the flapper has about ½ inch of slack in it.**

   When you push the lever, the flapper should rise high enough to stay open, but the chain shouldn't be so tight that it prevents the flapper from falling back into place.

2. **Check that the flapper moves freely up and down.**

   To do so, reach into the tank and lift the flapper by the chain and let go. It should fall back into the outlet pipe. To adjust it, loosen the screw holding the bracket around the overflow tube and move the flapper up or down, right or left as needed.

3. **Align the flapper with the outlet pipe.**

   If the flapper isn't aligned with the outlet pipe, loosen the clamp that holds the flapper in place and realign it so that it falls directly into the outlet pipe. Then retighten the clamp.

4. **Replace the flapper.**

   If the flapper falls into the outlet pipe but still doesn't stop the water flow, replace it. Loosen the screw that holds the bracket on the overflow pipe and pull the flapper assembly up and off the overflow pipe, as in Figure 7-4. Take it to your local home center and purchase a replacement. Reinstall the new flapper in the reverse order that you removed the old, following the installation instructions provided by the manufacturer.

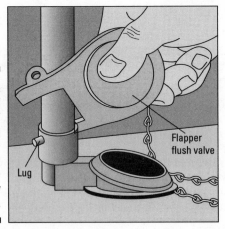

Figure 7-4: The new flapper valve slips over two lugs on the side of the overflow pipe.

Lug

Flapper flush valve

Floatball or Ballcock Problems

A ballcock that doesn't close completely is another possible cause of a leaking toilet. A misadjusted or damaged floatball, on the other hand, is usually the cause of water dribbling into the toilet tank, running out the overflow tube into the toilet bowl, and then going down the drain.

To determine whether your problem is with the floatball or ballcock, look into the tank and note whether the floatball is actually floating. If the floatball is partially submerged, it should be replaced. If the floatball is floating, reach into the tank and lift it up. The water should stop. If it does, follow the floatball adjustment instructions in the following section. If the water continues to flow even though you're pulling up on the floatball, the problem is in the ballcock valve.

Solving floatball problems

The floatball must, well, *float* in the water and resist any pressure to push it under. If it's partly full of water, replace it. Work through these steps to see how to replace and adjust the floatball:

1. **Unscrew the damaged floatball from the rod by turning it counterclockwise.**

2. **Take it to your home center or hardware store and purchase a plastic or copper replacement floatball.**

3. **Replace the floatball by threading it onto the end of the rod.**

   Turn it clockwise as you tighten it.

4. **If the water in the tank continues to run but the floatball is floating, lift up on the ball until the water stops.**

   Note the position and bend the rod down, lowering the floatball slightly and creating more pressure to close the valve as the water rises (see Figure 7-5). After bending the arm slightly, release the ball and check for running water. Repeat the process, increasing the bend in the arm, until the flow stops. Flush the toilet and check for leaking.

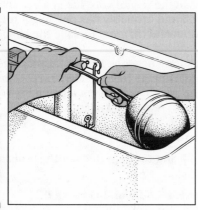

Figure 7-5: To adjust the floatball, grasp the rod close to the ballcock valve with one hand and bend the end with the floatball down.

Some toilets don't have a floatball on a rod, but instead have a floatball that surrounds the fill pipe. To adjust this type of floatball, loosen the screw on the side of the floatball and lower the floatball a bit on the connecting rod that leads from the floatball to the ballcock arm (see Figure 7-6).

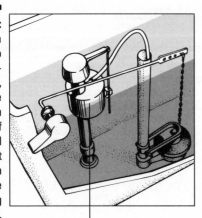

Figure 7-6:
To adjust a floating cup ballcock-type valve, loosen the setscrew on the side of the floatball and adjust the position of the connecting rod.

Floating-cup ballcock

Addressing ballcock problems

A ballcock that keeps on leaking even after you adjust the floatball probably has some sediment in the valve body or is just worn out. Fixing a clogged ballcock isn't a project that you should undertake. With many designs that all require special parts, you may spend the rest of your life in a plumbing supply store. A plumber can tackle this job and probably has or can get the parts, but he or she will most likely recommend that you replace the ballcock.

Now, swapping out an old ballcock for a new one is definitely a project that you can tackle. Most plumbing departments have a selection of toilet repair and rebuild kits to choose from that all come with installation instructions. Here are the general steps you take to replace a ballcock:

1. **Turn the water off below the toilet.**

   Flush the unit to drain the tank and then sponge out the remaining water from the bottom of the tank.

2. **Loosen the nuts securing the riser tube and remove it.**

   The riser tube is located under the toilet tank. It leads from the angle stop coming out of the wall up to the base of the ballcock valve coming out of the bottom of the toilet tank. *Be sure to turn off the water before you try to remove this tube, or you'll get wet.*

3. **Loosen the setscrew that holds the floatball rod in place on the top of the ballcock valve and then remove the floatball rod from the ballcock assembly and set it aside.**

4. **Loosen the large nut on the underside of the toilet tank that holds the ballcock assembly in place.**

   You may have to have a helper hold the ballcock inside the tank to keep it from turning as you loosen this nut.

5. **Pull the ballcock out of the toilet, take it with you to a home center, and purchase a replacement.**

   Also purchase a new flexible plastic riser tube in case the distance between the bottom of the new ballcock assembly and the stop valve has changed.

6. **Insert the replacement ballcock in the opening on the bottom of the toilet tank. Thread on the retaining nut from underneath the tank, as shown in Figure 7-7.**

   Follow the manufacturer's installation instructions. Don't overtighten.

Book VI

Plumbing

Figure 7-7:
Insert the ballcock into the tank and then thread on the retaining nut from the underside of the tank.

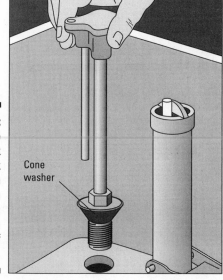

Cone washer

7. **Reinstall the riser tube between the stop valve and the new ballcock.**

8. **Reinstall the floatball arm if the ballcock you purchased requires one.**

   You will probably need to clip the bowl refill tube onto the overflow tube so that the refill tube is inside the overflow tube.

9. **Turn on the water and adjust the floatball so that the water fills to about ½ inch below the top of the overflow pipe.**

   The overflow pipe is in the center of the toilet tank and has the flapper valve attached to it. If the water level in the tank gets too high, the excess water runs out of the tube and into the toilet bowl.

10. **Flush the toilet to test your handiwork.**

    You may have to make some slight adjustments to the floatball to get the tank to fill.

Chapter 8

Fixing a Leaky Faucet

Stopping a leaking faucet is easy to do. The challenge is to determine what type of faucet you have. After you know that and have a replacement or the material to stop the leak, there isn't much to it.

Not only do you save water by stopping the leak, but you also get a sense of satisfaction — some may even call it smugness. You did it yourself, and the next time you notice a leak, you'll be ready and able to fix it, too.

Before you begin to repair a leak for any type of faucet, turn off the hot and cold-water shut-off valves under the sink by turning them clockwise.

Stopping a Compression Faucet Leak

A *compression faucet* is so called because a rubber washer, actually made from *neoprene* (a form of synthetic rubber), is forced against a metal seat to choke off the water flow. As you turn the handle, the washer is pushed against (and thus compresses) the valve seat. If the washer or valve seat becomes damaged, a seal isn't made, and the faucet leaks.

If your compression faucet is dripping, the rubber washer has most likely worn away. Less common is a worn metal seal that the washer presses against when it's closed. The metal (usually brass) valve seat can become damaged if you don't change the washer before it's too worn — metal then grinds against metal and chews up the seat. Hard foreign matter can become trapped between the valve seat and the washer. If this happens, closing and opening the faucet grinds the particles inside, damaging it beyond a simple washer replacement.

Replacing a worn washer

To replace a worn washer, follow these steps, using Figure 8-1 as a guide:

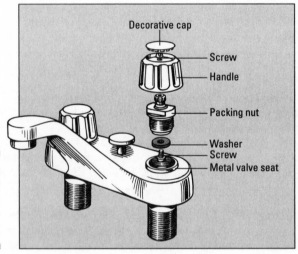

Figure 8-1:
The major parts of a compression faucet.

1. **Turn off the water to the faucet.**

2. **Remove the decorative cap, if there is one, on top of the faucet handle.**

   Depending on its design, you pull it up or unscrew it.

3. **Unscrew or pull off the handle and remove it.**

   If the handle sticks, gently nudge it up with a screwdriver. Wrap the screwdriver edge with a rag to prevent marring the finish.

4. **Remove the cover over the valve, called an *escutcheon,* if there is one.**

   Some types unscrew, while others are held in place by setscrews. Inspect the escutcheon to figure out how to remove it.

5. **Unscrew the packing nut that holds the body of the valve in place, turning it counterclockwise.**

   The valve stem should come out of the base of the valve. You may have to twist the valve-stem body several turns after you loosen the packing nut and the valve stem. If it's hard to unscrew, put the handle back on the stem and give it a twist. The stem then comes out of the valve.

6. **Unscrew the retaining screw and remove the washer.**

   On the other end of the stem is a rubber washer that's held in place by a screw. These valve washers come in many shapes and sizes, so take the valve stem to the plumbing department of your local hardware store or home center and get a washer that matches the old one. This task may be more difficult than it sounds, because the old washer is usually damaged and deformed. The best clue to the original shape of the washer is to look into the valve body and take a look at the metal opening that the washer presses against — the valve seat. If the side of the valve seat is angled, replace the washer with a cone shape; if the valve seat is flat, get a replacement washer that's flat.

7. **Replace the old washer with the new one and reassemble the faucet.**

Book VI

Plumbing

Replacing the valve seat

If the faucet still leaks after reassembly, the seat may be damaged. To replace a damaged valve seat, follow these steps:

1. **Disassemble the unit.**

   See the preceding "Replacing a worn washer" section for instructions.

2. **While the stem is out, look into the valve body and inspect the faucet seat.**

   Look for a brass insert inside the valve body that the rubber washer presses against to stop the flow of water. If this seat is rough, it will tear up the new washer and the valve will begin to leak again. A rough valve seat should be replaced. If the faucet doesn't have replaceable valve seats, you can grind the seat smooth with a valve seat grinder.

3. **If the valve has a removable seat, remove it.**

   If the seat has a hexagonal or grooved opening in its center, remove the seat with a screwdriver or an Allen wrench.

   If the seat isn't removable (it will have a round hole), you have a really old faucet. You can grind it smooth with a seat-grinding tool, found in the plumbing departments of hardware stores and home centers and shown in Figure 8-2. The tool, also known as a *faucet seat reamer,* comes with instructions and is easy to use. The tool fits over the valve seat (where the washer usually rests) and grinds the seat with the tool. The idea is to reshape the damaged seat to accept the new washer. When using this tool, take care to keep it perfectly aligned or the seat will be dressed unevenly.

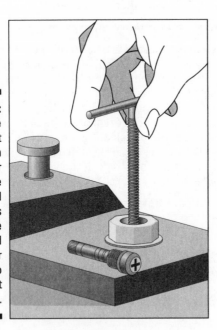

Figure 8-2:
Align the valve seat grinder in the center of the valve body and then press down on the handle and turn three or four times to grind it smooth.

4. **Take your old faucet to a well-stocked plumbing department or supplier, along with the faucet stem, and purchase the correct replacement.**

   Faucet seats come in many sizes and with many different thread patterns — a perfect match is critical.

5. **Replace the valve seat, being careful not to cross-thread the connection.**

6. **Coat the washer and all moving parts — including the handle stem — with heatproof grease.**

   This type of grease doesn't break down in hot water and keeps the stem and faucet working smoothly for a long time.

7. **Replace the stem washer and packing as necessary.**

8. **Reassemble the faucet in the reverse order that you removed it.**

Stopping a stem leak

If you have a leaky handle rather than a drippy faucet, the water is leaking past the *stem packing* — see Figure 8-3 — or the washer. Older faucets have a stringlike substance wrapped around the handle stem to hold the water back. The packing eventually wears, and water can sneak between the stem and the packing. Newer faucets stop the water leak with an o-ring or a washer.

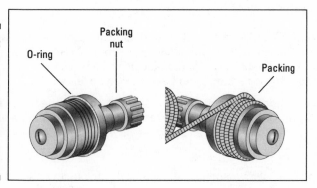

Figure 8-3:
Replace the packing around the valve stem and retighten the packing washer.

Older faucets with packing are more likely to leak. Here's how to fix them:

1. **Turn off the water to the faucet.**

2. **Remove the handle from the shaft.**

3. **Tighten the packing nut.**

   Turn it clockwise about ½ turn. This may be all that's necessary to stop the leak.

4. **If tightening the packing nut doesn't work, loosen the packing nut with slip-joint pliers or a wrench and then unscrew the nut by hand and remove it.**

5. **Remove the old packing from around the stem.**

6. **Replace the old packing with new packing.**

   You can find new packing in the plumbing departments of hardware stores and home centers.

7. **Reassemble the faucet.**

Keep a supply of various sized o-rings, packing washers, packing rope, and washers handy to save you a trip to the store at the first sign of a leak.

Stopping a Washerless Faucet Leak

The new variety of washerless faucet is easier to fix than a compression faucet. The hardest part of this project is figuring out what type of washerless faucet you have. The three sections that follow explain how to fix the three most common types of washerless faucets currently on the market.

The best tip-off as to what type of faucet you have is how the handle that controls the water moves:

- If the control handle moves all around in an arc (generally up and down to control the water flow and sideways to control temperature), is attached to a domelike top of the faucet, and has a small setscrew in the base of the control handle, you have a *ball-type faucet*.

- If the handle moves directly up and down to control the water flow and directly right or left to control the temperature (but not in an arc like the ball-type), you have either a *cartridge-type faucet* or a *ceramic disk-type faucet*.

If you can find the user's manual that came with the faucet (a small miracle!), you may find the manufacturer's name and model number. Most manufacturers sell repair kits, which home centers and large hardware stores usually stock. These kits have all the necessary parts, including any special tools needed to take the faucet apart and repair it.

Ball-type faucet

Follow these steps to fix a single-handle ball-type faucet, shown in Figure 8-4.

1. **Turn off the water to the faucet (see Chapter 2).**

2. **Remove the handle.**

   Loosen the setscrew that secures the handle to the shaft coming out of the ball valve. The screw head is on the underside of the lever. This setscrew requires an *Allen wrench* (an L-shaped hex wrench that fits into the recessed socket in the head of the setscrew) to loosen. Some faucets are manufactured in Europe and may have metric-sized parts. If you can't find an Allen wrench that fits the setscrew, chances are the screw has a metric head. In that case, you need to purchase a set of metric Allen wrenches, which aren't expensive.

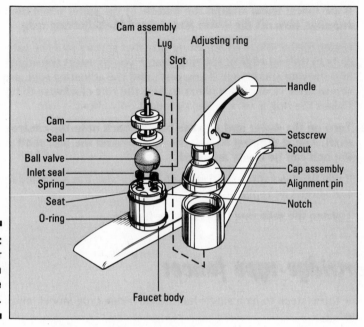

Cam assembly
Lug
Slot
Adjusting ring

Handle

Cam
Seal
Ball valve
Inlet seal
Spring
Seat
O-ring

Setscrew
Spout
Cap assembly
Alignment pin
Notch

Faucet body

Figure 8-4:
The major
parts of a
ball-type
faucet.

3. Remove the ball valve and spout.

Wrap tape around the jaws of your wrench or slip-joint pliers to protect the valve parts. Loosen the *cap assembly* (the dome-shaped ring at the top of the faucet) by turning the adjusting screw counterclockwise. Grab the shaft to which the handle was attached, move it back and forth to loosen the ball valve assembly, and then pull it straight up and out of the faucet body.

4. Replace the valve seats and o-rings.

When you look inside the faucet body, you see the valve seats and rubber o-rings. Behind them are springs. Remove the seats, o-rings, and springs from the faucet body and take them to a hardware store or home center to get the correct repair kit.

5. Replace the parts and reassemble the faucet in the reverse order that you took it apart (or follow the directions in the repair kit).

Make sure to reinstall the ball in the same position from which you removed it.

6. Turn the water back on to test the faucet.

7. **If the faucet leaks around the handle or the spout when the water is running, turn off the water and tighten the adjusting ring.**

   Under the handle is an adjusting ring that screws into the valve body. Slots in the top edge of the ring enable you to insert the adjusting tool into the ring and turn it. If you can't find the adjusting tool, use a large screwdriver or slip-joint pliers to turn the ring clockwise to tighten it. Unless the ring is very loose, tighten it only about ⅛ turn.

8. **Turn on the water and slip the handle back onto the control ball's shaft. Adjust the ring so that the leak around the ball shaft stops but the ball can be easily adjusted.**

   If you can't get the leak to stop, the seal under the adjusting ring is bad and should be replaced.

9. **Tighten the setscrew to secure the handle.**

Cartridge-type faucet

Follow these steps to fix a single-handle cartridge-type faucet, shown in Figure 8-5:

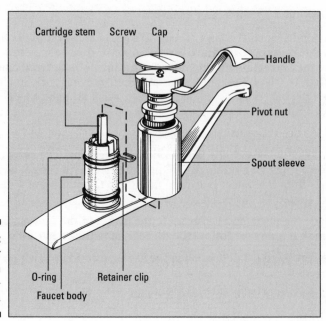

Figure 8-5:
The major parts of a cartridge-type faucet.

Cartridge stem   Screw   Cap

Handle

Pivot nut

Spout sleeve

O-ring   Retainer clip

Faucet body

1. **Turn off the water to the faucet (see Chapter 2).**

2. **Remove the handle.**

   Remove the cover on the top of the handle to expose the screw that holds the handle to the valve stem. Pop off the cover by placing the tip of a screwdriver between the cover and the handle housing and prying up. To remove the handle, turn the screw in the center of the cap counterclockwise; remove it and then pull the handle up and off the valve assembly. This exposes the valve stem coming out of the valve cartridge.

3. **If your faucet has a movable spout, remove the pivot nut.**

   Use an adjustable wrench or slip-joint pliers to loosen (turning counterclockwise) to remove the pivot nut at the top of the faucet body. This nut holds the spout sleeve in place and prevents water from coming out the top of the faucet.

4. **Remove the spout assembly by twisting it back and forth as you pull up.**

5. **Remove the cartridge clip and replace the cartridge.**

   To remove the cartridge, you have to pull out the small U-shaped clip that holds the valve cartridge in the faucet body. Pry the clip loose by placing the tip of your screwdriver between the faucet body and the U-section of the clip.

   Twist the screwdriver, and the clip comes out. Grab the clip with your pliers and remove it. Pull up on the cartridge stem with a twisting motion. If it doesn't twist out easily, reinstall the handle so that you can get a good grip on the shaft to pull the cartridge out. Take the old cartridge to your hardware store or home center and purchase a replacement kit.

6. **Reassemble the faucet according to the directions.**

Be sure to replace the cartridge in the correct position — there may be a notch in the valve body that the cartridge fits into. How the cartridge is inserted into the valve body determines which side the hot and cold water is on. Usually you move the lever right for cold and left for hot. If you reverse the position of the cartridge, the hot and cold will be on opposite sides. If this happens, take the faucet apart and reverse the cartridge position.

Ceramic disk-type faucet

A ceramic disk-type faucet is reliable and usually doesn't require much maintenance. If you do need to repair one, however, these faucets can be a bit tricky to take apart. Older models are held together by screws underneath the faucet,

Book VI

Plumbing

so if you can't figure out how to get the handle off, look under the counter, and you should see a couple of brass screws. Loosen them and the whole cover and handle will come off the faucet, revealing the valve cartridge — see Figure 8-6.

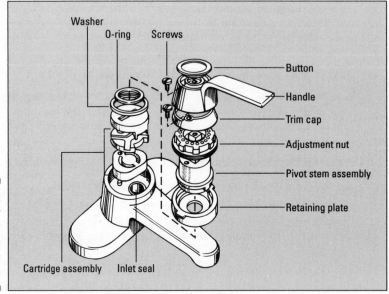

Figure 8-6:
The major parts of a ceramic disk-type faucet.

1. **Turn off the water to the faucet.**

2. **Remove the handle.**

   Lift the handle to its highest position to expose the setscrew holding it in place. Use an Allen wrench or a screwdriver to turn the setscrew counterclockwise and then lift off the handle.

3. **With the handle off, pull the decorative trim cap up and off the cartridge body.**

4. **Remove the valve seals and cartridge assembly.**

   Loosen the two screws on the top of the valve cartridge and lift the assembly off the faucet body.

5. **Replace the rubber seals.**

   You can find several rubber seals under the cartridge — replacing them stops most leaks. If you replace these seals and the faucet still leaks, the valve cartridge, which contains the ceramic disks, is worn and must be replaced.

6. **Take the cartridge assembly to your local hardware store or home center and purchase a replacement kit.**

7. **Install the new cartridge according to the instructions in the kit.**

   The kit will contain new o-rings to seal around the faucet body. Be sure to replace these o-rings even if the old ones look like they're in good shape.

Fixing a Dish Sprayer

If you notice that the water flow out of your kitchen sink's dish sprayer isn't what it used to be, you can't use it as an excuse not to do the dishes. The fix is easy. Here's how to clean the spray head, which is probably stopped up (see Figure 8-7):

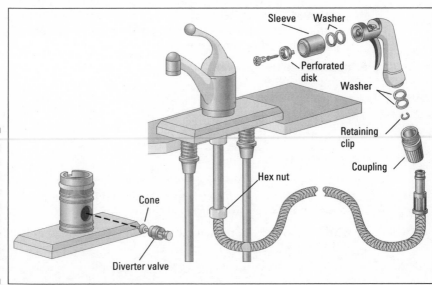

Figure 8-7: Remove the spray head and clean the deposits out of the small spray holes in the head.

1. **Turn the water off from under the sink.**

2. **Remove the spray head.**

   Untwisting the head disassembles some models; a screw holds other types together.

3. **Clean out any blockage in the small holes of the spray head.**

4. **Check the spray hose for kinks.**

   Look under the sink and check the condition of the spray hose. It may become entangled with objects stored under the sink, restricting the water flow. Replace a badly kinked hose. You can purchase replacement sprayer assemblies at most home centers, but take the hose and spray head with you when you shop for a replacement: Turn off the water supply and then unscrew the hose from the base of the faucet.

5. **Check the diverter valve.**

   If the spray head and hose look okay, a malfunctioning diverter valve may be the problem. A *diverter valve* is a simple device that's activated by water pressure. When the sprayer is off, the water is diverted to the spout. When you press the sprayer trigger, the water pressure in the hose drops, and the valve closes off the water flow to the spout and directs water to the sprayer. To do so, it must move freely. A sure sign of a bad diverter valve is that water flows from both the faucet and the dish sprayer at the same time. This valve is located in the base of the faucet behind the swivel spout, if one exists. Refer to Figure 8-7 for the location of this part. To service it, make sure that the valve moves freely and that all the rubber parts are in good shape. Replacement parts are available, including the entire spray head.

6. **Reassemble the sprayer.**

Index

• B •

• *M* •

• *T* •

Notes

Notes

Notes

Notes

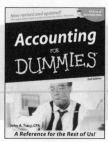

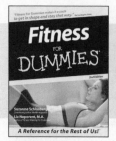

FOR DUMMIES®

A world of resources to help you grow

HOME, GARDEN & HOBBIES

0-7645-5295-3

0-7645-5130-2

0-7645-5106-X

Also available:

Auto Repair For Dummies
(0-7645-5089-6)

Chess For Dummies
(0-7645-5003-9)

Home Maintenance For Dummies
(0-7645-5215-5)

Organizing For Dummies
(0-7645-5300-3)

Piano For Dummies
(0-7645-5105-1)

Poker For Dummies
(0-7645-5232-5)

Quilting For Dummies
(0-7645-5118-3)

Rock Guitar For Dummies
(0-7645-5356-9)

Roses For Dummies
(0-7645-5202-3)

Sewing For Dummies
(0-7645-5137-X)

FOOD & WINE

0-7645-5250-3

0-7645-5390-9

0-7645-5114-0

Also available:

Bartending For Dummies
(0-7645-5051-9)

Chinese Cooking For Dummies
(0-7645-5247-3)

Christmas Cooking For Dummies
(0-7645-5407-7)

Diabetes Cookbook For Dummies
(0-7645-5230-9)

Grilling For Dummies
(0-7645-5076-4)

Low-Fat Cooking For Dummies
(0-7645-5035-7)

Slow Cookers For Dummies
(0-7645-5240-6)

TRAVEL

0-7645-5453-0

0-7645-5438-7

0-7645-5448-4

Also available:

America's National Parks For Dummies
(0-7645-6204-5)

Caribbean For Dummies
(0-7645-5445-X)

Cruise Vacations For Dummies 2003
(0-7645-5459-X)

Europe For Dummies
(0-7645-5456-5)

Ireland For Dummies
(0-7645-6199-5)

France For Dummies
(0-7645-6292-4)

London For Dummies
(0-7645-5416-6)

Mexico's Beach Resorts For Dummies
(0-7645-6262-2)

Paris For Dummies
(0-7645-5494-8)

RV Vacations For Dummies
(0-7645-5443-3)

Walt Disney World & Orlando For Dummies
(0-7645-5444-1)

Available wherever books are sold. Go to www.dummies.com or call 1-877-762-2974 to order direct.

FOR DUMMIES

Helping you expand your horizons and realize your potential

INTERNET

0-7645-0894-6

0-7645-1659-0

0-7645-1642-6

DIGITAL MEDIA

0-7645-1664-7

0-7645-1675-2

0-7645-0806-7

GRAPHICS

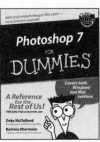

0-7645-0817-2

0-7645-1651-5

0-7645-0895-4

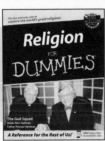

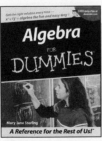